THE *DIDACHE* IN MODERN RESEARCH

ARBEITEN ZUR GESCHICHTE DES ANTIKEN JUDENTUMS UND DES URCHRISTENTUMS

HERAUSGEGEBEN VON

Martin Hengel (Tübingen), Peter Schäfer (Berlin),
Pieter W. van der Horst (Utrecht), Martin Goodman (Oxford),
Daniël R. Schwartz (Jerusalem), Cilliers Breytenbach (Berlin)

XXXVII

THE *DIDACHE* IN MODERN RESEARCH

EDITED BY

JONATHAN A. DRAPER

E.J. BRILL

LEIDEN · NEW YORK · KÖLN

1996

The paper in this book meets the guidelines for permanence and durability of the Committee on Production Guidelines for Book Longevity of the Council on Library Resources.

Translations from German and French by Jonathan A. Draper
Translation from Modern Hebrew by Atalia Ben-Meir
Translation from Italian by Lynda Palazzo

ISSN 0169-734X
ISBN 90 04 10375 9

PRINTED IN THE NETHERLANDS

CONTENTS

ACKNOWLEDGMENTS

The editor gratefully acknowledges the kind permission to use or reprint materials from the following sources, cited in the order of their appearance:

Schöllgen, G. 1986. "Die Didache als Kirchenordnung. Zur Frage des Abfassungszweckes und seinen Konsequenzen für die Interpretation", *Jahrbuch für Antike und Christentum* 29, 5-26. Used with permission.

Draper, J.A. "The Jesus Tradition in the Didache" in *Gospel Perspectives V: The Jesus Tradition Outside the Gospels*, ed. D. Wenham. Sheffield: JSOT, 1985 pp. 269-289. Used with permission. This article has been slightly reworked and updated.

Tuckett, C. M. 1989. "Synoptic Tradition in the Didache", in J.-M. Sevrin, *The New Testament in Early Christianity*, 197-230. Leuven: University Press. Used with permission.

Audet, J.-P. 1952. "Affinités Littéraires et Doctrinales du "Manuel de Discipline"". *Revue Biblique* 59, 219-238. Used with permission.

Rordorf, W. 1972. "Une chapitre d'éthique judéo-chrétienne: les deux voies". *Recherches de science religieuses* 60, 109-128. Used with permission.

Alon, G. 1958. [דידאכי] ה השליחים ׳׳ב שבתורת ההלכה, in *Studies in Jewish History in the Times of the Second Temple, the Mishna and the Talmud* I, 274-294. Tel Aviv: Hakibbutz Hameuchad. Used with permission.

Flusser, D. 1987. "Paul's Jewish-Christian Opponents in the Didache", in S. Shaked, D. Shulman & G. G. Stroumsa (eds), *Gilgul: Essays on Transformation, Revolution and Permanence in the History of Religions, Dedicated to R. J. Zwi Werblowsky*, 71-90. Leiden:Brill. Used with permission.

Rordorf, W. 1972. "Le Baptême selon la *Didaché*", in *Mélanges Liturgiques offerts au R. P. Dom Bernard Botte O.S.B.*, 499-509. Louvaine: Abbaye du Mont César. Used with permission.

Draper, J. A. 1992. "Christian Self-Definition against the "Hypocrites" in Didache 8", in E. H. Lovering, *Society of Biblical Literature 1992 Seminar Papers*, 362-377. Atlanta, Ga.: Scholars. Used with permission.

Betz, J. 1969. "Die Eucharistie in der Didache". *Archiv für Liturgiewissenschaft* 11, 10-39. Used with permission.

Mazza, E. 1979. "Didaché IX-X: Elementi per una interpretazione Eucaristica", *Ephemerides Liturgicae* 92, 393-419. Used with permission.

Halleux, A. de 1980. "Les ministères dans la Didachè", *Irénikon: Revue des Moines de Chevetogne* 53, 5-29. Used with permission.

Niederwimmer, K. 1977. "Zur Entwicklungsgeschichte des Wanderradikalismus im Traditionsbereich der Didache". *Wiener Studien* 11, 145-167. Used with permission.

Draper, J. A. 1991. "Torah and Troublesome Apostles in the Didache Community", *Novum Testamentum* 33/4, 347-372. Used with permission.

Bammel, E. 1961. "Schema und Vorlage von *Didache* 16". *Studia Patristica* 4/2 (*TU* 79), 253-262. Used with permission.

Seeliger, H. R. 1989. "Erwägungen zu Hintergrund und Zweck des apokalyptischen Schlusskapitels der *Didache*" in E. A. Livingstone (ed), *Studia Patristica 21: Papers presented to the Tenth International Conference on Patristic Studies held in Oxford 1987*, 185-192. Leuven:Peeters. Used with permission.

PREFACE

The recent collection by C. N. Jefford of articles in *The Didache in Context: Essays on its Text, History, and Transmission* (Leiden: Brill, 1995) has indicated that research into the *Didache* is entering a new and constructive phase. However, much of the work of modern scholars on this elusive but important text remain in journals and collections which are difficult to access, or in languages other than English. This book seeks to make a representative selection in English of the key essays on the *Didache* published in recent decades available in one volume.

The essays have been chosen because they each in some way represent a key position or a seminal advance on some aspect of research into the *Didache*, or else because they summarize and evaluate work in a particular area. The initial overview of the history of research is intended to provide a framework within which the essays may be read.

Mrs. Atalia Ben-Meir provided the translation of the Hebrew text of Alon's essay, which I have subsequently worked over. Mrs. Lynda Palazzo produced the draft of the translation of the Italian article by Mazza, but the final version is my own responsibility. While much of Mazza's essay is included in his recent book, *The Origins of the Eucharistic Prayer* (Collegeville, Minnesota: The Liturgical Press, 1995), the translation here is our own and is used because the article is more focussed and stands alone. Professor Mazza has kindly allowed me to use it in its original form.

I would like to thank all the contributors who were able to check the translations and proofs of their own articles. In addition a number of people have assisted in checking the translations. Among them I need to mention my colleagues, Professor Gunther Wittenberg, Professor Klaus Nürnberger and Dr. Philippe Denis, as well as as graduate assistant, Dieter Clackworthy. Father Paul Decock kindly read the final draft and made a number of helpful corrections. Professor James Pasto graciously checked the translation of the article by Alon.

A special mention should also be made of my graduate assistant, Mr. Ian van Tonder, who has worked so hard in producing the indexes, abbreviations and bibliography, as well as checking the references. I would also like to thank Dr. David Orton of E. J. Brill for his encouragement and advice in the project.

Finally, but by no means least, I would like to thank my wife Marion for her patience and understanding, especially in the final throes of publication.

The referencing systems of the articles have been reduced to a single format. In some cases it has not been possible to trace the references. In particular, the article by G. Alon has not always provided clear references, probably because of the difficulties and dislocation he suffered in moving to Israel.

Where possible reference has been made to the English translation of a work cited, where one exists. This is for the convenience of readers.

However, where no English translation exists, quotations are left in the original language. An attempt has been made to stay close to the literal sense of the original language without sacrificing readability, but sometimes one or the other has had to suffer.

Jonathan A. Draper

ABBREVIATIONS

I. Primary Sources

ACO	*Apostolic Church Order*
ActsJn	*Acts of John*
ActsPaulThec	*Acts of Paul and Thecla*
ActsPet	*Acts of Peter*
AdJud	John Chrysostom, *Adversus Judaeos*
AdNat	Tertullian, *Ad Nationes*
AdVir	Pseudo-Clement, *To the Virgins*
AdvHaer	Irenaeus, *Adversus omnes Haereses*
AJ	Josephus, *Antiquitates Judaicae*
Am	Amos
An	Tacitus, *Annales*
ApocMos	*Apocalypse of Moses*
ApocPet	*Apocalypse of Peter*
ApocZeph	*Apocalypse of Zephaniah*
Apol	Aristides of Athens, *Apologia*
1 *Apol*	Justin Martyr, *Apologiae*
ApTrad	Hippolytus, *Apostolic Tradition*
ARN	*Abot de Rabbi Nathan*
AscenIs	*Ascension of Isaiah*
b.AZ	Babylonian Talmud, tractate *Abodah Zarah*
b.Bek	tractate *Bekhorot*
b.Ber	tractate *Berakhot*
b.BM	tractate *Baba Mesia*
b.BQ	tractate *Baba Qamma*
b.Git	tractate *Gittin*
b.Hag	tractate *Hagiga*
b.Jeb	tractate *Jebamoth*
b.Ket	tractate *Ketubbot*
b.Mak	tractate *Makkot*
b.Meg	tractate *Megillah*
b.Men	tractate *Menahot*
b.MQ	tractate *Moed Qatan*
b.Naz	tractate *Nazir*
b.Ned	tractate *Nedarim*
b.Nidd	tractate *Niddah*
b.Pes	tractate *Pesahim*
b.Qid	tractate *Qiddushin*
b.San	tractate *Sanhedrin*
b.Shab	tractate *Shabbat*
b.Shebu	tractate *Shebuot*
b.Taan	tractate *Taanit*
b.Tam	tractate *Tamid*

b.Tem	tractate *Temurot*
b.Yeb	tractate *Yebamot*
Bapt	Tertullian, *De Baptismo*
BJ	Josephus, *Bellum Judaicum*
2 Bar	Syriac Apocalypse of Baruch
Barn	*Epistle of Barnabas*
CD	Cairo (Genizah text of the) *Damascus Document*
1-2 Clem	*1-2 Clement*
Col	Colossians
Comm	Origen, *Commentarii*
ConApion	Josephus, *Contra Apionem*
ConCels	Origen, *Contra Celsum*
Const	*Apostolic Constitutions*
1-2 Cor	1-2 Corinthians
Dan	Daniel
DE	Eusebius of Caesarea, *Demonstratio Evangelica*
Decal	Philo, *De Decalogo*
DeutR	*Deuteronomy Rabbah*
Dial	Justin Martyr, *Dialogus cum Tryphone Judaeo*
Dial	Origen, *Dialogue (with Heraclides)*
Did	*Didache*
Dida	*Didascalia*
Doct	*Doctrina Apostolorum*
Dt	Deuteronomy
Ec	Ecclesiastes
EcclR	*Ecclesiastes Rabbah*
EpFest	Athanasius, *Epistula Festivalis*
Eph	Ignatius of Antioch, *Letter to the Ephesians*
1 En	Ethiopic Apocalypse of Enoch
2 En	Slavonic Apocalypse of Enoch
Esdr	Esdras
Ex	Exodus
ExodR	*Exodus Rabbah*
Ez	Ezekial
4 Ezr	4 Ezra
Gal	Galatians
GBasilides	*Gospel of Basilides*
Gen	Genesis
Ger	*Gerim*
GPh	*Gospel of Philip*
GTh	*Gospel of Thomas*
GTr	*Gospel of Truth*
Haer	Irenaeus, *Adversus Haereses*
HE	Eusebius, *Historia Ecclesiastica*
Heb	Hebrews
HermMan	*Shepherd of Hermas, Mandates*

HermSim	*Shepherd of Hermas, Similitudes*
HermVis	*Shepherd of Hermas, Visions*
Hom	John Chrysostom, *Homiliae*
Hom	Pseudo-Clement, *Homiliae*
Hos	Hosea
Hyp	Philo, *Hypothetica*
In Dan	Hippolytus, *Commentary on Daniel*
Inst	Lactantius, *Divinae Institutiones*
Is	Isaiah
j.Ber	Jerusalem Talmud, tractate *Berakhot*
j.Ket	tractate *Ketubbot*
j.Kil	tractate *Kilayim*
j.MQ	tractate *Moed Qatan*
j.Qid	tractate *Qiddushin*
j.RH	tractate *Rosh ha-Shanah*
j.San	tractate *Sanhedrin*
j.Shab	tractate *Shabbat*
j.Yeb	tractate *Yebamot*
Jas	James
Jer	Jeremiah
Jn	John
Jon	Jonah
Jub	Jubilees
Jud	Judith
Judg	Judges
Josh	Joshua
LAB	Pseudo-Philo, *Liber Antiquitatem Biblicarum*
LegAll	Philo, *De Legum Allegoriae*
Lev	Leviticus
LevR	*Leviticus Rabbah*
Lk	Luke
m.Abot	Mishnah, tractate *Abot*
m.Ber	tractate *Berakhot*
m.BQ	tractate *Babba Qamma*
m.Eduy	tractate *Eduyot*
m.Hag	tractate *Hagiga*
m.Hal	tractate *Hallah*
m.Meg	tractate *Megillah*
m.Miqw	tractate *Miqwaot*
m.San	tractate *Sanhedrin*
m.Shab	tractate *Shabbat*
m.Shek	tractate *Shekalim*
m.Sot	tractate *Sota*
m.Taan	tractate *Taanit*
m.Tem	tractate *Temurot*
m.Yad	tractate *Yadayim*

1-4 Macc	1-4 Maccabees
Mal	Malachi
Mek	*Mekhilta de Rabbi Ishmael*
MidrPss	*Midrash on Psalms*
MidrTann	*Midrash Tannaim*
Mk	Mark
Mt	Matthew
Neh	Nehemiah
Num	Numbers
OdesSol	*Odes of Solomon*
OfMin	Ambrose, *De Officiis Ministrorum*
Orat	Tertullian, *De Oratione*
OrGr	Tatian, *Oratio ad Graecos*
Paed	Celement of Alexandria, *Paedagogus*
Pan	Epiphanius, *Panarion*
PE	Eusebius, *Praeparatio Evangelica*
PergMort	Lucian, *De Peregrini Morte*
PesR	*Pesiqta Rabbati*
1-2 Pet	1-2 Peter
Phld	Ignatius of Antioch, *Letter to the Philadelphians*
Plant	Philo, *De Plantatione*
PolyC	Ignatius of Antioch, *Letter to Polycarp*
POx	Papyrus Oxyrhynchus
Pr	Proverbs
PraescrHaer	Tertullian, *De Praescriptione Haereticorum*
PRE	*Pirqe de Rabbi Eliezer*
Protr	Celement of Alexandria, *Protrepticus*
Ps	Psalms
PssSol	*Psalms of Solomon*
4QFlor	*Florilegium (A messianic anthology)*
1QH	*The Thanksgiving Psalms*
1QpHab	*Commentary on Habakkuk*
1QS	*The Community Rule (Manual of Discipline)*
11QT	*Temple Scroll*
4QTestim	*Testimonia* (messianic references)
Recog	Pseudo-Clement, *Recognitions*
Ref	Hippolytus, *Refutatio omnium haeresium*
Rev	Revelation
Rom	Romans
2 Sam	2 Samuel
Sat	Juvenal, *Satire*
SibOr	*Sibylline Oracles*
Sir	Sirach
Smy	Ignatius of Antioch, *Letter to the Smyrneans*
SpecLeg	Philo, *De Specialibus Legibus*
Str	Clement of Alexandria, *Stromata*

Symp	Methodius, *Symposion*
t. Ber	Tosepta, tractate *Berakhot*
t. Git	tractate *Gittin*
t. Hul	tracate *Hullin*
t. San	tractate *Sanhedrin*
t. Shab	tractate *Shabbat*
t. Suk	tractate *Sukkah*
t. Taan	tractate *Taanit*
t. Yeb	tractate *Yebamot*
TestAsh	*Testament of Asher*
TestBenj	*Testament of Benjamin*
TestDan	*Testament of Dan*
TestDom	*Testamentum Domini*
TestGad	*Testament of Gad*
TestJos	*Testament of Joseph*
TestLevi	*Testament of Levi*
Tit	Titus
Tra	Pliny, *Epistulae ad Traianum*
1-2 Thess	1-2 Thessalonians
1-2 Tim	1-2 Timothy
Tob	Tobit
Trall	Ignatius, *Letter to the Trallians*
VitCon	Philo, *De Vita Contemplativa*
WisdSol	Wisdom of Solomon
Zech	Zechariah

II. Secondary Sources

AB	The Anchor Bible
ACh	Antike und Christentum
AF	The Apostolic Fathers, R.M. Grant (ed.)
ALW	*Archiv für Liturgiewissenschaft*
ASTI	*Annual of the Swedish Theological Institute*
AThANT	Abhandlungen zur Theologie des Alten und Neuen Testaments
AThR	*Anglican Theological Review*
BAGD	*A Greek-English Lexicon of the New Testament*, W. Bauer, W.F. Arndt, F.W. Gingrich, F.W. Danker
BBB	Bonner Biblische Beiträge
BDF	*A Greek Grammar of the New Testament*, F. Blass, A. Debrunner, R.W. Funk
BEThL	Bibliotheca ephemeridum theologicarum lovaniensium
Bibl	*Biblica*
BFCTh	Beiträge zur Förderung christilicher Theologie
BHTh	Beiträge zur historischen Theologie

BJRL	*Bulletin John Rylands Library*
BKV	Bibliothek der Kirchenväter
BRThAM	*Bulletin des recherches de Théologie ancienne et médiévale*
BS	*Bibliotheca sacra*
BSt	Biblische Studien
BStR	Brown Studies in Religion
BThAM	*Bulletin de Théologie ancienne et médiévale*
BTS	*Bible et terre sainte*
BZNW	Beihefte zur Zeitschrift für die neutestamentliche Wissenschaft
CahRB	Cahiers de la Revue Biblique
CBQ	*Catholic Biblical Quarterly*
ChQR	*Church Quarterly Review*
CSCO	Corpus scriptorum christianorum orientalium
CSEL	*Corpus scriptorum ecclesiasticorum latinorum*
DRev	*Downside Review*
DThC	Dictionnaire de Théologie Catholique
DViv	*Dieu Vivant*
ÉBib	Études bibliques
EphLiturg	*Ephemerides liturgicae*
Er	*Eranos*
EThL	*Ephemerides theologicae lovanienses*
ETSE	Estonian Theological Society in Exile
FC	Fontes christiani
FGThIL	Forschung zur Geschichte der Theologie und des innerkirchlichen Lebens
FRLANT	Forschungen zur Religion und Literatur des Alten und Neuen Testaments
FzB	Forschung zur Bibel
GCS	*Die griechischen christlichen Schriftsteller der ersten Jahrhunderte*
GTA	Göttingen Theologische Arbeiten
HDG	Handbuch der Dogmengeschichte, hg. v. M. Schmaus, J. Geiselmann und H. Rahner, 1951ff
HNT	Handbuch zum Neuen Testament
HNT.E	Handbuch zum Neuen Testament. Ergänzungsband
HTR	*Harvard Theological Review*
HUCA	*Hebrew Union College Annnual*
JAC	*Jahrbuch für Antike und Christentum*
JBL	*Journal of Biblical Literature*
JE	Jewish Encyclopaedia
JEC	*Journal of Early Christian Studies*
JLW	*Jahrbuch für Liturgiewissenschaft*
JQR	*Jewish Quarterly Review*
JR	*Journal of Religion*
JSNT	*Journal for the Study of the New Testament*

JSOT	*Journal for the Study of the Old Testament*
JTS	*Journal of Theological Studies*
KAV	Kommentar zu den apostolischen Vätern
KlT	Kleine Texte für theologische und philologische Vor-lesungen und Übungen
KuD	Kerygma und Dogma
Leiturgia	*Leiturgia*. Hanbuch des evangelischen Gottesdienstes, 1954ff
LThK	Lexikon für Theologie und Kirche (2nd ed), M. Buchberger (ed.)
LQF	Liturgiewissenschaftliche Quellen und Forschungen
MGWJ	Monatsschrift für Geschichte und Wissenschaft des Judentums
NGG.PH	*Nachrichten von der Gesellschaft der Wissenschaften zu Göttingen. Philologisch-Historische Klasse*
NGSt	New Gospel Studies
NHC	*The New Schaff-Herzog Encyclopaedia of Religious Knowl-edge III. 1909*
NovTest	*Novum Testamentum*
NovTest.S	*Novum Testamentum* Supplements
NTA	Neutestamentliche Abhandlungen
NTS	*New Testament Studies*
ÖBS	Österreichische biblische Studien
OCA	Orientalia Christiana analecta
OrChr	*Oriens Christianus*
PETSE	Papers of the Estonian Theological Society in Exile
PFLUS	Publications de la Faculté des Lettres de l'Université de Strasbourg
PG	*Patrologia graeca*, J. Migne (ed.)
PL	*Patrologia latina*, J. Migne (ed.)
PoTH	Le point theologique
RAC	*Reallexikon für Antike und Christentum*, Th. Klauser (ed.)
RadRel	*Radical Religion*
RB	*Revue biblique*
RDC	*Revue de droit canonique*
RE	*Realencyklopädie für protestantische Theologie und Kirche (3d ed. 1896 to 1913)*, J. Herzog (ed.)
RechSR	*Recherches de science religieuse*
REJ	*Revue des Études Juives*
RGG	Die Religion in Geschichte und Gegenwart
RHPhR	*Revue d'Histoire et de Philosophie Religieuses*
RHR	*Revue de l'histoire des religions*
RivAc	*Rivista di archeologia cristiana*
RQ	*Römische Quartalschrift für christliche Altertumskunde und für Kirchengeschichte*
RSR	*Religious Studies Review*

SANT	Studien zum Alten und Neuen Testament
SBFA	Studium Biblicum Fransicanorum Liber Annus
SC	Sources chrétienne
ScrCop	Scriptores coptici
SecCent	*Second Century*
SGKA	Studien zur Geschichte und Kultur des Altertums
SNTSMS	Society for New Testament Studies - Monograph Series
SQS	Sammlung augewählter kirchen- und dogmengeschichtlicher Quellenschriften
StAW	Studienhefte zur Altertumswissenschaft
StBTh	Studies in Biblical Theology
StLiturg	*Studia Liturgica*
StPatr	*Studia patristica*
SUC	Schriften des Urchristentums
TDNT	ed. Kittel, trns. G. W. Bromiley. Grand Rapids: Eerdmans, 1964.
ThB	Theologische Bücherei
Theol	*Theology*
TheolGl	Theologie und Glaube
ThH	Théologie historique
ThJ	*Theologische Jahrbücher*
ThLZ	*Theologische Literaturzeitung*
ThQ	*Theologische Quartalschrift*
ThR	*Theologische Rundschau*
ThSt	*Theological Studies*
ThW	*Theologisches Wörterbuch zum Neuen Testament*, G. Kittel & G. Friedrich (eds.)
ThQ	*Theologische Quartalschrift*
TRE	*Theologisches Realenzyklopädie*, Berlin 1976ff
TSAJ	Texte und Studien zum Antiken Judentum
TU	Texte und Untersuchungen zur Geschichte der altchristlichen Literatur
TZ	*Theologische Zeitschrift*
VetChr	*Vetera christianum*
VigChr	*Vigiliae christianae*
WdF	Wege der Forschung
WMANT	Wissenschaftliche Monographien zum Alten und Neuen Testament
WSt	*Wiener Studien*
WUNT	Wissenschaftliche Untersuchungen zum Neuen Testament
ZKG	*Zeitschrift für Kirchengeschichte*
ZNW	*Zeitschrift für neutestamentliche Wissenschaft und die Kunde der älteren Kirche*
ZThK	*Zeitschrift für Theologie und Kirche*

THE DIDACHE IN MODERN RESEARCH: AN OVERVIEW

JONATHAN A. DRAPER
Pietermaritzburg

1. The Text

In 1873 Archbishop Philotheos Bryennios, metropolitan of Nicomedia, discovered a manuscript in the library of the patriarch of Jerusalem at Constantinople, which contained a number of texts. The first to be published by Bryennios was the First Epistle of Clement in 1875, but it was not until ten years after the discovery of the Jerusalem manuscript that he realized the significance of another of the ancient texts entitled ΔΙΔΑΧΗ ΤΩΝ ΔΩΔΕΚΑ ΑΠΟΣΤΟΛΩΝ, which he published in 1883.[1] A facsimile of the Jerusalem text was printed by J.R. Harris in his commentary,[2] but there is essentially nothing to add to or subtract from the transcription of Bryennios. It is a clear and accurate, albeit relatively late, copy made by a scribe and dated precisely to 1056 C.E.

At first the reliability of the text, which was accepted by Adolf von Harnack[3] in his more accessible and hugely influential edition of the *Didache*, published within a year of the edition of Bryennios, remained unquestioned. Gradually, however, a body of direct textual evidence accumulated which led to a change in this perspective. A substantial portion of an Ethiopian version, containing 11:3-13:7 and 8:1-2, was found preserved in the Ethiopic Church Order published by G. Horner in 1904.[4] A fragment of the Greek text, containing 1:3b-4a and 4:7b-3:2a, was discovered among the Oxyrhynchus Papyri and published in 1922.[5] A Coptic version, containing 10:3b-12:2, was published by G. Horner in 1924,[6] substantially corrected by C. Schmidt,[7] and again corrected by L.-Th. Lefort.[8] A collation of a supposed

---

[1] Bryennios, P. Διδαχὴ τῶν δώδεκα ἀποστόλων (Constantinople: S. I. Boutura, 1883).

[2] *The Teaching of the Apostles* (London: Clay / Baltimore: John Hopkins University Press, 1887).

[3] A. von Harnack, *Die Lehre der zwölf Apostel* (Leipzig: Hinrichse, 1884 [TU 2,1-2]) p. 13.

[4] *The Statutes of the Apostles or Canones Ecclesiastici* (London: Williams & Norgate, 1904).

[5] B.-P. Grenfell & A. S. Hunt, *The Oxyrhynchus Papyri* 15 (London: Egyptian Exploration Society, 1922) p. 14.

[6] "A New Fragment of the Didache in Coptic", *JTS* 25 (1924) pp. 225-231.

[7] "Das koptische Didache-Fragment dere British Museum", *ZNW* 24 (1925) pp. 81-99.

[8] *Les Pères apostoliques en copte* I (Louvain: Durbecq, 1952 [CSCO 135-136, ScrCop 17-18]) pp. ix-xi.

Georgian version was published by G. Péradzé in 1932,[9] but has never been verified and must be discounted from text critical analysis. The text is also largely preserved in the *Apostolic Constitutions* VII.1-32.

Besides these direct textual sources, there is the indirect evidence of the text of the Two Ways in a number of different recensions. *Barnabas* was seen alternatively as a source for the *Didache* or as dependent on it. The Latin text of the *Doctrina apostolorum* was first published in its entirety by J. Schlecht in 1901.[10] There was considerable debate about whether it constituted an abbreviation of the *Didache* or its source. The *Apostolic Church Order* was available already in the edition of O. von Gebhardt in 1884.[11] In 1903, T. Schermann published the text of the *Epitome*.[12]

However, it was not until the study of E. Peterson was published in 1959,[13] that the reliability of the Jerusalem text was substantially questioned. Peterson begins with the assumption that the text of the Jerusalem manuscript is a corrupt Novatian recension and that the text of the Coptic version and indeed of the *Apostolic Constitution* is more reliable. His suspicion has been echoed by J.-P. Audet.[14] Both Peterson and Audet make substantial changes to the text in the light of their suspicions.

Audet has allowed his suspicion of the Jerusalem text and his theories of the development of the *Didache* to strongly influence the critical text in his commentary. For instance, he omits ταῦτα πάντα προειπόντες in 7:1 in favour of βαπτίσατε in the *Apostolic Constitutions*, which changes the whole perspective of the text. He also inserts various styles of brackets to indicate supposed subtractions and additions at various stages of the history of the text's development. K. Wengst[15] has also taken up this suspicion about the value of the Jerusalem manuscript into his

---

[9] "Die "Lehre der zwölf Apostel" in der georgischen Überlieferung", *ZNW* 31 (1932) pp. 111-116.

[10] *Doctrina XII Apostolorum, die Apostellehre in der Liturgie der katholischen Kirche* (Freiburg im Breisgau: Herder, 1901).

[11] "Ein übersehenes Fragment der Didache in alter lateiner Übersetzung" in A. von Harnack, *Die Lehre* (Leipzig: Hinrich, 1884 [TU 2]) pp. 275-286.

[12] *Eine Elfapostelmoral oder die Christliche Rezension der "beiden Wege"* (München: Lentner, 1903 [SGKA.E 3]).

[13] "Über einige Probleme der Didache-Überlieferung", *RivAC* 27 (1951) pp. 37-68, also in *Frühkirche, Judentum und Gnosis: Studien und Untersuchungen* (Rome: Herder, 1959) pp. 146-182.

[14] *La Didachè. Instructions des Apôtres* (Paris: Gabalda, 1958 [ÉBib]) pp. 52-78.

[15] *Didache (Apostellehre), Barnabasbrief, Zweiter Klemensbrief, Schrift an Diognet* (Darmstadt: Wissenschaftliche Buchgesellschaft, 1984 [SUC 2]). See especially his remarks on p. 6.

critical edition of the text. In particular, he has excluded the gospel section (1:3b-2:1), included the thanksgiving prayer for the myrrh (10:8) and completed the ending of the apocalypse from the witness of the *Apostolic Constitutions* (16:8). He has also made a large number of other changes from the Jerusalem text. His work has been essentially affirmed recently by B. Dehandschutter.[16]

Most modern critics have preferred to take a more moderate position, accepting the fundamental integrity of the Jerusalem manuscript in general, but testing it in particular instances. This is the line taken, for instance, by A. Vööbus,[17] A. Tuilier,[18] K. Niederwimmer,[19] and G. Schöllgen[20] Caution about the text remains and each case must be judged on its merits. The critical text produced by Tuilier in the *Sources Chretiennes* edition is a particular achievement, providing a clear, cautious and usable text with full notes on the variants.[21] Schöllgen has paid Tuilier the complement of adopting his text in its entirety in his commentary.[22]

C. N. Jefford and S. J. Patterson[23] have recently argued that the Coptic version is from a roll made for liturgical use and indicates an earlier recension than the Jerusalem text, which ended at 12:2a. However, their conclusions have been challenged in a thorough analysis of the Coptic version by F. S. Jones and P. A. Mirecki.[24] They argue that this text is from a double leaf not a roll, and consitutes a limited scribal exercise by an experienced scribe. The Coptic text seems to be reasonably accurate and indicates that it should be taken seriously as a witness alongside the Jerusalem text. Few today share the confidence of Peterson in the

---

[16] "The Text of the *Didache*: Some Comments on the Edition of Klaus Wengst", in C. N. Jefford (ed.), *The Didache in Context: Essays on its Text, History and Transmission* (Leiden: Brill, 1995) pp. 37-46.

[17] *Liturgical Traditions in the Didache* (Stockholm: Estonian Theological Society in Exile, 1968 [PETSE 16]) pp. 29-33.

[18] W. Rordorf & A. Tuilier, *La doctrine des Douze Apôtres (Didachè)* (Paris: Les Éditions du Cerf, 1978 [SC 248]) pp. 102-110.

[19] *Die Didache* (Göttingen: Vandenhoeck & Ruprecht, 1989 [KAV 1]) pp. 35-36.

[20] *Didache—Zwölf-Apostel-Lehre. Einleitung, Übersetzung und Kommentar* (Freiburg: Herder, 1991 [FC 1]) pp. 85-94.

[21] See Tuilier's introduction in *La Doctrine*, pp. 102-128; cf. "Une nouvelle édition de la Didachè (Problèmes de méthode et de critique textuelle)" in *Studia Patristica* 15 (Berlin: Adademie-Verlag, 1984 [TU 128]) pp. 31-36.

[22] *Didache Zwölf-Apostel-Lehre*, p. 86.

[23] "A Note on *Didache* 12.2a (Coptic)", *SecCent* 7 (1989-1990) pp. 65-75. Cf. also Patterson's recent article, "*Didache* 11-13: The Legacy of Radical Itinerancy in Early Christianity" in *Didache in Context*, pp. 313-329, esp. 319-324.

[24] "Considerations on the Coptic Papyrus of the *Didache* (British Library Oriental Manuscript 9271)" in *Didache in Context*, pp. 47-87.

reliability of the fourth century *Apostolic Constitutions*, unless it is confirmed by the reading of other witnesses.

2. The Titles

The work carries two titles: a shorter title (διδαχὴ τῶν ἀποστόλων) and a longer title (διδαχὴ κυρίου διὰ τῶν δώδεκα ἀποστόλων τοῖς ἔθνεσιν). Bryennios[25] and Harnack[26] accepted the longer title as the older and original title of the work, while the shorter title was an abbreviation. For Bryennios it indicated the nature of the *Didache* as catechesis of the Jewish Christian Church. Harnack, on the other hand, saw it as addressed to pagans newly converted to Christianity. This represented the initial concensus.

However, J.-P. Audet notes that ancient citations of the *Didache* fluctuate between the singular and plural of διδαχὴ / διδαχαί. The Coptic version of 11:2 also has the plural, and Audet argues that this stood in an original short title διδαχαὶ τῶν ἀποστολῶν.[27] The adjective "twelve", missing in many citations, was seen as a later addition. This for him indicated the nature of the work as a collection of instructions provided by itinerant evangelists / apostles of the primitive church. The long title, on the other hand, refers to the Jewish Two Ways teaching. Rordorf agrees with this assessment, adding the refinement that the reference to the κυρίου must have been added at the same time as 1:3b-2:1.[28] Wengst goes so far as to banish the long title altogether to the footnotes.[29] For Niederwimmer,[30] neither title stood in the original text; for him, as for Schöllgen,[31] the short title originated as a title for the Two Ways and thus came to be attached to the *Didache*, while the longer title is a later development.

3. The Early Years of Research

Bryennios's thorough notes and discussion of the text set the agenda for early research, noting that it was taken up in the

---

[25] Διδαχὴ, p. 3.

[26] *Die Lehre: Prolegomena*, pp. 24-37; cf. R. Knopf, *Die Lehre der zwölf Apostel; Die zwei Clemensbriefe* (Tübingen: Mohr, 1920 [HNT.E 1]) p. 3.

[27] *La Didachè*, pp. 91-103. The original work had no title, he argues, but came to be referred to in this way.

[28] *La Doctrine*, pp. 13-17.

[29] *Didache (Apostellehre)*, p. 66.

[30] *Die Didache*, pp. 81-82; cf. P. Vielhauer, *Geschichte der urchristlichen Literatur. Einleitung in das Neue Testament, die Apokryphen und die Apostolischen Väter* (Berlin: de Gruyter, 1975) pp. 722-725.

[31] *Didache Zwölf-Apostel-Lehre*, pp. 25-26.

Apostolic Constitutions and a number of other ancient Christian texts. He also argued that the *Didache* itself utilized the Two Ways material from *Barnabas* and quoted from the *Shepherd* of Hermas, and for this reason dates the work between 120 and 160 C.E. He sees it as a Jewish Christian work designed for the instruction of catechumens.

Harnack's commentary has been so central in the subsequent history of research, that it is important to set out his perspective in some detail. He also initially accepted the supposed dependence of the *Didache* on *Barnabas* and the *Shepherd* as a starting point for dating the text. Nevertheless, he recognized its early date and importance for the study of the Christian origins. He rather rashly celebrated it as providing clear and uncontroversial evidence for the life of the early Church, in contrast to the problematic nature of most early sources:

> Um so erfreulicher ist es, dass wir in der nun publicierten διδαχή eine Quelle erhalten haben, die nicht neue Trümmerstücke zu den alten fügt, sondern die sich formell und materiell aufs engste an den Ausschnitt der Überlieferung anfügt, der für uns der hellste und zugleich der wichtigste ist.[32]

Unfortunately, it was not to be the case. The *Didache* has proved to be one of the most enigmatic and contested of early Christian writings, and Harnack himself contributed to the controversy in no small manner by seeing in this text the key to settling the quarrel between the Reformation and the Roman Catholic Church on the question of church order.

The *Didache* enabled Harnack to put forward a threefold order of apostles, prophets and teachers against the Catholic order of bishops, priests and deacons as the earliest order of ministry. The *Didache*, he argues on the basis of 4:1, knew only one class of dignitaries in the community, namely those who were ministers of the gospel, and this vindicated Article V of the Augsburg Confession.[33] The Catholic order is the result of a two hundred year development, in which the "service of the Word" degenerated into the ministry of "Priester und Hierarchen":

> Der Katholicismus hat Recht, wenn er behauptet, dass alle wesentlichen Elemente seiner Kirchenordnung in der apostolischen Zeit vorgebildet seien, aber eine Fiktion ist es, wenn er daran fest hält, dass in der Kirche ursprünglich nur die selbständige, nicht von Menschen declarirte Würde der λαλοῦντες τὸν λόγον δοῦ θεοῦ, der διακονία τοῦ λόγου gegolten hat, und dass alle übrigen Einrichtungen, die getroffen wurden, die Constitution der Kirche, sofern sie eine ἐκκλησία τοῦ θεοῦ ist, nicht berühren.[34]

---

[32] *Did Lehre: Prologommena*, p. 38.
[33] *Ibid.*, pp. 94f.
[34] *Ibid.*, p. 157.

Harnack used the *Didache* as the fulcrum of his account of the development of the early Church in his major work, *Die Mission und Ausbreitung des Christentums in den ersten drei Jahrhunderten*.[35] The oldest Church order consisted of the threefold ministry of apostles (who were engaged in the *kerygma*) and prophets and teachers (who were engaged in teaching or *didache*). In the face of a decline and growing corruption in these ministries, the bishops and deacons originated secondarily within the local communities as a settled order of ministry. In other words, after the publication of Harnack's commentary the newly discovered *Didache* was assured a place at the forefront of controversy about the nature of the early Church.

The date of the work clearly has a major import on the relevance and significance of the information it contains and naturally has also been an important feature of debate. Harnack's commentary dates it on the basis, on the one hand, of its use as authoritative text in Clement of Alexandria. A reasonable time lapse from its composition to its use by Clement suggests 165 C.E. as a *terminus ad quem*, and, on the other hand, on the basis of its supposed dependence on *Barnabas* and the *Shepherd of Hermas*, works whose own dating is disputed, but suggest a *terminus a quem* of around 135 C.E.

The primitive conditions of community organization are, he argues, unthinkable at such a late date in Asia Minor or Syria, so that he is led to posit a rural backwater in Egypt, where older traditions clung stubbornly on against the trend towards Catholicization. This corresponds with the fact that external attestations of the use of the text point overwhelmingly towards Egypt. Internal features confirm this dating in his opinion, especially the lack of a dogmatic *regula fidei* and of any trace of the extensive schisms (particularly Marcion and Montanism) which characterized the end of the second century. The text still envisages Christianity as a universal spiritual unity rather than a Church with a common political organization of particular local congregations.

In terms of its nature, Harnack sees the *Didache* as a collection of ethical teaching and ordinances which were held to derive from the apostles, not as authors of the text but as tradents of its content. Thus the longer title of the work is the more ancient and accurately describes its nature. It was thus not a literary fraud but

---

[35] First published in 1902. For the relevant section, see the English translation, *The Mission and Expansion of Christianity in the First Three Centuries* (London: William & Norgate, 1908) pp. 319-368.

as particular instruction for Gentile Christians, a short manual for
Christians by which they can direct their general life-style. The
confession of faith is not found in dogmatic teaching, but is
embedded in the cultic worship of the community. The polemic
against the hypocrites in chapter 8 is regarded as confirmation that
this is a Gentile Christian work heralding the final rejection of any
commerce with Jews.

Harnack is particularly impressed by the solidarity of scattered Christian communities, in terms of their hospitality and self-
sacrifice. Everyone who comes to a community in the name of the
Lord must be received, without the necessity of letters of com-
mendation, simply the requirement that no Christian should live
without work. Christians still regard themselves as mere
sojourners on earth, so that wandering brothers are not abnormal
but representative. This is a clear indication for Harnack that the
Didache belongs to the period of "Christianity" and not to the
period of the "Church"—an observation heavy with value judgment and connected to the Catholic—Protestant debate in
Germany.

Despite his relegation of the *Didache* to the mid second
century, Harnack is also clear that much depends on the context of
the writing. He is only able to argue for 140-165 C.E. on the basis
of a backward community in rural Egypt. The ecclesiological conditions portrayed by the text would, he concedes, be inconceivable
at such a late date in Asia Minor or Syria. Harnack's position on
the date and origin of the *Didache* has been enormously influential
and was substantially affirmed by two other early critics of the
text, namely Adam Krawutzcky[36] and Adolf Hilgenfeld.[37]

A quite different position was taken in the first French commentary by P. Sabatier.[38] Sabatier argued from internal evidence
that the *Didache* originated in the mid first century C.E. in Syria.
He argued that the undeveloped baptismal and eucharistic
liturgies, the emphasis on charismatic leadership, the strong
Jewish influence and the eschatological immediacy, could only be
possible in the earliest stage of the development of the church.

Whereas Harnack viewed the *Didache* as deriving from a
Gentile Christian community, which had broken completely from
its Jewish roots, and read especially ch. 8 in this light, a majority

---

[36] A. Krawutzcky, "Über die sogenannte Zwölfapostellehre, ihre
hauptsächlichsten Quellen und ihre erste Ausnahme", *TQ* 4 (1884) pp. 547-606. His
article provides the variation that the Jesus tradition was derived from the lost
Gospel of the Hebrews.

[37] A. Hilgenfeld, *Novum Testamentum extra canonem receptum, Evangeliorum*
4,2 (Leipzig: Weigel, 1884) pp. 88-94.

[38] ΔΙΔΑΧΗ ΤΩΝ ΙΒ´ ΑΠΟΣΤΟΛΩΝ: *La Didaché ou l'Ensignement des douze
apôtres* (Paris: Noblet, 1885).

of early critics followed Bryennios in identifying it as the product of a Jewish Christian community. Most English critics in the years immediately following the publication of the *Didache*, with the notable exception of C. Bigg,[39] saw in it a Jewish Christian document from the first century, among them Bishop J. Wordsworth,[40] F. W. Farrar,[41] J.R. Harris,[42] H. de Romestin,[43] and Canon Spence.[44] All argue for a Jewish Christian origin around the end of the first century, as does J. B. Lightfoot in his landmark collection of the Apostolic Fathers.[45] The German scholar F. X. Funk in a commentary published in 1887 took a similar position, arguing for a first century composition in Egypt.[46]

Charles Taylor[47] read the text consistently against the background of the Talmud and found extensive similarities, concluding

---

[39] C. Bigg, *The Doctrine of the Twelve Apostles* (London: SPCK, 1898). Who argues that it was a romance from the fourth century. His position did not find much support, and indeed it was rejected by A. J. Maclean, who produced the second edition of his work in 1922.

[40] "Christian Life, Ritual, and Discipline at the Close of the First Century" in *The Guardian* 39/1998 (1884) pp. 422-423. Wordsworth sees in it a Jewish Christian writing of the last years of the first or early years of the second century from Egypt. This essay, together with the essays by Farrar, Harris and Taylor which follow have been conveniently reprinted by B. S. Walters, *Didachè (ΔΙΔΑΧΗ ΤΩΝ ΔΩΔΕΚΑ ΑΠΟΣΤΟΛΩΝ) The Unknown Teaching of the Twelve Apostles* (San Jose: Bibliographics, 1991).

[41] Farrar published two widely read critical articles and a translation of the text in 1884: "The 'Teaching of the Apostles' An Ancient Christian Treatise, Discovered and Edited by Philotheos Bryennios, Metropolitan of Nicomedia, 1883", *The Expositor* series 2, vol. 7 (1884) pp. 374-392; "The Bearing of the 'Teaching' on the Canon", *The Expositor* series 2, vol. 8 (1884) pp. 81-91; "The Teaching of the Lord by the Twelve Apostles to the Gentiles", *The Contemporary Review* 45 (1884) pp. 698-706. Farrar argues for 90-100 C.E. from Syria/Palestine.

[42] *Teaching of the Apostles*. In his article, "The Genuineness, Priority, Source and Value of 'The Teaching'" (*Journal of Christian Philosophy* [1885] reprinted in Walters, *Unknown Teaching*, pp. 115-144), Harris sees it as a Jewish Christian writing from Northern Syria, perhaps Antioch, from the beginning of the second century.

[43] *The Teaching of the Twelve Apostles*. ΔΙΔΑΧΗ ΤΩΝ ΔΩΔΕΚΑ ΑΠΟΣΤΟΛΩΝ *With Introduction, Translation, Notes and Illustrative Passages* (Oxford & London: Parker, 1884¹). De Romestin makes no suggestion for place of origin but argues for a date in the last quarter of the first century and no later than the first quarter of the second.

[44] *The Teaching of the Twelve Apostles*. Διδαχὴ τῶν δώδεκα Ἀποστόλων. *A Translation with Notes; And Excursus (I. to IX.) Illustrative of the "Teaching;" and the Greek Text* (London: Nisbet, 1885). Spence somewhat fancifully argues for a Jewish Christian origin in Pella under Symeon, the successor of James, about 80-90 C.E., though note the later thoughts of A. Adam below.

[45] *The Apostolic Fathers* (London: Macmillan, 1893) pp. 215-216.

[46] *Doctrina duodecim apostolorum* (Tübingen: Laupp, 1887).

[47] C. Taylor, *The Teaching of the Twelve Apostles* (Cambridge: Deighton Bell, 1886. The lectures were originally given originally in mid-1885. See also *An Essay on the Theology of the Didache* (Cambridge: Deighton Bell, 1889).

that it is "a genuine fragment of the earliest tradition of the church" from Palestine. He reverses Harnack's position on the sources of the *Didache*, arguing that it was used not only by *Barnabas* and the *Shepherd*, but also Justin Martyr's *Apologies*.[48] Harris provided a thorough-going analysis of patristic parallels to the text, together with further Jewish background material, and emphasized its early and widespread use. However, he argues for the integrity of the text and claims that, if a Jewish original lies behind it, then "this may very well have covered the same ground as the Teaching (Ethics, Baptism of proselytes, Passover, Day of Atonement, Signs of Messiah)".[49] Exploration of the Jewish roots of the *Didache* was taken still further by G. Salmon.[50]

Although Taylor and Harris argued for the Jewishness of the whole text, their argument was most convincing with respect to the Two Ways and succeeded in persuading Harnack that a Jewish source lay behind the Two Ways in both *Didache* and *Barnabas* although he continued to maintain that the former knew the latter.[51] Successive studies of the Two Ways[52] confirmed the independence of the Latin version of the Two Ways, which must have served as the source of both the *Didache* and *Barnabas*, although, as we shall see there was an attempt to view it as an abridgement of the former.

A full summary of the "torrent" of research into the problems of the *Didache* prior to 1900 is provided by A. Ehrhard.[53]

Beginning in 1903, Alfred Seeberg argued in a series of books [54] that the *Didache* was representative of the earliest Christian catechesis, which was taken over and appropriated by the earliest Church from Jewish traditions. G. Klein took this further in 1909 in an ambitious book seeking to trace the origins of Jewish propaganda literature and its appropriation by the earliest Christians.[55] He argues that the Latin text of the Two Ways pub-

---

[48] The question of the relation between Justin and the *Didache* remains an open one. Cf. M. A. Smith, "Did Justin Know the Didache?", *StPatr* 7 (1966) pp. 287-290.

[49] *Teaching of the Apostles*, p. 92.

[50] G. Salmon, *A Historical Introduction to the Study of the Books of the New Testament* (London: Murray, 1894)

[51] A. Harnack, *Die Apostellehre und die jüdischen Beiden Wege* (Leipzig: Hinrichse, 1886).

[52] L. E. Iselin, *Eine bisher unbekannte Version des ersten Teiles der "Apostellehre"* (Leipzig: Heusler, 1895 [TU 13,1b]); J. Schlecht, *Die Apostellehre in der Liturgie der katholischen Kirche* (Freiburg: Herder, 1901); L. Wohleb, *Die lateinische Übersetzung der Didache* (Paderborn: Schöningh, 1913 [SGKA 7,1]).

[53] *Die Altchristliche Literatur und irhe Erforschung von 1884-1900 I: Die Vornicänische Literatur* (Freibourg im Breisgau: Herder, 1900), pp. 37-68.

[54] A. Seeberg, *Der Katechismus der Urchristenheit* (Leipzig: Deichert, 1903); *Die Beiden Wege und das Aposteldekret* (Leipzig: Deichert, 1906).

[55] G. Klein, *Der Älteste Christliche Katechismus und die Jüdische Propaganda-Literatur* (Berlin: Reimer, 1909).

lished by Schlecht had established the existence of an independent, pre-existent Jewish text, substantially in the form in which it occurs in *Didache* 1-6, including ch. 16 as its eschatological conclusion.[56] Klein saw the *Didache* as based on oral Jewish ethical and legal tradition explicating the Old Testament tradition of the way of righteousness and love.[57] He attempts to trace its development as Jewish propaganda literature directed towards the Gentile God-fearers, containing the legal principles applicable to all human beings.[58]

By 1920 it seemed that a scholarly consensus had emerged, which is well-represented by Rudolf Knopf in his edition of the text for the *Handbuch zum Neuen Testament*.[59] The first part of the *Didache* was not taken from *Barnabas* and *Hermas*, but from a common source in a Jewish proselyte catechism, which contained chs. 1-6 without 1:3-2:1, and probably also most of ch. 16 as an eschatological conclusion. While many of the community relations point to an early age, others point to a post-Apostolic age, particularly the decline of the charismatic ministry and the emergence of the church spread throughout the world. Hence a date between 90 and 150 C.E. is all that can be stated with confidence. Contrary to Harnack, Knopf argues that it could not have originated in Egypt because of the mention of mountains (9:4), the close, albeit conflictual, relationship with Judaism, and the absence of presbyters. He allocates it instead to a rural backwater in Syria-Palestine.[60]

4. *Didache as a Pious Fiction*

However, 1920 also saw the publication of J. A. Robinson's Donnellan Lectures on the relationship between *Barnabas*, *Hermas* and the *Didache*, which reshaped scholarly opinion on the text for decades.[61] Robinson argued that the author of the *Didache* was merely imaginatively reconstructing what he considered to

---

[56] *Ibid.*, p. 157. See below for a discussion of ch. 16 as an eschatological warning to conclude the Two Ways.

[57] *Ibid.*, p. 160.

[58] Klein identifies this with the *Derech Eretz, Ibid.*, pp. 243f.

[59] *Die Lehre der Zwölf Apostel-Zwei Clemensbriefe* (Tübingen: Mohr, 1920 [HNT.E 1]).

[60] *Ibid.*, pp. 2-3.

[61] J. A. Robinson, *Barnabas, Hermas and the Didache: Being the Donnellan Lectures Delivered before the University of Dublin in 1920* (London: SPCK, 1920). Robinson builds on an earlier article on the second half of the *Didache* published much earlier: "The Problem of the Didache", *JTS* 13 (1912) pp. 339-356. He defended his thesis again in "The Epistle of Barnabas and the Didache", *JTS* 35 (1934) pp. 113-146, 225-248.

have been "the teaching of the Lord through the Twelve Apostles to the Gentiles", derived from Matthew 28:20. Consequently it has little historical value for the reconstruction of the life of the early church. The Two Ways section is founded on *Barnabas*, the original author of the Two Ways, interpolated from Matthew, who is conflated with Luke to disguise the borrowing. Use is also made by the Didachist of *Mandate* 2 of the *Shepherd* of Hermas. At every point, the Didachist is held to have garbled, misunderstood, obscured or grossly distorted the material he borrowed. Final proof of the use of *Barnabas* is that ch. 16 uses *Barnabas* 4:9, which is outside the Two Ways teaching.[62] The Latin *De Doctrina Apostolorum* is an abbreviation of the *Didache* which has made further use of *Barnabas* and the *Shepherd* to supplement the *Didache*. Robinson dismisses the supposed use of the *Didache* by Clement of Alexandria and others as "scripture" by seeing both dependent on a third source. With these impediments to a late dating removed, he is able to view it as a third century document intending to construct an "apostolic monument".[63]

Robinson's hypothesis was taken a step forward by the substantial Yale thesis of James Muilenburg in 1927.[64] Muilenburg's careful literary analysis argued that the two parts of *Barnabas*, namely 1-17 and 18-21, shared the same literary and stylistic traits and undoubtedly came from the same author.[65] *Didache*, on the other hand, is a compilation from different sources. Since *Barnabas* also provides the "clearer and more original form", whereas the *Didache* provides a more logical, improved form, it follows that *Barnabas* is simply the source for the Two Ways in the *Didache*. In addition, the latter is held to have used material found scattered throughout the epistle. Even the use of the *Didache* in Clement of Alexandria is disputed and the writing again relegated to the end of the second century.[66] This position was supported also by the highly respected patristic scholar R. H. Connolly, who added the refinement that the *Didache* was a Montanist text.[67] The most extreme representative of this growing

---

[62] *Barnabas, Hermas and the Didache*, pp. 67f.

[63] *Ibid.*, p. 82.

[64] J. Muilenburg, *The Literary Relations of the Epistle of Barnabas and the Teaching of the Twelve Apostles* (Marburg, 1929).

[65] *Ibid.*, p. 140.

[66] *Ibid.*, pp. 165-168.

[67] R. H. Connolly, "The Use of the Didache in the Didascalia", *JTS* 24 (1923) pp. 147-157; "The Didache in Relation to the Epistle of Barnabas", *JTS* 33 (1932) pp. 327-353; "Agape and eucharist in the Didache", *DRev* 55 (1937) pp. 447ff; "Canon Streeter on the Didache", *JTS* 38 (1937) pp. 364ff; "The Didache and Montanism", *DRev* 55 (1937) pp. 339-347. The idea that the *Didache* represented a Montanist theological position was mooted already by Hilgenfeld, Bonet Maury and J. R. Harris (see Ehrhard, *Altchristliche Literatur*, p. 61).

consensus among English scholars that the writing was a late and archaizing fiction designed to support the Montanist heresy was F. E. Vokes,[68] although he later modified and eventually retracted this position.[69] Part at least of this determined assault on the authenticity of the *Didache* by these Anglican High Churchmen may relate to the use of its evidence to support a Protestant ecclesiology by Harnack, which we have already described. This is the conclusion of their colleague, C. H. Turner, who takes a different position and emphasizes the Jewish Christian origin of the work. Commenting in 1931 on the position of Bigg and Robinson, he writes:

> Something odd there must be about the *Didache* which negatived, in the minds of these two distinguished scholars, the *prima facie* impression of a very primitive date: but in fact we need not look further than its surroundings for the explanation. It has none of the characteristics of the great Church at the end of the first century: it is Jewish Christian through and through.

There was, however, a vigorous opposition to this demotion of the *Didache* from its position of importance in the reconstruction of the development of early Christianity. In 1929 the eminent source critic, B. H. Streeter, contrasted the "high" Alexandrian Christology of *Barnabas* with the primitive Christology of the *Didache*.[70] He argues for echoes of the text in the letters of Ignatius, for clear dependence on Matthew. He emphasizes the reference to "mountains" in the eucharistic prayers as evidence against Egypt. Streeter also rejects the argument originating with Harnack that the *Didache* is from an isolated rural area, by pointing to its enormous and widespread influence and authority in the early centuries. He posits an origin about 100 C.E. in Syria and probably Antioch.[71] Others continuing to maintain an early date for the work were J. V. Bartlet,[72] J. M. Creed[73] and T. Klauser.[74]

---

[68] F. E. Vokes, *The Riddle of the Didache* (London: SPCK, 1938).

[69] "The Didache Re-examined", *Theol* 58 (1955) pp. 12-16; "The Didache and the Canon of the New Testament" in *Studia Evangelica* 3 (Berlin: Akademie-Verlag, 1964 [TU 88]) pp. 427-436; "The Didache—Still debated", *ChQR* 3 (1970) pp. 58f.

[70] B. H. Streeter, "Origin and Date of the 'Didache'" in *The Primitive Church* (London: Macmillan, 1929) pp. 279-287; "The Much Belaboured Didache", *JTS* 37 (1936) pp. 369-374.

[71] "Origin", p. 286.

[72] J. V. Bartlet, "The Didache Reconsidered", *JTS* 22 (1921) pp. 239-249.

[73] J. M. Creed, "The Didache", *JTS* 39 (1938) pp. 370-287.

[74] T. Klauser, "Taufet in Lebendigem Wasser! Zum religions- und kulturgeschichtlichen Verständnis von Didache 7,1-3" in *Pisciculi. Studien zur Religion und Kultur des Altertums (Fst. F. J. Dölger)*, ed. T. Klauser & Rükker (Münster: Aschendorff, 1939) pp. 157-164. Also in *Gesammelte Arbeiten zur Liturgiegeschichte, Kirchengeschichte und Christlichen Archäologie*, ed. E. Dassmann

However, Robinson, Muilenburg, Connolly and Vokes had spread sufficient doubt about the historical reliability of the *Didache* that it dropped off the scholarly agenda. The question of the Two Ways in *Barnabas* and the *Didache* seemed most easily solved by a straightforward dependence of the latter on the former.

5. The Dead Sea Scrolls and the Two Ways

The discovery of the Dead Sea Scrolls in 1948 has had a profound impact on many areas of early Christian studies. The *Didache* is no exception. The concrete evidence they provide for at least one form of Jewish life and thought in the first century has provided a benchmark against which other material from the period can be measured.

The Canadian scholar Jean-Paul Audet was the first to recognize the significance of the Scrolls for the debate about the origin of the Two Ways. His ground-breaking essay, "Affinités littéraires et doctrinales du "Manuel de Discipline"",[75] established beyond dispute that the *Doctrina apostolorum* could not be an abbreviation of the *Didache* and that *Barnabas* could not be the author of the Two Ways material. This changed the nature of the debate and laid the foundation for the modern study of the *Didache*. It is for this reason that the essay is included in this collection.

Audet points out that the question of the literary unity of *Barnabas* is not the same as the question of the source of the Two Ways. He accepts that Robinson and his followers have proved the literary unity of the epistle, but points out that there is nevertheless a tell-tale transition between the second person plural used in chapters 1-18 and 21, where the author is clearly at work, and the second person singular in 19-20 in the Two Ways material. Further, he points to the markedly Jewish character of the material in the *Didache*, which is even stronger in the Latin *Doctrina apostolorum*, which in many points is closer to the *Manual of Discipline* from Qumran than it is to the *Didache*, although both share a common literary framework with the *Manual*. This rules out the possibility that the *Doctrina* is a translation of the *Didache*, and indicates that it is an independent source.

Audet has convinced most scholars that the *Didache* was not dependent on *Barnabas* but on a source common to both, which is best represented by the *Doctrina apostolorum*. Few today would

---

(Münster in Westfalen: Aschendorff, 1974 [JAC.E 3]) pp. 177-183.

[75] "Affinités littéraires et doctrinales du "Manuel de Discipline"", *RB* 59 (1952) pp. 219-238.

go so far as to accept his proposition of a literary dependence of the Christian Two Ways tradition on the *Manual of Discipline*. However, the link between the *Manual of Discipline* and the Two Ways tradition has been further explored by K. Baltzer[76], building on the work of A. Vögtle[77] and S. Wibbing[78] on the lists of virtues and vices in the New Testament. Baltzer tries, not entirely successfully, to identify an ancient Covenant formula beneath the various forms of the Two Ways teaching. While his thesis has not been convincing in establishing the precise formal elements, he is undoubtedly right in seeing the background of the Two Ways in covenantal theology and practice. E. Kamlah[79] examines the form of the Two Ways teaching in its various sources to demonstrate the way in which the covenantal material has been influenced by Iranian dualism to a greater or lesser extent. The dualistic element is strong in the *Manual of Discipline*, *Barnabas* and *Hermas*, but not in the *Didache*.

M. J. Suggs[80] seeks to trace a progressive development in the Two Ways tradition, from the advanced dualism of the Qumran Literature through the more ethical and individualistic *Testament of the Twelve Patriarchs* and *Barnabas* to the purely ethical usage in the *Didache*, which he regards as standing at the end of the process. He sees the *Sitz im Leben* of the Two Ways form in the teaching of catechumens to prepare them for initiation into the community. Its function is to emphasize group exclusiveness and solidarity against non-members. Hence, the removal of the dualistic elements of the tradition in the *Didache* represents a retreat from the more sectarian nature seen in the other representatives of the tradition, a sign of a later provenance according to Suggs.

Willy Rordorf's fine study of the Two Ways tradition,[81] which is also included in this volume, was published in the same year as that of Suggs. Rordorf has cautioned against a too simplistic solution to the problem of the different forms of the

---

[76] K. Baltzer, *Das Bundesformular* (Neukirchen: Neukirchner Verlag, 1960 [WMANT 4]).

[77] A. Vögtle, *Die Tugend- und Lasterkataloge im Neuen Testament* (Münster: Aschendorff, 1936).

[78] S. Wibbing, *Die Tugend-und Lasterkataloge im Neuen Testament und ihre Traditionsgeschichte unter besonderer Berücksichtigung der Qumran-Texte* (Berlin: de Gruyter, 1959 [BZNW 25]).

[79] E. Kamlah, *Die Form der katalogischen Paränese im Neuen Testament* (Tübingen: Mohr, 1964 [WUNT 7]).

[80] "The Christian Two Ways Tradition: Its Antiquity, Form, and Function" in D. E. Aune (ed.), *Studies in New Testament and Early Christian Literature: Essays in Honor of Allen P. Wikgren* (Leiden: Brill, 1972 [NovTestSupp 33]) pp. 60-74.

[81] "Un chapitre d'éthique judéo-chretienne. Les deux voies", *RSR* 60 (1972) pp. 109-128.

Two Ways. For instance, the *Manual of Discipline* is directed by Jews to other Jews, whereas the *Didache* is directed towards Gentiles. Moreover, it is not clear that the Two Ways of the *Didache* is any closer to the Two Ways of the *Manual of Discipline* than to the same tradition found in Rabbinic writings. Using Kamlah, he argues that the dualistic and non-dualistic traditions existed side by side in late Judaism and were both inherited by early Christianity. In the early centuries, the non-dualistic form was used for catechesis given to proselytes to Judaism and subsequently in pre-baptismal catechesis given to Christian converts from paganism. Rordorf also traces the subsequent history of the Two Ways tradition in Christian asceticism through to the Rule of Saint Benedict. This study has been taken further in a recent study by C. Davies.[82]

My own detailed comparison of the Two Ways material in the *Didache* with the *Manual of Discipline*[83] has uncovered a number of interesting parallels in the lists of virtues and vices, e.g. between 3:7-10 and 1QS 4:2-8[84] and between 5:1 and 1QS 4:9-11,[85] but never at points where characteristic emphases of the Scrolls emerge. Instead, in important respects, the *Didache* is closer to remnants of the Two Ways tradition found in the Rabbinic writings, as in links between 3:1-6 and the *Derek Eretz*, which reflects the five "fundamental laws" of the Noachide Precepts.[86] This link with the *Derek Eretz* has been persued further in a fine study by H. van de Sandt.[87] These points of contact between the *Didache* and Rabbinic writings have increasingly interested Jewish scholars, notably G. Alon[88] and D. Flusser,[89]

---

[82] "The *Didache* and Early Monasticism in the East and West", *Didache in Context*, pp. 352-367.

[83] *A Commentary on the Didache in the Light of the Dead Sea Scrolls and Related Documents* (Unpublished Cambridge PhD Dissertation, 1983).

[84] *Commentary*, pp. 76-80.

[85] *Commentary*, 116-120.

[86] *Commentary*, pp. 65-76.

[87] "Didache 3,1-6: A Transformation of an Existing Jewish Hortatory Pattern", *JSJ* 23 (1992) pp. 21-41.

[88] ההלכה שבתורת י"ב השליחים [דידאכי], in *Studies in Jewish History in the Times of the Second Temple, the Mishna and the Talmud* I (Tel Aviv: Hakibbutz Hameuchad, 1958) pp. 274-294.

[89] "The Two Ways", in *Jewish Sources in Early Christianity* (Tel Aviv: Sifriat Poalaim, 1979) pp. 232-252; "Paul's Jewish Christian Opponents in the Didache" in S. Shaked, D. Shulman & G. G. Stroumsa (eds.), *Gilgul: Essays on Transformation, Revolution and Permanence in the History of Religions: Dedicated to R. J. Zwi Werblowsky* (Leiden: Brill, 1987) pp. 71-90; "The Ten Commandments and the New Testament" in B. Segal (ed.), *The Ten Commandments in History and Tradition* (Jerusalem: Magnes, 1990) pp. 219-246; D. Flusser & S. Safrai, "Das Aposteldekret und die Noachistischen Gebote", *Wer Tora vermehrt mehrt Leben: Festgabe für Heinz Kremers zum 60. Geburtstag* (Neukirchen-Vluyn: Neukirchener-Verlag, 1986) pp. 173-192.

whose essays have been included in this volume. This is an exciting development for Patristic studies, and promises to unlock further resources for the understanding of early Christian literature. It seems that the early indications of a Jewish Christian background to the text, which had been eclipsed by the work of Robinson and his colleagues, are being vindicated by modern research into the Judaism of the first century C.E.

The work of Audet and Rordorf on the Two Ways tradition has succeeded in removing any possibility that the *Didache* is dependent on *Barnabas*. A major stumbling block in the path of research has been removed and it is no accident that this resulted in a flood of new commentaries on the text, not least by these two scholars themselves, attempting a major re-evaluation of the *Didache*. However, the question of the relationship between the *Didache* and *Barnabas* may not yet be closed. In a recent article[90] I have focussed on the question of the *Sitz im Leben* of the Two Ways teaching in pre-baptismal catechesis and asked whether the transformation of the tradition into post-baptismal gnosis may not have been polemical in origin. A further open question concerns the extent of the Two Ways tradition and whether ch. 16 originally formed its conclusion, as argued by several scholars.[91]

6. The Question of the Gospel Tradition

Once the possibility of a dependence of the *Didache* on *Barnabas* had been ruled out by the discovery of the Dead Sea Scrolls, the only other major possibility of sources to be found in the text remained the question of the use of the Synoptic Gospels. This now offered the only secure point of reference for the dating of the work. The earliest commentators on the text usually assumed the use of at least Matthew's gospel, especially since the *Didache* itself four times refers to "the gospel" in 8:2; 11:3; 15:3, 4. Representative of those who affirm such a dependence is E. Massaux[92] in his monumental study published in 1950 of the use of Matthew in Christian literature.

---

[90] J. A. Draper, "Barnabas and the Riddle of the Didache Revisited", *JSNT* 58 (1995) pp. 89-113. A rather sceptical response to this may be found in J. Carleton-Paget, *The Epistle of Barnabas: Outlook and Background* (Tübingen: Mohr, 1994 [WUNT ns. 64]) pp. 49-51.

[91] Especially E. Bammel, "Schema und Vorlage von Didache 16" in F. L. Cross (ed), *Studia Patristica* IV (Berlin: Akademie-Verlag, 1961 [TU 79]) pp. 253-262. See below.

[92] *Influence de l'Évangile de saint Matthieu sur la littérature chrétienne avant faint Irénée* (Louvain, 1950); an English translation is now available: *The Influence of the Gospel of Saint Matthew on Christian Literature before Saint Irenaeus I: The First Ecclesiastical Writers*, trns N. J. Belval & S. Hecht. Leuven: Peeters; Macon, Ga: Mercer University Press, 1990-1993 [NGSt 5,1-3].

The debate was thrown wide open with the publication of the important study of Helmut Köster[93] in 1957, which argued that although the reference to the εὐαγγέλιον might point to a knowledge of a written gospel by the "compiler" of the *Didache*, the latter did not himself use such a source. The *Didache* did not stand after the gospel writers but alongside them, utilizing the same traditions.[94]

A similar, but rather more fanciful conclusion was reached by Audet in his important commentary, published in 1958.[95] He argued that the text was written in three phases: 1:1-3a, 2:2-11:2 (D1) was written before the emergence of a written gospel; 11:3-16:8 (D2) was written by the same author under the pressure of changed circumstances, who now knew of but did not use a written gospel; finally various interpolations made by a single interpolator (I), including 1:3b-2:1, which were made at a later date but still independently of the final form of any of the gospels. This thesis, which allowed Audet to date the composition of the *Didache* entirely between 50 and 70 C.E., has not won many followers.

Nevertheless, independence of the gospel tradition on the part of the *Didache* has been affirmed by a growing number of scholars since then, including R. Glover,[96] W. Rordorf[97] and my own study included in this volume.[98] The most recent sustained study of the issue by C. N. Jefford also concludes concerning 1:3b-2:1 that

> in most cases the relationship between the sayings collection in the Didache and the collection in the Matthew Gospel is best explained by the hypothesis that the Didachist and the Matthean redactor have shared a common sayings source.[99]

---

[93] *Synoptische Überlieferung bei den apostolischen Vätern* (Berlin: Akademie-Verlag, 1957 [Tu 65]), 159-241.

[94] *Ibid.*, p. 240.

[95] *La Didachè*, pp. 166-186.

[96] "The Didache's Quotations and the Synoptic Gospels", *NTS* 5 (1958) pp. 12-29; cf. "Patristic Quotations and Gospel Sources", *NTS* 31 (1985) pp. 234-251.

[97] Rordorf & Tuilier, *La doctrine*, pp. 83-91; "Le problème de la transmission textuelle de "Didachè" 1:3b-2:1", in F. Paschke (ed.) *Überlieferungsgeschichtliche Untersuchungen* (Berlin: Akademie-Verlag, 1981 [TU 125]) pp. 499-513; "Does the Didache Contain Jesus Tradition Independently of the Synoptic Gospels?" in H. Wansbrough (ed.), *Jesus and the Oral Gospel Tradition* (Sheffield: Sheffield Academic Press, 1991 [JSNTSupp 64]) pp. 394-423.

[98] J. A. Draper, "The Jesus Tradition in the Didache" in D. Wenham (ed.), *Gospel Perspectives V: The Jesus Tradition Outside the Gospels* (Sheffield: JSOT, 1985) pp. 269-289.

[99] *The Sayings of Jesus in the Teaching of the Twelve Apostles* (Leiden: Brill, 1989 [*VigChr.E* 11]), p. 91.

The parallels to the gospel material in 7-16 are attributed to the
Matthean, Synoptic or Lucan "traditions" rather than to a direct
literary dependence.[100]

There have been a number of attempts to counter this growing consensus concerning the Jesus tradition in the *Didache*. B.
Layton[101] argued that the structure of the Jesus sayings in 1:3b-2:1
betray secondary rhetorical heightening compared with the Synoptic gospels and that this indicates that the *Didache* is dependent on
them. M. Mees[102] countered this by pointing out that the gospels
themselves treat the tradition in the same way, and the *Didache*
could simply be using the same tradition differently.

W.-D. Köhler[103] and K. Wengst[104] argue for a dependence of
the *Didache* on Matthew and situate it in the region of Syria/
Palestine. The extremely thorough redaction-critical study of C.
M. Tuckett,[105] which is also reprinted in this book, attempts a
case by case analysis of each occurrence of the Jesus tradition and
concludes that the *Didache* is dependent on both Matthew and
Luke.

K. Niederwimmer[106] points out, in a careful and balanced
consideration, that references to the "gospel" only occur in passages attributable to the redactor of the *Didache*, and that the
word does not refer to the proclamation of the salvation events but
only to the *sayings of Jesus* from the Synoptic tradition. The
"words of the Kurios" become a new law of Christ, to regulate
the life and conduct of the community. Yet there is nothing to
prove one way or another whether the redactor of the *Didache*
knew and used a written gospel text. Thus the question of the relationship of the *Didache* to the Jesus tradition must be held to
remain unresolved. Its resolution will depend on the dating of the
work obtained on other grounds. My own position, argued in a
number of papers, is that the *Didache* and Matthew evolved
together in the same community, the former as the manual of discipline of the community and the latter as a record of the Jesus
tradition mediated by the prophets. The influence, then, could run

---

[100] See the Table of Sources Jefford provides in *Sayings*, pp. 160-161.

[101] "The Sources, Dates and Transmission of Didache 1:3b-2:1", *HTR* 61 (1968)
pp. 343-383.

[102] "Die Bedeutung der Sentenzen und ihrer Auxesis für die Formung der
Jesuworte nach Didache 1:3b-2:1", *VetChr* 8 (1971) pp. 55-76.

[103] *Die Rezeption des Matthäusevangeliums in der Zeit vor Irenäus* (Tübingen:
Mohr, 1987 [WUNT 2,24]) pp. 29-30.

[104] *Didache (Apostellehre)*, pp. 24-32, 61-63.

[105] "Synoptic Tradition in the Didache" in J.-M. Sevrin (ed.), *The New Testament in Early Christianity* (Louvain: Louvain University Press, 1989 [BEThL 86])
pp. 197-230.

[106] *Die Didache*, pp. 71-77.

in either direction, depending on the redactional layer of the text.[107]

7. The Didache as "Evolved Tradition"

The re-awakening of interest in the *Didache* in the years following the work of Audet was characterized by a new emphasis on form-critical analysis.

P. Prigent[108] argues that the composition of *Barnabas* is chaotic as a result of an eclectic and undigested arrangement of traditional material. In the same way, R. A. Kraft has described these writings as "evolved literature", in which an author is almost incidental:

> He has not consistently digested his materials so that they become part of him; he has not integrated them by means of a perspective which may be called, in a special way, his own. Rather, his tradition speaks through him. *It* is of prime importance. He is its *vehicle*, but the focus remains on the traditional material, not on the author-editor.[109]

Kraft[110] and K. Wengst[111] (following a suggestion of W. Bousset) have proposed that *Barnabas* is a collection of material from a school of legal interpreters.[112] On this understanding of the origin of the paraenesis in the text, it would be fruitless to try to identify any concrete purpose or context.

The *Didache*, meanwhile, is "in the form of an impersonal community manual", so that it is the product of a community and not an individual.[113] It stands in "the church manual tradition" and has a complex and rather haphazard history of accumulation:

---

[107] See J. A. Draper, "Torah and Troublesome Apostles in the Didache Community", *NovT* 33/4 (1991) pp. 347-372, esp. 372; "The Development of 'the Sign of the Son of Man' in the Jesus Tradition", *NTS* 39 (1993) pp. 1-21, esp. 14f; "Christian Self-definition against the "Hypocrites" in *Didache* VIII", in *Society of Biblical Literature: 1992 Seminar Papers (No. 31, 128th Annual Meeting, San Francisco, November 21-24, 1992)*, ed. E.H. Lovering. Atlanta, Ga.: Scholars Press, 1992 pp. 362-377, esp. 372-374.

[108] *Les testimonia dans le christiniasm primitif. L'épître de Barnabé I-XVI* (Paris: Études bibliques, 1961).

[109] Robert A. Kraft *The Apostolic Fathers III: Barnabas and the Didache* (London: Nelson, 1965) p. 2.

[110] Kraft, *Ibid.*, pp. 19-22.

[111] *Tradition und Theologie Des Barnabasbriefes* (Berlin: de Gruyter, 1971).

[112] Cf L.W.Barnard ("The Epistle of Barnabas and the Tannaitic Catechism" [*AThR* 41, 1959] 177-190) and M.B.Shukster & P.Richardson ("Temple and *Bet Ha-midrash* in the Epistle of Barnabas" in S.G.Wilson, *Anti-Judaism in Early Christianity 2: Separation and Polemic* [Waterloo, Ont.: Wilfrid Laurier University Press, 1986 (*Studies in Christianity and Judaism* 2)] 17-31).

[113] Kraft, *Barnabas and the Didache*, p. 4.

> Neither simplicity nor straight-line development characterize the production of such church manuals. We are not dealing with a copyrighted document, which is the result of one man's endeavors, but with a conservative, *living* community tradition which can occasionally (sometimes rather accidentally) be glimpsed in a state of suspended animation, as it were, by means of the various pieces of surviving Christian "literature" which represent these interests.

In this, Kraft has undoubtedly grasped something essential about the nature of the *Didache*. However, in two respects this perspective is problematic. In the first place, there is no "church order tradition" *per se* in the period in which the *Didache* was produced. It is a dubious procedure to read back into this early Christian document the characteristics of the *Didascalia* (probably third century) and the *Apostolic Constitutions* (probably fourth century), both of which know and use the *Didache*. If any comparison is made, it should be made with comparable Jewish literature, such as the *Manual of Discipline*.[114] Secondly, there is no evidence either in the *Manual* or in later church orders, that they were innocent of theology or intentionality as Kraft contends:

> And we must be constantly aware of the fact that the ideas which are simply reproduced from older materials preserved with little change, in the present form of the Didache do not necessarily represent the main interests and beliefs of the community for which *this form* of the Didache manual was produced. Repetition of traditional beliefs does not always imply conscious agreement with which the originators of the tradition had in mind.[115]

This approach to the structure and purpose of *Barnabas* undoubtedly reflects the influence of Martin Dibelius' form critical analysis of *paraenesis*.[116] Dibelius cites as characteristics of *paraenesis* eclecticism, lack of continuity, repetition of identical motifs in different places within a writing and more generally that "the admonitions...do not apply to a single audience and a single set of circumstances; *it is not possible to construct a single frame into which they will all fit*."[117] Such paraenesis has no "theology" and, since the units of tradition are simply taken over untouched, "it is not always possible to deduce from adopted concepts the intellectual environment of the author who appropriates them."[118]

---

[114] As I set out to do in my *Commentary*.

[115] *Barnabas and the Didache*, p. 65.

[116] M. Dibelius, *James: A Commentary on the Epistle of James*, revised H. Greeven; translated M. A. Williams, and edited H. Koester (Philadelphia: Fortress 1976) 1-55.

[117] *Ibid.*, p. 11.

[118] *Ibid.*, pp. 21.

The author of a paraenetical work is thus "not a thinker, a prophet, or an intellectual leader, but rather a pedagogue, one among many, who appropriates and distributes from the property common to all."[119] So

> one should not try to find the allusions to which an actual letter might make to its milieu, to missionary activity, to the life of the community, to controversies over matters of faith or to divisions in the community. Nor can one ask about the addressees. Since more specific information is lacking, one can deal only with the question of what sort of Christians [the writer of paraenesis] expected and wished to read his letter.[120]

A consequence of this position taken by Kraft is that the final form *Didache* is again dated from the mid second century C.E., even though it is conceded that it contains ancient tradition preserved because of the "conservative nature of the church manual tradition".[121]

Like Kraft, S. Giet[122] in a book which was published only posthumously, but was the fruit of many years of study of the *Didache*, argues that it is "living literature" which unfolds progressively in response to external circumstances rather than the work of one author. There continue to be interpolations added to the text until its present state, but these are in the nature of organic development rather than corruption of the text.[123] This means that one should think of a different date and context for each layer of the tradition. Giet attempts to unravel a complicated patchwork of sources underlying the present text. On the whole, he argues, the *Didache* reproduces its sources faithfully. Some of the traditions may even have been used as source material in the New Testament itself, while other material, for example chs. 14-16 which he attributes to a second redaction, is held to derive from the first decade of the second century.[124]

The somewhat exaggerated view of paraenesis as "decontextualized tradition", arising from form criticism, has been discounted by recent studies of the function of *paraenesis*, such as that provided by Leo G. Perdue[125] in a recent collection of

---

[119] *Ibid.*, pp. 25.

[120] *Ibid.*, p. 46.

[121] *Ibid.*, p. 76.

[122] *L'Énigme de la Didachè*. Paris: Ophrys, 1970 [PFLUS 149]. Cf. "Coutume, évolution, droit canon. A propos de deux passages de la "Didaché"", *RDC* 16 (1966) pp. 118-132; "La Didachè, enseignement des douze apôtres?", *Melto* 3 (1967) pp. 223-236.

[123] *L'énigme*, pp. 257-262.

[124] *Ibid.*, p. 262-265.

[125] Leo G. Perdue, "The Social Character of Paraenesis and Paraenetic Literature", *Semeia* 50 (1990) pp. 2-39.

essays on the genre. Perdue argues that the setting of paraenesis is in periods of *liminality*, times of marginalization leading to a change of life-style and re-incorporation.[126] It serves the purpose of either confirming and legitimating the *status quo* or, alternatively, of subverting it. Either way there is a deliberate theological and practical purpose, utilizing tradition but deliberate reshaping it for particular ends.[127]

8. The "Didachist" as a Redactor of Tradition

The emergence of redaction criticism in New Testament studies has naturally influenced the study of the *Didache* also. Several recent studies have focussed less on the question of sources and forms than on the way the underlying tradition has been shaped by the redactor.

The text and commentary of W. Rordorf and A. Tuilier, published in 1978, represents something of a milestone in the study of the *Didache*, drawing together the research of the preceding decades of scholarship, including many important studies by Rordorf himself.[128] Following the suggestions of Giet, Rordorf argues that an unknown author took an ancient Jewish and primitive teaching and added 1:3b-2:1 and 6:2-3, in order to make if represent the ideal of Christian perfection. To this the same author added the liturgical part, connecting it with 7:1 and adding material on baptism, but including chs. 9-10 from ancient Syrian liturgical usage. The same author again added ancient disciplinary material available to him, but adding material on problems of corruption in his own time. Chs. 14 and 15 were added by a second redactor of the work, and reflects a different situation. Ch. 16 was probably added at the same time and was not the original conclusion to the Two Ways, even though it contains ancient material. The whole collection was made by the end of the first century C.E.

U. Mattioli[129] argues that the Didachist redacted three principal sources: the Two Ways with an Eschatological Conclusion, New Testament material and the Eucharistic Prayers. The rest is the work of the Didachist. K. Wengst[130] holds to a minimal intervention of the (single) redactor, arguing that the work is constructed out of single blocks of tradition. It is only in 7:2f, and 11-15 that the hand and particular interest of the redactor emerges,

---

[126] *Ibid.*, 9-11.

[127] Draper, "Barnabas and the Didache Revisited", pp. 90-92.

[128] *La Doctrine*, pp. 91-99.

[129] *Didachè—Dottrina dei dodici apostoli: Introduzione, traduzione e note* (Rome: Edizioni Paoline, 1980³) pp. 20-29.

[130] *Didache (Apostellehre)*, pp. 14-23.

and that the conditions of the community are visible. However, the redactor is at work in making an orientation to the traditional blocks of material in chs. 1-10 the condition for the reception of itinerant teachers into the community. In any case, the Didachist does not create *de novo*, but simply sets down as regulations what was the existing practise of his community.[131]

The most thorough-going redaction critical analysis of the *Didache* is provided by K. Niederwimmer's important new commentary.[132] He argues that a Christian author originating from a Jewish Christian milieu compiled a sort of community rule at the beginning of the second century. A fundamental distinction should thus be drawn between the sources and the redactor. The sources he used were: a superficially Christianized Jewish Two Ways treatise, an archaic liturgical tradition of baptism and eucharist, an archaic tradition on the reception of itinerant charismatics, and a short apocalypse. The Didachist compiled, added and interpreted this tradition, especially by the addition of chs. 12-15, which he composed himself. His intention was to compose a rule book for his community, as far as possible from existing tradition. But the tradition needed to be updated to meet the new, altered circumstances of the community.[133] While the Two Ways is taken up *en bloc* (1:1-6:1), it is also made into a baptismal catechesis (7:1) and Christianized further by the addition of the Jesus tradition in 1:3b-6, which is made into a "council of perfection" by 6:2. A special problem is addressed in 6:3. In the liturgical section, only 7:1, 4b, 9:5, 10:7 are redactional. While 11:1-3 is composed by the Didachist, 11:4-12 is a piece of (written) tradition. The rest of the disciplinary section is also composed by the Didachist, except for a later gloss in 13:4. In the Apocalypse, only 16:7 is from the hand of the redactor. In a recent article,[134] Niederwimmer has provided a helpful text setting out clearly the sources and redaction for which he argues in his commentary.

The work of G. Schöllgen also begins from a redaction critical analysis in broad agreement with Niederwimmer. However he addresses in particular the question of the nature of a "church manual / order", which is raised by Kraft,[135] Wengst[136] and others. In an essay published in this book,[137] and in a series of

---

[131] "Dieser Überblick zeigt, daß bei der Beschäftigung mit der Didache weniger die Einzelpersönlichkeit ihres Verfassers in den Blick kommt als vielmehr das Leben der Gemeinde, aus der dieser Verfasser kommt und für die er das, was in ihrschon weitgehend Praxis war, kodifiziert hat." *Ibid.*, p. 23.

[132] *Die Didache.*

[133] *Ibid.*, pp. 66-67.

[134] "Der Didachist und seine Quellen", *The Didache in Context*, pp. 15-36.

[135] *Barnabas and the Didache*, p. 60.

[136] *Didache (Apostellehre)*, p. 18.

[137] G. Schöllgen, "Die Didache als Kirchenordnung", *JAC* 29 (1986) pp. 5-26.

other articles,[138] Schöllgen argues against the idea that the *Didache* is a comprehensive church order, seeking to regulate the whole life of the church. Instead, it is only a selective, collection of rules dealing *ad hoc* with particular burning issues of the day, even if it is often utilizing traditional material. Thus no conclusions may be drawn from what the *Didache* does not mention, as if this proves its absence in its community. Schöllgen also argues that there are no governing tendencies in the text. There seems to be something of a contradiction here, as if a text could deal with particular burning issues of the day and yet provide no coherent picture of its own situation. Nevertheless, the warning against any *argumentum e silentio* is a timely one. So too is his focus on the nature of a church order: particularly since we have no evidence for such a genre prior to the *Didache*. The ongoing debate between Schöllgen and B. Steimer[139] on the issue of the genre of church orders is to be welcomed.

Niederwimmer[140] accepts that the Didachist had no models to copy, but that he was no original composer. He takes the basic framework provided by his sources and seeks to compile a rule book for baptism, eucharist and community order, with an eschatological conclusion as suggested by his source. We do not know what occasion led to this compilation, except that the author wishes to apply old tradition to new circumstances in a time of transition. It is not intended to be comprehensive.

9. The Didache and Liturgical Traditions

Baptism

From its first publication, the liturgical section of the *Didache* excited the interest of scholars because of its archaic nature. Although the section on baptism has received less attention than it deserves, a number of particular issues have emerged.

R. Reitzenstein[141] argued that the prayer over the μύρος in the Coptic Version of the *Didache* and in the *Apostolic Constitu-*

---

[138] G. Schöllgen, "Die literarische Gattung der syrischen Didaskalie" in H. J. W. Drijvers *et al* (eds.) *IV. Symposium Syriacum 1984. Literary Genres in Syriac Literature* (Rome: Pontifical Institutum Studiarum, 1987 [OCA 229]) pp. 149-159; "Pseudapostolizität und Schriftgebrauch in den ersten Kirchenordnungen. Anmerkungen zur Begründung des frühen Kirchenrechts" in *Stimuli. Exegese und ihre Hermeneutik in Antike und Christentum: Festschrift Ernst Dassmann.* (Münster, 1996 [*JbAC Erg.-Bd* 23]) pp. 96-121; "Der Abfassungszweck der frühen Kirchenordnungen. Anmerkungen zu den Thesen Bruno Steimers", *JbAC* 40 (1997) forthcoming.

[139] B. Steimer, *Vertex Traditionis. Die Gattung der altchristliche Kirchenordnungen* (Berlin/New York: de Gruyter, 1992 [BZNW 63]).

[140] *Die Didache*, pp. 13-15.

[141] *Die Vorgeschichte der christlichen Taufe* (Darmstadt: Wissenschaftlicher Buchgeseloch, 1929) pp. 177ff.

tions VII.27 was originally concerned with baptismal unction and has been omitted by the Jerusalem text. This thesis was taken up again in E. Peterson's significant, although controversial, study of the liturgical aspects of the *Didache*.[142] On the basis of the supposed inaccuracy of the Jerusalem text, he argues that the text originally knew a pre- and post-baptismal unction, which was suppressed in a Novatian redaction.

The high valuation of running water and the interest in kinds of water (7:1-3) observable in the *Didache*, which had already interested Harnack,[143] was made the study of a monograph by T. Klauser.[144] E. Barnikol[145] observed that 9:5 has baptism only εἰς ὄνομα κυρίου, whereas 7:1 and 3 have baptism in the name of the Trinity. He connected this with the absence of the Trinitarian baptism in the Eusebian form of Mt 28:19,[146] to argue that an original baptism in the "name of the Lord [Jesus]" has been redacted by the emergent early catholic church to reflect its Trinitarian theology.

A. Benoit's important 1953 study on baptism in the second century[147] demonstrated a renewed interest in the significance of the *Didache* for the study of the development of Christian baptism in the first centuries. He argues that 7:1 indicates that catechetical instruction preceded baptism, namely 1-6; agrees that baptism "in the name of the Lord" was the original formula; emphasizes the importance of running water as purificatory and the antiquity of the pre-baptismal fast, and argues that the baptism was followed by the eucharist as its culmination. He finds striking resemblances between the baptismal instructions of the *Didache* and the Jewish proselyte baptism which he reconstructs, both in form and ideas. For this reason and also because he considers Mandaeanism a later development than the *Didache*, he rejects Reitzenstein's hypothesis. Thus baptism in the *Didache* is seen as having escaped

---

[142] "Einige Probleme", *Frühkirche, Judentum und Gnosis*, pp. 146-182.

[143] *Die Lehre*, pp. 22f.

[144] "Taufet in Lebendigem Wasser! Zum religions- und kulturgeschichtlichen Verständnis von Didache 7,1-3" in T. Klauser & Rükker (eds.) *Pisciculi. Studien zur Religion und Kultur des Altertums* (Fst. F. J. Dölger) (Münster: Aschendorff, 1939) pp. 157-164 (now also in E. Dassmann (ed.) *Gesammelte Arbeiten zur Liturgiegeschichte, Kirchengeschichte und Christlichen Archäologie* (Münster in Westfalen: Aschendorff, 1974 [JAC.E 3]) pp. 177-183.

[145] "Die triadische Taufformel: Ihr Fehlen in der Didache und im Matthäusevangelium und irh altkotholischer Ursprung", *ThJ* 4-5 (1936-1937) pp. 144-152.

[146] Cf. F. C. Conybeare, "The Eusebian Form of the Text Matth. 28,19", *ZNW* 2 (1901) pp. 275-288.

[147] *Le Baptême Chrétien au Second Siècle* (Paris: Presses Universitaires de France, 1953) pp. 5-33.

the Pauline current and remained within the Jewish milieu. In his view it may well attest the earliest stage of Christian baptism.[148]

Benoit apparently did not have access to Peterson's essay, but his findings refute it. Very vociferous in his condemnation of Peterson is the monograph of A. Vööbus.[149] In particular, Vööbus argues that the prayer for the μύρος is originally a prayer for the "aroma [of myrrh]" and that it was constructed by analogy with the eucharistic prayers of 9-10, although it misses the spirit of the latter in that the prayer is said over the vehicle of the spiritual gift rather than for the gift itself.[150] W. Rordorf's study of baptism in the *Didache* is included in this volume as a sober evaluation of the current findings of research.

While most studies conclude that the material in ch. 8 is a secondary addition to the baptismal instructions, occasioned by the mention of fasting in 7:3, my own study included here[151] asks whether there is not a structural and functional connection between initiation, the stationary fast, thrice daily Lord's Prayer of ch. 8 and the ritual process of baptism in the *Didache*.

Eucharist

Unlike the paucity of studies on baptism, there have been numerous major studies of the eucharist in the *Didache*. Harnack[152] considered that the eucharist was celebrated inside the agape. He also considered the absence of any reference to the death of Christ to be a sign of its post-apostolic provenance. The similarity of the prayers in chs. 9-10 to Jewish Berakoth was observed already by Taylor and Turner. E. von der Goltz[153] made a full study of the Jewish tradition behind these prayers. G. Klein[154] pointed to the influence of the Sabbath *Kiddush* prayers on chapter 9 and of the *Birkath Ha-Mazon* on chapter 10.

The problem posed by the double reference to the eucharist in chs. 9-10 and 14 soon drew the attention of scholars. P. Drews[155] and M. Goguel[156] argued that these two sections referred to different kinds of celebrations. The former reflected communal

---

[148] Benoit, *Baptême Chrétienne*, p. 32f.

[149] *Liturgical Traditions*, 30-33.

[150] *Ibid.*, pp. 56f.

[151] "Christian Self-Definition against the "Hypocrites" in Didache 8", in E. H. Lovering, *Society of Biblical Literature 1992 Seminar Papers* (Atlanta, Ga.: Scholars, 1992) pp. 362-377.

[152] *Die Lehre:*, pp. 28-36; *Ibid.: Prolegomena*, pp. 58-60.

[153] *Tischgebete und Abendmahlsgebete in der altchristlichen und in der griechischen Kirche* (Leipzig: Hinrichs, 1905).

[154] *Älteste Christliche Katechismus*, pp. 214-219.

[155] "Untersuchungen zur Didache", *ZNW* 5 (1904) pp. 53-79, esp. 76.

[156] *L'Eucharistie des origines á Justin Martyr* (Paris: Fischbacher, 1910).

meals in private homes on any day of the week, while the latter describes the formal eucharistic liturgy of the whole church on the Sunday presided over by the bishop and deacons. Drews and Goguel suggest that ch. 14 deliberately attacks the practise of private house eucharists in chs. 9-10. This opposition between the different sections of the *Didache* cannot really be substantiated, as W. Rordorf rightly points out.[157]

While early critics like P. Sabatier recognized the primitive nature of the liturgy, it was the major study of H. Lietzmann[158] which set the *Didache* at the centre of the study of the origin of the Christian eucharist as the "oldest extant formulary".[159] Lietzmann made a comprehensive and detailed study of the ancient liturgies and sources for the eucharist. The *Didache* is the key text in his construction of a theory of two types of the eucharist, a Pauline type which emphasizes the sacrificial nature of the eucharist as a sharing in the body and blood of Christ,[160] and an Egyptian tradition, in which the *Didache* also stands, which did not have a narrative of the institution and did not mention the death of Jesus, and emphasizes eschatological expectation.[161] Based on his analysis of other liturgical texts, Lietzmann argues that the *Didache* envisages a eucharist followed by an agape meal, and that the sentences in 10:6 have been misplaced from their original position before 9:5. They are a responsive dialogue between celebrant and people before the communion.[162]

The thesis of Lietzmann was rejected in an article in 1938 by M. Dibelius[163] on the basis of both the Coptic text and also of an analysis of Jewish table prayers. Dibelius argues that the prayers over the cup and fragments depend on a spiritualized form of the Jewish prayers current in the Hellenistic Jewish synagogues. Likewise the prayers after the meal, which end with 10:4. There follows a new Christian prayer in 10:5, followed by a short liturgy in 10:6 of the coming of the Lord, who was conceived not only as returning at the end but also approaching in the eucharist proper, which now follows but is not described. This is the eucharist described as $\theta\nu\sigma\acute{\iota}\alpha$ in 14:1-2.

The position of Lietzmann was strongly opposed by a number of Anglican high churchmen, who were also associated with

---

[157] "The Didache" in W. Rordorf *et al* (eds.) *The Eucharist of the Early Christians* (New York: Pueblo, 1978) pp. 1-23, esp. pp. 4-5.

[158] *Messe und Herrenmahl: Eine Studie zur Geschichte der Liturgie* (Bonn: Marcus & Weber, 1926); Eng. translation *Mass and Lord's Supper: A Study in the History of the Liturgy*, trns. D. H. G. Reeve. Leiden: Brill, 1953-1964.

[159] *Mass and Lord's Supper*, p. 188.

[160] *Ibid.*, pp. 172-187, 204-208.

[161] *Ibid.*, pp. 152-160.

[162] *Ibid.*, pp. 192f.

[163] "Die Mahl-Gebete der Didache", *ZNW* 37 (1938) pp. 32-41.

the assertion that the *Didache* was a late and unreliable witness. R. H. Connolly[164] and F.E. Vokes.[165], following the suggestion made by Drews and Goguel, argued that these prayers are remnants from the ancient Christian agape and not the eucharist proper. They are followed in this by their colleague, Dom Gregory Dix, in his influential work on the structure of the eucharist first published in 1945.[166] The *Didache* would not fit his reconstruction of an original fourfold action of the eucharist—take, give thanks, break and distribute—but fortunately can be relegated to the status of agape.[167] For him ch. 14 represents the authentic eucharist of the second century *Didache* community, regarded as a sacrifice and celebrated on Sunday by ordained officials of the church, whereas 9-10 represent prayers at everyday fellowship meals which may be said by the laity, or even varied at will by lay prophets. Secondly, the word εὐχαριστία, εὐχαριστεῖν does not refer to the eucharist proper, but is used interchangeably with ευλογία, εὐλογειν.[168] The work of Dix was developed further by L. Bouyer in terms of Jewish influence on the genesis of the eucharist.[169]

In line with his mistrust of the Jerusalem text of the *Didache* and his higher valuation of the *Apostolic Constitutions*, E. Peterson argued that this "Novatian recension" changed prayers which were originally eucharistic into everyday table prayers.[170] This thesis was taken up and argued in detail by J. Betz, in the essay included in this volume.[171]

The strong indications of a Jewish basis for the eucharistic prayers of the *Didache* were again investigated by J.-P. Audet.[172] Audet sought to formulate the underlying rules governing the Jewish *Berakoth*: first the short exclamatory "benediction proper", then the elaboration of the particular divine act which

---

[164] "Agape and Eucharist in the Didache", *DR* 55 (1937) pp. 477-489.

[165] *Riddle of the Didache*, pp. 177ff.

[166] *The Shape of the Liturgy* (Westminster: Dacre, 1945).

[167] *Ibid.*, p. 48.

[168] *Ibid.*, pp. 90-93.

[169] *L'eucharistie. Théologie et spiritualité de la prière eucharistique: Spiritualité d'hier et d'aujour'hui* (Tournai: Descleé, 1966 [BiblTh]); English translation by C. U. Quinn, *Eucharist: Theology and Spirituality of the Eucharistic Prayer* (Notre Dame, Ind.: University of Notre Dame Press, 1968).

[170] "Einige Probleme", *Frühkirche, Judentum und Gnosis*, pp. 169, 170, 181.

[171] "Die Eucharistie in der Didache", *ALW* 11 (1969) pp. 10-39.

[172] "Esquisse du genre littéraire de la bénédiction juive et de l'eucharistie chrétienne", *RB* 65 (1958) pp. 371-399; also "Literary Forms and Contents of a Normal Εὐχαριστία in the First Century", in *Studia Evangelica* (Berlin: Akademie-Verlag, 1959 [TU 73]) pp. 643-662; *La Didachè*, pp. 643-662; "Genre littétaire et formes cultuelles de l'Eucharistie. 'Nova et Veteras'", *EphLiturg* 80 (1966) pp. 353-385.

evoked the cry of wonder, then an encapsulating return to the original benediction. Like Dix, however, his thesis depends on treating εὐχαριστεῖν, εὐλογεῖν and ἐξομολογεῖσθαι as synonyms. This position cannot be sustained in the light of more detailed study of Jewish sources, especially the Dead Sea Scrolls, as the work of R. J. Ledogar,[173] T. J. Talley,[174] and my own study[175] have shown. Talley argues that the *Didache* is a Christianizing of the Jewish *Birkath Ha-Mazon* by means of deliberate insertions and deviations.[176] A similar position is taken by J. W. Riggs,[177] who also draws conclusions from "absence", "additions" and structural deviations from Rabbinic texts. The problem with this trend in research is that the Rabbinic text of the *Birkath Ha-Mazon* is only available from the ninth century and can scarcely be considered to be a rule applicable to first century Jews, however much it may reflect ancient traditions.

Audet also argued that the prayers of chs. 9-10 were not those of the agape nor the eucharist "major", but a novel form called the "breaking of the bread", a kind of eucharist "minor" which included a full meal, a celebration of the coming of the kingdom and the return of the Lord.[178] This "breaking of the bread" was then followed by a transition to the eucharist proper in another room, introduced by the "rituel de transition a l'eucharistie majeure" in 10:6: "If anyone is holy, let him come; if anyone is not, let him repent. Maranatha! Amen!"[179] This view of the matter is essentially confirmed by W. Rordorf in his article on the eucharist in the *Didache*,[180] which takes up again the study of von der Goltz on Jewish table prayers. The *Didache* represents

---

[173] *Acknowledgement: Praise Verbs in the Early Greek Anaphoras* (Rome: Herder, 1968).

[174] "De la "berakah" à l'eucharistie, une question à réexaminer", *La Maison-Dieu* 125/1 (1976) pp. 11-39, Eng. translation in "From *Berakah* to *Eucharistia*: A Reopening Question", *Worship* 50/2 (1976) pp. 115-137); "The Eucharistic Prayer: Tradition and Development" in K. Stevenson (ed.) *Liturgy Reshaped* (London: SPCK, 1982); "The Literary Structure of Eucharistic Prayer", *Worship* 58 (1984) pp. 404-420.

[175] *Commentary*, pp. 182-188.

[176] "De la 'berakah' a l'eucharistie", pp. 126f.

[177] Riggs, J. W. 1984. "From Gracious Table to Sacramental Elements: The Tradition-History of Didache 9 and 10", *Second Century* 4 (1984) pp. 83-102. Cf. "The Sacred Food of Didache 9-10 and Second Century Ecclesiologies", *Didache in Context*, pp. 91-101.

[178] *La Didachè*, pp. 406f.

[179] Audet, *La Didachè*, pp. 410-424. Audet appeals, rather unconvincingly, to evidence from the archaeological discoveries at Dura-Europos.

[180] "L'eucharistie selon la *Didachè*" in *L'eucharistie des premiers chrétiens* (Paris: Beauchesne, 1976 [PoTh 17]) pp. 7-28. Eng. translation, "The Didache" in W. Rordorf *et al* (eds.), *The Eucharist of the Early Christians* (New York: Pueblo, 1978) pp. 1-23.

a transition between the Jewish table prayers and the preface of the Christian anaphora. Rordorf sees ch. 14 as describing the same event, so that the eucharist is seen as preceded by confession of sins. The use of "sacrifice" to describe the eucharist is seen as a reference to thanksgiving, in contrast to blood sacrifice, and should not be taken in a later theological sense with reference to the eucharist.

K. Wengst[181] returns to the position of Dibelius, as far as the influence of the Greek-speaking Hellenistic synagogues is concerned, but rejects the idea that the prayers of chs. 9-10 are a prelude to a eucharist proper. They describe a real meal designated a eucharist, which is the same as what is described in ch. 14. The thanksgiving prayers differentiate the meal from everyday meals, but it does not stand in the tradition of the Lord's Supper in Paul or the Last Supper tradition of the Synoptics at all. Instead it is a lightly Christianized Jewish meal. The problem posed to such a theory by 10:6 is resolved by the suggestion that this was originally a piece of genuine tradition from the Last Supper, which is now in a different context.[182] In his commentary, K. Niederwimmer[183] rejects this rather contorted explanation and returns to the theory that 10:6 introduces the eucharist proper. Nevertheless, he considers the absence of the words of Institution to remain an open problem.

The most recent work on the eucharist in the *Didache* by E. Mazza has argued for a very early date for the prayers. In a paper published here,[184] Mazza argues that the term "holy vine of David" implies a Christology prior to the Council of Jerusalem. The eucharistic prayers in chs. 9-10 are not for an agape, but derive from a time before the eucharist and the meal were separated. Thus the meaning of the prayers must be found within the Jewish thought world of the *Berakah*. Word and act in the blessing combine into a new sacral reality, in which God is present at the meal. Mazza explores the absence of the account of the institution in the prayers, which is often used to argue that they do not constitute a eucharist proper. He finds in various ancient liturgies (e.g. *Addai and Mari*) a similar absence of any account of the last supper, and concludes that it is not the account of the Last Supper which constitutes the sacramental validity of the eucharistic anaphora, but rather the intention to fulfill the command of the Lord, "Do this in memory of me". He finds this intention in 10:3,

---

[181] *Didache (Apostellehre)*, pp. 43-57.
[182] Ibid., pp. 46-47.
[183] *Die Didache*, pp. 173-209, esp. 179-180.
[184] "Didaché IX-X: Elementi per una interpretazione Eucaristica", *Ephemerides Liturgicae* 92 (1979) pp. 393-419.

where thanks is given for the "grace of spiritual food and drink and eternal life through your Servant", which replaces the constitutive element of the Jewish sacral meal in Deuteronomy 8:10. In a subsequent essay, Mazza argues on the basis of 1 Corinthians 10:1-4, 16-17 that Paul was familiar with the Cup-Bread-Unity sequence of ch. 9.[185] He thus dates the prayers in 9-10 to between 50-52 C.E. These conclusions form the keystone of Mazza's recent book on the origins of the eucharist.[186] They are certain to stimulate a new look at the questions related to the *Didache*.

10. Didache and Itinerant Radicalism

As early as Harnack[187] and Knopf[188] *Didache* 6:2-3 was given an ascetic interpretation. The ascetics were those who kept the "whole yoke" of the Lord and became "perfect", while ordinary Christians did the best they could. This was combined with speculation about the homeless radicalism and possible spiritual marriage of the charismatics in 11:3-12. Harnack also, as we have seen, saw a threefold order of itinerant charismatics—apostles, prophets and teachers—as the earliest form of Christian ministry, which was gradually replaced by local bishops and deacons as the earlier order became corrupt. This set the scene for a continuing interest in asceticism and itinerant radicalism.

E. Peterson's 1951 study of the *Didache*[189] argued that the Jerusalem text was a late recension influenced by the Novatian heresy and relied heavily on the *Apostolic Constitutions* in establishing the original text. He also re-orders the text, arguing that ch.7 is a dogmatic revision of a prayer originally over prebaptismal ointment, which was removed by the Novatian redaction. This rather dubious procedure has rightly been criticized by most subsequent scholars.[190] However, Peterson also argued that the original text of the *Didache* stands within the stream of Syrian asceticism, something which has found resonance with a number of critics. He sees a twofold development of asceticism: a philosophical dualistic asceticism in the West, which had already been taken up within Western diaspora Judaism, and an eschatological asceticism in Syria and the East, which sees the

---

[185] "L'Eucaristia di 1 Corinzi 10:16-17 in rapporto a Didache 9-10," *Ephemerides Liturgicae* 100 (1986) pp. 193-223.
[186] *The Origins of the Eucharistic Prayer* (Collegeville, Minnesota: The Liturgical Press, 1995 [Pueblo]).
[187] *Die Lehre*, pp. 19-22.
[188] *Ibid.*, pp. 20-21.
[189] "Einige Probleme", *Frühkirche, Judentum und Gnosis*, pp. 146-182.
[190] E.g. A. Vööbus, *Liturgical Traditions*, pp. 17-60.

kingdom as already in the process of realization in the present world. [191]

Although he was not concerned with the *Didache* at this point, A. Vööbus also gave an impulse to a revival of interest in the origins of asceticism in Syria in a number of publications, beginning in 1951.[192] Vööbus argues that Syrian Christianity is a product of the mission of the Palestinian church. He sees the developmental of asceticism as passing from Essenism through Aramaic-speaking Jewish Christianity into the Syrian Church, strengthened in the time of Tatian and Marcion by ascetic trends coming from the West. However, Vööbus sees the *Didache* as a product of Egyptian Christianity, thus excluding it from his consideration of the development of Syrian asceticism.[193]

In 1957, a year before the publication of Audet's commentary, A. Adam published an important and influential essay taking up again the question of the ascetic origins of the *Didache*.[194] He argued that the Coptic version of the *Didache* was a translation exercize from a Syriac original. Linguistic evidence in the Greek text also, in particular the term χριστέμπορος, as well as the instructions on the stationary fast, indicate that the *Didache* originates from some part of the Syrian region. This suggestion is further supported on the basis of *Didache* 11:11, which Adam sees as referring to the ancient ascetic practise of "spiritual marriage". The Coptic text has κοσμικὸν παράδοσις in place of the Jerusalem text's μυστήριον κοσμικόν, and the Coptic also does not have the μὴ διδάσκων δὲ ποιεῖν ὅσα αὐτὸς ποιεῖ. Lying behind the word παράδοσις Adam sees the Syriac word 'šlem linked to the concept of syzygy, the spiritual union between Christ and the church, which is present in Ephesians 5:26-32. The prophets were those who realized on earth this heavenly reality, by an ascetic marriage.[195] This concept is understood by Tatian *Oratio ad Graecos* (esp. 15:1) as referring to the reunion of the human body and the (female) holy spirit forfeited at the Fall, and allegorized

---

[191] "Einige Beobachtungen zu den Anfängen der christlichen Askese", in *Frühkirche, Judentum und Gnosis*, pp. 209-220.

[192] "Celibacy a Requirement for Admission to Baptism in the Early Syrian Church", *ETSE* 1 (1951); See also *History of Asceticism in the Syrian Orient* I (1958 [CSCO 184 = subs. 14]).

[193] He specifically rejects Adam's thesis (*Liturgical Traditions*, p. 13) because the *Didache* is silent about Paul and his work. This may not be so, if my own hypothesis about chapters 11 and 16, in an essay included in this volume, is valid. See J.A. Draper, "Torah and Troublesome Apostles in the *Didache* Community", *NovT* 33/4 (1991): 347-372, esp. 372.

[194] "Erwägungen zur Herkunft der Didache", *ZK* 68 (1957) pp. 1-47. Adam's interest is in the origin of monasticism; cf. his "Grundbegriffe des Mönchtums in sprachlicher Sicht", *ZKG* 65 (1953/4) pp. 209-239.

[195] "Erwägungen", 20-25.

by Hermas in *Similitudes* 10:6-11:8. Since this practise was rejected at an early time (e.g. Ps. Clement, *Ad. Virg.*), Adam dates the *Didache* between 70, or more likely 90, and 100 C.E. and places it in Adiabene. He speculates that it was composed as a manual for this young Christian church by the Jerusalem church, which had been driven out to Galilee or Pella.

Adam's work has been taken further by an essay of G. Kretschmar's in 1964.[196] Kretschmar emphasizes the diversity of ascetic origins in different areas. He believes that the ascetic impulse was earlier in Syria than the West, since abstinence from marriage or virginity within marriage came to be a requirement for baptism in some circles in the second century C.E. He tests the hypotheses of Peterson and Adam, by bringing into the picture the itinerant prophets and ascetics, which Peterson had seen as aberrations from the great church.[197] He sees *syneisactum*, the spiritual cohabitation of prophet and prophetess already in *Didache* 11:11, and finds chs. 11-13 as evidence for itinerant apostles, prophets and teachers, whom he sees to be self-evidently ascetics.[198] These three groups are subsumed under the designation "prophets". In the period of the *Didache*, he argues, these itinerant charismatics were supported by "settled" Christians in the villages, for whom they constituted the pastors and community officials. While the text allows for the possibility that a prophet may wish to settle, they are expected from outside. This is very different from the Pauline communities, where the charismatics were local and settled. It is only at the end of the developmental process of the text that the communities become self-sufficient and appoint their own officials in the bishops and deacons, who gradually replace the declining order of charismatics.[199]

Kretschmar sees the Two Ways, despite its undeniable Jewish origins, as a Christian composition, the oldest Christian rule of life disseminated by charismatic teachers through the villages of Galilee, Samaria and Judaea. These teachers are still to be regarded as "charismatics", although the spirit is receding in the face of the didactic emphasis as in Matthew. Kretschmar seeks to trace this development from the first circle of disciples, for

---

[196] "Ein Beitrag zur Frage nach dem Ursprung frühchristlicher Askese", *ZThK* 61 (1964) pp. 27-67; now also in: *Askese und Mönchtum in der alten Kirche*, ed. K. S. Frank. Darmstadt: Wissenschaftliche Buchgesellschaft, 1975 [WdF 409] pp. 129-179; cf. "Das christliche Leben und die Mission in der frühen Kirche" in H. Frohnes & U. W. Knorr (eds.) *Kirchengeschichte als Missionsgeschichte I: Die Alte Kirche* (München: Kaiser, 1974) pp. 94ff.

[197] "Ein Beitrag", pp. 32f.

[198] While asceticism is not expressly described, it is, he argues clearly implied ("aber es versteht sich wohl von selbst", *Ibid.*, p. 36).

[199] *Ibid.*, p. 36ff.

whom personal union to Jesus means following him in a life of
wandering. He sees in the question as to what discipleship means
in the post-Easter time the origin of the Syrian form of early
Christian asceticism.[200] In the connection between following
(ἀκολουθεῖν) and the "Way" as a binding rule of life, we see the
importance of a Two Way teaching. The Christian response to the
breaking in of the Eschaton is a new way of "walking" or conduct. This walking is seen as "perfection" (τέλειος), as in the
Dead Sea Scrolls. However, discipleship as "perfection" is contrasted with keeping the law as fulfilled in the Double Love Command in Mt 19:16-26 (cf. *Didache* 1:2 and 6:2). This means
ultimately that there is a double way to life: law and discipleship,
in which discipleship is irreversible progress to the fulfillment of
the law in the "perfection" of discipleship. Matthew remains
strongly still within the Jewish community. However, the *Didache*
presupposes the separation of church and synagogue and seeks to
order the life of the settled local Christian communities which now
emerge. The "disciples" of Matthew live on in the itinerant
apostles, prophets and teachers of the *Didache*, but the settled
members of the local communities are no longer called to this life
of "discipleship" in this narrow sense. The *Didache* merges the
double way of Matthew into one: the way of the Double Love
Command is merged with and explicated by the teaching of Jesus
and the Decalogue as a first and second διδαχή. *Didache* 6:2 is
not a two tier ethic, but rather preserves the gospel freedom.
However, since perfection is something which can be gradually
learnt and achieved, it is understood quantitatively and not qualita-
tively. "Perfection" does not yet seem to have an ascetic colouring
in the *Didache*, though it is understood that way in the *Liber
Graduum*.[201]

Kretschmar essentially affirms the thesis of Adam that the
origin of Syrian asceticism lay in a continuation of primitive
Christian itinerant discipleship among the charismatic prophets
and teachers who worked as missionaries in the Palestinian-Syrian
Jewish communities under the new apocalyptic conditions
inaugurated by the Messiah. Thus the thesis of Peterson is also
largely confirmed by his research. After the separation of church
and synagogue, Syrian Christianity sought to reshape the call of
Jesus to discipleship into a rule of life, which in the end produced
a destructive tension between radical asceticism as a requirement
for all Christians and the compromise of a two tier ethic. This tension was never resolved in the Syrian church; indeed there is no

---

[200] *Ibid.*, pp. 41-49.
[201] *Ibid.*, pp. 49-62.

answer, according to Kretschmar, and it remains a "healthy troubler of the church".[202]

This work of Kretschmar lies behind the much more well-known and enduringly influential work of G. Theissen.[203] Theissen uses the sociological theory of Max Weber[204] to develop a typology of the Jesus movement, in which Jesus is viewed as a model of charismatic authority: the "bearer of revelation", who initiated a movement of "wandering charismatics", who were dependent on and pastored a network of "local communities".[205] These wandering charismatics continue the itinerant ministry of Jesus and manifest the τρόπους τοῦ κυρίου of which the *Didache* speaks (11:8). This lifestyle of ethical radicalism is characterized by itinerancy, renunciation of marriage and property. Theissen links this life-style with the "Q"-tradition, and argues that the prophets mentioned here were the mediators of the Jesus tradition, in a way analogous to the work of itinerant Cynic philosophers.[206] The thesis of Theissen has been criticized by a number of recent scholars for his selective use of sources, most recently by W. Stegemann[207] and R. A. Horsley.[208] Theissen also neglects to distinguish the redactional layers of the *Didache*, which distorts his use of this text as historical evidence for the earliest period.

---

[202] *Ibid.*, pp. 63-67.

[203] Theissen acknowledges that his thesis is a "Weiterentwicklung" of the work of Kretschmar in his "Wanderradikalismus. Literatursoziologische Aspekte der Überlieferung von Worten Jesus im Urchristentum", *ZThK* 70 (1973) pp. 245-271, esp. p. 86 note 20; this paper is reprinted in *Studien zur Soziologie des Urchristentums* (Tübingen: Mohr, 1979 [WUNT 19]) pp. 70-105, English translation, "Itinerant Radicalism: The Tradition of Jesus Sayings from the Perspective of the Sociology of Literature", trans. A. Wire, *RadRel* 2 [1976] pp. 84-93); *Soziologie der Jesusbewegung* (München: Kaiser, 1977), English translation, *The First Followers of Jesus: a sociological analysis of earliest Christianity*, trans. J. Bowden (London: SCM, 1978). The American edition has a different title: *Sociology of Early Palestinian Christianity*, (Philadelphia: Fortress, 1978).

[204] See "Zur forschungsgeschichtlichen Einordnung der soziologischen Fragestellung", in *Studien zur Soziologie*, pp. 3-34, esp. 23f; cf. his further use of the three forms of legitimation in Weber in "Legitimation and Subsistence: An Essay on the Sociology of Early Christian Missionaires", in *The Social Setting of Pauline Christianity: Essays on Corinth by Gerd Theissen*, trans. J. H. Schütz (Philadelphia: Fortress, 1982) pp. 27-67.

[205] This thesis is first developed in "Wanderradikalismus", pp. 245-271, and then more substantially in *Soziologie der Jesusbewegung*.

[206] "Wanderradikalismus", pp. 83-92.

[207] "Vagabond Radicalism in Early Christianity?: A Historical and Theological Discussion of a Thesis Proposed by Gerd Theissen" in W. Schottroff & W. Stegemann (eds.), *God of the Lowly* (Maryknoll: Orbis, 1984) pp. 148-168. Stegemann also questions the underlying desire/dream of the West for *voluntary* renunciation of property, arguing that the Jesus movement was property-less because of economic disintegration and not by choice.

[208] *Sociology and the Jesus Movement* (New York: Crossroad, 1989) pp. 15-64.

However, it could also be criticized for an inappropriate use of
Weber, in that Weber himself envisaged the period of radicalism
as only occurring during the life-time of the charismatic leader.
What happens *immediately* after the death of the leader is not a
continuation of radicalism but routinization, including settling in
one place and control over the financial resources of the movement.[209]

The influence of Kretschmar and Theissen is clear in the
important paper of K. Niederwimmer on itinerant radicalism in
the *Didache* which is included in this volume.[210] However, unlike
Theissen, Niederwimmer utilizes the insights of redaction critical
analysis to distinguish the ancient tradition he finds in *Didache*
11:4-12 from the redactional material in 11:1-3 and 12:1-13:7
(and a later gloss in 13:4). He observes that the standpoint of the
redaction is that of the local communities and not that of the
itinerant radicals. The ancient tradition points to a time when two
different kinds of itinerant charismatics moved from one community to another in a dense network of local Christians, dependent on their support. The apostles in the text are a larger group
than the "twelve" and are itinerant missionaries pledged to homelessness, renunciation of possessions and marriage. The prophets
are also itinerants whose task is ecstatic speech in the Spirit. They
may have been accompanied by a prophetess in a spiritual marriage. However, the rules in this ancient tradition are not so much
intended to describe their function as to provide criteria to correct
abuses. In other words decay had corrupted the institution of
itinerant charismatics.

According to Niederwimmer, the material provided by the
redactor provides a different picture. The local hosts for the
itinerant charismatics are solidifying into formally constituted
local communities who elect their own officials (15:1f). Ordinary
"non-charismatic" itinerant Christians are also now visiting the
communities (12:1ff), often with the intention of settling. Apostles
fade from the scene, and while prophets continue to visit the community, alongside teachers (13:1-7), they are now in the process
of settling also and in need of provision. This means that tensions
between the local emerging bishops and deacons and the prophets
and teachers need to be resolved. The solution is that both groups
are engaged in the same *leitourgia* and should receive the same
honour (15:1-2). In other words, the leadership of worship which

---

[209] I have argued this in a paper presented to the 1989 meeting of the Society of
Biblical Literature, Anaheim, "Weber, Theissen and the Wandering Charismatics of
the *Didache*".

[210] "Zur Entwicklungsgeschichte des Wanderradikalismus im Traditionsbereich
der Didache", *WSt* 11 (1977) pp. 145-167, esp. 10 notes 1 & 2.

was in the hands of the charismatics is now shared by the local functionaries. A process of integration and stabilization between the itinerant charismatics and the local officials is taking place, which is none other than the process of early catholicization. The thesis of Harnack is re-affirmed![211]

In another essay included in this book,[212] A. de Halleux attempts to roll back the influence of Harnack by a fresh examination of the evidence in the *Didache*. De Halleux proposes to read the text as it stands as the product of the same historical situation. Most importantly, he challenges the assumption that the prophets are itinerant by nature, rather than simply occasionally coming from outside as guests.[213] He sees the "ones teaching" of 11:1-2 as none other than prophets. The instructions concerning apostles are more concerned to warn the community against impostors than to describe their nature and ministry. While the rules pre-suppose some degree of travel and poverty for apostles, they do not need to be interpreted as requiring asceticism and permanent vagabondage. As with the titles "teacher" and "prophets", the title "apostle" does not so much describe an office as a function. Indeed, the absence of the definite article before προφητῶν in 11:3 indicates that the *Didache* does not envisage two groups here but one group designated in two different ways. Thus there is no ministerial trilogy of ministers: apostles, prophets and teachers.[214] de Halleux also denies that the prophet is an ecstatic, but rather concerned with prayer, teaching and charity. The rules of ch.13 do not show an order of itinerant charismatics settling down, although in the case of the apostolic function of the prophet this might be so, but are only concerned to ensure sustenance for the prophets. Nothing suggests that the bishops and deacons are a new institution.

In a recent article reproduced in this book,[215] I have argued that a form and redaction critical analysis should be taken in a different direction. Based on a form critical analysis of the rules

---

[211] This position is affirmed also by W. Rordorf and A. Tuilier, *La Doctrine*, pp. 49-64. The influence of the work of Kretschmar, Theissen and Niederwimmer continues in the modern quest for the historical Jesus in the work of scholars such as J. D. Crossan (*The Historical Jesus: The Life of a Mediterranean Jewish Peasant* [San Francisco: Harper & Rowe, 1991]), esp. 345ff. It merges with the popular theory that Jesus was a wandering Cynic teacher or prophet.

[212] "Les ministères dans la Didachè", *Irenikon* 53 (1980) pp. 5-29. I have been informed by Dom Emmanuel Lanne, the colleague of the late Fr. de Halleux at Louvain, that he was no longer entirely convinced by the thesis he defended in this paper. Nevertheless, it presents important insights and its challenge should continue to be heard.

[213] *Ibid.*, p. 10.

[214] *Ibid.*, pp. 22f.

[215] "Torah and Troublesome Apostles", pp. 347-372.

introduced by the περὶ δέ formula, the rules concerning apostles in 11:3-6 are seen to be the oldest core of the material, which is modified by the insertion of 11:1-2 in the face of the emergence of "false" apostles from within the community who advocate the abandonment of the requirement of Torah observance. This is later again redacted by the insertion of καὶ προφητῶν κατὰ τὸ δόγμα τοῦ εὐαγγελίου in 11:3 and the material on prophets in 11:7-12 at a period when these had begun to dominate the community. The false teaching against which a warning is given in 11:1-2 is linked to the nature of "perfection" and the "whole yoke of the Lord" in 6:2-3, as referring to the acceptance of the Torah by Gentile converts, or at least as much of it as they could bear. The minimum requirement was to observe the prohibition of eating food sacrificed to idols. This is linked to indications in the eschatological conclusion in ch. 16 that the final trials were associated with false teaching emerging from within the community and causing division and "lawlessness".

This thesis is taken further in and essay in *Didache in Context*,[216] where I utilize models from Mary Douglas's anthropological theory of witchcraft in order to analyze the nature of the conflict in the community of the *Didache*. I argue that the strong community boundaries, together with weak and ambiguous social structure, creates the condition for the emergence of a so-called "witch-believing" society, where individuals within the community are believed to be agents of demonic forces seeking to destroy it, and are driven out. The conflict between the untestable charismatic prophets coming from outside the community and the local patrons of the community, the bishops and deacons, is ameliorated and resolved by the production of text from the words and tradition mediated by the prophets, but collected by the teachers, by which they can be tested. This developing situation is linked to the development of the text of the *Didache* itself and its submission to and gradual replacement by the "gospel".

In the same volume, S. J. Patterson also addresses the question of radical itinerancy in the *Didache*, utilizing this time the Coptic version to argue that the text originally ended at 12:2a.[217] At this redactional stage the text was concerned to regulate aspects of the behaviour of teachers, apostles and prophets, which were felt to be problematic. It is written from the perspective of the

---

[216] "Social Ambiguity and the Production of Text: Prophets, Teachers, Bishops,and Deacons and the Development of the Jesus Tradition in the Community of the *Didache*", *Didache in Context*, pp. 284-313.

[217] "*Didache* 11-13: The Legacy of Radical Itinerancy in Early Christianity", in *Didache in Context*, pp. 313-329. Patterson takes up the thesis elaborated earlier in C. N. Jefford & S. J. Patterson, "A Note on *Didache* 12.2a (Coptic)", *SecCent* 7 (1989-1990) pp. 65-75.

settled community and views the behaviour of the itinerants as the source of the problem, whether false teaching, greed or false prophecy. Patterson suggests that the original response of the community was to exclude these itinerants, but that the rules admit them now under strict conditions. Later, in a time of social dislocation, the problem of refugees forces the community to add 12:2b-13:7. Apostles have disappeared now, and prophets and teachers are more welcome than before. In 15:1-2, a new set of officials is introduced, the bishops and deacons, whose legitimacy and equality is established. They represent the new order, while the prophets and teachers are a nostalgic reminder of the bygone era of radical itinerancy, which survived on the fringes in the West but more strongly in the East. Patterson thus essentially reaffirms the position of Theissen and Kretschmar. However, the textual reconstruction based on the Coptic manuscript has been challenged by F. S. Jones and P. A. Mirecki as we have seen and Patterson's theory remains unsubstantiated.[218]

11. Eschatology in the Didache

It is regrettable that the short apocalypse in *Didache* 16 has not received much attention from scholars. The main interest has been in whether or not this forms the original conclusion to the Two Ways. This was suggested already by P. Savi,[219] P. Drews,[220] G. Klein, J. M. Creed[221] and taken up by E. Bammel in the essay included in this volume. There have, however, been strong objections from P. Vielhauer,[222] T. H. C. van Eijk and[223] Rordorf.[224] Bammel, in the essay included here, argues that collections of Jewish paraenesis invariably end with an eschatological warning to re-inforce the ethical imperative. Even if Bammel is right that such a warning originally stood at the end of the Two Ways, it may not have been the same as ch. 16. Niederwimmer concedes that the Two Ways probably concluded with an eschatological warning, but that the Didachist has replaced this original conclu-

---

[218] "Considerations on the Coptic Papyrus of the *Didache* (British Library Oriental Manuscript 9271)", *The Didache in Context*, pp. 47-87.

[219] *La dottrina degli apostoli. Richerche critiche sull'origine del testo con una not intorno all'eucharistia* (Rome, 1893) pp. 55f; cited by Ehrhard, *Altchristliche Literature*, p. 51.

[220] "Untersuchungen", p. 68ff.

[221] "The Didache", *JTS* 39 (1938) pp. 370-387, esp. 379.

[222] *Geschichte der urchristlichen Literatur. Einleitung in das Neue Testament, die Apokryphen und die Apostolischen Väter* (Berlin: de Gruyter, 1975) pp. 730-733.

[223] *La Résurrection des Morts chez les Pèrres Apostoliques* (Paris: Beauchesne, 1974 [ThH 25]) pp. 20-21.

[224] Rordorf & Tuilier, *La Doctrine*, pp. 80-83

sion with tradition obtained from elsewhere, since ch. 16 shares
no material with the eschatological ending of *Doct.*[225]

A second focus of interest in the text has been its relation to
the apocalyptic tradition in the Synoptic Gospels. While some
have seen a dependence on Matthew and/or Luke,[226], H. Köster
has argued that the *Didache* reflects the Ur-text of a Jewish
apocalypse used also by Mark.[227] Glover[228] argues that "Q" is the
ancient source lying behing ch. 16. J. S. Kloppenborg[229] has
demonstrated that the *Didache* only uses material found in Matthew's special source "M" and does not cite Matthew where Matthew can be seen to be using Mark. For him the *Didache*
represents an independent tradition under whose influence Matthew altered his Markan source.[230] My own study of the "sign of
the Son of Man" in 16:6 comes to the same conclusion on the
basis of development of the symbol.[231]

A number of studies have taken up the question of resurrection in the *Didache*. An unpublished thesis by G. Ladd[232] takes up
again Harnack's contention that the Didachist is a millenarian.[233]
A. P. O'Hagan[234] concedes that this may be possible, especially
on the basis of the prayers for the gathering of Israel in chs. 9-10.
Even in 'a Christian framework, this hope would have a
materialistic sense of the re-establishment of the land of Israel
centred on Jerusalem. However, as he rightly points out, this hope
in itself does not consitute millenarianism unless there is also the
expectation of the one thousand year reign. This can certainly not
be derived from the text of the *Didache*, as van Eijk points out in
his thorough study.[235] In continuity with Jewish tradition, the
Didache envisages a resurrection of the righteous only, justified
on the basis of Zechariah 14:5, probably to share in and witness
the judgment of the world.[236]

---

[225] *Die Didache*, pp. 247-248.

[226] E.g. B. C. Butler "Literary Relations", pp. 265-283.

[227] *Überlieferung*, pp. 187-189.

[228] "Quotations", pp. 25-28.

[229] "Didache 16:6-8 and Special Matthean Tradition", *ZNW* 69-70 (1978-1979) pp. 54-67.

[230] "Tradition", p. 63. A reservation concerning Glover's conclusion needs to be made, in that the *Didache* may reflect at this point an underlying Jewish tradition rather than the Jesus teaching in particular, which may draw on the same tradition.

[231] J.A. Draper, "The Development of the "Sign of the Son of Man" in the Jesus Tradition", *NTS* 39 (1991) pp. 1-21.

[232] *The Eschatology of the Didache* (Unpublished Harvard Thesis, 1949).

[233] *Lehrbuch der Dogmengeschichte* I (Tübingen: Mohr, 1909⁴) pp. 186-187.

[234] *Material Recreation in the Apostolic Fathers* (Berlin: Akademie Verlag, 1968 [TU 100]) pp. 18-30.

[235] *La Résurrection*, pp. 25.

[236] *Ibid.*, pp. 25-28. The Jerusalem text ends abruptly and is probably to be reconstructed on the basis of *Const.*

Wengst[237] argues that ethics are given the first place in the way of salvation offered by the *Didache*, as in the Jewish proselyte catechesis from which it derives. Ethical behaviour or "perfection" in the present moment is the key to salvation in 16:2, and the return of the Lord is for judgment according to works (according to the ending reconstructed from *Const*). Eschatology thus becomes a subordinate aspect of ethics, a simple piece of instruction about the "Last Things". This, he maintains, represents a significant shift over against Jesus and earliest Christianity, where the expectation of the end included the hope of worldwide, fundamental upheaval, while ethics were an interim arrangement overshadowed by the eschatological horizon. The apocalypse of the *Didache* is half-way towards the kind of accommodation to the pressures of the world found in later Christian literature, although its community has not completely surrendered its Christian identity.

A number of recent articles have indicated a renewed interest in the eschatological section of the *Didache*. H. R. Seeliger,[238] in a study included in this book, has shown that the apocalypse of the *Didache* does not match the definition propounded by recent research into apocalyptic as a genre. The spatial element of a transcendent world has fallen away and only the temporal element of imminent catastrophe remains. Since this time of trouble revolves around false prophets, and 11:6, 9 also envisages such false prophets, he suggests that ch. 16 preserves an important part of the content of the apocalytic prophecy of the early church, to guard against imposters and to supply material to those communities which did not have prophets (13:4). Two studies in *Didache in Context* by A. Milavec[239] and N. Pardee[240] take up the study of the time of testing in 16:5. In response, I have taken up again the question of the resurrection of the righteous only in a recent paper,[241] and argued that it relates to the so-called "martyr-cult" theology emerging after the Maccabean revolt, and that this was already associated with Zechariah 14:5 in Jewish tradition.

---

[237] *Didache (Apostellehre)*, pp. 59-61.

[238] "Erwägungen zu Hintergrund und Zweck des apokalyptischen Schlusskapitels der *Didache*" in E. A. Livingstone (ed), *Studia Patristica 21: Papers presented to the Tenth International Conference on Patristic Studies held in Oxford 1987* (Leuven: Peeters, 1989) pp. 185-192.

[239] "The Saving Efficacy of the Burning Process in *Didache* 16.5", *Didache in Context*, pp. 131-155.

[240] "The Curse that Saves (*Didache* 16.5)", *Didache in Context*, pp. 156-176.

[241] "Resurrection and Zechariah 14.5 in the Didache Apocalypse", forthcoming in *JEC*.

12. New Currents in Research into the Didache

The collection of essays in *The Didache in Context* indicates that the proliferation of methods which have recently been applied to the New Testament are now being turned towards the *Didache*. Sociological or anthropological studies, begun already in the work of G. Theissen and M. J. Suggs mentioned above, include recent work by R. S. Ascough,[242] A. Milavec,[243] J. W. Riggs[244] and myself.[245] Literary analyses influenced by the theory of orality or rhetoric have been undertaken by I. H. Henderson,[246] J. Reed,[247] and J. S. Kloppenborg.[248] It remains to be seen to what extent these new methodologies will transform our understanding of this much debated writing. Research into the Jewish roots of the *Didache* also continues to develop, as we have seen, and this promises to be an important area for further work in the light of new discoveries and understandings.[249]

---

[242] "An Analysis of the Baptismal Tirual of the *Didache*", *StLiturg* 24 (1994) pp. 201-213 (utilizing the initiation model of Victor Turner).

[243] "The Social Setting of "Turning the Other Cheek" and "Loving One's Enemies" in the Light of the *Didache*", *BTB* 25 (1995) pp. 131-143 (utilizing a variety of models, especially Theissen).

[244] "The Sacred Food of *Didache* 9-10 and Second Century Ecclesiologies", in *The Didache in Context*, pp. 256-283 (utilizing Malinowski, Radcliffe-Brown and Mary Douglas).

[245] J. A. Draper, "Christian Self-Definition", pp. 362-377; "Social Ambiguity and the Production of Text: Prophets, Teachers, Bishops,and Deacons and the Development of the Jesus Tradition in the Community of the *Didache*", *Didache in Context*, pp. 284-313

[246] "*Didache* and Orality in Synoptic Comparison", *JBL* 111 (1992) pp. 283-306; "Style-switching in the *Didache*: Fingerprint or Argument", *Didache in Context*, pp. 177-209.

[247] "The Hebrew Epic and the *DIDACHE*", *Didache in Context*, pp. 213-225.

[248] "The Transformation of Moral Exhortation in *Didache* 1-5", *Didache in Context*, pp. 88-109.

[249] Besides the authors mentioned above on pp. 15, see M. del Verme, *Giudaismo e Nuovo Testamento: Il Caso delle Decime* (Naples: D'Auria, 1989) pp. 216-228 (on tithes); "Medio giudaismo e *Didaché*: il caso della comunione dei beni", *VetChr* 32 (1995) pp. 293-320 (on community of property).

THE DIDACHE AS A CHURCH ORDER: AN EXAMINATION OF THE PURPOSE FOR THE COMPOSITION OF THE DIDACHE AND ITS CONSEQUENCES FOR INTERPRETATION

GEORG SCHÖLLGEN

Aachen

Despite the intensive investigation the *Didache* has undergone since its *editio princeps* in 1883, it has remained an object of many controversies. Beside the question of its place and time of origin, this is true especially concerning the literary integrity and state of development of the church constitution which is mirrored in the writing.

Among the few points of consensus in research one may mention the formal structure: "Über die literarische Gattung der Did(ache) herrscht im übrigen Einigkeit: die Did(ache) ist eine Kirchenordnung, und zwar die älteste ihrer Art."[1] A first glance at the text already confirms this conclusion: catechesis, liturgy and church offices with very detailed rules are its main subject, generally typical themes of ancient Christian church orders. In addition there is an absence of any interest in dogmatic questions: the text deals with the external ordering of the community, not its theology.[2]

The obvious plausibility of this conclusion concerning the formal limitation of the thematic field has, however, misled most interpreters not to examine more closely the purpose for the composition of the text, and consequently to be in danger of working unconsciously with assumptions which correspond to modern conceptions of a church order, but are not applicable without further qualification to ancient representatives of this form, like the *Didache*, the *Apostolic Tradition*, the Syriac *Didascalia* and the *Apostolic Constitutions*.

Along with the question of the scope of the regulations, which is closely bound up with questions concerning the purpose of composition, one of these premises will be more closely examined here. The great majority of the interpreters of the *Didache*—seldom explicitly as in Vielhauer and Harnack, more often implicitly as in the newer commentaries of Rordorf and

---

[1] P. Vielhauer, *Geschichte der urchristlichen Literatur* (Berlin: de Gruyter, 1975) p. 725; compare also A. Harnack, *Die Lehre der zwölf Apostel nebst Untersuchungen zur ältesten Geschichte der Kirchenverfassung und des Kirchenrechts* (Leipzig: Hinrichs, 1884 [TU 2,1/2]), Prolegomena, p. 32.

[2] Cf. K. Wengst, *Didache (Apostellehre), Barnabasbrief, Zweiter Klemensbrief, Schrift an Diognet* (Darmstadt: Wissenschaftliche Buchgesellschaft, 1984 [SUC 2]) p. 17.

Wengst—assume that the *Didache* proceeded, according to its self-understanding, to regulate comprehensively the institutional life of the church in its essential areas, and did not simply deal with isolated contentious questions of community discipline.[3]

In my opinion, the consequences of this unfounded assumption in the previous literature are more far-reaching than may appear at first sight. If one follows the understanding of the *Didache* as a comprehensive church order, then the text—as the only source from the post apostolic period—is in the position to give an untruncated picture of the whole external life of an early Christian community. In other words, the criterion of comprehensiveness allows one not only to utilize the positive provisions which the text gives its addressees, but also allows the interpreters to go beyond this to the rare opportunity of a methodically legitimate use of the otherwise rightly rejected argument from silence: if the *Didache* is a comprehensive church order, then one can conclude—at least in the areas with which it deals more closely (eg. catechesis, liturgy and church offices)—that whatever it does not deal with was not practiced at the time of its composition. The reverse conclusion from the argument from silence raises the value of the text as a source considerably.

Most of the literature has eagerly seized on this possibility and given the argument from silence in the Didache more room than for any other pre-Constantinian text; moreover, most interpretations cannot do without this presupposition—which is not usually acknowledged.

The value of the *Didache* as a source would, however, be much reduced if it was not a comprehensive, but simply a selective church order, if it was thus not a matter of a regulation of the general institutional life of the community, but only of the clarification of contested particular issues from the thematic field "external rule of the community" and remained without reference to the wide area of uncontested praxis. In this case, completeness

---

[3] A. Harnack, *Die Apostellehre und die jüdischen beiden Wege*[2] (Leipzig: Hinrichs, 1896) p. 6: "Alles is darauf angelegt, in übersichtlicher, leichtfasslicher leicht behaltlicher Form die wichtigsten Regeln für das christliche Leben, die διδάγματα τοῦ κυρίου, zusammenzustellen. In dem, was die Schrift enthält und was sie nicht enthält, ...ist sie ein kostbarer Kommentar zu den ältesten Zeugnissen, die wir für das Leben, den Interessenkreis und die Ordnungen, die sich als nützlich erwiesen und als notwendig herausgebildet hatten, zu kodifizieren." Cf. as well J.-P. Audet, *La Didachè. Instructions des apôtres* (Paris: Gabalda, 1958) pp. 436-9, who rejects the title "Church Order" for the *Didache* and already discerns the essentially more modest goal of the writing, without proposing an exact designation of form. The objections of W. Rordorf & A. Tuilier (*La doctrine des douze apôtres (Didachè)* [Paris: Les Éditions du Cerf, 1978 (SC 248)] p. 21 n. 2) against the designation "Church Order" do not affect the definition of Vielhauer. In what follows the text will be cited according to this edition.

would not have been not intended, the argument from silence would thus be worthless to a large extent, and the interpretation would have to limit itself to positive regulations which are rather rare, as closer observation reveals.

In the following study, the question of the extent of the rules will be examined in the details of the text. Attention will be drawn to five aspects or questions in particular:

1. the *Didache* is structured into a large number of clearly separated thematic sections, which as a rule put forward one essential argumentation. To determine the extent of the rules it is necessary first to work out the respective goals of the argumentation of these single sections.

2. Since the text often rejects deviant practices, it must be asked whether its regulation is directed against a recognizable abuse or dissent, which may be attested elsewhere as well.

3. Is it clear from the context whether the text reacts to changed circumstances, in that it modifies the previously valid praxis in the sense of an adaptation?

4. To what extent is the particular area of the life of the community regulated? Is it restricted to the problematic, contentious issues or also to what no-one contests?

5. In what manner are the particular sections of argumentation connected to each other? Does the text have a tight construction, or do the sections stand next to each other in a merely associative or unconnected manner?

1. Chapters 1-6

We can dispense with a closer consideration of 1-6 in the present context, since it offers a piece of tradition. It is widely recognized today[4] that it represents a widely disseminated pre-existing Christian Two Ways teaching with few additions,[5] which possibly

---

[4] Of the more recent literature, one only need mention: J.-P. Audet, "Affinités littéraires et doctrinales du "manuel de discipline"", *RB* 59 (1952) pp. 219-238; also *Didachè*, pp. 121-163; S. Giet, *L'énigme de la Didachè* (Paris: Ophrys, 1970 [PFLUS 149]) pp. 39-170; R. A. Kraft, *Barnabas and the Didache* (New York: Thomas Nelson, 1965 [AF 3]) pp. 4-16; W. Rordorf, "Un chapitre d'éthique judéo-chrétienne. Les deux voies", *RSR* 60 (1972) pp. 109-128; also Rordorf & Tuilier, *La Doctrine*, pp. 22-34; Wengst, *Didache (Apostellehre)*, pp. 20-22.

[5] It is hard to determine whether these additions derive from the composer of the nucleus of the *Didache*; cf. on this B. Layton, "The Sources, Date and Transmission of Didache 1,3b-2,1", *HThR* 61 (1968) pp. 343-383, esp. 380-382; Giet, *Énigme*, pp. 189-191; A. Stuiber, ""Das ganze Joch des Herrn" (Didache 6,3-3)" in F. L. Cross (ed.), *Studia Patristica* 4 (Berlin: Akademie-Verlag, 1961 [TU 79]) pp. 323-329; W. Rordorf, "Le problème de la transmission textuelle de Didachè 1,3b-2,1" in F. Paschke (ed.), *Überlieferungsgeschichtliche Untersuchungen* (Berlin: Akademie-Verlag, 1981 [TU 125]) pp. 499-513; Wengst, *Didache (Apostellehre)*, pp. 18f; K. Niederwimmer, "Textprobleme der Didache", *WSt* 95 (1982)

goes back to a Jewish prototype. It is uncertain whether it was included with the rest of the *Didache* from the beginning, or was added only later. In any case the transition, ταῦτα πάντα προειπόντες,[6] is intended to integrate the Two Ways teaching into the context of the prescription for baptism in such a way that it had to precede the baptismal ceremony as pre-baptismal catechesis.[7]

2. Chapter 7:1-4

The first two sections deal with themes from the sphere of baptism.[8]

a. The main issue in the first three verses is the kind of baptismal water to be used. In accordance with local conditions, the author determines what kinds of water could be used for baptism. He shares the high preference of his Jewish and pagan environment and the early church for living (=flowing) water in rivers, springs and sea[9] and prescribes it as baptismal water.[10]

In vv.2-3 he nevertheless deems it necessary to make a series of qualifications. In accordance with local or seasonal circumstances,[11] he permits also water of a lesser quality[12] and finally

---

pp. 116-119.

[6] Did 7:1; with good reasons P. Nautin ("La composition de la "Didachè" et son titre", *RHR* 78 [1959] pp. 206f) and Rordorf ("Chapitre", pp. 116f) reject the conjecture of Audet (*Didachè*, p. 58) that ταῦτα πάντα προειπόντες was a late interpolation which had its origin in the praxis of the Egyptian church, to utilize the Two Ways Teaching as the foundation for pre-baptismal catechesis.

[7] προλέγειν is here better translated "explain" than "say beforehand", i.e. it is rather to be thought of as a pre-baptismal catechesis than as a recitation in the baptismal liturgy; cf. in this regard Rordorf, "Chapitre", pp. 115-122; A. Vööbus, *Liturgical Traditions in the Didache* (Stockholm: Estonian Theological Society in Exile, 1968 [PETSE 16]) PP. 17-20; A. Benoit, *Le baptême chrétien au second siècle* (Paris: Presses Universitaires de France, 1953) pp. 6f, 21-23.

[8] Cf. in this connection W. Rordorf, "Le baptême selon la Didachè" in *Mélanges liturgiques offerts au R. P. Dom Bernard Botte O.S.B.* (Louvain: Abbaye du Mont César, 1972) pp. 499-509; Vööbus, *Liturgical Traditions*, pp. 17-60; Benoit, *Le baptême*, pp. 5-33; S. Giet, "Coutume, évolution, droit canon. A propos de deux passages de la Didachè", *RDC* 16 (1966) pp. 118-132; R. Pillinger, "Die Taufe nach der Didache", *WSt* 88 (1975) pp. 152-160, whose inference about Didache 7-10 as a baptistry in in any case very questionable.

[9] Cf. in this regard T. Klauser, "Taufet in lebendigem Wasser! Zum religions- und kulturgeschichtlichen Verständnis von Didache 7,103" in E. Dassmann, *Gesammelte Arbeiten zur Liturgiegeschichte, Kirchengeschichte und Christlichen Archäologie* (Münster in Westfalen: Aschendorff, 1974 [JAC.E 3]) pp. 177-183; Rordorf, "Baptême", pp. 505-507; Vööbus, *Liturgical Traditions*, pp. 22-27; Benoit, *Le baptême*, pp. 8f.

[10] Did. 7:1.

[11] Possibly the rule that warm water may also be used refers not so much to the cold season but rather to sick baptisands; cf. F. J. Dölger, "Nilwasser und Taufwasser", *ACh* 5 (1936) pp. 175-183 and Benoit, *Le baptême*, p. 8.

[12] Cf. in this regard the detailed argument in Rordorf, "Baptême", p. 506.

even allows baptism by the threefold sprinkling of water over the head in place of immersion, though only when there is a great shortage of water.[13] The argument of the section is clear: while adhering strictly to the preference for flowing water and baptism by immersion, necessary concessions are made to local circumstances. One must assume that the author wants to solve a particularly pressing question for the communities in waterless regions. It is striking that, as the only other element of baptismal liturgy, the threefold baptismal formula is introduced. Whether the author—as is often assumed—turns against another formula,[14] remains uncertain. Perhaps one must assume that a second concern, albeit of subordinate significance, underlies the argument.

b. The fourth verse is devoted to the pre-baptismal fast.[15] Here the fast has clearly a higher level of obligation for the baptismal candidate than for the other participants: the baptisand is obliged to fast for one or two days,[16] while the baptizer and other congregands are merely recommended to fast for an unspecified period of time. The express requirement, expressed by the term κελεύεις, suggests that the author wants to oppose with his regulation a neglect of the baptismal fast.

In the four verses referred to, the instructions of the *Didache* concerning baptism are exhausted. The reader learns nothing about the actual rite of baptism, about the baptismal confession, about the person of the baptizer, about the conditions of admission of candidates (age, occupation etc.) or about the baptismal day. We do not argue that all of these questions—widely contested[17] —were already regulated in detail at the time of the composition of the *Didache*. This is still very controversial.[18] Yet it is certain

---

[13] G. Kretschmar, *Die Geschichte des Taufgottesdienstes in der Alten Kirche* (Kassel, 1970 [Leiturgia 5]) p. 47, understands the different kinds of water as equally graded alternatives and so misunderstands the argumentational goal of the text.

[14] Cf. in this regard Vööbus, *Liturgical Traditions*, pp. 35-39; Audet, *Didachè*, p. 352; Rordorf, "Baptême", p. 504f; the theory that Did. 9:5 preserves an (older) baptismal formula, remains hypothetical; cf. Rordorf & Tuilier, *La Doctrine*, p. 44, n. 2.

[15] Cf. Rordorf, "Baptême", pp. 503f; Vööbus, *Liturgical Traditions*, pp. 20f; J. Schümmer, *Die altchristliche Fastenpraxis mit besonderer Berücksichtigung der Schriften Tertullians* (Münster, 1933), p. 165.

[16] According to the thrust of the argument, κελεύεις must express a higher grade of duty than the imperative προνηστευσάτω; otherwise the necessity of the continuation in v.4b would be scarcely comprehensible.

[17] The datings extend from the apostolic time (Audet, *Didachè*, pp. 187-210) into the late second century: e.g. R. H. Connolly, "Agape and eucharist in the Didache", *DRev* 55 (1937) p. 489.

[18] One can be sure that there already was a baptismal confession; cf. in this regard A. Stenzel, *Die Taufe: eine genetische Erklärung der Taufliturgie* (Innsbruck: Rauch, 1958 [FGThUL 7/8]) p. 41.

that, in the case of concern with the baptismal water and the requirement of the pre-baptismal fast, matters of secondary importance are discussed and that the decisive questions, which a comprehensive church order would have had to settle with respect to baptism, are not dealt with, with the exception of the baptismal formula.[19] On these grounds any argument from silence[20] is forbidden, such as, for example, one which concludes from the fact that nothing more is specified about who conducts baptism, that the community has formed no rules or even preferences in the matter.[21]

With vv.2, 3, 4b, which differ from the context in their use of the second person singular address, the author may well have worked in pre-existent traditional material.[22] The comparison with ch.13 makes it probable that this is not a later interpolation, since in that case four verses which are written in second person singular are clearly to be identified as traditional material which has been worked in.[23]

3. Chapter 8:1

The pre-baptismal fast is connected with the stationary fast by conceptual association.[24] In this it is exclusively a matter of the specification of fast days in polemical differentiation from Jewish[25] or Jewish Christian[26] practice. Against members of the

---

[19] Similarly also Benoit (La baptême), who points out that the Didache overlooks "certains éléments essentiels et constants du baptême chrétien" Vööbus (Liturgical Traditions, p. 25): "Nothing is recorded about the way in which the act itself was conducted."

[20] Rordorf, for example, violates this principle ("Baptême", p. 509), and concludes from the absence of different elements of the baptismal liturgy, that they were unknown to the author, which he considers to be an argument for the "archaic character" of the Didache; similarly also Vööbus (Liturgical Traditions, p. 26).

[21] So e.g. Rordorf, "Baptême", p. 502, for Did. 7:1, 4a; Wengst, Didache (Apostellehre), p. 97, n. 62; more cautiously Vööbus, Liturgical Traditions, pp. 26f and Benoit, Le baptême, pp. 9f.

[22] Nevertheless, Vööbus (Liturgical Traditions, pp. 34f) expresses himself sceptical; besides the change of number, the repetition of the triadic baptismal formula also speaks for the separation of sources.

[23] Cf. below [p. 16, n. 88] with a comment on Audet's interpretatio nof the passages in the second person plural; Giet Le Énigme, p. 195f wants to distinguish inside vv.2 and 3 different "redactional touches", which is not necessary in my opinion.

[24] Cf. in this regard Schümmer, Altchristliche Fastenpraxis, pp. 82-150; R. Arbesmann, Art. "Fasttage", RAC 7 (1969) pp. 500-524.

[25] So the majority of commentators: e.g. Kraft, Barnabas and the Didache, p. 164; R. Knopf, Die Lehre der zwölf Apostel; Die zwei Clemensbriefe (Tübingen: Mohr, 1920 [HNT.E 1]) p. 23; Harnack, Die Lehre, Text p. 25; Audet, Didachè, p. 368; Wengst, Didache (Apostellehre), p. 97, n. 64.

[26] So Rordorf & Tuilier, La Doctrine, pp. 36f; in any case the argument that the Didache could not express itself very strongly against Jews, because it owes so

community who continue to keep the Jewish fast days[27]—Monday and Thursday—the *Didache* 8:1 asserts Wednesday and Friday as the Christian fast-days.

Again only one aspect of the practice of fasting in the ancient church is regulated. The reader learns nothing e.g. about the length,[28] intensity or even the degree of compulsion of the stationary fast, the extent of its applicability to people (with exemptions for sick, aged and children) and the Paschal fast.[29] All this is assumed as known.

4. Chapter 8:2-3

Again with the help of conceptual association,[30] the transition is made to a further differentiation against a Jewish or Jewish-Christian praxis. The prayer practice of the ὑποκριταί, which is not described in more detail, is replaced by the Lord's Prayer as a obligatory prayer. The occasion is clearly the practice of Christians using the prayer formulae of Jewish[31] or Jewish-Christian origin for private prayer,[32] which is regarded by the author as an abuse. Based on the authority of the Lord, he prescribes instead the Lord's Prayer, which must be prayed three times a day analogously to the Jewish custom.[33]

5. Chapter 9:1-10:7

The question as to which kind of community meals the "eucharistic" prayers, which chs.9-10 make obligatory, are designed to regulate does not need to be discussed here. The controversies over this, which have not yet reached final consensus,[34]

---

much to the Jewish tradition, bears little weight.

[27] Cf. Schümmer, *Altchristliche Fastenpraxis*, pp. 51-81; Arbesmann, pp. 512f.

[28] Cf. *Ibid.*, pp. 100-105; the theory of Rordorf & Tuilier, *La Doctrine*, p. 173, n. 6, that the accusative, τετράδα και παρασκευήν could refer to a continuation for a whole day, dispenses with the fundamentals.

[29] Cf. Schümmer, *Altchristliche Fastenpraxis*, pp. 51-81; Arbesmann, pp. 512f.

[30] Why Giet (*L'énigme*, p. 203) attributes chapter 8 to a "section consacrée à l'initiation baptismale", remains unclear; Pillinger ("Die Taufe", p. 156) also gives no evidence for this opinion.

[31] Cf. in this regard P. F. Bradshaw, *Daily Prayer in the Early Church* (London: SPCK, 1981) pp. 1-22.

[32] So too Knopf, *Die Lehre*, p. 23; P. Drews, "Untersuchungen zur Didache", *ZNW* 5 (1904) p. 74.

[33] Cf. Bradshaw, *Daily Prayer*, p. 2; Rordorf & Tuilier, *La Doctrine*, p. 37; J. Jeremias, *The Prayers of Jesus* (London: SCM [StBTh 2,6]), pp. 69-72.

[34] A detailed summary of the discussion is provided by W. Rordorf, "The Didache" in W. Rordorf et al (eds.), *The Eucharist of the Early Christians* (New York: Pueblo, 1978) pp. 1-23, esp. 3-9.

are already an indication that this section, even if one adds chapter 14, is not designed to provide a comprehensive regulation of the liturgical communal gathering.[35]

Instead, only three points are explained:

1. Provision of binding formulae for three "eucharistic" prayers:

    a. first, prayer[36] over the cup (9:2)

    b. then over the broken bread (9:3-4)

    c. finally after the ending of the meal (μετὰ δὲ τὸ ἐμπλησθῆναι 10:2-6)

2. Prohibition of the consumption of the wine and bread of the "eucharist" by unbaptized persons (9:5).

3. Instruction to give the prophets the right to formulate and use "eucharistic" prayers themselves without limitation (10:7).

It is clearly the chief intention of the passage to prescribe as binding the given "eucharistic" prayers, which probably do not originate from the pen of the author.[37] Possibly the communities had at their disposal formulae which were aberrant or insufficient; many perhaps had no fixed formulae, and the author considered it necessary to change this situation, which he considered an abuse.[38] The high valuation of talking in the Spirit, which ch.11 attests, however, makes it necessary to make an exception in the case of the prophet.[39] *Didache* 10:7 thus stands in direct connection with the chief intention of the passage.

This is not the case with the limitation of the consumption of the "eucharist" to the baptized, a prescription which the author has put immediately after the prayers over wine and bread. The harsh formulation of the reason: "Since the Lord has said about this: "Do not give what is holy to the dogs!" indicates that non-baptized[40] also participated at the "eucharistic" meals and the author wishes to reject this abuse.[41]

Since further regulations in the area of community meals follow in ch.14, we will only address the issue of whether the

---

[35] This becomes clear, e.g. if one assumes, with Rordorf & Tuilier (*La Doctrine*, pp. 40f) among others, that Did 10:6b announces a continuation of the "Eucharist", which is not regulated by the *Didache*.

[36] For the Jewish origin of the sequence of the first three prayers, cf. Rordorf, "Didache", pp. 8f.

[37] Cf. in this regard Rordorf, "Didache", 9-14; Audet, *Didachè*, p. 375; Wengst, *Didache (Apostellehre*, p. 23.

[38] Similarly also Drews, "Untersuchungen", p. 74.

[39] That the prophets presided over the "Eucharist", cannot simply be asssumed from this passage; it remains unclear who possessed the presidency; so too Vööbus, *Liturgical Traditions*, p. 111.

[40] Similarly also Drews, "Untersuchungen", p. 77; Knopf, *Die Lehre*, p. 27.

[41] Similarly also Drews, "Untersuchungen", p. 77; Knopf, *Die Lehre*, p. 27.

Didache offers a consistent, comprehensive, regulation of this area of community life at that point.

Chs.11 and 12 address themselves to a further problematic area. Common to them is that they provide regulations for the handling of Christians arriving from outside, who seek reception in the community as strangers. Christian and non-Christian sources of especially the second century give a graphic picture of the extent to which the well-known Christian hospitality was exploited.[42] The *Didache* now seeks to give the community criteria with which they can separate out the impostors, without having to abandon the institution of hospitality, and without cutting off the rights of particular church offices. Since the different offices were allocated differential qualifications and rights, they must be dealt with one by one.

6. Chapter 11:1-2

The *Didache* has a fairly simple solution for "those who teach".[43] Although the term διδάσκαλος is not used in the present passage,[44] one could well agree with Rordorf, among others, that it deals with the office of teacher.[45] The criterion for their acceptance is the agreement of their teaching with that of the *Didache*. Ταῦτα πάντα τὰ προειρημένα probably refers rather to the Two Ways teaching than to the detailed community rules of 7-10. If the new arrival teaches another διδαχή which contradicts the latter, which is liable to destroy the community, one must refuse him a hearing and indeed also accommodation; but if he teaches in the sense of our text "to add to righteousness and to the knowledge of the Lord", then he must be received as the Lord himself.[46]

---

[42] Cf. in this regard the collection of references in Harnack, *Die Lehre*, Text, pp. 43f; Prolegomena, pp. 125-127; K. Niederwimmer, "Zur Entwicklungsgeschichte des Wanderradikalismus im Traditionsbereich der Didache", *WSt* 90 (1977) p. 158, n. 36.

[43] Cf. in this regard H. A. Stempel, "Der Lehrer in der "Lehre der zwölf Apostle", *VigChr* 34 (1980) p. 209; A. von Harnack, *Die Mission und Ausbreitung des Christentums in den ersten drei Jahrhunderten* I (Leipzig: Hinrichs, 1924⁴) ppl 365-377; also *Die Lehre*, Prolegomena, p. 131-137.

[44] Cf. however Did 13:2; 15:1-2, where διδάσκαλος is explicitly used as a designationfor a church office.

[45] Did 11:2 ὁ διδάσκων is translated by Rordorf & Tuilier (*La Doctrine*, p. 183) as "docteur"; so too Stempel ("Der Lehrer", pp. 210, 213); hesitantly Harnack (*Die Lehre*, Text, p. 37). This interpretation is likely, because in the development of the chapter the question of conduct is directed to arrivals of the two remaining statuses which are not bound to the community; differently Wengst, *Didache (Apostellehre)*, p. 37.

[46] Cf. Mt 10:40; Lk 10:16.

The subject of the short passage is thus simply the criteria which allow one to discern the true from the false teacher in the understanding of the *Didache*. There is no regulation, one would expect from a comprehensive community rule, of the organizational scope of his activity: does he operate in baptismal preparation, or does he only take care of the catechesis of the candidates, or of the homily in the service?[47] Later in the *Didache*, in another context, we meet the simple claim of the true teacher to provision from the community, if he settles.[48] Further, in yet another context, he is numbered next to the bishops, deacons and prophets among the τετιμημένοι ὑμῶν, the honoured of the community.[49] A concrete description of his activity, which made him worthy of his wages,[50] is absent.[51]

7. Chapter 11:3-12

In v.3 two further groups of arrivals are singled out, whose condition demands individual treatment: apostles and prophets.[52] For instructions about conduct with them, the *Didache* explicitly appeals to the δόγμα τοῦ εὐαγγελίου.[53] The author must clearly

---

[47] How Stempel ("Der Lehrer", p. 212) concludes from Did 15:1f about the leadership of the liturgy by the teacher, remains unclear. Similarly also H. von Campenhausen, *Kirchliches Amt und geistliche Vollmacht in den ersten drei Jahrhunderten* (Tübingen: Mohr, 1963² [BHTh 14]) p. 79.

[48] Did 13:2; one need not necessarily conclude from this that they were without possessions or even that they were required to be so; differently Stempel, "Die Lehre", p. 212.

[49] Did 15:1-2.

[50] Did 13:2.

[51] Stempel ("Die Lehre", p. 210) relates a passage from the Two Ways teaching, Did 4:1, to the office of the teacher. That remains still uncertain. It could be related to the other offices in the context of the *Didache* just as well, especially the apostle and the prophet. That the writing had a teacher as author, as Stempel ("Die Lehre", pp. 210-212) suggests, remains in any case uncertain. Impermissible is the thorough-going identification of the teacher with the prophets, which Stemple ("Die Lehre", p. 213) proposes it in conjunction with Kraft. Likewise there is no certain evidence that "die Lehrer als die regulären geistlichen Führer einer Gemeinde angesehen werden" (Stempel, *Ibid.*). The attempt of A. de Halleux also ("Les ministères dans la Didachè", *Irenikon* 53 [1980] pp. 10f) to relate the two verses to the prophets, is not convincing, since other distinguishing criteria are given for them in the space of the same unit of argumentation (Did 11:7-12). Moreover, their speaking in the Spirit is not permitted to be tested—unlike the διδαχή discussed here.

[52] Cf. in this regard esp. G. Sass, "Die Apostel in der Didache", in W. Schmauch (ed.), *In memoriam E. Lohmeyer* (Stuttgart: Evangelisches Verlagswerk, 1951) pp. 233-239, esp. 235 on the differentiation of the title of apostle in chp. 11 of the *Didache* from the Twelve Apostles of the title; G. Schille, "Das Recht der Propheten und Apostel—gemeinderechtliche Beobachtungen zu Didache Kap. 11-13", in P. Wätzel & G. Schille (eds.), *Theologische Versuche* (Berlin: Akademie-Verlag, 1966) pp. 84-103; Niederwimmer, "Entwicklungsgeschichte", pp. 145-167.

[53] Cf. also Did. 8:2 with a similar formulation; the question as to whether this implies one of the synoptic gospels, cannot be discussed here.

cite this high authority, because, as a result of the high prestige of the two offices, the limitation of hospitality he is seeking will be hard to implement.

a. The Apostles (11:4-6)

As with the teachers, the duty to receive each apostle as the Lord stands at the beginning of the section. Yet the goal of the argumentation is to put an end to the obvious abuses to which the exploitation of this hospitality has led, while preserving the duty.

First the stay of the travelling apostle is limited to one, at most two days; a third day, which was granted to a normal Christian arrival,[54] already shows him to be a false prophet.[55] The short stay makes it impossible for the apostle to teach in the community or to do any other work.[56]

The author confronts the practice of false apostles, who demand gifts or at least expect them, with his demand that they should only be given bread or provision for a day's journey when they go, which does no more than fulfill a command of general hospitality.[57] If the apostle demands money, he has unmasked himself as a charlatan. About the task of the apostle, who probably must have been engaged in the mission outside already existing communities,[58] the Didache gives just as little explicit information[59] as over the nature and circumstances of his commis-

---

[54]Did. 12:2; on the background of Graeco-Roman and Jewish hospitality, which knew similar rules, cf. Audet, Didachè, pp. 444f.

[55]Cf. Rordorf & Tuilier (La Doctrine, p. 52) for the evidence that the expression, ψευδοπροφήτης in the LXX and early Christian literature is used "pour désigner une personne qui prétend être un envoyé de Dieu sans l'être véritablement", and does not simply refer to a false prophet (similar also Niederwimmer, "Entwicklungsgeschichte", p. 155 note 26). De Halleux could not refute this; with this the chief argument for the identity of apostles and prophets (and teachers), for which he argues, falls away. Elsewhere as well, the Didache distinguishes these three offices clearly from one another. The fact that the writing does not introduce the three offices together as a "trilogy" (de Halleux, p. 13) is no argument for identifying them.

[56] So they are also not preachers, who—like modern revivalists—seek out already existing communities, as de Halleux ("Les ministères", p. 13) thinks.

[57] Cf. in this regard Audet, Didachè, p. 446.

[58] This is probably also the reason why the apostles in Did. 15:2 are not introduced among the τετιμημένοι; unlike the prophets and teachers, they no longer have any function in already existing communities; for a different point of view, see Niederwimmer ("Entwicklungsgeschichte", p. 154 note 21), who does not see the apostles (and prophets) as community founders or organizers, but as eschatologically motivated drop-outs from the contemporary society. Howver, there are no bases to be found for this in the text.

[59]De Halleux ("Les ministères", p. 12) also demonstrates this. He rightly refutes the assumption that one can deduce anything from the text about the ascetic lifestyle of the apostle.

sion;[60] it is simply a matter of providing the community with criteria to distinguish the false apostle, and in this way overcome abuses.

b. The Prophets (11:7-12)

The subject of vv.7-12 is the office of prophet;[61] again the author has tried to give the community criteria which will put them in the position to differentiate true from false holders of this office.[62] With prophets this is particularly difficult because, in talking in the Spirit,[63] they have at their disposal a gift of divine origin, which is, in principle, impervious to human judgment.[64] Therefore the passage begins with the prohibition against putting prophets to the test[65] while they speak in the Spirit. Clearly this command had come to be widely disregarded, since the *Didache* finds it necessary to understand testing of speaking in the Spirit as a sin against the Holy Spirit and expressly indicates it to be unforgivable.

Since speaking in the Spirit, as a kind of technique, can be mastered not only by true but also by false prophets, it cannot by itself be a mark of differentiation. Instead of this, agreement with the lifestyle of the Lord[66] serves as the criterion of the true

---

[60] Schille ("Das Recht", p. 93) thinks that the apostles carried out a messenger service; there is no support for this in the text either.

[61] That it is a matter of wandering prophets, cannot be deduced from ch.11; but it is assumed implicitly in Did. 13:1; cf. also Niederwimmer, "Entwicklungsgeschichte", pp. 156f.

[62] Cf. the same problem in *HermMan* 11.7:21 (SC 53*bis*, 194-8 Joly).

[63] What the *Didache* understood by speaking in the Spirit is only promoted in a limited way. In terms of content it is a matter of demands spoken out aloud in comprehensible form (vv.8, 12) and teaching (vv.10f) from the realm of community discipline and ethics. In terms of its form, it is obviously a recognizable manner (or technique) of speaking instantly recognizable as such by every member of the community, which governed not only the true but also the false-prophet (v.8). Cf. D. E. Aune, *Prophecy in Early Christianity and the Ancient Mediterranean World* (Grand Rapids, Mich.: Eerdmans) p. 310. Perhaps it is distinguished from the speech of the teachers in that the listener gets the impression that it is not the prophet himself who speaks, but another, the Spirit, is serving his own. In this sense speaking in the Spirit presupposes ecstasy as "getting worked up".

[64] It is, strictly speaking, not a matter of a prohibition on testing prophets. Only the testing of speaking in the Spirit is forbidden. Thus there is no contradiction between vv.7 and 8, as Giet (*Énigme*, p. 222) assumes.

[65] What exactly is meant by παιράζω—test, put to the test—and διακρίνω—judge, speak a judgment—is made clear by a parallel in Eusebius, *HE* 5.16:16f and 5.18:13 (GCS 9,1,466. 478 Schwartz), where the attempt of bishops in the ecumenical church to refute montanist prophecies by internal contradictions and to move prophets to disputations is reported. Certainly it is not simply the interruption of speaking in the Spirit which is prohibited, as de Halleux ("Les ministères", p. 15) rightly objected against Rordorf & Tuilier (*La Doctrine*, p. 53 note 3).

[66] What the author understood by the lifestyle of the Lord, is not more precisely explained; the example of vv.9-12 simply gives an—admittedly fragmentary—example; Knopf (*Die Didache*, p. 31) sees behind this the thoughts of the "imitatio

prophet. "For by their lifestyle the false prophet will be known from the true prophet".[67] The area of doctrine clearly plays no role in this context—in contrast to the case of the teachers.

In vv.9-12 the principle set out in v.8 is developed in particular examples.[68] The demand of the prophet to prepare a meal, given while speaking in the Spirit,[69] must indeed be complied with by the community;[70] but if the prophet himself eats from it, he misuses speaking in the Spirit to his personal advantage—as this obviously often happened—and then he shows himself to be a false prophet.

As a further principle, the *Didache* sets out the agreement of true—obviously ethical—teaching and conduct. The cryptic sounding (to modern ears) v.11, which has not yet been satisfactorily explained,[71] limits this principle and so the community's possibility of testing in a special case—though only for the person who has already proved himself to be a genuine prophet. The last verse of this section tries once more to safeguard against an abuse of the regulation. Obviously false prophets misused speaking in the Spirit to make demands on the community for money; the Shepherd of Hermas attests similar abuses.[72] Again the criterion is use for oneself, which characterizes the speaking in the Spirit of the false prophets. Demands for money for others if they are poor, lies beyond the competence of the community to judge. The goal of the argument of vv.7-12 is clear: while strictly preserving the high valuation of speaking in the Spirit, which is beyond human judgment and testing, the author puts forward criteria which allow the community to trace the false usage of the technique of speaking in the Spirit by false prophets, with the help of the examination of their lifestyle, in which the criterion of use to one's own benefit plays a major role.

---

gerade des armen Lebens Christi"; similarly also Wengst (*Didache (Apostellehre)*, p. 40) and Aune (*Prophecy in Early Christianity*, p. 215). Cf. in this regard, however, Did. 13:3-7.

[67] Did. 11:8.

[68] So too Giet, *Énigme*, p. 223.

[69] While it is not unlikely that it is a matter of a liturgical meal, perhaps an agape for the poor, as Rordorf & Tuilier (*La Doctrine*, p. 53) suggest, there is nevertheless insufficient evidence in the text; cf. also Knopf (*Die Lehre*, p. 31).

[70] *Ibid.*

[71] Rordorf & Tuilier (*La Doctrine*, pp. 186-188 note 5) and Wengst (*Didache (Apostellehre)*, p. 98 note 99) provide an overview of the different attempts at interpretation; cf. also A. Frank (*Studien zur Ekklesiologie des Hirten, 2 Klemems, der Didache und der Ignatiusbriefe mit besonderer Berücksichtigung der Idee einer präexistenten Kirche*, Diss. Munich, 1975, pp. 333-343) and Aune (*Prophecy in Early Christianity*, p. 266).

[72] *HermMand* 11:12 (SC 53bis, 196 Joly); cf. with further parallels M. Dibelius, *Der Hirt des Hermas* = HNT.E 4 (Tübingen: Mohr, 1923) pp. 541f.

8. Chapter 12:1-5

After these three offices, the author now turns to ordinary Christians,[73] who come to a community as strangers.[74] All arrivals who make the claim to be Christians[75] have a right to hospitable reception. However, the *Didache* demands subsequent testing—probably to determine whether the traveler is really a Christian.[76] The motive for this would probably be to prevent the exploitation of hospitality by non-Christians.[77] In what follows, a different procedure is laid out, according to whether the traveler, who has proved to be a Christian, is only on a journey, or whether he wants to settle permanently in the community.

In the first case, he enjoys extensive support from the community; their hospitality is, however, limited to two, at most three, days. This rule is also obviously directed against a misuse of the claim to hospitality. A believer coming from elsewhere is not, however, forbidden to settle in the community. Yet then he must support himself with his own labour;[78] if the occasion demands it the community must provide work for him.

V.5 shows clearly that this provision is directed against misuses:[79] the person who refuses to work will be characterized as one who makes a trade of being a Christian, i.e. of belonging to the church.[80] The community is told to exclude him from their midst.

9. Chapter 13:1-7[81]

This general regulation must now be limited in the case of two groups of persons, who have a traditional claim to provision, if

---

[73] For a different interpretation see J. Roloff (*Art. Amt, Ämter, Amtsverständnis* 4: TRE 2 (1978) p. 515), who sees in them wandering prophets who are in the process of becoming settled. This conjecture is, however, as little explained as the difficulties which are then thrown up by the following chapter.

[74] Cf. in this regard M. Puzicha, *Christus peregrinus. Die Fremdenaufnahme (Mt 25:35) als Werk der privaten Wohltätigkeit im Urteil der Alten Kirche* (Münster: Aschendorff, 1980), esp. pp. 11-13, 60-65.

[75] This is how Knopf understands ἐν ὀνόματι κυρίου (*Die Lehre*, p. 33); similarly Kraft (*Barnabas and the Didache*, p. 172).

[76] Cf. Harnack, *Die Lehre: Text*, p. 48; Knopf, *Die Lehre*, p. 33.

[77] So too Harnack, *Die Lehre: Prolegomena*, p. 92; Puzicha, *Christus peregrinus*, p. 63.

[78] On the command to work, cf. Harnack, *Die Lehre: Prolegomena*, pp. 92f; H. Holzapfel, *Die sittliche Wertung der körperlichen Arbeit im christlichen Altertum* (Würzburg, 1941) p. 48.

[79] So too Knopf, *Die Lehre*, p. 34; Niederwimmer, "Entwicklungsgeschichte", p. 160.

[80] On the expression, χριστέμπορος, cf. Harnack, *Die Lehre: Text*, pp. 49f.

[81] On this passage, cf. Giet, "Coutume", pp. 122-124, 126-130.

they settle[82] and place themselves entirely at the disposal of the community: the prophets and teachers, inasmuch as they have been shown to be ἀληθινοί. To address this question, the author had at his disposal a clearly identifiable piece of traditional material. It is clearly discernible, for one thing, in that it is in Second Person Singular,[83] in contrast to the context; in addition it forms a stylistic and material unity:

3a. Every firstfruit of the product of the vine and of the threshing floor, of the cattle and of the sheep, take now and give the firstfruit to the prophets.
5. If you make dough, take the firstfruit and give it according to the law.
6. In the same way, if you open a jug of wine or oil, take the firstfruit and give it to the prophets.
7. But of gold and of clothes and of every possession take the firstfruit, as it seems appropriate to you, and give it according to the law.

In terms of content, all four verses are concerned with how the ἀπαρχή is to be provided.[84] Formally they are constructed according to the same schema: τὴν ἀπαρχήν (with concrete specification) λαβὼν δός + τοῖς προφήταις and κατὰ τὴν ἐντολήν, alternating according to an ABAB-Scheme.[85]

The author fits this piece of tradition into his argument, without altering it stylistically.[86] The first verse of the chapter makes it clear that this regulation does not relate to all prophets, but only to those who are already known as ἀληθινοί and want to settle permanently in the community. The second verse extends the traditional material, which was limited to the prophets, to the true teachers.[87] For both, the reason taken from the synoptic tradition is valid, that the person who works for the community is worthy of his wage.

---

[82] The initiative clearly comes from the prophets (and teachers).

[83] This would obviously not suffice as a criterion for a piece of traditional material.

[84] Cf. G. Schöllgen, "Die Didache—ein frühes Zeugnis für Landgemeinden?", *ZNW* 76 (1985) pp. 140-143.

[85] Giet (*Énigme*, pp. 228f) resolved the question of the piece of traditional material in a similar fashion; his conjecture that it is to be identified as oral teaching material on account of carefully observed rhythmic patterns, remains just as hypothetical as the assumption of the non-Christian origin. The interpretation of Schille ("Das Recht", pp. 99-101) overlooks the unity of the piece of traditional material and is also as usual without sufficient evidence in the text.

[86] Possible because of the high esteem enjoyed by the tradition from which this piece of tradition is taken.

[87] The conjecture of Rordorf & Tuilier (*La Doctrine*, p. 190 note 2), that 13:2 documents a development in the course of which the prophets were replaced by the teachers in catechesis and instruction, finds no evidence in the text.

The piece of tradition itself is still further extended by an interpolation. V.3b gives an Old Testament scriptural foundation for the prophets' right to support:[88] just as the high priests had the right to claim the ἀπαρχή, in the same way today the prophets have the right to support.[89]

V.4 takes up the question as to what a community, which is temporarily or permanently without settled prophets, should do with their ἀπαρχή, which they now are accustomed to collect, and it allocates them to the poor.[90]

The goal of the argument in ch.13 is purely and simply to authorize the claim of the prophets and teachers to support, and to regulate it concretely. This clarification had become necessary in the context because, in the preceding section, the author had refused all Christians, who wished to settle in a different community, a permanent claim to provision. Possibly the right of the prophets and teachers to support was also much contested. The *Didache* is no evidence for a slow integration of an originally nomadic prophetic ministry into particular communities, as de Halleux has rightly observed.[91] The settled state is rather only one lifestyle of Christian prophets—which, as the piece of traditional material shows, had already been long practiced and recognized.[92]

---

[88] V.3b, which betrays that it belongs with vv.1-2, 4 through the ὑμῶν, clearly indicates that the traditional piece of material 3a, 5-7 cannot be a later interpolation, as Audet (*Didachè*, pp. 105-110)(he inconsequentially allocates v.3b, despite the ὑμῶν, to the interpolation) and Rordorf & Tuilier (*La Doctrine*, pp. 190f note 5) think, or rather conjecture; the γάρ of v.3b provides the basis for the regulation in v.3a; in the same way v.4 gives an instruction which can only be understood as supplementary rule to 3a. Vv.3b, 4 thus provide a later expansion. In addition: why should an interpolation, which provides a developmental rule of vv.1-2, limit itself to the prophets and allow the teacher introduced by v.2 to disappear? One can conclude from ch.7: on the plausible but not necessary hypothesis that the chpters 7 and 13, which are both composed in the Second Person Plural, spring from the same source (as e.g. Audet (*Didachè*, p. 108 suggests), then Did. 13:2-3, 4b is also a pre-existing piece of traditional material reworked by the author of the *Didache*.

[89] What we have here is a simple comparison between prophets and highpriests with respect to the ἀπαρχή, a particular form of right to support. One can conclude nothering from this passage concerning the specific liturgical function of the prophets; so also de Halleux ("Les ministères", p. 19) *contra* Schille ("Das Recht", p. 93) and Rordorf & Tuilier (*La Doctrine*, p. 53).

[90] That the prophets take precedence over the poor, as Harnack thinks (*Die Lehre: Text*, p. 52), cannot be concluded from the verse: It is clearly only a matter here of an additional source for the care of the poor, which presents itself if the firstfruits are not claimed by the prophets. Niederwimmer ("Textprobleme", p. 121) wishes to see a gloss in v.4, which presupposes a later situation; this is, however, not explained in more detail.

[91] De Halleux, "Les ministères", p. 17.

[92] *Contra* Niederwimmer ("Entwicklungsgeschichte, p. 160-166), for example, who concludes from the fact that apostles are not mentioned in ch. 13 that only prophets and teachers existed at that stage, who were moreover no longer itinerant, but had become settled in local communities.

The *Didache* leaves one question unsettled, which one would wish to be answered by a comprehensive church order: what work is it that makes the prophets and teachers worth their upkeep? We know of the prophets, from a different context, only that they had the right to formulate the eucharistic prayers freely, and that they stood in high esteem on account of the gift of speaking in the Spirit. Whether they presided at the celebration of the eucharist; whether they had functions of community leadership; which tasks they generally performed in the community; these matters remain in the dark. The author of the *Didache* presupposes this knowledge in his readers and, since they clearly present no difficulties, sees no need for a regulation.

10. *Chapter 14:1-3*

Ch.14, which does not stand in close relation with what precedes,[93] has two argumentational goals. In the first place the concern of the author is directed at the purity of the "eucharistic" meal,[94] which is understood as an offering.[95] The Scriptural attestation in v.3 is intended to legitimate this concern. Purity will be attained through the communal confession of sins[96] in the eucharistic celebration, over whose concrete form the *Didache* is silent.[97] The purity is endangered by intra-communal strife; so the *Didache* prescribes that warring fellow Christians must be excluded from the celebration of the eucharist, until they have been reconciled. One would be right to conclude the presence of abuses in the background.[98]

The second goal of the argumentation is not so clear. The author emphasizes that the gathering of the community for the breaking of bread and thanksgiving should take place κατὰ κυριακὴν δὲ κυρίου. The doublet, "Lord's day of the Lord", may be interpreted, as Rordorf suggests, as directed against judaizing

---

[93] So too Knopf (*Die Lehre*, p. 35); Kraft (*Barnabas and the Didache*, p. 173) sees an associative relation between the firstfruits of ch.13 and the sacrificial thought of ch.14, which seems to me at least to be far-fetched.

[94] Cf. Rordorf, "Didachè", pp. 22-27 on the relationship of Did. 14 to Did. 9-10 and on the question of which ritual meal is intended here.

[95] Cf. in this regard Giet, *Énigme*, pp. 233f; Rordorf & Tuilier, *La Doctrine*, pp. 70f; Rordorf, "Didachè", pp. 26f; H. Moll, *Die Lehre von der Eucharistie als Opfer* (Köln: Hanstein, 1975 [*Theophaneia* 26]) pp. 104-115, esp. 109-113.

[96] On this see Rordorf, "Didachè", pp. 24f, esp. on the connection with Did. 4:14; the same, "La rémission des péchés selon la Didachè", *Irénikon* 46 (1973) pp. 283-297; B. Poschmann, *Paenitentia secunda* (Bonn: Hanstein, 1940 [*Theophaneia* 1]) pp. 87-97.

[97] Cf. Rordorf, "Didachè", p. 25.

[98] Cf. Did. 15:3, which signals something similar. On this see Harnack, *Lehre: Text*, p. 54.

Christians who preferred the sabbath,[99] so that it affirms Sunday
as the day of eucharistic celebration.[100] These verses are, together
with chs. 9 and 10, all that the *Didache* offers on the theme of the
eucharist, agape etc. Again it is clear that the text only regulates
particular controversial points; from the point of view of liturgical
studies, it raises more questions than it answers. Decisive aspects
remain unclear or are not dealt with, as e.g. the relation of the
actual meal to the eucharistic celebration in a narrower sense.[101]
Of the whole course of the eucharistic community gathering, only
fragments, i.e. the three eucharistic prayers, are regulated. The
ministry of the word is almost completely disregarded. The author
makes no mention of the topics of the origin and nature of the
sacrificial gifts, the place and time of assembly, the leadership of
the assembly and seating.

11. Chapter 15:1-2

This section also stands in no close relation with the preceding
chapter.[102] The two verses, are in my opinion, generally mis-
interpreted, because people have neglected to work out the real
goal of the argumentation. It is uncontested that the offices of
bishop and deacon stood in low esteem in the community. The
author feels forced to warn against despising them.[103] The ques-

---

[99] On this see Rordorf, "Didachè", p. 23; *Ibid.*, note 31, for further contemporary testimony for this kind of tendency.

[100] With the doublet the author wishes to exclude a possible Jewish Christian
misunderstanding, that κυριακή could also be taken as a designation for the sabbath
as the day of the Old Testamental κύριος. Cf. in this regard *Ibid.*, p. 23; Rordorf,
Der Sonntag: Geschichte des Ruhe- und Gottesdienstages im ältesten Christentum
(Zürich: Zwingli, 1962 [AThANT 43]) pp. 207f; Knopf, *Die Lehre*, p. 36; for a
different point of view see Giet, *Énigme*, p. 232, with very hypothetical elaborations.

[101] Cf. Kraft (*The Didache and Barnabas*, p. 173), "The description of early
Christian worship is frustratingly vague"; Knopf (*Die Lehre*, p. 35), "Sehr wichtige
Teile des Gemeindegottesdienstes fehlen, die Erbauung durch das Wort wird mit
keinem Blicke gestreift."

[102] The οὖν of Did. 15:1 is generally understood in the sense that it establishes
the connection between the rules of ch.14 on the celebration of the "Eucharist" and
the election criteria for the celebrants of the liturgy (so Rordorf & Tuilier, *La Doctrine*, p. 193 note 10; Knopf, *Die Lehre*, p. 37; Giet, *Énigme*, p. 239). Such an
interpretation seems to me to be even more unlikely. For one think, οὖν does not
have to point to a consequent, but can simply have the function, "to indicate a
transition to something new" (*BAGD*, p. 597); so perhaps in Did. 11:1; cf. Nautin
("La composition", p. 194). It is hard to accept that the provision of election
ciriteria for bishops and deacons could be a consequence of Did. 14:1-3, where it is
a matter of the purity of the sacrifice. Moreover, τὴν λειτουργίαν λειτουργεῖν in
Did. 15:1 should not be translated "to celebrate the liturgy"; cf. in this regard note
109 above.

[103] Did. 15:2.

tion is why they are so poorly esteemed. The first verse gives the decisive clue for this: he prescribes that only men who are worthy of the Lord should be chosen as bishops and deacons.[104] Clearly there were unworthy occupants of the offices, who did not meet the demands set out and so had brought the two offices into disrepute. In my opinion, the passage is best understood against the background of this abuse. The provision of criteria serves to prevent the selection of unsuitable candidates in the future. The requirements for the office reflect in part the duties of both offices:

a. πραΰς—gentle friendliness—in early Christian literature means, as a qualification for office, mostly the virtue of a person who resolves strife.[105] The *Didache* attests intra-communal strife in many places;[106] the selection criteria should be understood in this sense as a moderating, or community leadership, function in the widest sense.

b. ἀφιλάργυρος—refers, as Rordorf correctly supposes,[107] to the future function of the candidate in the administration of the community resources.

c. ἀληθινός—probably means that he must be a true, that is, an honest Christian.[108]

d. δεδοκιμασμένος—he must be a proven member of the community (i.e. not a newly baptized).

V.1b provides the reason (γάρ) for these qualitative demands: they too (i.e. bishops and deacons) provide the community with the work of the prophets and teachers.[109] Beyond that, as shown above, the *Didache* provides only meagre information about what the task of the prophets and teachers was. In addition, that form of

---

[104] On the meaning of χειροτονεῖν cf. Rordorf & Tuilier, jp. 193 note 9; G. Deussen, "Weisen der Bischofswahl im 1 Klemensbrief und in der Didache", *TheolGl* 62 (1972) pp. 131-134.

[105] Cf. in this regard F. Hauck & S. Schulz, Art. πραΰς, πραΰτης· TDNT 6 (1959) pp. 645-651; for the virtue necessary to hold office for the correction of recalcitrants: 2 Tim 2:25 (cf. also Tit 3:2); similarly *IgnTrall* 3:2; *IgnPol* 2:1; 6:3 (174, 217, 222 Fischer).

[106] E.g. Did. 4:3; 14:2; 15:3.

[107] Rordorf & Tuilier, *La Doctrine*, p. 193 note 11; cf. also 1 Tim 3:3, 8 with the same qualifications fo rthe office of the bishop and a similar (αἰσχροκερδεῖς) for the deacons; cf. Knopf, *Die Lehre*, p. 37.

[108] Cf. *BAGD*, p. 36.

[109] Nothing points to an exclusive liturgical meaning for τὴν λειτουργίαν λειτουργεῖν, which would, however, be lexically possible (cf. *BAGD*, pp. 471f); in addition the four election criteria of v.1a, for which v.2a indeed provides the basis, point to an essentially broader sphere of activity for bishops and deacons. Beyond this it is uncertain whether the teachers had a specifically liturgical function; the *Didache* at least does not attest it.

the λειτουργία of the prophets about which the *Didache* provides information, i.e. freedom in the formulation of "eucharistic" prayers[110] and speaking in the Spirit, is tied to their office.[111] It is therefore closed to bishops and deacons. Those tasks which can be recognized behind the first two criteria of choice—leadership of the community and administration of the community chest—are not mentioned in connection with prophets and teachers. Therefore one can only assume a partial identification of the tasks of the prophets and teachers and bishops and deacons. Since, however, there were clearly overlaps —perhaps in the area of teaching—the high esteem of the prophets and teachers—those who are true and tested of course—serves the author as the foundation for the qualitative demands the *Didache* makes for bishops and deacons.

It is thus not the intention of the author to provide a definition of the roles of bishops and deacons—the *Didache* mentions nothing specific about their tasks—nor to introduce two new community officials,[112] as is often asserted.[113] Rather he proceeds, analogously to the chapter on prophets, teachers and apostles, to rule out the abuses whereby the choice of unqualified candidates had led to low esteem for the position of bishops and deacons, and to place them together with the others among the τετιμημένοι of the community.

12. Chapter 15:3

Perhaps by association with the criterion of office, πραΰς, closely connected with the two preceding verses,[114] the author turns now to failings of Christians, especially against the neighbour. If this question had been handled in ch.14 from the point of view of the purity of the eucharistic offering, the author now insists on the *correctio fraterna*, which was probably extra-liturgical.[115] It remains unclear in what context it occurs.[116] The argumentational goal of the two verses is clear: if the *correctio fraterna* does not lead the person who has transgressed against his neighbour to discernment, he is excluded from the community until he repents. There is also no description of how the latter was to be carried out.

---

[110] Did. 10:7.
[111] Did. 11:7-12.
[112] So also de Halleux, "Les ministères", pp. 20-22.
[113] E.g. Giet, *Énigme*, p. 241; Rordorf & Tuilier, *La Doctrine*, p. 64.
[114] Cf. in this regard note 106 above; such a connection nevertheless remains very hypothetical.
[115] Cf. in this regard Rordorf & Tuilier, *La Doctrine*, pp. 78-80; Rordorf, "Rémission", pp. 293-296; Harnack, *Lehre: Text*, pp. 59f.
[116] So too Rordorf, "Rémission", p. 294.

13. Chapter 15:4

This verse forms the real conclusion of the church order provisions of the *Didache*, in the form of a summary: the author puts the whole of the community life, especially prayer and alms, under the authority of the gospel "of our Lord".[117]

Results of the First Part

The *Didache* is no comprehensive church order: its intention is not to order the life of the community as a whole, nor even in its most important areas.

The correct observation is that the text only concerns the external forms of the community in already established communities, and that theological problems play no role explicitly. Inside this framework it pursues only a limited goal: it is concerned to correct abuses and to address new rules to changed circumstances—often in the face of resistance. Large parts of the community life, in which the author sees no problems, remain unconsidered. The misinterpretation of the *Didache* as a comprehensive church order, in the modern sense, certainly rests for the most part on the fact that the text takes its themes from the whole breadth of early Christian community life: from the realm of catechesis, liturgy (baptism, prayer, "eucharist"), church offices and community charity. This interpretation overlooks the fact that the author does not provide a general order for these topics, not even dealing with the most important questions, but simply provides an authoritative regulation on controversial points. This is especially clear from the fact that it is often questions of the second order which are clarified, while the important ones are not handled because the author sees no difficulty there.

The *Didache* thus has a limited purpose in its composition and is, as a selective church order, a polemical text on particular problems of community life.

---

[117] Ch.16 can here be bracketed out, since it is irrelevant for the determination of the form of the *Didache*. Essentially it provides an eschatological warning to watchfulness (vv.1-2), bound up with a little Apocalypse, and thus falls out of the framework of the rest of the sections of the writing, which provide particular rules for contentious questions of community discipline. Possibly it originally formed a unity with the Two Ways teaching of chs.1-6; cf. indeed, in this regard, the objections of Vielhauer, *Geschichte*, pp. 730-733 and Rordorf & Tuilier, *La Doctrine*, pp. 80-83; see there also arguments for the idea that it is a matter of a pre-existing piece of traditional material. Possibly its function in the framework of the *Didache* lies in the concluding heightening of the particular rules of the writing; cf. in this regard E. Bammel, "Schema und Vorlage von Didache 16", *Studia Patristica* 4 (Berlin: Akademie-Verlag, 1961 [TU 79]) pp. 253f, for the Jewish parallels. The possibility that it is a matter of a later addition should in any case not be ruled out.

This specific definition of the purpose for the composition of the *Didache*, which is true also in similar manner for other early Christian church orders, especially the Syriac *Didascalia*, does not allow one to expect a systematic structure to the text. The solution of particular problems, which do not hang together as a rule, provides—if at all—only a very crude order. One can observe a certain concentration of liturgical themes in chapters 7-10, although it is questionable whether the author of the *Didache* already knew the category "liturgy" in its present sense and saw in it the connection between the complexes "baptismal water", "baptismal fast", "stationary fast", "private prayer", and "formula for the 'eucharistic' prayer". It is only clear that these sections are connected by association, mostly through word association. Only chapters 11-13 form a unity on the theme "conduct with regard to fellow believers who arrive in the community from outside". The following sections again stand alongside each other mostly without closer connection.

One seeks in vain in the *Didache* for even one or more fundamental tendencies, such as found in the Syriac *Didascalia*, which wishes especially to promote the claim of the monarchical bishop in all areas of the community life. The text struggles in many places against judaizing practices and shows, despite all abuses, a thoroughgoing esteem for speaking in the Spirit by prophets, yet neither of these becomes a governing theme. The details of the text, which seek nothing other than the solution of particular problems, do not allow this to happen.

II

The consequences of the forgoing study are more far-reaching than might at first appear. It is less a matter of new, startling insights, which are to be gained from this short writing, than a limitation of wild hypotheses which try to gain more historical information from the text than it is able to provide. This will be demonstrated with regard to two controversial interpretations of the *Didache*.

1. The Literary Integrity of the Text

Hardly any question, especially in recent literature, has been answered so differently as that of the origin of the text. If the older interpreters[118] start mostly from the assumption of a single person

---

[118] E.g. Harnack, *Lehre: Prolegomena*, pp. 24-63; so also Knopf, *Die Lehre*, *passim*.

as author of the *Didache* (who simply drew on a limited number of traditions), today only a minority—albeit growing[119]—hold that kind of simple theory of origin. The rest, proceeding by the literary critical method,[120] reconstruct a differentiated number of phases of development, into which the particular sections of the text are then ordered.[121] It is significant that there is neither a consensus nor even only a limited number of types of solution between these sometimes extraordinarily complex theories of origin. Nearly every attempt to solve the problem stands by itself, and forms its own criteria for the supposed division of sources. So one cannot avoid the impression of arbitrariness, especially if even the smallest stylistic differences must serve as signs of a change of author.[122]

A detailed account of all the proposals cannot be given here, any more than a final solution of the question of literary integrity. The recognition that the *Didache* is a selective church order allows us simply to demonstrate that the chief arguments for the differentiation of different phases of origin are groundless.

Unlike a clearly constructed church order, a collection of different regulations on particularly controversial questions in the

---

[119] De Halleux, "Les ministères", p. 22; Nautin, "La composition", pp. 209f; L. Alfonsi, "Aspetti della struttura letteraria della Διδαχή", in *Studi classici in onore di Q. Cataudella* 2 (Catania: Università di Catania, 1972) pp. 465-181, esp. 480f; Wengst, *Didache (Apostellehre)*, pp. 18-20.

[120] In withdrawing from the literary critical method, which he—without justification—considers out of date, Schille ("Das Recht", pp. 84f) attempts a redaction critical examination of the *Didache*. He separates the writing into small and smallest pieces of tradition and orientates himself in this expressly to the research into the synoptics, since the *Didache* as a collected work would have had a similar history of development as the synoptic gospels. This methodological assumption is not more extensively justified. Schille thus overlooks the fundamental difference in form between the gospels and the *Didache*; an unreflective borrowing of exegetical methods is thus not permissible from the outset. It denies the unique character and the clear orientation fo the individual units of argumentation.

[121] Here Audet (*Didachè*, pp. 104-120) should particularly be mentioned; he differentiates, apart from the pre-existing Two Ways teaching, four phases of development of the *Didache*; he has received a sufficient refutation from Nautin ("La compostition", pp. 191-214). Cf. further Giet (*Énigme*, p. 262) with four "niveaux principaux" of development, which are in themselves still more widely differentiated and differ essentially from those of Audet. Rordorf & Tuilier distinguish—apart from the Two Ways teaching—essentially chs. 7-13 from the later continuation of chs. 14-15 (16); Niederwimmer ("Entwicklungsgeschichte", above note 42) who only deals with chs. 11-13, 15, reckons on two chief levels—tradition and redaction—as well as a later gloss. Kraft (*The Didache and Barnabas*, pp. 63-65) accepts a profusion of successive developments and reworkings of the original Jewish Two Ways teaching, which indeed cannot always be reconstructed with certainty into their different phases.

[122] This is true especially for the Commentary of Giet, who posits a change of author for the smallest inconsistencies and irregularities (*Énigme*, esp. pp. 181-188).

sphere of community discipline, without recognizable systematic construction, does not allow one to evaluate the discussion of questions from the same set of circumstances in different sections, or breaks between particular units of argumentation as clear indices for interpolation or even change of author. So, for instance, the fact that "eucharistic" meals are handled in ch.9-10 as well as ch.14, is often taken as proof for a later origin of ch.14;[123] this ignores the fact that neither section provides a general order for the "eucharistic" meals, but simply provides regulations on particular questions, which are not dependent on each other and consequently need not be settled together.

In similar fashion, the handling of church offices in 11-13 on the one hand and 15 on the other has falsely been taken as evidence for two or three successive developmental phases of 11-15;[124] here too it is a matter of two independent complexes of questions, and there was no need to handle them together.

It must not be overlooked that the brief composition of the *Didache* offers, in principle, fewer difficulties in the way of interpolating additional units of argumentation into the text to address problems as they arise, or to add them on, than would be the case in a systematic construction. The greater openness to later interpolation thus offers a correspondingly great difficulty for the historian to demonstrate such interpolations satisfactorily. This methodological presupposition is not generally taken into account in the sometimes very superficial hypotheses about its origin.

If one wishes to escape from the danger of arbitrary source hypotheses against this background, there remain very few indices which can make a change of author probable; the most important are briefly enumerated here:

a. Unequivocal stylistic differences, inasmuch as they cannot be explained by a use of traditional material. Here strict criteria must be applied. If one ignores chs.1-6, where it can hardly be decided whether it is a matter of integration of traditional material or a later addition, as well as the eschatological concluding chapter, the following passages come into consideration in my opinion:

1. *Didache* 7:2-3, 4b
2. *Didache* 8:2 (Our Father)
3. *Didache* 9:2-4; 10:2-6 ("eucharistic" prayer)
4. *Didache* 13:3a, 5-7

They are best explained as interpolated traditional material, as we have tried to show above.

b. Explicit and clear contradictions between particular units

---

[123] Examples are presented by Rordorf ("Didachè", pp. 12-17), who also himself advocates this position; cf. also Rordorf & Tuilier, *La Doctrine*, p. 64.

[124] Cf. in this regard below pp. 23f.

of argumentation; nothing like this can be demonstrated, in my opinion.

Particular sections are often attributed to different phases of the development of the community discipline. The two most important presuppositions for this exercise are absent. In the first place, the *Didache* can still not be dated and localized. In the second, the parallel material from other sources in the first one and a half centuries, concerning the external order of the community, is already so fragmentary that clear developmental phases, to which particular sections of the *Didache* could be ordered, cannot be satisfactorily reconstructed, i.e. sufficiently defined in their temporal and spatial differentiation.[125]

c. Hiatuses can only be taken into account if they emerge inside a unit of argumentation and explode the sequence of the thought. Even such hiatuses are absent.

Obviously this still does not prove that the *Didache*, as it has been received in the *Codex Hierosolymitanus*, originates from the pen of a single author. In principle it remains possible that it represents a collection of problem-solving material from different origins, which has been reworked by one or more redactors, put together and placed under the authority of the apostles. However, there are great and, in my opinion, insoluble problems in the way of the demonstration of that kind of complex history of origin, in the face of such loose composition of the text. So it seems appropriate to me to take a conservative line, to give precedence to the simplest hypothesis of origin, until someone provides convincing evidence for a complex explanation.

2. The Church Offices

Most interpreters see in the *Didache* one of the most powerful witnesses for the process of the general supersession of charismatics by officials in the leadership of the communities. The presupposition is generally the allocation of the chapter in question to two or more phases in the development of the text, which for their part mirror different developmental phases in the constitution of the community.

Starting from this basic theory, however, the relevant passages are interpreted very differently in detail.[126] Since we cannot test all the claims one by one here, the commentary of Rordorf

---

[125] Cf. in this regard esp. the following section on the church offices.

[126] References to the relevant literature are provided in the discussion of chs. 11-15; in addition see A. Lemaire, *Les ministères aux origines de l'église: Naissance de la triple hiérarchie: eveques, presbytres, diacres* (Paris: Les Éditions du Cerf, 1971 [*Lectio divina* 68]) pp. 139-144.

will be examined as one of the newest and relatively cautious representatives of this type of interpretation, with respect to the consistency of his argument.

He differentiates two developmental phases in the formation of the *Didache* community, which he tries to delineate with the help of source criticism.[127] Chapters 11-13 reflect the original situation; they still do not know any local hierarchy. The decisions are generally taken together; only apostles, prophets and teachers are known as church officers. Chs.14f reflect a later stage of development: the community has, in the meantime, found it necessary to choose local officials. For one thing, prophets and teachers have become rare, as the rule of *Didache* 13:4 already shows; as a consequence of this the divine worship can no longer be offered everywhere without officials. In the second place, ch.11 already shows clear signs of the deterioration of wandering charismatics. Their declining numbers and dubious integrity now forces the community to introduce an innovation and to choose two colleges of officials out of their own ranks—bishops and deacons. The *Didache* mirrors the difficulties of this way of solving the problem, since the officials were not accepted as of the same worth as the charismatics.

This thesis of Rordorf's, concerning two developmental steps in the composition of the community, depends on the hypothesis that chs. 14 and 15 are a later addition. What Rordorf brings as evidence for this is not very convincing. From the provision of 13:4, that the first fruits should go to the poor (and not to the bishops and deacons) if the community had no settled prophets, he concludes that ch.11-13 still knew no local officials.[128] It is implicitly assumed that local officials possessed the right to support from the beginning.[129] A look at the sources shows, however, that this only happened from the turn of the second to the third century, mainly in large communities.[130] The assumption that chs.11-13 does not mention the bishops and deacons because it did not yet know these officials,[131] is thus an argumentation from silence, which might perhaps have some justification in a comprehensive church order, but must be regarded as unacceptable in a selective one. If one takes into account the limited goal of the argument in chs.11-13—dealing with the reception of Christians of various offices arriving from elsewhere—one cannot see why

---

[127] Cf. Rordorf & Tuilier, *La Doctrine*, pp. 63-80 on what follows.

[128] *Ibid.*, p. 63.

[129] De Halleux ("Les ministères", p. 19) also viewed this critically.

[130] Cf. in this regard G. Schöllgen, *Ecclesia sordida? Zur Frage der sozialen Schichtung frühchristlicher Gemeinden am Beispiel Karthagos zur Zeit Tertullians* (Münster: Aschendorff, 1985 [*JAC.E* 12]) pp. 307f.

[131] Rordorf & Tuilier, *La Doctrine*, p. 63.

this section should consider bishops and deacons, who—unlike apostles, prophets and teachers—were uncontested local officials.

Furthermore, there is nothing in the text to suggest that the elected offices of bishops and deacons constitute an innovation.[132] On the contrary, the text battles against the decline of these offices as a result of the choice of unsuitable candidates, and so indicates that both offices had already existed for a long time. The *Didache* does not attest a declining number, or a collapse, of the prophets and teachers either.[133] Did. 13:4 simply specifies what to do when a community is without a resident prophet. The assumption that in a previous time all communities had resident prophets and teachers with right to subsistence in their midst, is nowhere attested in the text or even suggested. Furthermore, while steps are taken against impostors who give themselves out as Christians, teachers, apostles or prophets, it is not permissible to conclude from this a general collapse of the "charismatic office". The whole text, especially *Didache* 15:2 testifies rather that they still stand in high esteem.

The thesis of collective communal leadership by all local Christians[134] also appears to me at least questionable. It is mostly based on the fact that those to whom the disciplinary steps of the *Didache* are directed are mostly addressed in Second Person Plural, and that the text, with one possible exception,[135] does not explicitly mention a church hierarchy. But this is easily explained by the pseudepigraphical fiction of the text.[136] The Jerusalem manuscript carries as its second title the following address: Διδαχὴ κυρίου διὰ τῶν δώδεκα ἀποστόλων τοῖς ἔθνεσιν. It is only natural then that the Apostles often speak to their Gentile Christian addressees in the Second Person Plural in the course of the text. Even if the second title was not original as a whole or in the present form,[137] it remains an impermissible argument from

---

[132] *Ibid.*, p. 64.

[133] *Ibid.*, p. 72.

[134] *Ibid.*, p. 64.

[135] Did. 7:4; the subject of κελεύεις remains unclear; it could be a matter of a community member provided with authority to instruct; v.4b belongs in any case most probably to a pre-existing tradition.

[136] On the hypothesis which Audet (*Didachè*, pp. 91-103) has presented on the two titles, cf. the compelling refutation in Nautin ("La composition", pp. 210-214), obviously unknown to Vielhauer (*Geschichte*, pp. 722-725); cf. also Rordorf & Tuilier (*La Doctrine*, pp. 13-17).

[137] Cf. in this regard Nautin ("La composition", p. 213); the older editors such as Bryennios and Harnack (*Lehre: Prolegomena*, pp. 24-32), as well as Knopf (*Die Lehre*, pp. 3f), consider the second title to be the original. Vielhauer's thesis (*Geschichte*, p. 725; similarly also Wengst [*Didache (Apostellehre)*, pp. 14f]) of a writing originally without a title is improbable. On whose authority could the author of the *Didache* then have founded and pushed through his rules? Cf., hower, S. Giet, "La Didachè, enseignement des douze apôtres?", *Melto* 3 (1967) pp. 223-236.

silence,[138] namely from the fact that the apostles directed none of their particular rules to the church officials, to deduce that all decisions were made collectively, or that there were still no officials. The fact that chs.14 and 15 speak to their addressees in Second Person Plural speaks against this last assumption, although this section, even according to Rordorf's theory, concerns officials.

Altogether the respective passages on the constitution of the community, with their limited argumentative goals, are to be taken as of much more limited value for the history of the early Christian offices and officials than is generally assumed.[139] They give simple, momentary, interventions into particular and actual problems, which are mostly of secondary significance both for the liturgy and for the field of church constitution. Evidence for an evolution in the sense of a general supersession of charismatics by officials cannot be drawn from the text. Rather, both groups existed alongside each other for a long time, without recognizable conflict between them.

Finally, the fragmentary information of the text on church offices can be summarized again:

1. There were wandering teachers, apostles and prophets who, with the exception of the apostles, worked temporarily in the communities—in what form remains generally unclear. They probably exercised no functions of community leadership.[140] The task of the apostles lay outside the already established communities, probably in mission.

2. Prophets and teachers had the right to decide to stay permanently in a community, where they could receive payment for their unspecified work. It remains unclear whether they led the community while they were present. How numerous such settled prophets and teachers were, whether their number at the time of the composition of the *Didache* was growing or declining, cannot be determined. It is only certain that not every community had prophets at their disposal.

3. By way of contrast, bishops and deacons should be elected by all communities—in what number is uncertain. It is possible in

---

[138] This is true also for the position, which in any case rests on different presuppositions, of Wengst (*Didache (Apostellehre)*, pp. 36f), who tries to demonstrate the concept of the priesthood of all believers in the writing.

[139] Cf. e.g. the enthusiastic valuation of Did. 15:1-2 in Harnack (*Lehre: Prolegomena*, p. 141): "...daß es in der gesamten urchristlichen Literatur keine zweite Stelle gibt, die für die Entstehungsgeschichte des katholischen Episkopats so wichtig ist wie die unsrige". Similarly Lemaire, "Les ministères", p. 142; essentially hesitantly de Halleux, "Les ministères", *passim*.

[140] Cf. in this regard Niederwimmer, "Entwicklungsgeschichte", p. 159.

principle, though not very probable, that there was even the monepiscopate, since one can not conclude for sure, from the fact that the apostles command their addressees to choose bishops and deacons, that both of the two groups formed a college in every particular community.[141] The qualification for office makes it clear that, among other things, their tasks lay in the sphere of community leadership and community finance, without that being certain. There was a partial overlap of their tasks with that of the resident prophets and teachers, with whom they formed the group of the "honoured".[142]

---

[141] Cf. my article, "Monepiskopat und monarchischer Episkopat", *ZNW* 77 (1986) pp. 146-151.

[142]*Addendum: January 1996*: It is, of course, not possible to elaborate here on ten years of research. Reference will be simply be made to a few publications of the author, which have carried the thoughts of the article further, as well as to a critical opinion concerning his position and a dispute with this criticism in a forthcoming publication. The author's subsequent publications include:

1. *Didache—Zwölf-Apostel-Lehre. Einleitung, Übersetzung und Kommentar* (Freiburg: Herder, 1991 [FC 1]).
2. "Die literarische Gattung der syrischen Didaskalie" in H. J. W. Drijvers & others (ed.), *IV. Symposium Syriacum 1984. Literary Genres in Syriac Literature* (Rome, 1987 [OCA 229]) pp. 149-159.
3. "Wandernde oder seßhafte Lehrer in der Didache?", *Biblische Notizen* 52 (1990) pp. 19-26.
4. "Pseudapostolizität und Schriftgebrauch in den ersten Kirchenordnungen. Anmerkungen zur Begründung des frühen Kirchenrechts" in *Stimuli. Exegese und ihre Hermeneutik in Antike und Christentum: Festschrift Ernst Dassmann* (Münster, 1996 [*JbAC Erg.-Bd* 23]) pp. 96-121.

The following book has interacted critically at length with the article printed above as well as with the addition mentioned under (2) above:

B. Steimer, *Vertex Traditionis. Die Gattung der altchristlicher Kirchenordnungen* (Berlin/New York, 1992 [BZNW 63]).

An answer to this will shortly appear as:

"Der Abfassungszweck der frühen Kirchenordnungen. Anmerkungen zu den Thesen Bruno Steimers", JbAC 40 (1997).

THE JESUS TRADITION IN THE DIDACHE

JONATHAN ALFRED DRAPER

Pietermaritzburg

I.

Since it was rediscovered in a monastic library in Constantinople and published by P. Bryennios in 1883, the Didache or *Teaching of the Twelve Apostles* has continued to be one of the most disputed of early Christian texts. It has been depicted by scholars as anything between the original of the Apostolic Decree (c. 50 C.E.)[1] and a late archaizing fiction of the early third century.[2] It bears no date itself, nor does it make any reference to any datable external event, yet the picture of the Church which it presents could only be described as primitive, reaching back to the very earliest stages of the Church's order and practice in a way which largely agrees with the picture presented by the New Testament, while at the same time posing questions for many traditional interpretations of this first period of the Church's life. Fragments of the *Didache* were found at Oxyrhyncus (POxy 1782) from the fourth century and in Coptic translation (PLond Or 9271) from the 3/4th century. Traces of the use of this text, and the high regard it enjoyed, are widespread in the literature of the second and third centuries, especially in Syria and Egypt. It was used by the compilator of the *Didascalia* (c. 2/3rd)[3] and the *Liber Graduum* (c. 3/4th), as well as being absorbed *in toto* by the *Apostolic Constitutions* VII (c. 3/4th) and partially by the Coptic and Ethiopic Church Orders,[4] after which it ceased to circulate independently.

---

[1] A. Seeberg argued for this connection in various books, e.g. *Die Beiden Wege und das Aposteldekret* (Leipzig: Deichert, 1906). More recently C. N. Jefford ("Tradition and Witness in Antioch: Acts 15 and Didache 6" in E. V. McKnight, *Perspectives on Contemporary New Testament Questions* [Lewiston: Mellen, 1992 (Perspectives in Religious Studies 19)] pp. 409-419, esp. 87; cf. "An Ancient Witness to the Apostolic Decree of Acts 15?" in *Proceedings: Eastern Great Lakes and Midwest Biblical Societies* 10 [1990] pp. 204-213) has raised the issue of the relationship between the *Didache* and the Apostolic Decree of Acts again in a modified form, "...it seems apparent that some form of the Apostolic Decree has been utilized as the foundational structure for Didache 6".

[2] E.g. J. A. Robinson, *Barnabas, Hermas and the Didache* (London: SPCK, 1902); R. H. Connolly, "The Didache in Relation to the Epistle of Barnabas", *JTS* 33 (1932) pp. 327-353; J. Muilenburg, *The Literary Relations of the Epistle of Barnabas and the Teaching of the Twelve Apostles* (Marburg: no publisher given, 1929 [Yale Dissertation]); C. Bigg (*The Doctrine of the Twelve Apostles* [London: SPCK, 1922] pp. xxvi-xxvii) dates it as late as the fourth century.

[3] See R. H. Connolly, "The Use of the Didache in the Didascalia", *JTS* 24 (1923) pp. 147-157.

[4] See G. Horner, *The Statutes of the Apostles or Canones Ecclesiastici* (London: Williams & Norgate, 1904).

Athanasius describes it as "appointed by the Fathers to be read by those who newly join us, and who wish for instruction in the word of godliness".[5] Hence a date for the *Didache* in its present form later than the second century must be considered unlikely, and a date before the end of the first century probable.[6]

In the absence of external criteria for dating the *Didache* more closely, the problem resolves itself into a question concerning possible sources, and especially concerning its relation to the Jesus tradition in the Gospel and to the *Epistle of Barnabas*, to which it presents extensive parallel material in chs. 1-6. Robinson, Connolly and Muilenburg, among others, saw the *Didache* as having borrowed and re-arranged the so-called "Two Ways" material from *Barnabas* 18-20. This would make the *Didache* a second century work, whose object was to codify and order material it considered to be "apostolic", so that any echo of the New Testament may be taken as evidence of literary dependence. A. Harnack had already taken such a position, declaring the *Didache*'s purpose to be a harmony of the gospel material on the basis primarily of Matthew.[7] A number of scholars preferred to see *Barnabas* as dependent on the *Didache*,[8] and the *Didache* as being thus contemporaneous with the formation of the written gospels. The Two Ways material was held to be derived from an earlier Jewish work of catechesis for proselytes, which was taken up and modified by the Christian community. The discovery of a Latin document entitled *Doctrina apostolorum* consisting of Did. 1-6 without 1:3b-2:1, gave considerable weight to this argument.[9]

---

[5] *Festal Letters* 39:7.

[6] A new consensus is emerging for a date c.100 C.E. This is represented for instance by W. Rordorf and A. Tuilier, *La Doctrine des Douze Apôtres* (Paris: Les Editions du Cerf, 1978 [SC 248]).

[7] *Die Lehre der zwölf Apostel* (Leipzig: Hinrichs, 1884 [reprint 1893, TU 2,1-2]) pp. 63-88. Harnack later changed his mind about the origin of the Two Ways, seeing it as derived from a Jewish catechetical document. See *Die Didache und die jüdischen beiden Wege* (Leipzig: Hinrichs, 1886 [reprint 1896])

[8] E.g. P. Schaff, *The Oldest Church Manual Called the Teaching of the Twelve Apostles* (Edinburgh: Clark, 1885) p. 119-125; C. Taylor, *The Teaching of the Twelve Apostles* (Cambridge: Deighton Bell, 1886); C. H. Turner, "The Early Christian Ministry and the Didache", in *Studies in Early Church History* (Oxford: Oxford University Press, 1912) pp. 1-31; G. Klein, *Der älteste christliche Katechismus und die jüdische Propaganda-Literatur* (Berlin: Reimer, 1909).

[9] See E. J. Goodspeed, "The Didache, Barnabas and the Doctrina", *AThR* 27 (1945) pp. 228-247 for the argument that the *Doctrina* represents the direct source for the Two Ways in the other two documents. There are substantial problems in the way of this hypothesis, since it differs at key points from both of them, e.g. the dualist tradition of the two angels set over the Two Ways in the *Doctrina*, where the *Didache* has a purely ethical framework (cf. Rordorf & Tuilier, *La Doctrine*, pp. 27f). The document was first published by J. Schlecht, *Doctrina XII Apostolorum. Die Apostellehre in der Liturgie der katholischen Kirche* (Freiburg im Breisgau: Herder, 1901). Opponents of the theory of a Jewish source held this to be an abridgement of the *Didache*, e.g. J. Muilenburg (*Literary Relations*, p. 42) calls

However, it was not until the discovery of the Dead Sea Scrolls that the study of the *Didache* was able to move out of the impasse over its use of sources. The so-called *Manual of Discipline* (1QS 3:13-4:26) proved to present a Two Ways teaching remarkably close to the material in *Barnabas*, the *Didache* and the *Doctrina*, both in content and in structure. It was demonstrated by J-P. Audet[10] that the *Doctrina* was closer in several respects to the *Manual of Discipline* than either *Barnabas* or the *Didache*. Hence, while the recension of the Two Ways evidenced by these three works may already have received Christian modifications, the teaching as a block existed already as Jewish catechetical material.[11]

This discovery led Audet to a radical re-assessment of the relationship between the *Didache* and the Jesus tradition.[12] He argued for a composition of the *Didache* in three phases: 1:1-11:2 (without 1:3b-2:1) written before the emergence of a written gospel; 11:3-16:8 written by the same author under the pressure of changed circumstances in the knowledge of a written pro-Gospel, and finally various additions (including 1:3b-2:1) made at a later date by an interpolator, who nevertheless did not have any gospel as we know it today. Audet's theory sets the origin of the *Didache* entirely between 50 and 70 C.E. This is somewhat of a romantic over-simplification, since a closer examination of the text shows signs of considerable redactional activity, which defies any theory of a unity of composition, even allowing for the activity of an interpolator.[13] The *Didache* is a composite work,

---

it "a homiletical extract and not a true copy or translation".

[10] "Affinités littéraires et doctrinales du "Manuel de discipline"", *RB* 59 (1952) pp. 219-238.

[11] R. A. Kraft (*Barnabas and the Didache* [New York: Nelson, 1965 (AF 3)] p. 9) argues that the *Doctrina* represents "the immediate source upon which the final author-editor of the Didache drew for his Two Ways material", while *Barnabas* is "the most primitive offshoot from the ancient common stock". The question of the relationship between *Barnabas* and the *Didache* has been re-opened by J. A. Draper, "Barnabas and the Riddle of the Didache Revisited", *JSNT* 58 (1995) pp. 89-113. This article suggests that *Barnabas* may be deliberately polemicizing against the Jewish Christian use of the Two Ways for catechesis, as epitomized by the *Didache*.

[12] *La Didachè* (Paris: Gabalda, 1959) pp. 166-186.

[13] Note, for example, the fluctuation between the singular and plural of the Second Person in chs. 7 and 13. Although Audet notices this, he draws the wrong conclusion. It is the Second Person Plural which is the mark of the later redaction, modifying the intimate tone of catechesis in favour of the collective plural of liturgical use in the community. See further my argument in *A Commentary on the Didache in the Light of the Dead Sea Scrolls and Related Documents* (Cambridge Dissertation, 1983) pp. 145-148, 258-259. J. A. T. Robinson (*Redating the New Testament* [London: SCM, 1976] pp. 322-327) agrees with Audet in his dating of the *Didache* before 70 C.E.

which has evolved over a considerable period, from its beginning as a Jewish catechetical work, which was taken up and developed by the Church into a manual of Church life and order. The text was repeatedly modified in line with changes in the practice of the communities which used it.[14] Thus the core of 1-6 is Jewish and pre-Christian (c. 100 B.C.E. to 50 C.E.) and the work as a whole had probably received its present form by the end of the first century C.E. However, the full text of the *Didache*, apart from its use in the *Apostolic Constitutions* and the various fragments, is available only in a manuscript (H54) from the eleventh century. It cannot be assumed that this text, accurate as it may be, does not contain alterations made considerably later than the first or even second century. Moreover the tendency in the transmission would always be towards harmonization with the written gospels and with the later practice of the Church. Thus divergence in the *Didache* with regard to the Jesus tradition in the Synoptic Gospels must be held to be specially significant and indicative of an independent witness, unless it can be demonstrated that a later redactor would have had a motive in altering the form of the text.[15] Here I disagree with C. M. Tuckett, who bases his discussion of the dependence of the *Didache* on Matthew and Luke on a detailed and admirably thorough examination of whether its text is dependent on "Q" itself or on the Matthean and Lukan redactions of "Q". However, this is a tenuous procedure, since we do not possess "Q" and even its existence in written form is questionable.[16] It could equally well be argued, for instance, on the assumption

---

[14] J. A. Draper, "Torah and Troublesome Apostles in the Didache Community", *Novum Testamentum* 33/4, 347-372." Cf. Kraft, *Barnabas and the Didache*, p. 2.

[15] Cf. W. Rordorf, "Problème de la transmission" in F. Paschke, *Überlieferungsgeschichtliche Untersuchungen* (Berlin: Akademie-Verlag, 1981 [TU 125] pp. 499-513; reprinted in W. Rordorf, *Liturgie, foi et vie des premiers chrétiens. Études patristiques* [Paris: Beauchesne, 1986 (ThH 75)]) p. 503. C. M. Tuckett ("Synoptic Tradition in the Didache" in J.-M. Sevrin, *The New Testament in Early Christianity* (Louvain: Louvain University Press, 1989 [BEThL 86]) p. 197-230, esp. 199 n. 11) argues against me here that the *Didache* is not "quotation" but a free allusion to the written Gospel tradition. This reasoning, however, seems to me to beg the question of literary relationship, since we do not know, in fact, which writing came first, the *Didache* or Matthew. The reference to the use of the Old Testament in Paul raised by K. Wengst (*Didache (Apostellehre)—Barnabas-Zweiter Klemensbrief—Schrift an Diognet* [Darmstadt: Wissenschaftliche Buchgesellschaft, 1984 (SUC 2)] p. 30) and cited by Tuckett, is not apposite, since there is no question that Paul knew and used the Old Testament.

[16] Cf. W. Rordorf, "Does the Didache Contain Jesus Tradition Independently of the Synoptic Gospels?" in H. Wansbrough, *Jesus and the Oral Gospel Tradition* (Sheffield: Sheffield Academic Press [JSNTSup 64]) pp. 398-401, esp. pp. 411-412; Niederwimmer, *Die Didache* (Göttingen: Vandenhoeck & Ruprecht [KAV 1]) p. 108.

that the *Didache* is independent of both gospels, that an agreement of either with the *Didache* establishes the original form of "Q".

II.

Because the *Didache* is a composite work, its evidence concerning the Jesus tradition must be evaluated differently for different sections of the work. The bulk of the tradition is found in 1:3b-2:1; 8 and 15:3-4, which appear to represent the latest redactional phase of the *Didache*, although still added before the end of the first century.[17] Here the concern is to subordinate the teaching contained in the *Didache* to the authority of the written Gospel (ὡς ἐκέλευσεν ὁ κύριος ἐν τῷ εὐαγγελίῳ αὐτοῦ, 8:2; ὡς ἔχετε ἐν τῷ εὐαγγελίῳ, 15:3; καὶ πάσας τὰς πράξεις αὐτῶ ποιήσατε, ὡς ἔχετε ἐν τῷ εὐαγγελίῳ τοῦ κυρίου ἡμῶν, 15:4),[18] just as the teaching of Jesus becomes the "first teaching" of the Way of Life (1:3), displacing the Torah to a "second teaching" (2:1). However, it cannot be assumed without more ado that the reference is to a written and not an oral Gospel, or that we have to do here with our Synoptic Gospels. Further important material relating to the Jesus tradition is contained in the "apocalypse" of chapter 16, although here the basis of the teaching may well derive, all or in part, from the original schema of the Two Ways and may not be simply equated with the Jesus tradition.[19] Apparent echoes of the Jesus tradition outside these sections should be examined with great caution, since they may well derive from a Jewish *Urtext*, and even if they are the product of a Christian community, they may reflect the general milieu of the

---

[17] W. Rordorf ("Problème de la transmission", pp. 499-513, esp. 509-513) has argued that 1:3b-2:1 was inserted by the Didachist (compiler) who added chs. 7-13 to the Two Ways. He evokes two key pieces of evidence. The first is the relation between νηστεύειν in 1:3b to the twice weekly fast in 8:1. This is a somewhat tenuous link it seems to me. The other is more convincing: the link between καὶ ἔσῃ τέλειος and οὐδὲ γὰρ δύνασαι in 1:4 with the same expressions in 6:2. This provides evidence that both pericopes come from the same Jewish milieu. The other connections cited by Rordorf are more circumstantial than inherent.

[18] I regard the phrases καὶ προφητῶν, κατὰ τὸ δόγμα τοῦ εὐαγγελίου οὕτω ποιήσατε in 11:3 to be a redactional insertion to the instructions on apostles, along with the rest of the material relating to prophets. This material may also derive from the same redactional layer, in that the prophets are the purveyors of the Jesus tradition. See further my articles, "Torah and Troublesome Apostles in the Didache Community", *Novum Testamentum* 33/4 (1991) pp. 347-372; "Social Ambiguity and the Production of Text: Prophets, Teachers, Bishops, and Deacons and the Development of the Jesus Tradition in the Community of the *Didache*" in C. N. Jefford, *The Didache in Context: Essays on its Text, History and Transmission* (Leiden: Brill, 1995) pp. 284-313.

[19] See E. Bammel, "Schema und Vorlage von Didache 16" in F. L. Cross (ed.), *Studia Patristica* IV (Berlin: Akademie-Verlag, 1961 [TU 79]), pp. 253-262.

earliest Christian communities rather than a use of the Jesus tradition.

The possible parallels in the Two Ways (1-6) material prove mostly to be independent of the Jesus tradition. 2:2 forms part of midrashic expansion of the Decalogue; 3:7 forms part of the *Tugendkatalog* from the earliest stratum of the Way of Life (cf. 1QS 4:3) which has been embellished from Psalm 36:11.[20] The reference of 6:2 is to the yoke of the Torah and not the "easy" yoke of Jesus, as the reference to the ritual food laws in 6:3 shows.[21] Only in 1:2b does it appear that the teaching of Jesus has influenced the text of the Two Ways. The original reference in the Jewish tradition was in the first instance to ἀγαπήσεις τὸν θεὸν τὸν ποιήσαντά σε, since a stress on God as Creator is an essential part of the Two Ways, subordinating the incipient dualism to the requirements of Jewish monotheism (as in 1QS 3:15f; 9:26f; 11:6, 11, 18; CD 2:21; 3:8). Then the second component of the Way of Life referred to the keeping of God's commandments, as in Deuteronomy 30:16. The combination of these two elements survives in *Barnabas* 19:2, ἀγαπήσεις τὸν ποιήσαντά σε...οὐ μὴ ἐγκαταλίπῃς ἐντολὰς κυρίου. The use in 1:2b of πρῶτον and δεύτερον to describe God and neighbour love as a summary of the Law seems to require the influence of the Christian tradition found also in Matthew 22:37-39, despite the fact that a deep rooted Jewish tradition lay behind the teaching of Jesus.[22] The question of literary dependence is raised acutely, but not settled, by this pericope.[23]

---

[20] The *Doctrina* makes it clear that it belongs within the context of Jewish hope by its addition of *sanctam terram* (Audet, *Didachè*, pp. 132f; S. Giet, *L'énigme de la Didachè* (Paris: Ophrys [PFLUS 149]) p. 112 n. 67.

[21] See A. Stuiber, "Das ganze Joch des Herrn (Didache 6:2-3)", in F. L. Cross, *Studia Patristica* IV (Berlin: Akademie-Verlag, 1961 [TU 79]) pp. 323-329. Stuiber argues that this represents a part of the purely Jewish *Urtext* of the Two Ways, which has been taken over by the redactor of the *Didache*. I have argued elsewhere that this represents the stance of the Jewish Christian community of the *Didache* ("Torah and Troublesome Apostles", p. 360-367); *contra* the ascetic interpretation of R. Knopf, *Die Lehre der zwölf Apostel. Die zwei Clemensbriefe* (Tübingen: Mohr [HNT.E 1]) p. 21; cf. K. H. Rengstorf, "ΖΥΓΟΣ", *TDNT* II, pp. 896-901, esp. 901.

[22] See K. Berger, *Die Gesetzesauslegung Jesu. Ihr historischer Hintergrund im Judentum und im Alten Testament* (Neukirchen-Vluyn: Neukirchener Verlag [WMANT 40]) pp. 136f; A. Nissen, *Gott und der Nächste im antiken Judentum* (Tübingen: Mohr [WUNT 15]) pp. 230-244.

[23] C. M. Tuckett ("Synoptic Tradition in the Didache", *The New Testament in Early Christianity*, pp. 210-211) sees dependence on Matthew as the "simplest solution" to this. C. N. Jefford (*The Sayings of Jesus in the Teaching of the Twelve Apostles* [Leiden: Brill, 1989 (VigChr.E 11)] pp. 36-37) has argued, however, that this represents "a common tradition of scriptural interpretation". His conclusion is supported by Rordorf ("Jesus Tradition", pp. 398-401).

III.

In the liturgical instructions of Did. 7, 9-14, there are few direct parallels with the Jesus tradition. The Trinitarian baptismal formula in 7:1 is probably a later redactional retouch, since a slightly different formula is given in 7:3, and the earlier formula εἰς ὄνομα κυρίου has survived in 9:5. Both formulae are taken from current liturgical practice and not from any written source.[24] The eucharistic prayers of Did. 9-10 seem close to the language of John 6:14, but they are closer still to the language of the Jewish *Berakoth* (see *b.Ber* 35a) and to the Jewish hope for the eschatological ingathering of the diaspora.[25] Moreover, the "Johannine" language of "life" and "knowledge" is now well attested in the Dead Sea Scrolls, so that they can be seen to form part of the milieu in which the *Didache* originated. In any case, the eucharistic prayers in the *Didache* were likely already to have been long an accepted part of the life of the Church and were certainly not a literary composition of the Didachist. The saying in 9:5 (μὴ δῶτε τὸ ἅγιον τοῖς κυσί) is attributed to the "Lord", but the meaning is quite different to Matthew 7:6, since it is used in a cultic purity sense to justify exclusion of the unbaptized from the eucharistic meal. A similar saying is found also in *m.Tem* 6:5, where it seems to be cited as an authoritative saying, and it is matched by Essene practice recorded by Josephus in *AJ* XVIII.22 and by 1QS 5:13. It may thus represent a Jewish *mashal* which was attributed to Jesus by the Matthean Redactor in Matthew 7:6. The use of the saying in the *Didache* seems to argue against its having been taken from Matthew, but rather from the Jewish milieu.[26]

The saying in 11:1-2 concerning false teachers seems to have connections with Mt 5:17-20, and to be directed towards the problem of the status of the Torah in the Christian movement. There is no certainty, however, that a literary dependence of the *Didache*

---

[24] The liturgical usage may well have influenced the text of Matthew also at this point, so that the original reference of Mt 28:19 was to "the name" only, as in most citations by Eusebius. See among others, F. C. Coneybeare, "The Eusebian Form of the Matt 28:19 Text", *ZNW* 2 (1901) pp. 275-288; E. Lohmeyer, "Mir ist gegeben alle Gewalt!" in W. Schmauch (ed.), *In Memoriam Ernst Lohmeyer* (Stuttgart: Evangelisches Verlagswerk, 1951) pp. 22-49. For a fuller bibliography, see Draper, *Commentary*, p. 146 n. 8.

[25] See L. Clerici, *Einsammlung der Zerstreuten. Liturgiegeschichtliche Untersuchung zur Vor- und Nachgeschichte der Fürbitte für die Kirche in Did. 9:4 und 10:5* (Münster: Westfalen, 1966 [LQF 44]).

[26] The "Lord" referred to would then be the Lord of the Old Testament and not Jesus. Cf. Audet, *Didachè*, p. 173; Rordorf, "Jesus Tradition", p. 422.

on Matthew would solve the problem, and it may even be more easily explained by a reverse influence of Matthew on the *Didache*, as I have argued elsewhere.[27] Although 11:3 refers specifically to τὸ δόγμα τοῦ εὐαγγελίου, the only echoes of the written Gospel in what follows are very faint. In 11:7 there is a parallel with Mt 12:32, but the sense is different, since it identifies blasphemy against the Holy Spirit with refusing to accept the authority of a prophet speaking ἐν πνεύματι. On the other hand 13:1-2 is close to the wording of Mt 10:10, πᾶς προφήτης-/διδάσκαλος....ἄξιός ἐστι τῆς τροφῆς αὐτοῦ. This saying of Jesus seems to have circulated independently of the written Gospels as we know them today, since it is found also in 1 Cor 9:13f and 1 Tim 5:18. It may also be rooted in Jewish wisdom tradition. The instruction of 14:2 is close to the sense of Mt 5:23f, although the wording is clearly independent. In all these examples, there is no proof of a dependence on Mt, rather a suggestion of independence.

IV.

Turning now to the Jesus tradition in 1:3b-2:1, it is important to notice first of all that the material is not attributed to a written Gospel, indeed it is not even cited as the teaching of Jesus. Moreover, it is interspersed with material from the Wisdom tradition (1:5-6), given all together as the distilled essence of the Way of Life. While the wording of the sayings is closest to Mt 5-7, they are given in a quite different order, with significant differences of wording, and interwoven with other material, some of which is found in Lk 6, and some of which is independent of both Gospels. In some respects the *Didache* is closer to the collection of material in Justin, *Apology* I.16 than to either Matthew or Luke. In other words, this material in Did. 1:3b-2:1 draws on material found also in the collection of sayings which is often referred to as the source "Q" in Matthew and Luke. The question arises as to whether it derives the material from the written gospels and harmonizes it, or whether it draws directly on "Q" or a similar source. For ease of reference, the material is set out below:

A.

Did. 1:3b εὐλογεῖτε τοὺς καταρωμένους ὑμῖν καὶ προσεύχεσθε ὑπὲρ τῶν ἐχθρῶν ὑμῶν, νηστεύετε δὲ ὑπὲρ τῶν διωκόντων ὑμᾶς. Ποιά γὰρ χάρις ἐὰν φιλῆτε τοὺς φιλοῦντας ὑμᾶς; οὐχὶ καὶ τὰ ἔθνη τὸ αὐτὸ

---

[27] Draper, "Torah and Troublesome Apostles", p. 357-360.

	ποιοῦσιν· ὑμεῖς δὲ φιλεῖτε τοὺς μισοῦντας ὑμᾶς, καὶ οὐχ ἕξετε ἐχθρόν.
Mt 5:44, 46	ἀγαπᾶτε τοὺς ἐχθροὺς ὑμῶν καὶ προσεύχεσθε ὑυπὲρ τῶν διωκόντων ὑμᾶς. ἐὰν γὰρ ἀγαπήσητε τοὺς ἀγαπῶντας ὑμᾶς τίνα μισθὸν ἔχετε; οὐχὶ καὶ οἱ τελῶναι τὸ αὐτὸ ποιοῦσιν;
Lk 6:27, 28, 32	ἀγαπᾶτε τοὺς ἐχθροὺς ὑμῶν, καλῶς ποιεῖτε τοῖς μισοῦσιν ὑμᾶς, εὐλογεῖτε τοὺς καταρωμένους ὑμᾶς, προσεύχεσθε περὶ τῶν ἐπηρεαζόντων ὑμᾶς. καὶ εἰ ἀγαπᾶτε τοὺς ἀγαπῶντας ὑμᾶς, ποία ὑμῖν χάρις ἐστίν; καὶ οἱ ἁμαρτωλοὶ τοὺς ἀγαπῶντας αὐτοὺς ἀγαπῶσιν.
Justin, *1 Apol* 15:14	εὔχεσθε ὑπὲρ τῶν ἐχθρῶν ὑμῶν, καὶ ἀγαπᾶτε τοὺς μισοῦντας ὑμᾶς, καὶ αὐλογεῖτε τοὺς καταρωμένους ὑμῖν, καὶ εὔχεσθε ὑπὲρ τῶν ἐπηρεαζόντων ὑμᾶς.
Justin, *1 Apol* 15:13	εἰ ἀγαπᾶτε τοὺς ἀγαπῶντας ὑμᾶς, τί καινὸν ποιεῖτε; καὶ γὰρ οἱ πόρνοι τοῦτο ποιοῦσιν.

B.

Did. 1:4a	ἀπέχου τῶν σαρκικῶν ἐπιθυμιῶν. ἐὰν τίς σοι δῷ ῥάπισμα εἰς τὴν δεξιὰν σιαγόνα, στρέψον αὐτῷ καὶ τὴν ἄλλην, καὶ ἔσῃ τέλειος.
Mt 5:39, 48	ἀλλ' ὅστις σε ῥαπίζει εἰς τὴν δεξιὰν σιαγόνα, στρέψον αὐτῷ καὶ τὴν ἄλλην· ἔσεσθε οὖν ὑμεῖς τέλειοι.
Lk 6:29a	τῷ τύπτοντί σε ἐπὶ τὴν σιαγόνα πάρεχε καὶ τὴν ἄλλην.
Justin, *1 Apol* 16:1	τῷ τύπτοντί σου τὴν σιαγόνα πάρεχε καὶ τὴν ἄλλην.

C.

Did. 1:4b	ἐὰν ἀγγαρεύσῃ σέ τις μίλιον ἕν, ὕπαγε μετ' αὐτοῦ δύο· ἐὰν ἄρῃ τις τὸ ἱμάτιόν σου, δὸς αὐτῷ καὶ τὸν χιτῶνα ἐὰν λάβῃ τις ἀπὸ σοῦ τὸ σόν, μὴ ἀπαίτει· οὐδὲ γὰρ δύνασαι.
Mt 5:41, 40	καὶ ὅστις σε ἀγγαρεύσει μίλιον ἕν, ὕπαγε μετ' αὐτοῦ δύο· καὶ τῷ θέλοντί σοι κριθῆναι καὶ τὸν χιτῶνα σου λαβεῖν, ἄφες αὐτῷ καὶ τὸ ἱμάτιον.

Lk 6:29b, 30

καὶ ἀπὸ σου τὸ ἱμάτιον καὶ τὸν χιτῶνα μὴ
κωλύσῃς, καὶ ἀπὸ τοῦ αἴροντος τὰ σὰ μὴ
ἀπαίτει.

Justin, *1 Apol* 16:2, 1b

παντὶ δὲ ἀγγαρεύοντί σε μίλιον
ἀκολούθησον δύο. καὶ τὸν αἴροντά σου τὸν
χιτῶνα ἤ τὸ ἱμάτιον μὴ κωλύσῃς. ὃς δ᾽ ἂν
ὀργισθῇ ἔνοχός ἐστιν εἰς τὸ πῦρ.

D.

Did. 1:5a

παντὶ τῷ αἰτοῦντί σε δίδου καὶ μὴ ἀπαίτει.
πᾶσι γὰρ θέλει δίδοσθαι ὁ πατὴρ ἐκ τῶν
ἰδίων χαρισμάτων.

Mt 5:42

τῷ αἰτοῦντί σε δός, καὶ τὸν θέλοντα ἀπὸ
σοῦ δανίσασθαι μὴ ἀποστραφῇς.

Lk 6:30

παντὶ αἰτοῦντί σε δίδου.

Justin, *1 Apol* 15:15

παντὶ τῷ αἰτοῦντι δίδοτε, καὶ τὸν
βουλόμενον δανείσασθαι μὴ ἀποστραφῆτε.

E.

Did. 1:5b

μακάριος ὁ διδοὺς κατὰ τὴν ἐντολήν·
ἀθῷος γὰρ ἐστιν. οὐαὶ τῷ λαμβάνοντι· εἰ
μὲν γὰρ χρείαν ἔχων λαμβάνει τις, ἀθῷος
ἔσται. ὁ δὲ μὴ χρείαν ἔχων δώσει δίκην
ἱνατί ἔλαβε καὶ εἰς τί.

Cf. Acts 20:35.

F.

Did. 1:5c

ἐν συνοχῇ δὲ γενόμενος ἐξετασθήσεται
περὶ ὧν ἔπραξε, καὶ οὐκ ἐξελεύσεται
ἐκεῖθεν μέχρις οὗ ἀποδῷ τὸν ἔσχατον
κοδράντην.

Mt 5:25, 26

καὶ εἰς φυλακὴν βληθήσῃ. ἀμὴν λέγω
ὑμῖν, οὐ μὴ ἐξέλθῃς ἐκεῖθεν, ἕως ἂν
ἀποδῷς τὸν ἔσχατον κοδράντην.

Lk 12:58f

καὶ ὁ πράκτωρ σε βαλεῖ εἰς φυλακήν.
Λέγω σοι οὐ μὴ ἐξέλθῃς ἐκεῖθεν, ἕως καὶ
τὸ ἔσχατον λεπτὸν ἀποδῷς.

G.

Did. 1:6

ἀλλὰ καὶ περὶ τούτο δὲ εἴρηται· ἱδρωσάτω
ἡ ἐλεημοσύνη σου εἰς τὰς χειράς σου,
μέχρις ἂν γνῷς τίνι δῷς.

Cf. Sirach 12:1

The peculiarities of the *Didache*'s version of these sayings cannot
be attributed to late glosses, since no doctrinal point is implied in

any of them, and the Greek of the *Didache* is often clumsier than that of the Synoptic Gospels, so that they cannot be derived from stylistic corrections. The first groups of sayings (A) agrees first with the Lukan text, and then with Justin against Matthew/Luke in the saying: (προσ)εὐχεσθε ὑπὲρ τῶν ἐχθρῶν ὑμῶν and presents a third member found nowhere else, which forms a climax: νηστεύετε δὲ ὑπὲρ τῶν διωκόντων ὑμᾶς.[28] The connection between prayer and fasting (which is seen as increasing the potency of prayer) is a common Jewish understanding.[29] The *Didache* gives φιλῆτε...φιλοῦντας...φιλεῖτε against the Synoptic ἀγαπᾶτε... ἀγαποῦντας...ἀγαπᾶτε; this reading is attested by the POxy fragment and the *Apostolic Constitutions*, which otherwise harmonizes the text of the *Didache* with Luke at this point. The tendency of the tradition was inexorably towards the use of ἀγαπάω, so this reading is important (cf. also *IgnPol* 2:1). The Didache uses ἔθνη for ἁμαρτωλοί in Luke and τελῶναι in Matthew (cf. ἐθνικοί in 5:47) and πόρνοι in Justin. In this the *Didache* presents most clearly the Jewish perspective, which is surprising in a work directed towards the Gentiles, a the longer title of the work suggests: Διδαχὴ κυρίου διὰ τῶν δώδεκα ἀπόστολων τοῖς ἔθνεσιν.[30] It may well attest a very old tradition.

Finally, the *Didache* includes a puzzling sentence not attested elsewhere: καὶ οὐχ ἕξετε ἐχθρόν. This is best taken as a prohibition climaxing the teaching.[31] Tuckett[32] argues that ποία γὰρ χάρις is dependent on Lk 6:32-34, which evidences an attack on "the morality determined by a reciprocity ethic". However, again, the wording is not identical to Luke's ποία ὑμῖν χάρις ἐστίν; and, while we may prefer Luke's sophisticated critique of this ancient ethic, this is no evidence for its priority. If the *Didache* "fails to see its significance" it may be simply that it does not know the Lukan text, rather than because it is obtuse.[33] This style of argu-

---

[28] H. Köster (*Synoptische Überlieferung bei den Apostolischen Väter* [Berlin: Akademie-Verlag, 1957 (TU 65)] p. 224) sees this as a sign of a late date.

[29] See Behm, ΝΗΣΤΙΣ, TDNT IV, p. 928; G. G. Moore, *Judaism in the First Centuries of the Christian Era: The Age of the Tannaim* II (New York: Schocken, 1958) p. 261; M. Mees, "Die Bedeutung der Sentenzen und ihrer Auxesis für die Formung der Jesuworte nach Didache 1:3b-2:1", *VetChr* 8 (1971) pp. 55-76, esp. 68f.

[30] Cf. Rordorf, "Jesus Tradition", pp. 402-403, *contra* Tuckett, "Synoptic Tradition", pp. 222-223; Jefford, *Sayings of Jesus*, pp. 46-47.

[31] Cf. Audet, *Didachè*, p. 264. R. Knopf (*Die Lehre der zwölf Apostel* [Tübingen: Mohr (HNT.E 1)] p. 7) sees here a lost gospel tradition.

[32] "Synoptic Tradition", pp. 223-224, citing the argument of W. C. van Unnik, "Die Motivierung der Feindesliebe in Lukas VI 32-35", *NT* 8 (1966) pp. 288-300.

[33] Rordorf ("Jesus Tradition", p. 403-404) accepts the presence of the "reciprocity ethic", but argues that the *Didache* does indeed critique it in that, "my enemy's conduct should not give me any pretext to give him a dose of his own medicine, namely hate; rather should I seize the initiative by loving him, so that he also may learn to love me".

ment depends on the dubious assumption that the earliest text is the most insightful and theologically sound, before the *Frühkatholisierungsprozess* corrupted the vision of the nascent church.

In this group of sayings (A), the *Didache* thus presents an independent text which cannot realistically be viewed as a harmony of the Gospels. It seems to have independent access to the traditions on which the Gospels also draw.

In the second group of sayings (B), the *Didache* contrasts the desires of the flesh[34] with the way of perfection, which is that of turning the other cheek. This sophisticated setting for the saying is not to be found in other witnesses.[35] However, the form of the text, while close to Matthew, appears the more primitive since δῷ ῥάπισμα is clumsy Greek compared with Matthew's ῥαπίζει.[36]

In the third group (C), the *Didache* presents a text close to Matthew in wording, but following Luke in the order ἱμάτιον/ χιτῶνα against Matthew. As in Luke, this saying is followed by the heightening saying ἐὰν λάβῃ τις ἀπὸ σοῦ τὸ σόν μὴ ἀπαίτει (Luke ἀπὸ τοῦ αἴροντος τὰ σά...μὰ ἀπαίτει) and its has further climax in οὐδὲ γὰρ δύνασαι (whose exact meaning is problematic, perhaps, "You are in any case not able to do so").[37] In this section, as in the others which have been examined, the *Didache* has the longest text. Glover sees in this the sign of a greater faithfulness to a source which Matthew and Luke abbreviate and refine.[38] Against this it has been asserted that the *Didache* arranges the material in a deliberately climactic style to heighten its effectiveness as catechesis.[39] This does not, however, prove which arrangement of the material is the earlier one.

---

[34] καὶ σωματικῶν should be omitted since it is absent from POxy and *Const* has a different reading also, καὶ κοσμικῶν.

[35] Note however Gal 5:16f.

[36] See R. Glover, "The Didache's Quotations and the Synoptic Gospels", *NTS* 5 (1958-1959) pp. 14f. It is interesting to note also Jn 18:22, ἔδωκεν ῥάπισμα τῷ 'Ιησοῦ. Tuckett ("Synoptic Tradition", pp. 225-226) argues that this may simply be the result of the *Didache's* freedom in the use of his sources.

[37] Cf. Giet, *Énigme*, p. 59; Mees, "Auxesis", p. 64. Tuckett ("Synoptic Tradition", pp. 229-230) again implies a (from his perspective necessarily later) backsliding from a difficult original saying, to provide a "worldly comment on the slightly puzzling preceding clause". Tuckett argues that the *Didache* is here dependent on the Lukan redaction of the "Q" tradition.

[38] "The greater brevity and stylistic improvements of the synoptics again recall the changes they made in the text of Mark when he was their source" ("Quotations", p. 15).

[39] Cf. B. Layton ("The Sources, Date and Transmission of Didache 1:3b-2:1", *HUCA* 61 [1968] pp. 343-383) who takes this approach. However his assertion that the *Didache* deliberately disguised his "plagiarization" of Scripture is absurd. The tendency was not to disguise but towards harmony with the Gospels, unless an author had theological motives. Moreover, Layton's assumption that rhetorical climax is a mark of later redaction is dubious. It is found already within the Gospels.

The fourth section (D) in the *Didache* turns to the question of alms giving, which preoccupies the rest of the material (E-G). In doing so, the *Didache* applies a saying to entreaty for alms which in Luke applies to what is demanded by force (παντὶ τῷ αἰτοῦντί σε δίδου). Matthew has a similar saying applied to lending in 5:42 with quite different wording: τῷ αἰτοῦντί σε δός καὶ τὸν θέλοντα ἀπὸ σοῦ δανίσασθαι μὴ ἀποστράφῃς. The *Didache* amplifies this saying with material drawn from the Two Ways: πᾶσι γὰρ θέλει δίδοσθαι ὁ πατὴρ ἐκ τῶν ἰδίων χαρισμάτων. (See *Doctrina* 4:8, *omnibus enim dominus dare uult de donis suis*. Cf. *HermMan* II.4; *Dida* 4:3). Its original reference, as the *Doctrina* shows, was to alms giving within the community, but the *Didache* universalizes its reference to include even ones enemies, as the context suggests (1:4).

A further saying, attested also in *HermMan* II.5-6, is introduced (E) in the form of a macarism. It seems to be reflected also in Acts 20:35 and 1 Clem 2:1, where it is attributed to the Lord Jesus Christ.[40] Köster[41] is skeptical of its origin as a saying of Jesus, preferring to see in it a Jewish proverb.

The short pericope concerning prison (F) has an eschatological reference in Matthew and Luke. Judgment is coming and it is imperative to put one's affairs right while there is still time. The eschatological context is clearest in Luke. The same context probably lies behind the *Didache*. The person who takes alms without needing them shall give account not to a human court but to the heavenly judge before whom he shall be examined (ἐξετασθήσεται κερὶ ὧν ἔπραξε). The use of the word σύνοχη in the *Didache* is striking, since it is a rare word meaning literally "compression" and hence "distress".[42] Only one possible instance of a use cognate with φυλακή is recorded (*PLond* 354.24) and even this is debatable. The word may rest on an Aramaic word such as מצר which could be rendered either φυλακή or σύνοχη. The wording differs considerably throughout the pericope from that in Matthew/Luke. The final saying (G) draws on a version of Sirach 12:1 which is independent of LXX, as a proof text from Scripture for the teaching.[43]

In none of these sayings from the Jesus tradition and the wisdom tradition can a dependence on either Matthew or Luke be demonstrated. Rather, the variation in order and wording seen in

---

[40] Cf. Glover, "Quotations", p. 15f.

[41] *Überlieferung*, pp. 231-237.

[42] BAG, p. 799.

[43] See P. W. Skehan, "Didache 1:6 and Sirach 12:1", *Bib* 44 (1963) pp. 533-536.

both the *Didache* and Justin indicates an independence over against the written sources in Matthew/Luke which is indicative of a time when the Gospel tradition was still in the process of formation. It may be that such collections of material had long been used in catechesis before they were finally inserted into the *Didache*, and indeed, such collections may well lie behind the Sermon on the Mount/Plain in Matthew/Luke.[44] Most important, for our purposes, is that all these parallels are from what is traditionally called "Q" material in Matthew/Luke, and there is no trace of Markan material. If the *Didache* had our Synoptic Gospels in their present form before it, it seems hard to understand how he could consistently have excluded Markan material present in Matthew and Luke and only drawn on "Q" material. It would seem a more likely inference that the *Didache* had access directly to the so-called "Q" material, either in a written or an oral form.

V.

Didache 8 does seem to know a written or oral gospel close to the present text of Matthew. This is indicated by ὡς ἐκέλευσεν ὁ κύριος ἐν τῷ εὐαγγελίῳ αὐτοῦ, as also by the reference to the ὑπόκριται (cf. Mt 6:1-6) and by the closeness of the text of the Lord's Prayer to that of Mt 6:9-13. Moreover Did. 8 appears to be a later addition to the earliest text of the *Didache*. It is inserted after the reference to the baptismal fast in 7:4, but it has a quite different reference to "stationary fasts" and daily prayer. It breaks up the natural flow in the catechetical manual from baptism to the eucharist. Moreover, it is not introduced by the formula which characterizes the liturgical sections of the *Didache* (περὶ δέ), and in the Ethiopian version it is set after 11:3-13. Nevertheless, the text of Did. 8 exhibits a certain independence with regard to Matthew, which may raise questions as to a simple direct dependence on the present form of the text.[45] The sense given to "hypocrites" is quite different to that in Matthew, where it is insincerity which is under attack. Here the term simply designates the Jewish opponents of the community.[46]

---

[44] "Nous sommes à l'intérieur d'une tradition du Sermon sur la montagne, orale ou écrite relativement uniforme quant à l'expression et relativement homogène quant au contenu", Audet, *Didachè*, p. 266.

[45] For a more thorough examination of this section of the *Didache*, see J. A. Draper, "Christian Self-Definition against the Hypocrites in *Didache* 8", in E. H. Lovering, *Society of Biblical Literature 1992 Seminar Papers*, 362-377. Atlanta, Ga.: Scholars Press.

[46] Cf. Rordorf, "Jesus Tradition", p. 422.

The differences in the text of the Lord's Prayer, though minor, may be significant, since it is clearly derived from the liturgy of the community, where it was known by heart (it was to be repeated three times daily, 8:3).[47] The *Didache* has ἐν τῷ οὐρανῷ for Matthew's ἐν οἷς οὐρανοῖς, and the plural is characteristic of Matthew's editorial activity (5:12=Lk 6:23; 7:11=Lk 11:3; 19:21=Mk 10:21).[48] The *Didache* also has the singular τὴν ὀφελήν for Matthew's τὰ ὀφειλήματα, where the tendency in the tradition may be away from the more primitive idea of collective "debt" towards an understanding of the number of particular sins (Lk τὰς ἁμαρτίας ἡμῶν). Finally the *Didache* has ἀφίεμεν for Matthew ἀφήκαμεν (Lk ἀφίομεν).[49] Here Matthew may be concerned to emphasize with the Aorist the requirement of forgiveness as a pre-requisite to divine forgiveness, in view of the logion which follows in Mt 6:14f. The presence of the doxology in the *Didache* indicates a liturgical use of the Lord's Prayer, and this usage gradually began to invade the text of Matthew also.[50] Did. 15:2-4 seems to have been added at the same redactional stage as Did. 8.

VI.

The "apocalypse" of *Didache* 16 presents many parallels to Mt 24 and yet demonstrates a clear independence with regard to its text. It is likely that the basis of Did. 16 was formed by the original eschatological conclusion to the Jewish Two Ways instruction of 1-6.[51] Ethical parenesis is underscored by the warning concerning the imminent judgment. This Two Ways tradition appears most clearly in 16:2, which is paralleled by *Barnabas* 4:9-10 almost verbatim, but may well be behind 16:1 also. Did. 16:1 uses material found in the Jesus tradition in Matthew and Luke, but in a form which could hardly be a harmonization, since it agrees with neither in order or context.[52] The *Didache* agrees with Mt 24:42 in γρηγορεῖτε and 24:44 (=Lk 12:40) in γίνεσθε ἔτοιμοι. It is not likely that the *Didache* has drawn this material directly from Matthew, since the short admonitions would be easily memorized

---

[47] Cf. *Ibid.*, p. 422.

[48] See Köster, *Überlieferung*, 206.

[49] Köster (*Ibid.*, pp. 208f) sees this agreement between the *Didache* and Luke as indicating what lay in "Q".

[50] Cf. Did. 9:2, 3; 9:4; 10:2, 4, 5.

[51] See E. Bammel, "Schema und Vorlage", p. 253-262; cf. Rordorf, "Jesus Tradition", pp. 412f.

[52] See J-P. Audet, *Didachè*, pp. 180-182. B. C. Butler ("The Literary Relations of Didache ch xvi", *JTS* ns. 11 (1960) pp. 265-283), on the other hand, sees the *Didache* as dependent on Luke.

and used in catechism.[53] There is a further agreement between the *Didache* and Lk 12:35, although the wording and the context are different:[54]

Didache	Luke
οἱ λύχνοι ὑμῶν μὴ σβεσθήτωσαν καὶ αἱ ὀσφύες ὑμῶν μὴ ἐκλυέσθωσαν	ἔστωσαν ὑμῶν αἱ ὀσφύες περιεζωμέναι καὶ οἱ λύχνοι καιόμενοι
Cf. Methodius, *Symposium* V.2	

This imagery seems to have been drawn in part from the general fund of eschatological imagery from Exodus 12:11.[55] See *Mekhilta* Pis. VIII.15-20 on this passage and *j.Kil* IX.32b.9; *j.Ket* XII.35a.9; *New Year Amidah*, Petition 3 in the Jewish tradition, as well as Ephesians 6:11f and 1 Peter 1:13 in the Christian tradition. B. C. Butler[56] thinks that the *Didache* is here dependent on Luke, but this is unlikely. Rather Luke is here drawing on "Q" material. The same must be said for the relation between 16:3-4 and Mt 24:10-11, where the sense is the same but the wording independent. The picture of the eschatological woes is a common ingredient of Jewish writings.[57] The only image which particularly calls for comment is that of the sheep and the wolves.

Didache	Matthew 7:15
καὶ στραφήσονται τὰ πρόβατα εἰς λύκους	προσέχετε ἀπὸ τῶν ψευδοπροφητῶν οἵτινες ἔρχονται πρὸς ὑμᾶς ἐν ἐνδύμασιν προβάτων ἔσωθεν δὲ εἰσιν λύκοι ἅρπαγες
Cf. *AscenIs* 2:24f	
	Cf. Mt 10:16
	ἰδοὺ ἐγὼ ἀποστέλλω ὑμᾶς ὡς πρόβατα ἐν μέσῳ λύκων

Here the text of the *Didache* could hardly be dependent on Matthew, but the image is undoubtedly related. It may be that an

---

[53] See Köster, *Überlieferung*, pp. 176f. On the other hand, R. Bauckham ("Synoptic Parousia Parables and the Apocalypse", *NTS* 23 (1976-1977) pp. 162-176, esp. 169) has seen the *Didache* saying as a "deparabolized" form of the "Thief in the Night" saying.

[54] Cf. Methodius, *Symposium* V.2. See R. Bauckham, "Synolptic Parables Again", *NTS* 29 (1983) pp. 129-143, esp. 131f. The wording in the *Didache* and Methodius may reflect LXX Job 18:5.

[55] Cf. Rordorf, "Jesus Tradition", p. 415; *contra* Tuckett, "Synoptic Tradition", pp. 201-203.

[56] "Literary Relations", pp. 265-283.

[57] See for instance 1QH 4; 1QS 3:21-24; 4QFlor 1:8f; *SibOr* II.165f; AscenIs 3:27ff; ApocPet 1:1; OdesSol 38; Rev 19:2; 16:13; 2 Pet 3:3; 1 Tim 3:1f; 1 Jn 2:18; 4:1. See Further Köster, *Überlieferung*, pp. 177-182.

Aramaic saying lies behind these texts, such as ומסבב הצאן אל זאבים, where the root סבב would explain στραφήσονται and ἐν μέσῳ as well as the extended interpretation of the saying in terms of a disguise. Whatever the semantic background to the saying, it breathes an atmosphere of betrayal and conflict which is absent from the saying in Matthew.[58]

There is a much closer relationship between the material in 16:5-8 and Mt 24.

Didache	Matthew 24:10, 13
καὶ σκανδαλισθήσονται πολλοὶ καὶ ἀπολοῦνται	καὶ τότε σκανδαλισθήσονται πολλοι....
οἱ δὲ ὑπομείναντες ἐν τῇ πίστει αὐτῶν σωθήσονται ὑπ᾿ αὐτοῦ τοῦ καταθέματος	ὁ δὲ ὑπομείνας εἰς τέλος οὗτος σωθήσεται

	Matthew 24:30, 31
καὶ τότε φανήσεται τὰ σημεῖα τῆς ἀληθείας πρῶτον σημεῖον ἐκπετάσεως ἐν οὐρανῷ εἶτα σημεῖον φωνῆς σάλπιγγος καὶ τὸ τρίτον ἀνάστασις νεκρῶν οὐ πάντων δέ... τότε ὄψεται ὁ κόσμος τὸν κύριον ἐρχόμενον ἐπάνω τῶν νεφελῶν τοῦ οὐρανοῦ	καὶ τότε φανήσεται τὸ σημεῖον τοῦ υἱοῦ τοῦ ἀνθρώπου ἐν οὐρανῷ καὶ τότε κόψονται πᾶσαι αἱ φυλαὶ τῆς γῆς καὶ ὄψονται τὸν υἱὸν τοῦ ἀνθρώπου... ἐρχόμενον ἐπὶ τῶν νεφελῶν τοῦ οὐρανοῦ...μετὰ σάλπιγγος μεγάλης καὶ ἐπισυνάξουσιν τοὺς ἐκλεκτοὺς αὐτοῦ ἐκ τῶν τεσσάρων ἀνέμων ἀπ᾿ ἄκρων οὐρανῶν ἕως τῶν ἄκρων αὐτῶν

There are a number of details in the *Didache* which show it to be independent of Matthew and perhaps even help to explain the background behind the text of Matthew. In 16:5 (cf. 4Esdr. 6:25), for example, the difficult phrase ὑπ᾿ αὐτοῦ τοῦ καταθέματος seems to be faithful to the tradition in which the faithful remnant is purged by suffering like a refiner's fire (Mal 3:2-4). The "curse" which saves is the πύρωσις τῆς δοκιμασίας (16:5) as is seen in the closely parallel texts of Hermas, *Vis* IV.3, 4 and 1 Peter 4:12.[59]

---

[58] See J. A. Draper, "Social Ambiguity and the Production of Text: Prophets, Teachers, Bishops,and Deacons and the Development of the Jesus Tradition in the Community of the *Didache*" in C. N. Jefford, *The Didache in Context: Essays of Its Text, History and Transmission* (Leiden: Brill, 1995 [*NT.E* 77]) pp. 284-313, esp. 284f.

[59] For a further discussion of this passage see A. Milavec, "The Saving Efficacy of the Burning Process in *Didache* 16.5", in *The Didache in Context*, pp. 131-155; N. Pardee, "The Curse that Saves (*Didache* 16.5)", *Ibid.*, pp. 156-176; J. A. Draper, "Resurrection and the Cult of Martyrdom in the Didache Apocalypse",

The σημεῖα of the *Didache* are also true to the tradition on which Mt 24:30f depends.[60] The meaning of the *Didache* is somewhat obscured by the translation of two Hebrew words את and נס respectively by the same Greek word σημεῖον (as also in LXX). The σημεῖα of the *Didache* are also true to the tradition on which Mt 24:30f depends. The σημεῖα τῆς ἀληθείας are the אותות האמת, true signs by which the heavenly Son of Man will be known, as opposed to the false signs given by the World Deceiver to pervert the world (16:4). The first sign (σημεῖον ἐκπετάσεως ἐν οὐρανῷ), however, is the נס פרש בשמים, the totem promised by Isaiah 11:10 which the Messiah would raise to rout the nations and gather in the exiles of Israel.[61] This is confirmed by the extensive commentary in the Targum to Isaiah whenever נס appears in the Old Testament (eg. Is 10:11ff; 18:3; 31:9). Jn 3:14 makes the same connection between the serpent set up as a נס (Num 21:4-9) and the cross as the sign of the Son of Man. The reason the nations mourn at the appearing of the sign of the Son of Man in Matthew is because the banner of the Messiah has been set up to rout the nations and gather in the diaspora. This banner was identified by the Church with the cross of Christ, and indeed even the word ἐκπετάσις, like the Hebrew פרש suggested crucifixion (cf. *Dida* 26 [Lagarde p. 107 ll 27-9] *SibOr* V.257; VIII.302; *OdesSol* 27:2f; *Gospel of Philip* [NgH II.3] 63:21ff).

The trumpet and the rising of the dead follow the raising of the sign, the gathering in of the scattered tribes being held to include the saints who had died (see 1QH 6:34; cf. 2:13). The whole schema is accurately reflected in the Jewish *Shemoneh Esreh*, Petition 10, which is widely regarded as being very ancient, probably going back to the late first or early second century AD: תקע בשופר גדול לחרותנו ושא נס לקבץ גליותינו וקבצנו יחד מארבע נפות הארץ.

Finally, the *Didache* in its present form has the quotation from Dan 7:13 found also in Mt 24:30. An older text of the *Didache* may be represented by *Const* which has καὶ τότε ἥξει ὁ κύριος καὶ πάντες οἱ ἅγιοι μετ' αὐτοῦ ἐν συσσεισμῷ ἐπάνω τῶν νεφελῶν, since *Const* usually harmonizes the text of *Didache* with the Gospels. The H54 text of the *Didache* like Matthew cites Dan 7:13, but the survival of ὁ κύριος indicates its independence of Matthew. Köster[62] has argued that the *Didache* draws here upon

---

Paper Delivered at the Society of Biblical Literature Congress, Philadelphia, 1995.

[60] See further on this passage, J. A. Draper, "The Development of the "Sign of the Son of Man" in the Jesus Tradition", *NTS* 39 (1991) pp. 1-21.

[61] See Draper, *Commentary*, pp. 319-325; also A. Stuiber, "Die Drei Semeia von Didache xvi", *JAC* 24 (1981) pp. 42-44.

[62] *Überlieferung*, pp. 187-189.

the Ur-text of a Jewish apocalypse used also by Mark. However, J. S. Kloppenborg[63] has demonstrated that the *Didache* only uses the material parallel to Matthew's special source "M" and at no point cites Matthew where Matthew can be seen to be using Mark. He concludes from this that the *Didache* represents an independent tradition under whose influence Matthew altered his Markan source.[64] This conclusion reached by Kloppenborg concerning Did. 16 is similar to that reached by Glover,[65] who goes so far as to say that "the case for the Didache being a witness to some source, or sources, of our Lord's teaching more primitive than the synoptic Gospels appears very strong indeed".[66]

VII.

The above assessment of the Jesus tradition in the Didache allows some tentative conclusions to be drawn. It suggests, firstly, an independence over against the Synoptic Gospels which often throws light on the Gospel material. Secondly, it shows that firm dependence on the Jesus tradition, rather than what can be attributed to the Jewish milieu, is limited to the tradition which is found mainly in the Sermon on the Mount in Matthew and the Sermon on the Plain in Luke, besides the "apocalypse" of Mt 24. The *Didache* is usually closer to Matthew but sometimes closer to Luke. While this might at first suggest a knowledge of Matthew and Luke, in which the Synoptic Gospels are harmonized on the basis of Matthew, this must be considered unlikely. The context, order and wording of the sayings is independent and cannot be derived from either.

The material the *Didache* has in common with Matthew and Luke *never* includes material these evangelists have drawn from Mark.[67] It co-incides with what is normally described as the "Q" Source in these Gospels, and seems to confirm the hypothesis that sayings of Jesus were collected and circulated in a more or less fixed form, whether oral or written, before the collection was incorporated into the Gospels as we have them. It may be that

---

[63] "Didache 16:6-8 and Special Matthean Tradition", *ZNW* 69-70 (1978-1979) pp. 54-67.

[64] "Tradition", p. 63. A reservation concerning Glover's conclusion needs to be made, in that the *Didache* may reflect at this point an underlying Jewish tradition rather than the Jesus teaching in particular, which may draw on the same tradition.

[65] "Quotations", pp. 25-28.

[66] *Ibid.*, p. 27.

[67] Tuckett ("Synoptic Tradition", p. 201) puts forward the material on the Antichrist performing "signs and wonders" in 16:4 as a case where the *Didache* echoes Mk 13:22=Mt 24:24; Mk 13:19=Mt 24:21; *contra* Köster, *Überlieferung*, p. 182; Rordorf, "Jesus Tradition", p. 415.

these collections were already referred to as τὸ εὐαγγέλιον (Did. 8:2, 11:3, 15:3, 4). The context of such a collection of sayings in Did. 1:3-2:1 strongly implies the use to which the collection was put—the instruction of catechumens: ταῦτα πάντα προειπόντες.[68]

Thirdly, the differences in wording and context of the Jesus sayings in the *Didache*, Matthew and Luke are of the same kind. They indicate an independent use of a common source at a time when that source was still fluid.

---

[68] The same explanation can be given for the collection of sayings of Jesus in Justin, *1 Apol* 15-16, which set out the kernel of Christian teaching which was to precede baptism.

SYNOPTIC TRADITION IN THE DIDACHE

CHRISTOPHER M. TUCKETT
Manchester

In recent years a substantial body of opinion has agreed in general terms about the problem of synoptic tradition in the *Didache*. The three studies of R. Glover, H. Köster and J.-P. Audet which appeared in the 1950's, apparently independently of each other, argued that the presence of synoptic tradition in the *Didache* was not to be explained by direct dependence of the *Didache* on the finished synoptic gospels.[1] Rather, the Didachist used prior traditions available both to himself and to the synoptic evangelists. This view has been endorsed in recent years by Rordorf, Tuilier, Kloppenborg and Draper in various studies devoted to the *Didache* and by other scholars in passing.[2] Some have been more specific about the nature of the common traditions: for example, Glover argued that the synoptic Sayings Source Q was one source of the *Didache*'s synoptic tradition.[3] It is true that there have

---

[1] H. Köster, *Synoptische Überlieferung bei den Apostolischen Vätern* (Berlin: Akademie-Verlag, 1957 [TU 65]) pp. 159-241; J.-P. Audet, *La Didachè: Instructions des apôtres* (Paris: Gabalda, 1958) pp. 166-186. R. Glover, "The *Didache*'s Quotations and the Synoptic Gospels", *NTS* 5 (1958) pp. 12-29; cf. also his "Patristic Quotations and Gospel Sources", *NTS* 31 (1985) pp. 234-251.

[2] See W. Rordorf & A. Tuilier, *La Doctrine des douze Apôtres* (Paris: Les Éditions du Cerf, 1978 [SC 248]); J.S. Kloppenborg, "*Didache* 16:6-8 and Special Matthean Tradition", *ZNW* 70 (1979) pp. 54-67; W. Rordorf, "Le problème de la transmission textuelle de Didachè 1,3b-2,1" in F. Paschke (ed.), *Überlieferungsgeschichtliche Untersuchungen* (Berlin: Akademie-Verlag, 1981 [TU 125]) pp. 499-513; J. Draper, "The Jesus Tradition in the *Didache*" in D. Wenham (ed.), *Gospel Perspectives V: The Jesus Tradition outside the Gospels* (Sheffield: JSOT, 1985) pp. 269-287; also his *A Commentary on the Didache in the Light of the Dead Sea Scrolls and Related Documents* (Ph.D. Dissertation, Cambridge University, 1983); cf. also D. A. Hagner, "The Sayings of Jesus in the Apostolic Fathers and Justin Martyr" in Wenham (ed.), *Gospel Perspectives V, op.cit.*, pp. 233-268, on p. 241f (though this represents a change of view from Hagner's earlier position: see his *The Use of the Old and New Testament in Clement of Rome* [Leiden: Brill, 1973 (NT.S 34)] p. 280: "It seems clear enough, however, that the Gospel of Matthew is used in the *Didache*.") Thus in a recent dictionary article, Tuilier summed up the present state of opinion with the words: "Die neuere Forschung ist sich darin einig, daß die Didache als Ganzes die Schriften des Neuen Testaments in ihrer heutigen Gestalt nicht kennt" (A. Tuilier, art. *Didache* in TRE 8 [1981] p. 735).

[3] Glover, "*Didache* Quotations", *passim* esp. p. 29. (In his later article, Glover seems to have changed his views slightly; he now postulates another source [the "Terse Source"] known to Matthew, Mark, Luke, Clement, *Didache*, Polycarp and Justin, which overlapped extensively with Q. However, he still maintains his view that the *Didache* knew Q: see p. 239). Cf. also Rordorf & Tuilier (*Doctrine*, p. 91), who say that the silence of S. Schulz in his monograph on Q in omitting any reference to Did is "regrettable."

always been those who have disagreed, arguing that the *Didache* presupposes the finished form of the synoptic gospels, or least that of Matthew.[4] The conclusions of this paper are intended to support this latter view.

Any discussion of the problem of synoptic tradition in the *Didache* must take note of the question of the unity of the text usually referred to as "the *Didache*". This text is available to us in its entirety in only one 11th century Greek MS published in 1883 by P. Bryennios.[5] It is almost universally agreed that the present text[6] is, in some sense at least, "composite". *Didache* 1-6 incorporates an earlier Two Ways tradition attested also in the *Epistle of Barnabas* 18-20, *Doctrina Apostolorum* and elsewhere; further, within this Two Ways tradition, the section 1:3-2:1 is probably a secondary, Christianising addition.[7] Other seams within our text have been suggested: for example, chapters 8 and 15 may be secondary additions to an earlier *Vorlage*.[8] The precise number of stages of redaction which one should postulate is much debated. Nevertheless it is clear that any theories about the origins of synoptic tradition in one part of the *Didache* will not necessarily apply to the *Didache* as a whole.[9] Each part of the text must therefore be examined separately and, to a certain extent, independently.

---

[4] See E. Massaux, *The Influence of the Gospel of Saint Matthew on Christian Literature before Saint Irenaeus* III, trns. N. J. Belval & S. Hecht (Macon, Georgia: Mercer University Press, 1993 [NGSt 5/3, trns. BETL 75]) pp. 144ff; B.C. Butler, "The Literary Relations of *Didache*, Ch. XVI", *JTS* 11 (1960) pp. 265-283; also "The 'Two Ways' in the *Didache*", *JTS* 12 (1961) pp. 27-38; P. Vielhauer, in E. Hennecke (ed.), *New Testament Apocrypha* II (London: Lutterworth, 1965) pp. 628f; B. Layton, "The Sources, Date and Transmission of *Didache* 1.3b-2.1", *HTR* 61 (1968) pp. 343-383; S. Giet, *L'Énigme de la Didachè* (Paris: Ophrys, 1970 [PFLUS 149]); K. Wengst, *Didache (Apostellehre), Barnabasbrief, Zweiter Klemensbrief, Schrift an Diognet* (Darmstadt: Wissenschaftliche Buchgesellschaft, 1984 [SUC 2]) pp.25-30; U. Luz, *Matthew 1-7: A Continental Commentary* (Minneapolis: Fortress, 1989), p. 93. W. D. Köhler, *Die Rezeption des Matthäusevangeliums in der Zeit vor Irenäus* (Tübingen: Mohr, 1987 [WUNT 2/24]) pp. 19-56. This was certainly the dominant view in the earlier period of research, prior to the 1950's.

[5] Other witnesses include versions in Ethiopic, Georgian and Coptic, a fragment from one of the Oxyrhynchus papyri, POxy 1782, as well as later writers who used the *Didache*, notably the author of Book VII of the Apostolic Constitutions.

[6] By this I refer to the text of the Bryennios MS.

[7] For this section, see part III below.

[8] Rordorf & Tuilier, *Doctrine*, pp. 36, 63; cf. Draper, *Jesus Tradition*, p. 271. For doubts about the reliability of the Bryennios text, see too E. Petersen, "Über einige Probleme der Didache-Überlieferung", in *Frühkirche, Judentum und Gnosis* (Rome: Herder, 1959) pp. 146-182. Cf. also n. 82 below.

[9] Thus, for example, Köster argues that most of the *Didache* is independent of the synoptic gospels, but that 1:3-2:1 presupposes our gospels and represents a much later addition to the *Didache*.

One further preliminary point to be made is that it is quite clear that, for the most part, the *Didache* does not "quote" the synoptic tradition. There are a few instances where the *Didache* clearly indicates its intention to quote something (from whatever source): cf. Did 1:6; 9:5; 16:7. Elsewhere there are references to a εὐαγγέλιον (8:2; 11:3; 15:3, 4) which may be a written source.[10] However, the remaining links between the *Didache* and synoptic tradition are at the level of allusion only. It is thus inappropriate to judge the *Didache*'s use of synoptic tradition as if it were a case of explicit quotation and to expect exact agreement between the quoted version and the source used. The *Didache*'s use of synoptic tradition is more one of free allusion. Hence disagreements between the *Didache* and the gospels in, for example, the context and application of synoptic tradition need not imply that the *Didache* cannot have known our gospels.[11] Indeed it can be argued that precisely such freedom in the use of synoptic tradition is to be expected if the *Didache* is using our gospels as, in some sense, authoritative texts.[12] How then can one determine whether or not the Didachist presupposes the finished gospels?

In terms of methodology, Köster's approach remains exemplary. Not only did he set out the relevant texts clearly in

---

[10] For a discussion, see Köster, *Überlieferung*, p. 10f. It is a key point of Wengst's argument against Köster that εὐαγγέλιον must refer to a written gospel and that gospel can only be Matthew: hence all the verbal similarities between the *Didache* and the synoptic tradition are due to dependence on Matthew. This however demands that the references to a εὐαγγέλιον, especially in 15:3, 4, bear a lot of weight in the argument: it ignores the possibility that ch. 15 may belong to a later stratum within the present text. It also does not deal with the possibility that the *Didache* might be using a written source which lies behind Matthew, rather than Matthew's gospel itself. Wengst does not discuss whether the parallels to the *Didache* in Matthew are redactional or traditional.

[11] This applies especially to the work of Glover (n. 1 above) who frequently argues that the *Didache* cannot be dependent on our gospels because the same material is used in such widely differing ways. (Glover even speaks of "the Didache's *Quotations*" in the title of his article). In any case, the different contexts imply freedom and change by at least one person, be it the Didachist or the synoptic evangelist. But the different contexts and uses of the same material cannot really be used in the argument here. Much the same can be said about Draper who argues that *any* difference between the *Didache* and the gospels may imply that the *Didache* is using independent traditions, since the tendency in the MS tradition was to harmonize the text of the *Didache* with that of the gospels ("Jesus Tradition", p. 271 and cf. his argument on Did 16:8 and the text of Did 1:3 discussed below). But again this seems to assume that the *Didache*'s practice is one of careful quotation, rather than alluding to, and using freely, the synoptic tradition. Wengst's comment is apt: "Nach diesem Argumentationsmuster müßte man etwa Paulus die Benutzung des AT absprechen" (*Didache*, p. 30).

[12] Cf. F.E. Vokes, "The *Didache* and the Canon of the New Testament" in *Studia Evangelica* 3 (Berlin: Akademie-Verlag, 1964 [TU 88]) pp. 427-436.

parallel;[13] he also worked with a clearly defined criterion: if material which owes its origin to the redactional activity of a synoptic evangelist reappears in another work, then the latter presupposes the finished work of that evangelist. Such a criterion must of course be applied with care, and one must not rule out the possibility that a feature could have been added to the tradition by two independent redactors. Nor should one assume that any dependence which is established on the basis of this criterion is necessarily direct: the later document may be several stages removed from the earlier one. Nevertheless, this criterion is really the only one which ultimately can determine whether a text like the *Didache* presupposes the finished gospels or whether it uses traditions which lie behind our gospels. Such an approach differs from that of, say, B. Layton who, in his study of Did 1:3-2:1 (cf. n. 4 above) effectively assumed dependence and sought to clarify the *Didache*'s redactional activity on that assumption. This certainly has great value in recognizing the importance of the Didachist's own intentions and contributions in producing his text. But Layton's approach is open to the criticism that what is "coherent" does not necessarily reflect historical fact. Thus, whilst Layton has shown how a later writer could have altered the synoptic gospels in the way suggested, his argument does not really show that this actually happened.

One must therefore supplement Layton's approach by a close analysis of the synoptic parallels to the text of the *Didache* to see if any elements are redactional there. Part of the weakness of the approach of some of those who have advocated the independence of the *Didache* from the synoptic gospels is that they fail to offer any sustained analysis of the synoptic data on its own terms. (This applies, for example, to the studies of Rordorf and Draper). If, for example, the *Didache* is using Q material in a form that existed prior to its use by Matthew and Luke, then the synoptic parallels to the *Didache* should all occur in elements which are pre-redactional in the gospels. Conversely, if the *Didache* shows agreement with redactional elements in the gospels, then this will be an indication that the *Didache* presupposes our gospels.

I. DIDACHE 16

Did 16 is widely recognized as containing a significant cluster of links with synoptic tradition and it may be regarded as an important test case in the discussion of the problem of synoptic tradition in the *Didache*.

---

[13] Cf. the praise of Layton, "Sources", p. 241; see too n. 102 below.

Many who have argued against any dependence of the *Didache* on Matthew's gospel have appealed to a peculiar pattern in the parallels between the *Didache* and the synoptic gospels. It is said that Did 16 only shows links with material peculiar to Mt 24 in the synoptic tradition: the *Didache* does not have any links with material from Mt 24 which Matthew has derived from Mark.[14] Hence, it is argued, the *Didache* is more likely to be dependent on the source(s) which lie behind Mt 24 and which were available to Matthew alone; if the *Didache* were dependent on Matthew, one would expect some of Matthew's Markan material to be reflected as well.[15] Such an argument is in danger of ignoring some of the evidence of Did 16 itself. For the text of Did 16 contains possible allusions to synoptic material in four verses common to Matthew and Mark (and which Matthew presumably derived from Mark).

Did 16:4

Did 16:4 mentions the κοσμοπλανής who, it is said, will do (ποιήσει) signs and wonders (σημεῖα καὶ τέρατα) and will perform iniquities ἃ οὐδέποτε γέγονεν ἐξ αἰῶνος. The language used is similar to that of Matthew and Mark. Mk 13:22/Mt 24:24 refers to the coming of false messiahs and false prophets who will perform[16] σημεῖα καὶ τέρατα, "leading astray"[17] the elect; and in Mk 13:19/Mt 24:21 the coming tribulation is said to be such as never has been (οὐ γέγονεν) since the creation of the world.[18] It can be argued, of course, that these parallels are not very significant. Both the *Didache* and the synoptists could be reflecting standard eschatological motifs and using OT language.[19] However, it is

---

[14] I am assuming through the discussion the theory of Markan priority, as indeed do most other scholars in their discussion of synoptic tradition in the *Didache*. This applies even in the articles of Butler. Butler himself is well-known as favouring the theory of Matthean priority, but he wrote his articles on the *Didache* taking care not to presuppose any particular solution to the synoptic problem, though see nn. 63, 89 below.

[15] See Glover, "Didache's Quotations", pp. 22-25; Köster, *Überlieferung*, p. 184f (on Did 16:6); Audet, *Didache*, p. 182; Rordorf & Tuilier, *Doctrine*, p. 90; Kloppenborg, "*Didache* 16,6-8", *passim*; Draper, *Dissertation*, pp. 325f; "Jesus Tradition", p. 283.

[16] Mark ποιήσουσιν, Matthew δώσουσιν. The *Didache* is in fact marginally closer to Mark here, though this verbal agreement is scarcely significant enough to show anything.

[17] Mark ἀποπλανᾶν, Matthew πλανῆσαι—hence the same root as the *Didache*'s κοσμοπλανής.

[18] *Didache*'s ἐξ αἰῶνος is not verbally the same as Mark's / Matthew's phrase ἀπ᾽ ἀρχῆς κτίσεως κόσμου, but the idea is the same.

[19] The language is close to Dt 13:2 and Dan 12:1 Θ': see Köster (*Überlieferung*, p. 182) who also refers to 2 Thess 2:9; Rev 13:13. Glover ("Didache's Quotations", p. 24) refers to the differences between the *Didache* and the gospels: e.g. in the *Didache* the single "world-deceiver" performs the signs and wonders,

clear that the verbal links between Did 16 and Mt 24 are not confined to material peculiar to Matthew.

Köster recognizes these parallels but asserts that, since Mk
13:19, 22 come from the *Vorlage* used by Mark in Mk 13, the
Didache here shows links only with Mark's source and not with
Mark's gospel itself.[20] This argument raises a number of critical
problems. First there is a question about criteria. The argument
here is that if the *Didache* shows links with Mark's source, it cannot be dependent on Mark's gospel. Elsewhere, however, Köster
argues that since the *Didache* does not have allusions to material
in Matthew's source (Mark), the *Didache* cannot be dependent on
Matthew's gospel.[21] Clearly there are dangers of possibly contradictory criteria being applied and it would be better to consider
the whole pattern of agreements between the *Didache* and the
synoptic material in relation to synoptic sources before making
premature judgments about individual verses. Second, the appeal
to a *Vorlage* of Mk 13 raises complex issues of Markan study
which can only be touched on briefly here. Köster appeals almost
exclusively to the claims of Bultmann and Klostermann about the
content of Mark's alleged source here. In recent years there have
been several important studies of Mk 13,[22] though not all would
agree in assigning the relevant verses in this discussion to Mark's
source. V. 19 probably is as likely as any verse to have been in
whatever *Vorlage* there might have been, but opinions differ about
v. 22. According to Pesch, Hahn and others, v. 22 is part of the
pre-Markan source. According to Brandenburger, the verse is one
of a number which come to Mark from traditions other than that
of the basic apocalypse which underlies the present chapter, so
that although the wording may be pre-Markan, the positioning of
v. 22 here may be due to MkR.[23] However, Lambrecht and
Laufen have argued very persuasively that v. 22 is due to MkR.[24]

---

whereas in the gospels it is the (many) false prophets. However, this is an example
of confusing quotations and allusions: cf. n. 11 above.

[20] *Überlieferung*, *op.cit.*, p 182.

[21] *Überlieferung*, pp. 184f, on Did 16:6.

[22] To mention only a few, see J. Lambrecht, *Die Redaktion der Markus-
Apokalypse. Literarische Analyse und Structuruntersuchung* (Rome: Pontifical Biblical Institute, 1967 [AB 28]); R. Pesch, *Naherwartungen. Tradition und Redaktion in
Mk 13.* (Dusseldorf: Patmos, 1968) and his *Das Markusevangelium II. Teil*
(Freiburg: Herder, 1980²); F. Hahn, "Die Rede von der Parusie des Menschensohnes Markus 13" in R. Pesch & Schnakenburg (eds.), *Jesus und der Menschensohn* (Fs. Anton Vögtle), Freiburg: Herder 1975) pp. 240-256; E. Brandenburger *Markus 13 und die Apokalyptik* (Göttingen: Vandenhoeck & Ruprecht, 1984
[FRLANT 134]).

[23] Brandenburger, *Markus 13*, pp. 147ff and see his "Übersicht" on p. 166f. The
problems of assigning v. 22 to the *Vorlage* are discussed on p. 24.

[24] Lambrecht, *Redaktion*, p. 170f; R. Laufen, *Die Doppelüberlieferungen der
Logienquelle und des Markusevangeliums* (Bonn: Hanstein, 1980 [BBB 54]) pp.
379-382. V. 22 is of course also very important as evidence of Mark's concerns in

It is thus precarious to build too much on the alleged pre-Markan nature of v. 22.

Did 16:5

Another possible link between the *Didache* and Markan material occurs in Did 16:5: οἱ δὲ ὑπομείναντες...σωθήσονται cf. Mk 13:13/Mt 24:13; 10:22 ὁ δὲ ὑπομείνας εἰς τέλος...σωθήσεται. Again it can be argued that the parallel is not by itself very significant.[25] Köster again ascribes it to Mark's *Vorlage* and argues, somewhat strangely, that since Matthew's wording is dependent here on Mark, this cannot prove dependence of the *Didache* on Matthew.[26] By itself, such an argument is true though it appears to concede in passing that the *Didache does* have verbal links with material in Matthew which Matthew derives from Mark. The language is not unusual in such an eschatological context: cf. Dan 12:12; 4 Ezra 6:25,[27] though the verbal agreement between these texts and the *Didache* is not as close as that between the *Didache* and Matthew/Mark.[28] The problem of the origin of Mk 13:13 is a complex one. Many regard the verses as pre-Markan and it is certainly not easy to point to any clear Markan characteristics.[29] But whatever its origin, it is clear that Did 16:5 provides another instance where the *Didache* shows verbal links with material which Matthew shares with Mark.

Did 16:8

The most significant connection between the *Didache* and material in both Matthew and Mark occurs in Did 16:8 (τότε ὄψεται ὁ κόσμος τὸν κύριον ἐρχόμενον ἐπάνω τῶν νεφελῶν τοῦ οὐρανοῦ).

---

the theory of T.J. Weeden, *Mark--Traditions in Conflict* (Philadelphia: Fortress, 1971) esp. pp. 72ff: "Mark's hand is most visible in the formation of sections 5-6, 9-13, 21-23, 28-37" (p. 72).

[25] Glover does not even mention it.

[26] *Überlieferung*, p. 183.

[27] So Köster, *ibid*; Kloppenborg, "*Didache* 16,6-8", p. 66.

[28] Despite Köster's claim that 4 Ezr is "almost word for word the same as Mk 13:1b par" (my translation), Dan 12:12 θ' has ὁ ὑπομένων but no exact parallel to σωθήσεται. 4 Ezr 6:25 has *omnis qui derelictus fuerit...saluabitur* but *derelictus* is rather weaker than the meaning of ὑπομένω here which probably has a meaning of more active endurance and is not just a reference to simply surviving (so Bauer's *Lexicon, ad loc.*)

[29] See R. Kühschelm, *Jüngerverfolgung und Geschick Jesu* (Klosterneuburg: Verlag Österreichisches Katholisches Bibelwerk, 1983 [ÖBS 5]) p. 22. The verse is in Mark's *Vorlage* according to Pesch and Hahn. However, Brandenburger assigns it to other traditions included here by Mark.

The allusion to Dan 7:13 here is very similar to that in Mt 24:30 (cf. Mk 13:26). The very close relationship between the *Didache* and Matthew has often been noted. In particular the *Didache* shares with Mark and Matthew the use of ὄψεται / ὄψονται and the inversion of the order of "coming" and "clouds" as compared with Dan 7. Further, the *Didache* agrees with Matthew's redaction of Mark in using ἐπάνω (Matthew ἐπί) for Mark's ἐν with the "clouds", and adding τοῦ οὐρανοῦ. A priori there is a strong case here for seeing the *Didache* reflecting MattR of Mark and hence presupposing Matthew's finished gospel.

Glover explains the agreement as due to "joint borrowing from Dan. vii 13",[30] but he offers no explanation for the unusual features (ὄψεται and the relative order of the "clouds" and "coming") mentioned above. Köster claims that Matthew is unlikely to have changed the text of Mark in the way suggested and hence Matthew's text is based on a *Vorlage* of Mark which read ἐπὶ τῶν νεφελῶν.[31] However the basis for such a claim is unconvincing. Kloppenborg, who is also defending the thesis of the independence of the *Didache* and Matthew, rightly criticizes Köster here and says that there is no justification for postulating an earlier version of Mark's text used by both the *Didache* and Matthew.[32] Yet Kloppenborg also denies that the *Didache* shows any dependence on MattR here. He appeals to the lack of any reference in the *Didache* to the signs of heaven of Mt 24:29; however, the *Didache* does have its own version of (admittedly quite different) signs in 16:6. Kloppenborg also appeals to the fact that the words which follow the allusion to Dan 7 in Matthew/Mark, μετὰ δυνάμεως καὶ δόξης πολλῆς, do not appear in the *Didache*, and asserts that "there is no reason for the author's avoidance of this phrase."[33] However, an argument from silence here is very precarious. It is universally agreed that the text at the end of the *Didache* here is in some disarray and that some further text has probably got lost.[34] It is thus very dangerous to base any theory on the absence of material after Did 16:8 in our Greek MS. Kloppenborg's claim is that "Did 16:8 agrees with Mt 24:30 at those points where Matthew disagrees with Mark";[35] this however

---

[30] "Didache's Quotations", p. 24.

[31] *Überlieferung*, p. 188.

[32] "Didache 16,6-8", p. 61f.

[33] *Ibid*, p. 63.

[34] See Audet, *Didache*, p. 73f; Rordorf & Tuilier, *Doctrine*, pp. 107, 199; Draper, Commentary, p. 326; Wengst, *Didache*, p. 20; Wengst even prints (p. 90) a further clause as the ending of the text (ἀποδοῦναι ἑκάστῳ κατὰ τὴν πρᾶξιν αὐτοῦ) on the basis of the text in *Const*, though the latter is considerably longer and more complex than this.

[35] "Didache 16,6-8", p. 63.

ignores the agreement between Matthew and Mark in using ὄψονται and in inverting the "clouds" and the "coming" of Dan 7[36] as well as the features common to the *Didache*, Matthew, Mark and Daniel. Kloppenborg's conclusion is that "Did 16:8 represents an independent tradition under whose influence Matthew altered his Markan source, namely by substituting ἐπὶ for ἐν and adding τοῦ οὐρανοῦ".[37] However, a much simpler explanation is available. Matthew's differences from Mark here serve to align his version of Dan 7:13 with that of the LXX. A tendency by Matthew to conform OT allusions to the form of the LXX is well-documented.[38] The "tradition under whose influence Matthew altered his Markan source" need only be the LXX text of Dan 7. There is no need at all to postulate a tradition very closely parallel to Mk 13, but independent of Mark and known only to Matthew. Such a theory is a totally unnecessary complication.

A different appeal to textual criticism is made by Draper. Draper refers to the text of *Const* VII which reads ἐν συσσεισμῷ as the equivalent of the Bryennios MS's τότε ὄψεται ὁ κόσμος τὸν κύριον ἐρχόμενον. He argues that, since *Const* has a tendency to conform the text of the *Didache* to that of Matthew's Gospel, this reading in *Const* which differs from Matthew's text may represent a more original version of the text of the *Didache*; the reading in the Bryennios MS would then be the result of secondary scribal assimilation to the text of Matthew.[39] All this is somewhat speculative. It is not the case that the text of *Const* is uniformly closer to Matthew than that of the *Didache*.[40] Further, Draper's suggestion that the use of κύριος in the Bryennios text betrays the vestige of an independent tradition (Matthew has "Son of Man") is also unconvincing. The κύριος of 16:8 in the Bryennios MS presumably arises by assimilation to the κύριος of 16:7 (citing Zech 14:5). In fact the use of κύριος is quite characteristic of the *Didache* (it is used 18 times elsewhere, at times clearly referring to Jesus, cf. 8:2). Hence it is quite easy to ascribe the usage of κύριος in the Bryennios text at 16:8 to the "original author" of the

---

[36] Kloppenborg argues that both these features may be pre-Markan since they can be paralleled elsewhere (though not all his evidence is equally valid e.g. the text of Justin *Dialogue* 51:9 [wrongly cited as "15,9" consistently] could be due to influence of the gospel tradition). But again this excludes a piece of evidence prematurely. The fact that the features *may* be pre-Markan cannot settle the issue of how they are to be explained in the *Didache* itself.

[37] "Didache 16,6-8", p. 63.

[38] See K. Stendahl, *The School of St. Matthew and its Use of the Old Testament* (Philadelphia: Fortress, 1954) pp. 147ff; G. Strecker, *Der Weg der Gerechtigkeit* (Göttingen: Vandenhoeck & Ruprecht, 1971 [FRLANT 82]) pp. 21ff; W. G. Kümmel, *Introduction to the New Testament* (London: SCM, 1975) pp. 110f.

[39] "Jesus Tradition", p. 283; *Commentary*, p. 325.

[40] E.g. Did 16:4 has παραδώσουσιν as in Matthew; *Const* has προδώσουσιν.

Didache. In any case, it would probably be precarious to rely too much on such a indirect source as *Const* for reconstructing the text of the *Didache*.

None of the arguments considered appears to provide a convincing alternative to the theory that the *Didache* here presupposes knowledge of Matthew's revision of Mark. Thus Did 16 has links not only with Matthew's special material, but also with material common to Matthew and Mark and, in the last instance considered, presupposes Matthew's redaction of Mark. I now consider the links between Did 16 and material peculiar to Matthew.

Did 16:3-5.

The existence of links between Did 16 and material peculiar to Mt 24 is accepted by all. In Did 16:3-5 there is a cluster of similarities between the language of the *Didache* and Mt 24:10-12 and other Matthean passages. 16:3 πληθυνθήσεται οἱ ψευδο-προφῆται uses similar language to Mt 24:11f. (ψευδοπροφῆται in v. 11; πληθυνθῆναι in v. 12); "sheep becoming wolves" in Did 16:3 uses imagery similar to that of Mt 7:15; "ἀγάπη turning to μῖσος" reflects Mt 24:10, 12 (μισήσουσιν in v. 10, ἀγάπη in v. 12); ἀνομία increasing (Did 16:4) is similar to Mt 24:11 (ἀνομία multiplying); and διώξουσι in Did 16:4 links with διώκωσιν in the very closely related context of Mt 10:23. Finally σκανδαλισ-θήσονται πολλοί of Did 16:5 recalls the identical words in Mt 24:10.

It is noteworthy that the parallels to Did 16:3-5 in Matthew include the three Matthean references to ψευδοπροφῆται (Mt 7:15; 24:10-12; 24:24).[41] This is readily explained if the author of the *Didache* were attempting to cull from Matthew all the available material about false prophets. This provides a reasonable explanation for what might appear at first sight to be a rather random set of parallels in Matthew.

If the existence of these parallels is universally accepted, their significance is disputed. Much depends on one's beliefs about the origin of the material in Mt 24:10-12. Methodologically, the problem should perhaps be one of synoptic study before one considers the *Didache* itself.[42] Within Matthean scholarship there

---

[41] For the parallel between Did 16:4 and Mt 24:24 see above. Glover ("Didache's Quotations", p. 23) ascribes these references to three different sources in Matthew; but the multiple references are much more likely to be due to MattR.

[42] Cf. the comments of F. Neirynck ("John and the Synoptics", in *Evangelica: Collected Essays* [Leuven: Leuven University Press, 1982 (BETL 60)] p. 379) in relation to the not dissimilar problem of the relationship between John and the synoptic tradition: "The question whether John depends upon Mark or upon the sources of Mark is primarily a problem of Synoptic criticism".

is widespread agreement that these verses are due to MattR.[43] If this is the case, then it would appear to provide clear evidence of the *Didache*'s presupposition of Matthew's redactional activity and hence of Matthew's gospel.

This conclusion has however been disputed from the side of Didachean scholarship. Some have appealed to the fact that the same words are used in different ways in the *Didache* and Matthew as evidence of their independence: for example, in Matthew it is the lawlessness which is multiplied in the *Didache* it is the false prophets.[44] However, this kind of argument tends to assume that the *Didache* is quoting synoptic tradition, whereas in fact there is at best here only an allusion and use of common language. Appeal is also made to the fact that much of the common

---

[43] See J. Lambrecht, "The Parousia Discourse. Composition and Content in Mt XXIV-XXV", in M. Didier (ed.), *L'Evangile selon Matthieu* (Gembloux: Duculot, 1972 [BETL 29]) p. 320: "Matthew has formed these verses himself ... He has used words and ideas which the context has offered. The result is typically Matthean". See too G.D. Kilpatrick, *The Origins of the Gospel according to St. Matthew* (Oxford: Oxford University Press, 1946) p. 32; F. W. Burnett, *The Testament of Jesus Sophia* (Washington, 1979) p. 247; Kühschelm, *Jungerverfolgung*, pp. 124f; R. H. Gundry, *Matthew. A Commentary on his Literary and Theological Art* (Grand Rapids: Eerdmans, 1982) p. 479. Cf. the typical Mattheanisms καὶ τότε, σκανδαλίζομαι (14-8-2), πλανάω (8-4-1), ψευδοπροφήτης (3-1-1), ἀνομία (4-0-0) etc.

Very few have argued explicitly that this is traditional in Matthew. One exception is D. Wenham: see his *The Rediscovery of Jesus' Eschatological Discourse* (Sheffield: JSOT, 1984) pp. 256-259, and in more detail in "A Note on Matthew 24:10-12" in *TynB* 31 (1980) pp. 155-162. Wenham appeals to an allegedly clear chiastic structure (ABBCCA) though this is scarcely obvious (e.g. the alleged "A" elements, v. 10a and v. 12, are parallel only in the most general terms: a quite different chiastic structure for vv. 9-14 is proposed by Kühschelm, *Jüngerverfolgung*, p. 63). He claims too that the paratactic style is uncharacteristic of Matthew: however, Mt 4:23-25; 17:18 (cf. Mk 9:25); 27:11-14 all owe a lot to MattR and are equally paratactic. (Cf. also instances where Matthew adds καί to Mark, as listed by F. Neirynck, *The Minor Agreement of Matthew and Luke against Mark* [Leuven: Leuven University Press, 1974 (BETL 37)] p. 204). Wenham also appeals to allegedly non-Matthean vocabulary. Some of this may be due to allusions to the language of Daniel which would be consistent with an origin in MattR, but he claims that ἀγάπη and ψυγήσεται are unexplained. (Cf. especially "Note", p. 159 n. 4, where these are said to be the most significant). However, the importance of "loving" is widely recognized as of vital importance for Matthew's ethic and hermeneutic: cf. Mt 19:19; 22:40 (see R. Mohrlang, *Matthew and Paul* [Cambridge: Cambridge University Press, 1984 (SNTS MS, 48)] pp. 94-96, with full supporting bibliography). Hence, even though it is the noun rather than the verb which is used here, it would be precarious to base too much weight on this grammatical difference. Thus the only possible indication of non-Matthean vocabulary is the hapax ψύχω, and in view of the large number of Matthean features elsewhere in these verses it seems easiest to ascribe the whole section to MattR.

[44] See Glover, "Didache's Quotations", p. 23; Köster, *Überlieferung*, pp. 178, 180f.

vocabulary here may be reflecting stock motifs, though it is certainly the case that the verbal and contextual links between Did 16 and Mt 24 are much closer than those with other texts proposed as parallels here.[45]

In a significant part of his argument, Köster recognises the parallels between Mt 24 and the *Didache* here. However, he claims that the verbal agreement is insufficient to show dependence on Matthew; rather, both depend on common tradition and indeed Did 16 itself may provide evidence that Mt 24:10-12 is a piece of pre-Matthean tradition.[46] Such an argument raises at least two major difficulties. First, the measure of verbal agreement between the *Didache* and Matthew cannot be used to determine whether that agreement is due to direct dependence of one on the other or to common dependence on a prior source. Common dependence on a prior source does not necessarily involve less close verbal agreement.[47] Second, and more important, the claim that Did 16 itself may provide evidence that Mt 24:10-12 is pre-Matthean is a case of *petitio principii* here. If the question is whether the *Didache* depends on Matthew's Gospel or on a pre-Matthean source, one cannot use the evidence of the *Didache* itself to solve the source problem of Matthew's text. Köster's argument is thus dangerously circular.

Did 16:6.

Parallels between Did 16:6 and Mt 24:30a, 31 are also widely recognized (e.g. the common use of φανήσεται, σημεῖον, ἐν

---

[45] Glover ("Didache's Quotations", p. 23) refers to ἀνομία occurring also in 2 Thess 2:3 (though the usage in the *Didache* is much closer to Mt 24 than to 2 Thess's more specialized ὁ ἄνθρωπος τῆς ἀνομίας). Köster (*Überlieferung*, p. 173) refers to 2Bar 48:35 for the idea of love turning to hate (though neither love nor hate are explicitly mentioned there); he also appeals to ApocPet 1:1, though this text is almost certainly dependent on Matthew: see R. J. Bauckham, "The Two Fig-Tree Parables in the Apocalypse of Peter", *JBL* 104 (1985) pp. 271-273. (Bauckham is discussing the Ethiopic version; the Achmim fragment, referred to by Köster, is an even less reliable witness to the text of ApocPet and assimilation to Matthew is even more likely there. The textual tradition of ApocPet is discussed by Dr. Bauckham in a forthcoming article the contents of which he has kindly communicated to me). Köster also claims that Matthew's idea of love growing cold is secondary to Did's "kräftiger und ursprünglicher" phrase: but this is difficult to establish with any precision.

[46] *Überlieferung*, pp. 181, 184: "...drängt sich die Frage auf, ob nicht Did. 16,4 beweist, daß Mt. 24,10ff keine Schöpfund des Mt., sondern ein selbstständiges Traditionsstück ist, das Mt. und Did. unabhängig voneinander verwendet haben" (p. 181).

[47] Cf. the situation in discussion about the synoptic problem: close verbal agreement between Matthew and Luke does not of itself exclude the Q hypothesis. Equally, a measure of verbal disagreement in triple tradition material does not preclude the possibility of direct dependence of one evangelist on another.

οὐρανῷ, σάλπιγξ). Again many would ascribe this material to
MattR in Matthew,[48] though the limited extent makes any certainty
impossible. In defending the theory of the independence of the
Didache and Matthew, some have pointed to the differences
between the two texts here,[49] though one must again note that the
Didache here is not explicitly quoting any source at this point.
The *Didache* develops its own idea of the three "signs",[50] though
this could well have been prompted by Matthew's "sign of the Son
of Man". Several too point to the fact that Did 16:6 shows links
only with material peculiar to Matthew.[51] However, this is valid
only if one confines attention to 16:6; in 16:8 the *Didache* does
use material common to Matthew and Mark, as we have seen. As
before, it is possible to appeal to the fact that many of these motifs
may be stock apocalyptic ideas (e.g. the trumpet),[52] though the
connection between, for example, the eschatological trumpet and
Dan 7:13, as in both Did 16:6, 8 and Mt 24:30, is not easy to
attest elsewhere.

The conclusion of this section is that there is nothing peculiar
in the pattern of parallels with Did 16 in Mt 24. Did 16 shows
verbal links with the material peculiar to Matthew in this chapter,
with material common to Matthew and Mark and with Matthew's
redaction of Mark. there is little convincing evidence to show that
Matthew had access to any extensive source other than Mark for
this chapter. The pattern of parallels between the *Didache* and
Matthew is thus most easily explained if the *Didache* here presupposes Matthew's finished gospel.

II. OTHER TEXTS
Did 11:7.

The saying about the unforgivable sin in Did 11:7 πᾶσα γὰρ
ἁμαρτία ἀφεθήσεται, αὕτη δὲ ἡ ἁμαρτία οὐκ ἀφεθήσεται may
provide further support for this thesis. The evidence here is very
small in extent and so certainty is not possible. However, the

---

[48] See Lambrecht, "Parousia Discourse", p. 324; Gundry, *Matthew*, p. 488. For
a pre-Matthean origin, see Wenham, *Rediscovery*, pp. 318ff. Clearly Matthew is
using traditional ideas and phraseology so that in that sense Matthew's language is
traditional; the question is whether Matthew himself has supplied this traditional
language.
[49] See Glover, "Didache's Quotations", p. 24f; Köster, *Überlieferung*, pp. 184f.
[50] On which see Draper, *Commentary*, pp. 319-325; also A. Stuiber, "Die drei
Semeia von Didache xvi", *JAC* 24 (1981) pp. 42-44.
[51] Glover, "Didache's Quotations", p. 24; Köster, *Überlieferung*, pp. 184f;
Kloppenborg, "Didache 16,6-8", pp. 64f.
[52] Glover, "Didache's Quotations", p. 25; Köster, *Überlieferung*, p 186.

Didache's wording agrees exactly with Matthew's redaction of Mark in Mt 12:31/Mk 3:28. (Matthew πᾶσα ἁμαρτία...ἀφεθήσεται; Mark πάντα ἀφεθήσεται...τὰ ἁμαρτήματα). The second half of the saying in Did has been modelled very precisely on the first half. ἁμαρτία in the second half has no precise parallel in any synoptic version, though οὐκ ἀφεθήσεται agrees with Matthew again (Mt 12:31b, 32b also Lk 12:10b). Köster admits that the *Didache* is closer to Matthew than to the other synoptic versions here, but denies direct dependence in view of the lack of any significant features;[53] however, any links between the *Didache* and Matthew's version are with redactional features in Matthew. Glover too denies any direct dependence here and seeks to find support for his general theory that the *Didache* is dependent on Q. He claims that the *Didache* here rejects words common to Matthew and Mark alone but not in Luke (e.g. βλασφημία). Further, Did shares some words with Matthew which are not from Mark (πᾶσα ἁμαρτία); but since Matthew is carefully conflating Mark and Q here, these words are probably words from Q and omitted by Luke.[54] This is however unconvincing. It is almost universally agreed that the Q version of the saying has "whoever/everyone who speaks a word against the Son of man" in the first half[55] and has nothing equivalent to the πᾶσα ἁμαρτία of Mt 12:31a which is almost certainly MattR of Mark's πάντα τὰ ἁμαρτήματα (Mk 3:28). Hence the verbal links with the *Didache* in the synoptic versions occur in Matthew's redactional material, not in Q. Köster also refers to Jewish parallels for the idea of speaking against the prophetic Spirit as being the unforgivable sin.[56] However, such an idea is not peculiar to non-Christian Judaism either.[57] It is thus difficult to decide the question of literary dependence just on *traditionsgeschichtlich* grounds.

Certainly there is nothing here to tell against the theory that the *Didache* is using language which is derived (perhaps at more than one stage removed) from Matthew's finished gospel.

Did 13:1.

This is probably also implied by the saying in Did 13:1, that every true prophet ἄξιός ἐστι τῆς τροφῆς αὐτοῦ. This recalls the language of the saying in the mission charge Mt 10:10/Lk 10:7. The

---

[53] *Überlieferung*, p. 216.

[54] "Didache's Quotations", p. 20.

[55] See my *The Revival of the Griesbach Hypothesis* (Cambridge: Cambridge University Press, 1983 [SNTS MS 44]) p. 88, with further bibliographical references. Cf. Mt 12:32a/Lk 12:10a.

[56] *Überlieferung*, p. 216f; also Rordorf & Tuilier, *Doctrine*, pp. 53, 88.

[57] Cf. Glover, "Didache's Quotations", p. 20, referring to Ignatius and Justin.

Didache again shows links with Matthew's version rather than Luke's. (Luke has μισθοῦ not τροφῆς). Certainty is not possible but it seems most likely that Luke's version is more original and that Matthew's τροφῆς is MattR.[58]

Köster argues that the saying may have been a stock proverb,[59] though none of the non-Christian examples he gives offers a precise parallel. He also refers to 1 Tim 5:18 and 1 Cor 9:14 as evidence that the saying must have circulated in isolation of its synoptic context. However, 1 Tim 5 may well be dependent on 1 Cor itself (at least indirectly) and so may not provide independent evidence here. 1 Cor 9 probably presupposes a version with μισθοῦ rather than τροφῆς, and Paul may indeed only know the saying as an isolated one.[60] But Paul's lack of knowledge of the synoptic context does not necessarily tell us anything about the form in which the saying was known to the Didachist. The fact that the *Didache* betrays links with Matthew's redacted form of the saying must provide some evidence that the *Didache* only knows the saying as mediated through Matthew's gospel.

Did 1:2.

I now consider the version of the double love command in Did 1:2a and the negative form of the golden rule in 1:2b. The commands to love God and one's neighbour are well-known separately in non-Christian Judaism, and at times together, notably in *Testaments of the Twelve Patriarchs*.[61] However, the use of πρῶτον ...δεύτερον is not easy to parallel in non-Christian sources, and may well betray Christian influence.[62] In view of what has been established so far, the simplest solution is to postulate dependence on Matthew's πρώτη...δευτέρα in Mt 22:38f. The "first...second" formulation is not confined to Matthew: Mark also has πρώτη ...δευτέρα (Mk 12:28, 31) in a slightly different relation to the

---

[58] See my "1 Corinthians and Q" in *JBL* 102 (1983) pp. 607-619, on p. 612; also S. Schulz, *Q--Die Spruchquelle der Evangelisten* (Zürich: Theologische Verlag, 1972) p 406; P. Hoffmann, *Studien zur Theologie der Logienquelle* (Münster: Aschendorff, 1972 [NTA 8]) p. 274; Laufen, *Doppelüberlieferungen*, p.219. Wengst also agrees that Did is here dependent on Mt, though he gives no justification in terms of any argument that Mt's version here is redactional: he simply points to the fact that Mt's version is different from the Lukan parallel (*Didache*, p. 28).

[59] *Überlieferung*, p. 212; Rordorf & Tuilier, *Doctrine*, p. 88, appeal to Köster.

[60] See my "Paul and the Synoptic Mission Discourse?" in *ETL* 60 (1984) pp. 376-381.

[61] See R. H. Fuller, "The Double Commandment of Love: A Test Case for the Criteria of Authenticity", in Fuller (ed.) *Essays on the Love Commandment* (Philadelphia: Fortress, 1978) pp. 41-56.

[62] This is admitted even by Köster, *Überlieferung*, p. 172.

two love commands themselves.[63] This tells against Glover's thesis that the *Didache* tends to follow Matthew only when Matthew is not following Mark and hence that the *Didache* is dependent on Q rather than Matthew.[64] There may well have been a Q version of this pericope but it is very doubtful if the πρώτη...δευτέρα comes from such a Q version here.[65] It is not present in any form in Lk 10:25-28 and is thus probably in Matthew from Mark. Köster argues that the ordering and numbering of the commands is pre-redactional in the gospels and hence one need not deduce dependence on our gospels.[66] This may be the case, but we have already seen that there is a lot of material in the *Didache* which does presuppose Matthew's finished gospel. It seems therefore an unnecessary complication to presume that this feature of the text of the *Didache* is not also derived from Matthew's gospel.

The version of the golden rule in Did 1:2b may also be derived from Matthew. It is true that the version given here uses the negative form which is found elsewhere in Jewish sources, though it is not found in some other sources of the Two Ways tradition (e.g. Barnabas and 1QS).[67] However, Butler has shown very clearly how several unusual features of Did 1:2b can be easily explained if the *Didache* is based on Mt 7:15.[68] Again, knowledge of Matthew's finished gospel is the simplest solution to explain Did's text.

Others.

The evidence from the rest of the *Didache* is less clear-cut for the present purposes. In the *Lasterkatalog* of Did 5:1f, Butler has shown how the order of vices in Did is explicable if the Didachist were editing a list similar to that of Barn 20:1f in the light of the list of Mt 15:19.[69] Other links between the *Didache* and Matthew

---

[63] Butler, "Two Ways", p.29, goes too far in claiming that all the references to the "first ... second" commandments derive from his "M(g)" (i.e. the Matthean form of synoptic tradition). Perhaps this is a case of Butler's unconsciously assuming his own solution to the synoptic problem.

[64] Here, "Didache's Quotations", p. 13. Glover sees a reflection of Luke's version of the pericope in the reference to the way of "life" in Did 1:1; but this seems rather fanciful.

[65] See Fuller, "Double Commandment", p. 45.

[66] *Überlieferung*, p. 172.

[67] See Butler, "Two Ways", p. 31, arguing against Audet.

[68] Butler, "Two Ways", p. 30. Note that again the *Didache* is not quoting. Hence Glover's assertion that the *Didache* here "is so different that it would be hard for anyone to write it if he were intending to quote our Gospel" ("Didache's Quotations", p. 13) is beside the point.

[69] Butler, "Two Ways", p. 33.

are easily explained if the *Didache* is dependent on Matthew, but they do not demand such a theory. The saying "the meek shall inherit the earth" in Did 3:7 could derive from Mt 5:5, though position and presence of that beatitude in Matthew is textually uncertain and common dependence of the *Didache* and Matthew on Ps 36:11 is equally likely. The baptismal commands in Did 7 are clearly similar to Mt 28:19, though a common milieu with similar liturgical practice will explain this as well. Agreements in the versions of the Lord's Prayer in Did 8 and Mt 6 may also be explicable in the same way. It may be significant that Did 8 links injunctions about prayer (including the Lord's Prayer) with those about fasting and inveighs against opponents as "hypocrites", just as Mt 6:5-16 does. Certainly the text of Did 8 is readily explicable if the *Didache* knew Matthew, but perhaps does not compel such a belief. So too the saying in Did 9:5 about not giving what is holy to dogs, which is one of the few explicit quotations in the *Didache*, is verbally identical with Mt 7:6. However, Mt 7:6 is not clearly MattR and the saying looks very like a stock proverb;[70] hence one cannot lay too much weight on this parallel.

Did. 16:1.

One final synoptic parallel should be noted. Did 16:1 ("Watch over your life: let your lamps be not quenched and your loins be not ungirded, but be ready, for you do not know the hour in which our Lord comes") recalls various synoptic parallels. The introductory γρηγορεῖτε is parallel to Mt 24:42 (MattR of Mk 13:33 though the word occurs elsewhere in Mark). The saying about the lamps and loins is close to Lk 12:35; and the saying about being "ready for you do not know..." is close to the ending of the parable of the thief at night in Mt 24:44/Lk 12:40 and the similar saying in Mt 24:42/Mk 13:35.

Certainty is not possible here. One must again bear in mind the fact that this is not an explicit quotation but a piece of exhortation perhaps using traditional language. Thus it is not unexpected that the uses of individual words may have shifted slightly from their synoptic contexts. There is nothing here that is so clearly MattR that it could only have derived from Matthew's gospel.[71]

---

[70] Cf. R. Bultmann, *The History of the Synoptic Tradition* (Oxford: Blackwell, 1968) p. 103.

[71] Mt 24:44 is very closely parallel to Lk 12:40. γρηγορεῖτε in Mt 24:42 can scarcely count as significant enough to show dependence on Matthew in view of the common nature of the word, especially in eschatological contexts (so Köster, *Überlieferung*, p. 176); the parallel between the final clause of Did 16:1 and Mt 24:42 is perhaps more significant in this context though the verbal agreement is not exact (*Didache* has ὁ κύριος ἡμῶν where Matthew has ὁ κύριος ὑμῶν, MattR for Mark's ὁ κύριος τῆς οἰκίας). However, Bauckham has shown that a shift from the

More difficult is the question about the parallel between Did 16:1a and Lk 12:35. Some have seen this as clear evidence of the *Didache*'s dependence on the gospel of Luke.[72] Others have disagreed, arguing variously that Lk 12:35 may be Q material so that the *Didache* is here dependent on Q rather than Luke,[73] that the imagery is stereotyped (cf. 1 Pet 1:13; Eph 6:14),[74] that the verbal agreement between the *Didache* and Luke is not close enough to imply direct dependence,[75] or that the *Didache* nowhere shows knowledge of Luke's gospel and hence is unlikely to do so here.[76]

It must be said that none of these arguments is absolutely convincing. Certainly the last argument is a case of *petitio principii*: the question of the dependence of the *Didache* on Luke at this point is precisely what is in question and can scarcely be solved by assuming the answer initially. The degree of verbal parallelism is also not a problem provided one remembers that the *Didache* is not explicitly quoting here. As far as the allegedly stereotyped imagery is concerned, it is true that the use of the "girding up loins" metaphor can be paralleled elsewhere, but the conjunction of this with the "lamps" motif is harder to parallel outside these two texts.[77] Whether Lk 12:35 belonged to Q is more debatable.

---

synoptic version of this parable to the application as found in the *Didache* is thoroughly typical of early Christian use of this parable: see his "Synoptic Parousia Parables and the Apocalypse" *NTS* 23 (1977) pp. 162-176, esp. 169 in relation to this passage. Bauckham himself, referring to Audet, finds it incredible that the author of the *Didache* could have constructed his saying with the gospels in front of him (which may well be true, but one must remember that the *Didache* is not quoting here: cf. n. 11 above); however, he does say that "it is unlikely that his [the Didachist's] tradition was wholly independent of the specifically Matthean redaction" (*ibid*).

[72] So Butler, "Literary Relations", who appeals to the parallels between Did 16:1a, 1b and Lk 12:35, 40 respectively and argues that the link between Lk 12:35 and 12:40 is LkR.

[73] Glover, "Didache's Quotations", pp. 21f; Draper, "Jesus Tradition", p. 280.

[74] Köster, *Überlieferung*, pp. 175f; Draper, *ibid.*; Wengst, *Didache*, p. 99.

[75] Cf. Audet, *Didache*, p. 181; Köster, *ibid*. See too R. Bauckham, "Synoptic Parousia Parables Again", *NTS* 29 (1983) pp. 129-134, on p. 131, who refers to a very similar form of saying in Methodius, *Symp* V.2. He writes: "This agreement cannot be accidental... Methodius' text could be influenced by the *Didache*, or it may be independent testimony to the same non-Lukan version of the saying which the *Didache* quotes. In that case it would confirm the *Didache*'s independence of our Gospels at this point". However, dependence of Methodius on Did is equally possible. Methodius' work dates from the end of the 3rd century, not the 2nd century as Bauckham claims (n. 13 on p. 133), and this was a period when the *Didache* must have enjoyed some popularity: cf. H. Von Campenhausen, *The Formation of the Christian Bible* (Philadelphia: Fortress, 1972) p. 213.

[76] Köster, *Überlieferung*, pp. 175f.; Rordorf & Tuilier, *Doctrine*, pp. 89f.

[77] Parallels in *j.Kil* IX, 32b.9 or *j.Ket* Xll, 35a.9 (Draper, "Jesus Tradition", p. 280; *Commentary*, p. 299) are not close. Both metaphors may derive from Passover symbols (Draper, *ibid.*) but the conjunction of both in a single saying in still striking.

More recent study has suggested that whilst Lk 12:36-38 may (in part at least) derive from Q, v. 35 is more likely to be LkR.[78] This would imply that the *Didache* is dependent on LkR material and hence presupposes Luke's finished gospel. This last conclusion is not certain in view of the very limited extent of the evidence available. Nevertheless it seems perhaps the least problematic solution.

No attempt has been made to provide a fully comprehensive analysis of all possible parallels between the text of the *Didache* and the synoptic gospels in this section.[79] Only the parallels which are perhaps most significant for the present discussion have been noted. However, the analysis given suggests that these parallels can be best explained if the *Didache* presupposes the finished gospel of Matthew (and perhaps also of Luke). One section of the *Didache* which has not yet been considered is the small section in 1:3-2:1. In view of its peculiar problems, this section deserves a separate and detailed study.

III. DIDACHE 1:3-2:1

By almost universal consent, Did 1:3-2:1 is a passage of great complexity, posing critical problems at a number of different levels.[80] It occurs at the start of a sub-section of the *Didache*, namely chs. 1-6, which itself almost certainly had a history prior to its incorporation into the present text of the *Didache*. This section comprises the teaching about the "Two Ways" in a form which is closely paralleled in other texts, in particular in the *Doctrina Apostolorum* and in Barn 18-20. Further, in both these texts, there is nothing corresponding to Did 1:3-2:1 although the texts run closely parallel to the rest of Did 1-6. This Two Ways tradition is almost devoid of specifically Christian features, so that a Jewish *Vorlage* has long been suspected. Such a theory has now received considerable support from the evidence given by the

---

[78] See my *Revival*, p. 181, with further references. Certainly the link between v. 35 and vv. 36-38 looks to be secondary in view of the καὶ ὑμεῖς at the start of v. 36. For the theory that Lk 12:35 is a vestige of Mt 25:1-13 and part of an earlier source, see Wenham, *Rediscovery*, pp. 77ff. However, this seems rather fanciful: J. A. Fitzmyer, *The Gospel according to Luke X-XXIV* (New York: Doubleday, 1985 [Anchor 28A]) p. 988, points to several differences between this verse in Luke and the Matthean parable and calls the theory of a link between them "far-fetched": cf. also I. H. Marshall, *The Gospel of Luke* (Exeter: Paternoster, 1977) p. 535.

[79] For a full list of possible parallels see Köhler, *Rezeption*, pp. 30ff.

[80] This section III was not part of the paper given at the 1986 Leuven Colloquium, the text of which comprises Sections I and II here. Research for it was undertaken during a period of study in 1987 in the University of Marburg, financed by the Alexander von Humboldt Stiftung, Bonn. It is included here by kind permission of the Editor of the Colloquium volume.

Dead Sea Scrolls, since it has been shown that the Two Ways teaching in the Qumran Manual of Discipline (1 QS 3:13-4:26) shows many common features with the Two Ways tradition in the *Doctrina Apostolorum, Barnabas* and the *Didache*.[81]

The small section in Did 1:3-2:1 clearly interrupts this Two Ways teaching. The textual evidence provided by *Doctrina Apostolorum* and *Barnabas* strongly suggest that Did 1:3-2:1 is a later addition to an earlier Two Ways *Vorlage*. In terms of content too, the section stands out from its immediate context since the large number of parallels to the synoptic tradition in such a short compass of text contrasts strongly with the rest of Did 1-6 where explicitly Christian features are so strikingly absent. Thus Did 1:3-2:1 is generally accepted as a later, Christianizing addition to an earlier *Vorlage* lying behind Did 1-6.

Whether Did 1:3-2:1 is secondary in relation to the rest of Did 1-16 is another matter. The parallels to Did 1-6 suggest that the latter may have been taken over from an earlier, Jewish *Vorlage* by the Didachist to form the start of the present work. Hence the fact that 1:3-2:1 is a secondary addition to the *Vorlage* of Did 1-6 cannot in itself determine whether the section was added before, at the same time as, or after the time when the rest of Did 1-6 was combined with chs. 7-16.[82]

Recent studies of the problem of synoptic tradition in this section of the *Didache* have reached widely differing results. Contrary to his general conclusions about the lack of dependence on the synoptic gospels by many of the apostolic fathers (including the rest of the *Didache*), Köster argued that Did 1:3-2:1 does presuppose the finished gospels of Matthew and Luke (perhaps via a post-synoptic harmony).[83] The same conclusion was proposed in the detailed analysis of this section by B. Layton.[84] However, other recent studies of this section have argued in detail that the text of the *Didache* here is not dependent on the synoptic gospels and that the *Didache* represents a line of the tradition which is independent of the synoptic evangelists.[85] Draper is even more

---

[81] See J.-P Audet, "Affinités littéraires et doctrinales du 'Manuel de discipline'", *RB* 59 (1952) pp. 219-238; Rordorf & Tuilier, *Doctrine*, pp. 22ff; Draper, "Jesus Tradition", p. 270.

[82] See Rordorf, "Problème" (n. 2 above) pp. 499f. However, Wengst is so convinced that the section is a later addition to the text of the original *Didache* that he assigns it *en bloc* to a footnote in his edition of the text (*Didache*, p. 66).

[83] *Überlieferung*, pp. 217ff.

[84] Cf. n. 4 above For others supporting the dependence of the *Didache* here, see Massaux, *Influence* III, pp. 150-157: Butler, "Two Ways", p. 31; Wengst, *Didache*, p. 19: F. Neirynck, "Paul and the Sayings of Jesus" in A. Vanhoye (ed.) *L'Apôtre Paul* (Leuven: Leuven University Press, 1986 [BETL 73]) pp. 265-321, on p. 298f.

[85] See especially Rordorf, "Problème", and Draper, "Jesus Tradition"; also Audet and Glover (as in n. 1 above); see too H. T. Wrege, *Die Überlieferungsges-*

specific about the point at which the trajectory which leads to the text of Did 1:3-2:1 diverged from the synoptic trajectories: "It would seem a more likely inference that *Didache* had access directly to the so-called "Q" material, either in a written or an oral form".[86] Such a theory needs rigorous testing especially in the light of contemporary interest in Q.

Part of the complexity of the section 1:3-2:1 arises from the text itself. Despite its small compass, the section may well have had a complex tradition-history: editorial comments, and possible textual corruption, have long been suspected.[87] However, this is not the only factor which makes the problem of synoptic tradition in this section so difficult. The parallels in the synoptic gospels are mostly confined to one small section of the Great Sermon, viz., the sayings about non-retaliation and love of enemies in Mt 5:39-48/Lk 6:27-36. This is a Q passage which is itself one of notorious complexity. The section has been analyzed in great detail many times in recent years (usually without reference to the *Didache*, though see nn. 93, 117 below).[88] There is no absolute certainty about where precisely tradition and redaction are to be

---

chichte der Bergpredigt (Tübingen: Mohr, 1968 [WUNT 9]); H. Conzelmann, art. χάρις, TDNT IX, p. 400; Köhler, *Rezeption*, pp. 46f. (Köhler is thus rather different from Köster in advocating dependence on Matthew by the *Didache* elsewhere, but listing this passage as one where "Mt-Abhängigkeit eher unwahrscheinlich ist" [p. 421]. However, he does not make clear how he thinks the "Herrenwortsammlung", which he believes to be the immediate source used here, is related to the gospel of Matthew). It may be noted too that sometimes the independence of the *Didache* is assumed and then used to solve traditio-historical problems within the synoptic tradition: see nn. 93, 117 below.

[86] "Jesus Tradition", p. 279.

[87] See Layton, "Sources", and Rordorf, "Problème", *passim*, also n. 111 below.

[88] To name but a few, see H. Schürmann, *Das Lukasevangelium* (Freiburg: Herder, 1969 [HTKN 3/1]); Wrege, *Bergpredigt*; S. Schulz, *Q*; D. Lührmann, "Liebet eure Feinde (Lk 6,27-36/Mt 5,39-48)", *ZTK* 69 (1972) pp. 412-438; D. Zeller, *Die weisheitlichen Mahnsprüche bei den Synoptikern* (Würzburg: Echter-Verlag, 1977 [FzB 17]); H. Merklein, *Die Gottesherrschaft als Handlungprinzip. Untersuchung zur Ethik Jesu* (Würzburg: Echter-Verlag, 1978 [FzB 34]); G.Strecker, "Die Antithesen der Bergpredigt", *ZNW* 69 (1978) pp. 36-72, and *Die Bergpredigt: Ein Exegetischer Kommentar* (Göttingen: Vandenhoeck & Ruprecht, 1984); J. Piper, *Love Your Enemies. Jesus' Love Command in the Synoptic Tradition and the Early Christian Paraenesis* (Cambridge: Cambridge University Press, 1979 [SNTS 38]); R. A. Guelich, *The Sermon on the Mount* (Waco: Word, 1982); P. Hoffmann, "Tradition und Situation. Zur 'Verbindlichkeit' des Gebots der Feindesliebe in der synoptischen Überlieferung und in der gegenwärtigen Friedensdiskussion", in K. Kertelge (ed.), *Ethik im Neuen Testament* (Freiburg: Herder, 1984), pp. 50-118; J. Sauer, "Traditionsgeschichtliche Erwägungen zu den synoptischen und paulinischen Aussagen über Feindesliebe und Wiedervergeltungsverzicht", in *ZNW* 76 (1985) pp. 1-28; D. R. Catchpole, "Jesus and the Community of Israel--The Inaugural Discourse in Q" in *BJRL* 68 (1986) pp. 296-316; J. Schlosser, *Le Dieu de Jésus* (Paris: Les Éditions du Cerf, 1987 [LD 129]), and many others.

located here. The fact that this is a Q passage means that (on the basis of the Two Source theory) either Matthew or Luke could preserve the Q wording at any point and there is no clearly definable criterion for determining which version is original. Further, the version which is deemed not to preserve the Q original at any one point is not thereby guaranteed to be redactional. The "Q" available to Matthew and Luke could have been expanded independently in the pre-redactional tradition, so that one might have to think in terms of a Q^{mt} and a Q^{lk}.[89]

Nevertheless, despite the uncertainty inherent in the synoptic analysis, the method of trying to identify redactional elements in the gospel, and then comparing these with the text of the *Didache*, remains the best way of determining whether this section of the *Didache* presupposes the finished gospels or not. (Since this paper is concerned primarily with synoptic tradition in the *Didache*, attention will be confined here to Did 1:3-5a and the parallels in the synoptic gospels dealing with love-of-enemies and non-retaliation. Other problems associated with this passage, e.g. the parallel between Did 1:5 and *HermMand* IV.2 and the parallel between Did 1:6 and Sir 12:1 will therefore not be discussed here).

For the sake of convenience, the relevant section of the *Didache* is divided into six smaller sub-sections which are examined in turn.

A.   Did 1:3a   Mt 5:44   Lk 6:27-28

^{44}ἀγαπᾶτε τοὺς ἐχθροὺς ὑμῶν	^{27}ἀγαπᾶτε τοὺς ἐχθροὺς ὑμῶν καλῶς ποιεῖτε τοῖς μισοῦσιν ὑμᾶς

---

[89] So Strecker, *Antithesen*. Although the Two Source theory has been assumed throughout here, the whole argument could be repeated almost verbatim on the basis of the Griesbach hypothesis (the main rival today to the Two Source theory of synoptic relationships). Many modern defenders of the Griesbach hypothesis would argue that at times, Luke has access to traditions which were parallel, but independent, to those of Matthew, and this effectively reduces to a form of the Q hypothesis. If one adopts a very "strong" form of the Griesbach hypothesis, and argues that Luke is always dependent on Matthew for the material they have in common, the present discussion becomes much simpler, with an identical result: every agreement between the *Didache* and Luke can be taken as an agreement with LkR and hence an indication that the *Didache* presupposes at least Luke's finished gospel. Cf. also the argument of Butler (on the basis of his preferred Augustinian hypothesis rather than the Griesbach hypothesis, though both hypotheses assume Luke's dependence on Matthew here): the fact that Did 1:3-2:1 "borrows some of the specifically Lukan modifications of the M(g) material" [for Butler "M(g)" is Matthew] shows that *Didache* is dependent on Luke here ("Two Ways", p. 31).

εὐλογεῖτε τοὺς   ²⁸εὐλογεῖτε τοὺς
καταρωμένους ὑμῖν   καταρωμένους ὑμᾶς
καὶ προσεύχεσθε ὑπὲρ   καὶ προσεύχεσθε ὑπὲρ   προσεύχεσθε περὶ
τῶν ἐχθρῶν ὑμῶν
νηστεύετε δὲ ὑπὲρ
τῶν διωκόντων ὑμᾶς   τῶν διωκόντων ὑμᾶς   τῶν ἐπηρεαζόντων
                                                            ὑμᾶς

The evidence from this section is mostly ambiguous for the present purposes. Did 1:3a presents a version of the "love of
enemies" saying which is closer to Lk 6:27f than to Mt 5:44: the
Didache has an exact parallel to the "Bless those who curse you"
clause of Lk 6:28a which has no parallel in what are regarded as
the best manuscripts of Matthew (though the extra words are contained in several other manuscripts of Matthew).[90] Further,
although Did 1:3a has no explicit statement here that one is to
"love one's enemies" (Mt 5:44a/Lk 6:27a), the rhetorical question
which follows in the next section ("if you love those who love
you") suggests strongly that the *Didache* presupposes a command
here to "love" people who are not well-disposed to one. Moreover, the *Didache* has a clause a the end of the next section ("love
those who hate you") which is parallel to both halves of Lk 6:27
("*love* your enemies and do good to *those who hate you*"). The
whole of the longer, four-fold command to love one's enemies
thus seems to be presupposed by the *Didache*.

It is not certain whether Luke's four-fold form, or Matthew's
two-fold form, most accurately represents the Q version of the
command to love one's enemies.[91] Several scholars remain
undecided.[92] However, even if one could establish that Matthew's
shorter version represents the Q version, the presence of a (rough)

---

[90] Notably in the Western text of Matthew and in several later manuscripts. One
must always bear in mind the obvious fact that the version of the gospels which may
have been known to the Didachist will not necessarily the identical with the version
printed in the 26th edition of the Nestle-Aland text! Still, Glover's claim that the
Didache agrees with Luke only when *Didache* "is covering ground common to both
Luke and Matthew" ("Didache's Quotations", p. 14), which he uses to posit some
relationship between *Didache* and Q, is clearly true only in the most general terms
here.

[91] Luke's version is regarded as more original by J. Schmid, *Matthäus und
Lukas* (Freiburg: Herder, 1930 [BSt 23/2-4]) p. 229: Schürmann, *Lukasevangelium*,
p. 346; Merklein, *Gottesherrschaft*, p. 225; Sauer, "Feindesliebe", p. 8; Schlosser,
Dieu, p.225. Matthew is regarded as more original by Lührmann, "Liebet", pp.
416f; Zeller, *Mahnsprüche*, p. 102; Hoffmann, "Tradition", p. 52f; J. A. Fitzmyer,
The Gospel according to Luke I-IX (New York: Doubleday, 1981 [Anchor 28]), p.
637.

[92] Piper, *Love your Enemies*, p. 56f; others cited in Hoffmann, "Tradition", p.
52 n. 9.

parallel to Lk 6:28a in Rom 12:14 may suggest that Luke has added a traditional saying here, rather than creating the clause himself.[93] The strongest argument for the activity of LkR concerns the use of καλῶς ποιεῖτε. This links with the use of ἀγαθοποιεῖν later in this context in Luke, and this is widely regarded as LkR.[94] But it is just this phrase of Lk 6:27f. which does not have a parallel in Did 1:3. The *Didache* does have a parallel to Luke's "those who hate you" (cf. above), but Luke's use of μισέω here may well reflect the use of his source: many would argue that the "love of enemies" complex in Q followed immediately after the last beatitude in view of the close parallels in wording and substance between them, and it is probably the Q version of the final beatitude which referred to "hating".[95] Thus the longer form of the command to love one enemies in the *Didache* can probably not tell us very much in the present discussion.

The Didache's version differs from both the synoptic version in making the "enemies" the object of the verb "pray for" the command to "pray for your enemies" can be found in several other places in early Christian literature (cf. Justin, *1Apol* 14:9; 15:3; *Dial* 35:8; 96:3; 133:6; POxy 1224; *Dida* 108:14; PsClem*Hom* XII.32). Some have seen here evidence of an independent saying.[96] However, Köster has shown that the saying probably reflects later church practice of praying for enemies, and Polycarp *Phil* 12:3 may show an intermediate phase of the tradition: here an exhortation to pray for various people is combined with a clear reference to the gospel saying in Mt 5:44/Lk 6:28, so

---

[93] Cf. F.W. Horn, *Glaube und Handeln in der Theologie des Lukas* (Göttingen: Vandenhoeck & Ruprecht, 1983 [GTA 26]) p. 105. However, Horn also adduces the evidence of Did 1:3 itself to show that the longer Lukan text is not LkR. Clearly such an appeal would be circular in the present context. Cf. the discussion of the parallels between Mt 24:10-12 and Did 16:3-5 at nn. 42, 46 above. For doubts about the parallel between Lk 6 and Rom 12, see Neirynck, "Paul and the Sayings of Jesus", p. 303. One may note that the verb "to curse" is used differently: in Luke it describes the behaviour of the opponents ("those who curse you"); in Paul it describes behaviour which the Christian is to shun ("do not curse"). Cf also Neirynck, *ibid.*, p. 299: "the contrast between blessing and cursing appears in both texts but in biblical language this can scarcely be cited as a significant contact".

[94] See n. 114 below and the discussion in the text there. Sauer's argument that καλῶς ποιεῖτε is a Lukan hapax, different from the Lukan ἀγαθαποιεῖν and hence pre-Lukan (cf. also Horn, *Glaube*, p. 105) seems unnecessarily restrictive of Luke's ability to vary his terminology. Cf. Neirynck, *ibid.*, p. 297.

[95] Cf. Schürmann, *Lukasevangelium*, p. 346; Lührmann, "Liebet", pp. 414f. Lührmann postulates that μισέω stood in Q in the second half of the original 2-fold saying as the object of προσεύχεσθε. This seems plausible, though Neirynck (*ibid.*, pp. 297f) sees the link as more probably Lukan.

[96] Glover especially makes much of parallels between the *Didache* and Justin as evidence of independent traditions.

that the general saying in the form "pray for your enemies" is probably due to later developments in the tradition.[97]

The same may apply to the command to "fast" for one's persecutors which has no synoptic parallel. Prayer and fasting were connected in several contexts in Christian (and Jewish) texts.[98] Hence a reference to fasting, secondarily added to an injunction to prayer, would not be unexpected in a later development of the tradition.[99]

One small feature which may be more significant in this section is the use of διώκω which agrees with Mt 5:44b against Lk 6:28b. Many would argue that διώκω in Mt 5 is due to MattR. Luke's parallel here has ἐπηρεάζω which is not a Lukan word (it occurs only here in Luke-Acts). ἐπηρεάζω also occurs in 1 Pet 3:16 in a not unrelated context, which may indicate that the word had its place in a Christian paraenetic tradition of this nature.[100] Further, Luke uses διώκω three times in his gospel and nine times in Acts, so there is no clear reason why he should avoid using the word here if it lay in his source. The word may well be a Matthean favourite (cf. the use in the penultimate beatitude Mt 5:10, which is widely regarded as due to MattR). Hence the likelihood is that it is due to MattR here.[101] One could argue that the word is too general to carry much weight here; but against this is the fact that the motif of persecution is not one that really dominates this, or any, section of the *Didache*. It is therefore unlikely to have been added by the Didachist himself. This small agreement between the *Didache* and Matthew may thus be an instance where the *Didache* presupposes MattR and hence Matthew's finished gospel.

B.   Did 1:3b   Mt 5   Lk 6

ποία γὰρ χάρις

---

[97] Köster, *Überlieferung*, p. 224; also A. Bellinzoni, *The Sayings of Jesus in the Writings of Justin Martyr* (Leiden: Brill, 1967 [NT.S 17]), pp. 79f.

[98] Cf. Köster, *Überlieferung*, p. 224; Draper, "Jesus Tradition", p. 276; Massaux, *Influence* III, p. 154.

[99] Layton, "Sources", p. 353, refers to similar expansions to the references to prayer in Mk 9:29 and 1 Cor 7:5 in the manuscript tradition of the NT. Rordorf, "Problème", pp. 501f, thinks that the persecutors are Jews, but this says nothing about the relation of the passage to the synoptic tradition.

[100] The question of the relation of 1 Peter to gospel tradition is of course much debated.

[101] So Schürmann, *Lukasevangelium*, p. 333; Schulz, *Q*, p. 128; Merklein, *Gottesherrschaft*, p. 225; Sauer, "Feindesliebe", p. 11. For the evidence from the beatitudes see my "The Beatitudes: A Source-Critical Study", *NT* 25 (1983) pp. 193-207, on p. 203. Cf. also n. 95 above.

ἐὰν ἀγαπᾶτε τοὺς ἀγαπῶντας ὑμᾶς	⁴⁶ἐὰν γὰρ ἀγαπήσητε τοὺς ἀγαπῶντας ὑμᾶς τίνα μισθὸν ἔχετε· οὐχὶ καὶ οἱ τελῶναι τὸ αὐτὸ ποιοῦσιν; ⁴⁷καὶ ἐὰν ἀσπάσησθε τοὺς ἀδελφοὺς ὑμῶν μόνον τί περισσὸν ποιεῖτε;	³²καὶ εἰ ἀγαπᾶτε τοὺς ἀγαπῶντας ὑμᾶς ποία ὑμῖν χάρις ἐστίν; καὶ γὰρ οἱ ἁμαρτωλοὶ τοὺς ἀγαπῶντας αὐτοὺς ἀγαπῶσιν ³³καὶ γὰρ ἐὰν ἀγαθοποιῆτε τοὺς ἀγαθοποιοῦντας ὑμᾶς ποία ὑμῖν χάρις ἐστίν;
οὐχὶ καὶ τὰ ἔθνη τὸ αὐτὸ ποιοῦσιν; ὑμεῖς δὲ ἀγαπᾶτε τοὺς μισοῦντας ὑμᾶς καὶ οὐχ ἕξετε ἐχθρόν	οὐχὶ καὶ οἱ ἐθνικοὶ τὸ αὐτὸ ποιοῦσιν	καὶ οἱ ἁμαρτωλοὶ τὸ αὐτὸ ποιοῦσιν... (v. 34) ³⁵πλὴν ἀγαπᾶτε τοὺς ἐχθροὺς ὑμῶν...καὶ ἔσται ὁ μισθὸς ὑμῶν πολὺς καὶ ἔσεσθε υἱοὶ ὑψίστου
	⁴⁵ὅπως γένησθε υἱοὶ τοῦ πατρὸς	

In this section the *Didache* is once again close to Luke's version without being identical to it. Did 1:3b has only one rhetorical question, set in terms of "loving those who love you", as do both Matthew and Luke. The *Didache* agrees with Mt 5:47 in mentioning Gentiles as the "opposing group" from whom the readers are to distinguish themselves.[102] The *Didache* then enunciates a version of the love command, and in doing so follows the structure of Lk 6 where the love command is repeated after the rhetorical questions (Lk 6:35). Finally the *Didache* agrees with both Matthew and Luke in enunciating a consequence for those who obey the love command; but the consequence is not that of divine sonship (as in the synoptics) but the more mundane "you will not have an enemy".

One should perhaps first deal with a peculiar problem of the text of the *Didache* at this point. The word used for "love" here is uncertain. The Bryennios manuscript uses ἀγαπάω three times. However, POxy 1782 uses φιλέω in the last instance (the earlier instances do not appear on that part of the papyrus which has been

---

[102] Draper, "Jesus Tradition", p. 277, is slightly confusing in saying "the *Didache* uses ἔθνη for ἁμαρτωλοί in Luke and τελῶναι in Matthew", though he concedes in a bracket "(cf. ἐθνικοί in 5:47)". The *Didache* is parallel to Mt 5:47 here, not 5:46. Audet, *Didachè*, pp. 184f, simply prints Mt 5:38-47 *in toto* without even considering v. 47 and makes no attempt to determine which part of the *Didache* is parallel to which part of the synoptic versions. He also appeals to the very different order in the *Didache* as compared with the synoptics, but fails to analyze Didache's own structure at this point.

preserved). Further, the text of *Const* VII, which takes up the text of the *Didache* almost wholesale whilst commenting on it and adding to it, has φιλέω on these three occasions. It is argued by some on the basis of this evidence that the original text of the *Didache* read φιλέω all three times. *Const* has a tendency to conform the text of the *Didache* to that of the canonical gospels; hence in this instance, the disagreement between *Const*'s reproduction of the *Didache*'s text and the synoptic versions is all the more striking. (There is no manuscript evidence for a text of the gospels reading φιλέω here). Also the Bryennios manuscript shows a tendency elsewhere to conform its text to that of well-known Biblical versions.[103] Hence, it is argued, the three-fold ἀγαπάω in this manuscript may represent a later scribal assimilation to the text of the gospels, and the original text of the *Didache* used φιλέω. Further, since this is unlike both the Matthean and Lukan forms of the saying, this may indicate that the *Didache* preserves an independent version of the saying.[104]

This evidence is however of uncertain value. The text of *Const* is not a manuscript of the *Didache*: it represents the use of the *Didache* by a later author, not a scribe.[105] Further, although the tendency of *Const* generally is to conform the text of the *Didache* to that of the gospels, this has not happened at every point. (Cf. n. 40 above). There are thus other occasions when *Const* makes the text of the *Didache* less like that of the canonical gospels, and hence one cannot rule out the possibility that the same has happened here. One must also note that φιλέω and ἀγαπάω are almost synonymous, or, even if they are not, that the author of *Const* seems quite happy to regard them as synonymous. On two occasions he adopts the pose of the beloved disciple of the fourth gospel and uses φιλέω to describe his special relationship to Jesus: V.14:3 φιλούμενος πλεῖον τῶν ἄλλων ὑπ'αὐτοῦ, VIII.16:1 ἐγὼ ὁ φιλούμενος ὑπὸ τοῦ κυρίου. Although these could have been inspired by Jn 20:2 (ὃς ἐφίλει ὁ Ἰησοῦς), the more usual Johan-

---

[103] Cf. J.B. Lightfoot, *The Apostolic Fathers. Part I. Clement of Rome Vol. I.* (London: Macmillan, 1890) pp. 124ff, in relation to the text of 1 Clement in the Bryennios manuscript.

[104] See Audet, *Didachè*, p. 54; Draper, "Jesus Tradition", p. 276f; Köhler, *Rezeption*, p. 44; cf. also R. Bauckham, "The Study of Gospel Traditions outside the Canonical Gospels: Problems and Prospects", in *Gospel Perspectives* (n. 1), pp. 369-403, on p. 389, who then uses the parallel in Ignatius *Pol* 2:1 (which also uses φιλέω) as a key point in his argument that Ignatius is demonstrably independent of Matthew at at least one point. It is, however, not clear how such a theory would relate to the *Didache*'s alleged use of Q (cf nn. 3, 86 above): is the variation due to independent translations of an Aramaic original? If so, is Q thought to be an Aramaic document? Or are we to think of variations in the oral tradition?

[105] Massaux, *Influence* III, p. 148 n. 11, is slightly misleading when he says "some *codices* read φιλεῖτε" (my italics) at the first use of ἀγαπάω.

nine verb to use for Jesus' relationship to the beloved disciple is
ἀγαπάω (13:23; 19:26; 21:7, 20). One could even argue that
these instances might indicate a slight preference by the author of
Const for φιλέω over against ἀγαπάω (though he uses ἀγαπάω
frequently elsewhere). At another point it seems clear that the
author regarded the two verbs as synonymous: at V.15:2 he refers
to the Gentiles in words clearly influenced by the use of Hos 2 in
1 Pet 2 and Rom 9; but whereas Paul uses ἀγαπάω twice here,
Const uses φιλέω in the second instance (οἵτινές ποτε οὐκ
ἠγαπημένοι νῦν δὲ πεφιλημένοι). The use of φιλέω in VII.2:2
(the parallel to Did 1:3) may therefore simply reflect the readiness
of the author of *Const* to use the verbs φιλέω and ἀγαπάω interchangeably. The evidence of the POxy 1782 fragment must retain
its value, but this only supplies the reading for the last occurrence.
(The papyrus is not extant earlier). It may be that the author of the
Didache wanted to avoid having three uses of ἀγαπάω very close
together. His use of his tradition (whatever that was) meant that
with only one rhetorical question here, the two ἀγαπάω's of the
question and the "love" command itself are very close together.
The use of φιλέω in the third instance (*if* that is the correct reading) could then be due to the Didachist's desire to avoid repetition.
In all, the textual evidence is too uncertain for us to be sure that
the *Didache* used φιλέω all three times here. The indirect nature
of the witness of the text of *Const* must be borne in mind, and it
would be very precarious to build too much on the use of two
words here which are clearly regarded by the final author in the
chain of witnesses as synonymous.[106]

Turning to other features of the *Didache*'s text in this section, the reference to "Gentiles" is probably indecisive for the
present purposes. Almost all agree that Luke's "sinners" here
represents a secondary alteration of the tradition and that Matthew's οἱ ἐθνικοί is most likely to represent the Q wording.[107]
Thus the *Didache*'s use of τὰ ἔθνη here only shows agreement
with a pre-redactional element in the synoptic versions.[108] Glover

---

[106] Layton, "Sources", p. 373f, points out that if the Bryennios readings are due
to scribal assimilation, then such assimilation has not gone very far (e.g. not as far
as *Const*'s other assimilations of the *Didache* here). He thus prefers to see the readings as "separative errors". However, his further remark that "adoption of the *H*
[i.e. Bryennios] variants also obviates the necessity of postulating a more complex
and far less elegant hypothesis on the relationship of the *Didache* passage to its
parallels" (p. 374) is perhaps less fortunate. One cannot assume that the least complex and most elegant hypotheses always correspond to historical reality

[107] Schürmann, *Lukasevangelium*, p. 35; Schulz, *Q*, p. 129f; Hoffmann,
"Tradition", p. 55; Sauer, "Feindesliebe", p. 12; Catchpole, "Inaugural Discourse", p. 304, who also refers to a similar disparaging reference to Gentiles in
another Q passage, *viz.* Mt 6:32/Lk 12:30.

[108] It is dubious whether one can place too much weight on the difference
between ἔθνη and ἐθνικοί (so Rordorf, "Problème", p. 503, who claims that the

and Rordorf both appeal to the allegedly "tactless" way in which
the Didachist refers to Gentiles here, and they deduce from this
that the *Didache* is here preserving an old tradition which is at
odds with a work addressed to Gentiles.[109] However, it is doubtful
whether we can deduce too much from the title. There are, after
all, two titles and it is not certain which, if either, is original and
reflects the aim of the work as a whole.[110] One may also say that
the Didachist is not renowned for his consistency of thought: cf.
the tension between 1:5 and 1:6 on the question of whether one
should ask questions before giving alms.[111] Thus an alleged tension between the title and this reference to Gentiles is not
impossible in a work such as the *Didache*.

The one feature which is more noteworthy in this section is
the introductory question ποία γὰρ χάρις; this agrees closely with
Luke's form of the rhetorical questions in Lk 6:32f. (ποία ὑμῖν
χάρις ἐστίν;). Further, it has become clear in recent Lukan study
that Luke's version here is heavily indebted to LkR. Köster
ascribed χάρις to LkR simply on the basis of a word count.[112]
However, others have pointed out that word counts in themselves
may be misleading in that the word in question may well have different meanings elsewhere: in this case χάρις elsewhere in Luke
tends to mean divine grace.[113] Nevertheless, the redactional nature
of the word here can be established via another route. In a
programmatic article, van Unnik has shown how Luke has
adapted his tradition in order to address the morality determined
by a reciprocity ethic;[114] an ethic of doing good to others in order
to receive reciprocal favours in return was widespread in the
ancient world. Further, the language of "doing good" and χάρις

Didache is close to Matthew but not verbally identical, and therefore probably independent). The two are almost synonymous and one must remember that the *Didache*
is not a scribe's copy of the text of the gospels (cf. above). In fact it is Matthew's
ἐθνικοί which is unusual and invites a change to ἔθνη: cf. Layton, "Sources", p.
355.

[109] Glover, "Didache's Quotations", p. 14; Rordorf, "Problème", p. 502f; also
Draper, "Jesus Tradition", p. 277.

[110] Layton, "Sources", p. 382, referring to the reference to "the twelve apostles" in the title, says: "the literary fiction in the title is, unless the date of composition be extremely early, a clear example of archaism, used here to lend authority to
the document". The τοῖς ἔθνεσιν is probably intended to reflect Mt 28:19f and has
the same aim. One need not therefore see any great significance in the intended
readership in the phrase.

[111] The tension is so great that Petersen, "Probleme", pp. 147ff, ascribes 1:6 to
a marginal gloss.

[112] *Überlieferung*, p. 224f.

[113] Cf. Wrege, *Bergpredigt*, p. 89; Piper, *Love Your Enemies*, p. 192 n. 146.

[114] W.C. van Unnik, "Die Motivierung der Feindesliebe in Lukas VI 32-355",
NT 8 (1966) pp. 288-300.

had a firm place in such talk. Thus Luke's use of ἀγαθοποιεῖς and χάρις here are almost certainly redactional adaptations of the older tradition, addressing this ethos and criticizing it sharply. (The fact that very similar ideas recur in the almost certainly redactional verses Lk 14:12-14 indicate that this is a peculiarly Lukan theme).[115] Luke's language is striking: ποία ὑμῖν χάρις ἐστίν should probably be translated "what kind of a reward do you have?", to which the implied answer is that one has a human reward but not a divine one.[116] Luke's language thus belongs within a closely constructed framework of thought and needs that framework to make sense.

The *Didache* shares some of the same language but not the framework of thought. For the *Didache* too has ποία γὰρ χάρις; but the conclusion is the rather lame καὶ οὐχ ἕξετε ἐχθρόν. However, this is now precisely the ethos of the reciprocity ethic which Luke's language was designed to oppose: love others and they will love you back. Thus the formulation of the χάρις question, which makes excellent sense in the Lukan context, becomes confused when repeated verbatim in the slightly different context of the *Didache*. The fact that the agreement between the *Didache* and Luke goes beyond that of just the common use of χάρις alone suggests that there is some literary relationship involved here.

Some have appealed to the possibility that χάρις and μισθός may simply be translation variants of an Aramaic original, and that the parallel with Lk 6:32 in Did 1:3 and 1 Pet 2:20 suggests a common catechetical tradition.[117] However, the χάρις vocabulary in the Hellenistic tradition suggests that Luke's choice of vocabulary here is deliberate. Further, the appeals to the *Didache* and 1 Peter to solve the problem of the synoptic tradition-history create difficulties here. 1 Pet 2:20 is perhaps not relevant: although the idea in 1 Pet 2 is not dissimilar to that of Lk 6 (a contrast between something which is not particularly worthy of divine praise and something which is), the vocabulary is different: the negative statement is cast in the form ποῖον κλέος, and χάρις is used positively. The use of the *Didache* here is a case of *petitio principii* in the present context. We cannot use the *Didache* itself to establish the pre-Lukan nature of Lk 6:32f and then use this "result" to establish the conclusion that the *Didache* betrays no links with redactional elements in the Gospel. The fact remains

---

[115] See also the detailed discussion by Horn, *Glaube*, pp. 100-102. For LkR here see too Schmid, *Matthäus und Lukas*, p. 229f; Schürmann, *Lukasevangelium*, p. 353; Schulz, *Q*, p. 129; Lührmann, "Liebet", p. 420; Hoffmann, "Tradition", p. 55; Sauer, "Feindesliebe", p. 12, and many others.

[116] Horn, *Glaube*, p. 102.

[117] Cf. Wrege, *Bergpredigt*, p. 89; Piper, *Love your Enemies*, p. 156; Guelich, *Sermon*, p. 231.

that the author of this section of the *Didache* seems to presuppose Luke's version here in a way that goes beyond simply using the word χάρις: he takes over the Lukan rhetorical question, but fails to see its significance and hence betrays the secondary nature of his own text.

C. Did 1:4a	Mt 5	Lk 6
ἀπέχου τῶν σαρκικῶν		
καὶ σωματικῶν		
ἐπιθυμιῶν		
ἐὰν τίς σοι δῷ	³⁹ὅστις σε ῥαπίζει	²⁹τῷ τύπτοντί σε
ῥάπισμα		
εἰς τὴν δεξιὰν σιαγόνα	εἰς τὴν δεξιὰν σιαγόνα	ἐπὶ τὴν σιαγόνα
στρέψον αὐτῷ	στρέψον αὐτῷ	πάρεχε
καὶ τὴν ἄλλην	καὶ τὴν ἄλλην	καὶ τὴν ἄλλαν
καὶ ἔσῃ τέλειος	(cf. v. 48)	

The textual (and other) problems associated with the opening phrase will be left on one side here,[118] as they do not affect the question of the *Didache*'s possible use of synoptic tradition. The main part of this section represents a version of the saying about turning the other cheek. The evidence here is probably indecisive. Did 1:4 agrees very closely with the Matthean form of the saying, specifying the "right" cheek, using διδόναι ῥάπισμα (cf. Matthew's ῥαπίζει as opposed to Luke's τύπτω) and στρέψον (Luke πάρεχε). However, it is not clear if any of these features are due to MattR. The technical nature of the reference to the "right" cheek is often noticed: such a blow implies a back-handed slap which, according to the Mishnah (*m.BQ* 8:6), was regarded as extremely insulting and worthy of double recompense. But whether such a detail belonged to Q and was omitted by Luke as irrelevant, or whether it was added by Matthew (or in a Q^mt form of the tradition) is hard to say.[119] Matthew's other features mentioned above (i.e. the use of ῥαπίζω and στρέψον) are widely regarded as more original than Luke's τύπτω and πάρεχε.[120] Thus the *Didache* does not have any clear links with MattR.

---

[118] Cf. Layton, "Sources", p. 376f.

[119] For MattR, see Schmid, *Matthäus und Lukas*, p. 229; Schürmann, *Lukasevangelium*, p. 347; Hoffmann, "Tradition", p. 59f; Guelich, *Sermon*, pp. 221f; Fitzmyer, *Luke*, p. 638; Sauer, "Feindesliebe", p. 12. It is regarded as pre-Matthean by Wrege, *Bergpredigt*, p. 76; Schulz, *Q*, p. 122; Merklein, *Gottesherrschaft*, p. 269; Catchpole, "Inaugural Discourse", p. 306. Köster, *Überlieferung*, p. 226f, takes it as MattR and evidence of the dependence of the *Didache* on Matthew, but he offers little justification for the redactional nature of the word.

[120] So Schulz, *Q*, p. 122; Sauer, "Feindesliebe", p 12f, and others cited there.

One feature that is often adduced by supporters of the *Didache*'s independence of the synoptics is the allegedly clumsy nature of the *Didache*'s Greek phrase δῷ ῥάπισμα. This, it is argued, must tell against the theory of dependence on Matthew as Matthew has the more usual simple verb ῥαπίζει.[121] However, this need only show that the *Didache* is exercising an element of freedom at this point and that, *if* the usage is clumsy,[122] the Didachist is capable of writing poor Greek. This may say something about the Didachist's style, but it does not solve the problem of whether the *Didache* is presupposing our gospels or not.[123] In fact, as Draper points out, the *Didache*'s language is also that of Jn 18:22 and not dissimilar to that of Is 50:6. Thus the *Didache* here may simply reflect further "biblical" influences. One must also allow for a greater element of freedom on the part of the Didachist in using his sources than in the case of a scribe seeking to copy a manuscript.

It is possible that the very last phrase of this section in the *Didache*, καὶ ἔσῃ τέλειος, may show a link with MattR. Mt 5:48 closes the series of antitheses in Matthew with an exhortation to be "perfect" (τέλειος) and there is almost complete scholarly agreement that this is due to MattR of the more original Lukan version "be merciful" (Lk 6:36).[124] On the other hand, it could be argued that a very similar exhortation in Did 6:2 after the end of the Two Ways section, indicates that this language of "perfection" is of some importance for the Didachist. Thus the exhortation here could be due to independent redaction by the Didachist.[125] So whilst this feature looks at first sight to be a clear example of an agreement between the *Didache* and MattR, its value should probably not be over-estimated.

D.   Did 1:4b   Mt 5

ἐὰν ἀγγαρεύσῃ σέ τις μίλιον ἕν   [41]καὶ ὅστις σε ἀγγαρεύσει μίλιον ἕν
ὕπαγε μετ᾽ αὐτοῦ δύο   ὕπαγε μετ᾽ αὐτοῦ δύο

---

[121] Glover, "Didache's Quotations", p. 14f; Rordorf, "Problème", p. 504; Draper, "Jesus Tradition", p. 277.

[122] Layton, "Sources", p. 357, suggests that the *Didache*'s usage is perhaps to avoid four utterly parallel sentences.

[123] Cf. the similar problem in discussions of the Synoptic problem in relation to Mark's allegedly rough style, and the remarks of W. R. Farmer, *The Synoptic Problem* (Dillsboro, 1976²) p. 122.

[124] Schulz, *Q*, p. 130; Lührmann, "Liebet", p. 421, and many others.

[125] Cf. Rordorf, "Problème", p. 505. He also rightly notes that the reference in 6:2 (along with other agreements with different parts of the *Didache*, must cast some doubt on theories that the section 1:3-2:1 was added after the rest of the text was completed. Cf. n. 142 below.

Did 1:4b is parallel to Mt 5:41, which has no Lukan parallel. One cannot say with any certainty whether this verse is due to MattR, whether it was part of Q but omitted by Luke, or whether it originated in a Q[mt] expansion of Q.[126] An origin in Q seems the least likely option on literary-critical grounds: the examples of non-retaliation in Lk 6:29f constitute a reasonably neatly balanced pair of couplets; the presence of Mt 5:41 makes for five examples and this seems rather overloaded. (On the other hand, it could be argued that the two last examples are distinctly anticlimactic,[127] so that an original trio of examples in the pre-Q tradition was secondarily expanded by the sayings about giving.[128]) The situation presupposed here is probably that of Roman troops forcing service from native Jews; but whether this already reflects the situation of the Q "community", or the later Matthean community, or a stage of the tradition in between, is very hard to say without arguing in a circle.[129] Certainly the situation presupposed does not seem to be particularly "Didachean" and hence the presence of the saying here is almost certainly due to the writer's use of his tradition, but the evidence is not definite enough to enable us to identify that tradition accurately.

---

[126] For MattR see Schulz, *Q*, p. 123; for Q, see Piper, *Love Your Enemies*, p. 58; Hoffmann, "Tradition", p. 61; Sauer, "Feindesliebe", p. 9; for Q[mt], see Strecker, *Bergpredigt*, p. 87; Zeller, *Mahnsprüche*, p. 55.

[127] Cf. Lührmann, "Liebet", pp. 418, 427; Zeller, *Mahnsprüche*, p. 55; Sauer, "Feindesliebe", p. 15.

[128] The sayings about non-retaliation and about giving are thus regarded as of separate origin by Schürmann, *Lukasevangelium*, p. 349; Schulz, *Q*, p. 13; Lührmann, "Liebet", p. 427.

[129] Cf. Theissen argues that it is the Matthean situation: see his "Gewaltverzicht und Feindesliebe (Mt 5,38-48/Lk 6,27-38) und deren sozialgeschichtlicher Hintergrund", in *Studien zur Soziologie des Urchristentums* (Tübingen: Mohr, 1979 [WUNT 19]) pp. 160-197, esp. p. 176f. Hoffmann, "Tradition", p. 61, argues strongly that this is the situation of the Q- "Gruppe" as well. Against Hoffmann it must be said that there are virtually no other direct references to worries about contact with *Roman* troops in Q, whereas Matthew does reflect on the theological implications of the events of the Jewish war (cf. Mt 22:7). The preceding two examples about non-retaliation in Mt 5:39f have to do with personal insult, and, if it is justified to connect the love-of-enemies complex in Q with the final beatitude (cf. n. 95 above), then the people addressed are those who are facing persecution for their Christian commitment. See L. Schottroff, "Gewaltverzicht und Feindesliebe in der urchristlichen Tradition. Mt 5,38-48; Lk. 6,26-27" in *Jesus Christus in Historie und Theologie:* Fs. H. Conzelmann (Tübingen: Mohr, 1975) pp. 197-221. Merklein, *Gottesherrschaft*, p. 272, and Zeller, *Mahnsprüche*, p. 59, both argue that the non-retaliation sayings refer to quite general, typical situations of violence; however, it would seem that Schottroff is justified in her claims at least at the level of Q where the context gives a rather more precise application of the saying.

E.   Did 1:4c

Did 1:4c	Mt 5	Lk 6
ἐὰν ἄρῃ τις τὸ ἱμάτιόν σου	τῷ θέλοντί σοι κριθῆναι καὶ τὸν χιτῶνα σου λαβεῖν	καὶ ἀπὸ τοῦ ἄροντός σου τὸ ἱμάτιον
δὸς αὐτῷ καὶ τὸν χιτῶνα	ἄφες αὐτῇ καὶ τὸ ἱμάτιον	καὶ τὸν χιτῶνα μὴ κωλύσῃς

The *Didache* here reveals close affinities with the Lukan version. Further, the differences between Matthew and Luke are quite considerable, though again it is difficult to know which version is more original. Matthew's version presupposes the situation of a law-suit where the person addressed is being sued for his shirt (χιτών) and is told to surrender even his cloak (ἱμάτιον), the one item which the Jewish Law expressly forbade anyone else to take (cf. Ex 24:25f; Dt 24:13).[130] Luke's (and the *Didache*'s) version reverses the order of the χιτών and the ἱμάτιον and seems to presuppose a robbery situation: if a person is robbed of his cloak (the first thing a robber would grab) he is to surrender his shirt as well. Again the argument about originality can go (and has gone) either way. Luke could be generalizing Matthew's more technical language for a non-Jewish audience;[131] or it could have been Matthew who has introduced the legal ideas here (cf. Mt 5:38).[132] Once again the evidence is indecisive and the agreement between the *Didache* and the Lukan version cannot be taken any further here.

F.   Did 1:4d-5a

Did 1:4d-5a	Mt 5	Lk 6
ἐὰν λάβῃ τις ἀπὸ σοῦ τὸ σόν μὴ ἀπαίτει οὐδὲ γὰρ δύνασαι παντὶ τῷ αἰτοῦντί σε δίδου καὶ μὴ ἀπαίτει	[42b]καὶ τὸν θέλοντα ἀπὸ σοῦ δανείσασθαι μὴ ἀποστραφῇς [42a]τῷ αἰτοῦντί σε δός...	[30b]καὶ ἀπὸ τοῦ αἴροντος τὰ σὰ μὴ ἀπαίτει [30a]παντὶ αἰτοῦντί σε δίδου...

The final section to be considered here again shows agreement between the *Didache* and Luke. Did 1:4f has the sayings in the

---

[130] Guelich, *Sermon*, p. 222.

[131] So Schürmann, *Lukasevangelium*, pp. 349, 351; Schulz, *Q*, p. 123; Hoffmann, "Tradition", p. 60; Sauer, "Feindesliebe", p. 13.

[132] Cf. Guelich, *Sermon*, p. 222; Catchpole, "Inaugural Discourse", p. 306. Theissen, *Studien*, p. 184, argues that Luke is primarily interested in the idea of borrowing, and hence would not have altered his tradition here. This is not altogether convincing. Luke may well have omitted the borrowing reference here (see below), perhaps simply because he wanted to generalize and make things more relevant for a non-Jewish audience, and also to develop the lending motif later.

reverse order to that of the synoptics (probably so as to end with a saying about "giving" to lead on to 1:5). The last clause in the section given above, "give to everyone who asks", agrees with Luke in having παντί and δίδου. Both are probably LkR in Luke,[133] though one cannot build too much on this here: Luke's aim is to generalize the idea of giving, but the *Didache* has exactly the same idea and hence the παντί and the present imperative δίδου could just as easily be seen as independent redaction of the tradition by the Didachist.

More significant in the present context is the opening sentence here, where the *Didache* agrees with Luke against Matthew in referring to someone who takes, rather than someone who wants to borrow; there is also agreement between the *Didache* and Luke in using ἀπαίτει in the final part. Now it is almost certain that Matthew's reference to "borrowing" represents the Q version here: Luke uses the same (rather rare) verb in vv. 34, 35 and this seems to constitute a reminiscence of the earlier saying.[134] Luke is above all here interested in the idea of generous giving, and he appears to save up the borrowing reference to develop it considerably in v. 34f. Further, it is of considerable importance to Luke to stress the idea that one should expect nothing in return. (This is, of course, part of his critique of the reciprocity ethic.) Hence Luke's "lending" to a borrower is virtually equivalent to a gift.[135] However, the "not expecting anything back" idea dominate Luke's version here.[136] Thus the Lukan ἀπαίτει in v. 30 is much more likely to be redactional than Matthew's ἀποστραφῇς.[137] In v. 30 Luke appears to have continued the robbery idea from v. 9, and saved the reference to the "borrower" for later; but he starts to introduce the idea of not asking for anything in return (μὴ ἀπαίτει) here.

The result is that Luke's version is rather uneven. For the Lukan text exhorts someone who has just been robbed not to demand his property back. But whatever means one might employ to recover stolen goods, simply demanding is unlikely to have any

---

[133] See Schulz, *Q*, p. 121; Sauer, "Feindesliebe", p. 13 and others cited there Köster, *Überlieferung*, p. 228, sees this as evidence of dependence of the *Didache* on LkR, but this is probably over-pressing the evidence.

[134] See Schulz, *Q*, p. 123; Lührmann, "Liebet", p. 418; Sauer, "Feindesliebe", p. 13; Catchpole, "Inaugural Discourse", pp. 306f. The attempt of Schürmann, *Lukasevangelium*, p. 357f (followed by Guelich, *Sermon*, p. 223) to see the connection as pre-Lukan is unnecessary: see the critique in Hoffmann, "Tradition", p. 66f.

[135] Schottroff, "Gewaltverzicht", p. 217; Horn, *Glaube*, p. 102.

[136] See Piper, *Love Your Enemies*, p. 157f.

[137] So Schürmann, *Lukasevangelium*, p. 349; Schulz, *Q*, p. 123; Guelich, *Sermon*, p. 223; Hoffmann, "Tradition", p. 63; Sauer, "Feindesliebe", p. 13; *Contra* Catchpole, "Inaugural Discourses", p. 307.

effect at all.[138] It may be that it is precisely this incongruity in the Lukan text which is reflected in the notorious little clause, οὐδὲ γὰρ δύνασαι, which is appended at this point in the *Didache*. The clause has caused immense perplexity.[139] However, it may be that it is simply the Didachist's comment on the preceding exhortation which he recognizes as somewhat incongruous: if you have been robbed, do not demand back[140] your property, "for you cannot"--you will have no success![141] The perplexity of commentators on the *Didache* may simply be a reflection at one stage removed of the Didachist's (or perhaps a later scribe's) worldly comment on the slightly puzzling preceding clause.

If this suggestion has any value, it may indicate that the Didachist was using his sources here with a certain degree of faithfulness: he was primarily interested in the exhortation to "give"; but he found this in his tradition coupled with another exhortation not to demand back stolen property, and although he found this difficult, he nevertheless reproduced it faithfully (albeit adding a comment of his own). This may then imply that the author of this clause regarded his source with some considerable respect. The source may thus have had something of the status of a "canonical" work, and this is clearly easier to envisage if this section of the *Didache* (at least in its present form) has a relatively late origin.

The net result of the discussion of this section is that the *Didache* here appears to presuppose Luke's redactional work and hence Luke's finished gospel.

The result of this detailed analysis of Did 1:3-5a in relation to the synoptic parallels in Mt 5 and Lk 6 shows that this section of the *Didache* appears on a number of occasions to presuppose the redactional activity of both evangelists, perhaps Luke more clearly than Matthew. This suggests very strongly that the *Didache* here

---

[138] Catchpole, *op.cit.*, p. 307, is one of the very few who have noted the incongruity of the Lukan text here: he speaks of the Lukan ending as providing "an unduly weak sequel" here.

[139] See the discussion of older views in Layton, "Sources", pp 346ff, together with his own proposed emendation of the text.

[140] Lake's translation of the text in the Loeb edition ("if any man will take from thee what is thine, refuse it not") is probably misleading: the idea is of demanding back what one has not got, not refusing to give what one has.

[141] Rordorf, "Problème", p. 505, also seems to hint at the strange nature of the Lukan version, reproduced in the *Didache*: "Or à las différence du cas du vol (1,4e) où une réclamation serait illusoire, elle serait possible dans le cas d'un prêt (1,5a)". However he resorts to the interpretation of the extra phrase in the *Didache* as referring to the spiritual impossibility of the Christian filled with love for his enemies to engage in such action. The *Didache* may be rather more mundane!

presupposes the gospels of Matthew and Luke in their finished forms.

IV. CONCLUSIONS

This paper has analyzed some of the parallels between material in different parts of the *Didache* and material in the synoptic gospels. The result has been that these parallels can be best explained if the *Didache* presupposes the finished gospels of Matthew and Luke. Further, this result seems to apply to all parts of the *Didache* examined here.[142] Precisely how the gospels were available to the author of the *Didache* is impossible to say: they may have been available as separate texts; they may have been already combined to form a single harmonized text. However, the evidence of the *Didache* seems to show that the text is primarily a witness to the post-redactional history of the synoptic tradition. It is not a witness to any pre-redactional developments.

---

[142] I have not discussed in detail the problem of the unity of the *Didache*, in particular the question of whether the section 1:3-2:1 should be regarded as an integral part of the text of the *Didache* (cf. n. 82 above). I remain unpersuaded that it should not be so regarded. Rordorf, "Problème", pp. 509ff, gives an impressive list of links between Did 1:3-2:1 and the rest of the *Didache*. The fact that there is no parallel to this section in the Two Ways teaching of the so-called "Church Order" (regarded by Wengst as decisive evidence that Did 1:3-2:1 is a secondary addition) may be explained by the latter being dependent on the Didachist's *Vorlage*: cf. Rordorf, *ibid.*, p. 513. In any case the Church Order only parallels part of Did 1-6, omitting the "Way of Death" in Did 5-6.

LITERARY AND DOCTRINAL AFFINITIES OF THE "MANUAL OF DISCIPLINE"

† JEAN-PAUL AUDET

My purpose is less ambitious than my title, taken in a general sense, might lead one to believe. On the one hand I only want, for the moment, to look at the second section of the "Manual" (1QS 3:13-4:26). It is a moral instruction which, in spite of its obvious affinities with the rest of the writing or writings the scroll contains, may be considered in itself and can, to a certain extent, receive independent treatment. On the other hand, the comparisons which I would like to suggest only concern the *Duae viae* and the *Shepherd of Hermas*, two works which met with very different fates, which nevertheless have this fact in common, that they show a very singular Jewish colour, which is so singular that at this point it certainly goes beyond what might be expected in primitive Christian literature. The great difficulties which they present so far to the numerous attempts at explanation which have been made, are now gaining some clarity it seems to me, from the moral instruction of the "Community of the Covenant"—of which a part of the standard library has been rediscovered near Khirbet Qumran.

In itself, if one accepts that the "Community of the Covenant" was living in Palestine at the very least in the first century of our era, that its origin may be put at a date considerably earlier than this period, and that it has known, so it seems, a certain expansion in space as well as in time, then it is not impossible that one should find, even in the literary heritage of the first Christian generations, so varied in thought and expression, some literary and doctrinal affinities with works like the moral instruction of the "Manual of Discipline". One should not forget that Christianity had been pent up in Palestine for many years, and that the complete separation with Judaism occurred relatively slowly, and not without allowing many points of personal contact to continue here and there, even if not full communion. And that is already more than is necessary to make the facts that we are about to analyze perfectly natural. In the mid second century, whatever allowances one may need to make to take account of literary fiction, a real dialogue was still possible between Justin and Trypho. This fact is very significant in itself. It is also through authentically Christian hands and not through Jewish hands that so many pseudepigraphical writings have come down to us, of whose authentic origin there could be no serious doubt, without speaking of Philo and Josephus, nor the Greek versions collected by Origen for his *Hexapla*. One could even think that if they had had the *Manual of Discipline* and the *Damascus Document* accessible to them in Greek, the Christians would not have hesitated to transcribe them, as they actually transcribed *Enoch*, *Jubilees* and the *Testaments of the Twelve Patriarchs*, which must have been part of the regular library of the "Community of the Covenant", if they did not owe their very birth to them. It is only by the chance of an extraordinary find that we possess today the *Manual of Discipline* in Hebrew: the comparisons which I wish to propose with the *Duae viae* and the *Shepherd of Hermas*, do not have to be explained by a Greek version of the *Manual* which probably never existed, and with good reason!

THE "DUAE VIAE"

At the risk of appearing to be long winded, I must begin by discussing a very widely agreed opinion on the origin of the early history of the *Duae viae*. This opinion owes its acceptance to the work of Robinson, Muilenburg and Connolly, taken up recently on a large scale by Vokes.[1] Through all the amplifications which it has undergone since it was proposed for the first time, the essential line of the argument on which this opinion is based has, however, remained the same as that in which it was found originally in the study of Robinson himself. It will not be necessary then to undertake here a separate discussion of the minute analyses of Muilenburg and Connolly.

---

[1] The literature in question is quite extensive. Here at least are the main references: J.A. Robinson, "The Problem of the Didache", *JTS* 13 (1912) pp. 339-356 (on this important article, see the observations of Harnack in *TLZ* and the notes of Swete in the appendix to his work, *The Holy Spirit in the Ancient Church* [London: Macmillan, 1912] pp. 414ff); *Barnabas, Hermas and the Didache* (London: SPCK, 1920 [Donnellan Lectures, 1920]); "The Epistle of Barnabas and the Didache", published posthumously by Connolly in *JTS* 35 (1934) pp. 113-146, 225-248; J. Muilenburg, *The Literary Relations of the Epistle of Barnabas and the Teaching of the Twelve Apostles* (Marburg: no publisher given, 1929), with a good review by F.C. Burkitt in *JTS* 33 (1932) pp. 25ff; R.H. Connolly, "The Didache in Relation to the Epistle of Barnabas", *JTS* 33 (1932) pp. 246ff; "The Didache and Montanism", *DRev* 55 (1937) pp. 339ff; "Canon Streeter on the Didache", *JTS* 38 (1937) pp. 364ff; F.E. Vokes, *The Riddle of the Didache* (London: SPCK, 1938). In a different direction, one can see J.V. Bartlet, "The Didache Reconsidered", *JTS* 22 (1921) pp. 239ff; A.S. McLean, *The Doctrine of the Twelve Apostles* (London, 1922) esp. pp. xll-xvi and xxxi-xxxv; B.H. Streeter, "The Much Belaboured Didache", *JTS* 37 (1936) pp. 369ff; J.M. Creed, "The Didache", *JTS* 39 (1938) pp. 370ff; E.J. Goodspeed, *A History of Early Christian Literature* (Chicago: University of Chicago Press, 1942) pp. 31ff (cf. his "The Didache, Barnabas and the Doctrina", *AThR* 27 [1945] pp. 228-247, which unfortunately I only know about indirectly from bibliographies which I have come across).

The force of the argument is cumulative. Every summary must therefore be handled with care. But, with this caution, I do not believe that I will betray the thought of Robinson in presenting it briefly as follows: The moral part of the *Epistle* of Barnabas (18-20) has been regarded by a certain number of critics as a spurious addition (*"addition d'origine étrangère"*), borrowed from an already existing manual of moral instruction (*Duae viae*). But one can show by constant reading and analysis of the *Epistle* that it is all by one and the same hand. Everywhere, it has the same spirit, the same clumsiness of composition, the same manner of using literary sources, the same habit of repeating on various occasions the formulae already used. *A priori*, there is no reason to think that the moral part of the *Epistle* was from an earlier author. On the contrary, all the evidence of the internal examination tends to show that the *Duae viae* is the original work of Barnabas himself.[2]

On the other hand, if the *Duae viae* of the *Didache* differs noticeably from that of Barnabas, all the differences can be explained by the peculiar literary habits and peculiar intention of the "Didachist". After having borrowed the theme, he treats it with the greatest freedom: he amplified it with precepts drawn from the Old Testament, from the Sermon on the Mount, from the *Shepherd of Hermas*, and other more obscure sources; he arranges it, he interprets it, he explains it, ridding it of some inappropriate or useless sentences. On the whole, he aims to produce the baptismal catechesis which he needs to respond, according to Matthew 28:19-20, to the intention he has expressed in the title, "Teaching of the Lord through the Twelve Apostles to the Gentiles."[3]

On all sides, it then continues to be established that the *Epistle* is entirely from the same author, and that there is no valid reason to question its literary unity: "The description of the Two Ways is an integral part of the document."[4]

With all the array of analyses which support it, this argument may have seemed unassailable. If it were to be accepted, it would make the *Duae viae* a Christian writing, whose already peculiar history would be even more difficult to explain now that we have the *Manual of Discipline* before our eyes. In reality, however, I do not believe that the argument of Robinson stands up to a rigorous examination.

This is no place to take up these problems in all their fullness: they are perhaps the most difficult of the whole of ancient Christian literature. It would be necessary to take the *Didache*

---

[2] Cf. Robinson, "Barnabas and the Didache", pp. 132, 142, 146.
[3] Cf. Robinson, *Barnabas, Hermas and the Didache*, p. 70.
[4] Cf. Robinson, "Barnabas and the Didache", p. 146.

together with all the related documents, which would take us well beyond the acceptable limits of one article. But, to upset the argument of Robinson, it is sufficient here to consider its theoretical implications. The proof rests mainly on the affinities which connect the two parts of the *Epistle* of Barnabas (1-17 and 18-20, or 21). But, putting these things in their best light, what do these affinities prove by themselves in the question of sources? Very little, if they prove anything at all. For it is clear as soon as one thinks of it, that the facts mentioned by Robinson could be exactly the same if one assumed a source used from memory and known for a long time. What would prevent this source (*Duae viae*), which Barnabas would have had in his mind before the writing the first line of his letter, from having established in the first seventeen chapters the affinities of thought and style which connect them to the two following chapters? The extensive usage in chs. 18-20 does not mean that they could not be used occasionally and partially in the previous chapters. A word, an expression, a turn of phrase or style, a distinctive idea can recur here and there, but they only prove one thing, which it was natural to guess, and that is that the author has not made a sudden acquaintance with the writing used in chs. 18-20 just at the moment when he had finished writing ch. 17. Thus the more one points out affinities of all kinds between the two parts of the *Epistle*, the more one will have shown that the possible source of the last part was already familiar to the author of the first part. But in doing this, one will have left intact the problem of a dependence of the *Duae viae* of the *Didache* on the *Duae viae* of the *Epistle*, or, perhaps, in regard to the independent *Duae viae* which would be the common source of both.

It is, on the other hand, a dubious procedure to force together, as Robinson does, the question of the literary unity of the *Epistle* and the question of its sources. To show that the *Epistle* proceeds entirely from one and the same hand, is obviously not equivalent to showing that the author has drawn everything from his own resources. The question of the literary unity is a preliminary one; beyond this the question of sources remains open. Thus, an argument from affinities, such as presented by Robinson, would be absolutely efficacious in resolving the question of literary unity, if it is posed again, but it says nothing by itself on the question of its sources. Barnabas could have used a *Duae viae* of which he was not the author, as he has used the Old Testament, without placing the unity of the authorship in doubt. These things are obvious. One also asks why a critic of Robinson's quality could have fallen into such confusion.[5]

---

[5] The confusion is obvious in a passage like the following: "If this point shall seem to have been somewhat unreasonably laboured, it should be borne in mind that

Robinson's argument makes use, besides, of what is only in reality a trick of perspective. It labours on a *Duae viae* which it conjectures and which it presumes to come from Barnabas. It uncovers a certain number of affinities with the rest of the *Epistle*. But then, precisely, it has begun by illogically ruling out the possibility that the *Duae viae* of Barnabas could have been in reality a *Duae viae* utilized from elsewhere and then already made to conform to the literary tastes and customs and personal ideas of the author of the *Epistle*. Noone today would wish to deny that the *Duae viae* has passed through the hands of Barnabas: it is another thing to demonstrate that he is purely and simply the author. The affinities are deceptive: they could have come, at least in part, as much from the fact that Barnabas has used the *Duae viae* as from the fact that he was its author. For the argument to remain fully effective, it would have to distinguish with enough certainty between the affinities which derive from the one or the other case. But internal criticism has no hope of making this distinction, so that if one avoids allowing oneself to be deceived, one finds oneself back where one started from, in the presence of a question to be resolved and not of a question already resolved. We wonder always whether Barnabas has not used a pre-existing *Duae viae*, on which he would have left his own particular mark.

The affinities are not, moreover, the only things to be considered. There is the counterweight of undeniable literary hiatuses from the first to the second part of the *Epistle*. The most apparent is that of the abrupt transition from the second person plural to the second person singular in ch. 19, with the return to the second person plural for ch. 21. With the hypothesis that Barnabas was the author of the *Duae viae*, as Robinson proposes, such a literary procedure could not be explained without difficulty, even by making an appeal to the practice of the diatribe, which is, however, in reality, completely irrelevant. Indeed, one could understand a short reflection or question in this form. But for a long development of this kind, in the context of an epistle, one asks oneself how the idea could have come to its author, unless it had been somehow imposed from outside. In any case, in all the passages where it is certain that Barnabas is left to himself, it is

---

the literary unity of the Epistle has been called into question in recent controversy and the latter portion which we are now considering (the *Duae viae* of chs. 18-20) has been regarded by some critics as a spurious addition derived form an already existing manual of instruction. But in view of what has been here said, can any one doubt that the passages which we have cited are all by one hand?" ("Barnabas and the Didache", p. 132. Cf. Muilenburg, *Literary Relations*, p. 9; and M. Vokes, *Riddle*, pp. 42-47).

the plural which appears, as one would expect. It is so, in particular, for ch. 21 which continues the moral instruction of chs. 18-20 with an exhortation. To all appearances, Barnabas has returned to his particular habits, abandoned momentarily for an accidental reason.

Thus, all things considered, it seems to me that the labours of Robinson and those who have followed him, have left the real problem of the provenance and original form of the *Duae viae* intact. It has not at all been shown that Barnabas was himself its author, still less that the "Didachist" was only a secondary and later editor. Only one thing has been clarified, and that one completely: the literary unity of the *Epistle* of Barnabas. This is all that one has been able to show, in a straightforward way, in the line of analysis in which one has been engaged, and this is all that has been really shown.

Thus, at least in this matter, the path is clear. A second hypothesis, defended long ago by Funk in particular, should be examined here, attributing the original *Duae viae*, which includes *Didache* 1:3b-2:1, to the "Didachist" himself.[6] But a discussion of this point would raise all the literary problems of the *Didache*, a problem which it would, however, be vain to think we would be able to resolve by indirect means. Will the reader excuse me if I content myself here a simple remark? On the one hand, the *Duae viae* of the *Didache* breathes altogether the air of Judaism in its literary genre, in its expression and in its spiritual content. This feature of its appearance has long been noticed, and it is, for the most part, incontestable. On the other hand, a hypothesis such as that of Funk leads necessarily to making the *Doctrina apostolorum* of Schlecht some kind of translation of the *Duae viae* of the *Didache*.[7] Now when one compares the so-called Latin version (i.e. the *Doctrina apostolorum* of Schlecht) attentively with the Greek text which it is supposed to translate (i.e. the *Duae viae* of the *Didache*), one is faced with a fact which is very strange for a translation: whereas the (Christian!) translator would naturally

---

[6] For Funk's opinion see, besides his own separate edition of the *Didache* (*Doctrinae duodecim apostolorum, Canones ecclesiastici ac reliquae doctrinae duarum viarum expositiones veteres* [Tübingen: Henrici Laupp, 1887]), the introductions to the successive editions of the Apostolic Fathers: *Opera Patrum apostolicorum* (Tübingen: Henrici Laupp, 1887, 1901); "Der Barnabasbrief und die Didache", *ThQ* (1897) pp. 617ff; *Didascalia et Constitutiones apostolorum* II (Paderborn: F. Schöningh, 1906), (less assertively than in the former studies on the authenticity of *Did* 1:3b-2:1).

[7] It is well known that the full text of the *Doctrina apostolorum* was published for the first time by J. Schlecht, who discovered the manuscript of the document (J. Schlecht, *Doctrina XII apostolorum*, Freiburg im Breisgau: Herder, 1900). The exact title of the MS of Schlecht is *De doctrina apostolorum (Monacensis 6264)*, but the *Mellicensis (Q. 52=914)* simply bears the title *Doctrina apostolorum*.

have manipulated the text he had to translate, it would appear, on the contrary, that he has worked hard to make it hark back to its distant origins, in such a way that the alleged translation of the *Duae viae* of the *Didache* seems still more strongly coloured by Judaism than is the *Duae viae* of the *Didache* itself. This sounds very unlikely. But these things could easily be explained, on the other hand, if the so-called partial version of the *Didache* were actually a version of the *Duae viae*, not as we find it incorporated in the *Didache*, but as it could have circulated independently of its accidental insertion into the latter. If the *Duae viae* originated directly from Judaism, then there would be nothing very surprising in the fact that the very ancient Latin version, which has fortunately preserved it for us, reveals here and there the spiritual origins of the writing more clearly than the *Duae viae* incorporated into the edition of the *Didache* itself.

The solution is then simple, although common opinion does not expect it: to all appearances, the *Doctrina apostolorum* of Schlecht has nothing to do, as far as being a version is concerned, with the *Duae viae* of the *Didache*. It represents a text of the *Duae viae* independent of that of the *Didache* and of Barnabas, in many respects more marked by a Jewish point of view than either of them, which must in that case be the Judaism of its origins.

Moreover, the title *Doctrina apostolorum*, which the *Duae viae* of Schlecht carries, does not present any serious difficulty to this explanation. Because, on the one hand, the *Duae viae* designated in this way by Rufinus[8] did not have its own title, and because, on the other hand, it appeared in almost identical form at the beginning of a writing bearing the title Διδαχὴ τῶν ἀποστόλων,[9] it could have been enough that the two writings intersected in the course of their distribution in the same milieu for the title of the *Didache* to have passed to the Greek *Duae viae* and then, naturally, to its Latin version.[10]

---

[8] Rufinus, *Comm. in Symb. apost.*, p. 38; *PL* 21, 274. The Latin tradition adorned the *Duae viae* with a title which is known to us only indirectly: *Iudicium secundum Petrum* (Rufinus, *loc.cit.*), or *Iudicium Petri* (Jerome, *De viris ill.*, 1; *PL* 23, 609). This ambitious description confirms, if there is any need of it, the primitive anonymity of the writing. If, as seems likely, the vague reference of Optatus of Milevis must be intended to refer to the *Duae viae*, then this would only confirm this (*De schism. Donat.*, I,21; *CSEL* 26, 23).

[9] This is the title by which Athanasius, in particular, designates the *Didache* (cf. *EpFest* 39; *PG* 26, 14); the same title after him in the canonical list that the transmission has taken in the *SynScrSac* of Pseudo-Athanasius (*PG* 28, 432), and in the *Stichometry* attributed to Nicephorus (text in Zahn, *Gesch. des neutest. Kanons*, II, 297ff.

[10] One can get an idea of the freedom which has prevailed in the transmission with respect to the ascriptions and titles of this gnomic literature with an example borrowed from the Greek world. The *Delphic Precepts*, of which many recensions exist, were at first an anonymous collection. In spite of Apollo, they have sub-

Now we are ready to begin our work. It would be simplest to begin by placing the texts opposite each other: they already speak for themselves. In order that the comparison should not hide any problems, I will transcribe the two texts in question in full.[11]

1QS 3:13 For the master (of initiation),[12] to transmit to all the sons of light

---

sequently been attributed *en bloc* to the Seven Muses, then divided out in sections and attributed in this form to each one of them (cf. Dittenberger, *Sylloge*, III[3], 1268, noted by Diels). The *Duae viae* has suffered exactly the same fate. At first anonymous, it has subsequently been attributed to Peter and to the Twelve (the *Iudicium Petri* of Rufinus and St. Jerome and the *Doctrina apostolorum* of Schlecht), then, naturally, it was divided up into little sections to be distributed between the Apostles (the recension of the *Ecclesiastical Canons*). To complete the comparison, I add that the *Delphic Precepts*, having passed into the Egyptian gnomic tradition, have been taken under the local patronage of Amenhotep, just as the *Duae viae* has much later, in passing from Judaism into Christian, been placed under the name of the "masters of wisdom" of the latter. One could take many other examples of such treatment. It is a serious illusion on Goodspeed's part to have accepted the suggestion of the title of the *Doctrina apostolorum*. I am equally astonished that he has been so easily persuaded that he was obliged to ignore its Jewishness (*History of Early Christian Literature*, p. 32). C. Taylor, who was sensitive to these things and who was not a bad judge, has from the beginning thought very differently (*The Teaching of the Twelve Apostles, with illustrations from the Talmud* [Cambridge: Deighton Bell, 1886]). And Taylor has not been alone. Goodspeed recognizes this, but he adds that the "historians of Jewish literature" have not accepted the *Duae viae*. I don't know what this allusion, which is not strictly true, has in mind (cf. *The Jewish Encyclopedia* IV, 585ff; *Encycl. judaica* III, 11ff; G. F. Moore, *Judaism* I, p. 188). Besides, strictly speaking, one only needs in addition to read for example the *Duae viae* (in the recension of the *Doctrina apostolorum*) and the *Testaments of the Twelve Patriarchs* (in Greek).

[11] For the *Doctrina apostolorum* (= *Doct*), I have used the text of L. Wohleb, *Die lateinische Übersetzung der Didache* (Paderborn: F. Schöningh, 1913 [SGKA 7.1]) pp. 90-102. For the text of the *Manual of Discipline* (= 1QS), I acknowledge with pleasure the help which I have found in the careful work of my predecessors (Brownlee, van der Ploeg, Milik, Lambert), but, in the form presented here, the translation of 3:13-4:26 is my own work.

[12] משכיל must be taken here in an institutional sense, in accordance with the general context: it is a matter of a juridical collection, of which the very particular literary genre recalls the compilation of the *Apostolic Constitutions*, just to take an eastern example. The laws, the simple customs, the moral exhortation, prayer itself, link up and back each other up, without too much concern for the consequences which a similar mixture may have for the distinctness of discipline. Nevertheless, the overall intention of works of this sort, in Judaism as in Christianity, is to provide rules of conduct for an institution taken as it is. In the present case, the preposition which introduces the term (ל) indicates the particular destination of the instruction which follows (3:13-4:26). For lack of a better translation, I propose: "For the Master of Initiation". This is, it seems, the suggestion of the context: it is about the transmission of foundational instruction. Moreover, it could not be an accident that the instruction comes in the scroll immediately after the ritual of acceptance into the community. In the OT שכל is the gift of the ruler and teacher: the insight, the ability to discern what is good and right in matters of collective or individual behaviour (so Jer 3:15; Dan 1:17 and one can add Job 34:35; Prov 1:3 and 21:16 in this sense, the parallels have generally derived from ידע). He who

insight and knowledge concerning the lineages[13] of humanity, **14** all the varieties of spirits which deceive the human works throughout the generations, the evil visitations at the same time as **15** the ages of peace.

From the God of all knowledge (proceeds) all which is and all which has been.[14] Before anything even existed, he has established the design of all things, **16** and when they came into being, at the summons received,[15] according to the design of his magnificent power, they (began to) produce their works. Nothing ought to be changed. From him **17** (emanate) the laws of all things which exist, and it is he who sustains them in all their inclinations.

Doct **1:1** Uiae duae sunt in saeculo uitae et mortis, lucis et tenebrarum. in his constituti sunt angeli duo,	But he has created man to rule **18** the world, and he has appointed in it two spirits, so that he might behave

---

possesses the gift is the משכיל, who by the very fact that he possesses it, finds himself virtually designated by God to fill the corresponding function in the service of his people (cf. Dan 11:33; 12:3; also very important in 1QS itself in 11:12-21 or with respect to the משכיל one moves imperceptibly from the personal quality to a title with a function in the service of the community). It would be interesting to compare, from this point of view, the double ministry of the teacher and prophet in the very first Christian generations (see especially the very stange texts of *Did* 11-13, again very imperfectly explained in other respects).

[13] תולדות should be translated "lineages" rather than "generations" (Brownlee, Lambert, van der Ploeg, *histoires*), as can be seen from דורות in the following line. Milik, at least, saw clearly that in our text there could only be two תולדות, but he has translated it by *genera* so vague that he has lost the force of the image. It is really a collection which shows the totality of the generations that one can attach to a common ancestor, real or fictional. Here, of course, the term has only a metaphorical value, in the same vein and in the same taste as "sons of light, sons of darkness" etc. He enters into a general explanation of the moral problem and through that, indirectly, of the problem of good and evil, of retribution and thus of the course of the history of Israel from its origins until the final consummation.

[14] נהיה. This is a *Niphal* participal used substantively, and therefore atemporally in itself. It is only the immediate context which could here determine the temporal relation. One could not therefore reason in this regard as one would do purely and simply for a verb. Thus, although Brownlee seems to be right in one or other of the examples which he brings, I am not sure that it is permissible to link the term to the future so closely. It must be determined in each case. I have preferred here the past tense, but I admit that it is only a preference founded, in my opinion, on the general orientation of our text. It is from history that all the experience on which the small moral system presented by the Master of initiation is taken (cf. Dan 3:1ff).

[15] תעורות. The variety of translations presented until now reflects the awkwardness one finds here. In returning to the probable sense of the root, "to declare distinctly or solemnly", could we not see in this noun an allusion to the creative word of God and hear in it the order which has called all things into existence? The verb itself can also mean, "to address an exhortation, give a solemn reprimand" and hence "to direct", which is not far from the sense proposed in the translation. The suffix may indicate, nevertheless that one should take the correlative from the side of the creatures: a summons received rather than an order given.

unus aequitatis, alter iniquitatis. dis-
tantia autem magna est duarum
uiarum.

himself according to them until the
time appointed for his visitation.—These are the spirits **19** of
truth and of falsehood.—Under a
cover of light (is conceived) the
lineage of faithfulness, and out of
the depth of a pit of darkness, the
lineage of falsehood.[16] **20** To the
hands of the prince of lights (is
remitted) the government of all the
sons of righteousness: they walk in
the ways of light; but to the hands of
the angel **21** of darkness (is trans-
ferred) all power over the sons of
falsehood: they walk in ways of
darkness.

It is from the angel of darkness that bewilderment (comes) **22** to all the sons
of righteousness: their sins, their iniquities, their offences and the transgressions of their conduct (are due) to his power, **23** according to a secret plan of
God, until his demise. All their afflictions and their times of distress (are
explained) by his malevolent rule, **24** and all the spirits that fell to his lot (are
only designed) to lay snares for the sons of light. But the God of Israel, and
his angel of truth, have become the refuge of all **25** the sons of light. For it is
he who has created the spirit of light and the spirit of darkness; on them he
has established every work, **26** and on their ways all religion. God loves the
first one completely **4:1** for eternity and in all that he does he takes his
pleasure for ever; as for the other one, he has had its counsel in loathing and
to all its ways he has devoted an eternal hatred.

1:2 uia ergo uitae haec est: primo
diliges deum aeternum qui te fecit,
secundo proximum tuum ut te
ipsum. omne autem, quod tibi fieri
non uis, alio non feceris. **3** interpretatio autem horum uerborum haec
est. **2:2** non moechaberis, non homi-
cidium facies, non falsum testi-
monium dices, non puerum uiol-
aberis, non fornicaberis, non magica
facies, non medicamenta mala
facies, non occides filium in abortum
nec natum succides, non concupisces

2Here then are their (respective)
ways in the world: to enlighten the
heart of a man and to make straight
before him all the ways of righteousness and faithfulness; to make his
heart responsive to the fear of the
judgments **3** of God. It is a spirit of
humility and of slowness to anger,
of great compassion and of unending
goodness, of sagacity, of discernment and of lofty wisdom, well-tried
in all **4** the works of God, relying on
the richness of his goodness. It is a

---

[16] This obscure phrase seems to me to make an allusion to the role of the spirits
in the birth of the two lineages.

quicquam de re proximi tui. **3** non periurabis, non male loqueris, non eris memor malorum factorum, **4** non eris duplex in consilium dandum neque bilinguis; tendiculum enim mortis est lingua. **5** non erit uerbum tuum uacuum nec mendax. **6** non eris cupidus nec auarus nec rapax nec adolator nec contentiosus nec mali moris.

spirit which knows the way to do everything, which has the zeal for just judgments, a holy **5** intent with a firm purpose, a great gentleness towards all the sons of faithfulness and of radiant purity, detestation of impure idols, with humble manners, **6** intelligent in all things and, concerning what is of the truth, throwing the veil upon the mysteries of knowledge. These are the counsels of the spirit for all the sons of faithfulness in the world.

non accipies consilium aduersus proximum tuum. **7** neminem hominum odieris, quosdam amabis super animam tuam. **3:1** fili, fuge ab homine malo et homine simili illius. **2** noli fieri iracundus, quia iracundia ducit ad momicidium. nec appetens eris malitiae nec animosus, de his enim omnibus irae nascuntur. **4** noli esse mathematicus neque delustrator, quae res ducunt ad uanam superstitionem; nec uelis ea uidere nec audire. **5** noli fieri mendax, quia mendacium ducit ad furtum; neque amator pecuniae nec uanus; de his enim omnibus furta nascuntur. **6** noli fieri murmuriosus, quia ducit ad maledictionem. noli fieri audax nec male sapiens; de his enim omnibus maledictiones nascuntur. **7** esto autem mansuetus, quia mansueti possidebunt sanctam terram. **8** esto patiens et tui negotii, bonus et tremens omnia uerba quae audis. **9** non altiabis te nec honorabis te apud homines nec dabis animae tuae superbiam. non iunges te animo cum altioribus sed cum iustis humilibusque conuersaberis. **10** quae tibi contraria contingunt pro bonis excipies sciens nihil sine deo fieri. **4:1** qui loquitur tibi uerbum domini dei, memineris die ac nocte, reuerberis eum quasi dominum; unde enim dominica procedunt, ibi et dominus est. **2** require autem facies sanctorum, ut te reficias uerbis illorum. **3** non facies dissensiones, pacifica litigantes, iudica iuste sciens quod tu iudicaberis, non deprimes quemquam in casu suo. **4** non dubitabis uerum erit an non erit. **5** noli esse ad accipiendum extendens manum et ad reddendum subtrahens. **6** si habes per manus tuas redemptionem peccatorum, **7** non dubitabis dare nec dans murmuraberis sciens quis sit huius mercis [mercedis] bonus redditor. **8** non avertes te ab egente, communicabis autem omnia cum fratribus tuis nec dices tua esse; si enim mortalibus socii sumus, quanto magis hinc initiatntes esse debemus! omnibus enim dominus dare uult de donis suis. **9** non tolles manum a filiis sed a iuuentute docebis eos timorem domini. **10** seruo tuo uel ancillae, qui in eundem sperant dominum in ira tua non imperabis, timeat utrumque, dominum et te. non enim uenit ut personas inuitaret, sed in quibus spiritum inuenit. **11** uos autem, serui, subiecti dominis uestris estote, tamquam formae dei, cum pudore et tremore. **12** oderis omnem affectationem et quod deo non placet non facies. **13** custodi ergo, fili, quae audisti neque appones illis contraria neque diminues. **14** non accedas ad orationem cum conscientia mala. haec est uia uitae.

1QS 4:6 The visitation of all those who behave themselves according to him (the spirit of faithfulness), is complete health, **7** abundance of well-being in length of days, increase of descendants, and in addition all blessings for eternity, joy without end in a life incorruptible, a crown of glory **8** and a garment of honour in eternal light.

Doct **5:1** mortis autem uia est illi contraria, primum nequam et maledictis plena. Moechationes, homicidia, falso testimonia, fornicationes,desideria mala, magicae, medicamenta iniqua, furta, uanae superstitiones, rapinae, affectationes, fastidia, malitia, petulantia, cupiditas, impudica loquela, zelus, audacia,superbia, altitudo, uanitas, non timentes, **2** persequentes bonos, odio habentes ueritatem, amantes mendacium, non scientes mercedem ueritatis, non applicantes se bonis, non habentes iudicium iustum, pervigilantes non in bono, sed in malo, quorum longe est mansuetudo et superbia

As for the spirit of falsehood, it is breaking up of the heart and carelessness of hands in the service of righteousness, wickedness and lies, pride and self-conceit from within, fraud and merciless cunning, **10** thorough dishonesty, ill-temper, great folly, rivalry in insolence, abominable deeds at the will of the spirit of fornication and filthy conduct in the service of uncleanness, **11** a tongue (fertile) in blasphemy, blindness of eyes and heaviness of ears, stiffness of neck and hardness of heart to walk in all the ways of darkness and in the ability for evil.

proxima, persequentes remuneratores, non miserantes pauperum, non dolentes pro dolente, non scientes genitorem suum, peremptores filiorum suorum, abortuantes, avertentes se a bonis operibus, deprimentes laborantem, aduocationem iustorum deuitantes. abstine te, fili, ab istis omnibus. **6:1** et vide, ne quis te ab hac doctrina auocet, et si minus extra disciplinam doceberis. **4** haec in consulendo si cottidie feceris, prope eris uiuo deo; quodsi non feceris, longe eris a ueritate. **5** haec omnia tibi in animo pone et non deceperis de spe tua, sed per haec sancta certamina perueneris ad coronam.

1QS 4:11 The visitation **12** of all those who behave themselves according to him (the spirit of falsehood), is a multitude of diseases[17] from the side of all the angels of affliction, down to eternal ruin under the furious wrath of the

---

[17] It seems to me that גיעים has the sense indicated by מרפא which comes at the beginning of the "visitation" of the sons of truth (4:6). The latter passage does not, moreover, suggest a purely metaphorical sense for מרפא. To healing or health, naturally, sickness is opposed.

God of vengeance, perpetual anguish and endless **13** disgrace, with the ignominy of destruction in the flames of the places of darkness. All the flow of their generations will be sad lamentation and bitter adversity in the disaster of darkness, until **14** there does not remain either survivor or remnant from among them.

15 To these lineages (belongs) humanity and all the human mass throughout the generations shares their (mutual) opposition as a heritage. They follow their proper ways and every retribution **16** for their works (will fulfill) their lines of division, following the portion inherited by each, great or small, until the end of time. God has, for that purpose, assigned their respective share until the final **17** consummation and he has vowed to their tribes an endless hostility. The works of falsehood are an abomination in the eyes of faithfulness, and all the ways of faithfulness are a horror to false-hood. A jealous **18** rivalry inspires their decision, for their ways never meet. God, nevertheless, in the mystery of his prudence and in the magnificence of his wisdom, has set a term to the existence of falsehood, and in the time **19** of his visitation, he will annihilate it for ever. Then faithfulness will enter the world for ever, for it had allowed itself to turn aside into the way of iniquity under the power of wickedness until **20** the hour of the final judgment. In that time, God will purify with his truth all human actions, and out of regard for himself, he will place in the crucible some from among the sons of man, destroying every spirit of falsehood in the coils **21** of his flesh, and, by a spirit of holiness, purifying it of every evil action. He will sprinkle it with a spirit of truth as with a water of purification to wash it of all abomination of falsehood; and he will turn around to him and return **22** in (the waters) of a spirit of purification, to give to the righteous the knowledge of the Most High and the wisdom of the sons of heaven, and to give understanding to those who are perfect in their ways. For God has chosen them for an eternal covenant, **23** and it is to them that all the human glory will go. There will be no more falsehood, to the disgrace of all the workers of fraud. Until now the spirits of faithfulness and falsehood confront one another in the heart of man: **24** (thus) they walk in wisdom or folly. According to his personal heritage of faithfulness and of righteousness, so one hates falsehood; but according to his portion of falsehood, so one is committed to evil, thus conceiving **25** a hatred of faithfulness. For God has established them in equal measure, until the moment of decision and of making all things new. He knows the result of their works throughout **26** their [times], and he distributes them as a heritage to men, in order that they may know what is good [and what is evil, and in order that he may assign] a destiny to every living being according to his spirit [...in the time] of the visitation.

From this parallel reading of the *Duae viae* and from the moral instruction of the *Manual of Discipline*, there emerges first an important fact: that is that the two texts have a literary framework which is closely related, and therefore also a general line of development which is almost identical. Of course, this general observation should not make us forget the differences which separate the two writings so clearly in the treatment of detail, and it will be necessary to give place to a positive explanation of this fact also. But it is the similarity in the general outline of the construction which constitutes the principle fact: the particular differences, despite their number, are only a secondary and derived phenomenon. One could more easily perhaps put these things in perspective by hypothetically reversing the order of the facts. From resemblances of detail, unless they are proportionally numerous, would be less significant for the origin of the writing. It would always be possible to take account of them by relatively remote relationship, indirect and distended. If one wishes, the explanation to present will be of such a kind as suffices to take effective account of the encounter of the *Syntagma doctrinae* of Pseudo-Athanasius,[18] on the one hand, and of the *Duae viae* itself, on the other hand. But it is precisely because the *Syntagma* has escaped from the literary framework which the *Duae viae* has provided for it, that it has only retained very small details in the precepts and a vague general resemblance in phraseology. I insist somewhat on this distinction, because, very curiously, the *Duae viae*, which decisively resembles the *Manual* for its literary framework, must be compared, on the contrary, with the moral exhortations of the *Testament of the Twelve Patriarchs* for the details of the precepts and for the phraseology. And is not even this itself again very significant? Indeed there is no absence of reasons for thinking that the *Testaments* have for their own part some relationship with the "Community of the Covenant". On both sides then, one would remain always in the same spiritual milieu or, in any case, in its very close environs.

One must try, nevertheless, to see things more precisely. Let us put aside the title (1QS 3:13-15), which only indicates the themes. The instruction of the *Manual* begins with a reminder of creation (3:15-18). When one thinks of the community to which this instruction was destined, one can wonder that there is not the least direct reference to the covenant. Indeed, this only appears later (4:22) and in the eschatological perspective of the plan of God for the final restoration of all righteousness. But one should indeed see that this solemn declaration on the origin of things in general, and of man in particular, is already really in the best Jewish taste of the second and then of the first century B.C.E., for us to keep here to this limit for it.[19] Usually, however, we would

---

[18] Text in PG 28, 836ff.

[19] Cf. J. Bonsirven, *Palestinian Judaism in the Time of Jesus Christ*, trns. W. Wolf (New York: Holt, Rinehart & Winston, 1964 [= *Le Judaisme palestinien* I, 136f]).

not expect an affirmation as pronounced as that of the *Manual*.
One finds rather the formulae analogous to that of Sirach: ἐν ὅλῃ
δυνάμει ἀγάπησον τὸν ποιήσαντά σε,[20] or of the *Testament of
Benjamin*: νῦν οὖν, τέκνα μου, καί ὑμεῖς ἀγαπήσατε κύριον τὸν
θέον τοῦ οὐρανοῦ καὶ τῆς γῆς, καὶ φυλάξατε ἐντολὰς αὐτοῦ.[21] It
is faith in the creation which is the ultimate foundation of the
moral obligation, and the thought refers instinctively to it in the
exhortation to keep the commandments. One should not then consider the very brief allusion of the *Duae viae* to be negligible:
primo diliges deum aeternum qui te fecit (1:2). One could be sure,
on the contrary, that it was considered as a capital affirmation
which actually justified all the rest. Thus, one should not allow
oneself to be deceived by a superficial consideration of the texts:
the *Duae viae* and the instruction of the *Manual* begin indeed from
the same characteristic point of the faith of Israel, and if the feature is not unique to the teaching of the Community of the
Covenant, it is not however without literary significance, and that
is all that matters here.

But what follows is much more marked. In the instruction of
the *Manual*, just as there are two lineages of humanity, there are
also two qualities of moral ways: the way of light and the way of
darkness; inspired by two opposing spirits: the spirit of faithfulness and the spirit of falsehood; presided over by two hostile
angels: the prince of light and the prince of darkness; leading
respectively to life or to death (3:18-23, to which one could add
for the final point 4:6-8, 11-14). This is the framework which
determines the whole development until the end. But, except for
the two spirits of faithfulness and falsehood, this framework is
found identically in the *Duae viae* and it plays, though indeed
more discretely, the same literary role: two ways of life and
death, of light and darkness, to which have been appointed two
angels: an angel of righteousness and an angel of iniquity (1:1).
But, before drawing any conclusion, let us examine it in detail.

One must first recognize that the image of the two ways, to
symbolize the choice of the conscience between virtue and vice,
does not permit any literary inference in itself. It is found already
in Jeremiah 21:8 and it was current in the Judaism contemporary
with our documents.[22] It is actually universal: it suffices to cite
here, for the Greek world, the celebrated myth of Hercules at the
crossroads.[23] But our texts are far from holding to this element

---

[20] *Sir* 7:30; from our point of view, we should re-read all of ch. 39.

[21] *TestBenj* 3:1 (Charles, p. 216); cf. from an equally decisive point of view the
recompenses promised to the one faithful to the commandments in 2 Macc 7:23; 4
Macc 5:25.

[22] *TestAsh* 1:5-9 (Charles, pp. 172ff); 2 Enoch 30:15.

[23] For other examples see R. Knopf, *Die Lehre der zwölf Apostel. Die zwei
Clemensbriefe* (Tübingen: Mohr, 1920 [HNT.E 1]) pp. 4f.

which, in itself, could be neutral. The double qualification of each
of the ways: light and darkness, life and death (the latter explicitly
in the *Duae viae*, implicitly in the *Manual*), constitutes an indication of literary relations already much less equivocal: way of light
and way of darkness is found in 2 Enoch 30:15; way of life and
way of death in Jeremiah 21:8, but nowhere else, to my knowledge, are they united as in the *Duae viae* and the *Manual of Discipline*. If one adds to this now the two angels set over each of the
ways, one could no longer think that the similarities could be for-
tuitous. Finally, and this, taken with the rest, seems to me to be
decisive: it is not only metaphors and ideas which are identical in
each, but it is a literary framework which determines the whole
development of the two texts. Facts so clearly determined are
inexplicable, unless one admits a certain literary relation between
the *Duae viae* and the moral instruction of the *Manual of Discipline*.

That is not all. One could raise again more characteristic
similarities between the two texts, and always at points which
define their common literary framework. Thus, to the beginning
of the *Duae viae*: "*viae duae sunt in saeculo*" (1:1), corresponds
the beginning of the description of the ways of the two spirits in
the *Manual*: "These then are their ways in the world (בתבל)"
(4:2; cf. 6). The Latin *Duae viae* is the only one of all the recensions to have preserved this "*in saeculo*". But it has all the air of
being original, and also of echoing the בתבל of the *Manual of Discipline*. Of course, the detail is in itself a very banal matter, and I
would not have raised it if it had not been linked on both sides to
more important elements of the literary framework of the two
writings. In this respect it does not appear to be without significance.

The *Manual*, at the end of the description of each of the
ways, briefly develops the theme of retribution (4:6-8 and 11-14).
The *Duae viae* simplifies all this still further, but at least it refers
to it, and this is already significant. The theme of rewards promised to those who observe the commandments, goes to the end of
the writing to serve it as a conclusion: "*haec in consulendo si cottidie feceris, prope eris uiuo deo; quodsi non feceris, longe eris a
ueritate. haec omnia tibi in animo pone et non deceperis de spe
tua, sed per haec sancta certamina pervenies ad coronam*" (6:4f).
When one has read the instruction of the *Manual*, the "*sancta
certamina*" of the *Duae viae* are not surprising to us (cf. in particular 1QS 4:23f), and even less the "crown", which is explicitly
named in the same context (1QS 4:7). The theme of the chastise-
ments is abbreviated in the same way as the theme of rewards in

the *Duae viae*, but it is not completely absent: it introduces the
way of death: "*mortis autem uia est illi* (the way of death) *contraria, primum nequam et maledictis plena*" (5:1).

Nevertheless, there remain some secondary difficulties,
which must not be passed over in silence. I am depending on the
Latin *Duae viae* to compare the texts. If one excludes the title and
the final doxology, of which the adventitious character is evident,
this recension does not seem to have been subjected to serious
retouches. But it would require a long and minute examination to
show it. We must content ourselves here with confirming two particular readings in the recension of Barnabas, which is not a very
reliable witness when it is alone, but in which one can place one's
confidence when it is supported by others. Thus, the qualification
of the two ways as *lucis et tenebrarum* (1:1) is absent from the
Didache, from the *Epitomes of the Ecclesiastical Canons* and the
Ecclesiastical Canons themselves. It is found, however, in
Barnabas, who has not invented it as by chance.[24] One must say
the same for the angels set over each of the ways, except that
Barnabas this time takes his habitual liberty with his source: the
angel of righteousness and the angel of iniquity have become for
him the φωταγωγοὶ ἄγγελοι τοῦ θεοῦ and the ἄγγελοι τοῦ
σατανᾶ (18:1). Moreover, the two angels who watch over each of
the ways are not described in exactly the same terms as in the
Duae viae and the *Manual of Discipline*. For the latter it is the
"Prince of lights" and the "Angel of darkness" (3:20f), while for
the *Duae viae* it is the "*(angelus) aequitatis*" and the "*(angelus)
iniquitatis*" (1:1). But the divergence is more apparent than real,
for the "Prince of lights (שֹׂר אורים)" is actually put in charge of
the "sons of righteousness (בני צדק)" and the "Angel of darkness
(מלאך חושך)" in charge of the "sons of iniquity (בני עול)", which,
simplified, suggests quite naturally the angel of "righteousness"
and the angel of "iniquity", or perversion, of the *Duae viae*.
Moreover, it suits our purpose to make, with respect to this particular divergence, a more general remark. One could ask oneself
whether the moral instruction of the *Manual of Discipline* has ever
intended to impose itself itself in a form *ne varietur* to the "master
of initiation". Is it necessary to repeat that we must take care not
to project into antiquity, and above all perhaps into Jewish antiquity, our modern understanding of the transmission of texts and of
literary propriety? There has, doubtless, been space for many

---

[24] It is not absolutely impossible, moreover, that the double qualification: "life
and death, light and darkness", which characterises the Latin *Duae viae* among all
the recensions, is the result of the encounter of two distinct currents in the transmission which carry the one or the other. But one could admit it without the indications
of literary relationship which we have raised being perceptibly weakened.

modifications of the received composition. It would have been natural to think that the usage would have pretty nearly succeeded in fixing the framework but that a considerable freedom was operative for the rest. In this genre of literature especially, the transmission has always had the tendency to create new recensions. Without leaving the circles of writings which occupy us, one has only to think of the history of the *Duae viae* in Christian literature. Few writings have been more muddled from the "Didachist" and Barnabas to the panegyrist of Shenoude, leaving aside the obstinate revisers of the *Ecclesiastical Canons*. For those who have familiarized themselves a little with this literary genre, there is nothing surprising in the fact that it should be above all the framework and the general line of development of the moral instruction of the *Manual of Discipline* which is found in the *Duae viae*: this is rather appropriate in the order of things.

The accumulation of points of literary connection, which have been raised between these two writings, leaves little place for doubt then. The first owes to the second the entire framework of its construction. The *Duae viae* is only a variation on a known theme. Where has its author taken it from? One would not know what to say. It is not impossible that he himself belonged to the "Community of the Covenant". But it is not necessary to go that far. It suffices that he must have come into contact with it, or that he has only known part of its special writings. The instruction which we read in the collection of the *Manual of Discipline* is moreover only loosely tied to it. It could, then, have circulated by itself, especially since it had a more general interest than that of the rule properly speaking. A Jew who knew Hebrew and Greek could have mastered it, while making use of the idea in a way which, while respecting entirely a literary framework established by usage, was original in his treatment of particular precepts. The more so since, according to all appearances, the *Duae viae* was originally written in Greek and not in Hebrew. It was probably not destined for the "Community of the Covenant". Did it not then come out of it previously, before entering another milieu? That would explain in a positive way how it has been deprived of its eschatological material and its doctrine of the spirits to take on the genre of moral exhortation of which we have typical examples in the *Testaments of the Twelve Patriarchs*. Compared to the instruction of the *Manual of Discipline* this is in every way a step towards universality. Must one think moreover that the *Duae viae* originally had proselytes in mind? It has often been proposed with respect to the *Didache* when one sought a Jewish origin for its *Duae viae*. But it goes without saying that such an intention has not proved entirely convincing.

But be that as it may for the moment with regard to this particular matter, a first indirect consequence becomes clear from the totality of observations made and the conclusions drawn: that is that there is less chance than ever that Barnabas was the author of the *Duae viae*, as Robinson proposed. How then do we get back from the Latin *Duae viae* of Schlecht to that of the *Didache*, then to that of Barnabas, then finally to that of the *Manual of Discipline*? One might as well say immediately that it is impossible. The recension most closely related to the prime source by its internal characteristics would then be at the same time the most distant in date and most indirectly derived. And, indeed, the literary problem of the *Didache* is not settled by all this, but the least that one could say is that it comes close to solving the impasse in which it was locked up by attributing the primitive *Duae viae* to Barnabas.

A second consequence concerns the moral instruction of the *Manual of Discipline*. It seems to me that a resumption of the whole textual and literary problem of the *Didache* would show, on the one hand, with a high degree of probability, if not certainty, that the *Duae viae* which is incorporated in it, must have been in circulation in Syria-Palestine from the first half of the first century of our era. On the other hand, there is hardly any place for entertaining seriously the hypothesis that the moral instruction of the *Manual of Discipline* could have been derived from the *Duae viae*, rather than the other way round. Clearly one could always think that a common source has been used in two different ways. But that remains a simple possibility. As long as it is without support, it could not prevail against this positive fact: as far as its literary framework is concerned, the *Duae viae* is easily explained by the existence of such a writing as the moral instruction of the *Manual of Discipline*. The conclusion is self-evident. One must take care, however, that it is limited: it only applies directly to the moral instruction of the *Manual*, not to the entire collection; obviously, it also only applies to its text and not to the manuscript which conveys it to us. What one can say is that the moral instruction of the *Manual of Discipline* is not a late text, that it must already have been known at a date at least as early as the turn of the Common Era.

AN ASPECT OF THE JUDEO-CHRISTIAN ETHIC: THE TWO WAYS

WILLY RORDORF

Neuchâtel

It is well known that the *Didache*, discovered by P. Bryennios and published by him in 1883, opens with this phrase: "There are two ways, one of life and one of death." The teaching of the two ways, which is an ethical teaching, essentially takes up chapters 1-5 of the writing.[1] Very soon, people began to designate it as a *manual of the Two Ways*,[2] as *die beiden Wege*[3] or *zwei Wege*,[4] or more simply as the *duae viae*.[5] The teaching of the two ways, preserved in different forms in many Christian writings of the first centuries,[6] has not ceased exciting the curiosity of scholars. The research undertaken over almost a century has, among other things, concentrated on two problems: 1. The question of the provenance of the *duae viae*; 2. The question of the *Sitz im Leben* of the *duae viae*; to which I intend to add a third problem, that of the *Nachleben* of the *duae viae* in Christianity which, it seems to me, has been somewhat neglected. In what follows, I allow myself to take up each of these problems, one after the other; I apply myself to take account of past research and to draw the conclusions indicated by the present research.

I. THE QUESTION OF THE PROVENANCE OF THE DUAE VIAE[7]

The resemblance between *Didache* 1-5 and the *Epistle of Barnabas* 18-20 already struck the first editor of the *Didache*. At

---

[1] For the moment we leave aside the question as to whether or not chapter 6 forms the conclusion of the *duae viae*, or whether chapter 16 also originally belongs to the *duae viae* (cf. below, nn. 32, 36, and p. [10]).

[2] So C. Taylor, *The Teaching of the Twelve Apostles with illustrations from the Talmud* (Cambridge: Deighton Bell, 1886).

[3] So A. Harnack, *Die Apostellehre und die jüdischen beiden Wege* (Leipzig: J. C. Hinrichs, 1886, 1896²).

[4] So R. Knopf, *Die Lehre der zwölf Apostel. Die zwei Clemensbriefe* (Tübingen: Mohr, 1920 [HNT.E 1]).

[5] The *Doctrina apostolorum*, known already in part in 1884, begins in fact with the words: *Viae duae sunt in saeculo, uitae et mortis...*

[6] Apart from *Did* 1-5, one must point especially to *Barn* 18-20, *Doctr*, *EccCan* 4-13 and *EpEccCan*, *Const* VII.1-18, *Vie de Chenoute* (Arabic), and various Pseudo-Athanasian texts. Cf. S. Giet, *L'énigme de la Didachè* (Paris: Ophrys, 1970 [PFLUS 149]) pp. 19-26.

[7] One finds summaries of the history of research in J.-P. Audet, *La Didachè. Instructions des apôtres* (Paris: Gabalda, 1958 [ÉBib]) pp. 2-21; P. Prigent-R.A. Kraft, *Épître de Barnabé* (Paris: Les Éditions du Cerf, 1971 [SC 172]) pp. 12-20. Cf. also A. Turck, *Évangélisation et catéchèse aux deux premiers siècles*, 1962.

first, people thought there were only two possible solutions to the problem: either the *Didache* follows the *Epistle of Barnabas* in the *duae viae* section (so Bryennios, Harnack), or the other way round, and *Barnabas* here depends on the *Didache* (so Zahn, Funk). It was C. Taylor[8] who advanced the hypothesis of a common source which he believed to be Jewish; Harnack was won over to his point of view.[9]

Since the complete text of the *Doctrina apostolorum* has been known and published,[10] there is a new problem to be resolved: is it a translation of the *Didache* or an independent text which was even closer to the supposed common source of *Didache* and *Barnabas*? The second response seems more plausible.[11] But it has not helped to determine whether the common source was of Christian or Jewish provenance.

A fervent defender of the Jewish origin of the *duae viae* was A. Seeberg. In several publications,[12] he tried to prove the existence of a primitive Christian catechism containing the two ways, instructions concerning food (cf. *Did* 6!), instructions concerning baptism, prayer, the eucharist (cf. *Did* 7-10!) and a doctrinal teaching, in imitation of the catechism that the Jews used to initiate their proselytes, and which was inspired partly by the "Holiness Code" (Lev 17ff).[13] Because of their boldness, these theses of Seeberg have not found the hearing that they deserve;[14] the fact remains that P. Carrington[15] and, following him, E.G. Selwyn[16] were clearly inspired by him in their much better known

---

[8] *Teaching of the Twelve Apostles*; before Harnack, so it seems, J. Wordsworth, "Christian Life, Ritual and Discipline at the Close of the First Century", *The Guardian*, London, 19 March 1884, Supp., cited by J.-P. Audet, *Didachè*, p. 12, n. 3.

[9] *Apostellehre*; cf. *Die Apostellehre*, in RPThK I (1896³) pp. 723ff; *Didache*, in *The New Schaff-Herzog Encyclopaedia of Religious Knowledge* III (1909) p. 423.

[10] By J. Schlecht, *Doctrina XII apostolorum* (Freiburg im Breisgau: Herder, 1901); cf. L. Wohleb, *Die lateinische Übersetzung der Didache kritisch und sprachlich untersucht* (Paderborn: Schöningh, 1913 [SGKA 7]).

[11] Cf. E. Hennecke, "Die Grundschrift der Didache und ihre Rezensionen", *ZNW* 2 (1901) pp. 58-72; E.J. Goodspeed, "The Didache, Barnabas and the Doctrina", *ATR* 27 (1945) pp. 228-247; B. Altaner, "Zum Problem der lateinischen Doctrina apostolorum", *VgChr* 6 (1952) pp. 1-47.

[12] *Der Katechismus der Urchristenheit* (Leipzig: A. Deichert, 1903); *Das Evangelium Christi* (Leipzig: A. Deichert, 1905); *Die beiden Wege und das Aposteldekret* (Leipzig: A. Deichert, 1906); *Die Didache des Judentums und der Urchristenheit* (Leipzig: A. Deichert, 1908).

[13] G. Klein, *Der älteste christliche Katechismus und die jüdische Propaganda-Literatur* (Berlin: G. Reimer, 1909), goes still further: according to him, all the Christian moral teaching rests in actual fact on Gen 6:12 and Ps 34 (33)!

[14] Cf. F. Hahn, in his introduction to the book, *Der Katechismus der Urchristenheit* reprinted in 1966; cf. also A. Turck, *Evangélisation*, pp. 20ff.

[15] *The Primitive Christian Catechism. A Study in the Epistles* (Cambridge: Cambridge University Press, 1940).

[16] *The First Epistle of St. Peter* (London: Macmillan, 1947²) Essay II, pp. 363-466.

work on the primitive Christian catechism; but these two authors
have not included the *duae viae* in their research (at least not
directly).

After Seeberg, the question of provenance—Jewish or
Christian—of the *duae viae* has not been much in the foreground.
This disinterest is due to J.A. Robinson who, since 1912,[17] took
up again the thesis of the first editors of the *Didache*, namely that
the *duae viae* of the *Didache* depends on that of the *Epistle of
Barnabas* since the latter is an integral part of the *whole* Epistle
which forms a literary unity. Robinson has been followed by the
majority of scholars.[18] In one stroke, the problem of the
provenance of the *duae viae* seemed to be resolved: it was quite
simply the creation of the author of the *Epistle of Barnabas*. Few
were the critical voices who dared to say that the problem of the
possible common source for *Barnabas* and the *Didache* remained
completely unanswered.[19]

The discoveries of Qumran forced scholars to return to the
problem left suspended. In fact, the *Manual of Discipline* (3:13-
4:26) contains an instruction on the two spirits which resembles at
many points the *duae viae* that we find in the *Epistle of Barnabas*
and in the *Didache*; it even seems that the form of the *duae viae*
represented by the *Doctrina apostolorum* is closer to it, which
confirmed, after the event, the warning given long ago by Hennecke, Goodspeed, Altaner.[20] Audet has the merit of having been
the first to turn to this problem and to have shown in detail that
the Christian *duae viae* must have depended, in one way or
another, on his Qumran model.[21] His demonstration has found a
largely positive response.[22] Daniélou, in various publications,[23]

---

[17] "The Problem of the Didache", *JTS* 13 (1912) pp. 339-356; cf. *Barnabas,
Hermas and the Didache* (London: SPCK, 1920); "The Epistle of Barnabas and the
Didache", *JTS* 35 (1934) pp. 113-146; 225-248.

[18] Besides J. Muilenburg, *The Literary Relations of the Epistle of Barnabas and
the Teaching of the Twelve Apostles* (Marburg: no publisher given, 1929); R.H.
Connolly, "The Didache in Relation to the Epistle of Barnabas", *JTS* 33 (1932) pp.
237-253; "The Didache and Montanism", *DRev* 55 (1937) pp. 477-489;
F.E.Vokes, *The Riddle of the Didache. Fact or Fiction, Heresy or Catholicism?*
(London: SPCK, 1938). M. Vokes has recently said to me that he no longer holds
his thesis of the Montanist origin of the *Didache*.

[19] J.-P. Audet (*op. cit.*, pp. 20f) cites the following names: J.V. Bartlet, B.
Capelle, A.J. McLean, C.H. Turner, B.H. Streeter, J.M. Creed, Th. Klauser.

[20] Cf. n. 11.

[21] Cf. his article, "Affinités littéraires et doctrinales du *Manuel de discipline*",
RB 59 (1952) pp. 219-238; and his weighty commentary on the *Didache* (*op.cit.*),
pp. 121-163.

[22] Cf. the most recent editions of the *Didache* and the *Epistle of Barnabas*, in
R.A. Kraft, *Barnabas and the Didache* (New York: Thomas Nelson & Sons, 1965
[AF 3]), and P. Prigent & R.A. Kraft, *Épître de Barnabé* (Paris: Les Éditions du
Cerf, 1971 [SC 172]). Cf. also J. Liebaert, *Les enseignements moraux des Pères
apostoliques*, 1970, pp. 99f.

has shown the same point of view. S. Wibbing[24] has supported this thesis in proving that the Christian lists of vices and virtues depends on the same section of the *Manual of Discipline* from Qumran. In his turn, E. Kamlah[25] has uncovered the *religionsgeschichtlich* background of this form of paraenesis in the writing of late Judaism and early Christianity.

Light thus seems to have been cast on the provenance of the *duae viae*: it issued from a dualistic Essene tradition and has made its way into Christianity.[26] However, there are still questions which pose themselves and which future research must take into consideration if it wishes to come to solid established results. Here are the questions:

1. One must not lose the unique perspective that the comparison between the *Manual of Discipline* from Qumran and the different forms of the Christian *duae viae* brings concerning the *dualistic framework* (which is absent in the *Didache*!) and concerning the general literary genre of instruction which places side by side a list of virtues and a list of vices; but in the detail of content and vocabulary, resemblances are missing. Moreover, if Audet is to be believed, the *duae viae* of the *Didache* was addressed "to the Gentiles"[27] and consequently is situated in a universalist and not in a particularist orientation (as in Qumran). One is then forced to admit, with Audet,[28] that "the *duae viae* has known, doubtless in

---

[23] Cf. for example, "Une source de la spiritualité chrétienne dans les manuscrits de la Mer Morte: la doctrine des deux esprits", *DViv* 25 (1953) pp. 127ff; *The Dead Sea Scrolls and Primitive Christianity*, trns. S. Athanasio (Baltimore, Md: Helicon, 1958) pp. 41ff; *The Theology of Jewish Christianity* I (London: Darton, Longman & Todd, 1964) pp. 28ff, 315ff; and again more recently, *La catéchèse aux premiers siècles* (1968) pp. 127ff.

[24] *Die Tugend- und Lasterkataloge im Neuen Testament* (Berlin: de Gruyter, 1959 [BZNW 25].

[25] *Die Form der katalogischen Paränese im Neuen Testament* (Tübingen: Mohr, 1964 [WUNT 7]). Cf. previously A. Wlosok, *Laktanz und die philosophische Gnosis* (Heidelberg, 1960 [Abh. HAW, Philhist. Kl.2]) pp. 107ff.

[26] H. Braun, *Qumran und das Neue Testament* II (Tübingen: Mohr, 1966), pp. 184ff, 286ff, summarizes the discussion in a very nuanced and competent manner. According to E. Robillard ("L'Epître de Barnabé: trois époques, trois théologies, trois rédacteurs", *RB* 78 (1971) pp. 184-209), it was Barnabas, the companion of Paul, who took up the Jewish *duae viae* for his own missionary purposes!

[27] In fact, J.-P. Audet, *Didachè*, pp. 91ff, places confidence in the long title of the writing which he believes would have had, in a Jewish milieu, the following sense: Διδαχὴ κυρίου (= God!) τοῖς ἔθνεσιν.

[28] *Didachè*, p. 158. So too Prigent in Prigent & Kraft, *Épître de Barnabé*, p. 20. Cf. the critical remarks of F. E. Vokes, "The Didache—Still debated", *ChQR* 3 (1970) pp. 58f, 62.

the first period of its history (pre-Christian?), a very active
recensional phase."

2. On the whole, the relationship between the *Manual of Discipline* and the *duae viae*, dazzling because recently discovered,
does not seem to be much closer than one had established, before
the "new wave" from Qumran, between Jewish proselyte
catechetical instruction and the *duae viae* that one believed to be a
Christian catechetical instruction.[29] Although we might be poorly
informed on the baptism of Jewish proselytes in the primitive
Christian epoch, the parallels which it presents to Christian baptism are undeniable.[30] Future research must not neglect this aspect
of the problem.

3. There is another matter: that is the Old Testament background
of the *duae viae*. I am not thinking here of the allusions to the
theme of the two ways which are found in the Old Testament, but
I am thinking of the very specific genre of the *Bundesformular*
which K. Baltzer[31] has revealed in certain Biblical texts, and that
he has uncovered, in new forms, precisely in the *Manual of Discipline* at Qumran and the Christian *duae viae*. One must be careful to take this view of things seriously in future.[32]

Given the complexity of the problem of the provenance of the
duae viae, one should above all avoid simplistic, unilateral solutions; it does not seem, in fact, that the *duae viae* (in *all* its forms)

---

[29] Cf. in particular A. Benoît, *Le baptême chrétien au second siècle* (Paris:
Presses Universaires du France, 1953) pp. 5-33, but also D. Daube, *The New Testament and Rabbinic Judaism* (London: University of London Athalone, 1956), pp.
106ff. The Golden Rule and the Household Code incorporated into the *duae viae*
are also situated rather in this context: cf. A. Dihle, *Die goldene Regel* (Göttingen:
Vandenhoeck & Ruprecht, 1962 [StAW 7]), and D. Schroeder, *Die Haustafeln des
Neuen Testamentes* (Thesis, Hamburg, 1959). A. Adam ("Erwägungen zur Herkunft
der Didache", *ZKG* 68 [1957] pp. 30ff), is very specific: he sees in the *duae viae*
the catechetical manual of the Jewish proselytes of Adiabene.

[30] M. Dujarier (*Le parrainage des adultes aux trois premiers siècles de l'Eglise*,
1962) while dealing entirely with the possible background in Qumran (pp. 103ff),
has not ignored this problem (pp. 73ff). Cf. also J. Jeremias, *Infant Baptism in the
First Four Centuries*, trns. D. Cairns (London: SCM, 1958) pp. 28ff.

[31] *Das Bundesformular* (Neukirchen, Vluyn: Neukirchner Verlag, 1964[2]
[WMANT 4]). Cf. the good summary in French in J. L'Hour, *La morale de
l'alliance*, in CahRB 5 (1966). See also J. Becker, *Untersuchungen zur Entstehungsgeschichte der Testamente der zwölf Patriarchen* (Leiden: Brill, 1970).

[32] E. Kamlah, *Paränese*, p. 163 n. 1, has made the criticism very easily! We
should note, however, that the two authors agree in saying that chapter 16 of the
Didache belongs to the primitive *duae viae*. Cf. H. Köster, *Synoptische
Überlieferung bei den apostolischen Vätern* (Berlin: Akademie-Verlag, 1957 [Tu
65]) pp. 160, 173, 189f, and R.A. Kraft, *Barnabas and the Didache*, pp. 12ff.

comes from Qumran, nor that it is derived uniquely from the instruction given to Jewish proselytes, nor again that it was a late expression of the covenant morality rooted in the *Bundesformular*. By way of hypothesis, I see the evolution rather in the following manner: the Old Testament ethical tradition attached to the *Bundesformular* has undergone in certain circles of late Judaism (not in all) a clearly dualistic modification under Persian influence (in this area, I freely follow Kamlah). Christianity has inherited both these currents, dualistic and non-dualistic. In the New Testament, we find both these traditions.[33] Is it not possible that the different forms of the Christian *duae viae* also reflect the *two* traditions? From this point of view, the *Doctrina apostolorum* and the *Epistle of Barnabas* take their place in the *dualistic* lineage of moral instruction that is found in the *Manual of Discipline*, while the *Didache* and the documents derived from it represent the non-dugalistic lineage of moral instruction which was formed in the course of the history of Israel and which has passed into the sapiential and synagogal teaching of Judaism (and eventually into the catechism given to proselytes).[34] A study of the question of the *Sitz im Leben* will, perhaps, provide us with further light on this subject.[35]

II. THE QUESTION OF THE SITZ IM LEBEN OF THE DUAE VIAE

In *Didache* 7:1 we read as follows: "On the subject of baptism, baptize thus: after having taught all which precedes ($\tau\alpha\hat{\upsilon}\tau\alpha$ $\pi\acute{\alpha}\nu\tau\alpha$ $\pi\rho o\varepsilon\iota\pi\acute{o}\nu\tau\varepsilon\varsigma$), baptize in the name of the Father and of the Son and of the Holy Spirit." The words $\tau\alpha\hat{\upsilon}\tau\alpha$ $\pi\acute{\alpha}\nu\tau\alpha$ $\pi\rho o\varepsilon\iota\pi\acute{o}\nu\tau\varepsilon\varsigma$ must refer back to chapter 1-5(6)[36] of the *Didache*, which contains

---

[33] Roughly (I take this with a grain of salt!), the synoptic gospels represent the non-dualistic tradition, while the Johannine and Pauline literature reflects the dualistic tradition.

[34] Cf. Audet, *op.cit.*, pp. 255f. R.A. Kraft (*Barnabas and the Didache*, p. 136) places the accent on the criteria of eschatological intensity to distinguish between the traditions; he comes close to my point of view. In my opinion, however, the criterion of the presence or absence of the dualistic framework goes more to the heart of the problem.

[35] It is quite useless to try to say what the exact *content* of the pre-Christian *duae viae* was. Of course, the "gospel section" (*Did* 1:3-2:1) was not included. Giet (*op.cit.* (n. 6), pp. 153ff) wishes to be more specific: the Jewish *duae viae* did not contain the *double* love commandment, nor the "instruction of the wise" (*Did* 3:1-6), nor even (possibly) the way of death. There is no space here to discuss this thesis. As far as the double love commandment is concerned, cf. the implicit critique of C. Burchard in *Der Ruf Jesu und die Antwort der Gemeinde, Festschrift für Joachim Jeremias*, ed. E. Lohse (Göttingen: Vandenhoeck & Ruprecht, 1970) pp. 39-62.

[36] *Didache* 6:1 seems to be the end of the *duae viae*. However, the precept concerning foods (6:3) has its roots in an equally ancient tradition; cf. the apostolic

properly the *duae viae*. Consequently, the first editors of the
Didache, Bryennios and Harnack, thought that the *duae viae* was
without doubt a part of the *catechetical* teaching preparatory to
baptism, in the milieu from which the writing emerged.[37] At first
this interpretation was unanimously accepted by the scholarly
world. It was Audet who first, as far as I know, questioned this
assumption.[38] He begins with the observation that the words
ταῦτα πάντα προειπόντες are only found in the manuscript discovered in Constantinople (from A.D. 1056) and in the Georgian
version, but not in the remains of the *Didache* in book VII of the
Apostolic Constitutions, from the end of the fourth century. He
can see only one possible explanation for this fact: the compiler
of the *Apostolic Constitutions* did not find the words in question in
the text of the *Didache* which he used. Moreover, he sees in the
words ταῦτα πάντα προειπόντες a stylistically awkward insertion
into the text from a second hand, which he does not hesitate to
omit from his edition of the Greek text.[39] This particular reading
of the manuscript from Constantinople would then be a gloss of a
copyist, who reflected the usage of the Egyptian church, to
appropriate the *duae viae* for the instruction of catechumens.[40]

The thesis of Audet is very fragile. As far as the question of
the style of the *Didache* is concerned, P. Nautin[41] has already
shown it. One could also remark that the style of the "addition"
does not seem strange to the manner of expression of the editor of
the *Didache*, since he utilizes in 11:1 a formula virtually identical:
ταῦτα πάντα τὰ προειρημένα. But what is more serious, is that
Audet does not even ask the question whether the compiler of

---

decree which is reflected , in an archaic form and in a catechetical context in the
Pseudo-Clementines; cf. on this subject the work of E. Molland, in *Opuscula
Patristica* (1970), pp. 25-60; A.F.J. Klijn, in *NT* 10 (1978) pp. 305-312; M.
Simon, in *BJRL* 52 (1969-1970) pp. 437-460; and Y. Tissot, in *RB* 77 (1970) pp.
321-346. One could even ask the question as to whether *Didache* 6:2-3 does not
show that the *duae viae* is addressed originally to the God-Fearers (cf. the Noachic
precepts of the Rabbinic tradition: Billerbeck III, 36ff); this is the thesis of M.
Simon (cf. already J.-P Audet, *op.cit.*, p. 354, and A. Stuiber, "Das ganze Joch des
Herrn (Didache 6,2-3)" in *Studia Patristica* IV, ed. F. L. Cross (Berlin: Akademie-
Verlag, 1961 [TU 79]) pp. 323-329). But, in Christianity, the unit of 6:2-3 belongs
rather to an ascetic tradition: cf. below, pp. 161f.

[37] A. Harnack (*Did Lehre der zwölf Apostel* [Leipzig: J. C. Hinrichs Verlag,
1884 (TU 2,1-2)] p. 22) leaves open the question of whether it was a matter of a
baptismal discourse immediately preceding baptism or of actual catechetical instruction.

[38] *Didachè*, pp. 58ff; cf. p. 358f.

[39] *Ibid.*, p. 232.

[40] Cf. Athanasius, *EpFest* 39, but also *Ce* 12.

[41] "La composition de la "Didache" et son titre." *RHR* 78 (1959) pp. 206f. Cf.
also B. Botte, in *BTAM* 8 (1958) pp. 168.

the *Apostolic Constitutions* could not have had an interest in changing the text of the *Didache* for the reason that *in his time and in his church* the *duae viae* was no longer used for the instruction of catechumens.[42] One has the impression that this is the right answer when one reads an account of the baptismal catechesis in the *Apostolic Constitutions* VII.39ff.

If the critique of *Didache* 7:1 by Audet seems unjustified, then,[43] the question of the *Sitz im Leben* of the *duae viae* is not resolved for all that. In fact, it remains true that the *duae viae* was not used exclusively in catechesis preparatory to baptism. Proof is provided by the *Epistle of Barnabas*: in all probability it was addressed to Christians already baptized;[44] at the end it takes them back to the teaching of the two ways.[45] In the *Didache*, the *duae viae* then has its place in prebaptismal teaching; in the *Epistle of Barnabas*, on the contrary, it has its place in postbaptismal teaching. Can we speak about it any longer as a *pre*baptismal ethical instruction and its *Sitz im Leben*?

Let us first pose a preliminary but important question: to whom was the *duae viae* addressed? To Jewish-Christians? Or to Gentile-Christians? Can the titles of the *Didache* give us the information we want? In fact, the manuscript of Constantinople carries two titles: "*Didache* of the Twelve Apostles" and "*Didache* of the Lord to the Gentiles through the Twelve Apostles." It is not a matter of solving here the problem of the relation of these two titles to each other and to the rest of the writing, a problem which is very complicated.[46] It is beyond doubt, however, that the long title (which seems inspired by Mt 28:19f) intends to present the *Didache* as a teaching given to converts coming from paganism.[47] A passage of the *duae viae* itself confirms this interpretation: in *Didache* 2:2 it is said, "You shall not commit murder; you shall not commit adultery.[48] You shall not

---

[42] A linguistic indication that tends to support this assumption: why does he express himself just here in the following way: ἤδη μὲν καὶ πρότερον διεταξάμεθα?

[43] Daniélou, in his publications on the subject (cf. n. 23), has always had confidence in the text of *Did* 7:1.

[44] Cf G. Schille, "Zur urchristlichen Tauflehre. Stilistische Beobachtungen am Barnabasbrief", *ZNW* 49 (1958) pp. 31-52.

[45] Cf. the allusions to the *duae viae* in *1 & 2 Clement* and in the *Shepherd of Hermas*, thus in writings which are addressed to baptized Christians.

[46] Audet (*Didachè*, pp. 91ff) complicates it still more; cf. P. Nautin, in *RHR* 155 (1959) pp. 210ff.

[47] So already Harnack, *Die Lehre*, pp. 27ff, *contra* Bryennios.

[48] *Doct* places the sin of adultery at the beginning, following in this the order of the Decalogue in the Septuagint (cf. also Philo, *Decal* 121; Clement of Alexandria, *Protr* 108; *Paed* II.89:1). This order must be early (cf. S. Giet, *L'énigme*, p. 103). This is again an indication of the situation of origin of the *duae viae* in a milieu of "diaspora" Judaism and Christianity.

commit sodomy; you shall not commit fornication; you shall not
steal; you shall not use magic; you shall not use sorcery; you shall
not kill the child in the womb and you shall not kill the child
already born." The precepts envisaging pederasty, magic, abortion and exposure of babies, which are opposed to the commandments of the Decalogue, are more comprehensible if they are
addressed to ancient Pagans.[49] The *duae viae* seems then to have
been destined for God-fearers or proselytes in a Jewish milieu,
and to Gentile Christians in a Christian milieu.

This conclusion can help us to understand why the *Didache*
speaks of the *duae viae* as part of the catechetical instruction in
preparation for baptism. Often, in fact, one has the impression
that this testimony of the *Didache* was absolutely unprecedented in
early Christian literature. The New Testament (apart from Heb
6:1ff) does not seem to say anything to us of a prebaptismal
catechesis; most of the moral instruction of the New Testament
seems linked to post-baptismal paraenesis;[50] the accounts of baptism contained in Acts suggests to us that one was baptized
without losing any time with a preliminary catechesis. However,
we should not forget that the first baptisms were the baptisms of
Jews or God-fearers converted to Christianity. These did not have
any further need to be initiated into the morality of the Covenant,
they knew it and practised it even before they came to be
Christians. Consequently, their faith in Christ Jesus was sufficient
for them to be admitted to baptism. Quite different was the situation of those first converts from Paganism seeking baptism: it was
necessary to instruct them, prior to their baptism, in the rudiments
of ethical behaviour in accordance with faith in one God. Saint
Irenaeus, apparently knowing of this problem, writes as follows:

Wherefore also Paul, since he was the apostle of the Gentiles, says, "I
laboured more than they all" (1 Cor 15:10). For the instruction of the former, [viz., the Jews,] was an easy task...But although they who were of
the circumcision still did not obey the words of God, for they were
despisers, yet they were previously instructed not to commit adultery, nor
fornication, nor theft, nor fraud; and that whatsover things are done to our
neighbours' prejudice, were evil, and detested by God. Wherefore also
they did readily agree to abstain from these things, because they had been
thus instructed. But they were bound to teach the Gentiles also this very
thing, that the works of such a nature were wicked, prejudicial,and useless, and destructive to those who engaged in them. Wherefore he who
had received the apostolate to the Gentiles, did labour more than those
who preached the Son of God among them of the circumcision.[51]

---

[49] Cf. Audet, *Didachè*, pp. 286ff. See also *Did* 3:4.

[50] Cf. for example F. Hahn, Introduction to Seeberg, *Der Katechismus*, p.
xxviii; this is one of the criticisms he makes of the studies of A. Seeberg.

[51] *Haer* IV.24:1-2; trns. W.H. Rambaut, *The Ante-Nicene Fathers* I (Grand
Rapids, Mich.: Eerdmans), p. 495. Is there an allusion to the *duae viae* in this text?

Not only must we postulate that such was indeed the situation of the mission among the Gentiles, already in the first century, but we have indications which confirm this point of view. In addition to what Dujarier[52] has provided, with respect to the New Testament, one could cite two texts from the beginning of the second century which, in all likelihood, pre-suppose prebaptismal ethical instruction. These are the letter of Pliny the Younger, on the one hand, and a passage from the Book of Elchesai, on the other. In his well-known letter to Trajan (X.96:7, trans. in J. Stevenson, *A New Eusebius* [London: SPCK, 1957], 13), Pliny says, speaking of the Christians whom he has interrogated:

> They maintained, however, that the amount of their fault or error had been this, that it was their habit on a fixed day to assemble before daylight and recite by turns a form of words to Christ as god; and that they bound themselves with an oath, not for any crime, but not to commit theft or robbery or adultery, not to break their word, and not to deny a deposit when demanded.

According to the interpretation of this passage given by H. Lietzmann,[53] and which still remains the most plausible, the "binding oath" (sacramental) of which the text speaks, was the baptismal oath. In that case, we must suppose that an ethical instruction has preceded baptism. The same conclusion is supported by the passage of the Book of Elchesai which Hippolytus[54] as follows:

> (The one who dips himself in the water says:) "Behold, I call to witness the heaven and the water, and the holy spirits, and the angels of prayer, and the oil, and the salt, and the earth. I testify by these seven witnesses that no more shall I sin, nor commit adultery, nor steal, nor be guilty of injustice, nor be covetous, nor be actuated by hatred, nor be scornful, nor shall I take pleasure in any wicked deeds.

Although it is here a question of a second baptism, as an act of penitance, which was made by self-immersion, it is beyond doubt that it belongs strictly to the rite of first baptism.

We must add to this the testimony of the Pseudo-Clementine *Preaching of Peter*, a little later, it is true.[55] These preachings of

---

[52] *Le parrainage*, pp. 117ff. Cf. J. Daniélou, *La catéchèse*, pp. 37ff.

[53] "Die liturgischen Angaben des Pliniusbriefs", in *Geschichtliche Studien für A. Hauck zum 70. Geburtstag*, pp. 34ff.

[54] *Rev. omn. haer.*, IX.15:5-6 (ANF V, p. 133). Cf. with respect to this passage E. Peterson, *Frühkirche, Judentum und Gnosis* (Rome: Herder, 1959) pp. 221-235. G. Kretschmar (*Studien zur frühchristlichen Trinitätstheologie*, 1956, p. 212) rightly also refers to the baptism of Jewish proselytes. Cf. moreover the Ps.Clem. *Contestatio* (1:1).

[55] Cf. G. Strecker, "Die Kerygmata Petrou", in *New Testament Apocrypha* II,

Peter's are particularly interesting for our purpose since they
reflect without doubt a prebaptismal ethical teaching which proves
to be very close to the *duae viae*. We need only cite *Homily* VII:[56]
Peter preaches first to Tyre. As elsewhere,[57] it underlines the
importance of following the precepts of the Apostolic Decree and
further gives an explanation of the Golden Rule which takes up
part of the Ten Commandments (cf. *Did* 1:2; 2:2-3). After this
catechesis (the Greek text already uses the verb κατηχεῖν!) which
lasts many days, the hearers are baptized *en masse*. Peter goes on
to Sidon, where he takes up his catechetical teaching which leads
to a large number of baptisms, speaking as follows:

> But I shall not refuse to show you the way in which you must be saved.
> For I have learned from the Prophet of truth the conditions fore-ordained
> of God...Knowing, then, these good and evil deeds, I make known unto
> you as it were two paths, and I shall show you by which travellers are lost
> and by which they are saved, being guided by God. The path of the lost,
> then, is broad and very smooth—it ruins them without troubling them; but
> the path of the saved is narrow, rugged, and in the end it saves, not
> without much toil, those who have journeyed through it.[58] And these two
> paths are presided over by unbelief and faith.

I believe that it is also necessary to mention, in this context, the
baptismal rite of *abrenuntiatio*. Although it is attested explicitly
only at the end of the second century,[59] its roots must go back far
in time. In fact, it is unthinkable that one could have created, at
the end of the second century, a rite of renunciation of Satan, of
his angels and his works, a rite which expresses a very marked
eschatological dualism. This rite must be connected to a Jewish
and Jewish Christian dualistic conception, to which was attached
in its turn, as we see it, certain forms of the *duae viae*. But the
right of renunciation of Satan implies the existence of a prior ethical catechesis.[60]

   That is to say that there was, without doubt, an uninterrupted
tradition of prebaptismal ethical instruction in the Christian church
of the first two centuries, a tradition which has its roots in

---

ed.   E. Hennecke & W. Schneemelcher (Philadelphia: Westminster, 1965) pp.
102ff.

[56] One could also cite *Hom* XI and XVIII.

[57] Cf. the works mentioned in note 36. The translation given is from ANF VIII,
269.

[58] The influence of Mt 7:13f is obvious here.

[59] Cf. H. Kirsten, *Die Taufabsage*, 1960; G. Kretschmar, in *Leiturgia* 5 (1970)
pp. 72, 96ff.

[60] Tertullian, *De cor.* 3:2 tells us, moreover, that the first renunciation was
already made some time before the baptism. To this should be added the testimony
of Justin, *1Apol* 64 (cf. also *2 Clem* 17:1).

Judaism, which has its *Sitz im Leben* in the context of the intiation of Gentile converts, and which led to the institution of the Christian catechumenate at the end of the second century. The *duae viae* has its place in this tradition.[61]

To end this section, I would like again to make a plea. The interest in "catechetical" traditions in the nascent church has grown appreciably in these last few years. One asks about the catechetical structure of the Sermon on the Mount,[62] one looks for it in the Synoptic Gospels in their entireties;[63] likewise, one studies again, after Carrington and Selwyn, the catechetical elements in the epistolary paraenesis of the New Testament.[64] But one generally forgets to specify whether one is speaking of pre- or post-baptismal catechesis. It would be wise, it seems to me, to distinguish these things more, and to reserve the term catechesis for the instruction which one is sure was given *before* baptism. The application of a certain methodical rigour in this domain would clarify the situation and would, at the same time, I am convinced, cast new light on the ethical instruction prior to baptism.[65]

III. THE NACHLEBEN OF THE DUAE VIAE
IN CHRISTIANITY

In the first decades which followed the discovery of the *Didache*, people turned up all the passages in the Christian literature of the

---

[61] It is difficult to say whether one can compare the Christian catechumenate and the Qumran "catechumenate" (affirmatively, J. Daniélou, in *RHPhR* 35, 1955, 105ff); the context is in any case very different.

[62] Cf. E. Massaux, *The Influence of the Gospel of Saint Matthew on Christian Literature before Saint Irenaeus* I (Macon, Ga.: Mercer University Press, 1990-1993); G. Bornkamm, *Überlieferung und Auslegung im Matthäusevangelium* (Neukirchen-Vluyn: Neukirchner Verlag, 1965⁴ [WMANT 1] p. 15 (Cf. *idem*, in *Mélanges Dodd*, 1956, p. 225); J. Jeremias, *The Sermon on the Mount*, trns. N. Perrin (Philadelphia: Fortress, 1963 [*Biblical Series* 2]) pp. 19ff; C.H. Dodd, "The primitive Catechism and the Sayings of Jesus", in *New Testament Essays in Memory of T.W. Manson*, 1959, pp. 106-118; W.D. Davies, *The Setting of the Sermon on the Mount* (Cambridge: Cambridge University Press, 1964) pp. 370ff; O. Hanssen, in Lohse, *Der Ruf Jesu (op.cit.)* pp. 94-111.

[63] Cf. G. Schille, in *NTS* 4 (1957-1958) pp. 1-21; 101-114.

[64] C.H. Dodd, *Gospel and Law: the Relation of Faith and Ethics in Early Christianity* (Cambridge: Cambridge University Press, 1965⁶); W. Schrage, *Die konkreten Einzelgebote in der paulinischen Paränese*, 1961; K. Wegenast, *Das Verständnis der Tradition bei Paulus und in den Deuteropaulinen* (Neukirchen-Vluyn: Neukirchner Verlag, 1962 [WMANT 8]); cf. also G. Schille, in *ZNW* 46 (1955) pp. 81ff; *ZNW* 48 (1957) pp. 270-280; *ZNW* 51 (1960) pp. 112-131; F.L. Cross, *I Peter. A Paschal Liturgy* (London: Mowbray, 1954); M.E. Boismard, in *RB* 63 (1956) pp. 182-208; *RB* 64 (1957) pp. 161-183.

[65] The close relationship between the *duae viae* of the *Didache* and the Sermon on the Mount is undeniable (cf. the works mentioned in n. 62). Do they have the same *Sitz im Leben*? Cf. also J. Daniélou, *La catéchèse aux premiers siècles*, 1968, p. 134f.

first three centuries which cited the *duae viae* or seemed to allude to it.[66] Two texts have come to be added in 1907 and 1914. These are the *Demonstration of Apostolic Preaching* of St. Irenaeus,[67] and the Sermon *De centesima, de sexagesima, de tricesima.*[68] A. Turck[69] has the honour of having made the connection between the first text and the *duae viae*. As far as the Sermon is concerned, J. Daniélou[70] has seen that it cites *Did* 6:2; we shall come back to it.

It is not my intention to add to this list of citations and allusions; moreover one cannot always say with certainty whether the allusions that one believes one has found really refer to the *duae viae*. I intend rather to study those texts of the fourth, fifth and sixth centuries which seem to me to be influenced by the *duae viae* and which noone has taken much account of. These texts show us at the same time that the *Sitz im Leben* of the *duae viae* has changed in the course of its history.

The first text to cite is the *Epitome of the Divine Institutions* of Lactantius. In chapters 53-62, where Lactantius takes up book VI of the *Divine Institutions*, *De vero culto*, the influence of the *duae viae* is undeniable.[71] In fact, we not only find allusions to one or another passage from the *duae viae*, but—what is more—we find the entire framework of the *duae viae* as it is preserved for us in the *Didache* and the *Doctrina apostolorum*. At the beginning is placed the theme of the two ways of life and death. The way of life is explained in the following way: firstly, one must love God who made us, secondly, one must love one's neighbour. Love of the neighbour is explained, in its turn, by the Golden Rule (cf. *Did/Doct* 1:1-2). One must first combat vices, then plant virtues.[72] To combat vices, one must begin by tearing up their roots in the heart: the passions (*ira, avaritia, libido*); then, one will be able to keep the Decalogue and the other

---

[66] A. Harnack, in his edition of the *Didache* (n. 37), already presented a rich dossier of parallels, but it was above all A. Seeberg who, in his various publications (cf. n. 12), assembled a vast documentation on this subject; cf. also G. Resch, *Das Aposteldecret*, 1905, pp. 92ff.

[67] Published by Ter-Mekerttschian, in TU 31/1, 1907.

[68] Published by R. Reitzenstein, "Eine frühchristliche Schrift von den dreierlei Früchten des christlichen Lebens", *ZNW* 15 (1914) pp. 60-90.

[69] *Op.cit.* (n. 7) pp. 128ff.

[70] In his review of J. Liébaert, *Les enseignements moraux des Pères apostoliques*, in *RSR* 59 (1971) p. 68. Cf. now his article in *VigChr* 25 (1971) pp. 71-81.

[71] Despite the statement to the contrary by B. Altaner, "Zum Problem", p. 162. Cf. M. Gerhardt, *Das Leben und die Schriften des Lactantius* (Erlangen Thesis), 1924, pp. 121-128.

[72] But, as Lactantius says in a formula: *primum est enim non nocere, proximum, prodesse.* Ambrose, *OfMin* I, again follows this scheme, and in this exact way, he surpasses Cicero.

Christian precepts (cf. *Did/Doct* 2-4).[73] Finally, one can pass to the Christian virtue, which is love (cf. *Did* 1:3-2:1). Of course, Lactantius develops the primitive teaching of the *duae viae* in the light of the Christian philosophy which was his own; but it is all the more interesting to establish that an ancient manual of Jewish Christian ethics could have served him as the basis to do it, because this instruction proved so substantial that it could not be abandoned, and at the same time so supple that it could be transformed in its function for the needs of a new epoch. This endeavour of Lactantius, innovator and at the same time profoundly attached to the tradition, could perhaps inspire us today when it is also a matter of reformulating the Christian ethic in a new language.[74]

A second text which I wish to cite is the sermon which is found at the end of the *Canons of Hippolytus*.[75] Canon 38, the last of the collection, bears the title: "Concerning the night when our Lord was raised: that a person should not sleep on this night and that one should bathe (previously). Concerning the person who sins after baptism, and an explanation of this; concerning the prohibition of what one must not (do), and the practice of what one must (do)." In the list of titles, at the beginning of the collection, one reads as follows: "And if anyone wishes to imitate the angels." Very quickly, the author passes over to direct discourse; this part of Canon 38 seems then to be a sermon given during the Paschal Vigil. The preacher—the moment was well chosen to do it—repeats the baptismal liturgy in order to exhort his listeners.[76] If they have rejected Satan, they must persevere, as good soldiers, in their promise, and not return to evil deeds, or else the Lord will not recognize them as his in the time of judgment: they must "Walk in the precepts of Christ." Then follows a long list "concerning the things which one must not do," a list which, in both literary genre and in content, resembles very closely the *duae viae*; it is followed, at the end, by a list of things "which one must do" which, itself, recalls the "Gospel section" of the *duae viae*. The list of things "which one must not do" finishes in this way: "If the Christian perseveres in all this, that is to say imitates Christ, he will be at his right hand, he will be sent with the angels

---

[73] It is true that *Did/Doct* do exactly the opposite of Lactantius: they first repeat the sins condemned by the Decalogue and then show those passions pushing a person to commit these sins.

[74] Cf., in a general way, the fine remarks of J. Daniélou, *La catéchèse*, pp. 170ff.

[75] Cf. the recent edition of R.-G. Coquin, in *Patrologia Orientalis* 31/2 (1966) pp. 413ff. For the editor, the *Canons of Hippolytus* has been edited in Egypt, about A.D. 340.

[76] One must suppose that there were newly baptized among them also.

and will be honoured by him; since he has taken the crown of the good, has accomplished his duty and has kept the faith, he will receive the crown of life which has been announced to those who love him,"—a passage which recalls the end of the *Doctrina apostolorum*. However, the text continues thus: "If the Christian wishes to be of angelic rank, then he shuns women once and for all and determines in his heart neither to look at them nor to eat with them. He swiftly gives away all his goods to the poor, he has the rule of the angels in humility of heart and of body." The preacher addresses himself here to a different class of Christians, who go beyond what the ordinary faithful do; these select Christians live in celibacy and are voluntarily poor, give themselves to suffering and "give themselves to death every moment, because of Christ, for the faith," as the text says. They have to undergo the three temptations of Christ, "which are gluttony, pride and covetousness." It is interesting to note that this part of the sermon has close parallels in certain monastic texts belonging to the same milieu.[77] One must add to these texts the *Syntagma doctrinae* and the Pseudo-Athanasian *Faith of the 318 Fathers* which, as is well known, incorporates summaries of the *duae viae*. There also we find these two classes of Christians, but it receives a supplement reserved to the μονάζοντες which is in the same vein as the sermon preserved in the *Canons of Hippolytus*. If one reads these texts, one is tempted to say that chapter 6 of the *Didache* to which these texts refer, reflects the same ascetic tradition; it seems that the form of the *duae viae* attested by the manuscript of Constantinople has been marked by this tradition.[78]

If we turn towards the West, we find confirmation of what we have come to see. In his explanation of the Sower (Mt 13:1ff, par.), the author of the sermon *De centesima, de sexagesima, de tricesima*[79] distinguishes three classes of Christians: the martyrs

[77] It is a matter of the Pseudo-Athanasian *Treatise on Virginity* (which has, moreover, utilized the prayers of *Did* 9-10), of the two treatises of Evagrius of Ponticus and a text of John Cassian, pointed out by R.-G. Coquin, *Patrologia*, pp. 311ff.

[78] The relationship of this manuscript with the *Liber graduum* has been noted by A. Adam, "Erwägungen", pp. 25f, by E. Peterson, *Frühkirche*, pp. 150f, and by G. Kretschmar, "Ein Beitrag zur Frage nach dem Ursprung frühchristlicher Askese", *ZThK* 61 (1964) pp. 40f (the latter links the tradition in question to itinerant Syrian ascetics; it goes back to primitive Christianity and is reflected in the Gospel of Matthew and in the Apocalypse of John). In the other texts which reproduce the *duae viae* (cf. n. 6), the equivalent of *Did* 6:2-3 is missing; *Const* VII.19-21 also omits *Did* 6:2.

[79] According to R. Reitzenstein ("Frühchristliche Schrift"), the sermon was written as early as the end of the second century in North Africa (cf. also J. Daniélou, *op.cit.*); according to D. de Bruyne, in *ZNW* 15 (1914) p. 281, it is from the third century.

who produce fruit "one hundred-fold", the ascetics who produce fruit "sixty-fold", and the chaste who produce fruit "thirty-fold". To support his point of view, he slips in on behalf of the martyrs, the citation of *scriptura* which goes as follows: *si potes quidem, fili, omnia praecepta domini facere, eris consummatus; sin autem, uel duo praecepta, amare dominum ex totis praecordiis et similem tibi quasi [te ipsum]*. The beginning is an almost literal citation of *Didache* 6:2a;[80] the end is a valuable commentary on the very obscure phrase of *Did* 6:2b: "but if not, do what you can": we now hear that "what is possible" is the double love commandment, that is to say the very contents of the *duae viae* of which it is the explanation. The author of the sermon is eager to add that the fulfilment of the double love commandment is still not perfection, but that there are various stages (*gradus*) to pass through on the way (*uia*) which leads to perfection. We are in the same perspective that we have found in the sermon at the end of the *Canons of Hippolytus*: the *duae viae* is good for the mass of believers, but the "perfect" Christian goes further in his ascetic effort and in his readiness for martyrdom.

In the sixth century, the situation has evolved still further: the *duae viae* is no longer an instruction addressed to all believers and which receives in ascetic circles a characteristic supplement, but is has become part of the monastic rule itself, both in Egypt and in the West. For Egypt we have the well-known evidence of the Arabic *Life of Shenoude*;[81] for the West we have the *Regula Benedicti*.[82] In my opinion, it is undeniable that St. Benedict, in his prologue and fourth chapter of his *Rule*, was inspired by a form of the *duae viae*. In the prologue, the master addresses the sons and instructs them, in the manner of Psalm 34 (33), the "way of life" which tells us to do good and to avoid evil; this way of health is straight and narrow, expecially at the beginning, but it leads those who persevere to eternal life. Chapter 4 gives the list of things to do and to avoid; it begins with the double love commandment and also cites the Golden Rule (cf. *Did/Doct* 1:2), then

---

[80] The only change: ὅλον τὸν ζυγόν becomes *omnia praecepta*.

[81] Cf. L.E. Iselin, in TU 13/1, 1895, p. 10f. The Arabic text is only from the seventh century, but it is the translation of a Coptic text which goes back to the sixth century, if not the fifth century. The teaching of the two ways seems moreover already to have played a rôle in the earlier cenobitic tradition: cf. the first catechesis of Pachomius, edited and translated by L.-T. Lefort, in CSCO 159, 1965², pp. 1ff and CSCO 160, 1964², pp. 1ff. By contrast, the Rules of Saint Basil does not seem to have been inspired by the *duae viae* despite their use of the double love commandment.

[82] Cf. the recent edition of R. Hanslik, in CSEL 75, 1960. According to B. Steidle, *Die Regel St. Benedikts*, 1952, pp. 24ff, Benedict was eventually inspired by the rule of the monks of Lérins.

it makes one follow the precepts found in the second table of the Decalogue (cf. *Did/Doct* 2). The rest of the chapter also has many parallels of detail with *Did/Doct* 3-4 and with *Did* 1:3-2:1. Of course, precepts with a typically monastic character are now found mixed up with the primitive teaching of the *duae viae*, but the framework of the latter is still visible.[83] Once the *duae viae* had made its way into the monastic tradition, it ceased to exist outside it.[84] It could be that the Waldenses have tried to use the *duae viae* in their preaching which essentially calls for conversion; but it is not certain.[85]

Today when we know the importance that the *duae viae* has had for the ancient Church, one must pose the question as to whether it is not necessary for it to regain a place in our catechetical instruction. I do not know a better way to express the value of the *duae viae* than by availing myself of Cardinal Daniélou's own teaching:[86] "The theme of the two ways is much more than a pedagogical schema or a method of presentation. One would have believed it possible to see the description of the way of life presented as a treatise on virtues and that of death as a treatise on vices. It is, in fact, much more than that. To place the candidate for baptism before the two ways which open before him, is to place him before a decisive option: the renunciation of Satan or adherence to Jesus Christ. The whole Biblical tradition witnesses to it. The way of life is that of those who have chosen God. It is this which gives to the whole of the moral catechesis according to the schema of the two ways its character of conflict, of struggle, particularly at the time of preparation for baptism, and moreover for all the Christian life. But it then concerns every other matter in a "good education". This "moral" is indeed rather the exposure of a supernatural reality which shows that the soul must be wrested from the power of the forces of evil. It denotes the concrete path of the living faith. The theme of the two ways is then an essential catechetical *topos*."

---

[83]St. Benedict depends himself on the *Regula Magistri* (cf. SC 105, 1966, p. 290, 386).

[84] Besides the manuscript of Constantinople, which has preserved the text of the *Didache* itself, there are only a few medieval writings which keep the vague memory of this "apocryphal writing"; cf J. Schlecht, *Doctrina XII Apostolorum* (Freiburg-im-Breisgau: Herder, 1901) pp. 62ff, and J.-P. Audet, *op.cit.*, pp. 87ff.

[85] Cf. on this subject H. Böhmer, in RE 20 (1908[3]) p. 827.

[86] *La catéchèse*, pp. 130f.

THE HALACHA IN THE TEACHING OF THE TWELVE
APOSTLES

† GEDALIAH ALON

Jerusalem

The majority of the *Halachot* embedded in this ancient book[1], which was written a few years after the destruction of the Second Temple[2] in Israel or in Syria[3], are typical of those which were adapted by the early Christians, with modifications, from the tradition and the custom of Israel, although some of the quasi-*Halachot*, which are included in the first chapters of this exposition, originated in the Torah of the Jews in their substance and form. Inasmuch as these sections are "fundamental writings" of the book, and as an ancient *Mishnah* which was written in the times of the Temple by an Israelite, we shall, therefore, first of all examine the first document in order to acquaint ourselves with what it appertains to, as well as those statements analogous to *Halacha* which it contains, and afterwards return to discuss the body of *Halachot* which can be found in the remainder of the Christian chapters.

Most scholars have noted the uniqueness of the first six chapters in relation to the other chapters for the following reasons: a) the subject matter: while all the other chapters deal with the establishment of Christian ritual (baptism, prayers and fasts and blessings of the Lord's Supper), fixing the the order of leadership in the communities (authorities—supervisors over *kashrut* and cantors) and the reception of apostles, prophets, laymen-hosts and

---

[1] Mentioned only a few times in the first Christian writings, it disappeared and was discovered once more by Bryennios in 1875 and was published by him in 1883 (P. Bryennios, Διδαχὴ τῶν δώδεκα ἀποστόλων [Constantinople, 1883]). My text is taken from the Harnack's commentary, *Die Lehre der zwölf Apostel* (Leipzig: Hinrichs, 1893 [TU 2,1-2]) pp. 1-64. The orthography for the names of the Rabbis and the abbreviations of Rabbinic texts is taken from H. L. Strack & G. Stemberger, *Introduction to the Talmud and Midrash* (Edinburgh: Clark, 1991).

[2] There is no consensus in this regard, as there are some who attribute it to the first half of the second century. However, many scholars have situated it in the period between 80-100. See F. Zeller, *Die Apostellehre, 6-16*, (München: Kösel, 1918 [BKV 35]); R. Knopf, *Die Lehre der zwölf Apostel* (Tübingen:Mohr, 1920 [HNT.E 1]) p. 3; Harnack RE III, p. 712; Leclercq, *Dictionnaire d'archéologie chrétienne et de liturgie* 4,1, p. 777.

[3] Harnack (*Die Lehre*, pp. 168-170) and others presume that it was written in Egypt. However there are some details in the book itself which point to its place in Israel and in Syria. See Knopf, *Die Lehre*, p. 3, and especially A. Greiff, *Das älteste Pascharituale der Kirche, Did. 1-10, und das Johannesevangelium* (Paderborn, 1929) pp. 11-36 (although his arguments for Antioch are not decisive); Jordan, *Geschichte d. altchr. Literature* p. 342; E. Hennecke, *Neutestamentliche Apokryphen* (Tübingen: Mohr, 1964) p. 560

priestly gifts and gifts for the poor (chs. 7-10, 11-14), the above
mentioned chapters deal with "Two Ways", the Way of Life and
the Way of Death, and propose a paradigm for the principles of
religion which are based, in the main, on *Torat hamidot*, which
devolved from Scripture and which permeates the Tannaitic *Mishnah*, the Apocrypha and the books written by the scholars of Israel
in Greek, and which contain (except for Did 1:3-6 from the word
"bless" and 6:2-3)[4] not the slightest hint of Christianity; b) from
the wording: we can discern that the style of these chapters differs
completely from the language of the others; c) from the aspect of
their use, since we find these chapters embedded in the *Epistle of
Barnabas* 19-20 and other later writings[5], a fact which could possibly attest to the existence of "the Two Ways" as a book in its
own right, as well as to its antiquity relative to the final *Teaching
of the Apostles* (and relative also to the *Epistle* itself). On the basis
of these sections, scholars[6] have presumed that they have before
them a Jewish book which was written before the Destruction
(even antedating Paul, who uses it in some of his Epistles[7], as well
as being embedded in *Berachot*) and served as the foundation of
the exposition of the Christian writer, who made of it a quasi-
opening and an authoritative Torah for the Gentiles who came to

---

[4] These verses were added by the Christian writer; see P. Drews, "Untersuchung
zur Didache", *ZNTW* 5 [1904] pp. 53-79, esp. 54.

[5] See Hennecke, *Neutestamentliche Apokryphen*, pp. 556-7, to which should be
added the Coptic version of the *Didache* copied by C. Schmidt ("Das koptische
Didache-Fragment des British Museum", *ZNW* 24 [1925] pp. 81-99), and the
Georgian translated by G. Peradse ("Die 'Lehre der zwölf Apostel' in der georgischen Überlieferung", *ZNW* 31 [1932] PP. 111-116).

[6] Harnack RE III, pp. 193-196 on the basis of C. Taylor, *The Teaching of the
Twelve Apostles* (Cambridge: Deighton Bell, 1886) to which I did not have access;
as well as most scholars. However, there are those who advance the hypotheses that
it was written by a Jewish-Christian, and even though they admit that the Jewish
material had been embedded in it (Hennecke, *Neutestamentliche Apokryphen*, p.
558) nevertheless apparently this hypothesis is far-fetched, as is Harnack's interpretation (RE III, p. 718). It is superfluous to say that the claim that "the golden
rule", which is presented here, is Christian can be rejected. Even the proof of the
term ἅγιοι ("saints") in 4:2 is not decisive, nor is the expression οὓς τὸ πνεῦμα
ἡτοίμασεν in 4:10; since *Kadosh* and *Kedoshim* are found even among the scholars,
and in Enoch I.48:1 (*Tzadikim*, *Kedoshim* and *Bechirim*) and in the Syriac Baruch
66:2 (*Kedoshim*, *Tzadikim* and *Hachamim*). And in the Talmud it is written, "All
those who observe the words of Sages are called *Kadosh*" (*b. Yeb* 19a). Nevertheless, in regard to this and to the latter proof it must be said that testifying, "What
we have not seen can not be considered proof". Since so little is extant in the tradition of the latter generations prior to the destruction of the Temple, we can deduce
from the language of the early Christian writings that they originated with them (or
were unique to them), and did not belong to Israel.

[7] In addition, Drews ("Untersuchung", pp. 53-63) presumes that chapter 16 also
belongs at the end of the Two Ways document and derives from the same writing;
however this has not been proven, and perhaps it is from another Jewish source.

accept the Christian religion.

However, we must first discuss the very essence and purpose of this Jewish writing, inasmuch as it is the general opinion accepted by researchers that the book under discussion was written primarily for Gentiles who came to convert to Judaism, in order to teach them the fundamentals of religion and the *mitzvoth* of the religion, in accordance with what we have learnt in the tradition of the Sages about the *Mektzat mitzvoth* which were presented to each convert.[8] But this assumption, which depends on their use in the relevant chapters in the *Teaching of the Apostles* for training Gentile-Christians, has no basis in its contents. Not only is there no hint of this purpose in the book itself, but there is no allusion to it in the substance of those *mitzvoth* of the Torah which all those who wish to convert to Judaism are required to confess to, such as the Sabbath, Holy Days and forbidden foods etc., as these have been interpreted in the Tannaitic *Mishnah*.[9] On the other hand, we do find some matters in the document which are not *a priori* presented to the Gentiles who have come to take upon themselves the burden of the kingdom of God and *mitzvoth*.[10] Therefore, we must seek the orientation of the book in some another way.

Apparently, the facts which determine the essence and purpose of the exposition are as follows: a) the writer has set out to provide a brief manifesto of the fundamentals of life according to Judaism; b) these fundamentals are, on the whole, in the sphere of *mitzvoth* between man and man, and the minority refer to withdrawal from anything resembling idolatry; c) it begins with the writer committing himself to the Ten Commandments, which he presents in his opening, inferring that the remainder of his words can be considered mere commentaries; d) an account of the spe-

---

[8] Harnack RE III, p. 724; Drews, "Untersuchung"; K. Kohler, *s.v.* "Didache", JE IV, p. 585; I. Elbogen, *Der jüdische Gottesdienst in seiner geschichtlichen Entwicklung* (Frankfurt a. M., 1924[2]) pp. 71-74; Knopf, *Die Lehre*, p. 2; Zeller, *Apostellehre*; G. Klein (*Der älteste christliche Katechismus und die jüdische Propaganda-Literatur* [Berlin, 1909] p. 172) is of the opinion that this is a Torah for *Gerim Toshavim* but the writer can be counted among the "opposition to *Halacha*" and of "heirs of the prophets", who rescinded the *Mitzvoth* between man and God and accepted Gentiles who observe the moral *Mitzvoth* of Judaism. But he has no proof for his words.

[9] *b.Yeb.* 47a (and in Tractate *Gerim* 1:3 we find only eight minor *Mitzvoth* and see *Ruth Rabba*, end of chapter 1) for those who seek to complement the "Two Ways" with Halacha, which parallel the Christian Law—circumcision, sacrifices, purities, Sabbaths and Holy Days—there is no foundation for this in the book itself. See Hennecke, *Neutestamentliche Apokryphen*, p. 558.

[10] For example the warnings found in chapter 4 (to cover yourself with the dust from the feet of the *kedoshim*, to flee from doubt and from conflicts in the community).

cial transgressions in which the Gentiles of his day were mired (as
well as before and after his time), in other words the Greeks and
the Romans who sanctioned them, as well as flattery towards the
deeds of these nations.

First of all, we must illustrate the analogy between our document and other extant writings, which include comprehensive
expositions (in the opinion of their owners) of Judaism and its
essence, such as the sections which are embedded in *Contra Apion*
by Josephus, the end of the second book,[11] Philo's chapters in the
remains of his book Ὑποθητικά,[12] and the Jewish poetry attributed
to Phocylides.[13] However, the first two compositions mentioned,
although they are equivalent to the essay under discussion as far
as the generality of their exposition is concerned and even in some
of their details, nevertheless the evident differences obviate their
being reviewed together with this essay. First of all, although
hermeneutical principles occupy a major portion of these writings,
they also devote a prominent place to presenting the essence of
Judaism in the sphere of the fundamental *mitzvoth* between man
and God;[14] and secondly, most of the warnings in "the Two
Ways" cannot be found in these sections; and lastly, the language
of these writings attests to their having been, for all practical purposes, consciously written for the Gentiles to explain to them the
customs practised by Israel in order to vindicate them to the
enemies of Israel among the nations.

However, a comparison of our essay to that attributed to
Phocylides discloses an apparent close affinity between them, as
even the poetry leans towards the exposition of the *mitzvoth* of the
Ten Commandments as well as a warning against violations of the
mitzvoth between man and man (including incest), while avoiding
giving details in regard to the *mitzvoth* between man and God
(except in two verses which speak of the prohibition on corpses
and non-kosher food), and we find many sayings written in these
two books which are similar in their content and language.[15] Furthermore, to my mind it seems that we should pay attention to the

---

[11] Especially chs. 26-30.

[12] In Eusebius, *Praep. Evang.* VIII.7.

[13] In J. Bernays, *Gesammelte Abhandlungen* II (Berlin, 1885) pp. 254-261.

[14] Especially Josephus, but also Philo.

[15] Such as taking a vain oath (2:3)—Cf. ch. 16; avoiding witchcraft (3:4), ch.
149; fleeing doubt and conflict (4:3-4), ch. 184; abortion and discarding foetuses,
ch. 183; regarding the matter of justification (and the reason for it—partnership in
assets), ch. 30:59-60; giving wages and labour (missing in the Greek *Didache* but
found in the one copied by L. E. Iselin, *Eine bisher unbekannte Version des ersten
Teiles der "Apostellehre"* (Leipzig: Heusler, 1895 [TU 13,1b]) pp. 1-16 from *Vita
des Schenudi*, in Arabic,)(2:4)—"Do not oppress the wages of an employee", and
apparently it is one of the principles of the *Didache*. See fn. 28 below and others.

fact that in neither of them do we find an allusion to the uniqueness of God or a warning against idolatry (although it does contain several recriminations against other transgressions which were widespread among the nations) and against *abodah zarah* (the dust of idolatry).

J. Bernays sees in the Phocylidian poetry a quasi-Talmud arranged for the Gentiles as in the "Seven Noachide laws"; in other words, the Jewish writer had proceeded to teach the foreigners those Noachide laws which they are obligated by the Torah to observe, in accordance with tradition.[16] However, not only are some of his utterances inconsistent with the Gentile "Catechism",[17] but the absence of the cardinal principle of the seven Noachide laws, namely, the prohibition on idolatry, is decisive in refuting the explanation of this scholar. In fact Bernays himself grappled with this problem which undermined his methodology and forced him to resolve it by proposing that the writer had made a special effort to avoid offending what was so "dear and precious" to the foreign readers. Needless to say, his answer is far-fetched.

However, despite the fact that some of the sayings in the above poetry were deliberately[18] written for the nations, who were preoccupied with the major moral *mitzvoth*, the final chapter, where the writer sums up his commandments, namely, that these are the revealed and wise "mysteries" of Judaism as opposed to the secretive and magical "mysteries" of the ritual of the idol worshippers, attests to the fact that the words were deliberately aimed at the Gentiles. In any case, we cannot conclude from this that they were written for the purpose of constituting a Torah for them. It is more plausible that the book in its core is only an exposition of the principles and ways of life of the Jews,[19] invidiously comparing them to the foreign culture in which many Israelites were involved. This is why it did not specify the *Mitzvah* of the uniqueness of God and the prohibition on idolatry, as these were a "cardinal principal" among the Jews, even among the most distant, and it was superfluous to mention them. And when the author clothes the composition in foreign attire, by attributing it to a Gentile, it becomes obvious that he was aspiring to bring it to

---

[16] Bernays, *Abhandlungen*, p. 252, and Klein (*Katechismus*, pp. 144f) agrees with him.

[17] Such as V.95—"Don't put your faith in the crowd" etc.

[18] Abortion, discarding of newborn for predators, homosexuality, cruelty towards slaves and similar sayings.

[19] This refers to the essence of this document; since there were additions of chapters from the sphere of *halachot* of *Derech Eretz*, as well as wisdom literature from the books of homiletical sayings. It is also obvious that some of the sayings in it, both in the content as well as form, were influenced by Greek wisdom.

the attention of the Gentiles in order to praise Judaism, and to say
that in its essence it was reflected upon and learnt by an ancient
Greek scholar. Yet, the "Noachide Laws" cannot be found here;
whereas the "Two Ways" does not resort to any semblance of
subterfuge and even in its intimate language it supports our assertion that this is a presentation of the principles of Judaism, as conceived by the writer.[20]

This method of exhaustively presenting the principles of
belief of the nation was widespread in Israel in the times of the
Second Temple (and afterwards). There are a few aspects to this
way of thinking. There were those who distinguished between
mitzvoth which obtained for the individual, thus isolating them
from others for all practical purposes, such as the enactment in
Lod that idolatry, incest and bloodshed, which are subject to capital punishment, must not be transgressed. However, the uniqueness of these *mitzvoth* antedates the Destruction by many days,
since the purpose of the famous Apostolic Decree (Acts 15:2) that
Christian Gentiles must avoid idolworshipping and prostitution
and (meat) from what has been strangled and from blood was to
impose on the foreigners the above-mentioned three *mitzvoth*, and
"blood" does not refer to a prohibition on eating but on
bloodshed, as G. Resch has deduced from the precepts.[21] Needless
to say, James, the brother of Jesus, and his followers did not con-
trive this arbitrarily, but made a binding decision in regard to the
disagreement between Paul and the Elders of Jerusalem by effect-
ing a compromise, as was the custom in the tradition of the early
generations of Israel.

And there were those who saw the major *mitzvoth* as pro-
genitors of others, but these were no more than commentaries to
the "general principles", such as the Ten Commandments which
were regarded as "fathers" to the Torah, as Jesus replied to an
enquiry in Matthew 19:18-19, and as has been proven by the
words of Paul in Romans 13:10. We already know that this was
accepted by Philo, who took pains to propose the Ten Commandments and their commentaries as a *Halacha*, and even organized
his *Mishnah* as an elucidation of the *Halachot* of the whole Torah
and as an outcome of these Commandments, and therefore linked
the *mitzvoth* to each and every Commandment[22]. Furthermore,

---

[20] Idolatry was mentioned in the *Didache* only in enumerating crimes (5:1) and
not in the body of the *Mitzvoth*.

[21] G. Resch, *Das Aposteldekret nach seiner ausserkanonischen Textgestalt* (1905
[TU 13,3]). "Western version" and the word "the suffocated" does not appear in
the tradition which initially did not discuss prohibited food.

[22] And it is proven from the reading out in the Temple of the Ten Commandments together with the reading of the *Shema* (*b.Tam* 85, 41) and even the other
cities and villages in Israel wanted to read them but this was abolished in view of
"the resentment of the Minim" (*b.Ber* 12a; Jerusalem Talmud, *Ibid.*). And even

there were even those who enjoined being more stringent in observing the Commandment, and ruled that a death sentence should be imposed on transgressors, in contrast to those who transgress the other prohibitions of the Torah[23], and this is reminiscent of the endeavour to base the whole Torah on two great principles of loving God and loving humankind[24], and the way in which Jesus spoke to the Pharisee: Mt 22:37-40; Mk 12:30-32 (and from the reply of the scribe we can learn that these words were the transmission of the Oral Tradition); Lk 10:27 (here also it was Oral Tradition in the hands of the Sages). And there were those who attributed the whole Torah to one "great principle", loving humankind, as Hillel did in his reply to the convert and similarly we read what Paul has written in Galatians 5:14 and we can read the Epistle of James 2:8. Now, these principles in all their multiple aspects can be found in several places in the Apocrypha, in particular in those chapters where it is possible to regard them as a quasi-exposition on the fundamentals of life and Torah resembling the Two Ways; and even here we can discern differences which can be reduced to only one principle "loving humankind", and there were those who included the love of God and the *mitzvoth* obtaining to religion and ritual. Thus we read in the Book of Jubilees 20:2-3 about Abraham, who ordained justice and the love of one's neighbour, circumcision and idolatry, and also about Isaac (*Ibid.* 15:2-3, justice, love idolatry). And similarly the author of *Tzvaot Shevatim*, although the latter ultimately inclines towards the *mitzvoth* between man and man. And also the apocryphal Jeremiah[25] seeks in the streets of Jerusalem, in accordance with God's wishes, a man who performs *tzedek* (righteousness), loves his brother and neighbour and purifies the idols on the altars with his mouth.[26] Likewise, the

---

though there were those who adhered to this custom even afterwards, as we have learnt from the Nash Papyrus and from sections of the Genizah (Mann, *HUCA* 2, pp. 283-4). And Rabbi Levi (*j.Ber* 1:3a) stresses that the reason we read the portions of the *Shema* is because of the Ten Commandments that it contains.

[23] See I. Heinemann, *Philons griechische und jüdische Bildung* (reprinted Darmstadt, 1962) p. 357. We can even see this same tradition in Philo (He himself comments that there are divergent opinions) who supports the death sentence as punishment for making a vain oath, for the same above-mentioned reason.

[24] There are two aspects to our writing which have converged as one, since it begins, "This is the way of life, first love God your Creator, second your neighbour as yourself, and what you do not want to happen to you, do not do unto others"; he added to the "great principle", the love of humankind, the "Golden Rule" of Hillel and Rabbi Aqiba, which can be found in Philo in the in the extant parts of the Ὑποθητικά and in the Book of Tobit 4:15 (cf. the defence of Aristides I, Mingana 159, 14, 4 published by J. Geffcken p. 22) and concludes with the Ten Commandments.

[25] A. Mingana, *Woodbrooke Studies* I, 1927.

[26] P. 171.

wonderful verses which open with "Happy is he" in the Slavonic Enoch (2 Enoch 35-60), which speak of truth and justice and the love of peace and even *chasidut* towards heaven (although the former triumph) and in Enoch 1:94-99, where Enoch reads "from the books", presenting many sayings which combine to comprise one big unit which limits itself to a discourse on good qualities and justice (towards humankind). In general, these are the writings of Jews, expositions on Judaism, compelling us to regard them as the fruit of the indefatigable reflective thought of the nation, which sought exhaustively to derive for itself the principles of Torah and to assure its transmission for the benefit of its children.[27] Inasmuch as Judaism in the times of the Second Temple (as during the times of the Prophets) tended to see the essence of the Torah as justice and *tzedaka* and the love of humankind "the *mitzvoth* (between man and God) were not given except to unite all Israel together", therefore even these expositions, which were born and evolved with these thoughts in mind, include, on the whole, matters originating from the same sphere.[28]

We shall return to examine those *Halachot* which are embedded in the "Two Ways".

The Prohibition on Abortion

2.2 οὐ φονεύσεις τέκνον ἐν φθορᾷ οὐδὲ γεννηθὲν ἀποκτενεῖς
Do not destroy the foetus and do not murder the newborn.

---

[27] An outstanding example of this way of seeking the principles of *Mitzvoth* (without discussing the essence of belief) can be found in the article by Rabbi Simlai b. Abba (*b.Mak* 23b-24a) and it can be seen that even the common factor between Philo and Josephus in their above-mentioned expositions were not written to present the fundamentals of life to Israelites, but they rather aim it at the Gentiles for the purpose of defending Judaism, and in regards to Phocylides, I concur with E. Schürer, G. Vermes, G. Millar & M. Goodman, *The History of the Jewish People in the Age of Jesus Christ (175 B.C.-A.D. 135)* III.1 (Edinburgh: Clark, 1986) pp. 689-690).

[28] In the version "Two Ways" which was concealed in the *Vita des Schenudi* (Iselin, *unbekannte Version*, p. 1) there are verses which can be seen to have originated with this scholar, for example, "Do not oppress the salary of the employee so that he will not call for God's help and He will hear", as well as the warning that man should not be a "userer" (after "Do not steal", compare with the use of the term "the robbers and the userers" by the Tanaim). Similarly, in chapter 4:1-2, we can see the Arabic version which advocates the *Mitzvoth*—devotion to honouring "the speakers of God's words" and the "Kedoshim"—honour towards God's word itself as a principle. (With regard to the name of the book, see Klein, *Katechismus*, p. 184). "Didache" should be compared to the Jerusalem seal (Synagogue) which was published by R. Weil, *REJ* 71, p 30. and see L. H. Vincent (*RevBib* 30, p. 251) verse 4-5 on the Synagogue which was built εἰς ἀν(άγν)ωσ(ιν) νόμου καὶ εἰς (δ)ιδαχ(ὴ)ν ἐτολῶν for the reading of the Torah and for the study of *Mitzvoth*.)

This *Halacha*, whose contents are replicated by Clement of Alexandria from the Ten Commandments,[29] can be found in the *Sibylline Oracles*[30] attributed to Phocylides, and in Philo and Josephus;[31] and all its force is dedicated to warn against this Greek and Roman custom. It is not necessary to elaborate on the fact that the killing of babies by throwing them to wild animals, which was permitted by the majority of Gentiles, was prohibited by the laws of Israel and considered bloodshed, since once the head of the foetus has emerged into the air of the world, the law which applies to adults applies to him/her as well and capital punishment would be imposed on anyone who kills him/her. Similarly, this applies to the interdict against the destruction of a foetus to prevent a woman from giving birth, which is consonant with the *Halacha*. However, we have to discuss the seriousness of the transgression. Inasmuch as Josephus teaches of the woman who aborts her seed deliberately: "and if a woman should be found doing so, she would be adjudged in court as a killer of children because she has extirpated a soul...", we can derive from this that she has endangered herself by this act. Similarly, Philo resolved (as well as the Septaguint), that a person who hits a pregnant woman and destroys the foetus after its formation in her womb is complete, will have the death sentence imposed on him.[32] There is no doubt that these laws diverge from the *Halacha* which was current in the tradition of the Sages, which exempts from capital punishment the killing of a foetus as long as it has not emerged into the air of the world. There is therefore a basis to the premise that it is possible to learn from the Tannaitic teachings of the existence of a *Halacha* which had been incorporated, and which is consistent with the tradition of the above mentioned *Soferim*, and corresponds with what is recorded in the *Talmud*[33] in the name of Rabbi Ishmael, namely, that a Noachide is sentenced to death even if the victim was a foetus, as well being consistent with the other stringencies enumerated, all of which could possibly prove the existence of ancient *Halachot* which took a stringent attitude towards capital punishment in regards to Israelites,[34] and this needs further scrutiny.

---

[29] *Paedagogus* III.89:7 (Staehlin, p. 285); Is there a lack of precision in the citing of the source or is this an ancient Jewish-Greek "midrash-Torah", which served as a commentary to "Thou shall not kill"?

[30] Book Three, J. Geffcken, *Die Oracula Sibyllina* (Leipzig: Hinrichs, 1902 [GCS 8]) p. 87.

[31] See Heinemann, *Philons*, pp. 392-394.

[32] Compare with Heinemann, *Philons*, p. 390 (and perhaps in the Septaguint it is written "there shall be no loyalty", analogous to "loyalty to Torah" etc.).

[33] *b.Sanh* 57b, *Bereshit Rabba* 34. Theodor, p. 325 (See *j.Qid* 1:58b).

[34] Heinemann (*Philons*, pp. 352-357) discusses the multiplicity of death penalties which can be found in the Philonian *Hypothetica*, and even mentions the opinion

The Ways of the Amorites

3.4　Τέκνον μου, μὴ γίνου οἰωνοσκόπος, ἐπειδὴ ὁδηγεῖ εἰς τὴν εἰδωλολατρίαν, μηδὲ ἐπαοιδὸς μηδὲ μαθηματικὸς μηδὲ περικαθαίρων, μηδὲ θέλε αὐτὰ βλέπειν. ἐκ γὰρ τούτων ἀπάντων εἰδωλολατρία γεννᾶται

My son, do not be among those who look on birds, as this leads to idolatry, and [let there not be] incantations, and do not be an astrologer nor a sorcerer, and also do not lust after them to see them, because they are all idolatry.

With regard to the diviners, we can take it for granted that they are prohibited and thus consonant with the Torah and *Halacha*.[35] Nevertheless, during Temple times and after its destruction, sorcerers and magicians existed amongst the Israelites, both in Israel and abroad,[36] as well as "magicians' books" which were popular among the people. There were even Sages who were well versed in magic, and there were those who were engaged in it under compelling circumstances. However, there were those who prohibited the uttering of charms (on diseases) which was especially prevalent, and contrary to the fact that the majority of the Tanaim and the Amoraim had ruled that it was permitted. Rabbi Aqiba ruled in his *Mishnah* (*m. Sanh* 10:1):

> He that utters charms over a wound and says "I will put none of the diseases upon thee which I have put upon the Egyptians"...does not have a portion in the world to come.

However, in the *Tosephta* (*t. Sanh* 12:10) Abba Saul says in his name—"Even the diviner..." etc. The *Halacha* is not clear, inasmuch as it is possible to interpret it that he prohibited only the *Rokek*, but that which is not *rekika* is permitted (and this is the law

---

that both Philo's exposition and Josephus's *Contra Apion* were based on a common source, whose purpose was to convert Gentiles. In this manner it is also possible to explicate Josephus' allusion to the ruling that a death penalty should be imposed upon a woman who aborts her foetus. However, an examination of the early sources (and other even more obscure books) confronts us with the first *Halacha* which applied the death penalty with great stringency and imposed it for many transgressions, so that the *Halacha* (the Pharisaic and the later one) moderated them. And in the matter of the foetuses, it is necessary to examine other later writings which are in the tradition, although there is no need to expand on this.

[35] In regards to the divining using birds, compare with the story by Hikitus (was it invented? See H. Lewy, *ZNTW* [1934] pp. 117-132) in Josephus, *Contra Apion* 1:22, about Meshulam the Jew.

[36] See Schürer, Vermes, Millar & Goodman, *History of the Jewish People* III.1, pp. 342-347.

in the tradition transmitted in the name of Rabbi Yoḥanan ben Nuri in *Abot de Rabbi Nathan* chapter 36), and it is possible to interpret the *Baraita* as referring only to the present, whereas the uttering of charms is prohibited everywhere. Indeed, there are divergent opinions on this issue in the *Talmud*. In the opinions of R. Yoḥanan in the Babylonian *Talmud* (*b.Sanh* 101a) and Rab in the Jerusalem *Talmud* (*j.Sanh* 28:270b) Rabbi Aqiba only prohibited spitting "since you do not mention the Name of Heaven over spitting" (Babylonian *Talmud*). However, according to Rabbi Ḥanina (as well as Rab in the Babylonian *Talmud*), incantations are prohibited even when verses which do not mention the Name are uttered, in fact they forbid the uttering of charms under any circumstances, as Rabbi Joshua ben Levi said, "Do not heal through the words of the Torah".[37] While it is true that we can not derive an absolute teaching from the words of Rabbi Joshua ben Levi, and not even from Rabbi Aqiba's *Mishnah*, that indeed the uttering of charms was prohibited even with words not from the Torah; it appears that the bulk of Jewish incantations were based on the reading of verses from the Torah.[38] It is, therefore, reasonable to assume that their intention was to prohibit incantations totally, justifying this with the phrase "because of the ways of the Amorites", and this is compatible with the manner in which Rabbi Meir pronounced the prohibition in the *Mishnah* (*m.Shab* 6:10):

> They may go out with the egg of a locust or with a tooth of a fox or with a nail from the stake as a means of a cure even on ordinary week days [it is forbidden] for the same reason.

This premise, that there were scholars who categorically opposed the uttering of charms, can assist us in explaining the words of Origen against Celsus,[39] who recounts that Israel was preoccupied with divining and oaths, that he found people amongst the populace of Israel who did not know Torah, and he did not see *Hechsharim* who avoided what was prohibited. We must therefore consider the chapter which is replicated above from our book as expressing the opinion of those Sages who condemned the uttering of charms and regarded it as bordering on sorcery, which is related to idolatry.[40]

---

[37] *b.Shebu.* 15b. This was how the Rambam understood it, *Halachot Idolatry (Avodah Zara)*, 77, chapter 11, *Halacha* 12.

[38] See *b.Shab* 67a, and also the blessings and charms which include elements "from the Torah" (*b.Shab* 115b; *t.Shab* 13:4; *m.Yad* 2:12; *j.Shab* 17:15c—and in the latter two no charms are mentioned but nevertheless it seems that the allusion to "blessings" refer to the same type) also belong here.

[39] *Contra Celsum* V.9 (Koetschau II, p. 9).

[40] With regard to the astrologers, even though the Sages believed in them and relied on them (by approaching others), in any case, there were those who neverthe-

Concerning the Slaves

4.10 Οὐκ ἐπιτάξεις δούλῳ σου ἢ παιδίσκη, τοῖς ἐπὶ τὸν αὐτόν θεὸν ἐλπίζουσιν, ἐν πικρίᾳ σου, μήποτε οὐ μὴ φοβηθήσονται τὸν ἐπ᾽ ἀμφοτέροις θεόν

Do not impose[41] on your man-servant or your maid-servant who hope on God—the same God as you—with bitterness, lest they desist from fearing the God you both share.

Now through this admonition not to impose excessive fear on your slaves, the Sages drew a comparison with the *Agadah* in order to teach us that some of the Tanaim and Amoraim did not stand on their honour and protected them [the slaves] and acted towards them by the standard of mercy. However, as far as the *Halacha* is concerned, we must first discuss to what the documents refer, whether to Canaanites or Hebrews, as what is not written is not interpreted. However, there is no doubt that the reference here is only to Canaanite slaves, since the same tradition which testifies to the fact that there were no Hebrew slaves during the Second Temple period (*b.Qid* 69a and parallel editions), is true at least as far as the latter part of this epoch is concerned. Although explicit proof for this tradition is lacking, it seems that we can find corroboration in John 8:33, where "Jews who believe in Jesus" say to him after he had promised them freedom through the knowledge of the truth, "We are the seed of Abraham and in our lives we have never been slaves to anyone, so how can you say that we shall be freemen?" This is especially likely as the plain sense of what has been written informs us that "the sons of Abraham" were forever freemen. From this we have learned that common Canaanite slaves who were owned by Israelites do not remain Gentiles, but are slaves to Heaven, thus confirming the *Halacha*.[42]

---

less imposed a prohibition on it (*b.Pes* 113b, fortune tellers and diviners. In regards to Heter, allowing it, see *b.Shab* 156a-b). And we found a Gentile astrologer who converted who said, "Has this holiness not cleaved to this nation to isolate itself from these things?" (*j.Shab* 6:8d, and see Levi below). In addition, the early Christians were quite strict in not accepting converts from the astrologers (corresponding to the Israelites?).

[41] At first glance it may seem that it is difficult that it should warn against "commanding" the slaves, and perhaps embedded in the article a Hebrew basis—"Do not impose" etc, in order to tell us, do not punish, and read: do not impose (in Phocylides 224-226 it says that physical damage to slaves that must be avoided).

[42] We cannot rely here on the opinion of Rabbi Aqiba ("Do not keep slaves who are not circumcised") as opposed to the *Halacha* of Rabbi Ishmael (*b.Yeb.* 47b, and see *Mekhilta of Rabbi Ishmael* 7, Horowitz, p. 230) and even less so on the *Halacha* which permits forcing circumcision upon slaves (*b.Yeb.* 47b-48a; *j.Yeb.* 8:8d, as well as the article by Rabbi Abba bar Kahana, in *Genesis Rabba* 90 (Theodore-Albeck, p. 1106): "you impose circumcision" as did those Egyptians

What is the relevance of this embedded chapter?

3.1 Τέκνον μου, φεῦγε ἀπὸ παντὸς πονηροῦ καὶ ἀπὸ παντὸς ὁμοίου αὐτοῦ
My son, flee from all evil, and from anything else similar to it.

It seems that this concurs with the opinion of the majority of the Sages that the allusion is to not to a person but to an evil thing.[43] And this has already been brought to our attention in the edict of the Tanaim, "Distance yourself from ugliness and what is similar to it [or to ugliness]"[44]. However, it is necessary to assess whether the writer had encountered this Hebrew edict and misunderstood its subject matter and formulated it in a way which diverged from its substantial meaning. In our book the edict is conceived as having the purpose of teaching us that a person should isolate himself from the minor transgressions which lead to major ones, and then goes into more detail (do not get angry as anger leads to bloodshed, etc.). However, the Hebrew script, apparently conveys an admonition to avoid those deeds which in themselves are not transgressions but are liable to raise suspicions amongst the people towards himself. Since that is the literal meaning of the word "ugliness" or "ugly" in the language of the Sages, and this is its use in many places,[45] and even the sources which have transmitted this edict teach us this. The *Talmud* presents this as proof that the *Halacha* imposed a prohibition on eating an animal which a Sage had interdicted, even though it was permitted on the "basis of doubt". And we can find corroboration for this in *t.Yeb* 4:7 and in *Abot de Rabbi Nathan* Ashkenazi version, chapter 2, which inclines towards caution because of "complaints of the people". And *Derech Eretz* 5:12 (Higger, p. 63) concludes with "lest you be suspected of a transgression". This is so also in the *Mekhilta* to Deuteronomy (*Midrash Tanaim*, 134): Rabbi Ishmael says that what is written comes to teach us to distance ourselves

---

themselves who were the slaves of Joseph, Genesis 47:19, and we have already learned this *Halacha* from the Kingdom's commands as they were presented in *Codex Theodosianus* and therefore it is not necessary to proofread Albeck, in his remark—"*Kaspan*" (whose interpretation has been disallowed)—since we cannot derive proof from this that all the slaves were, indeed, God-fearers.

[43] In the section of the *Didache* which was published in *ZNTW* (1922) p. 238, the version is ἀπὸ παντὸς πονηροῦ πράγματος ("from every evil matter").

[44] In the *Mekhilta* to Deuteronomy (*Midrash Tanaim* 134) which is copied down by the words of Rabbi Ishmael and in *t.Hull* 2:24)—by Rabbi Eliezer.

[45] In *b.Yeb* 24b; *j.Ket* 7:32c and the above meaning was current in the School of Rabbi Elijah (*Tana debi Eliyahu*).

from the ugliness "so that others will not suspect you of a transgression". And this is interpreted in a chapter in Phocylides: "Flee from a bad rumour[46] (bad reputation)". It seems that the latter was referring to a ruling to avoid slander by distancing oneself from evil people (so that you will not be considered one of them), since he concludes with the verse, "keep away from depraved people". Or perhaps it is possible to interpret the Tosephta in *Hullin* along these same lines, where Rabbi Eliezer transmits this edict in order to rebuke himself for having enjoyed a sermon on the Torah given by an heretic (*min*). And it was interpreted similarly in *Schenudi*'s version, who added afterwards, "and do not join an evil person (*rasha*), lest your life be shortened and you die before your time." (as in Phocylides). However, it is has been proven from the rest of the section that the essence of the version in our book is, as we have said, an admonition to avoid minor transgressions which lead to major ones, and so it stands to reason that the basic significance of the adage has been distorted here. However, we have already found this in our sources, as he adds in *Abot de Rabbi Nathan* reference to that same edict, "Therefore the Sages have decreed keep afar from a minor sin lest it lead you to a grave sin." And below (Schecter, 6,2) he says

> (Where it is written, "and I shall observe the virgin")—it teaches that Job eschewed anything which was liable to lead to a transgression and from the ugliness and to anything resembling ugliness. And we have learned in the *Mishnah* ? (1, 26), in accord with our edict, (*Ibid.* 12)—Refrain from anything which could lead you to sin and anything resembling it etc.

And even in the *Mekhilta* to Deuteronomy he concludes after repeating the edict and elucidating it—that they should not suspect you of a transgression—"as if a man is wearing a woman's clothes—and we find ourselves having been impelled to commit a transgression", indicating that even in this tradition the edict had become obscured and confused with similar edicts. In any case, at the core of the adage, as it is formulated in the Hebrew parallels (and they are the most important), a foundation exists for many *Halachot* which were enacted on the grounds of "obviating suspicion" and *mareet ayin*, and the *Binyan-Av* to all of them can be found in Tractate *Shekalim* in the *Mishnah* (*m.Shek* 3:2), "he who made the appropriation did not enter with a hem...for a man must satisfy people just as he has to satisfy the Almighty".[47]

---

[46] The content of the document can be found in Paul also (1 Thess 5:22) ἀπὸ παντὸς εἴδους πονηροῦ ἀπέχεσθε ("Distance yourself from everything which resembles evil"), but is not sufficiently clarified.

[47] There is an ancient *Halacha* which recounts the divergent opinions between Rabbi Aqiba and Rabbi Ishmael in regard to to the *Midrasha* (*Sifre Deuteronomy* 10:9, *Midrash Tanaim* 61).

THE *HALACHA* IN THE CHRISTIAN CHAPTERS

Prayer

> 8.3 After he has commanded them not to pray in the manner of the flat-
> terers (Pharisees, Jews), but in the fashion conceived by Jesus ("Our
> Father in Heaven..."), he adds Τρὶς τῆς ἡμέρας οὕτω προχεύχεσθε:
> "Pray thus three times a day."

Ostensibly, from this we have irrefutable evidence for the
Halacha which fixed prayer three times a day, *Shacharit*, *Minha*
and *Aravit*, and corroboration for the opinion of Rabban Gamaliel
against Rabbi Joshua who says that the *Aravit* prayer is optional.
However, after examination we found that there is substance to his
opinion. According to Tertullian[48] the reference is to the the
prayer being at the third hour and the sixth hour and the ninth
hour of the day, and similarly, the author of *Didascalia
Apostolorum*;[49] in opposition to them Origen,[50] ruled that it should
be at *Shacharit* and at midnight and at *Aravit*. Thus it is not clear
what the intention of the writer of the *Didache* was. As to the
essence of the question in regards to the modifications introduced
by the early Christians, we must turn to and scrutinise ancient
sources in order to learn whether they were no more than custom-
innovations introduced by Israel. First of all, in Acts 10:9 we read
about Peter who prayed in the Temple at the sixth hour and about
Cornelius the Roman officer, a God-fearer, who prayed in his
house at the ninth hour (10:30), demonstrating beyond doubt that
they had comprehended the original way of the Jews, but only
with regard to the final prayer. From Luke we deduce that the
nation must pray at the time of [the burning of] the incense (at
dusk, 1:10). Similarly, we read in Judith (9:1) that she prayed in
her house at the time of the sacrifice of the incense[51] at the
Temple in the evening. Akin to these testimonies is the admonition
given by the writer of the Slavic Enoch (13:88): "morning, noon
and evening it is good to come to the house of the Lord and to
praise the Creator for everything." However, in all these sources
the time of the prayer of *Shacharit* was not interpreted as being at

---

[48] *De ieiunio* 10, *De oratione* 25, See Harnack, *Die Lehre*, p. 27.

[49] Gibson, p. 26.

[50] *On prayer* 12 (Koetschau, p. 325).

[51] In *j.Ber* 4:7b Rabbi Yose says in regards to the final time to pray the *Minha*
according to Rabbi Jehuda, that it is, in the opinion of the *Baraita*, "eleven hours
less a quarter"—בין הערבים של תמיד המנחה תפילת הזקשה לא see *t.Ber* 26:2
"*Debur Hamatcheel*" until *Peleg Hamanche*" (These are *Halachic* units of time. The
Minha).

the third hour (on the contrary, the connotation of "morning" in Enoch is exactly dawn). Moreover, in some of the sources we have learnt that the first prayer was set at the beginning of the day, since it says in the Songs of Solomon 6:4-5 "He shall wake up from his sleep and bless the name of God...and await the face of God for all his household" And so with the *Sibylline Oracles* (3:591-593)—"At dawn they lift up holy arms toward heaven, from their beds...and they honor only the Immortal who always rules" (Charlesworth, *Pseudepigrapha* I, p. 375). And even in Judith (12:8), apparently she prayed with the first rays of the sun. And the author of *Epistle of Aristeas*, testifies that the Elders prayed "as was the custom among all the Jews" at *Shacharit*, even though it was not the rule, with the first rays of the sun (*Ibid.*, *Pesiqta de Rab Kahana*, according to the simple meaning of the verse). However, the Therapeuts in Egypt used to pray twice a day, *Shacharit* and *Aravit*, as Philo attests, and the first prayer was recited with the first rays of the sun[52]. Now, in order to elucidate the custom of the *Shacharit* prayer at the third hour, for which explicit proof does not exist in the early sources[53], it is, perhaps, possible to allude to the *Halacha* enacted by Rabbi Joshua in the reading of the *Shema* at the third hour. And it is possible that the custom was established on the basis of its affinity to the dawn *Tamid*, whose deadline was the fourth hour, and this, in the opinions of Rabbi Jehuda ben Baba and Rabbi Judah, applies also to the prayer. In any case, it must be said first of all that those sources (*m. Eduy* 6:1 and *m. Ber* 4:1) which state that prayer is at the sixth hour and at the ninth, undoubtedly count three prayers, although they do not mention an evening prayer, and this is in accord with Rabbi Joshua's opinion. In regards to the two latter prayers, the middle one is intended approximately for the major *Minha*, and the latter for the minor *Minha*. However, there were those who ruled that this prayer should be delayed until after the *Minha*, to the hour of the dawn incense. Thus we have established that the tradition which ruled three prayers in a day (to the exclusion of *Aravit*) is based on the custom that definitively linked the prayer to the sacrifices and to the Temple. In contradistinction to this, the same tradition which ruled two prayers a day, *Shacharit* and the one at the beginning of the evening (precisely),

---

[52] *De vita contemplativa* 83 (with the first rays of the sun and its setting). Josephus provides similar testimony in regards to the Essenes (*Wars*, II.8:5) although he does not mention the Aravit prayer. And these prayers were aimed towards those who prayed "with the dimming of the sun", between the dawn prayer [*Shacharit*] and the evening prayer [*Aravit*] (Rabbi Yose, *b. Shab* 118, 2. See *j. Ber* 4:7b).

[53] However, we find that the Amoraim prayed at three different hours (Rabbi Yasa, Rabbi Ḥiyya bar Abba and also Rabbi Barchaya, Jerusalem Talmud *Ibid.*).

has no affinity to the Temple (*Avot Tikunam*).[54] From this we permit ourselves to state that the *Halacha* enacted by Rabban Gamaliel that the *Aravit* prayer is obligatory is comprised of both of these traditions simultaneously. And we have found a similar fusion with the early Christians, where in the opinion of Tertullian a man must pray not only the above-mentioned three prayers, at the third, sixth and ninth hours of the day, but also when he arises (with the sun's rays) and when evening commences. Similarly, the writer of the Syriac *Didascalia*.[55] Now, it is possible to state that this *Halacha* was renewed after the Destruction when a third prayer was added. In view of this, if we interpret the edict in the *Didache* in such a manner, then we have no choice but to defer the dating of the time our composition was written. However, as was mentioned above, the two customs existed side by side during Second Temple times.[56] Therefore, we cannot attribute this *Halacha* to the Destruction, but it must be interpreted under the assumption of a fusion of two different customs, a phenomenon which was common especially in regards to blessings and prayer. And in reference to the issue itself, although there is no evidence to support this, it is logical to assume that the writer of the book was referring to the dawn prayer (as the *Halacha* has ruled) and to *Minha* and to *Aravit*, thus conforming to Rabban Gamaliel's ruling.

The Prayer over the Meal

The whole of chapter 9 discusses the prayers over the meal, which apparently is "the Lord's Supper", to which he also devotes chapter 14. This is the manner in which he opens: περὶ δὲ τῆς εὐχαριστίας, οὕτως εὐχαριστήσατε. This wording can also be found in chapter 14 below. However, we shall return to clarify this matter afterwards; let us now examine the body of the text, which is reproduced here:

---

[54] In the opinion of the *Tosefta* the *Shacharit* and *Aravit* prayers are the substance of the "law", and with regard to the Syrian *Didache* it must be stated, that it adds another prayer which is "on the bed". Compare with the words of Rabbi Joshua ben Levi in the matter of the reading of the *Shema* in *b.Ber* 4b, and the words of other Amoraim in *j.Ber* 1:4d ("in order to avoid damages").

[55] Rabbi Yose and his son Rabbi Eliezer (*t.Ber* 3:2) subsume the closing prayer (*Neila*) under *Aravit* (and *Neila* is definitely "the closing of the gates of the Palace"). Rav also is of the opinion that *Neila* exempts from the evening prayer (*b.Yoma* 87b; *j.Ber* 4:7c). In any case, it is still far-fetched to see this as an Aravit prayer which comes during Neila (which previously was prayed even outside the "three chapters") and which has an affinity to the Temple.

[56] Holtzmann, *ZNTW* 12, pp. 90-107, deals with this matter, but his words are not clear to me.

Chapter 9 First over the cup: We thank you, our Father, for the holy vine of David your servant, which you have made known to us through Jesus your servant. To you be eternal honour.

And concerning the bread for breaking: We thank you; our Father for the life and knowledge, which you have made known to us through Jesus your servant. To you be eternal honour. As the broken [bread] was spread over the mountains and gathered and became one, so your congregation will gather together from the ends of the earth to your kingdom. Because to you be the honour and the might through Jesus the Messiah forever.

But let no one eat or drink from your εὐχαριστία, except those who baptise themselves for the Lord, because concerning this the Lord has said, "Do not give what is holy to the dogs."

Chapter 10 And after you have been filled then bless in this way: We thank you, holy Father, for your holy Name which resides in our hearts and for the knowledge and the faith and eternal life which have been made known to us through Jesus your servant. To you be honour forever. You, the Lord of all, you created everything for the sake of your Name; you have given food and drink to humankind for their support, so that they will thank you. However, upon us you have bestowed spiritual food and drink and eternal life through your servant. We thank you for everything, because you are great. To you be eternal honour. O God, remember your congregation, to save it from all evil and to consummate it with your love, and gather it, the holy one, from the four winds, into your kingdom, which you have established for it. Because to you be eternal might and honour. Let grace come and this world disappear. Hosanna to the God of David. If anyone is holy, let him come, and if he is not, let him repent. Let our Lord come, Amen. However, allow the prophets to give thanks as they will.

We find that scholars who have tried to elucidate the question of this meal,[57] argue that it cannot unequivocally be the "eucharist" (which is alluded to in chapter 10) since there is feasting here with not even a hint of a holy sacrifice (θυσία, as in chapter 14 below), as a symbol of the Lord's flesh and blood. Opinions are divided here, as there are those who argue that from its origin, the "Lord's Supper" (which was on Sunday) was comprised of actual food and drink, and it is with this issue that we are dealing. Whereas there are those who argue that the writings refer to the communal suppers in which the early Christians partook, the ἀγάπαι which eventually evolved into public meals for the poor, or it refers to "house suppers" which resembled a private eucharist (which took place at any hour)[58]. Nonetheless, to delve

---

[57] E. von der Goltz, *Tischgebete und Abendmahlsgebete in der altchristlichen und in der griechischen Kirche* (Leipzig, 1905 [TU 29,2b]) pp. 1 ff; H. J. Holtzmann, *ZNTW* 1904, pp. 89-120; Drews, "Untersuchung", pp. 74-79; W. O. E. Oesterley, *The Jewish Background of the Christian Liturgy* (Oxford: Clarendon, 1925) pp. 198-9; F. Gavin, *The Jewish Antecedents of the Christian Sacraments* (London: SPCK, 1928) pp. 80-81; Knopf, *Die Lehre*, p. 24; J. Weiss, *Das Urchristentum*, p. 510 n.1 (Eng. *Earliest Christianity* I-II [New York 1959]); Leclerq, *Dictionnaire*, p. 790.

[58] See Holtzmann, *Ibid.*, p. 95; Axel, *ZNW*, 1902, p. 138; Oesterley , *Jewish Background*, pp. 156-193; Gavin, *Jewish Antecedents*, pp. 64-66.

into the substance of the law it is necessary to state that even the eucharist, like the *agape*, was based on the communal-meals of Israel. In the beginning, since it was known that Jesus' Last Supper, according to the opinion of the tradition in the Gospel of John and in the (apocryphal) Gospel of Peter and in the opinion of researchers, despite being propounded in the tradition of Mark, was not Passover evening but took place on a weekday. Secondly, the Passover sacrifice is missing from the *Seder* of the eucharist and not even an allusion to a *Seder* exists, and therefore the theory which derives the "Lord's Supper" from the *Seder* of the evening of Passover *Seder* is totally refuted.[59]. Nevertheless, the alternative, which seeks to deduce it from the Sabbath meal and from the *kiddush*, is no better, because there is no mention of the holiness of the day in its blessings[60].

And we find with regard to these communal meals, that the law itself demonstrates that they took place, on the whole, on the Sabbaths (and on holy days and new months). And certainly Geiger is right when he interprets the foundations of the *Halachot* governing *Eruvay Hatzarot* (unification of courtyards on Sabbath so that food can be carried from courtyard to courtyard to permit everyone to bring their Sabbath food and eat together) on the basis of the custom of eating together on the Sabbaths in a large company[61] (and eventually, when the first custom took root, the *takannah* itself was not abolished even though its cause became obsolete). And apparently this process occurred in the matter of the meals of the same type, for whose existence we have found some evidence (of their content and even as to their semi-ritualistic quality) in the days of Julius Caesar (and before them). As we read in Josephus (*Antiquities* 14.10:8) that in the order

---

[59] G. Klein, "Die Gebete in der Didache", *ZNW* 9 (1908) pp. 134-144, and in *Katechismus*, pp. 216-217; Oesterley and Gavin rely on the whole on Elebogen (*Tiferet Yisrael*, 179-181) who relates that in the days of the Tanaim they would receive the Sabbath with a meal while it was still daytime (*Tosephet*), which he teaches in the Tosephta (*t.Ber* 5:31-33 and parallel ones) and to this must be added *b.Git* 38b. See there. However, Rabbi Judah disagrees and forbids eating "from the *Minha* and above". According to Rabbi Meir the time of reading the *Shema* in the evening falls "from the time that people enter to eat their bread on Sabbath evenings" (*t.Git* 1:1 and parallels) and even from the words of Rabbi Yose we can not learn that there was a fixed custom even among the "rich and the aristocratic". It seems that the *Baraita* which states that it was not the custom to blow the *shofar* on Sabbath evenings at these meals (*t.Suk* 4:11-12; *b.Shab* 35b) ("when they have filled the barrel with water and roasted the fish and lit the candle"). In any case, the Eucharist should not be linked to the *Kiddush*, as proposed by these scholars, since there is no mention in the blessing in the *Didache* to the holiness of the day (neither in the blessing over the wine nor in the blessing over the meal).

[60] Goltz, *Tischgebete*, p. 124.

[61] *j.MQ* 2:81b; *j.San* 8:26b.

given by the Roman Proconsul to the leaders and to the nation of
the Island of Pyrus with regard to the Jews; the Jewish people of
Dilus had complained against the Greeks that they were prevent-
ing them from observing their Torah and their customs:

ἐμοὶ τοίνυν οὐκ ἀρέσκει...κωλύεσθαι αὐτοὺς ζῆς κατὰ τὰ αὐτῶν ἔθνη καὶ
χρήματα εἰς σύνδειπνα καὶ τὰ ἱερὰ εἰσφέρειν...καὶ γὰρ Γαίος
καῖσαρ...κωλύων θιάσους συνάγεσθαι...τούτους οὐκ ἐκώλυσεν οὔτε
σύνδειπνα ποιεῖν...ὁμοίως, δὲ κἀγὼ...ἐπιτρέπω κατὰ τὰ πάτρια ἔθη καὶ
νόμιμα συνάγεσθαί τε καὶ ἑστιᾶσθαι.

We have learnt from this that there was a fixed custom among the
Israelites in the days of Caesar (and before them), whether in
Rome or in Dilus, to eat together in groups (assemblies) and for
this purpose they would collect money from the public and these
meals were considered a *Mitzvah*. Thus, in any case, it appears
that not only on the Sabbaths did the "*Mitzvah* groups", who are
mentioned in the tradition of the Tanaim, as well as being
permitted by Rabbi Yoḥanan to lend money with interest for the
purpose of providing for fulfilling the obligation of money for
these suppers[62], assemble together for these suppers with their
companions. And if we require proof that these parties (that sometimes took place at the synagogues or in the Midrashic schools[63],
and as was introduced by the Christians subsequently with the
eucharist), but even during the weekdays it was a religious act
with an ambience of holiness. Josephus attests to this in his
testimony about the Essenes and their suppers. And so we must
state that it was precisely the communal-supper (over which the
substance of the Blessing over the meal was devoted), as it was
taught in the *Mishnah* and arranged in the *Tosephta*,[64] with its
"manner of reclining" and sequence of eating, and with its many
cups, which constituted the source for both the Christian *Agape*
and the Eucharist, since the many modifications found in the early
Christian sources with regard to the order of blessings over the
cup and over the bread, which precedes the other, were
underpinned by the two cups which were always drunk in the
above-mentioned meals amongst the Israelites, a cup before the
food and a cup afterwards (a cup for the blessing). The Christians
maintained one, eliminating the second so that the first cup was
preserved by the former [Israelites] while the last cup (the blessing after the meal) was preserved by the latter.

---

[62] *j. Shab* 4:7a; 2:17c; *j. Ber* 7:11c.

[63] *m. Ber* 4:8, and the parallels in the *Talmudim*.

[64] Goltz (*Tischgebete*, pp 13-14) understands the cup of the blessing (after the
meal) as similar to the "cup of Elijah the prophet", but there is no sign of this cup
in the early sources, and in principle it symbolized the fifth cup of the passover evening, which was ultimately rejected.

As can be seen, the name itself, ἀγάπη (אהבה), proves its
Jewish origins. Although scholars have been doubtful and have
sought to clarify its origins, they have not been successful. For
example, Oesterley sought to explain it as a translation of the term
"communal" [*havurah*] from the linguistic term *hiba*;[65] however,
the word *havurah* is never used in this way. Closer to the truth is
that the *agape* is but the Hebrew term *meriyot*, which is found in
the *Baraita* in the *Talmud* (*b.Moed Qatan* 22b)[66], and its contents
refer to a supper with companions, which was initially,
undoubtedly, referred to as *seudat-reyim* (fellowship-meal), but
with time the name was shortened, as usual, and only the term
meriyot remained.

Now, after we have seen the affinity between the essence of
the Christian meals and the communal-meals of Israel, it will not
be difficult to appreciate the pattern of blessings in the portion
under discussion, and to see in them the foundations upon which
the Sages moulded the Grace after Meals. And here, the first
blessing over the cup, which is the blessing over the wine (the
Creator of the Vine), was transformed by the Christian writer into
thanksgiving for redemption by converting the vine into a symbol
of the kingdom of heaven and the Messianic days (which have
already arrived), and similarly with the rest of the blessings. And
the second blessing over the bread was also eliminated and in its
place a thanksgiving for spiritual good was introduced,[67] although
it is necessary to be precise with regard to its end. Inasmuch as
the same Christian prayer which speaks of the ingathering of the
exiles, which concludes the blessing, certainly does not cohere
with Christianity in its early days, and it is reasonable to assume
that the Jewish blessing-pattern was embedded here. However, the
version of the blessing which is in the *Halacha* is shorter, and, as
we learned in the *Tosephta* (1:6): "These are the blessings that
you shorten when blessing over fruit...", and there is no petition.
Similarly: "These are the blessings which do not end with blessed
be he who blesses over the fruit...". And here he concludes

---

[65] Oesterley, *Jewish Background*, p. 204.

[66] In this *Baraita*, *LeSimcha* and *Lemeriyot*, the *Meriyot* has its own meaning
although according to Rabba bar bar Ḥana—*Simchat Meriyot*.

[67] We should avoid regarding spirituality as a Christian innovation, as it is possible that even amongst Israel there were paradigms of similar blessings. M.
Dibelius ("Die Mahlgebete der Didache", *ZNTW* [1938] pp. 32-41) has already suggested that such a paradigm should be sought amongst the Hellenistic Jews. Bousset
demonstrated this in his exposition, *Eine Judische Gebetsammlung im siebenten
Buch der apostolischen Konstitutionen* (See Philo's testimony in regards to the
prayers of the Therapeuts "on the sereneness and the truth and the understanding
and the knowledge"), although we must not exclude the Jews of Israel, especially
certain circles, from similar concerns.

(doxology). From this it can be deduced that in early days a single *Halacha* or custom did not exist for the blessing over deriving benefits, since there is a fourth prayer for the Grace after Meals, it too is part of the same *Halacha* in the *Tosephta* (*Ibid.*), that can be shortened. You can conclude with it, but nevertheless: "Rabbi Yose ha-Gelili would conclude with the last blessing in the Grace after Meals and prolong it." Furthermore, it seems that from the *Epistle of Aristeas*, where we read about the Elder of the Priests who had made a blessing during the meal (with the king) before eating "as was the custom among the Jews". It was also the custom among the Essenes, where the priest blesses (*Jewish Wars* 2.8:5), blessing the king and his wife and his household. It seems that we can learn from this that they would prolong the Grace before the food and include a petition (here—a blessing for the host, which our *Talmud* and custom has fixed as part of the Grace and after it),[68] although we must discuss what determined the blessing over the breaking of the bread, namely, that it is said only after the breaking. Now in Matthew (15:36; 26:26) and in Mark (6:41; 8:6; 14:12) and in Luke (9:16; 22:19) and in Acts (27:35) and in Paul in 1 Corinthians (11:24) we read that the blessing preceded the breaking of the bread, as is the ruling which the *Halacha* ordained in the *Gemara* (*b.Ber* 39b). However, from the words of Rabbi Ḥiyya bar Ashi (39a) we learn that there were those who instructed that the blessing should be said over the bread which had been broken (Rabbi Ḥiyya's opinion, as recorded in *j.Ber* 6:10, 71, is the middle road between both of these opinions). At first glance, there seems to be a disagreement in this *Halacha* among the early Sages, and moreover, it seems from the words of Rab Papa that, "everyone agrees that on Passover you place pieces of bread both whole and broken", that we have before us a vestige of the meal of the Passover evenings (as well as several other customs) reminiscent of the ancient custom to bless over the broken bread (See above the statement made by Mar b. Rabina and the *Baraita*, which always tries to harmonise customs), since its reason ("because of the bread of the poor") is untenable.[69]

---

[68] *b.Ber* 46a. The *Rishonim* replicate the "Jerusalem" and to the "*Tosephta*" as also speaking of this custom.

[69] Even though the above *Halacha* of Passover was observed in Babylon only, we have fortuitously learned from the differences in customs between the people of Israel and the people of Babylon, that they acted in accordance to this custom in Israel also (M. Margoliyoth (ed.), *Encyclopedia of Talmudic and Geonic Literature* (Tel Aviv, 1960 [Hebrew]) p. 133). And J. Jeremias ("Das Brotbrechen beim Passahmahl und Mc 14,22 par.", *ZNTW 33* [1934] pp. 203-204) reprimands the scholars that have come to elucidate from the Gospels on the "Last Supper" which relate that Jesus blessed and afterwards broke the bread that was not a Passover meal, where the custom is precisely the converse, and claims that even on the Passover the blessing over the bread is said first and then the bread is broken. He

Let us now return to the blessings after the food. First of all we have learnt that there are three blessings, as is set out in the first *Halacha* of the *Mishnah* which speaks of three blessings and *Maayan Shalosh* (the prayer *al Hamehya* and other prayers said upon foodstuffs and cakestuffs and products of the land of Israel other than bread in *m.Ber* 6:1).[70] However, from the *Baraitot* we have learnt, according to the opinions of Rabbi Eliezer, Rabbi Ishmael and Rabbi Yose ha-Gelili, that a fourth blessing (the good and does good) can be found within the Grace after Meals. And contrary to the tradition of the Amoraim in the two *Talmudim*, which testifies to the existence of a fourth blessing introduced in memory of those killed at Betar, at their burial. There is no doubt that the blessing "the good and does good" existed during the meals at the Temple,[71] and if we want to reconcile this with the above tradition of the Amoraim, then we are compelled to state that after the Bar Kochba war the blessing was fixed in its place and the division of opinion ceased.[72] In any case, from this we find corroboration for the opinion of the early scholars who rejected the fourth blessing as being moulded into the Grace after Meals.

As to the contents of the blessings, we find the imprint of the pattern-of-blessings current in Israel, since the blessing on "the holy Name who resides in the hearts" and "the knowledge and the faith" etc. are intended for the second blessing (covenant, *Torah* and *Eretz*) and the blessing on "food and drink which God has given to humankind to support them" is intended as a blessing for sustainment, and the third (the petition for the ingathering and redemption of the congregation) is aimed at "the rebuilder of Jerusalem", but the Christian writer altered it for his purposes, and even deliberately stressed the spirituality of the Grace after Meals in the Christian prayer ("but you bestowed upon us spiritual food..."). However, it is necessary to explore the

---

however did not go into the depths of these particulars. On the other hand, this conjecture is rejected on the basis of Greiff's methodology, where he establishes that the *Didache* refers to Passover (*Das älteste Pascharituale*, p. 149).

[70] Perhaps we should learn about the three blessings especially from covenantal blessing in the *Book of Jubilees* 22:6.

[71] A. Büchler has dealt with this issue (*Studies in Sin and Atonement in the Rabbinic Literature of the First Century* London, 1928 [*Jews' College Publications* 11]) and so has C. Albeck ("Die vierte Eulogie des Tischgebets", *MGWJ* 78 [1934] pp. 430-437).

[72] Büchler is of the opinion that they fixed it after Betar as a fourth blessing in the house of mourning, while in all the other places it was already fixed and existed (although it is difficult to interpret the tradition as it is). Albeck believes that at first there was no fixed formula for this blessing, and after those killed in Betar were buried, it was fixed as the last rite.

changes in the arrangement introduced by the Christian mould,
which can be found in the second blessing (on the land) which
precedes the blessing "who sustains". It is not improbable that we
have before us a foundation upon which we can interpret the name
Eucharistia which pertains to the blessing after the food, whose
theme is thanksgiving. As we have learned in the *Baraita* (49a):
"R' Abba (=Rab) says that it is necessary that thanksgiving
should be said (in the second blessing) at the beginning and at the
conclusion and anyone diminishing should not diminish from any
one of them". This *Halacha* teaches us that thanksgiving occupies
a special place in the Grace after meals, and since according to the
tradition in the *Didache* the second blessing preceded the first
blessing, this indicates that thanksgiving, and an expectancy
towards God, were fixed features of the blessings over the food.
Nevertheless, the language of thanksgiving appears even in the
blessings before the food. It seems, therefore, that the early tradition was preserved here, and that the blessings over the meal have
always included thanksgiving, but this needs further investigation.

As to the matter of the verses after the blessings, the first one
reminds us of "May the All-Merciful send us Elijah the
Prophet...". And even in regards to the remainder, there are
scholars who propound the theory that they were said in a manner
of praise, similarly to the blessings said after the meal by the
Israelites.[73] Despite this, it is worthwhile to assess the language of
"Hosanna to THE GOD OF DAVID" which is rarely found in
Christian books (in Mt 21:9—to Jesus—to the son of David). As
is known, this resembles the formula "the rebuilder of Jerusalem"
found in the prayer of *Eretz Yisrael* ("the God of David and
rebuilder of Jerusalem"),[74] so it is possible that we can discern a
hint of this formula here. Or perhaps there were those who practised the custom of blessing in this manner in *Eretz Yisrael*, even
in the Grace after meals, in accord with the tradition which
existed among the *Rishonim*[75] .

The language of the final prayer of the *Apostolic Tradition* of
Hippolytus and in *Apostolic Church Order* and the Coptic version
indicates that its substance had already been fixed in the *Didache*,

---

[73] Goltz, *Tischgebete*, p. 16. There are those who link them with political peti-
tions against the Romans (Klein, *Katechismus*, pp. 222ff). From every aspect this
portion needs further investigation.

[74] As well as "in the prophet the God of David who sprouts redemption", *j.RH*
4:59c., and in *Midrash Shmuel* ch. 26, 126.

[75] See Z. W. Rabinowitz, *Sh°are Torat Eretz Jisrael: Notes and Comments on
the Yerushalmi*, ed. E. Z. Melammed (Jerusalem, 1940) pp. 10-11, and in the
ancient poems (Habermann,. blessings virtually three and virtually four) we find
"the God of David rebuilder of Jerusalem" or "the God of David he is..." several
times, as well as in proverb of the *Kalir*.

but had been misplaced, and this is the mould into which it was fixed:

> Concerning the oil of myrrh this is the way we give thanks: we thank you God [the Creator of everything] for the smell of the good myrrh, and for the eternal world which you made known to us through Jesus your servant. Because to you be the honour and the might forever. Amen.

And we have already had the privilege of deriving confirmation from the differences of opinion among the Sages, as we have learnt in *Tosephta* (*t.Ber* 6:5): "The School of Shamai say that with a glass of wine on his right and pleasant oil on his left he blesses the wine and afterwards the oil and the School of Hillel says you bless on the oil..." (the reference is to oil and wine after the food). And this blessing has not been elucidated, although we found several formulas in the *Talmud*[76] ("Creator of pleasant oil", "Creator of oil of our land", *b.Ber* 43a; "who infused good aroma into pleasant oil, who infused good aroma into the trees of spices, and others", *j.Ber* 6:10d). From this we can apparently establish that the blessing of Rabbi Zera ("who infused good aroma into pleasant oil") is the essence of the prayer.[77]

The Fast on the Second and Fifth Day of the Week

> 8.1 Αἱ δὲ νηστεῖαι ὑμῶν μὴ ἔστωσαν μετὰ τῶν ὑποκριτῶν. νηστεύουσι γὰρ δευτέρᾳ σαββάτων καὶ πέμπτῃ. ὑμεῖς δὲ νηστεύσατε τετράδα καὶ παρασκευήν
> And let your fasts not be with the flatterers; because they fast on the second day of the week and on the fifth; but you will fast on the fourth and on the eve of the Sabbath.

Now we have learnt in several places in the tradition, that it was the custom in Israel to fast on these very days (even though not in the majority, and not even regularly).[78] However later tradition pins the reason for the fasts on the destruction of the Temple. However, from this, and from Luke 18:12 (which is interpreted in

---

[76] 43:1 and compare with 43:2 (there were those who used it for lubrication, even though, apparently, you do not need to make a blessing over the "oil for filth" - *j.Ber* 6:10d; however, in "the Church reforms of Hippolytus, the blessing over the oil contains thanksgiving for lubrication.

[77] The researchers tried to interpret what the properties of this oil were, and there were those who said that it was oil for the lubrication of the sick which was mentioned in the *Epistle of James* 4:14, and others said that it was the oil of baptism. However, according to our sources it can be said with no doubt that it came after the meal for "good aroma" (and even for lubrication), but not everyone acted in accordance with this, and therefore there is no "torah" in the versions before us.

[78] See volume II of the *Studies*, לישובה של ברייתא אחת and S. Lieberman, *Hayerushalmi Kiphshuto* (Jerusalem, 1934).

accordance to our document) we learn that they acted accordingly
even at the time of the Temple. When we seek the cause of this, it
seems that the only way to interpret this is on the basis of the
premise that the fast was linked to the customs whereby in those
days the rural people came together (to the market), where they
used (until the destruction of *Betar*) to sit down with *Dayanim* and
read from the *Torah* (the reading of the *Torah* on Mondays and
Thursdays evolved especially for the people in the rural areas who
did not have anyone who could read for them on the Sabbaths).
Inasmuch as we know that they did not practice these fasts in
Babylon in the days of the Tanaim and the Amoraim, and
inasmuch as we have not heard of the reading of the Torah on
Mondays and Thursdays in the Diaspora (at least until the
Destruction), this would substantiate our conjecture that we can
locate the *Didache* either in Eretz Yisrael or adjacent to it.

BAPTISMAL *HALACHOT*

6:2-3 (Speaks of the baptism of converts to Christianity) Ἐὰν δὲ μὴ ἔχῃς
ὕδωρ ζῶν, εἰς ἄλλο ὕδωρ βάπτισον. εἰ δ' οὐ δύνασαι ἐν ψυχρῷ, ἐν θερμῷ.
Ἐὰν δὲ ἀμφότερα μὴ ἔχῃς, ἔκχεον εἰς τὴν κεφαλὴν τρὶς ὕδωρ εἰς ὄνομα
πατρὸς καὶ υἱοῦ καὶ ἁγίου πνεύματος
Even if you do not have fresh water [as is commanded], baptise in other
[waters]; and if it is impossible in cold water—in hot. And if you do not
have either of those or those, pour water over the head [of the person
being baptised] three times in the name of the Father and the Son and the
Holy Spirit.

We have before us a primary source for the introduction of
"baptism" among the Christians through the pouring of water,
over which reservations were raised later on; even though the
Gnostics, in the second century of their calender, used to baptise
in this way.[79] And in a *Baraita* which we studied (Berachot 22,1):

You pour nine portions of pure water over the one having nocturnal pollu-
tion; Naḥum of Gimzo whispered to Rabbi Aqiba who whispered to Rabbi
Azai and Rabbi Azai withdrew and there was hatred towards his disciples
in the market.

We learnt that this *Halacha* had only recently become known to
the public, and the progenitor of this *Halacha* was Naḥum of
Gimzu, and he himself only said it in a whisper (permission under
constraint).[80] It is possible, therefore, to conclude that the *Baraita*
originated at the time of the destruction of the Temple. And as far
as the *Hachamim* is concerned, we only heard that it was *kosher*

---

[79] Irenaeus, *Contra Haer.* I.21:4.
[80] See above, fn. 18.

from the words of the Amoraim (Babylonian Talmud *Ibid.*, Rab Huna) from which it is perhaps possible to ascertain that it is an early tradition.

THE *HALACHOT* GOVERNING PRIESTLY GIFTS

13:3 Πᾶσαν οὖν ἀπαρχή. γεννημάτων ληνοῦ καὶ ἅλωνος, βοῶν τε καὶ προβάτων λαβὼν δώσεις τὴν ἀπαρχὴν τοῖς προφήταις· αὐτοὶ γάρ εἰσιν οἱ ἀρχιερεῖς ὑμῶν. Ἐὰν δὲ μὴ ἔχητε προφήτην, δότε τοῖς πτωχοῖς. Ἐὰν σιτίαν ποιῇς, τὴν ἀπαρχὴν λαβὼν δὸς κατὰ τὴν ἐντολήν. Ὡσαύτως κεράμιον οἴνου ἢ ἐλαίου ἀνοίξας, τὴν ἀπαρχὴν λαβὼν δὸς τοῖς προφήταις· ἀργυρίου δὲ καὶ ἱματισμοῦ καὶ παντὸς κτήματος λαβὼν τὴν ἀπαρχήν, ὡς ἄν σοι δόξῃ

And all *Teruma* of the fruit of the winery and of the silo, the cattle and the sheep, take and give as a *Teruma* for the prophets; because they are your high priests. And if you do not have a prophet amongst you, give it to the poor. And when you make a compound[81] take the *Teruma* and give it to the prophets. And when you open a jar of wine or oil take *Teruma* and give it to the prophets. However, from the money, from clothing and from all property, take a *Teruma* as you will and give it as a *Mitzvah*.

Now first of all we must examine the issue of the source of these words. Harnack[82] and the scholar Drews believe that we cannot regard them as deriving from the *Torah*, but they must be interpreted as new Christian *Halacha*. They sustain their argument with two pieces of evidence, the first being the fact that tithes are not mentioned. And the second is that there is no substance in the *Torah* to the giving of money as *Teruma* etc. Therefore Drews[83] assumes that the writer derived this from a special source which contained "*mitzvoth* of the Lord", in other words Jesus (and he supplements this with 1:5 ("Happy is he who gives *tzedaka* as a *Mitzvah*"). However, the fact that it does not mention the tithes is not conclusive. Because, even if he had wanted to abolish them, this is not proof that everything that he observed was derived in its essence from a new Torah. Moreover, we have already found this in early sources (such as in Israel), where the tithes are subsumed under the generic name of *Terumot*.[84] In addition, a Jewish *sofer* who is well-versed in tradition, who wrote the *Book of Biblical Antiquities*, which is attributed to Philo, erred and explicitly altered the term from tithes to *Terumot*, for this reason. As he

---

[81] Is it possible that we have here extensive evidence of a *Halacha* which obligates the giving *halah* from a mixture which has not been baked, in contrast to a tradition we have from Philo, and was the custom among the Jewish inhabitants of Alexandria (*m.Hal* 4:10)?

[82] In his remarks to the same verses in his big publication.

[83] Drews, "Untersuchung", pp. 63-67.

[84] Philo undoubtedly subsumed the tithes under the portion of the priestly-gifts *SpecLeg* 1:132-141, and see also the *Letter of Aristeas* 158 (Wendland, p. 45).

writes (14:4), "since the Holy One, Blessed be He, saved one of
fifty Israelites (from Egypt)". In this manner he explicates "and
fifty Israelites went up" (see the Tannaitic *Midrash*), therefore, "I
command my people to tithe their fruit for me (changing *Teruma*
which is one of fifty, to a tithe [one in ten]). And in the matter of
the *Teruma* of oil and money etc., the *Halacha* derives its substance from the tradition of the *Rishonim*, as we shall see below. It
is not difficult to suppose that those *Halachot* which were renewed and added as accretions to the substance of *Torah*
(*Midrash*) were ultimately regarded as written *Mitzvah*, even if we
refuse to concur that the writer relied on the laws of the Torah,
since *Mitzvah* in the language of the Sages was regularly used to
express the words of the *Soferim* (such as "the *mitzvoth* of the
Elders"),[85] and it is not improbable to assume that this fixed language existed at the time of the writer (and before him). And perhaps we can discern in the wording *kemitzvah*, which only applies
to the *Halachot* obtaining to gifts for [their] priests and for the
poor, a hint of the word, *Mitzvah*, *metzavta* which is used by
Amoraim and the Tanaim in Israel, and denotes *ketzedaka*, the
giving of money.[86] As to the essence of the question, it cannot be
denied that the writer relied on Scripture, as evidenced by his language. Origen had already commanded that the priestly gifts mentioned in the *Torah*, are among those *mitzvoth* which were not to
be abolished, that even the Christians are obliged to observe (in
their fashion)[87]. Nevertheless Irenaeus opposes the tithes[88], and in
any case the writer of the Syriac *Didascalia* observes them *de jure*
(but not *de facto*) and imposes an obligation to give "to the true
Messiah the High Priest and his servants[89].

We shall return to discuss the *Halachot* themselves.

---

[85] See below, p. 311.

[86] *Mitzvat* in the *Halacha* of Rabban Gamliel (in the name of the *Rishonim*) and
in the tradition of *minyan Usha* (*j.Peah* 1:15b) and see *b.Ket* 51a; *Pesikata Rabati*
25 undoubtedly refers to *tzedaka*.

[87] *Sermon on the Book of Numbers* (Baehrens XI, pp. 75-80) refers to *primitiae*,
the firstfruits of the new wine and oil and all the fruit of the tree and the grain of
the field and a tithe of the animals, and he testifies that the Pharisees who do not eat
until they have separated— baptise!—and he says: How "shall our righteousness be
more than the Pharisees who do not enjoy the fruits until they have brought *terumot*
to the Priests—thus confusing separation with donating—and you separate the
TITHES to the LEVITES. *et ego nihil horum faciens fructibus terrae ita abitur ut
sacerdo nesciat, Levites ignorat divinum altare non sentiat?.*

[88] Harnack, *Die Lehre*.

[89] Gibson, Ch. 9, p. 85 (although at the beginning of the chapter p. 77 he is
inclined to intimate that the tithes had been abolished).

It is clear that the writer is of the opinion that the tithe of cattle is for the priests, in contrast to the *Halacha* which ordains that the tithe should revert to the owners. But corroboration for his view can be found in Jubilees 13:25-26 and the Book of Tobit (the long version, 1:6-7) and Philo (*SpecLeg* 141:1). Contrariwise, in the matter of *Teruma* which is not of the crops of the earth or cattle, this is not dealt with in the Bible and the writer himself confesses that there is no absolute obligation and has no measure, and we did find corroboration in our own sources. First of all, in the Jerusalem *Talmud* (*j.Demai* 1:21d) Rabbi Yoḥanan rules that,[90] in other words he tithed even from foods which were not of "the produce of your seed", and despite this the *Talmud* explains so that it can be discerned that the custom adhered to by Rabbi Yoḥanan was based on the tradition of the *Rishonim* who were stringent in the tithes, extending the range of the applicability of the *Mitzvah* even beyond what had been interpreted in the Torah (including fruits of the tree and vegetables).

However, the writers of the *Tosephot* transmit what is written (*t.Taan* 9:1) in *Sifre*: "Tithe—I do not have anything but the crops of my seed which must be tithed and merchandise". And nevertheless, in contrast to the *Sifre* which is before us, it is still far-fetched to conjecture, as proposed by the scholar Finkelstein,[91] that the *dictum* is from the Middle Ages as it suited the economic life of the Israelites in those days (there were fewer landowners and an abundance of merchansie), since already in the times of the Second Temple (in the times of the latter Hasmonaeans and afterwards) the number of businessmen grew in Israel (and even more so in the Diaspora). The law provides, especially in those days when priestly gifts were no more than a type of taxes for the kingdom of Israel that were sent to Jerusalem to the "treasury"[92], that a *takanah* be enacted which would devolve upon the owners of moveable property and monies so that they would not be exempt from the obligation which was imposed on everyone else. And indeed, Rabbi Abba demands (Bar Kahana?) in *Pesiqta de Rab Kahana* that a tenth be tithed (Buber, 90, 2): and it is reasonable to assume that these same "*terumot* and tithes" which were collected from the Diaspora by the messengers of the *Ne'siim* [head of the Sanhedrin] for their benefit (and appropriated for the benefit of "those who labour in Torah"), a phenomenon observed by Appian (*On Cilicia*), were undoubtedly subsumed under the *terumot* and tithes which were given first to the priests, so that

---

[90] When he would even eat meat, even an egg, he would rule (= מְעַשֵּׂר).

[91] On the same verse in his publication of *Sifre*.

[92] See G. Alon, *Studies in Jewish History* I (Tel Aviv: Hakibbutz Hameuchad, 1958) pp. 83-92.

even these gifts were not collected exclusively from the land-owners[93]. Support for this can be found in what Jubilees 32:2 has recorded, namely that Jacob had a Levi tithe for him "from man to animal and from the gold including all the tools and the clothes". Or perhaps we should be more precise by turning to Luke 18:12, who mentions a Pharisee who gives thanksgiving to the Holy-One, Blessed be He, who did not make him like other creatures who oppress etc. or like the tax collector, as he (the Pharisee) "fasts twice on Sabbath and tithes πάντα ὅσα κτῶμαι (from all his wealth)".

In any case, from the body of the *Halacha* which is found in the book which has been mentioned, it has been established that it was not an actual fixed *Mitzvah*, as was the *Teruma* for the harvest of the land (which is from the *Torah*), but had no measure, and someone can give more and someone else can give less, both having fulfilled their obligation. And this obviously was the opinion of the *Rishonim* in Israel.[94]

---

[93] *Panarion haer.* 30:4-30, 12, 9.
[94] Some of the books and research in the matters discussed in this article were not available for examination.

PAUL'S JEWISH-CHRISTIAN OPPONENTS
IN THE *DIDACHE*

DAVID FLUSSER
Jerusalem

The aim of the present paper is not to clarify the various facets of enmity between so called "Jewish Christianity" and Paul. The real purpose of our study is to show that *Didache* 6:2-3 reflects the position of the majority in the Mother Church towards the Gentile Christian believers while Paul's attitude was more unusual and therefore revolutionary. Both positions represent two genuine interpretations of the necessary obligations of Gentile God-fearers. We believe that both factions based their claims upon the Apostolic Decree. Paul's view became victorious but even so it is not without interest to learn what was the opposite view with the help of *Didache* 6:2-3, a position which was held, among others, by the apostle Peter. The text of *Didache* 6:2-3, it will be recalled, runs as follows: "If you can bear the whole yoke of the Lord (i.e. of the Law), you will be perfect; but if you cannot, do what you can. Concerning the food, bear what you will be able to bear. But be sure to refrain completely from meat which has been sanctified before idols, for it represents the worship of dead gods."

The Apostolic Decree is quoted three times in the Acts of the Apostles (15:20, 28-29 and 21:25). Already from the beginning of modern scholarship, the question was asked concerning the actual point of contact between the Apostolic Decree and the so called Noachic precepts in Judaism, because both contain a list of religious and moral obligations for non-Jews. The Noachic precepts were thus a Jewish non-Christian parallel to the Apostolic Decree, which was issued by a community of Jews believing in Jesus in order to lay upon the Gentile no greater burden than that which is necessary. The first step towards the solution of the problem was taken by the German scholar Adolf Resch already in 1905.[1] He rightly recognized the eminent value of the so called Western text of the Apostolic Decree. In contrast to the common text, where Gentiles are obliged to abstain from what has been sacrificed to idols, from blood, from what is strangled and from unchastity, in the Western text the prohibition to eat what is strangled is missing. Resch also succeeded in showing that for the most important of the Church Fathers only the three prohibitions—not including the one concerning that which is strangled—formed the text of the

---

[1] A. Resch, "Das Aposteldekret nach seiner ausserkanonischen Textgestalt Untersucht", (Leipzig: Hinrich's, 1905 [TU ns. 3]) pp. 1-179.

Apostolic Decree and that these three prohibitions were originally identical with the three capital sins in early patristic literature, namely idolatry, bloodshed and fornication. He also rightly argued that Paul in reality fulfilled the obligations of the original text and meaning of the Apostolic Decree.

It is not our task here to treat fully the problems of the text and the historical development of the Apostolic decision. This we have already done in another study.[2] Here we only have to mention the fact that the three capital sins, idolatry, bloodshed and fornication, are often mentioned in rabbinic literature and that, according to a decision from the beginning of the second century C.E., a Jew must choose death rather than let himself be coerced to transgress one of these three prohibitions. Some decades later, at the end of the second century C.E., perpetrators of these sins were excluded from the church and their penitence was not accepted. Here the main point which pertains to the present study is that idolatry, bloodshed and fornication are also three of the extant seven Noachic precepts. As has been demonstrated by Resch, the prohibition of the same three crimes formed the original content of the Apostolic Decree. The whole list of seven Jewish Noachic precepts is attested only from the mid-second century C.E. If so, it is more than probable that in the Apostolic Age the official Jewish position was to require the Noachites, the God-fearing Gentiles, to abstain from idolatry, bloodshed and fornication. Hence quite naturally this same rule was accepted by the Apostolic Church. I hope to show here that even if the basic rule was then accepted by the church, new problems arose in the interpretation of the Apostolic Decree. The two divergent approaches concerning the application and interpretation of the famous decree are represented by the Petrine and Pauline parties. Moreover one discovers some strong indications that the same problem—albeit probably not in such an earnest and clear formulation—also existed among Jews in the politics pertaining to God-fearing Gentiles.

Does *Didache* 6:2-3 express a "conservative" Jewish interpretation of the Noachic laws[3] or does the passage represent an analogous Christian position concerning the Apostolic Decree? I think that the function of our passage in the context of the *Didache* dispels all doubts about the Christian origin of *Didache* 6:2-3. The passage clearly reflects the Jewish-Christian understanding of the

---

[2] David Flusser and Shmuel Safrai, "Das Aposteldekret und die Noachistischen Gebote", *Wer Tora vermehrt mehrt Leben: Festgabe für Heinz Kremers zum 60. Geburtstag* (Neukirchen-Vluyn: Neukirchener-Verlag, 1986) pp. 173-192.

[3] This is the opinion of A. Stuiber in his excellent study "Das ganze Joch des Herrn (Didache 6,2-3)", in *Studia Patristica* 4,1 (Berlin: Akademie-Verlag, 1961 [TU 79]) pp. 323-329.

obligations of Gentile Christians towards Judaism, a position which was utterly unacceptable for Paul.

Almost as soon as the text of the *Didache*[4] was published in 1882 from a Greek manuscript, it was recognized that the first six chapters of the work are actually a Jewish treatise christianized by the author of the *Didache*; from chapter seven on, the book is of Christian provenance. It was only as a consequence of the discovery of the Dead Sea Scrolls that it was recognized that the Jewish treatise contained in the first six chapters of the *Didache* is indeed extant in an old Latin translation.[5] Its real title was *de doctrina Apostolorum*, but today it is commonly referred to as The Two Ways. This Jewish tractate—and not the Christian *Didache*—was used by the author of the apocryphal Epistle of Barnabas of the first half of the second century C.E. All this can lead only to one conclusion: the Jewish treatise The Two Ways[6] was already considered to be a manual of Christian ethics in the first decades of Christianity and often it was even viewed as the teaching of the Apostles. Whether the Didachist was aware of the original provenance of his source is not possible to determine with absolute precision. However it would seem that he was convinced that The Two Ways was a Christian work, and even one of "apostolic" authority because he did not permit himself to change the wording of his source very much. It is reasonable to believe that the *Didache* was written before the end of the first century C.E. The Two Ways was written earlier, there are indications that this Jewish treatise was known to Philo of Alexandria.[7]

The Jewish tractate ended originally with an admonition. Although the Didachist (6:1) abbreviated it, the text is more complete in the Latin version of the Jewish source (*Doct* 6:1-6). Nonetheless it is difficult to reconstruct the precise original wording of the admonition.[8] Even so, it is evident that the Latin translation of the ending reflects the original content of the conclusion of The Two Ways: "Beware lest anyone cause you to abandon this teach-

---

[4] The most recent editions of the *Didache* are Klaus Wengst, *Didache (Apostellehre)* (Darmstadt: Wissenschaftliche Buchgesellschaft, 1984 [SUC 2]) pp. 3-100; Willy Rordorf & Andre Tuilier, *La doctrine des Douze Apôtres (Didachè)* (Paris: Les Éditions du Cerf, 1978 [SC 248]). A pioneering book about the Jewish roots of the *Didache* was the treatise of G. Klein, *Der älteste christliche Katechismus und die jüdische Propaganda-Literatur* (Berlin: G. Reimer, 1909).

[5] J.-P. Audet, "Affinités littéraires et doctrines du Manuel de Discipline", *RB* 59 (1952) pp. 217-238.

[6] About the Two Ways treatise, see also my study, "The Two Ways," in D. Flusser, *Jewish Sources in Early Christianity* (Tel Aviv: Sifriat Poalim, 1979) pp. 235-252 (in Hebrew).

[7] See the preceding note.

[8] The last sentence of the Latin *Doct* (6:6) is surely a Christian medieval addition. It seems to me that *Doct* (6:5b) is a later addition too.

ing, otherwise you will be taught apart from the (true) instruction. If you do these things daily with deliberation,[9] you will be near to the living God. But if you fail to do them, you will be far from the truth. Store up all these things in your soul and you will not be beguiled from your hope."

This concluding admonition fits admirably well the ethical imperative and the dualistic vein of the Jewish Two Ways, and is an appropriate conclusion of the work. Neither in the Latin *Doctrina Apostolorum* nor in the paraphrastic *Epistle of Barnabas* was any other new precept added. Here the *Didache* differs. After the abbreviated form of the original conclusion and before the Christian "Manual of Discipline" that follows, in *Didache* 6:2-3 an addition to The Two Ways was inserted.

As has already been noted, the passage was absent from the original tractate of The Two Ways, but the appendix already existed in the copy of the treatise used by the Didachist. Theoretically the passage under question could have been a Jewish addition to the Jewish tractate,[10] but this is highly improbable. We hope to show further that, although *Didache* 6:2-3 was not composed by the Didachist, it was a Christian work, written by a man whose Christian Weltanschauung differed from the approach of the Didachist. On the other hand, the addition differs also from the preceding Jewish text. While the Two Ways is an inner-Jewish ethical treatise, only *Didache* 6:2-3 is addressed to Gentile believers.

Though The Two Ways is of Jewish origin, it was regarded as apostolic instruction not only by the Didachist,[11] but also by the *Doctrina Apostolorum*. If the apostolic ascription appears from the text's very beginnings in all the witnesses without any exceptions, it follows that from the first decades of Christianity, the Two Ways was considered a product of the Apostolic Mother Church. As such, the tractate began to be read also by Gentile believers in Christ, and thus it is no wonder that an appendix was added, reflecting the spirit of the majority of the Jewish Mother Church which sought to stipulate the obligations of Gentile Christian believers.

At this stage the tractate reached the Didachist. For him *Didache* 6:2-3 belonged to the Vorlage and was an authentic apostolic teaching that carried all the authority of his source. Did

---

[9] Was this written under the influence of the famous verse in Joshua 1:8?

[10] This is the opinion of A. Stuiber. See above note 3.

[11] I even venture that the supposed Apostolic origin of the Two Ways was the main impulse for the Didachist to compose his own book. He believed that the treatise is an apostolic message to the Gentiles. The Two Ways became for him a starting point for his *Didache*. About the titles of the work see Rordorf & Tuilier, *op.cit.*, pp. 13-17.

he notice that the passage was a child of a spirit different from his own? Even if he had some suspicions, the authority of his Vorlage dissipated them. One passage begins with the words: "If you can bear the whole yoke of the Lord, you will be perfect..." The "yoke of the Lord" means here the "yoke of the Law," but as we will see later, the term "the yoke of the Lord" is also Jewish and has the same meaning. The Didachist could understand the expression as describing common Christian duties.

But did the Didachist fully understand the passage? Certainly he did not need it when he adopted it from his source. For some of us, the tendency of the whole passage is clear enough, but for many who do not possess historical imagination—or knowledge— it will be easy to miss the central point of *Didache* 6:2-3. At least after the rediscovery of the *Didache* not a few modern scholars were misled.[12] They believed that the passage taught a Christian ascetic attitude concerning both food and sexual life: those who completely renounce sex are perfect. In this field, as also in ascetic dietetics the Christian believer has to try as far as possible to reach the ideal exigencies. If such a distorted exegesis could arise in modern scholarship, why was the Didachist obliged to understand his *Vorlage* better, even if its approach was more or less foreign to the Didachist, as it was surely foreign to such cognate contemporary Christian circles in which the three Pastoral Epistles were composed? The Didachist understood and accepted the general line of argument presented in the passage: try to reach the highest possible standard of Christian obligations! "If you can bear the whole yoke of the Lord, you will be perfect; but if you cannot, do what you can!"[13] A kind of contrast really does exist between the original exigencies embedded in our passage and the later regulations of the Gentile Christian Churches to which the *Didache* was addressed. Nevertheless, this difference was not felt by the Didachist himself. So he could incorporate *Didache* 6:2-3 into his treatise and at the same time admonish the Churches not to let their fasts fall on the same day as the hypocrites, who fast on Monday and Thursday, "Rather you should fast on Wednesday and Friday" (Didache 8:1). He also instructs them, "Nor should you pray as the hypocrites, but pray the Lord's Prayer thrice daily" (Didache 8:2-3). Nor does he refer to the Sabbath, but rather to the celebration of the Lord's Day, i.e. Sunday.

In order to proceed further in our investigation, we must make a few remarks concerning some philological questions. Our passage speaks about the bearing of the whole yoke of the Lord

---

[12] 12 See A. Stuiber, *op.cit.*, pp. 325-326; and Wengst, *op.cit.*, pp. 95-96, n. 52-53.
[13] Naturally also he abhors the meat connected with idolatry.

(or of the Law). It is evident that this terminology alludes to the atmosphere of the so called Apostolic Decree. According to Acts 15:10 it was Peter who said in this connection: "Now therefore why do you make trial of God by pulling a yoke upon the neck of the disciples which neither our fathers nor we have been able to bear?" And according to Acts 15:28 in the letter which announced the decisions of the Apostolic Church it was written: "For it has seemed good to the Holy Spirit and to us to lay upon you no greater burden than these necessary things," namely, the restrictions of the Apostolic Decree. And it was already recognized that a similar terminology appears also in the message to the church of Thyatira in Rev. 2:24-25. "I do not lay upon you any other burden; only hold fast what you have, until I come." According to *Didache* 6:2-3 those who are able to bear the whole yoke are perfect, but if anyone is not able to reach perfection, it does not matter: he shall bear what he is able to bear. This implies that those who are unable to fulfill all the commandments are somehow imperfect. I do not know any other good parallel for the use of the term "perfect," but perhaps the closest text is Mt 19:21. I will try to explain the strange attitude of our passage later.[14]

As we have seen, although it was recognized that the intended audience of *Didache* 6:2-3 was the believing Gentiles, the relevance of his unique text to this complex problem has not, as far as I know, been fully appreciated until now. The proposal contained in *Didache* 6:2-3 is one of the possible solutions to the question regarding the status of believing Gentiles, a problem which was then common to both Judaism and Christianity. The proposed solution is astonishing, but it makes good sense in the context of various trends within Judaism and the early Christian Church. Although the situation was already known in is broad outlines, *Didache* 6:2-3 throws light upon it, and thus the passage becomes a substantial help for understanding both Judaism and primitive Christianity.

It is surely not our task to describe the strong attraction of the Jewish faith among the Gentiles. "The masses have long since shown a keen desire to adopt our religious observances and there is not one city, Greek or barbarian, not a single nation to which our custom of abstaining from work on the seventh day had not

---

[14] It is an ironical paradox that the only parallel that contradicts the approach is the Pauline Romans 14:1-15:5. According to Paul, the weak in faith is a believer who is bound by religious and ritual restrictions. "I know and am persuaded in the Lord Jesus that nothing is unclean in itself; but it is unclean for anyone who thinks it unclean" (Rom 15:14). And Paul says (Rom 15:1); "We who are strong ought to bear with the failings of the weak and not to please ourselves." In both cases, in Romans and in *Didache* 6:2-3, the weak or the less perfect has to be fully respected.

spread, and where the fasts and the lighting of lamps and many of
our prohibitions in the matter of food are not observed"
(Josephus, *Contra Apion* 2:282-3; cf. ibid. 2:123). Many Gentiles
were fascinated not only by the theological spirituality and the
ethical values of Judaism, but also by its "ceremonial law". We
know from the sources that levels of observing the Jewish way of
life as embraced by Gentiles varied from one person to another, it
seems that the Gentile Godfearers were more and more eager to
accept and follow further Jewish obligations as they proceeded in
learning.[15] Since it was impossible in practice, and from the
Jewish point of view even undesirable, for all the God-fearing
Gentiles to become full proselytes, the Gentile "Judaizers" had to
decide, how great a burden they desired to assume. In their decisions they necessarily depended upon the advice and the instructions of their Jewish friends.

In this connection the story of the gradual progress of the
royal family of Adiabene towards full proselytism (Josephus, *AJ*
20:17ff) is instructive, but at the same time clearly atypical. The
obstacles to becoming full proselytes were far more restrictive for
persons of a high social position such as sovereigns of a state than
for other Gentiles who were not exposed to public censure. One
should moreover not forget that the story is narrated by Josephus
from the standpoint of his Gentile readers.

In the process of the full proselytization of the royal house of
Adiabene at least two Jews were involved. The first was a certain
Jewish merchant, named Ananias: "He taught them to worship
God after the manner of the Jewish tradition" (*AJ* 20:34), and it
happened, moreover, that the Queen, Helena, "had likewise been
instructed by another Jew and had been brought over to their
laws" (ibid 35). Finally Izates came to the conclusion, "that he
would not be genuinely a Jew unless he was circumcised and
therefore he was ready to act accordingly" (Ibid 38). Then
Ananias tried to dissuade the king from this last step. "The king
could, he said, worship God even without being circumcised if he
had fully decided to be a devoted adherent of Judaism, for it was
this that counted more than circumcision" (ibid 41). The final
decision to complete the process of proselytism was caused by
"another Jew, named Eleazar, who came from Galilee and who
had the reputation of being extremely strict when it came to the
ancestral laws" (ibid 43). The Greek wording that describes
Eleazar's Jewish way of life shows that he was a Pharisee.[16] In
Greek sources the technical term *akribeia* serves as a definition of

---

[15] See Juvenal, *Sat.* 14:96-106:1.

[16] See Josephus, *Ant* 20.43 about Eleazar: *panu peri ta partia dokon akribes
einai.* See also n. 21 below.

Pharisaic piety: the Pharisees "are believed to interpret the laws with strictness" (*met' akribeias*, Josephus, *BJ* 2.162). According to Acts 22:3 Paul was brought up in Jerusalem at the feet of Gamaliel the Pharisee (see Acts 5:34), "according to the strict manner of the law of our fathers" (*kata akribeian tou patroou nomou*). And in Acts 26:5 Paul says that he has lived as a Pharisee, "according to the strictest (*akribestate*) party of our religion."[17] But even if his Eleazar was a Pharisee, this does not mean that his approach represented the opinion of the majority within rabbinic Judaism.

In reality it should be well known already that in general, ancient Judaism neither wished nor required that all the Gentile God-fearers should become full proselytes. On the other hand, the Jews had no choice but to try and find, for the sake of the Gentiles, a formula which would establish the minimum of obligations indispensable for the Gentiles to be saved together with the Jews who were required to observe the whole Law. Today the obligations for the Gentiles are the so called seven Noachic precepts and we have shown elsewhere[18] that these seven obligations are the result of a long development. We also tried to show that in the earliest stage of development, these seven Noachic precepts originally consisted of only three commandments, he same ones as contained in the better reading of the Apostolic Decree.

Today the Jewish code strictly forbids a non-Jew to observe any Jewish commandment, no matter how minor. A Gentile has to live only according to the Noachic prescriptions and nothing more is required, unless he decides to "become a Jew." Only after passing all the prescribed ceremonies of proselytism and becoming legally Jewish, does he have to observe the whole Law. What happened in later Judaism is a historical paradox: medieval Judaism finally reached a solution not dissimilar to that which Paul more or less endeavored to enforce in Gentile Christian communities, i.e. Gentiles were not permitted to observe the Jewish commandments, but if they became Jews, then they were obliged to observe the whole law of Moses. In both cases, a similar approach led to similar results. Both Paul and the medieval Rabbis wanted to separate the Jews from non-Jews and the most dangerous obstacle in the way of achieving this aim was when Gentiles began to fulfill, even partially, the Jewish law. Such a constellation makes a com-

---

[17] From this small list follows that those who opposed the execution of James, Jesus' brother, were the Pharisees. Even if this designation does not appear explicitly in *Ant* 20:201, they are described there as those who were thought "to be strict in connection of the laws" (*peri ton nomon akribeis*).

[18] See above, n. 2.

plete separation of Jews from Gentiles and vice versa quite impracticable. Thus Gentile "Judaizers" became non desirable for both sides. The question is how far the medieval Jewish separatist solution was stimulated by the ecclesiastical politics of the Church which punished Judaizers and strictly prohibited all proselytism. Gentile Judaizers and possible proselytes were then a menacing danger for the very existence of the Jewish communities. Thus we cannot completely exclude the possibility that the parallelism between the Church and the Synagogue in their wish to achieve complete mutual separatism also had a hidden, hideous dimension.

Before returning to *Didache* 6:2-3, we have to make the following remark, though with some hesitation. According to Acts 16:4 Paul and Silas, "as they went on their way through the cities, they delivered to them for observance the decisions which had been reached by the apostles and elders who were in Jerusalem," i.e. the Apostolic Decree. I do not see any serious cause which would force us to reject this "harmonizing" information as non-historical, especially as we believe that the Apostolic Decree contained only the prohibitions against what was sacrificed to idols, bloodshed and unchastity. Another question is how deeply Paul was interested in imposing upon the churches the rule that the Jews believing in Jesus Christ should be forbidden to transgress the Law of Moses that they had been bound to fulfill before becoming Christians. I am aware of the present tendency of many outstanding Christian New Testament scholars to view Paul as a sincerely observant Jew who never doubted that it was the eternal will of God that all Jews, including naturally those saved by Christ, remain under the holy yoke of the Jewish Law. Personally I am not sure that Paul's mind was so simple and undialectical, but fortunately for me Paul's position about the Law is not the object of our present inquiry. In any case, in the extant epistles Paul never says in so many words that there is anything that can release a Jew from his observation of the Law and its works. On the other hand, we also never find an explicit statement by Paul to the contrary, namely that the belief in Christ for the Jew is incompatible with his life according to the ancestral laws. This became the official opinion of the Church only later, some hundred years after Paul's execution. What we read in 1 Corinthians 7:17-24 is: "Only let every one lead the life which the Lord has assigned to him, and in which God has called him. This is my rule in all the churches. Was any one at the time of his call already cir-' cumcised? Let him not seek to remove the marks of circumcision. Was anyone at the time of his call uncircumcised? Let him not seek circumcision... Every one should remain in the state in which he was called. Were you a slave when called? Never mind... So, brethren, in whatever state each was called, there let him remain

with God." Happily enough it is not our task to decide how great
is the theological weight of this passage. In any case, one is at
least obliged to recognize from the passage that Paul accepted and
delivered to the Churches the rule that Christians from Jewish
stock should practise what they did before their call and also that
the Gentiles should live as they did before becoming Christians.
Thus we are apparently not wrong when we assume that Paul
actually enacted the Apostolic Decree with its implications both
for the Gentiles and for the Jews, and we have already seen that
this was also the regulation of Judaism concerning the Gentile
God-fearers.

    The Apostolic Decree was evidently no more than a con-
firmation and reinforcement of the Noachic prescriptions as they
were then commonly understood. But this did not unequivocally
solve the whole "Gentile question." Are these prescriptions the
minimum obligations of the Gentiles or are they indeed the maximum rules for the God-fearers, as Paul and later the medieval rab-
binism decided? In a famous Jewish homily[19] from the second
century C.E., we read that a Gentile who does the (Mosaic) Law[20]
is considered to be in the same category as the Jewish High Priest
himself. It is not written that God's ordinances and statutes are
destined for the priests, Levites and Israelites; it is rather said:
"You shall keep my statutes and my ordinances which the man
(adam) shall do" (Lev 18:5). In 2 Sam 7:19, the Law is not given
only for the priests, Levites and Israelites, but rather, "This is the
Law for man (adam)." Moreover, the prophet Isaiah does not say
that God's gates are open for the priests, Levites and Israelites,
but he says: "Open the gates that the righteous nation (Hebrew:
goy, the Gentile) which keeps faith may enter in" (Is 26:2). So we

---

[19] *Sifra* to Lev 18:5 (*Ahare Moth*, Chapter 13, *Codex Assem ani*, ed. L. Finkelstein [New York, 1936] pp. 373-4); the same text appears in *Midrash Hagadol* to
Lev, ed. A. Steinsaltz (Jerusalem) p. 518. It is clear that the tradent is Rabbi
Jeremiah. W. Bacher, *Die Agada der Tannaiten* II (Strassbourg, 1890) p. 31, and n.
2, where he cites other parallels, *b.BQ* 38a, *b.San* 59a, where the tradent is Rabbi
Meir. This shows that the saying of a comparatively unknown sage, Rabbi Jeremiah
(see the materials collected by Bacher) was cited in the name of Rabbi Meir.

[20] About the Jewish expression, "to do the Law", see S. Abramson, *Leshonenu*
(Jerusalem, 1954) pp. 61-65. The expression occurs already in Sir 19:20 and in 1
Macc 2:67, 13:48, and in the Dead Sea Scrolls in lQpHab 7:11; 8:1; 12:4-5 and 4
QpPs 2:15, 23, cf. CD 16:8. For the expression "the works of the Law" in the
DSS, see E. Qimron and J. Strugnell, "An Unpublished Halachic Letter from Qumran", *Biblical Archaeology Today* (Jerusalem: Israel Exploration Society, 1985) pp.
401 and 406 n.5. In the *Testaments of the Twelve Patriarchs* "the works of the
Law" appear in *TDan* 6:9 and the expression "to do the Law" occurs in *TGad* 3:2
and *TJos* 11 :1. In the New Testament "to do the Law" occurs in Jn 7:19, Rom
2:12, 14, 25 and Gal 5:3. The "works of the Law" are Pauline. As to the Rabbinic
literature see also the preceding note and *Abot de Rabbi Nathan*, ed. S. Schechter,
p. 124, *DeutR, Zot Haberakha* 11 and the *Targum* to Is 1:27.

see that even a Gentile who practices the (Mosaic) Law is considered to be like the High Priest.

The author of our homily believes that in principle, the Mosaic Law is destined to be observed by all mankind. Therefore he considers a Gentile who 'does the Law' as having great merit, and it is undoubtedly not a proselyte who is meant. Thus there is no doubt that the circles to which the tradent belonged saw in the Noachic precepts no more than an indispensable prerequisite, a minimal obligation for the pious Gentiles. According to the spirit of the saying, a God-fearing Gentile is to be praised if he fulfills many commandments of the Mosaic Law. On the other hand, according to Paul and to later medieval Jewish legislation, a believing Gentile should not accept upon himself more obligations than the Noachic precepts. Did such a Jewish view exist already in Paul's day at least as a recommended suggestion? Until now I have not found any decisive Jewish text which would explicitly confirm this approach, but this position fits admirably well the divergent tendencies within Judaism of antiquity.

This 'dialectical' unity in Judaism is often inaccurately described as its universalism and particularism. It was an expression of the genuine Jewish universalistic tendency which regarded the Law as destined for all of mankind and thus came to hold the opinion that it is preferable for a pious Gentile to accept upon himself the Jewish obligations. It is superfluous to repeat here that Judaism was not and is not a missionary religion;[21] however, as it also has a universal message, Judaism in antiquity mostly welcomed proselytes, but logically this approach was not without some ambivalence. The open mindedness of the school of Hillel towards proselytes, and the reserve shown by the school of Shammai against them are well known.[22] No wonder that the prominent disciple of the school of Shamai, Rabbi Eleazar ben Hyrcanos thought that proselytes tended to possess a bad character.[23] Moreover, if sometimes one had to be careful even of full proselytes, how could one ever trust the Godfearing Gentiles? Rabbi Shimeon ben Yochai was pessimistic.[24] When Pharaoh decided to pursue

---

[21] The Pharisees in Mt 23:15 seem to be an exception or the saying has to be understood in the vein of the story of the gradual conversion of the kings of Adiabene. We already assumed that Eleazar from Galilee was a Pharisee (see n. 16 above). Jesus' saying possibly alludes to such Pharisees who "traverse sea and land" in order to convert the Gentile God-fearers to full proselytes.

[22] See e.g. b.Shab 31a and W. Bacher, Die Agada der Tannaiten I (Strassbourg, 1903) p. 4 and pp. 8-9.

[23] See Ibid, pp. 106-107, and about the original evil nature of proselytes, see also tractate Gerim 4:2.

[24] 24 See the Mechilta de-Rabbi Ishmael to Ex 14:7, ed. S. Horovitz and J.A. Rabin, (Jerusalem, 1970) p. 87.

the children of Israel, he "took six hundred chosen chariots" (Ex 14:7) but where did he get the beasts to pull the chariots? The beasts of the Egyptians and those of Pharaoh had already died during the ten plagues, and the cattle of the children of Israel remained with them (see Ex 10:26). To whom did they belong? The cattle belonged to the God-fearing Gentiles among the servants of Pharaoh. Their cattle was spared, since they had heeded the warning of Moses. We learn this fact from another biblical verse: "He who *feared the word of the Lord* among the servants of Pharaoh, made his slaves and his cattle flee into the houses" (Ex 9:20). So Pharaoh used these beasts which belonged to the God-fearers among his servants against the children of Israel. We thus learn that the God-fearing Gentiles constitute a snare for Israel.[25]

Rabbi Eleazar ben Hyrcanos thought that a proselyte did not cease to be attracted by his pagan past. In addition, Rabbi Shimeon ben Yochai believed the God-fearing Gentiles possessed an unstable and weak character and that they presented a danger for the Jewish people because one could not be sure that when Israel was persecuted they would not join their Gentile compatriots. The exaggerated suspicions of the two Jewish sages resulted from the basic ambivalent theological and psychological structure of Judaism which we have already mentioned. As to the God-fearing Gentiles, it is easy to imagine that besides those who welcomed their zeal for Jewish commandments, there were also many Jews in whose hearts the multitude of "half-Jews" evoked an uneasy feeling. Do these Gentiles observe parts of the Mosaic Law because they understand the Jewish call, or perhaps they perform Jewish customs as an act of superstition? Where is the line separating proselytes from God-fearing Gentiles? All who have experienced modern parallels to these ancient Gentile "Judaizers" will surely understand the ambivalent feelings concerning practising Gentiles: on the one hand, the high appreciation of a Gentile who "does the Law"[26]—and on the other, the negative attitude of Rabbi Shimeon ben Yochai against the Godfearing Gentiles.[27] In such a state of affairs, it is plausible to imagine that already in antiquity there existed among the Jews a tendency to recommend that Gentiles restrict themselves in their observance only to those prescriptions which are indispensable, namely the Noachic precepts. It is not too far-fetched even to suppose that Paul's warning to the Gentiles as regards the observance of the Law was

---

[25] The translation of the last sentence is according to the text in the edition of Horovitz & Rabin.

[26] See above, n. 19.

[27] See above, n. 24. Rabbi Jeremiah and Rabbi Shimeon ben Yochai were contemporaries (second half of the second century C.E.).

not merely a consequence of his conversion. It is possible that the point of departure for this component of his theology lies in Paul's "Pharisaic" past. But as we have already stated, the restriction calling on the Gentiles not to observe more than the Noachic precepts is not explicitly attested in ancient Jewish sources. Nevertheless, the view that the believing and already practising Gentiles should be permitted to perform specifically Jewish commandments is also unattested in ancient Judaism.

Shall we therefore accept the view that *Didache* 6:2-3 is a purely Jewish passage in which an anonymous Jewish maximalist appeals to the God-fearing Gentiles to observe the Mosaic Law as far as they can? This seems to me to be almost impossible. Already at first glance one has the impression that, if the passage is purely Jewish, its content is a very clumsy proposal. However, if the passage is Christian, then it is a directive addressed to the Gentile Christians and inspired by the position of the right wing of the Mother Church and in that case, *Didache* 6:2-3 makes good sense. There are two reasons why the passage is Christian and not purely Jewish. The first is decisive, namely the setting of the passage in the midst of the development of the *Didache* from the Jewish Two Ways towards our actual *Didache*. The second reason why *Didache* 6:2-3 has to be considered as a Christian work is that although the question of the Believing Gentiles was also a Jewish problem, it really became an urgent matter in the primitive Church, whose future and very nature depended upon the manner in which this decisive issue would be resolved.

Let us first requote the passage itself. "If you can bear the whole yoke of the Lord (i.e. of the Law),[28] you will be perfect; but if you cannot, do what you can. Concerning the food, bear what you will be able to bear. But be sure to refrain completely from meat which has been sanctified before idols, for it represents the worship of dead gods." The views expressed in the passage are indeed possible within the framework of ancient Judaism, but it is extremely difficult to imagine that a Jew, or a Jewish authority of the period, would address God-fearing Gentiles and beg them to be perfect and to observe the whole Jewish Law, or at least to observe as much as they can and recommend that their food should be as kosher as possible. I admit that the passage remains somehow grotesque even if it is Christian, but as a

---

[28] The whole yoke of the Lord was probably original. In the tractate *Gerim* 1:2 there is a *varia lectio* "if he (the future proselyte) says, "I am not worthy to place my neck under the yoke of Him Who spoke and the world came into being, blessed by He" they receive him forthwith, and if not, he is dismissed and goes his way." See *The Minor Tractates of the Talmud* II, A. Cohen (London: Soncino, 1971) p. 603 n.5. The passage quoted above is also pertinent to Acts 15:10, where the expression "putting a yoke upon the neck" of Gentiles appears.

Christian composition it becomes far less strange and incredible. Both Jews and Christians are sure that Gentiles will be saved under certain conditions, but as soon as Gentiles accepted the faith in Jesus Christ, the question of their unity with the Christian Jews in one Church was no more essentially identical with the original Jewish religious view about the pious Gentiles. Christians believe that the Messiah has already come and that his expiatory death saves all who believe in him and in this central point there is no difference between Jews believing in Christ and Gentiles. Moreover Christ unites the Jews who believe in him with Christian Gentiles and removes the Christian Jews from the rest of Jewry.

It is necessary to state these truisms in order to understand that a fast and unequivocal solution of the problem of the Christian Gentiles for the Church became from its very beginnings unavoidable. There were two possible kinds of solutions for the Gentile problem in the Church, and both were proposed. The points of departure were naturally the Noachic precepts, for which the Gentiles are held responsible. The first solution was obvious. In order to strengthen the ties of Gentile Christianity with the Jews believing in Christ who were "all zealous of the Law" (Acts 21:20), it was desirable for the Gentile Christian believers to observe all the Mosaic Law as far as they were able to do so. In this manner the difference between the Jewish believers and their Gentile brethren would be minimized. We have already seen that this solution was based upon Jewish patterns. The other solution was evidently dictated by the suspicion that if Gentile Christians "did the Law", the common bond with the non-Christian Jews would be so great that there would be a danger that Gentile Christians would finally become Jewish (non-Christian) proselytes. Therefore Gentile Christians should not be required to observe the special Jewish prescriptions.[29] Although no explicit Jewish parallel from antiquity is available to authenticate this approach, this Pauline solution fits certain tendencies in Judaism. This has become evident, among other things, from the fact noted above, that Paul's position conforms to the later Jewish legislation concerning Gentiles.

---

[29] For all the questions of the Law in the Church see the personal opinion of Justin Martyr, *Dial* 47. The whole chapter is very instructive. He says (97:21) that the "good" observant Jewish Christians observe the portions of the law of Moses which may now be observed (cf. possibly expression in Rom 14:1-7 and 1 Cor 8:9). He opposes such Jewish Christians who compel Gentile Christians to live according to the Law of Moses, *Ibid.* 47:3; the whole passage is evidently also influenced by Gal 2:11-14). Naturally Justin denies the salvation of those who believed in Christ, began to observe the Mosaic Law and finally abandoned their belief in Christ (*Ibid.* 47:4). The last category shows that there were really Gentile Christians who "did the Law" and for whom the Christian faith was only an intermediary stage. This happened to the famous proselyte Aquila.

Anyone reading Paul even once knows that he always warns Gentiles not to observe Jewish commandments. During the period, some God-fearing Gentiles evidently underwent circumcision without becoming full proselytes, because they thought that circumcision was only one important component of the Jewish way of life. To those who would adhere to this approach Paul answered, "I testify again to every man who receives circumcision that he is bound to keep the whole law" (Gal. 5:3).[30] Here Paul repeats the current Jewish position. However one cannot be sure that at the time some of the Jewish doctors did not think that for the Gentiles, as for Jews, circumcision was only one of the obligations of the Law. Therefore circumcision would not bind the Gentiles to keep the whole Mosaic Law. If such a view ever existed, it expressed the position of those who thought that Gentile God-fearers were permitted and even encouraged to live at least partially in the same manner as Jews. Such a demand was probably adopted by the majority of the Jewish Mother Church, because it evidently seemed to its members that it was the easiest solution to the urgent problem of the Gentile Christians. If they observed the Jewish commandments as far as possible, the ties between the Jewish and Gentile members of the Church would be strengthened. Such "Church-politics" did not contradict the so called Apostolic Decree, as it agreed with the Jewish viewpoint concerning the Noachic precepts.

Our considerations are based upon the general situation in the Apostolic Church. All its members accepted the authority of the Apostolic Decree but is application depended on two possible interpretations of the indispensable obligations of Gentile believers. The question was whether these obligations constituted a minimum or a maximum. Now we should understand Paul's vehement opposition to such Gentiles who wanted to take upon themselves a heavier Jewish burden. On the other hand, the approach of the faction to which Peter belonged no longer looks as absurd as it often used to do. They adhered to another interpretation of the Apostolic Decree, identical with the Jewish view that the "doing of the Law" by a Gentile is meritorious. Those who tried to persuade Gentile Christians to live more or less like the Jews wanted to reach a high goal, namely the creation of a single Church, composed of both Jews and Gentiles.

Now we can understand the incident which happened in Antioch (Gal. 2:11-14).[31] "For before a certain man[32] came from

---

[30] The whole passage of Gal 5:1-6 shows that Paul does not merely repeat a current Jewish opinion but that Gal 5:3 is also a part of Paul's Christological approach to the Law.

[31] The latest study about this incident is T. Holtz, "Der antiochenische Zwischenfall (Galater 2:11-14)", *NTS* 32 (1986) pp. 321-343.

[32] "A certain man" and "he came" is the original wording. This can be deduced

James, he (Peter) ate with the Gentiles; but when he came he drew
back and separated himself, fearing the circumcision party... I
said to Cephas (Peter) before them all, "If you, though a Jew, live
like a Gentile and not like a Jew, how can you compel the Gentiles
to live like Jews?"" Paul did not blame Peter because he had
never before, "eaten anything that is common or unclean" (Acts
10:14) but because he now makes concessions to the Gentiles and
at the same time he compels them to live like Jews. We have tried
to explain what it meant for Peter and the faction to which he
belonged to "compel" the Gentiles to live according to the manner
of the Jews. Peter and his tried to persuade the Gentile Christians
not to become full proselytes but to do some "works of the law
(see Gal 3:1-5). The argumentation of this faction of the Jewish
Mother Church was approximately as follows: "If you (i.e.
Gentile Christians) can bear the whole yoke of the Lord, you will
be perfect; but if you cannot, do what you can. Concerning the
food, bear what you will be able to bear. But be sure to refrain
completely from meat which has been sanctified before idols for it
represents the worship of dead gods" (*Didache* 6:2-3). Incidentally, one of the points that prove that the passage is indeed
Christian is the reference to "what has been sacrificed to idols"
which is mentioned in the Apostolic Decree (see also 1 Cor 8 and
10:25-29 and Rev 2:14, 20).[33]

We are sure that *Didache* 6:2-3 is of Christian and not
Jewish origin. It is a precious document from the first years of
Christianity. The passage fits the meagre and incomplete information about the tendencies and aims of the group in the Apostolic
Church which Paul opposed, and thus it enlarges and supplements
our knowledge about this trend which was once named the
"Petrine" faction. I believe that with the help of our passage one
can learn also something about Paul, since it casts light upon the
tendencies against which Paul was constrained to fight. If,
however, some doubts remain about the Christian origin of
Didache 6:2-3, it is the position of this passage within the final
arrangement of the *Didache* which unequivocally decides the
question.

We should like at this stage to repeat the main points of this
argument: (1) *Didache* 6:2-3 is addressed to Gentiles while the
preceding tractate the Two Ways is an inner-Jewish ethical
treatise. (2) *Didache* 6:2-3 did not belong to the Jewish treatise, as
it can be seen i.a. from the old Latin translation of this Jewish

from Martini's edition.
[33] See also K. Wengst, *op.cit.*, p. 96, n. 53 and A. Resch, *op.cit.*. See also
Justin Martyr, *Dial* 34:8-35:2.

source, where this addition is still absent. (3) Already in the first decades of Christianity the Two Ways was considered to be a product of the Apostolic Mother Church. The apostolic ascription of the Jewish source appears in all witnesses without exception. (4) Under such circumstances it is plausible that at the end of the treatise an appendix was added which regulated the obligations of the Gentile believers in the spirit of the majority of the Apostolic Mother Church. (5) The tractate together with the addition reached the Didachist who also believed in the apostolic origin of his *Vorlage*. He interpolated his source and adjoined it, from chapter 7 on, to his own Christian "Manual of Discipline." (6) The Didachist was a Gentile Christian similar to the author(s) of the Pastoral Epistles and his pastoral work concerns Gentile Christian Churches. On the other hand, the author of *Didache* 6:2-3 is a Christian Jew. *Didache* 6:2-3 is a child of a different spirit from the following Christian "Manual of Discipline." But as the Didachist believed that both the Two Ways and the addition are a product of the Apostolic Church, he did not pay attention to the different tendencies represented in *Didache* 6:2-3. (7) The progressive development of the text of the *Didache* shows that *Didache* 6:2-3 was written in a period between the Jewish Two Ways and the Gentile Christian treatise of the Didachist. Also in this respect, *Didache* 6:2-3 is not a Jewish but a Christian composition.

We have come to the end of our journey, which has led us through the birth pangs which finally produced the "historical" Christian church. There is no doubt that the plan of Paul's opponents was well meant, but in reality it was impractical. How could such a Gentile Christian Church have survived in the long run when it contained a membership of Gentile Christians on various levels of Jewish perfection? Paul was capable of imposing his solution upon the Church. But even the best human decision is potentially dangerous and tends to lead to strange consequences if no strong will exists to avoid the impending evil. So Paul's reasonable arrangement succeeded more or less in keeping Gentile Christians from observing the Jewish way of life. Later on, however, not only were Gentiles who observed the smallest Jewish commandment cruelly punished, but also Jews who became Christians were forbidden by the Christian Church to live according to the Law of Moses.

BAPTISM ACCORDING TO THE DIDACHE

WILLY RORDORF
Neuchâtel

The *Didache* gives the following instructions on the subject of baptism:

7:1 Περὶ δὲ τοῦ βαπτίσματος, οὕτω βαπτίσατε· ταῦτα πάντα πρειπόντες, βαπτίσατε εἰς τὸ ὄνομα τοῦ πατρὸς καὶ τοῦ υἱοῦ καὶ τοῦ ἁγίου πνεύματος ἐν ὕδατε ζῶντι.
2. Ἐαν δὲ μὴ ἔχῃς ὕδωρ ζῶν, εἰς ἄλλο ὕδωρ βάπτισον· εἰ δ'οὐ δύνασαι ἐν ψυχρῷ, ἐν θερμῷ.
3. Ἐαν δὲ ἀμφότερα μὴ ἔχῃς, ἔκχεον εἰς τὴν κεφαλὴν τρὶς ὕδωρ εἰς ὄνομα πατρὸς καὶ υἱοῦ καὶ ἁγίου πνεύματος.

4a. Πρὸ δὲ τοῦ βαπτίσματος προνηστευσάτω ὁ βαπτίζων καὶ ὁ βαπτιζόμενος καὶ εἴ τινες ἄλλοι δύνανται·
4b. κελεύεις δὲ νηστεῦσαι τὸν βαπτιζόμενον πρὸ μιᾶς ἢ δύο.

1. On the subject of baptism, baptize thus: after having taught all that precedes, baptize in the name of the Father and of the Son and of the Holy Spirit, in living water.
2. If for some reason you do not have living water, baptize in other water; and if you are not able to in cold water, in warm water.
3. If you do not have (enough) of one or the other, pour out water three times on the head, in the name of the Father and of the Son and of the Holy Spirit.

4a. Before the baptism, let the baptizer, the baptized and others who can, observe first a fast;
4b. as for the baptized, you must enforce a fast before-hand for one or two days.

This text is important since it is one of the first post-canonical texts which teaches us on the rite of Christian baptism. However, though it may be short—or rather because it is short—it creates a certain number of problems which are not easy to solve. It is thus not surprising that it has ever anew aroused the interest of scholars.[1] If I bend over the text in my turn, it is not that I will pretend to be able to propose an entirely new solution; I aim rather to take my bearings from previous research.

---

[1] To mention only the most recent studies: S. Giet, "Coutume, évolution, droit canon. A propos de deux passages de la "Didaché"", in *RDC* 16 (1966), pp. 118-132, republished (with modifications) in *L'Énigme de la Didachè* (Paris: Ophrys, 1970 [PFLUS]) pp. 192-197; A. Vööbus, *Liturgical Traditions in the Didache* (Stockholm: Estonian Theological Society in Exile, 1968 [PETSE 16]) pp. 17-60.

1. Literary Unity of Didache 7?

With this question we are already at the heart of the problem posed by the text. Indeed, *Didache* 7:1 begins by addressing itself to a group of persons: "You baptize..."; but *Didache* 7:2-4 is addressed to only one person. How can one explain this change?

The problem becomes still more complex, when one takes account of the context in which the chapter is found. *Didache* 1-6:1 presents, without any other introduction, the teaching of the "two ways" of life and of death, teaching which goes back essentially to a Jewish model.[2] Apart from *Didache* 1:3b-6—a passage which originates in turn from a source of the teachings of Jesus[3] —all the teaching of the "two ways" is given in the second person singular;[4] in several places (*Did* 3:1, 3, 4, 5, 6; 4:1[5]) the person to whom it is addressed is called τέκνον μου. But, curiously, at the end of the "way" of death (5:2), we find a phrase in the plural: ῥυσθείητε, τέκνα, ἀπὸ τούτων ἁπάντων.[6] The end of the "two ways" teaching returns again to the second person singular in *Didache* 6:1, the same as for the rest of chapter 6. But everything which follows after chapter 7, i.e. *Didache* 8-16, is written in the second person plural, except *Didache* 13:3a, 5-7.

Noticing that, Audet[7] has attributed the whole of the "you-singular passages" of the *Didache*, which do not belong to the teaching of the primitive "two ways", to the same "interpolator".[8] As far as *Didache* 6:2-3 and 7:2-4 are concerned, the hypothesis is seductive since it is supported by a supplementary stylistic

---

[2] Cf. W. Rordorf, "Un chapître d'éthique judéo-chrétienne: les Deux Voies", in *RSR* 60 (1972) pp. 109-128.

[3] Cf. W. Rordorf, "Le problème de la transmission textuelle de "Didachè" 1,3b-2,1", in *Überlieferungsgeschichtliche Untersuchungen*, ed. F. Paschke (Berlin: Akademie-Verlag, 1981 [TU 125]) pp. 499-513. Reprinted in W. Rordorf, *Liturgie, foi et vie des premiers chrétiens. Études patristiques* (Paris: Beauchesne, 1986 [ThH 75]).

[4] *Did* 4:11, which changes the point of view, must be an addition. In connection with this passage and in connection with *Did* 4:8b, cf. S. Giet, *L'énigme*, p. 184.

[5] The *Doctrina apostolorum* reads *fili* in *Did* 4:13 also; and the Sermon *De centesima, de sexagesima, de tricesima* (cf. on this subject J. Daniélou, "Le traité de centesima, sexagesima, tricesima et la judéo-chretianisme latin avant Tertullien", in *VigChr* 25 [1971] pp. 171ff) reads the same in *Did* 6:2!

[6] J.-P. Audet, *La Didachè. Instructions des apôtres* (Paris: Gabalda, 1958 [ÉBib]) p. 232, wished to emend the text. B. Botte, in his review of Audet's book in *BThAM* 8 (1958) p. 168, has rightly criticised this conjecture. He is probably right in saying, "It is not exactly true that *Doctr.* supports the singular. One can not only read *abstine te fili*, but also *abstinete fili[i]*, since *fili* was frequently written for the plural.

[7] *Didachè*, pp. 104ff.

[8] We will not discuss this thesis in its entirety; cf. the critical remarks of Giet, *L'énigme*, pp. 183f, and my own in the article cited in n. 3.

indicator: in the two passages we find several phrases constructed with the verb δύνασθαι; the two passages thus breathe the same spirit of concession.

But the problem is more complex.[9] In *Didache* 6:3, which is a "you-singular passage", we find the same construction with περὶ δέ as in the "you-plural passage" which introduces *Didache* 7:1: περὶ δὲ τῆς βρώσεως. One has the impression that this is only a pure co-incidence of style. If one compares it to the parallel text of the *Apostolic Constitutions* (VII.21), one is struck by the fact that it reads the *plural* for *Didache* 6:3: ἀπὸ δὲ τῶν εἰδωλοθύτων φεύγετε![10] This shows, it seems to me, that *Didache* 6:3-7:1 forms a literary unity.

I intend to propose the hypothesis that chapters 9-10 on the "eucharist", where the construction with περὶ δέ appears three times (in *Did* 9:1, 2 and 3) belongs to the same literary unity as *Didache* 6:3-7:1.[11]

The editor of the *Didache* would then have compiled two literary sources: the "two ways" teaching on the one hand, and several liturgical chapters introduced by περὶ δέ on the other.[12] He would have modified the latter source by adding the concessions made in *Didache* 6:3 and 7:2-3.[13]

Be that as it may, I do not believe that one could deny an important change of perspective between *Didache* 7:1 and 7:2ff, which is expressed precisely in the fact that the beginning of the chapter is addressed to a plurality of persons, whereas what follows is addressed to one person only. This fact alone proves that the chapter could not have been written by the same hand.

---

[9] R. A. Kraft (*Barnabas and the Didache* [New York: Nelson, 1965 (AF 3, ed. R.M. Grant)] pp. 161, 163) has seen this well.

[10] The plural is also attested in the Ethiopic version of the *Didache* (ed. G. Horner, *The Statutes of the Apostles* [London: Williams & Norgate, 1904] p. 193).

[11] I am less certain with regard to *Didache* 11:3 where the reading περὶ δέ is only attested by the *Apostolic Constitutions*. As for the prayer contained in *Const* VII.27 and in the Coptic version of the *Didache*, see below, p. [7].

[12] S. Giet (*L'énigme*, p. 203) attributes the phrases introduced by περὶ δέ to the redactional work of the "Didachist" himself, which seems at first sight to be the simplest solution. But S. Giet does not explain in a satisfactory way the transition from the second person plural to the second person singular in *Didache* 7.

[13] Obviously one could ask why the editor of the *Didache* has compiled these two sources. Conscious that I am advancing on the uncertain grounds of pure speculation, I would give the following answer: the editor found in his source a text very close to the apostolic decree of Acts 15 (cf. the Ethiopic version of *Did* 6:3!) which he "refines" in his own way (and the author of *Const* VII.20 in his!). He knows, moreover, that the "two ways" teaching was given to converts recruited from the ἔθνη to which the apostolic decree was addressed; he then joined the two documents (the Western text of Acts has proceeded in a similar way by adding the Golden Rule to the Apostolic Decree! Cf., on this subject, the article of Y. Tissot, in *RB* 77 (1970) pp. 321-346).

Didache 7:1 presupposes a situation where, in principle, every believer could baptize, and not just in the case of necessity either; *Didache* 15 teaches us that the traditional ministers of the local church for the administration of baptism, the bishop and the deacon, had not yet been instituted. The itinerant apostles, prophets and teachers could not be in mind in *Didache* 7:1, since chapters 11ff speak of those in the third person plural. Moreover, the same situation is reflected in *Didache* 7:4a, where the term ὁ βαπτίζων to designate the one who administers baptism indicates the absence of a specific minister; for this reason, it seems to me that *Didache* 7:4a is drawn from the same source as *Didache* 7:1.[14]

Didache 7:2-3, 4b, in turn, is addressed directly to the one who administers baptism. It is not specified who it is, but one has the clear impression that it is a matter of one person designated to do it in a regular manner; for it specifies several situations that the person concerned might encounter in carrying out his service (7:2-3), and the person in question had a certain power to give orders (7:4b).

The *Apostolic Constitutions* (VII.22) expresses itself clearly by saying, "On the subject of baptism, oh bishop or deacon,...baptize like this." In the *Didache*, we are not yet there. But it seems evident to me that *Didache* 7:2-3, 4b, compared to *Didache* 7:1, 4a, makes a stride in this direction.

Can these clues help us to date chapter 7 of the *Didache*? At the beginning of the Christian mission, it was the apostles and the evangelists themselves who baptized the converts (cf. Acts 2:41; 8:38; 9:18; 16:15, 33; 1 Cor 1:14ff); but later they delegated this task to others (1 Cor 1:16f; Acts 10:48). *Didache* 7:1, 4a seems to represent this stage of the tradition. But Ignatius of Antioch was already anxious to reserve the right to baptize to the institutional ministers of the local church; he says in his *Letter to the Smyrnians* 8:2, "It is not permitted for anyone to baptize or to celebrate the agape without the bishop, but everything which he approves is acceptable to God also." Does *Didache* 7:2-3, 4b move in this sense? It is difficult to say so with certainty.[15]

---

[14] Cf. S. Giet, *L'énigme*, p. 197, and A. Vööbus, *Liturgical Traditions*, p. 35, n. 19. It would be another way of proving that the criterion of Audet for distinguishing the layers of redaction (you-plural passages and you-singular passages) is not subtle enough.

[15] The person in question could also be a teacher (so A. Benoit, *Le baptême chrétien au second siècle* [Paris: Press Universitaires de France, 1953] p. 10); in fact, teachers administered baptism in certain regions until the end of the second century (cf. G. Kretschmar, "Die Geschichte des Taufgottesdienstes in der alten Kirche" in *Leiturgia* 5 [1970] pp. 64f).

2. Pre-baptismal Catechesis

I have shown elsewhere[16] that I could not follow Audet, who thinks that the words ταῦτα πάντα προειπόντες in *Didache* 7:1 are a later addition of fourth century Egyptian provenance. At the beginning of the second century, a pre-baptismal catechesis of the kind contained in the first six chapters of the *Didache* would have been nothing surprising. Since we have said that the editor of the *Didache* has compiled the two sources *Didache* 1-6 and 7ff, it would then have been him who would have added this remark in *Didache* 7:1.[17]

3. Preparatory Fasting

F. J. Dölger[18] and J. Schümmer[19] have already said what is necessary on the evolution and significance of the preparatory fast for baptism. A remark of J. Schümmer[20] seems particularly pertinent to me: "The custom of fasting with the person to be baptized is possibly even older than the general Easter fast (cf. Didache) and it could in its turn, after the transfer of the time of baptism to the Easter celebration, have contributed to first making the Easter fast into a general practice." The trajectory then passed from the *Didache* to Justin (*1Apol* 61), to Tertullian (*Bapt* 19f) and to Hippolytus (*ApTrad* 21).[21]

One could even ask whether the *Didache* does not presuppose that baptism is usually administered on Sunday. *Didache* 14 knows Sunday as the day of the Christian cult. From the second century we have several witnesses for an administration of baptism on Sunday.[22]

M. Dujarier[23] wishes to see in the expression εἴ τινες ἄλλοι δύνανται a beginning of the practice of sponsorship by god-

---

[16] "Les deux voies", *op.cit.* Botte is of the same opinion (*BThAM* 8, p. 168).

[17] I agree here with the observation of Audet, *La Didachè*, pp. 60f, on the stylistic awkwardness of this insertion; it seems justified (despite the criticism of P. Nautin ("La composition de la "Didachè" et son titre", *RHR* 155 (1959) pp. 191-214, esp. 206f).

[18] *Der Exorzismus im altchristlichen Taufritual* (Paderborn, 1909 [SGKA III,1-2]) pp. 80-86.

[19] *Die altchristliche Fastenpraxis. Mit besonderer Berücksichtigung der Schriften Tertullians* (Münster, 1933 [LQF 27], pp. 164-178.

[20] *Altchristliche Fastenpraxis*, p. 169.

[21] Let us not forget to mention the text of Pseudo-Clement, *Hom* 3:73; 13:9; *Rec* 7:34, 35f; 10:72.

[22] Cf. W. Rordorf, *Sabbat und Sonntag in der Alten Kirche* (Zürich, 1972 [Traditio Christiana]), p. 139 n. 5.

[23] *Le parrainage des adultes aux trois premiers siècles de l'Église*, 1962, pp. 292-297.

parents. This clearly remains hypothetical. But at any rate I believe that he is right to say that one must consider the participation of several people in the fast as a reality and not as a possibility. I have adopted his translation of the expression in question, "and others who can do it."

4. The Baptismal Formula

This is a very delicate problem. In fact we find three different baptismal formulae in the *Didache*. *Didache* 7:1 presents the complete trinitarian formula: εἰς τὸ ὄνομα τοῦ πατρὸς καὶ τοῦ υἱοῦ καὶ τοῦ ἁγίου πνεύματος; *Didache* 7:3 presents the trinitarian formula without articles: εἰς ὄνομα πατρὸς καὶ υἱοῦ καὶ ἁγίου πνεύματος; and *Didache* 9:5 knows the formula with one member: εἰς ὄνομα κυρίου.

When one approaches this problem, it is appropriate to repeat a remark of Cullmann[24]: "One must guard against the temptation to read back the later situation into the primitive time and to suppose that the trinitarian construction should be the only one possible from the beginning...One does not then have the right to allow that the writings of the New Testament and the early Church, where they only speak of Christ, cite only a *part* of the *trinitarian confession*." Without any doubt, *Didache* 9:5 has preserved the most ancient baptismal formula.[25] At the beginning of Christianity, one baptized "in the name of Jesus."[26]

In turn, if the trinitarian formula is the most recent, this does not mean that it only made its appearance in the milieu of the second century as some have tended to think.[27] One cannot argue from the textual variants of Matthew 28:19: they only prove that the two traditions existed simultaneously, but does not say anything about the date of their origin. The text of the *Didache* invites us to caution. In fact, we have seen that *Didache* 7:1 must be situated in a tradition which probably goes back to the first century. But we must go still further and say that the trinitarian baptismal formula has been imposed after the transition of the passage from the Jewish-Christian mission to the Gentile-Christian mission. In contrast to the Jews who, at their conversion to Jesus

---

[24] *La foi et le culte de l'Église primitive*, 1963, p. 67.

[25] Moreover it fits best with the Christology of the *Didache*: cf. A. Vööbus, *Liturgical Traditions*, pp. 38f.

[26] Cf Acts 2:38; 8:16; 10:48; 19:5; 22:16; 1 Cor 1:13; Gal 3:27: Jas 2:7; *Herm-Sim* 7.6.4; *ActsThec* 34. It is true that H. von Campenhausen (*VigChr* 25 [1971] pp. 1-16) is opposed to this consensus, but I do not find his arguments convincing.

[27] Cf. G. Kretschmar, *Die Geschichte*, pp. 18f; 32-36; *Idem, Studien zur frühchristlichen Trinitätstheologie* (1956) p. 207; A. Vööbus, *Liturgical Traditions*, pp. 36f.

received his Spirit with baptism, the Gentiles first had to confess the unique God, Father of Jesus Christ, to be able to be baptized. This situation is already given in the time of the Pauline mission (cf. 1 Thess 1:9-10), it emerges again in the *Didache* which is addressed to Gentile converts.[28]

5. The Water

There is no doubt that the instruction to baptize in "living water" in *Didache* 7:1 is archaic and goes back to the beginnings of the Christian mission.[29] It has a Jewish background[30] and was not unknown in the Greco-Roman world.[31] Although the expression "living water" could have taken a symbolic significance,[32] it does not seem that it had any other sense in the *Didache* than that of "running water."[33]

Didache 7:2-3 adds a series of exceptions to the rule. The first case envisaged is the absence of running water. In other words, there was no possibility of going for baptism to a place where there was running water.[34]Then one takes "other water". One should note: water which is not running, water which is no longer related to its natural source.[35]

If it is not possible to baptize in cold water, one should do it in warm water.[36] It seems clear to me that one is speaking here of

---

[28] Cf. also Irenaeus, *Haer* IV.24:1-2, and U. Luck, in *EvTh* 27 (1967) 494-508.--A. Benoît, *Le baptême*, p. 7; J.-P. Audet, *Didachè*, pp. 360ff; R. A. Kraft, *Barnabas and the Didache*, p. 164. H. von Campenhausen (*VigChr* 25, pp. 10f) is right then not to *oppose* Did 9:5 to Did 7:1, 3. I would say that Did 9:5 nevertheless reflects the situation of the Jewish Christian communities which is now adapted in *Did* 7:1 and 3 to the new situation of the Gentile Christian mission. One notes the same change of viewpoint in Justin: in *Dial* 39:2 when he addresses himself to Jews, he speaks of baptism in the name of Jesus alone; in *1Apol* 61:3, 10, 13, when he addresses himself to Gentiles, he uses the Trinitarian formula.

[29] Cf Acts 8:36; 16:13 and again Justin, *1Apol* 61. A. Vööbus (*Liturgical Traditions*, pp. 22ff) cites still further texts.

[30] Cf. baptism in the Jordan required by John the Baptist! A. Benoît (*Le baptême*, p. 16) makes reference, besides, to the baptism of proselytes, and S. Giet (*L'énigme*, pp. 193ff) to the Old Testament and to the "baptist movement".

[31] Cf. T. Klauser, "Taufet in lebendigem Wasser! Zum religions- und kulturgeschichtlichen Verständnis von Didache 7,1-3", in *Pisciculi* (1939) pp. 147-164.

[32] Cf. J. Daniélou, in *RSR* 39 (1958) pp. 337ff.

[33] *Contra* E. Peterson, *Frühkirche, Judentum und Gnosis* (Rome: Herder, 1959) pp. 310-333.

[34] The expression ἔχειν ὕδωρ ζῶν is not very well chosen. Apparently it implies "to have in the proximity." One cannot deduce, as E. Peterson (*op. cit.*, p. 159 n. 48) does, that the primitive text spoke of a washing for purification (cf. the justified criticism of A. Vööbus, *Liturgical Traditions*, pp. 29ff).

[35] Note that running water was always preferred: even in the interior of houses and, much later, of baptisteries, one kept to running water.

[36] The argument of S. Giet (*L'énigme*, p. 196), which sees in this phrase an interpolation by a second hand, seems too subtle to me.

water warmed for a particular reason.[37] It is a measure which would be necessary if baptism was to take place in extreme weather conditions.[38] It is not necessary to think here of sick people[39] and, of course, still less of infant baptism.[40]

The third case envisaged is that of baptism *per infusionem*:[41] it anticipates that one should pour water three times over the head of the baptized person. This rule is applied when one has "neither the one nor the other (kind of water)." The two kinds of water are clearly running water, on the one hand, and still water on the on the other. To grasp the sense of the passage, one must take into consideration the Georgian version of the text, which says this:[42] "If, however, you *do not have enough* of either, then pour out some water three times over the head." We learn then that baptism was normally a baptism by immersion;[43] but if there was not a sufficient quantity of water to practice immersion, baptism *per infusionem* was also permitted.[44] In *Didache* 7:3, the trinitarian

---

[37] A. Vööbus (*Liturgical Traditions*, p. 24) thinks that "the term "cold water" obviously refers to baptism with the use of water from a river or spring, that is, with water at its natural temperature. By contrast, the term "warm water" is not that enigmatic--it seems to be a general characterization for water of a different kind, the kind to be found in cisterns, pools and reservoirs. This is still water which has lost its natural temperature." The difference between cold water and "warm" would then be minimized!

[38] So A. Benoît, *L'baptême*, p. 8. One thinks about all of the northern Alps (p.ex. from Zurzach in Switzerland), of the baptisteries where one had to warm the water. But the Mandeans also criticized Christian baptism in warmed water (and perhaps in Elchasai: Hippolytus, *Ref* ix.16:1): "They bury a jug in the earth, steal water out of the Jordan, boil it with fire, pour it in the jug and let men and women go down into it stark naked. They baptized them in water and give them the same water to drink. They speak the name of the dead over them, the name of the Son and the Holy Spirit. They baptize them and speak there the name of Christ over them" (*Ginza. Der Schatz oder das grosse Buch der Mandäer*, ed. M. Lidzbarski [Göttingen, 1925 (Quellen der Religionsgeschichte 13)] p. 227). In many respects, this baptism resembles that described in the *Didache*! E. Peterson (*op. cit.*, p. 161) is wrong in thinking that it is a matter uniquely of baptism of a Christian sect in Mesopotamia.

[39] Cf. F. J. Dölger, in *JAC* 5 (1936), pp. 175-182, and the critique of E. Peterson, *Frühkirche*, p. 160f.

[40] Cf. the critique of A. Vööbus, *Liturgical Traditions*, p. 23.

[41] So S. Giet, *L'énigme*, p. 196. One must in fact avoid the term "by affusion" which leads to confusion.

[42] Ed. G. Péradzé, "Die "Lehre der zwölf Apostel" in der georgischen Überlieferung" in *ZNW* 31 (1932) pp. 111-116, esp. 115. Otherwise, one loses one's way in fantastic speculations, as in E. Peterson, *Frühkirche*, pp. 158ff.

[43] Cf. J. Jeremias, *Infant Baptism in the First Four Centuries* (London: SCM, 1960) p. *37.

[44] I do not believe that we have here the first example of baptism that was given much later to the sick (*clinici*) and that, in such a case, was baptism by aspersion. I would rather suggest here the origin of the rite practiced later by the universal Church: the baptized stands upright in the baptismal font and the baptizer pours water over his head (cf. Christian archaeology and iconography).

baptismal formula appears for the second time; the instruction to pour water "three times" over the head of the baptized seems to refer to it.

The exceptional situation envisaged by *Didache* 7:2-3 must have presented themselves very quickly in missionary practice. Nothing prevents one from saying that the measures prescribed by the *Didache* were already established in the first century.[45]

6. Baptismal Unction?

Let us again briefly speak of this question. In fact, R. Reitzenstein[46] already believed that the prayer preserved at the end of chapter 10, in the Coptic version of the *Didache* (cf. the *Apostolic Constitutions* VII.27), was a prayer over baptismal oil and that, consequently, the baptismal rite of the *Didache* knew the practice of anointing with oil.[47] R. Reitzenstein based his theory on the Mandaean rite which was, in his opinion, the "model" for the Christian rite. Today, we know that the influence was the other way round.[48] But recently E. Peterson[49] has accepted the testimony of the *Apostolic Constitutions* and proceeded to think that chapter 22 of book VII, which is parallel to *Didache* 7 and which knows the pre- and post-baptismal unction, is more original than the *Codex Hierosolymitanus* of the *Didache*; the latter is supposed to have modified the text to suppress the reference to baptismal oils, which revealed a Novatian tendency.[50] Both J.-P. Audet[51] and A. Vööbus[52] have energetically refuted this very audacious thesis of E. Peterson: the prayer in question has not been suppressed in the *Codex Hierosolymitanus* of the *Didache*

---

[45] We have already said that the Trinitarian baptismal formula agrees with this viewpoint. It is striking that the three divine names should have been used without definite articles. Is it accidental?

[46] *Die Vorgeschichte der christlichen Taufe* (*Leipzig, 1929) pp. 177ff.

[47] Here is the translation of the Coptic text proposed by L.-Th. Lefort, in CSCO 135 (1952) p. 26: "In the matter of perfumes say thanks like this and say: "Father, we give you thanks for the perfume that you have made known to us through the agency of your son Jesus: to you be glory for ever! Amen"."

[48] E. Segelberg, *Masbuta. Studies in the Ritual of the Mandaean Baptism* (Uppsala: Almqvist & Wiksell, 1958) pp. 148f; K. Rudolph, *Die Mandäer II: Der Kult* (Göttingen: Vandenhoeck & Ruprecht, 1961) p. 174.

[49] *Frühkirche*, pp. 156ff.

[50] He sees in the phrase ἐὰν δὲ ἀμφότερα μὴ ἔχῃς, ἔκχεον εἰς τὴν κεφαλὴν ὕδωρ in Did 7:3, the rudiment of the text of *Const* VII.22: εἰ δὲ μήτε ἔλαιον ᾖ μήτε μύρον, ἀρκεῖ τὸ ὕδωρ!

[51] *Didachè*, pp. 67ff. Botte, *BThAM* 8, p. 168, is in agreement with him.

[52] *Liturgical Traditions*, pp. 41-60, in a meticulous study of the whole problem. Cf. also S. Giet, *L'énigme*, p. 213, n. 76.

but, on the contrary, has been interpolated in the Coptic version of the *Didache* and in the *Apostolic Constitution*!

It remains to determine whether the prayer is truly a prayer over baptismal oil. It could also be a matter of oil for the use of the sick.[53] A. Adam[54] has even believed it possible to claim that the Coptic prayer goes back to a Syriac original and that it is really a prayer for the agape. One has also tried to reconcile several of these interpretations.[55] It seems to me that one must put aside the interpretation according to which the baptismal rite of the *Didache* knew an anointing with oil: *Didache* 7 does not say a word, and the prayer at the end of chapter 10 in the Coptic version and in the parallel text of the *Apostolic Constitutions* is situated in a different context.[56]

7. The Particular Characteristics of Baptism according to the "Didache"

The text is striking less for what it says than for what it does not say. One can clearly observe that this short text does not transmit the entire formula of the baptismal rite. But only those aspects of baptism which one could not assuredly pass over in silence, if one had known them. Let us try to summarize them.[57]

a) The renunciation of Satan is not mentioned. Moreover, one has the impression that this rite would have been included in the kind of work which sanctions the teaching of the "two ways" in *Didache* 1-6.[58]

b) The consecration of the water seems to be unknown in the *Didache*.[59]

---

[53] Cf. K. Bihlmeyer, *Die Apostolischen Väter* (Tübingen: Mohr, 1956[3]); A. Benoît, *Le baptême*, p. 6.

[54] "Erwägungen zur Herkunft der Didache", in *ZKG* 68 (1957) p. 8 (= *Sprache und Dogma: Untersuchungen zu Grundproblemen der Kirchengeschichte*, ed. G. Ruhbach [Gütersloh: G. Mohn, 1969] pp. 31ff). A. Vööbus, *Liturgical Traditions*, pp. 44f, has critiqued him.

[55] R. A. Kraft, *Barnabas and the Didache*, pp. 167f; G. Kretschmar, *Die Geschichte*, p. 30 n. 41.

[56] One can ask whether one should not study the "sacred meal" of the Jewish Egyptian romance of *Joseph and Aseneth* more closely, which could provide the background of the prayer in question in the Coptic version of the *Didache*. Cf. on this subject, M. Philonenko, *Joseph et Aséneth* (Leiden: Brill, 1968) pp. 89-98.

[57] Cf. also A. Benoît, *Le baptême*, pp. 30f. He believes that the idea of "remission of sins" is absent from the *Didache*. But given that Christian baptism probably goes back to the baptism of John the Baptist, and that one prepares oneself for baptism, according to the testimony of *Didache* 7:4, by a fast, I ask myself whether one can really maintain this view.

[58] Cf. on this subject F. J. Dölger, *Die Sonne der Gerechtigkeit und der Schwarze*, 1971[2]; H. Kirsten, *Die Taufabsage*, 1960.

[59] It first appears in texts from the end of the second century: Tertullian, *Bapt* 4; Hippolytus, *ApTrad* 21.

c) There is no trace of the Pauline theology of baptism.[60]
d) What is most striking is the absence of the laying on of hands
and of any mention of the gift of the Holy Spirit at the moment of
baptism. G.W.H. Lampe[61] has shown that this tradition was more
widespread, at the beginning of Christianity, than one would think
at first sight. The *Didache* must be linked to that stream of the
tradition, which is a sign of its archaic character.

---

[60] This is not surprising. All baptismal theology of the second century seems to
more or less ignore the apostle Paul. This is one of the findings of the study of A.
Benoît (*Le baptême*).

[61] *The Seal of the Spirit* (London: SPCK, 1967²) esp. pp. 64ff; cf. also G.
Kretschmar, *Die Geschichte*, pp. 23f.

CHRISTIAN SELF-DEFINITION AGAINST THE "HYPOCRITES" IN DIDACHE VIII

JONATHAN A. DRAPER
Pietermaritzburg

I. INTRODUCTION

While many aspects of the *Didache* have excited interest and debate among New Testament scholars, chapter 8 has occasioned little comment. It has been only as ammunition for the question of dependence or independence of Matthew's Gospel that it has been explored. The *function* of the passage within the text of the *Didache* as a whole is largely neglected. C. N. Jefford, for instance, although his analysis contains some interesting insights, sees the insertion of this material as somewhat arbitrary: "For the redactor, it is the incorporation of authoritative pericopae that is important in these chapters, not a concern for the actual flow of the text".[1] This assumption seems to me to be mistaken and a close analysis of the function of this chapter in the overall framework of the *Didache* sheds important light on the question of Christian self-definition against other Jewish groups in the first century of the Christian Era.

While the question of dependence on Matthew is obviously important, it will not be the concern of this paper. I have argued elsewhere,[2] that there is no evidence that the *Didache* used the text of Matthew as we have it today. On the contrary, there are indications that the gospel may be itself dependent on an earlier form of the *Didache*[3]. It is enough for the purposes of this paper, that the *Didache* is utilizing authoritative Jesus tradition for a particular purpose.

---

[1] C. N. Jefford, *The Saying of Jesus in the Teaching of the Twelve Apostles* (Leiden: Brill, 1989) p. 105. The use of terminology from literary composition is also anachronistic.

[2] J. A. Draper, "The Jesus Tradition in the Didache", in D. Wenham (ed), *Gospel Perspectives V: The Jesus Tradition Outside the Gospels* (Sheffield: JSOT, 1985) pp. 269-289; cf. R. Glover, "The Didache's Quotations and the Synoptic Gospels", *NTS* 5 (1958-1959) pp. 12-29; *contra* E. Massaux, *The Influence of the Gospel of Saint Matthew on Christian Literature before Saint Inenaeus III*, trns. N. J. Belval & S. Hecht (Macon, Ga: Mercer University Press, 1990-1993) pp. 144-176 "a sort of catechetical summary of the first gospel" (p. 180); B. Layton, "The Sources, Date and Transmission of Didache 1.3b-2.1", *HTR* 61 (1968) pp. 343-383; H. Köster, *Synoptische Überlieferung bei den Apostolischen Vätern* (Berlin: Akademie-Verlag, 1957) pp. 159-241, stands somewhere inbetween: *Didache* knew Matthew but did not use it.

[3] J. A. Draper, "Torah and Troublesome Apostles in the *Didache* Community", *NovT* 33/4 (1991) pp. 347-372.

The question of date and origin will also not be directly addressed. The consensus emerging in recent scholarship is that the text was in its present form by the turn of the first century C.E. and was produced either in Syria or Egypt.[4] My own position is that the text comes from the same community as Matthew, probably the community at Antioch which expelled Paul over the question of the Law, and that it developed in close interaction with the Gospel tradition which eventually replaced it.[5]

II. THE LITERARY SETTING OF CHAPTER 8

Didache 1-6 represents a block of catechetical instruction designed to be taught to converts to the Christian community before their baptism. As has been often noted, this is the implication of 7:1, "And concerning baptism, baptize in this way: having beforehand taught all these things, baptize...." (ταῦτα πάντα προειπόντες, βαπτίσατε).[6]

These instructions are also characterized by the sub-title of the writing as instruction given by the (twelve) apostles to the Gentiles (Διδαχὴ κυρίου διὰ τῶν δώδεκα ἀποστόλων τοῖς ἔθνεσιν). Early commentators often contended that this longer title was the original one and betrayed the milieu of pagans recently converted.[7] More recent commentators, however, argue for the shorter title, without the reference to the "twelve", as the original. Rordorf[8] sees the longer title as an amplification of the first after

---

[4] W. Rordorf & A. Tuilier, *La Doctrine des Douze Apôtres* (Paris: Les Éditions du Cerf, 1978) pp. 91-99; K. Niederwimmer, *Die Didache* (Göttingen: Vandenhoeck & Ruprecht, 1989 [KzdAV 1]) pp. 78-80.

[5] J. A. Draper, "Torah and Troublesome Apostles", pp. 269-289; cf. D. Flusser, "Paul's Jewish-Christian Oponents in the Didache", in S. Shaked, D. Shulman, and G. G. Stroumsa, *Gilgul: Essays on Transformation,Revolution and Permanence in the History of Religions* (Leiden: Brill, 1987) pp. 71-90.

[6] Cf. E. F. Harrison "Some Patterns of New Testament Didache". *Biblia Sacra* 119 (1962) pp. 118-128; Jefford, *Sayings of Jesus*, p. 104; Niederwimmer, *Didache*, pp. 158-160; A. Milavec, "The Pastoral Genius of the Didache: An Analytical Translation and Commentary, in J. Neusner, E. S. Frerichs, & A. J. Levine (eds.), *Religious Writings and Religious Systems* II (Atlanta: Scholars, 1989 [BStR]) pp. 105-110.

[7] P. Bryennios, Διδαχὴ τῶν δώδεκα ἀποστόλων (Constantinople: S. I. Boutura, 1883) p. 3; A. Harnack *Die Lehre der zwölf Apostel* (Leipzig: J. C. Hinrich's, 1884) pp. 24-37; C. Taylor, *The Teaching of the Twelve Apostles: With Illustrations from the Talmud* (Cambridge: Deighton Bell, 1886) p. 7). Some, however, have argued for dependence on Matthew 28:19f (e.g. J. A. Robinson, *Barnabas, Hermas, and the Didache* [London: SPCK, 1920] pp. 82, 87; Massaux, *Influence*, pp. 144f).

[8] "Le baptême selon la Didachè", in *Mélanges liturgiques offerts au R. P. Dom B. Botte O.S.B. de l'Abbaye du Mont César à l'occasion du cinquantième anniversaire de son ordination sacerdotale (4 Juin 1972)* (Louvain: Abbaye du Mont César, 1972) pp. 499-509; also *Doctrine*, 15f.

the insertion of the Gospel section. Audet[9], however, rightly points out that κύριος in these titles refers to Yahweh not Jesus. Rordorf's claim[10], dependent on Nautin[11], that κύριος without the definite article always refers to Christ in the *Didache*, is without foundation, since all his references are outside of the Two Ways section (1-6) to which this longer title belongs (i.e. 9:5; 11:2, 4; 14:1). Moreover, Audet's claim is supported by the title used in the Chinese, "Teaching of the Lord of Heaven", which seems to be derived from the *Didache*,[12] since Lord here is unequivocally Yahweh: "At that time, preaching the laws of Hiu-po (ie Jehovah) who is the Lord of Heaven, the Messiah spoke thus" (*The Lord of the Universe's Discourse on Almsgiving* 1).

In an important article on the *Didache*, David Flusser[13] has argued that chs. 1-6:1 are entirely "inner-Jewish" in their provenance. A recent paper by Peter Borgen[14] has also argued that virtue and vice lists were standard Jewish proselyte material leading to circumcision. This makes it likely that the longer title does relate specifically to the Two Ways. Indeed, the sub-title is an important indication that the Two Ways instruction is directed by a Jewish Christian community towards Gentile converts.[15] Its Jewish-Christian nature is underlined by the orientation of the subsequent instructions to the Torah[16].

---

[9] *Didachè*, pp. 252ff.

[10] *Doctrine*, p. 14 n. 5.

[11] P. Nautin, "La composition de la "Didachê" et son titre." *RHR* 78 (1959) pp. 191-214, esp. 211.

[12] J. H. Walker, "An Argument from the Chinese for the Antiochene Origin of the Didache", in *Studia Patristica* 8, ed. F. L. Cross (Berlin: Akademie-Verlag, 1966 [TU 93]) pp. 44-50.

[13] D. Flusser, "Paul's Jewish Christian Opponents in the Didache", in S. Shaked, D. Shulman & G. G. Stroumsa (eds), *Gilgul: Essays on Transformation, Revolution and Permanence in the History of Religions: Dedicated to R. J. Zwi Werblowsky* (Leiden: Brill, 1987) pp. 71-90.

[14] P. Borgen, "Catalogues of Vices, the Apostolic Decree and the Jerusalem Meeting", in J. Neusner, P. Borgen, E. S. Frerichs, R. Horsley (eds.), *The Social World of Formative Christianity and Judaism: Festschr. H. C. Kee* (Philadelphia: Fortress, 1988) pp. 126-141.

[15] Cf. C. Taylor, *The Teaching of the Twelve Apostles* (Cambridge: Deighton Bell, 1886), pp. 18-23; G. Salmon, *A Historical Introduction to the Books of the New Testament* (London, 1894) pp. 551-566; A. Seeberg, *Der Katechismus der Urchristenheit* (Leipzig: A. Deichert, 1903); G. Klein, *Der älteste christliche Katechismus und die jüdischen Propaganda-Literatur* (Berlin: G. Reimer, 1909) p. 184. On the other hand, it is not clear that δώδεκα stood in the original text. The textual evidence indicates that the short title originally read ΔΙΔΑΧΗ (or ΔΙΔΑΧΑΙ) ΑΠΟΣΤΟΛΩΝ (Audet, *Didachè*, pp. 19-25; cf. Niederwimmer, *Didache*, pp. 81-82), and the number twelve may have been introduced in both places.

[16] J. A. Draper, *A Commentary on the Didache in the Light of the Dead Sea Scrolls and Related Documents* (Cambridge Dissertation, 1983), pp. 11-142; also "Torah and Troublesome Apostles", pp. 347-372.

Chapter 7 gives instructions on the method of baptism, which is strongly concerned with the ritual purity of water understood in a Jewish fashion. It must be running water and cold to be ritually pure[17] except in special circumstances, but otherwise it should be poured over the head three times. The regulations have their parallels in Jewish halakic debates about ritual washing.[18] There is no theological explanation beyond the Trinitarian baptismal formula, repeated twice in slightly different form: εἰς τὸ ὄνομα τοῦ πατρὸς καὶ τοῦ υἱοῦ καὶ τοῦ ἁγίου πνεύματος (7:1) and εἰς ὄνομα πατρὸς καὶ υἱοῦ καὶ ἁγίου πνεύματος (7:3). The modified repetition and the use of a different formula altogether in 9:5, εἰς ὄνομα κυρίου, indicates that the words have been changed repeatedly to bring them into line with changing community praxis.[19] Finally, the baptismal instructions provide for a compulsory pre-baptismal fast by the baptizer and baptized for one or two days, and a voluntary fast on the part of any others who can (7:4). Again, these instructions have been extensively edited.[20]

The mention of the baptismal fast then introduces the subject of the so-called stationary fast in 8:1. This is followed by instruction on prayer in 8:2-3. 9:1 signifies a complete change of subject with the formula περὶ δὲ....οὕτω ποιήσατε as in 6:3, 7:1, 9:1,

---

[17] T. Klauser, "Taufet in Lebendigem Wasser! Zum religions- und kulturgeschichtlichen Verständnis von Didache 7,1-3", in T. Klauser & Rükker (eds.), *Pisciculi. Studien zur Religion und Kultur des Altertums* (Fst. F. J. Dölger) (Münster: Aschendorff, 1939) pp. 157-164; A. Vööbus, *Liturgical Traditions in the Didache* (Stockholm: ETSE, 1968 [PETSE 16]) pp. 22f; Niederwimmer, *Didache*, p. 161)

[18] Draper, *Commentary*, pp. 156-158. Niederwimmer (*Didache*, pp. 161-162) argues that the "redactor" of the *Didache* tradition has left this Jewish understanding behind in 7:2f, but this may be disputed, since what follows refers to the definition of "other water", the different kinds of water which, although not running, may yet be held to be used for ritual washing (*m.Miqw* 1:1-8; CD 10:10-13; cf. Draper, *Commentary*, pp. 158-159).

[19] The same thing probably occurred in the transmission of Matthew 28:19, where Eusebius preserves what may be an earlier form of the text F. C. Coneybeare, "The Eusebian Form of the Text of Matthew 28,29". *ZNW* 2 (1901) pp. 275-288; E. Lohmeyer, "Mir ist gegeben alle Gewalt!", in W. Schmauch (ed), *In Memoriam Ernst Lohmeyer* (Stuttgart: , 1951) pp. 22-49; H. B. Green, "The Command to Baptize and Other Matthaean Interpolations" *SE* 4 (Berlin: Akademie-Verlag, 1968 [TU 102]) pp. 60-63; H. Kosmala, "The Conclusion of Matthew", *ASTI* 4 (1965) pp. 132-147; Vööbus, *Liturgical Traditions*, pp. 36f; *contra* E. Riggenbach, *Der trinitarische Taufbefehl Matth. 28,19 nach seine ursprünglichen Textgestalt und Authentie untersucht* (Gütersloh, 1903 [BFCTh 7]); K. Kertelge, "Der sogenannte Taufbefehl Jesu (Mt 28,19)", in *Zeichen des Glaubens. Studien zu Taufe und Firmung* (Fst B. Fischer) (Freiburg im Breisgau: Einsiedeln, 1972) pp. 29-40; G. Barth, *Die Taufe in Frühchristliche Zeit* (Neukirchen-Vluyn: Neukirchener-Verlag, 1981) pp. 13-17.

[20] They are given first in the imperative third person singular (προνηστευσάτω), and then in the second person singular (κελεύεις), even though the introductory formula in 7:1 is in the second person plural (βαπτίσατε).

[10:8].[21] This is important, since it shows that the context of *Didache* 8 remains that of initiation into the community. Jefford argues that chapter 8 is part of a discussion on a "second institution", namely the community meal, and that the material on prayer thus "does violence to the flow of the text".[22] There is no doubt that ch. 8 presents a hiatus in structure, but not because it belongs to the material on the eucharist. Rather, the instructions on initiation in chapter 7 have called up the question of boundary definition of the community, in a time of change. The instructions in chapter 8 address the problem by reworking authoritative tradition. A. Milavec[23] includes *Didache* 9-10 with 8:2, under the rubric: "How to pray unlike the hypocrites", but his structure is open to the same objections. In particular, the absence of any reference to the "hypocrites" in the context of the instructions concerning eucharist is an important indication that they derive from a different context.

The Position of Chapter 8 in the Tradition

As has already been observed, this chapter appears to be an interruption to the logical progression of the liturgical section of Didache, in which baptism is followed by the Eucharist.[24] It surely represents a later stage in the evolution of the work. The Ethiopic version of the *Didache* puts 8:1-2 after 11:3-13, and this also indicates its uncertain status in the tradition, although the dislocation may reflect the work of an eclectic compiler. In any case, the chapter presents close parallels to the synoptic tradition and an appeal to the authority of the "gospel". *Didache* 8 thus belongs with the other sections of the work which refer to the gospel tradition, 1:3-2:1 and 15:3-4, probably representing the latest stage in the redaction of the work.

This section is clumsily joined to what precedes by the conjunction δέ, while the context is quite different. 7:4 describes the baptismal fast of the candidate, officiant and any others who are able, for one or two days before the event. 8:1 talks of the so-called "stationary fast" kept by pious Jews and now enjoined on Christians, albeit on different days of the week[25].

---

[21] Draper, "Torah and Troublesome Apostles", p. 351; cf. M. M. Mitchell, "Concerning ΠΕΡΙ ΔΕ in 1 Corinthians". *NovT* 31/3 (1989) pp. 229-256.

[22] Jefford, *Sayings of Jesus*, pp. 104-105.

[23] Milavec, "Pastoral Genius", p. 104.

[24] R. Knopf, *Die Lehre der zwölf Apostel. Die zwei Clemensbriefe* (Tübingen:Mohr, 1920) p. 23; Rordorf & Tuilier, *Doctrine*, pp. 36f; Niederwimmer, *Didache*, p. 165.

[25] Note that the reference to fasting is in the plural αἱ δὲ νηστεῖαι ὑμῶν, although the Ethiopic version gives the singular. The tendency to cite the topic in the singular appears to be later (cf. the variants at 6:3; 7:1).

The Reason for the Insertion of New Material

According to Victor Turner,[26] initiation into a new community is
achieved by so-called "rites of passage" in three temporal and
spatial phases: separation, margin and aggregation. In the
marginal or liminal situation, ritual actions and symbols are
oriented first towards the "death of their previous social identity
and its governing norms". "Paraenesis given in this first phase is
subversive, designed to undercut the validity of the prior social
world and to produce anomy, at least temporarily".[27] In a second
phase actions and symbols are oriented towards experiences of
new birth.

The paraenesis in *Didache* 1-6 functions primarily to cut the
convert off from her/his previous social identity, namely that of
pagan Graeco-Roman society, by means of the Two Ways instruction. The vices of this society are set out both in the Way of Life,
where they are incorporated into a vice list (2:2-7) and into the
"Fence about the Law" (3:1-6) and in the Way of Death in a further vice list (5:1-2). Accusations of sexual license[28], homosexuality and pederasty[29], magical practices[30] astrology and omens[31],
abortion and exposure of infants[32], constitute a Jewish perspective
on that pagan society.[33] This is the life-style from which converts
are to cut themselves off: "My child, flee from every evil person /
deed and from all like her / him / it" (3:1f); "You shall not associ-

---

[26] V. Turner, *The Ritual Process* (Ithaca: Cornell University, 1967); cf. L. Perdue, "The Social Character of Paraenesis and Paraenetic literature", in L. G. Perdue & J. G. Gammie, *Paraenesis: Act and Form*, *Semeia* 50 (1990) pp. 5-39, esp.
9-11.

[27] Perdue, "Paraenesis", p. 10.

[28] Cf. *b.San* 57b-58a on prohibited sexual behaviour associated with the so-
called "Noachic Precepts".

[29] Eg. Philo, *VitCon* 50-52; Jos. *ConApion* II.199; II.273; II.275; *AJ* III.275. In
Rabbinic writing, *b.Nidd* 13b links proselytes and pederasts: "Proselytes and those
that play with children delay the advent of the Messiah" (Cf. *b.Yeb* 47b).

[30] Eg. PsPhilo, *LAB* XXXIV.1-4. Such magical practice was widespread in Hellenistic society (N. G. L. Hammond & H. H. Scullard, *The Oxford Classical Dictionary* [Oxford: Clarendon, 1970²] pp. 637f), and also common in certain Jewish
circles (L. Blau, *Das altjüdische Zauberwesen* [Budapest, 1898]).

[31] Rabbinic tradition concerning the Noachic Precepts tended to elaborate on
such pagan practices in the same way as *Didache* 3:4, showing that prohibition of
sorcery in all its forms was considered to be a priority (*b.San* 56a; *m.Sot* 9:13).

[32] Which is usually equated with murder. See Josephus, *ConApion* II.202; Philo,
Hypothetica 7.7; Ps.-Phocylides, 183f; Tacitus, *An* V.5 (who sees a refusal to
comit infanticide as wickedness on the part of Jews). Cf. *b.San* 57b, "On the
authority of R. Ishmael it was said: He is executed even for the murder of an
embryo".

[33] Cf. Rordorf, "Le baptême", p. 117.

ate yourself with the proud, but conduct yourself with the righteous and humble" (3:9); "May you be delivered, children, from all these (people)" (5:2).

In the second phase of this initiatory process, the paraenesis is orientated towards reaggregation, and emphasizes inner community relationships: "some you shall love more than your life" (2:7); "seek daily the presence of the saints, so that you can rest in their words; do no seek schism but reconcile those who are in conflict" (4:2-3); share material goods with other community members, withholding nothing (4:5-8).

What is significant in both of these phases, is that no specifically Christian motivation is given, which would not equally serve a convert to Judaism. There is evidence that the outward movement of Judaism in the conversion of proselytes continued well beyond the first and second centuries C.E.,[34] so that it would have continued to be in competition with the growing Christian movement. In fact, it is not unlikely that the Two Ways material originates in Jewish proselyte instruction, though this cannot be proved.[35] It is only with the insertion of the Jesus material in 1:3-6 that any Christian emphasis emerges, and this is clearly a late stage in the development of the text, probably the same stage as that represented by chapter 8. The material is absent from the various recensions of the Two Way tradition outside of the *Didache* (e.g. *De doctrina apostolorum, The Epistle of Barnabas, The Epitome* and the various Church Orders).[36]

The instructions of 1-5 are largely haggadic expansion of Old Testament material, especially the Ten Commandments and the Holiness Code of Leviticus 17-19.[37] This is re-enforced in 6:2 with a reference to attempting to take on the whole yoke of the Lord, in my opinion a reference to the Torah.[38] If the whole

---

[34] M. Simon, *Verus Israel: A Study of the Relations between Christians and Jews in the Roman Empire (135-425)* (Oxford: Littman Library, 1986) p. 271-305.

[35] J.-P. Audet, "Affinités littéraires et doctrinales du "Manuel de Discipline"", *RB* 59 (1952) pp. 219-238; D. Flusser, "The Two Ways", in *Jewish Sources in Early Christianity* (Tel Aviv: Sifriat Poalaim, 1979) pp. 232-252.

[36] Indeed Wengst removes this passage from the text and relegates it to the critical aparatus in his recent edition (K. Wengst, *Didache (Apostellehre), Barnabasbrief, Zweiter Klemensbrief, Schrift an Diognet* [Darmstadt: Wissenschaftliche Buchgesellschaft, 1984 (FC 1)] p. 66). This, however, misses the point, in that it is part of the final form of the *Didache*, which has taken up the Two Ways and modified it. It is found in also in *Const* and POx1782.

[37] Draper, *Commentary*, pp. 50-62; cf. P. Carrington, *The Primitive Christian Catechism: A Study in the Epistles* (Cambridge: Cambridge University Press, 1940) ch. 6; E. G. Selwyn, *The First Epistle of St. Peter* (London: Macmillan, 1958²) pp. 369-375; D. Flusser, "The Ten Commandments and the New Testament", in B. Segal (ed), *The Ten Commandments in History and Tradition* (Jerusalem: Magnes, 1990) pp. 219-246.

[38] Draper, "Torah and Troublesome Apostles", pp. 347-372; cf. Flusser, "Paul's Jewish Christian Opponents", pp. 71-90.

Torah proves too much, at least the food laws and prohibitions on idolatry are mandatory (6:3), the common ingredients of the so-called Noachic code.

All of this material provides strong motivation for separation from the surrounding Graeco-Roman society, but provides a model of aggregation with strong links to Jewish law and tradition. Clearly, the original community of the *Didache* saw no need to differentiate itself from the Jewish community. They differentiated themselves not from Jews but from pagans.[39] The thanksgiving prayer of the community sees the soteriological work of Jesus in terms of "making known the vine of David your son" (9:2), bringing pagans into the eschatological community of Israel.

The paraenesis of 1-5 provides no hint of animosity towards Jews or the Torah, nor any sign of Christian self-definition over against them. A catachumen instructed in this way would see her/ himself joining a particular Jewish community with a strong apocalyptic hope. It would be one among several Jewish groups, and such Jewish proselytism was probably common in the first century C.E., at least in Pharisaic Judaism, as the jaundiced comment in Matthew 23:15 suggests.[40] Even baptism was probably a part of proselyte initiation to Judaism;[41] The Jewish Christian community was accommodating on the question of circumcision and Torah for Gentiles, but remained a faithful, Torah-observant Jewish community. The question of its relationship to the wider Jewish society is not raised in the chapters 1-7.

All of this makes the sudden intrusion of material against the "hypocrites" in ch. 8 all the more surprising and instructive. It clearly reflects the emergence of new social tensions and exigencies. The fact that it emerges in the context of baptism is also instructive. Members of the *Didache* community are now being required to separate themselves not only from the pagan Graeco-Roman world, but also from another Jewish community. One should hesitate to say "separate themselves from Jewish society as a whole", since Jewish society was at this stage a very amorphous and multi-faceted affair. Ethnic Jews in the Diaspora could be observant or non-observant; they were also probably

---

[39] Cf. Borgen ("Catalogues of Vices", pp. 126-141) who sees this as the root of the conflict in Galatians.

[40] Schürer, E., Vermes, G. & Millar, F. 1973 (rev.ed.). *The History of the Jewish People in the Age of Jesus Christ (175 B.C.-A.D. 135)* III (Edinburgh: T & T Clark, 1986) pp. 158-176; G. G. Moore, *Judaism in the First Centuries of the Christian Era* I (New York: Schocken) pp. 323-353.

[41] A. Benoit, *Le Baptême Chrétien au Second Siècle* (Paris: Presses Universitaires de France, 1953) pp. 5-19; Moor, *Judaism*, pp. 331-341; Simon, *Verus Israel*, pp.286-287; Schürer-Vermes, *History*, pp. 173-174.

responsible for the development of strands of Gnosticism which rejected both the Torah and the God of Torah.[42] There was, at this stage, no single overall authority able or competent to determine who was or was not a Jew! Not, at least, until the Council at Yavneh towards the end of the first century C.E. Even then, one must question the assumption that the authority of the Rabbis was accepted immediately or without question.

At any rate, it appears that the community of the ὑποκρίται was close and attractive enough to members of the *Didache* community to warrant this kind of attack. Isaac of Antioch is moved to preach vigorously against Christians who have received Christian baptism and go on to receive proselyte baptism of the Jews in addition (*Hom. de mag.*; in Simon 1986:356-238). Chrysostom preaches against similar practices in Antioch in the fourth century (*Jud* 5 & 6).[43] Flusser[44] argues that *Didache* 6:2-3 sets out the position of the (Petrine) Jewish Mother Church on the observance of the Torah by gentile converts, a position which was ultimately undermined by the attraction of full conversion to (non-Christian) Judaism. It seems that he is not so wide of the mark.

III. THE IDENTITY OF THE "HYPOCRITES"

Streeter[45] sees *Didache*'s reference to the ὑποκριτῶν in 8:1 as in agreement with the written letter of Matthew 6:16, but "in flagrant discord with the spirit". R. Glover[46] is surely right, however, in rejoining that it is not according to the letter but breaches "letter as flagrantly as spirit". The only thing the passage has in common with Matthew is the word ὑποκριτῶν and even there, μετὰ τῶν ὑποκριτῶν gives a different focus from the ὡς of the Gospel, (inserted by the Ethiopian version at this point also in the *Didache*). The focus is not on the manner of the fast, but only on the timing of it, which is intended to delineate Christians from Jews.

Even the sense of ὑποκριτῶν is different. Matthew 6:16 attacks some Pharisees for doing things for the sake of appearances only. Such a meaning would be absurd in the context

---

[42] B. Pearson, "Friedländer Revisited: Alexandrian Judaism and Gnostic Origins", in *Gnosticism, Judaism, and Egyptian Christianity* (Minneapolis: Fortress, 1990 [*Studies in Antiquity and Christianity*]) pp. 10-28.

[43] Cf. W. A. Meeks and R. L. Wilken, *Jews and Christians in the First Four Centuries of the Christian Era* (Missoula, Mont.: Scholars, 1978).

[44] Flusser, "Paul's Jewish-Christian Opponents", pp. 71-90.

[45] B. H. Streeter, *The Four Gospels: A Study of Origins* (London: Macmillan, 1936) p. 508; cf. K. Lake, *The New Testament in the Apostolic Fathers* (Oxford: Oxford University Press, 1905) p. 28.

[46] "Didache's Quotations", p. 18.

of the *Didache*. Massaux[47] sees the sequence of the whole block of Jesus material in 8:1-2 as proof of such a dependence. Köster sees it as a free use of the tradition represented also by Matthew and "eine nicht mehr verstandene Reminiszenz".[48] This assumes that Matthew's usage is the earlier one. Certainly it seems more likely that the *Didache* uses ὑποκρίτης in a different sense to Matthew.

In the LXX, the word group can render the root חנף[49] or עגה, both in very general senses of impiety or ungodliness.[50] It is certainly wrong to translate these passages automatically with the sense of the English "hypocrisy", as is done in various modern translations.

1QS 4:10 shows that רוב חונף can be used as a very general accusation in a vice-list against opponents. The sense of חנופה is very general also in 4QTestim (*175*) 28. חנופה can mean either "hypocrisy, dishonesty, flattery" or "faithlessness to religion, apostacy" (Jastrow 1950:482). It is thus likely that its Greek equivalent ὑποκρίτης could also be used in this general sense of ungodliness, as an accusation one might level against religious opponents (cf. *PssSol* 4:7). On the other hand, no doubt, the object of characterizing religious opponents in this way is to question their *bona fides*. They may appear to be behaving piously, but their motives are all wrong. This would be the way in which the transition was made to the use of the word to characterize them as doing things for outward show. Moshe Weinfeld[51] has shown that "preaching well but not practising well" was a common charge in Rabbinic admonitions against unworthy Pharisaic teachers, and may be described as חנפי תורה.[52]

In Greek, ὑποκρίτης can mean "interpreter" or "expounder", although it is usually used to mean "actor" or "hypocrite", especially in the Apostolic Fathers.[53] The *Didache*, however, does not seem to be using the word with reference to "play-acting", but rather in a general sense to characterize its opponents as ungodly and to question their good faith.

---

[47] *Influence*, pp. 154-155.

[48] Köster, *Überlieferung*, p. 203.

[49] P. Jouon, "YPOKRITES dans l'Evangile et hebreux HANEF", *RSR* 20 (1930) pp. 312-316; Audet, *Didache*, pp. 344, 368f; cf. Did 4:12; 5:1.

[50] E. Hatch and H. A. Redpath, *A Concordance to the Septuagint and the Other Greek Versions of the Old Testament* II (Oxford: Clarendon, 1897) p. 1414.

[51] M. Weinfeld, "The Charge of Hypocrisy in Matthew 23 and in Jewish Sources", *Immanuel* 24-25 (1990) pp. 52-58.

[52] E.g. Ecclesiastes Rabbah 4:1; Weinfeld, "Charge of Hypocrisy", pp. 57-58.

[53] H. G. Liddell and R. Scott, (rev. H. S. Jones) *A Greek-English Lexicon* (Oxford: Clarendon, 1968) p. 1886; G. W. H. Lampe, *A Patristic Greek Lexicon* (Oxford: Clarendon, 1961) p. 1450.

Rordorf and Tuilier[54] see a reference to a group of Judaizing Christian dissidents, but this is unlikely. The *Didache* nowhere else condemns Judaism, but everywhere shows its own closeness to Jewish roots. Their hypothesis has not found much acceptance, and most scholars continue to see the reference to Jews.[55] Harnack,[56] Audet[57] and more recently Niederwimmer[58] think that there is no need to see Pharisees in particular in this expression, but pious Jews in general, who refuse to accept the Gospel. It seems to me more likely to refer to Pharisees in particular, since there is no evidence that pious Jews "in general" kept the Monday and Thursday fast and prayed three times a day. The Essenes do not seem to have made a special point of regular fasting, since no mention is made of this, but seem to have prayed twice a day as a matter of principle.[59]

On the one hand, the targeting of Pharisaic Jews as ὑποκρίται is a measure of the closeness of the community of the *Didache* to its Jewish roots (because it accepts the act itself but questions the motives). As Weinfeld[60] has shown, it is a feature of inner-Jewish debate. On the other hand, no justification is given for the accusation of impiety or insincerity. It is simply stated as an unconditional, accepted fact. This indicates that the breach may be beyond repair. This must represent one further step in the gradual alienation of Christianity from its parent Judaism.[61]

IV. THE NATURE OF THE DIFFERENTIATION

The "Stationary" Fast

The characterization of the opponents of the *Didache* community as fasting on Mondays and Thursdays (νηστεύουσι γὰρ δευτέρᾳ σαββάτων καὶ πέμπτῃ) matches the evidence of the Rabbinic texts e.g. *m.Meg* 3:6; 4:1.[62] Some fasted on these days throughout the

---

[54] Rordorf & Tuilier, *Doctrine*, pp. 36f.

[55] Wengst, *Didache*, p. 34; Jefford, *Sayings of Jesus*, p. 106; Niederwimmer, *Didache*, pp. 165-166; G. Schöllgen & W. Geerling, *Didache Zwölf-Apostel-Lehre / Tradition Apostolica Apostolische Überlieferung* (Freiburg: Herder, 1991 [FC 1]) p. 47 n. 94.

[56] A. von Harnack, *Lehre der zwölf Apostel nebst Untersuchungen zur ältesten Geschichte der Kirchenverfassung und des Kirchenrechts* (Leipzig: J. C. Hinrich'se, 1884) pp. 24f.

[57] *Didachè*, pp. 367f.

[58] *Didache*, p. 166 n. 4.

[59] A. R. C. Leaney, *The Rule of Qumran and its Meaning* (London: SCM, 1966).

[60] "Charge of Hypocrisy", pp. 52-58.

[61] Cf. Schöllgen, *Didache Zwölf-Apostel-Lehren*, p. 48.

[62] Schürer-Vermes, *History* II, pp. 483-484.

year according to *b.Taan* 12a. In *m.Meg* 1:2, 3; 3:6 instruction
about the correct timing of the fast follows after the instruction to
read the blessings and curses of Leviticus 26:3-46 on fast days.
The two things may well be linked.[63] The men of the lay order or
Maamad, who supported their priestly course on duty in
Jerusalem with worship in the synagogue, also fasted from the
second to the fifth day according to *m.Taan* 4:2 and *b.Taan* 12a
(cf. 10a). Such fasting would be a public and visible witness to a
person's piety, but also to their adherence to the Pharisaic party.
Jewish fast days were observed in public in open places according
to *m.Taan* 2:1, a practice recorded also by Tertullian: *Iudaicum
certe ieiunium ubique celebratur, cum omissis templis per omne
litus quocumque in aperto aliquando iam precem ad caelum mit-
tunt* (*De ieiunio* 16; cf. *Ad Nationes* i.13). The public nature of the
solemn fast is also characterized by the blast on the *shofar* during
droughts. People would stop work to worship and resume their
work at this signal.[64] Matthew 6:16 attests the public nature of this
Pharisaic practice, although he impugns their motives and requires
members of his community to fast in secret. No such instruction to
secrecy is given in *Didache* 8:1. In the light of the function of the
text, it is more likely that it was intended to create a public differentiation between its community and the Pharisaic community.
For the Jewish Christian community to cease to join in the public
fasts of the Pharisaic Jewish community would be a sign of seces-
sion, especially if they celebrated their own fasts publicly on different days. Matthew's insistence on secrecy might be seen as
conciliatory.

The *Didache* asserts an alternative fast on Wednesdays and
Fridays (τετράδα καὶ παρασκευήν), which looks as if it might
have been compulsory, since it is couched in the imperative (ὑμεῖς
δὲ νηστεύσατε).[65] Fixed days or "stations" are attested in Hermas,
Similitude V.1, where their value without a life of good works is
rejected. Later attestation is provided by Clement of Alexandria,
Stromata VII.12; Tert. *De ieiunio* 14; Origen *Homily on Leviticus*
X.2. The *Apostolic Constitutions* (*Const* VII.23) require the fast
on Wednesday and Friday as a symbol of the betrayal and
crucifixion of Jesus.[66] *Didache*, however, remains silent on the
reasoning behind the choice of days, except that they were in
opposition to the "hypocrites". They marked off the Christian

---

[63] Cf. H. L. Strack & P. Billerbeck, *Kommentar zum NT aus Talmud und
Midrasch* II (München: C. H. Beck, 1926⁴) p. 241; *Ibid* IV, p. 89.

[64] Schürer-Vermes, *History* II, pp. 446-7).

[65] Schöllgen (*Didache Zwölf-Apostel-Lehre*, p. 48 n. 99) is more cautious, arguing that the goal of the passage is not to make the fast a binding duty, but to replace
the Jewish fast with a Christian one.

[66] Cf. *Didascalia* (Lagarde p 89, ll 13-15).

community from its Jewish rivals.[67] Audet argues that the fast on Friday represents a deliberate flouting of the Sabbath (cf. *m. Taan* 4:2) but this is not clear.[68]

Connolly[69] makes the rules for fasting in *Didache* a major plank in his theory of the Montanist origin of the *Didache*, since Tertullian in *De ieiunio* attacks the "Catholic" Church for having an optional fast, whereas the Montanists have a compulsory fast. However, Montanism was essentially a reactionary movement, and may well be re-asserting the tradition found in the *Didache*. Moreover, the genuinely ascetic *Liber Graduum*, which regards the *Didache* as "Scripture", rejects the stationary fast twice a week in favour of a continual fast (VII.20). Rather, the purpose for the instruction on fasting was to distinguish the Christian community from other Jewish groups with which it was in close contact and rivalry, as Niederwimmer points out:

> Die scharfe Polemik gegen die ὑποκριταί und die Notwendigkeit, sich von den Fastensitten der jüdischen Frommen durch the Wahl anderer Fastentage zu unterscheiden, setzt--auf der einen Seite--noch einen engen Kontakt der hier in Erscheinung tretenden Gemeinden mit der jüdischen Umwelt voraus.[70]

The Lord's Prayer

The prohibition against praying ὡς οἱ ὑποκριταί also implies a close contact with Jewish groups. The instruction τρίς τῆς ἡμέρας οὕτω προσεύχεσθε sets the Lord's Prayer in the context of the regular Jewish practice of prayer.[71] The obligation to recite the *Shema*c in the morning and the evening was laid on all men and boys from the age of twelve, and combined with the prayers three times a day, which were laid even on women, children and slaves (*b. Ber* 26b; *t. Ber* 3:6). The practice is justified from Daniel 6:10; Psalm 55:17.[72] The content of the daily *Tephilla* had crystallized by the end of the First Century at least into the *Shemoneh* c*Esreh*, the Eighteen Benedictions. Thus the Lord's Prayer is here laid on Christians as a replacement for the recital of the *Shemoneh* c*Esreh* which is prayed by the ὑποκρίται.[73] Audet[74] sees it as a later

---

[67] Cf. Taylor, *Teaching*, pp. 58-62.

[68] Audet, *Didachè*, p. 369.

[69] R. H. Connolly, "The Didache and Montanism", *Downside Review* ns 36 (1937) pp. 339-347, esp. 343-346.

[70] *Didache*, p. 166.

[71] Moore, *Judaism* I, pp. 291f; *Ibid.* II, pp. 212-238; cf. J. Jeremias, *The Prayers of Jesus* (London: SCM, 1967) pp. 66-72; Schürer-Vermes, *History* II, pp. 447-463.

[72] Cf. Klein, *Katechismus*, p. 215.

[73] P. Drews, "Untersuchungen zur Didache", *ZNW* 5 (1904) pp. 53-79, esp. 74ff; Klein, *Katechismus*, p. 215; Knopf, *Die Lehre*, p. 23; Rordorf & Tuilier,

imitation of the Jewish practice. Dugmore[75] denies the origin in Jewish prayer practice and claims it comes from the "hours on the Cross". This is unlikely. Later Christian tradition required a thrice daily recitation of the Lord's Prayer by catechumens in the preparation for baptism (Hippolytus *ApTrad* 18, 19). The *Apostolic Constitution* VIII.44 (cf. III.18) envisages the recital of the Lord's Prayer by the newly baptized on their arising from the water.

Schürer suggests that the recital of the *Shema*ᶜ was more in the nature of a confession of faith than a prayer, and thus was not "prayed" but "recited" (קריאת שמע).[76] The recital was also a very public affair, since the Mishnah provides rules for the circumstances in which someone reciting the *Shema*ᶜ in the street should act (*m. Ber* 2:1-2; cf. Matthew 6:5).[77] This would underline the need for a confessing Christian community, concerned to differentiate itself from Pharisaic Judaism, to find an alternative form of prayer, which was also in the nature of a confession. The prayer would be prayed aloud, perhaps also in the street if business required that (cf. Acts 3:1). In ancient "residually oral society" it is spoken words which are dynamic and infused with power. Silent reading was not as yet practised and one should imagine that silent prayer in words was also not known.[78] The whole point of Matthew's insistence on prayer in the inner chamber, is that the sounds of spoken prayer should not be heard by others. There is no suggestion that one could pray secretly in silence in a public place. Matthew's version sounds like a modification at a secondary level after the event.

It seems, then, that some Christians were still using the Jewish daily prayers, the *Shemoneh* ᶜ*Esreh* and the *Shema*ᶜ, for which the *Didache* urges the Lord's Prayer as a replacement.[79] This is cited as authoritative tradition, commanded by the Lord (ὡς ἐκέλευσεν ὁ κύριος ἐν τῷ εὐαγγελίῳ αὐτοῦ). This need not refer to a written gospel, but could refer to the oral material which constituted the Kerygma.[80] It should, however, be noted that the

---

Doctrine, p. 175. Schöllgen, *Didache Zwölf-Apostel-Lehre*, pp. 48f.

[74] *Didachè*, p. 371.

[75] C. W. Dugmore, *The Influence of the Synagogue upon the Divine Office* (London: Alcuin, 1964²) pp. 59-70.

[76] Schürer-Vermes, *History* II, p. 449.

[77] Cf. Schürer-Vermes, *History* II, p. 482.

[78] W. J. Ong, *Orality and Literacy: the Technologizing of the Word* (London/New York: Methuen, 1982) pp. 32f, 74f, 117ff. With reference to the culture of late antiquity, see P. J. Achtemeier, "*Omne Verbum Sonat:* The New Testament and the Oral Environment of Late Western Antiquity", *JBL* 109/1 (1990) pp. 3-27.

[79] Knopf, *Die Lehre*, p. 23; W. D. Davies, *The Setting of the Sermon on the Mount* (Cambridge: Cambridge Universityf Press, 1966) pp. 309-315.

[80] Köster, *Überlieferung*, pp. 203f; Audet, *Didachè*, p. 173.

εὐαγγέλιον in this case is rather a matter of paraenesis than of "kerygma". If this chapter forms part of the latest redactional stage of the *Didache*, it may also attest the beginning of an authoritative written Gospel in some form. Audet's hypothesis[81] that the emergence of a written Gospel intervenes between the first and second redactions by the same author, is an unnecessary elaboration. If, as is likely, the *Didache* is a composite work which has undergone several redactions, the latest redaction would be in a different situation with regard to the developing Jesus tradition. The important question is whether one of the canonical Gospels had emerged and attained an authoritative position in the *Didache* community by the time of the final redaction. Nothing allows such an assertion to be made without reservation. Audet sees *Didache* 8 as part of the first redaction, but it is more likely that it represents the latest stage of redaction. In any case, the *function* of the insertion of the "gospel" tradition is to lend the authority of the Lord to the new wording of the thrice daily prayer in opposition to the prevailing practice of the "hypocrites", the Jewish opponents of the community.

Although the texts of the Lord's Prayer in *Didache* and Matthew agree so closely, it is unnecessary to suppose literary dependence. According to *Didache* 8:3, the Prayer is repeated three times a day by every Christian, and it is absurd to imagine that the *Didache* would need a written source for a prayer so familiar to his community. The Prayer would already have had a fixed and tenacious liturgical form[82] such that even minor variations would be significant.[83]

The liturgical use of the Lord's Prayer in the community is indicated by the presence of the doxology (ὅτι σοῦ ἐστιν ἡ δύναμις καὶ ἡ δόξα εἰς τοὺς αἰῶνας).[84] The textual variants which add a doxology in varying forms to Matthew's text of the Lord's Prayer show how widespread and ancient this usage was. T. W. Manson[85] has shown that from earliest times the Lord's Prayer was linked to the reception of candidates into Church membership. In the teaching of Cyril of Jerusalem (AD 350), the Lord's Prayer is recited in the part of the eucharistic prayers reserved for the participation of the baptized, the *missa fidelium*. The *Apostolic Constitution* VII.44 envisages the newly baptized candidate rising from the water, facing East and reciting the Lord's Prayer. This

---

[81] *Didachè*, p. 176.

[82] E. Lohmeyer, *The Lord's Prayer* (London: Collins, 1965) p. 16; Köster, *Überlieferung*, p. 205.

[83] Lake, *New Testament*, p. 29; Glover, "Didache's Quotations", p. 19.

[84] T. W. Manson, *The Sayings of Jesus* (London: SCM, 1949) p. 171; "The Lord's Prayer", *BJRL* 38 (1955-1956) pp. 99-113, esp. 107f.

[85] "Lord's Prayer", pp. 99-113; cf. Jeremias, *Prayers of Jesus*, pp. 82-85.

agrees with the position of the Lord's Prayer in the *Didache*, after baptism and before Eucharist. The teaching is thus post-baptismal and the use of the prayer may have been reserved for full church members.[86] Liturgical rubrics also seem to require such a situation, as Jeremias has pointed out.[87] Particularly important is the presence of "*audemus dicere*" in the Western rite and a similar sentiment in the Liturgy of St. John Chrysostom. Thus the presence of the text of the Lord's Prayer in the *Didache* at this point is far from accidental. The indications are that it serves to encapsulate a specifically Christian theology, which would be memorized by the catechumens and then recited publicly at her/his baptism. The significance of repeating the prayer three times a day would then serve in part as a continuing reminder of this act of initiation and differentiation.

Social Pressures Reflected in Liturgy

In both these cases, of instructions on fasting and on prayer, it is clear that the practices are not new. The community was already fasting twice a week, in solidarity with other Jewish groups, or the Pharisees at least. The community was already using the Lord's Prayer liturgically, as the doxology and amen shows. What the instruction does is to use these two existing practices to differentiate between the Christian community and its opponents, Pharisaic Jews. The days are changed for fasting, and the Friday fast indicates that traditional observation of the Sabbath may also be under attack, perhaps because the community was already observing Sunday as the Lord's Day (κατὰ κυριακὴν δὲ κυρίου συναχθέντες κλάσατε ἄρτον καὶ εὐχαριστήσατε *Didache* 14:1), the new sabbath for Christians.[88] The prayer to be recited daily three times to replace the prayers of Pharisaic Judaism is the Lord's Prayer, thus providing a daily re-affirmation of the community's difference from other Jewish groups.

V. THE EFFECT OF THE INSERTED MATERIAL

The effect of the insertion of the material on fasting and praying into the framework of the instruction to catechumens, is to heighten a sense of the unique identity of the group. It could be termed an exclusion rule: this is the condition on which new members of the community are baptized. This in turn must have

---

[86] Manson, "Lord's Prayer", p. 102.

[87] *Prayers of Jesus*, p. 85.

[88] Cf. R. J. Bauckham, "The Lord's Day", in D. Carson (ed), *From Sabbath to Lord's Day* (Grand Rapids: Academie, 1985) pp. 221-250.

impacted on the normal table fellowship of the community. *Didache* 9:5 limits participation in the εὐχαριστία or B°rakah of its members to those who have been baptized. The terminology of the instruction indicates that this was originally directed against the admittance of unbaptized Gentiles, characterized as "dogs": καὶ γὰρ περὶ τούτο εἴρηκεν ὁ κύριος· μὴ δῶτε τὸ ἅγιον τοῖς κυσί.

This short saying has far-reaching implications in its present context. It refers to the bread and wine as τὸ ἅγιον. The use of the singular shows that it has not become simply a formula to denote the eucharistic elements as in later liturgies. Knopf[89] claims that τὸ ἅγιον refers to the eucharistic elements in the later liturgies, but the later liturgies use τὰ ἅγια, and Knopf seems to have missed the importance of this difference. Cyril of Jerusalem writes in his *Catechese mystagogicae*, "After this the Priest says, "Holy things to holy people (τὰ ἅγια τοῖς ἀγίοις)"". With this can be compared the *Liturgy of James* 40; *Liturgy of St. Mark* 20; *Liturgy of the Holy Apostles* 19; Chrysostom, *Homily on Matthew* vii.7. In all these instances, it is the elements themselves which receive emphasis, and not the cultic state of holiness, as in the Didache. The strength of the liturgical tradition is such, that it has interfered with the text of Matthew 7:6, where the Miniscules 118, 157, 209, 243, 245, 1689, and the text in Ephraem of Edessa have substituted τὰ ἅγια for τὸ ἅγιον. Methodius, *Symposium* IV.4, has τὰ ἅγια even though he interprets the saying to refer to the word of the Gospel.[90]

τὸ ἅγιον in Didache refers to the condition of cultic holiness as in LXX, where it is used for food offered in sacrifice which only the priests may eat (Ex. 29:33; Lev. 2:2f; 22:10-16; Num. 18:8-19). Leviticus 22:10 is especially pertinent: καὶ πᾶς ἀλλογενὴς οὐ φάγεται ἅγια....ὅτι ἐγὼ κύριος ὁ ἀγιάζων αὐτούς. (Cf. also PssSol 1:8; 2:3; 8:12). Because the meal is eaten in a state of cultic purity, those who have not been purified and sanctified by baptism are excluded. Holiness entails separation. The unbaptized are here described as κύνες, a word commonly used by Jews in the First Century AD to describe Gentiles, because dogs, like swine, were regarded as especially despicable and unclean animals.[91] (For examples see 1 Enoch 56:5; b.*Meg* 15b; b.*Bek* 20b; GenR 81:3; LevR 5:6; MidrPss 4:11.) A particularly apposite parallel to the *Didache* is provided by *Pirqe de*

---

[89] *Die Lehre*, p. 27.

[90] Cf. also *TestDom* I.18, 31. *Const* alters the whole section and omits the saying altogether, so that unauthorized communion is seen as a breach of Law, not of holiness (ὡς οὐ θέμις).

[91] O. Michel, "ΚΥΩΝ, ΚΥΝΑΡΙΟΝ", *TDNT* III, pp. 1101-1104; Strack-Billerbeck, *Kommentar* I, pp. 722-726; O. Böcher, "Wölfe im Schafspelzen: zum religionsgeschichtlichen Hintergrund von Matth. 7,15", *TZ* 24 (1968) pp. 405-426.

Rabbi Eliezer 29, "One who eats together with an idolater is like one who eats together with a dog" (cf. also Mt 9:11 (=Lk 15:12); Acts 10:28; 22:15; Phil 3:2, and POx840).

While the saying appears verbatim in Matthew 7:6, it has a quite different context, which applies it to the teaching of Jesus, which must be safeguarded from abuse. However the pericope sits uneasily in this context.[92] Bultmann[93] argues that it is among the sayings which "belong to the secular meshalim which have been made into dominical sayings in the tradition", and "do not have a specific meaning until they appear in a concrete situation". When the saying about holy things and dogs is combined with another saying about pearls and swine, it is given a new meaning. For, while τὸ ἅγιον refers primarily to what is ritually pure, ὁ μαργαρίτης refers to something very precious, usually a precious saying or Biblical word given to those unworthy of it.[94] The Babylonian tractate *Qiddushin* 39b has the saying "The mouth which produced pearls must now lick the dust" (Cf. *b.Hag* 3a). Jewish preaching with its stringing together of Scriptural citations was compared to a string of pearls. Later Gnostic texts make much of the saying to refer to secret wisdom, eg. *Acts of Peter and the Twelve Apostles* 6:1; *Gospel of Philip* (NgH II,3) 62:18f. The combination of the saying about holy things and the saying about pearls turns the former saying into a metaphor: although the Gospel is to be preached to all men, there must be a certain reservation with respect to those who reject and despise it, since it is holy and precious (cf. Mt 10:14). The effectiveness of the saying as a metaphor depends on its prior reference to cultic purity, so that *Didache* 9:5 seems to be using it in its more primitive and original sense.[95] Both interpretations of the saying continued to be current in the Church. The Gnostic Gospels according to Basilides and Thomas relate the saying to the Gospel, as do Cyprian, Pseudo-Clement, Methodius and Origen.[96] Tertullian teaches the necessity for excluding the unbaptized from communion (*PraescrHaer* 41:2). *Testamentum Domini* II.13 also contains a

---

[92] P. Gaechter, *Das Matthäusevangelium* (Innsbruch, 1962) pp. 236f; P. Bonnard, *L'Évangile selon St. Matthieu* (Neuchatel: Delachaux & Niestlé, 1970) pp. 97f; Köster, *Überlieferung*, p. 299.

[93] R. Bultmann, *The History of the Synoptic Tradition*, trns. J. Marsh (Oxford: Basil Blackwell, 1972) pp. 102f.

[94] Strack-Billerbeck, *Kommentar* I, pp. 447f; F. Hauck, 1967. "ΜΑΡΓΑΡΙΤΗΣ", in TDNT IV, *op. cit.*, pp. 472-273, esp. 472f.

[95] Audet, *Didachè*, pp. 173f; Rordorf & Tuilier, *Doctrine*, p. 87; *contra* Köster, *Überlieferung*, p. 199.

[96] *GBasilides* (*Pan* XXIV.5:2); *GTh* 93; Cyprian, *Test* 3; *Recog* III.1:5f; Origen, *CommExodus* XIII.1; Methodius, *Symp* IV.4; *GPh* (NgH II.3) 80:30-81:13; 82:20-24.

form of the saying to justify the exclusion of non-members from any meal eaten by believers, although the reference here is to wolves not dogs. The Pseudo-Clementine writings repeatedly forbid Christians to eat even their common meals with the unbaptized (*Hom* I.22; VIII.22, 24; XIII.4-5; *Recog.* I.19, 22; *AdVir* II.6; cf. Justin *Apol* I.66).

Sayings concerning holy things and dogs are found also in Rabbinic sources. Haninah b. Antigonus (T3) says, "All animal offerings that have been rendered *terafah* may not be redeemed, since animal offerings may not be redeemed in order to give them as food to the dogs (שאין פודים את־הקדשים להאכילן לכלבים" (*m. Tem* 6:5). Here the relative שׁ implies the citation of a generally accepted principle. This offers a very close parallel to Didache both verbally and in the cultic ritualistic application of the saying (cf. *b.Bek* 15a; *b.Tem* 30b; *b.Sheb* 11b; *b.Pes* 29a). The parallels are discussed in Strack-Billerbeck (1926a:447). Ritual purity, especially of foodstuffs and drink, was a major preoccupation of the Rabbis[97] and led to a complex system of graded purity well exemplified in the Mishnaic tractate *Hagiga* 2:7. It is likely that the Pharisees maintained these purity laws in their communal Haburah meals.[98]

The inclusion of such a rule in the *Didache* shows both a very Jewish concern with ritual purity and also a sectarian concern to exclude non members of the community. Initially, the exclusion was aimed at Gentiles, but the insertion of ch. 8 as a test for initiation turns this exclusion against other Jews as well. The process of differentiation between Jewish and Christian communities now seems complete.

V. RELATIONSHIP TO MATTHEW 6:1-18

A detailed study of the relationship between *Didache* 8 and Matthew's Gospel would be a labour beyond the scope of this essay. Nevertheless, some reference to the problem is inevitable and cries out for comment. Whereas the main concern of the material as it is arranged in the *Didache* lies in differentiation between Christians and the ὑποκρίται, the main concern of Matthew 6:1-18 lies in the need to avoid public display, as its preface suggests:

---

[97] H. Danby, *The Mishnah* (Oxford: Oxford University Press, 1933) pp. 714, 800-804.

[98] P. Seidensticker, *Die Gemeinschaftsform der religiösen Gruppen des Spätjudentums und der Urkirche* (Jerusalem: Franciscan Press, 1959 [*SBFLA*]) pp. 116f; M. Hengel, *Judaism and Hellenism* (London: SCM, 1974) p. 170; J. A. Draper, "The Social Milieu and Motivation of Community of Goods in the Jerusalem Church of Acts", in C. Breytenbach (ed), *Church in Context* (Pretoria: NG Boekhandel, 1988) pp. 77-88.

προσέχετε δὲ τὴν δικαιοσύνην ὑμῶν μὴ ποιεῖν ἔμπροσθεν τῶν
ἀνθρώπων πρὸς τὸ θεαθῆναι αὐτοῖς (6:1).

In the *Didache*, it is indeed the very public nature of fasting
and prayer, identifying marks of adherence to a particular religious community within the broader Jewish society, which have
resulted in their being targeted for differentiation. If the days of
public fasting and the words of the public prayers are changed,
then it provides a clear witness to adherence to the Christian community, without changing the essence of religious practice. The
Christian and Pharisaic Jewish communities are at the parting of
the ways, without as yet having clearly defined any theological
rationale for a separation. It heralds public confrontation between
the two communities. ὑποκρίται is a general and conventional religious accusation of ungodly conduct levelled at a rival community
within Jewish society.

In Matthew 6:1-18, a theological principle is at work: doing
religious works to earn earthly rewards must be avoided, because
the goal of religious behaviour is to earn treasure in heaven (6:19-
21).[99] Works of piety must consequently be done in secret: to do
otherwise is to imitate the ὑποκρίται who love to do their pious
works in public (6:2, 5, 16). Parallels can be found in Jewish and
pagan literature for such sentiments.[100] It is noteworthy, however,
that it takes no account of the public communal witness of fasting
and prayer, on which the *Didache* seems to depend. Almsgiving is
added to the list of activities which must be kept secret to avoid
doing as the ὑποκρίταις (6:2-4). Almsgiving plays a prominent
role also in the *Didache*, where it relates to inner communal relations (1:5-6; 4:5-8), and is thus only indirectly concerned with differentiation. While the Lord's Prayer is again presented in the
context of prayer "not like the hypocrites", it is more specifically
related to avoiding the verbose repetitive prayer (βατταλογία) of
the Gentiles (6:7-8). The difference between the fasting of the
Christians and the hypocrites is now a question of outward
appearances against secret fasting, not a question of days.

There is clearly a close relationship between the two texts.
The question of literary dependence cannot easily be settled, since
the great verbal similarity is accompanied by a different ethos.
The direction of dependence between two such texts will depend
on prior assumptions. The *Sitz im Leben* of the passage in the
Didache is clear and understandable, but it is theologically undeveloped. On the other hand, Matthew shows clear theological

---

[99] Cf. H. D. Betz, *Essays on the Sermon on the Mount* (Philadelphia: Fortress,
1985) p. 61.
[100] *Ibid*, p. 62; U. Luz, *Matthew 1-7: A Commentary* (Edinburgh: T & T Clark,
1989) p. 358; Weinfeld, "Charge of Hypocrisy", pp. 52-58.

development and includes the passage in an ordered collection of general paraenesis which shows signs of his own redactional concerns.[101] If there is a schema underlying Matthew's choice of material, which is not unlikely, then it is not unlikely that it would resemble *Didache* 8! Betz[102] entitles this section in Matthew a "cultic-*didache*", specifically citing the *Didache* as the rationale for this title, but tantalizingly does not comment on his choice beyond a despairing conclusion, "for want of sources, we can discover nothing more about this form of Judaism and Jewish Christianity".[103] This study contends that the *Didache* constitutes just such a "source" and is intended to call for further comment.

VI. CONCLUSION

This study of the redactional process at work in the *Didache* has revealed a community which started by defining itself primarily against the Gentiles. The material was originally collected for the catechesis of Gentile converts. Differentiation of the Christian community from the pagan world was a key part in preparation for initiation. However, the lack of clear differentiation from other Jewish groups seems to have caused problems for the community at a later stage, perhaps under attack from the Pharisees. Detailed study of the text shows the *Didache* to be closer to Pharisaic Judaism than to any other Jewish group.[104] This is confirmed in a negative way by the terms of the attack on the ὑποκρίται. No defence is given for their characterization as ungodly, nor are any possibilities of reconciliation left open. Instead, the instructions provide for Christian behaviour in the crucial and public areas of fasting and prayer which would differentiate them from their opponents. The insistence of Matthew's gospel that these things be done "in secret" marks a subsequent development, as does its understanding of the term ὑποκρίται in terms of insincerity and play acting.

---

[101] M. D. Goulder, *Midrash and Lection in Matthew* (London: SPCK, 1974) pp. 262-263; R. H. Gundry, *Matthew: A Commentary on his Literary and Theological Art* (Grand Rapids, Mich.: Eerdmans, 1982) pp. 101-111; R. A. Guelich, *The Sermon on the Mount* (Waco: Word, 1982) pp. 316-320; *contra* Betz *Essays*, pp. 55-69; W. D. Davies and D. C. Allison, *A Critical and Exegetical Commentary on the Gospel according to Saint Matthew* I (Edinburgh: T. & T. Clark, 1988) pp. 572-575.

[102] *Essays*, p. 57.

[103] *Ibid.*, p. 69.

[104] *Commentary*, p. 329.

THE EUCHARIST IN THE DIDACHE

† JOHANNES BETZ

Maria Laach

Since its discovery in 1873, the Teaching of the Twelve Apostles has posed questions to research, the discussion of which has lasted until the present time and still has not led to any assured, generally recognized finding. Above all, the circumstances of its origin remain problematic. Scholars have argued, ever more insistently, that it originates in Syria/Palestine.[1] But a more precise date of composition remains contested. Until recently the dominant viewpoint, which is still represented today, was that the *Didache* originated in the second century C.E., with many researchers arguing strongly for the second half or even later.[2] Meanwhile, however, the researches of A. Adam[3] and J. P. Audet[4] have introduced a turn-about. If Audet's early dating around the years 50-70 C.E.[5] has found few supporters, neverthe-

---

[1] Many researchers try for an even more far-reaching precision. A. Adam ("Erwägungen zur Herkunft der Didache", *ZKG* 68 [1957] pp. 1-47) argues for Pella; the following authors argue for the spiritually alive church in Antioch, which was active in mission and important for the development of the liturgy: J. -P. Audet, *La Didachè. Instructions des Apôtres* (Paris: Gabalda, 1958 [EBib]) pp. 209f; J. Daniélou *The Christian Centuries I: The First Six Hundred Years*, trns. V. Cronin (London: Darton, Longman & Todd, 1964) pp. 49, 52.

[2] It is above all English researchers who argue for the second half of the second century, eg. R. H. Connolly, "The Didache and Montanism", *DR* 55 (1937) pp. 339-347; F. E. Vokes, *The Riddle of the Didache* (London: SPCK, 1938); W. Telfer, "The Didache and the Apostolic Synod of Antioch", *JTS* 40 (1939) pp. 133-146, 258-271; M. H. Shepherd, "Smyrna in the Ignatian Letters", *JR* 20 (1940) p. 155); further E. Massaux, *The Influence of the Gospel of Saint Matthew on Christian Literature before Saint Irenaeus I: The First Ecclesiastical Writers*, trns N. J. Belval & S. Hecht (Leuven: Peeters; Macon, Ga: Mercer University Press, 1990-1993 [NGSt 5,1-3]) pp. 3-6; *Ibid. III: The Apologists and the Didache*, pp. 144-189. E. Peterson ("Über einige Probleme der Didache-Überlieferung" in *Frühkirche, Judentum und Gnosis* [Freiburg: Herder, 1959] pp. 146-182) considers our Greek Bryennios text, which comes from a manuscript of the eleventh century, to be a late revision, under the influence of ascetic circles, of an original text which can no longer be reconstructed. Among those who date the *Didache* earlier, namely in the first half of the second century, are J. Quasten, *Patrology I: The Beginnings of Christian Literature* (Utrecht: Spectrum, 1950) p. 37; J. Schmid, *RAC* III (1957) p. 1010; E. Molland, *RGG* I (1957) p. 508; B. Altaner, *Patrology*, trns. H. C. Graef (Freiburg: Herder, 1960) p. 51.

[3] Adam ("Erwägungen", p. 46) earlier placed the composition soon after 70 C.E., most probably shortly after 90 C.E.; in his *Lehrbuch der Dogmengeschichte I: Die Zeit der alten Kirche* (Gütersloh: Mohr, 1965) p. 83, he now specifies the date as about 95 C.E.

[4] His work (*Didachè*) represents the most extensive research into the *Didache*.

[5] *Loc cit.*; Daniélou (*First Six Hundred Years*, p. 37) follows Audet; so too J. Ortiz de Urbina, "Review of Audet, *La Didachè*, Paris, 1958", *OChrP* 25 (1959): 186-7.

less an ever growing number of authors put the origin of the text at the end or at the turn of the first century.[6] However, it is important to remember that this date, which has now been accepted, only applies to the final and overall editing of the text. It is well known, however, that the text is a compilation from different components: the first ethical section offers for the most part materials from the Two Ways teaching taken over from Judaism (chs. 1-6), followed by liturgical instructions (chs. 7-10), rules of church order (chs. 11-15), and concluded by a fragmentary apocalypse (ch. 16). Thus the overall date for the final redaction means very little. The individual elements already had an independent existence before their incorporation into the *Didache*, their own *Sitz im Leben* and corresponding meaning.[7] And so a more exact understanding of the text requires a tradition-historical study here also, which must examine in each case the extent, age, origin, sense of the unit of tradition, together with the way the meaning has been changed by its incorporation into the present text.

The famous Meal Prayers of chapters 9 and 10 are also among the most difficult and contested problems of *Didache* research. Their main content consists of prayers which are certainly older than the writing as a whole. That they already originated early and derive from the pre-*Didache* Aramaic community, is indicated by their formal and material proximity to Jewish formulae (*Berakoth*), from the Aramaic cries of *Hosanna* and *Maranatha*, from the baptism into the Lord (Jesus) attested here, from the ancient *Pais*-Christology, as generally from their Jewish Christian theology. The whole stands under the title "eucharist". In any case, what exactly is meant by this is, to this day, a contested question and a problem which continues to be posed.

Chapter 14 also concerns the eucharist. Here it is beyond doubt a matter of the sacramental Lord's Supper on the Lord's day, which is introduced by a confession of sins. It is described as

---

[6] So H. Lessig, *Die Abendmahlsprobleme im Lichte der ntl. Forschung seit 1900* (Diss. Bonn, 1953) p. 173; P. Cayré, *Patrologie et Histoire de la Théologie.* I (Paris: Desolée, 1953) p. 91 (c 90-110 C.E.); R. Stählin, *Die Geschichte und Lehre des evangelischen Gottesdienstes* (K. F. Müller-W. Blankenburg [eds.], *Leiturgia* I [Kassel: Stauda, 1954] p. 16); the reviews of Audet's work by P. Benoit, *RB* 66 (1959) p. 600; J. A. Fischer, *ThLZ* 85 (1960) p. 525; cautiously also J. N. D. Kelly, *JThS*, n. s. 12 (1961) pp. 332f. The following also argue for the above named period of composition: T. Camelot, *LThK* III² (1959) p. 369; L. Goppelt, *Apostolic and Post-Apostolic Times*, trns. A. Guelich (London: Black, 1970) p. 132; K. Baus, *Handbook of Church History I: From the Apostolic Community to Constantine*, ed. H. Jedin & J. Dolan (London: Burns & Oates, 1965) p. 139.

[7] For the details cf. Audet.

a "pure sacrifice" and as the salvation historical fulfillment of
Malachi 1:11, 14.

Our research here concerns the two chapters 9 and 10 on the
Meal. To facilitate the understanding of what follows they are
offered in translation:[8]

9:1 Concerning the eucharist you shall give thanks as follows: 2. first concerning the cup: We give you praise and thanks, our Father, for the holy
vine of your servant David, which you have revealed to us through Jesus,
your servant. To you be the glory for ever! [Amen]. 3. But over the
broken bread thus: We give you praise and thanks, our Father, for the life
and the knowledge, which you have revealed to us through Jesus, your
servant. To you be the glory for ever! [Amen]. 4. As this bread was scattered over the mountains and gathered together became one, so let your
church be gathered together from the ends of the earth into your kingdom. For yours is the glory and the power for ever! [Amen]. 5. But none
shall eat or drink from your eucharist except those who are baptized in the
Name of the Lord. For the Lord has also spoken concerning this, "You
shall not give what is holy to the dogs!"
10:1 After the repletion, you shall pronounce thanks in the following way:
2. We give you praise and thanks, holy Father, for your holy Name,
which you have allowed to dwell in our hearts, and for the knowledge and
faith and immortality, which you have revealed to us through Jesus, your
servant. To you be the glory for ever! [Amen]. 3. You, almighty Ruler,
have created all things for the sake of your Name. Food and drink you
have given to human beings for refreshment, so that they might pronounce
praise and thanks to you. But to us you have graciously granted spiritual
food and spiritual drink and (by this means)[9] eternal life, through Christ,
your servant. 4. For[10] everything we pronounce praise and thanks,
because you are mighty. To you be glory for ever! Amen. 5. Remember,
Lord, your church, to rescue it from all evil and to perfect is in your love,
and to gather it from the four winds, the sanctified, into your kingdom,
which you have prepared for it! For yours is the power and the glory for
ever! Amen. 6. Let grace come and let this world pass away! Hosanna to
the house[11] of David! Whoever is holy, let that person come here!
Whoever is not, let that person do penance! Maranatha! Amen. 7. Let the
prophets be permitted to pronounce thanks in whatever manner they wish.

I. THE MORE SPECIFIC LITURGICAL CHARACTER OF
THE CULT MEAL OF THE DIDACHE

The first question which confronts us is this: What kind of a meal
is it that these prayers frame? What is its peculiar character,

---

[8] We follow the critical text of Audet (Didachè, pp. 234-236). His conjectures
stand in []. Departures from Audet's text are in nn. 9 & 10.

[9] Previous studies read καὶ ζωὴν αἰώνιον, but Audet reads εἰς ζωὴν αἰώνιον.
Whether the latter is confirmed by a manuscript or is conjecture is not clear from
Audet.

[10] I consider the reading περί of the Coptic version to be the more probable,
along with M. Dibelius ("Die Mahl-Gebete der Didache", ZNW 37 [1938] p. 39)
and Peterson ("Probleme", p. 171).

[11] Here Audet follows the Coptic version. See n. 82.

which can be recognized on the basis of the text? In answering this question however, opinions diverge widely. It is sometimes seen as *a)* a simple, even though sacral, meal (agape)[12]; *b)* a sacramental eucharistic meal[13]; *c)* both in one, so that the enjoyment of a meal in the community is also experienced as a sacramental eucharist[14]. *d)* A more nuanced exegesis rightly finds in the cultic meal of *Didache* 9-10 a combination of a fellowship meal (9:1-10:5) with the sacramental Lord's Supper (10:6), and indeed in the order of agape-eucharist mentioned above.[15] *e)* Meanwhile, by rearranging 10:6 before 9:5, one idiosyncratic theory finds the succession of eucharist (9:2-4; 10:6) followed by *agape* (10:1-5).[16] *f)* Finally the opinion has also been expressed that the texts as we have them in *Didache* 9-10 today, are simply table prayers utilized in ascetic circles, although reworked out of originally eucharistic prayers.[17] This large number of interpretations shows the uncertainty of the state of the research, the hypothetical character of the explanations and the difficulty of the question.

An interpretation which seeks to be as unbiased as possible will begin from the present text form and not from a reconstruc-

---

[12] J. Jeremias (*The Eucharistic Words of Jesus* [London: SCM, 1966] p. 118) names the following representatives of this perspective: P. Ladeuze, F. Kattenbusch, P. Drews, Ermoni, van Crombrugghe, E. Baumgartner, P. Cagin, R. Knopf, T. E. J. Ferris, W. Goossens, J. Brinktrine, R. H. Connolly, F. J. Dölger, F. L. Cirliot, G. Dix.

[13] Jeremias (*Eucharistic Words*, p. 118) numbers older authorities, i. e. P. Batifoll, J. Bricout, K. Völker, A. Greiff, O. Casel. Further representatives see n. 27.

[14] Cf. B. Reicke, *Diakonie, Festesfreude und Zelos in Verbindung mit der altchristlichen Agapefeier* (Uppsala: Lundequistska Bokhandeln, 1951) p. 13; H. Lilje, *Die Lehre der Zwölf Apostel²* (Hamburg: Furche, 1956).

[15] The importance of this opinion already held by Th. Zahn was re-emphasized by M. Dibelius ("Mahlgebete", pp. 32-41). Jeremias (*Eucharistic Words*, p. 118) also follows them; he cites as authorities also E. v. d. Goltz, E. Hennecke, R. Stapper, R. Hupfeld, J. Quasten, A. Arnold, R. Bultmann, A. M. Schneider. Further representatives are Lessig, *Abendmahlsprobleme* p. 172; G. Stählin in K. F. Müller & W. Blankenburg (eds) *Leiturgia. Handbuch des evangelischen Gottesdienst* I (Kassel: Staude, 1954) p. 16; J. Betz, *Die Eucharistie in der Zeit der griechischen Väter I: Die Aktualpräsenz der Person und des Heilswerkes Jesu im Abendmahl nach der vorephesinischen griechischen Patristik* (Freiburg: Herder 1955) pp. 75f; Audet, *Didachè*, pp. 410-416, 423; J. A. Jungmann, *Missarum Sollemnia⁵* I (Freiburg: Herder, 1962 = *The Eucharistic Prayer: A Study of the Canon Missae*, trns. R. L. Batley [London: Challoner, 1956]; *The Mass: An Historical, Theological and Pastoral Survey* [Collegeville, Minn.: Liturgical Press, 1976]) p. 16; Goppelt, *Die apostolische und nachapostolische Zeit*, p. 31, 145; Daniélou, *First Six Hundred Years*, p. 73; Adam *Dogmengeschichte* I, pp. 83, 117.

[16] H. Lietzmann, *Mass and Lord's Supper: A Study in the History of the Liturgy*, trns. D. H. G. Reeve (Leiden: Brill, 1953-1964) pp. 189-194.

[17] Thus Peterson, "Probleme", pp. 169, 170, 181.

tion made by re-arranging it, and will seek to explore its sense. A quick overview of the two chapters provides the following chief points of procedure for the meal: in each case a blessing over cup and bread (9:2f), prayer for the gathering of the church (9:4), exclusion of unbaptized from the eucharist (9:5), meal (10:1), prayers after the meal which take up and expand the prayers before the meal (10:2-5). There follows (in 10:6) an emphatic call for the return of Christ and the instruction to the "holy, to come", i.e. to come forward to an act, which is clearly connected to the coming of the Lord referred to in *Maranatha*. In a strange manner, the conditions for admission in 9:5 and 10:6 are in conflict with each other.

If one looks at this composition as a whole, then only the interpretation *d)* which considers the cultic meal of the *Didache* as a combination of a proper meal and the sacramental Lord's Supper does justice to it: the words of 9:2-10:5 referring to the first and 10:6 to the last. The eucharistic celebration proper is only referred to in 10:6 in fragmentary fashion, not in its full course. The action of 10:6 is therefore often understood as a rite of entry or transition[18] to the full eucharistic sacrament. This basic viewpoint today rightly has many supporters.[19] Most regard the preceding meal proper as an *agape*, some try to characterize it more precisely. So Audet sees in it a phenomenon *sui generis*, a "breaking of the bread" only found in Jewish Christianity and disappearing with it, whose meaning would have been a liturgy of vigil, a feast of expectation of the coming *basileia*.[20] Daniélou speaks of a Christianized Passover meal in the framework of an Easter baptismal celebration during the Easter Vigil.[21] These attempts at a more exact characterization remain, however, questionable.

The commonly held theory, according to which we have in *Didache* 9-10 a combination of meal proper and eucharist, rests on the following grounds: the order cup-bread, found only here, is unusual for the sacramental Lord's supper, however more readily conceivable for an agape.[22] The blessing formula itself for the two elements does not lack a eucharistic colouring, to be sure, about which we will speak later, but reveals a clear disparity with the New Testament words over the bread and cup. The typical concepts like body (flesh), blood, covenant, together with an explicit

---

[18] Dibelius ("Mahl-Gebete", p. 40) speaks of "entry"; Audet (*Didachè*, p. 415) of "rite of passage".

[19] See under n. 15.

[20] *Didachè*, pp. 405-407.

[21] *First Six Hundred Years*, p. 72f.

[22] One can compare the (later) Sabbath Kiddush; see Jeremias, *Eucharistic Words*, p. 28f.

reference to the death of Jesus typical there, are missing in the *Didache*. Of particular importance is the expression ἐμπλησθῆναι in 10:1. It is a rubric, and so cannot be taken in an extended sense, but must rather be understood literally; but then it points to the preceding food and drink as a genuine meal. In the same way the command in 10:6, that only the holy should come while the unholy must do penance, presents the eucharist as only now happening, not as already having happened.

These are now weighty arguments for the above thesis. They concern, however, primarily the instructions over the external ritual sequence of the general celebration. On the other hand, up to now we have scarcely taken the theological peculiarities of the *agape* material in verses (9:2-5 and 10:2-5) into account. But if we consider these, the picture changes somewhat, or at least takes on new colours. That is, the sayings in these verses offer a pronounced eucharistic colour which can hardly be ignored. Thus the fact that the bread and cup, the specific eucharistic elements, are blessed, though not conclusive in itself, is nevertheless noteworthy. If, however, the text speaks of the holy "vine" of David, of κλάσμα, of life and immortality, of spiritual food and (likewise) drink, then it not only alludes distantly to the eucharist which only appears in 10:6, but reveals a close and immediate reference to a such a kind of sacramental Lord's meal. Although they show less contact with the Synoptic Lord's Supper proclamation, they still have an unmistakable material and verbal relationship with the Johannine tradition,[23] and remind one in certain respects of the sayings concerning the new Passover in Luke 22:16-18, which must be understood eucharistically.[24] In addition, the instruction in 9:5, which disagrees completely with 10:6, that only the baptized must eat and drink from the "eucharist", must be seen as old tradition, not first composed by the redactor of the *Didache* but taken over, and thus needs to be interpreted with reference to the sacramental communion.[25] Finally the origin of the prayers (in 9:2ff; 10:2-5) out of a eucharistic celebration is,

---

[23] See further below p. 255.

[24] See H. Schürmann, *Der Paschamahlbericht Lk 22,(7-14)* (Münster: Aschendorff, 1953 [NTA 19,5]) pp. 15-18.

[25] Audet (*Didachè*, pp. 414f) explains the instruction 9:5 as a redactional note of the Didachist and as his innovation, which disrupts the usual custom prevailing until then and excludes the unbaptized from the fellowship meal, the "breaking of the bread". Audet has only expressed his opinion in this thesis, but provided no evidence. Materially it seems questionable to me that one excluded all unbaptized guests, thus including novices, from the agape at such an early date. But this exclusivity then developed—perhaps under the influence of *Didache* 9:5; cf. *Recog* II 71 (CGS 93); *ApTrad* 25 (46 Dix). In Qumran according to 1 QS 6:16f, 20, novices were excluded from certain meals.

perhaps, corroborated by their later history: the blessing formulae
for cup and bread were understood and explained sacramentally-
eucharistically by the *Apostolic Constitutions* (VII.25f)(attesting
Antiochene tradition), and the prayer for gathering (9:4) is found
in Egyptian anaphorae.[26] If one considers the texts as isolated
units, in terms of their content and development, not according to
their external place in the framework of the *Didache*'s celebration,
then it leads to the conclusion that they are genuine eucharistic
prayers and that the meal ordered by them is a genuine Lord's
meal. They have also been evaluated in this way by a row of
reputable researchers for a long time.[27]

   Thus a more exact examination leads to two divergent conclusions: the prayers and the corresponding meal of *Didache* 9:2-
10:5 belong in one respect to an agape, and in another respect to a
sacramental Lord's supper—apart from vv.10:1, 3a, with which
we will busy ourselves later. For each of these points of view well
respected scholars have taken their stand, for each point of view
there are reasons which cannot be overlooked. So the question
arises: do the two conclusions exclude each other? Or can they be
harmonized? Can both be affirmed in a broader perspective?

   In fact, many researchers have already attempted such a
settlement. According to one account, the meal proper was
identified with the Lord's supper.[28] Yet each constitutes a fundamentally distinctive part inside one all-embracing general celebration. According to the testimony of the New Testament, they may
not be identified; the oldest report of the institution, 1 Corinthians
11:23f, already separates the eucharistic gifts from the meal. Also
the attempt of H. Lietzmann, by means of major re-ordering of
the text, specifically through the removal of 10:6 to 9:2-4, to con-

---

   [26] *Euchologium Serapionis* 13:13 (II 174, 17-22 Funk); *Euchologium of Dèr-
Balizeh* (26 Roberts-Capelle); *Eth. Gregorius-Liturgy* (26 Löfgren-Euringer).
   [27] G. Rauschen, *Eucharistie und Bußsakrament in den ersten sechs
Jahrhunderten*[3] (Freiburg: Herder, 1910) p. 96 (here older representatives); P.
Batiffol, *Études d'histoire et de théologie positive II: L'Eucharistie* (Paris: Lecoffre,
1920); K. Völker, *Mysterium und Agape* (Gotha: Klotz, 1927) 105ff; C. Ruch, *La
Messe* (DThC 10, 1 [1928] p. 867); O. Casel, *Prophetie und Eucharistie* (*JLw* 9
[1930] pp. 1-19 = *The Mystery of Christian Worship and Other Writings*, trns. B.
Neunheuser [Westminster, Md: Darton, Longman & Todd, 1963]); M. Goguel,
L'Église primitive (Paris: Payot, 1947) p. 366 = *The Primitive Church*, trns. H. C.
Snape (London: Allen & Unwin, 1963); Quasten, *Patrology* I, p. 32; G. Rietschel-
P. Graff, *Lehrbuch der Liturgik*[2] (Göttingen: Vandenhoeck & Ruprecht, 1951) pp.
232ff; Reicke, *Diakonie, Festesfreude und Zelos* pp. 13f; Cayré, *Patrologie* I, pp.
92f; Lilje, *Die Lehre der zwölf Apostel*, pp. 63ff. —That in *Didache* 9-10 "it is a
matter of a eucharistic Lord's supper", Lietzmann also recognized (*Mass and
Lord's Supper*, pp. 189-194), who in any case solved the problem in his own way
by re-ordering the text.
   [28] So Reicke and Lilje; cf. n. 14.

stitute a complete eucharistic act as the beginning of the celebration and to allow an *agape* to follow after[29], must be judged to have failed. The New Testament sources provide a different picture. According to 1 Corinthians 11:23f, there existed at the beginning the sequence bread-meal-cup; then according to 1 Corinthians 11:21, 34, Mark 14:22 the sequence meal-bread-cup appears. The sequence eucharist-*agape* meal is on the other hand hardly attested.[30] The point of view that the prayers were indeed spoken at an *agape*, but reflected the sacramental eucharist which followed, also remains unsatisfactory.[31] In reality they directly qualify the things to which they immediately relate, and indeed eucharistically, i.e. cup and bread, as a detailed exegesis will plainly confirm.

There is, however, a better solution to our dilemma, in my opinion. That is, on closer examination the two divergent interpretations largely result from viewing the same tradition at different stages of its development, and are not different interpretations of the tradition at the same moment in time, if one ignores 9:5. Indeed, on this view, the same prayers appear once to have belonged to an agape, and on the other occasion to have belonged to a eucharistic celebration. What makes the difference to the point of view, however, is that the material is considered on the one occasion in the overall framework of the two chapters, while on the other occasion loosed from this context, isolated by itself. If we keep these two things separate, we seem to have a useful solution based upon an analysis of the layers of tradition. The prayers cannot be simultaneously eucharistic and *agape* prayers, but they can be both of these side by side. They were previously and originally texts for a Lord's Supper and are now in the composition of the Didachist used at a meal proper. So we come to our thesis: the prayers of *Didache* 9:2-10:5 were transformed and revalued from original eucharistic prayers to mere agape prayers.[32] We will now explain how this happened.

This point of view, which is intended for the moment only to be considered as a working hypothesis, now makes one feature of the two chapters more readily understandable (and so demonstrates its usefulness). Perhaps it explains the introduction

---

[29] *Mass and Lord's Supper*, pp. 188-194.

[30] To my knowledge only the Coptic text of the *Epistula Apostolorum* (140/170 C.E.) has this sequence; cf. Jeremias, *Eucharistic Words*, p. 116.

[31] Thus Daniélou, *First Six Hundred Years*, p. 72.

[32] The further development in many places, eg. in Egypt, tended to reduce them completely into house table prayers in ascetic circles. That is clear in Athanasius, Λόγος σωτηρίας πρὸς τὴν παρθένον (*TU* 29/2a [1905] p. 47). Peterson incorrectly concludes from this that even our present Bryennios text may have been such a late version.

of the cup before the bread, unusual for the Lord's Supper. One could think that this goes together with the "degradation" of the prayers. Originally the sacramental bread was blessed and distributed first as shown by 1 Corinthians 11:24, while the cup was blessed and shared after the meal. Then when the originally eucharistic prayers were used for the *agape*, the passage 9:3-4 remained as the tightly composed unit which it was, while the cup was put before it. The observation that the same sequence appears in 9:5 and 10:3 speaks for an original sequence bread-cup.

Our theory also makes a satisfactory explanation of the saying in the prayer after the meal possible: "You, almighty Lord, have created all things for the sake of your name, you have given food and drink to human beings to enjoy" (10:3a). The half-verse is striking and rather out of order inasmuch as it breaks the previously uniform eucharistic orientation and gives thanks for the creation of everything and for the natural food and drink provided for all human beings. The continuation (3b) links immediately back into the eucharistic track, however, and gives thanks again for the spiritual food and drink offered to Christians alone ($\dot{\eta}\mu\hat{\iota}\nu$ $\delta\acute{\varepsilon}$).[33] This shows verse 3a to be a development of the old (eucharistic) *Vorlage*, as an insertion which takes account of the character of the introductory meal section, which now has more the character of an *agape*. A stylistic peculiarity also strengthens the case that v.3a is an insertion, namely the striking expression $\delta\acute{\varepsilon}\sigma\pi\sigma\tau\alpha$ $\pi\alpha\nu\tau\sigma\kappa\rho\acute{\alpha}\tau\sigma\rho$ instead of $\pi\acute{\alpha}\tau\varepsilon\rho$ $\dot{\eta}\mu\hat{\omega}\nu$ (9:2f) or $\pi\acute{\alpha}\tau\varepsilon\rho$ $\ddot{\alpha}\gamma\iota\varepsilon$ (10:2) in the ancient *Vorlage*. The mention of the "spiritual" food and drink could be left intact, so that a backward look at the past eucharist becomes indeed a look ahead to what is still to come (in 10:6). The old, pre-Didachist rule for the Lord's Supper, which excluded the unbaptized, could and probably did become the command in 9:5, and sounds like the exclusion from worship which appears already in the New Testament in 1 Corinthians 16:22 and Revelation 22:15. The formula of address ("your" eucharist) lets us recognize the editorial hand of the Didachist. So the eucharistic sayings of the verse group 9:2-4 distinguishes itself as ancient tradition, indeed also 9:5 and 10:2, 3b-5.

If one now takes the parts mentioned above as previously eucharistic texts which have been changed into an *agape*, then one can ask the question as to why the Christians of the oldest time—whether the Didachist himself or someone else before him?—at a certain point in time changed the pre-Didachist Lord's Supper prayers for the development of the *agape* meal. A plausible, if not certain, reason could be that the *agape* originally had no strict rule; from 1 Corinthians 11:21 one sees how freely

---

[33] The term $\chi\alpha\rho\acute{\iota}\zeta\varepsilon\sigma\theta\alpha\iota$ is chosen carefully and seems to refer to the eucharist.

and unliturgically it could be conducted, surely not just in Corinth but also elsewhere. The development, according to a general principle of growth of the church, pressed towards consolidation and defined ritual even for the fellowship meal. So one grasped at the old eucharistic formula, since this for its part did not describe the essence of the Lord's meal clearly and completely enough, and in this respect and function was no longer satisfactory. This formula was not simply discarded, but used for a better ritualization of the *agape* meal and, in so doing, used to order it more clearly in relation to the eucharist. The sentences have more to do with the confession of the community as a whole than the role of the liturgist.

If our thesis is correct, then the texts of *Didache* 9:2-5 and 10:2, 3b-5 had its original setting in life in a sacramental Lord's Supper; in this case, however, they are interesting witnesses for the early history, indeed reach back into the Aramaic epoch of the church in the ·earliest time. They are, however, interesting not only in the history of liturgy but also in respect of the history of dogma. We will understand their content better if we report and observe their theological standpoint more precisely.

II. THE POSITION OF THE DIDACHE PRAYERS IN THE HISTORY OF IDEAS

The old eucharistic celebration which, in our opinion, is still reflected in *Didache* 9:2-5; 10:2, 3b-5, has its own theological stamp and gives the impression at first sight of a striking intellectual distance from the eucharistic celebration of the New Testament accounts of its institution. Not that we have before us in *Didache* 9-10 a completely different action. Besides the above mentioned differences, the commonalities must also be emphasized. Even the celebration in the *Didache* revolves around bread and cup; the two elements are provided with a characteristic blessing, brought into particular connection with Jesus, are valued as holy and spiritual; the celebration effects the presence of the "Name" of God in the heart. Even if in veiled form, the institution of the meal by Jesus is reflected in the referral back of the stated mediums of salvation to revelation through Jesus as servant/son (*pais*) of God (9:2f; 10:2, 3b). Above all, however, the common eschatological direction binds the celebration here and there, like a strong bracket—like a common womb; it is the outstanding mark of the *Didache* meal, as appears in 9:4—about which more below—and 10:6; it is however also a particular and essential foundation of the Synoptic and Pauline eucharistic meal, as Luke 22:15-18, Mark 14:25 and 1 Corinthians 11:26 testify.

At the same time the difference from the New Testament eucharistic proclamation remains considerable. For its central

thought, the reference of the action to the death of Jesus and the
inauguration of a new covenant, the qualification of the gifts as the
body of Jesus given for us and his blood poured out for us, are not
mentioned in the *Didache*. Indeed, for this reason H. Lietzmann
wants to find in the *Didache* a witness for an independent
"Jerusalem" type of the eucharistic meal, which did not contain a
report of the institution, which was not a repetition of the Last
Supper of Jesus and memorial of his death, but was a continuation
of his earthly table fellowship with the disciples, joy over the
spiritual presence of the Exalted One and expectation of his
return.[34] Today this type is held to be the earliest stage of the
whole development of the Lord's Supper.[35] But the eucharistic
chapter of the *Didache* does not justify such conclusions at all. It
is improbable that the pre-*Didache* community celebrated a meal
in which they took account of Jesus as God's *pais*, but ignored the
particular institution of the meal which was already expressly
stamped by the *pais* Christology, according to the oldest recognizable tradition.[36] The texts of the *Didache* in no way exclude the
report of the institution. They indeed only offer a part, not the
whole, of what was spoken at the celebration, and draw more
from the prayer response of the community than the liturgy which
recited the account of the institution. The *Teaching of the Twelve
Apostles* in 10:7 expressly authorizes the prophets as appropriate
cultic officials for a thanksgiving going beyond the extent of the
accompanying formulae, and thus also leaves room for the recitation of the account of the institution, indeed considers it as the
duty of the prophets, "who add to the righteousness and knowledge of the Lord" (11:2). On the other hand even the pericopes on
Lord's Supper in the New Testament point back, for their part,
clearly enough through their extensive Aramaic and their liturgical
stylization[37] to the cultic usage in the primitive Palestinian community.[38] This all speaks against Lietzmann and for the assump-

---

[34] Lietzmann, *Mass and Lord's Supper*, p. 195. Its basis is said to be the
"breaking of bread"of the primitive community in Jerusalem. E. Lohmeyer ("Vom
urchristlichen Abendmahl", *ThR* 9 [1937] pp. 302ff; *ThR* 10 [1938] pp. 92ff)
provides a variation on Lietzmann's thesis and proposes a similar "Galilean" type,
based above all on John's Gospel.

[35] Cf. e.g. W. Marxsen, "The Lord's Supper as a Christological Problem" in
The Beginning of Christology, trns. P. Achtemeier & L. Nieting (Philadelphia:
Fortress, 1979).

[36] On this see J. Betz, *Die Eucharistie in der Zeit der griechischen Väter*. II.1:
*Die Realpräsenz des Leibes und Blutes Jesu im Abendmahl nach dem Neuen Testa-
ment* (Freiburg: Herder, 1964) pp. 26-35.

[37] Cf. Betz, *Die Eucharistie* I.1, pp. 5-13; 16f; Jeremias, *Eucharistic Words*, pp.
111-115; 173-186.

[38] Luke (22:15-20) and Paul (1 Cor 11:23ff) attest the liturgical usage of the
words of Institution even for Syria and Antioch, which many see as the homeland of
the *Didache* (cf. note 1). Luke is already closely linked with Antioch by his birth

tion that even the community of the *Didache* knew the account of
the institution.[39] However, it did not emphasize and elaborate it in
its Lord's Supper theology. The *Didache* offers no independent
Lord's Supper type, but an independent Lord's Supper theology.

The latter relates more closely to the Johannine tradition.
Typical concerns of this tradition echo, when our eucharistic
chapter describes Jesus as the revealer, when it speaks of the vine,
when it brings the bread into connection with life and immortality
and reckons it to the spiritual world, and when it prays for the
sanctification and gathering of the church (cf. John 11:52).
Beyond material parallels[40] the striking terminological agreements
deserve particular attention. A list of the material and verbal anal-
ogies give the following picture:[41]

Didache 9 compared with John		Didache 10 compared with John	
εὐχαριστεῖν	6:11	ἐμπλησθῆναι	6:12
ἄμπελος	15:1	πάτερ ἅγιε	17:11
γνωρίζειν	15:15; 17:26	ὄνομα	17:6, 11, 26
κλάσμα	6:12	κατασκηνοῦν	1:14
ζωή	6:35, 48	γνῶσις καὶ πίστις	6:69
ζωὴ καὶ γνῶσις	17:3	ζωὴ αἰώνιος	6:54
διεσκορπισμένον-ἕν	11:52	πνευματικὴ τροφή	6:63
ἕν	17:11, 21	ῥύσασθαι ἀπὸ πονηροῦ	17:15
συνάγειν	11:52	τελειοῦν ἐν ἀγάπῃ	17:23; 1 Jn 2:5, 4:12
		ἁγιάζειν	17:17, 19

This concordance, which does not show direct citations but
instead a close relationship, justifies the conclusion that the two
texts feed on the same eucharistic tradition, even from a common
local tradition,[42] which we might look for in North Palestine/
Syria. Now many of the roots, or at least influences, which also

(according to the old Prologue to the Gospel and according to Eusebius, *HE* III.4,
6), both are linked to it by their life history. Cf. Acts 11:25; 13:1; Gal 1:21; 2:11.

[39] The east Syrian Nestorian *Liturgy of the Apostles Addai and Mari* in any case
contains (in the manuscripts and editions originating from later centuries!) no
account of the institution. Its absence is an unsolved problem, but could be secondary, perhaps arising out of a fear of profanation of the holy words, perhaps also
out of a valuation of the Epiclesus as a form of consecration; for further information
see Jungmann, *Missarum Sollemnia*[5] II, p. 243.

[40] For the eucharistic colouring of John 13, 15 and 17, cf. Betz, *Die Eucharistie*
II.1, pp. 169f.

[41] Cf. W. von Löwenich, *Das Johannesverständnis im zweiten Jahrhundert* (Berlin: Töpelmann, 1932) pp. 19f.

[42] von Löwenich, *Johannesverständnis*, pp. 20-22, rejected by Audet, *La
Didachè*, p. 175.

stamp the fourth gospel, reach back to Syria.[43] If one seeks to define the relationship between *Didache* 9-10 and John's Gospel more exactly, then the early dating of the *Didache* eucharistic chapters does not permit *a priori* a literary dependence of this on John, nor does it establish its a-posteriority.[44] On the contrary, one should say that the Fourth Gospel knew and used the eucharistic prayers and formulations of the *Didache* tradition, even if from the oral stream of tradition. It cannot be shown that he had the *Didache* as a literary entity before him and used it, even if this could not be completely excluded. The relationship between the *Didache* and Johannine sayings can be expressed as follows: What the *Didache* says preliminarily and briefly, is amplified, clarified, and more strongly Christologized in the Fourth Gospel. We should not, however, without more ado, read back into the *Didache* the temporally later and amplified insights of the Fourth Gospel.

The theological principle of interpretation, with whose help the community represented by the *Didache* tradition made their cult meal understandable—how could it be otherwise—is the Old Testament. So they understood their eucharistic meal as the fulfillment of the Old Testament pronouncements and promises. In this context one can immediately point out that Scripture often refers to revelation and its gift with the picture of food and drink[45], the longing for these things as hunger and thirst[46], their reception as eating and drinking,[47] and so the existential meaning of these things is expressed. Even eschatological salvation is described as a rich and universal feast.[48] The observation, that in the late period of the Old Testament revelation was categorized as Wisdom and viewed as a meal, leads us still closer to the *Didache*. Wisdom appears as the embodiment of revelation: it is, on the one hand, identified with the Torah (Sir 24:23; Bar 4:1), but is, on the other

---

[43] Cf. R. Schnackenburg, *The Gospel According to St John* I (London: Burns & Oates, 1968) p. 152: "The Johannine tradition, originating in Palestine, was subjected to Syrian influences before it reached Asia Minor (Ephesus), where it was fixed and edited".

[44] Schnackenburg, *Gospel of John* I, p. 198: "There are undoubtedly formal similarities of language (e.g. between Did. 9:4, and Jn 11:52), but whether they are enough to prove direct knowledge of John remains questionable".

[45] According to Jeremiah 15:16, God's commands are food of the prophets; according to Isaiah 55:1-3, God's promises are an unusually given meal of bread and water; according to Psalm 16:5, Yahweh is the "portion of the cup".

[46] Am 8:11, 14; Sir 24:21; Mt 5:6.

[47] Sir 24:21.

[48] Is 25:6; 65:13; Ez 34:13f; 1 En 62:14f; 2 En 42:5; *ApocBaruch* 29:3-8; for the Rabbinic material see H. L. Strack & P. Billerbeck, *Kommentar zum NT aus Talmud und Midrasch* IV (München: C. H. Beck, 1926⁴) p. 840, pp. 1154ff. NT: Mt 8:11; 22:1-14; Lk 22:15-18, 29f; Mk 14:25; Rev. 3:20; 19:7, 9.

hand, seen as proclaimer and revealer (Pr 1-9; Sir 24:8f; Bar
3:38) and personified (Wisd 7-9). If an oriental myth indicates that
wisdom comes from above, seeks a resting place among human
beings, gives up and returns,[49] nevertheless the Old Testament
declares that the pre-existent Wisdom abiding with God seeks and
finds a home in Israel (Sir 24:8-11; Bar 3:37f), as it is identical
with the Torah. Its role is thus descent. Secondly, Wisdom, like
revelation, is expressed in terms of meal. On one occasion it is
itself presented as food and drink (Sir 24:23); another time it is
the provider of true sustenance, namely the "tree of life" (Pr
3:18). In Sirach 24:13-17 it is further compared with other trees,
among which are even the "vine, which brings $\chi\acute{\alpha}\rho\iota\varsigma$" (24:17
LXX). Finally it emerges also as host and provider of a meal.
According to Sirach 15:3 it feeds the wise with bread and gives
water to the insightful. Proverbs 9:1-6 sounds particularly
emphatic. There Wisdom gives a feast, invites the simple and the
unlearned to it, offers them their bread and their wine, provides
life, knowledge and wisdom (9:6 LXX: $\grave{\epsilon}\nu$ $\gamma\nu\acute{\omega}\sigma\epsilon\iota$ $\sigma\acute{\upsilon}\nu\epsilon\sigma\iota\nu$).[50]

If appearances do not deceive, the pre-*Didache* community
took over these ideas and with their help, freely and not in verbal
dependence, expressed their eucharistic meal which derived from
Jesus, indeed considered it as the fulfillment of the wisdom meal
mentioned in the Old Testament. It thus developed the Old Testament sophiological motif further, saw in the wisdom meal
expressed there not only an allegorical entity, not only a literary
form of expression,[51] but a true sacramental reality, which the ser-
vant/son of God, Jesus, had disclosed (Didache 9:2f; 10:2f). For it
is most easily understood against the background of wisdom ideo-
ogy if the liturgy of the *Didache* gives thanks especially for the
"vine" (9:2, cf. Sir 24:17), for "life and knowledge" (9:3; 10:2,
cf. Pr 9:6). Even the characteristic thought of the descent of Wisdom and its dwelling down below with human beings, together
with the corresponding term $\kappa\alpha\tau\alpha\sigma\kappa\eta\nu o\widehat{\upsilon}\nu$ echoes in *Didache*
10:2; it is then further developed in John 6, and so the eucharist is
proclaimed as sacramental incarnation (Jn 6:57f). The theology
coming to expression in *Didache* 9-10 thus has—this provides further support for our interpretation—done the same in the case of
the eucharistic meal as also is to be confirmed for the most ancient
Christology: in both a secret is illuminated by means of Old Testa-

---

[49] Cf. 1 En 42:1-2; for further attestations see G. Fohrer, "$\sigma o\phi\acute{\iota}\alpha$", *TDNT* VII,
pp. 490ff; U. Wilckens, *TDNT* VII, pp. 508f.

[50] If one may point to the Song of Solomon on the relationship of Wisdom to the
soul, then Song of Songs 5:1 could also count as evidence for the Wisdom meal.

[51] One could only raise the question as to whether the Christian community
could build on the foundation of an actual Jewish cultic meal in honour of Wisdom,
but not prove it; there were religious meals in Judaism, cf. e.g. at Qumran.

ment Wisdom teaching, in the one case the sacrament, in the other case the person of Jesus; so a Wisdom Christology is also developed and with its help, for example, the pre-existence of Jesus is brought to consciousness.[52]

This background in the history of ideas prevents one from taking the meal prayers of *Didache* 9f as a product of Hellenistic thought, as has often happened, on the basis of the concepts of life, knowledge, immortality which occur here. How typically Jewish Christian these texts are will become still clearer if we examine their dogmatic content.

III. THE EUCHARISTIC-DOGMATIC CONTENT OF THE TWO MEAL CHAPTERS

If, according to our thesis, the expressions in *Didache* 9:2-5; 10:2, 3b-5 go back in their original usage to the eucharistic meal, like the old call to repentance in 10:6, then the two text groups can complement and illuminate one another and can be used for mutual interpretation.

The general character of the celebration, its basis and essence, come to expression already in the concept which penetrates the whole like a *Leitmotiv* and stands in its substantive form as a title over the whole: εὐχαριστεῖν. The term possesses considerable dogmatic relevance. It is, like its equivalent in meaning εὐλογεῖν, with which it alternates in the Biblical institution accounts, a translation of the Hebrew ברך (*berak*, Aramaic: בריך) and must be interpreted on that basis from the *berakah* concept.[53] The Hebrew verb indicates on the one hand the blessing of human beings by God and understands by this the empowerment of human beings by him. It is however also used of the "blessing" of God by human beings. The human "blesses" God, in that s/he recognizes him as author of her/his well being and salvation and confesses in praise God's history-making power as decisive for him/her. From the spontaneous cry of praise to God the *berakah* developed in Israel to a reflected fixed doxological blessing used above all in the cult. At the time of the *Didache* it was used as such for different occasions; it governed also the official Jewish

---

[52] Cf. Mt 11:19; 12:42; Mk 6:2; Lk 11:49; 1 Cor 1:24-30; Col 2:3; on this see U. Wilkens, "σοφία" (*TDNT* VII, PP. 514-525); E. Schweizer, *Neotestamentica* (Zürich-Stuttgart: Zwingli, 1963) pp. 105-109.

[53] For the following see J. P. Audet, "Literary Forms and Contents of a Normal Εὐχαριστία in the First Century", in *Studia Evangelica* (Berlin: Akademie-Verlag, 1959 [TU 73]) pp. 643-662; also *Didachè*, pp. 276-402; L. Clerici, "Einsammlung der Zerstreuten. Liturgiegeschichtliche Untersuchungen über die Vor- und Nachgeschichte der Fürbitte für die Kirche in Did 9,4 und 10,5", *LQF* 44 (1966) pp. 5-47.

chief prayer, the *Shemone Esre*.[54] The particular "thanksgivings" of the *Didache* are Christianized developments of such Jewish blessings, from which they take over the formal structure, function and meaning. Like the Jewish *berakah* the Christian eucharist is an acknowledging praise of God for his beneficent power in history, a memorial of the redemptive activity of God and praise for that, anamnesis and confession, which break out at the existential wonder of God's deed. This existential moment comes up in particular in the Greek term εὐχαριστεῖν, since translated literally it means: "to behave as one who has received much". It expresses on the one hand praise for God's gracious act, and on the other hand the human's wonder at it and his answer to it.[55] The one giving thanks understands her/his concrete existence from the gracious power of God, s/he thinks not anthropocentrically nor individualistically but theocentrically.[56]

Besides the formal proximity, the material proximity of the *Didache* eucharistic prayers to the Jewish table blessing has already long been observed. The Jewish blessing for the cup is: "Blessed are you, Yahweh, our God, King of the World, because you created the fruit of the vine".[57] Over the bread the Israelite prays: "Blessed are you, Yahweh, our God, King of the world, who brings forth bread from the earth."[58] The prayer of thanks after the meal has the following content: (1) "Blessed are you, Lord, our God, King of the world, who provides the whole world with goodness, grace, mercy. (2) We thank you, Lord, our God, that you have given us for possession a good and wide land. (3) Have mercy, Lord, our God, over Israel, your people, and over Jerusalem, your city, and over Zion, the dwelling place of your glory, and over your Temple and over your dwelling and over the kingdom of the house of David, the messiah of your righteousness (of your righteous messiah). Blessed are you, Yahweh, God of David, who builds Jerusalem."[59] The thanksgiving for knowledge

---

[54] The "Eighteen Prayers", also called the *Tefilla*.

[55] We try to hold both aspects together when we translate εὐχαριστεῖν with "give thanks and praise" (see above).

[56] Audet, "Literary Forms", p. 644; *Didachè*, 378f, allows as the proper sense of εὐχαριστεῖν only the praise and the *anamnesis* of the action of God and rejects the rendering "thanksgiving", because this is only anthropocentric conduct; he is mistaken in this. C. Westermann (*Das Loben Gottes in den Psalmen*[3] [Göttingen: Vandenhoeck & Ruprecht, 1963] p. 23), and in conjunction with him also indeed Clerici (*Einsammlung der Zerstreuten*, p. 15), similarly considers the thanksgiving for an individualistic activity and mere sentiment.

[57] *m.Ber* 6:1; O. Holtzmann, *Der Tosephtatraktat Berakot* (Gießen: Töpelmann, 1912) p. 73; Strack-Billerbeck, *Kommentar* IV, p. 616.

[58] *m.Ber* 6:1; Holtzmann, p. 73; Strack-Billerbeck *Kommentar* I, p. 685.

[59] 14. *Berakoth* of the Palestinian recension (Strack-Billerbeck, *Kommentar* IV, p. 213).

in *Didache* 9:3 and 10:2 reminds one of the fourth prayer of the
Tefilla: "O favour us, our Father, with knowledge from you and
with understanding and discernment from your Torah. Blessed are
you, O Lord, gracious Giver of knowledge".[60] Here as everywhere the Jewish *Berakah* does not speculate abstractly over
God's essence, but reflects on Yahweh's all-powerful might which
works itself out in history. In the same way the Jewish Christian
prayers in the *Didache* give thanks for salvation-historical blessings, which only are made known through the revelation of Jesus
(9:2f; 10:2) and belong to revelation.

Exegesis of particular parts of the text, to which we now
turn, must bear this in mind. It is not the simple natural gift of
wine (which the Israelite could even consider as a salvation-
historical gift because it is a product of the God-given land) for
which thanks are given in the blessings over cup and bread, nor is
it "hellenistic" ideal gifts like knowledge and immortality: rather
these are concrete redemptive gifts based on salvation-historical
revelation. As far as the present sequence is concerned it is indeed
secondary.[61] Since, in our context, we are reading *Didache* 9-10
as a previously eucharistic text, we keep to the old order and
begin with the thanksgiving for the bread (9:3).

Particularly striking here is the terminological peculiarity,
κλάσμα, in the introductory remark. Even this will have
originated from the Didachist as a rubric, it is nevertheless
already found in the vocabulary of the prayer, as 9:4 shows. The
word hangs naturally together with the typically ancient Christian
usage of the "breaking of the bread". The expression κλάσις τοῦ
ἄρτου serves in the New Testament time, on the one hand, as an
expression for the combined general meal and sacramental cult
meal of the Christians (Acts 2:42, 46), indicating the breaking of
the bread in the wider sense, on the other hand, it becomes a special term for the nucleus of the celebration, the sacramental-
eucharistic act,[62] indicating the breaking of the bread in the narrow sense. The latter sense occurs also in *Didache* 14:1. We do
not exclude the possibility that the word κλάσμα, which means the
agape bread in the present text of *Didache* 9:1-4, was already used
for bread of the Lord's Supper. Then it would share the double
meaning with κλάσις τοῦ ἄρτου.

The blessing over the bread gives thanks for "the life and
knowledge" which have been revealed through the servant Jesus.
The naming of these salvation goods can lead to the assumption

---

[60] Palestinian recension (Strack-Billerbeck, *Kommentar* IV, p. 211).
[61] See above p. 254.
[62] So Acts 20:7, 11; 1 Cor 10:16; above all Mk 14:22; Mt 26:26; Lk 22:19; 1
Cor 11:24; dubious Lk 24:30, 35; cf. E. von Severus, *RAC* II (1954) pp. 620-626.

that hellenistic religiosity comes to expression here.[63] But these concepts do not only play an important role in hellenism but also in the Old Testament, and it is in the latter that the point of connection is to be sought. The predicate "life", as embodiment of God's gift, is identified especially with the Torah in the Old Testament[64] as also in the Rabbis,[65] which is identified with Wisdom. This Torah is allegorized as the bread and wine of its dependents—especially in connection with Proverbs 9:5f.[66] The above mentioned passage in Proverbs 9:5f (LXX) promises life and knowledge to partakers in the meal of Wisdom. In Proverbs 3:18 this functions as "tree of life". Behind this as the immediate reference point for *Didache* 9:3 lies that Old Testament passage in which the two salvation gifts of life and knowledge are expressly cited, indeed as real food: Genesis 2:9 tells of the tree of life and the tree of knowledge in Paradise, of those ominous trees on which the course of salvation history turned. The forbidden taste of the tree of knowledge led human beings to death (Gen 2:17; 3:19); the taste of the tree of life, which was intended but unfulfilled, should have brought them immortality (Gen 3:22). Significantly "immortality" appears together with "knowledge" and "faith" now also in *Didache* 10:2 as the fruit of the cult-meal. Through the naming of these salvation gifts in 9:3 and 10:2 the eucharist is presented as the renewed gift of paradise in Genesis 2:9. Their description as "holy" in 9:5 and as "spiritual food" in 10:3 confirms this interpretation. While it might at first seem surprising, it is supported by the following consideration.

The understanding of the Lord's Supper as a gift of paradise is rooted particularly in its eschatological character. The primitive community considered their Lord's Supper as the paradisal gift of salvation, because it considered it primarily as eschatological event and gift of salvation. Since, indeed, according to ancient belief, the end time repeats the first time, the *Didache* meal as an event of the end time repeats the gifts of the first time. The eschatological orientation comes most clearly into focus in the cry of 10:6 "Let grace come and let the world pass away! Maranatha!" By the "grace" which is implored is meant the com-

---

[63] M. Dibelius ("Mahlgebete", *ZNW* 37 [1938] pp. 34-41) postulates as the prototype of our *Didache* prayer (and the intermediary between this and the Hebrew table prayers) prayers of Hellenistic Judaism. L. Clerici (*Einsammlung der Zerstreuten*, p. 37) considers the salvatory blessings of life, knowledge, faith, immortality as "stark hellenistisch gefärbt".

[64] Sir 17:11; 45:4; Pr 8:35; cf. Acts 7:38.

[65] Attested by Strack-Billerbeck, *Kommentar* III, pp. 129ff. Cf. also P. Borgen, *Bread from Heaven* (Leiden: Brill, 1965) p. 148.

[66] Attested Strack-Billerbeck, *Kommentar* II, pp. 482ff. (*ExR* 25c); 483f (*GenR* 70, 44d, 44; *GenR* 54, 34c; *Pesiqta* 178a; 614 (*Pesiqta* 102b).

pleted eschatological salvation, which the Lord will bring with his
return. The prayer for the gathering and uniting of the church in
the coming kingdom also implores, intends and actualizes the
eschatological state of consummation. The one bread made out of
the many grains of corn is already a natural symbol for the present
unity of Christians in the Church. It points, however, still more to
the future perfect unity, because it is itself in its real essence
already a foretaste of the paradisal future gift.

What is new and unheard of in the belief of the Christian
community is that the end time has already started in Jesus. Corresponding with this is the idea that the paradisal gifts of life,
knowledge and immortality are being given as food in the
eucharist, which is only the translation of a late-Jewish apocalyptic expectation into a Christian one. In other words, apocalyptic
considered the end time salvation as the recurrence of paradise or
as the re-emergence of a paradise which has been hidden and kept
in readiness until now.[67] In this expectation the tree of life already
played an important role. The *Ethiopian Enoch* knew of a secret
tree, which stood in the eschatological world (24), invisible for the
mortal and preserved for the final judgment, but then given over
to those who have been judged and saved. "Its fruit serves then as
food for the elect; it will be planted in the holy Place, in the
Temple of the Lord, of the everlasting King" (35:4). According to
4 Ezra 8:52 "paradise is opened, the tree of life planted, the
future world prepared, the blessing made ready" for the elect. The
Apocalypse of Moses promises its hero that the gift of the tree of
life, immortality, would be given to him at the time of the resurrection (28:4). Finally the *Testament of Levi* 18:10 says of the new
priest-king: "He will open the door of paradise and take away the
sword which threatened Adam. And he will give the holy to eat of
the tree of life, and the Spirit of holiness will rest on them." If
here eating from the tree of life fills the partaker with the Spirit of
Holiness, then this reminds one of the "spiritual food" of *Didache*
10:3. The passage cited, and indeed according to many the whole
book of the *Testament of Levi*, probably comes from Jewish-
Christianity.

The New Testament also shows in a few texts of secret
revelation that the expectation of receiving a share in the tree of
life was really alive in primitive Christianity also. In Revelation
2:7 the promise goes: "To the victor I will give to eat of the tree
of life, which stands in the paradise of God." Above all in Ch. 22
the tree of life is mentioned three times (v.2, 14, 19). We have
good reason to believe that the reference to the tree of life in

---

[67] Besides the examples cited above, the following texts: 2 En 65:9-10; 4 Ezr
7:36, 123; *ApocBar* 4:6; *ApocMos* 13:2.

Revelation 22 is nourished by the liturgy,[68] especially as this was considered to be a pre-enactment of the end time salvation. On the other hand the brief formulation of the benediction of *Didache* 9:3, the brief proclamation of "life and knowledge", requires explanation and interpretation. Revelation 22 allows one to recognize, or at least to assume, that the tree of life really played a role in the liturgy, in a liturgy close to the *Didache*.[69] But then one must assume that the *Didache*'s salvation gifts of life, (knowledge) and immortality stand in connection with it, that the eucharistic bread was believed to be a gift of the renewed paradise.

A certain support for this understanding of the bread formulae of the Didachist could perhaps be offered by an early Christian writing. It concerns a eucharistically coloured homily in an appendix handed on with the *Letter of Diognetus* numbered as its eleventh and twelfth chapters. It introduces itself as from a (pseudepigraphal) pupil of an apostle and purports to offer traditional material. It also contains genuine elements of tradition, which one meets in the *Didache* prayers, but extensively reinterprets them. Its chief theme is the ever new birth of the Logos, which was from the beginning and appears anew in the hearts of Christians. This may be an echo of *Didache* 10:2. The words which the Logos preaches, through whom he chooses and when he chooses (11:7), remind one of *Didache* 10:7. Further, the inside of the participant is seen as a blissful paradise, because in him the tree of knowledge and the tree of life have been planted. And this is seen as the sense of the text of Genesis 2:9, that in the beginning God planted the tree of knowledge and the tree of life in the middle of paradise, by which he indicates that life is through knowledge. Gnosis is placed in connection with the heart, and life is placed in connection with the Logos. The value of these sayings for us lies in the fact that the sermon names knowledge and life as cultic fruits of salvation and bases this on Genesis 2:9. Here the tradition of *Didache* 9:3 may, circumstances permitting, be at work, but it is de-eschatologized and interpreted in a spiritual-moralizing way in the manner of Philo.[70] This composition could be perhaps a further Alexandrian development of old tradition in the manner of *Didache* 9f.

The blessing of the cup gives thanks for the "holy vine of David", which Jesus has proclaimed as a reality (9:2). The con-

---

[68] Cf. A. Hamman, "La Prière" (in *Le Nouveau Testament* [Tournai, 1959] pp. 348ff). O. Cullmann (*Salvation in History* [London: SCM, 1967] p. 319) makes the claim that, "The whole book [Revelation] could and should be explained in the light of early Christian worship."

[69] In Rev 22:20 we find the translated *Maranatha* of Did. 10:6; the "shoot of David" in Rev 22:16 is closely related to the "vine of David" in Did. 9:2.

[70] Philo already allegorizes in a similar sense; cf. *LegAll* III.59; *Plant* 8-9.

cept of the "vine" is directly bound up with the contents of the
cup, the eucharistic element in the cup, but names the *causa pro
causato*, the cause instead of the fruit. It is, however, not only a
matter of the natural product found in the cup, but of a salvation-
historical quantity, which is clearly used in connection with the
cup. The term "vine" is found also in the Jewish *Berakah* formula
for the wine. In the Old Testament the vine stands as a picture for
Israel,[71] but also for the royal house (Ez 19:10-14) and for the
(royal) representative of the people of Israel (Ez 17:6-10; Ps
80:16, 18). Wisdom is praised in Sirach 24:17 as a vine which
produces lovely shoots or, according to the LXX, χάρις. The picture of the vine is also found in the environment of the *Didache*.
In the roughly contemporaneous Syriac *Apocalypse of Baruch*
(c.100-130 C.E.), it describes the Messiah.[72] Occasionally,
Mandaism also uses the predicate "vine" for its heavenly sent
Manda dᵉ-Hayye.[73] Above all, however, John's Gospel should be
named in this context, where Jesus proclaims himself as the true
vine (15:1-10). Over against this *Didache* 9:2 offers no open comparison of the vine with Jesus, but only proclaims him as the
revealer of the vine. In any case, we cannot simply carry the clear
Johannine identification over into the *Didache*, but must rather
seek to bring out the peculiarity of the *Didache*'s understanding of
the picture. It is characterized by the genitive qualification "of
David". But what is to be understood by the "vine of David"? The
Christians of that time knew it or introduced it into the homily; we
must try to find an interpretation carefully.

A first interpretation[74] treats the mention of "David" as a
reference to the author [of Psalms], who gives us an explanation
of the vine cited here. David is seen as the composer of the
Psalms[75], and he speaks in Psalm 80 (79):8 of a vine which Yahweh brought out of Egypt and planted, but which now is laid low;
by this Israel is meant. In conclusion to this, the Psalmist prays
for Yahweh's protection for the son (LXX Son of Man), whom
this refers to (v.16, 18). This passage was messianically
understood. From Psalm 80, so many interpreters say, the
Didache community understood the "holy vine of David" as the
new Israel in itself, as well as the messiah Jesus. In this inter-

---

[71] Is 27:2-6; Jer 2:21; Ez 15:6; Hos 10:1; Ps 80:9. In *LAB* 12:8f Israel is interpreted as a cosmic vine; cf. TDNT VII, p. 1071.

[72] *ApocBar* 36:6f; 37:1; 39:7 with 40:1.

[73] On this cf. esp. R. Borig, *Der wahre Weinstock. Untersuchungen zu Jo 15,1-
10* (München: Kösel, 1967 [SANT 16]) pp. 135-198.

[74] In opposition to A. Harnack represented by Lietzmann, *Mass and Lord's Supper*, p. 190; R. Eisler, "Das letzte Abendmahl", *ZNW* 25 (1926) pp. 6-12.

[75] Cf. Mk 12:35f; Acts 2:25, 34; 4:25; Rom 4:6; 11:9; (perhaps also 2 Macc
2:13).

pretation the material understanding of the concept "vine" remains noteworthy; against this, it is less satisfactory that David here is seen primarily as literary author.

A second attempt at the interpretation of *Didache* 9:2 also considers David as author, but this time as guardian of belief in the resurrection. For primitive Christianity he was regarded, on the basis of Psalm 16:8-11, as the supreme prophet of the resurrection of Jesus. In Acts, Peter (2:25-28) and Paul (13:34f) point to the resurrection of Jesus with the help of the prophecy in Psalm 16:8-11, in that they relate to Christ the saying that the flesh does not remain abandoned in the underworld and the holy One need not see corruption. The resurrection of Jesus means, according to Acts 13:34, the realization of the salvation gifts promised to David in Isaiah 55:3. Connected to this idea many authors see in the *Didache*'s "vine of David" a remembrance of the resurrection.[76]

This interpretation is right, if it begins with the evaluation of the David-figure in the primitive community and emphasizes the salvation event bound up with this name. That corresponds also fully to the anamnesis meaning of a primitive Christian eucharist. Certainly the oldest meal fellowship was also deeply touched and determined by the resurrection of Jesus. (Even the "immortality" mentioned in the post-communion thanks is according to 1 Cor 15:33 a resurrection gift.) It is only unclear how the thought of the resurrection hangs together with the pictorial representation of the vine. The two interpretations set out above correspond more closely to the viewpoint of modern people, who occupy themselves in a literary way with the ideas of the *Didache* than the viewpoint of the oldest Christians, who lived in them.

The salvation-historical meaning of David is not exhausted by the fact that he speaks of the vine and prophesies the resurrection of Jesus. He is much more pre-eminent in himself, in his rôle as a salvation figure chosen by God and a sign of salvation, i.e. as the ancestor of the Messiah.[77] To this extent the messianic salvation derives from him and, where this is realized, David comes into view as a consequence (cf. Lk 1:69). The Old Testament presented the Messiah as the sprout of David, as the heir to David's throne or as the new David.[78] To this extent the New Testament also knew of the Davidic sonship of Jesus[79] as a factor, even if not

---

[76] So Audet, *Didachè*, pp. 425f.

[77] Cf. 2 Sam 7:12; Acts 2:30.

[78] Sprout of David: Is 11:1ff; Jer 23:5; Davidic claimant to the throne: Is 9:5; new David: Jer 30:9; Ez 34:23f; 37:24; Is 55:3f.

[79] Rom 1:3; 15:12; Mk 10:48; 12:35, 37; Mt 1:1, 6; 9:27; 12:23; 15:22; 20:30f; 21:9, 15; Lk 1:32; 1:69; 2:4, 11; 3:31; Acts 13:22f; Jn 7:42. On this see W. Michaelis, "Die Davidssohnschaft Jesu als historisches und kerygmatisches Problem" in H. Ristow-K. Mattiae (eds), *Der historische Jesus und der kerygmatische Christus*[2] (Berlin: Evangelische-Verlagsanstalt, 1962) pp. 317-330.

the essence, of his messiahship.[80] This fact can also be expressed in a picture, that comes closer to the expression "vine of David" in *Didache* 9:2: the Book of Revelation, which is bound up with the *Didache* tradition, twice calls Jesus the "root/sprout of David" (5:5; 22:16). From this it is a short step to the conclusion that the (pre)Didache description of the cup as "vine of David" is to be explained as a modification and concretization of the idea of Davidic sonship, as its translation into the Eucharist, conditioned by the particular character of the Lord's Supper. At the same time the description of Wisdom as a vine in Sirach 24:17 can also have conditioned the choice of the expression. This would then mean that the function of Wisdom has realized and fulfilled itself in the Davidic descendent Jesus and in the Lord's Supper proclaimed as a reality by him. To this extent the pre-*Didache* Lord's Supper acknowledges with its benediction of the cup that in Jesus the expected Davidic messiah and Wisdom have come, and that he makes present his coming sacramentally in the eucharistic drink; since the benediction is indeed said over the cup.

Our interpretation of the expression "vine of David" as the messianic son of David, Jesus, has indeed another support in the Hosanna cry of 10:6, which takes up the Davidic motif. Of course the exact form of this latter has not been unanimously handed down from a text-critical point of view.[81] The oldest reading, because it is the most difficult, would appear however to be the Coptic version: "Hosanna to the House[82] of David!" The content of this formulation fits well with the "vine of David", as it has been interpreted by us. The cry of praise is valid for the family of David because God "has erected in it a shield of salvation" (Lk 1:69), has chosen it as the way and means of his salvation plan.[83] Even the other readings "son of David" and "God of David" preserve at least the reference to David as salvation-historical figure.

---

[80] Cf. Mk 12:35-37.

[81] The Greek and Georgian version read θεῷ, the coptic οἴκῳ, *Const* VII. 26:5 reads υἱῷ.

[82] So also Audet, *Didachè*, p. 236; grounds for this pp. 62-67; cf. also p. 420. The reading θεῷ can be explained as an explanatory change or carelessness, υἱῷ as (consciously or unconsciously) parallelism to Mt 21:9. Audet (*ibid.*, p. 63) makes the further observation that Origen's reads οἴκῳ in Mt 21:9 (cf. the ed. of Tischendorf). The *Shemoneh Esreh* also calls on God for the kingdom of David (Palestinian edition fourteenth benediction) or for the sprout of David (Babylonian edition fifteenth benediction). Beyond Audet's reasons the reading οἴκῳ receives a support through our exegesis.

[83] Audet's further proposal, that by the House of David is intended not only the family but also the Temple and in our case the interior space in which the eucharist is celebrated (pp. 420-423), derives more from fantasy than from critical historical thinking.

Finally, in interpreting the image of the "vine", it must be still considered and taken into account that it has predominantly a collective meaning in the Old Testament and refers to the people of Israel, and further that the Jewish Christians who used it still preserved and kept this aspect in mind, even if they understood it primarily in a Christological sense. So it should be supposed that it referred at the same time both to Christ and to Christians. This assumption is all the more probable since the Lord's Supper is already the place where the one Christ unfolds to the multitude of Christians and draws this multitude back again into unity in himself. In Pauline terms, the one bread, the eucharistic body of Christ, is extended to the manifold ecclesial body of Christ and again drawn together (cf. 1 Cor 10:17). In fact our eucharistic prayers speak of the unification and "gathering of the church into the kingdom" (9:4 and 10:5) and at the same time see a symbolic representation of this event in the unification of the many grains into the bread (9:4). This present sense means at the same time a foretaste of the eschatological unification. So the ecclesial unification of Christians is thus expressly brought into connection with the bread in 9:4, while in 10:5 in any case it is referred generally to the meal event. But a collective, ecclesial note intrudes even in the image of the vine of David, i.e. the inclusion of the Christian in Christ. The Gospel of John brings this explicitly to expression when it speaks of the branches on the vine (15:2, 5).

Our study leads to the conclusion that the anamnesis thanksgiving for the "holy vine of David" refers primarily to the person of Jesus as the Davidic Messiah, but secondarily also to the meal fellowship constituted and actualized by him. So we come in fact close to the Johannine understanding of the vine,[84] without having started from this clear expression as a history of religions proof text. The *Didache* speaks in veiled form, John expresses the same conviction openly. The characterization of the vine as Davidic interprets the actual historical passage of the salvation event; it emphasizes that the messianic salvation which came in Jesus is the fulfillment of the promise given to David. The realization of this in the Old Testament, however, is represented as the constitution of a divine covenant, as an everlasting covenant in Isaiah 55:3, as a covenant of peace in Ez 34:25. So lines can also be drawn from the Davidic motif to the covenant thought, which the New Testament cup formula expressly and explicitly declares, though the accounts of the institution base the new covenant in the shed blood of Jesus and thus in the death of Jesus. For the pre-*Didache* liturgy, on the other hand, the messianic

---

[84] Cf. Borig, *Der wahre Weinstock*, pp. 248f.

event in general stands in the foreground; the death of Jesus echoes only softly in the concept of the servant of God.

We must come back once more to the expression "vine". This time we need to observe the peculiarity that the messianic event conjured up by the word is specifically expressed in this picture. It is clearly chosen with reference to the content of the cup, wine. In itself it allows other metaphors to be thought of also. The Messianic event remembered in the benediction is thus in conscious approximation to the contents of the cup, expressed in sacramental clothing, eucharistized. In view of this fact one can scarcely escape the conclusion that, even at that time in the Aramaic community, there was believed to be an ontic correspondence between the salvation event expressed in the word and the meal elements. The saying over the bread also gives just such a close ontic relation between the proclaimed gift of salvation and the meal element, even if this can also not be seen at first sight. That is, if "the life and knowledge" really are to be understood as the paradisal gifts according to Gen 2:9 and now are said over the bread, then everything suggests that those gifts were believed to be renewed here and that the present meal elements mediate those salvation gifts, even if in a more particularly qualitative fashion.

The particular ontic nature of the elements of the sacramental meal is revealed further in the instructions in 10:6 and 9:5. Certainly the command in 10:6, that only the holy may enter while the unholy must do penance, relates to the eucharist and shows this to be a numinous quantity. The command to be holy here is often understood from baptism, the warning to penance correspondingly to the command to receive baptism.[85] If, however, one considers the Pauline deliberations in 1 Corinthians 11:27-31 and the *Didache* instruction of 14:1 to confess sins before the eucharistic celebration, then it is more probable that in 10:6 the ethical holiness of the already baptized is required. In any case the eucharist appears itself as "holy" food, which places demands on the receiver.

We have a parallel to 10:6 in 9:5, according to which only baptized may eat from the "eucharist", because it is a matter of "the holy". Now of course the difficult question arises as to what then is meant by "eucharist" here. In the present framework of the *Didache* meal chapters the saying 9:5 stands inside the meal proper. That leads to the conclusion that the term εὐχαριστία refers here to the agape meal, which is thus given a highter value because it is reserved to the baptized.[86] Only that is not certain; it

---

[85] So Audet, *Didachè*, p. 415.
[86] This proposal is presented by Audet, *Didachè*, p. 415.

could also be that the injunction in 9:5, pronounced in the sequence of the agape, does not refer to the agape itself but serves as a prior warning for the following sacramental offering. The fact that it is valued as "the holy" speaks rather for the second interpretation. In addition the term εὐχαριστία has the tendency in the history of language to move from a wider meaning to an ever more technical term for the sacramental Lord's Supper. Is it likely that the Didachist at the end of the first century would have introduced the word expressly for the agape? However that may be, even if the term εὐχαριστία and the whole saying of 9:5 relates to the sacrament or to the agape in the *present* text, nevertheless, according to our theory developed above, the present text of the agape of *Didache* 9:1-10:5 contains earlier eucharistic sayings. If this is correct, then *Didache* 9:5 is also an early witness for the Lord's Supper and enlightens its essence: it presupposes baptism, that is membership of Christ; it is itself "the holy" and as εὐχαριστία is the objectivation of the remembered salvation event.

Furthermore, the Prayer after the Meal casts light on the eucharistic faith of the *Didache* tradition, also on the rest of its sayings, which bring further essentials to prominence. It begins with the thanks to the Father for his holy Name, which he has allowed to take up residence in the hearts of participants. This fact, pulled into the foreground, is clearly considererd to be a decisive aspect. Here it needs to be asked first of all what is to be understood by "holy Name". The qualifying σοῦ identifies it as belonging to the Father. What is meant, however, is hardly the personal name "Father" itself, with which we should address God according to the instruction of Jesus (Mt 6:9; Did 8:2) and consequently also not the indwelling of the "Father" personally, as proclaimed in John 14:23. This interpretation would break out of the otherwise consistent Christo-centric thought process. Rather the concept "the Name" in *Didache* 10:2, as also in many other primitive Christian sayings, serves as a circumlocution for Jesus the Son. This usage grew out of the Biblical Name-ideology. Here the Name stands for the person, insofar as s/he reveals her/himself, or becomes apparent. The "holy Name" for which the pre-*Didache* liturgy gives thanks relates now not to the person of the Father as such[87] but to the other person who reveals him, in whom he is recognizable and visible in the sense of the Johannine Jesus: "He who sees me, sees the Father" (John 14:9). The term "the' Name" used in an absolute sense appears also in the New Testament, especially in old Palestinian layers of tradition, in Acts,[88]

---

[87] Audet (*Didachè*, p. 431) affirms this.

[88] Cf. Acts 4:18 v.1; 5:41; probably also Acts 4:17; 5:28; further 1 Pet 4:16 (?); 3 Jn 7.

further in early Christian writing in Ignatius of Antioch,[89] also in
the Gnostic literature.[90] Of particular importance for us is the witness of Irenaeus of Lyon, because he uses it in the eucharistic
context. He interprets the saying about the Name which would be
glorified among the peoples in Malachi 1:10f, the early Christian
locus classicus for the Lord's Supper, as "no other than that of
our Lord, through whom the Father is glorified and the human
being. Because it is the name of his own Son, however, and
because he has made human beings, so he names him with his
own Name".[91] One would not be much in error if one sees in this
exegesis of the Church Father an old exegetical tradition, which
reaches back into *Didache* 10:2. It is further noteworthy that the
prophecy of Malachi in abbreviated form occurs also in *Didache*
14:3, but in the context of the mention of the Name marveled at
by all peoples also. So it seems to us sufficiently justified to
understand the "holy Name" in *Didache* 10:2 as the person of the
Son Jesus.[92] This interpretation fits—and that also speaks for
it—perfectly into the eucharistic context.

The κατασκηνοῦν of the Name mentioned in the text also
points in the same direction. The term is significant. With it the
Old Testament expresses the particular dwelling of the Name of
God in a particular place.[93] It is also a key concept of the Old
Testament theology of Wisdom and allows us to see this as the
theological background of the *Didache* prayers. According to
Sirach 24, Wisdom had its home in heaven, but then found its particular dwelling and rest in Israel (v. 8) in the realization of salvation history. Identical with the Torah (Bar 4:1), she became
visible in Israel (Bar 3:37: ὤφθη). The root σκηνοῦν describes the
incarnate existence of the Logos in John 1:14, so that
(κατα)σκηνοῦν reveals an incarnationally oriented perspective. On
the basis of *Didache* 10:2, the eucharist[94] is recognizable as the
sacramental descent and indwelling of Jesus in the heart of human
beings, and indeed, since the saying serves as thanks for the meal,

---

[89] *Eph* 3:1; 7:1; *Phld* 10:1.

[90] *GospTruth* 80:6f; 81:25f (M.Malinine-H.C.Puech-G.Quispel [Zürich, 1956]
pp. 38-40).

[91] *AdvHaer* IV.17:6 (II.200 Harvey).

[92] This interpretation of "the Name"=Jesus is also represented by J. Daniélou,
*A History of Early Christian Doctrine Before the Council of Nicaea I: The Theology
of Jewish Christianity* (London: Darton, Longman & Todd, 1964) pp. 155ff, but
rejected on unconvincing grounds by Audet (see n. 86) and J. Ponthof ("La signification religieuse du "Nom" chez Clément de Rome et dans la Didachè", *EThL*
35 [1959] pp. 359ff).

[93] Cf. 2 Esdras 11:9 (LXX); Jer 7:12; Ez 43:7.

[94] The interpretation of the saying in Did. 10:2 as referring to baptism by W.
Michaelis, TDNT VII, p. 389 is off course.

by means of the food. That is exactly the position of the Gospel of John, which also speaks more clearly than the *Didache*: "This is the bread which has come down from heaven" (John 6:58). "As the Father who sent me is living and I live through the Father, so everyone who eats me lives through me" (John 6:57). This verse proclaims the eucharist as the sacramental realization of the previous incarnation of Jesus.[95] In the *Didache* the present eucharistic indwelling of Jesus is fairly clearly expressed (10:2); the reminder of his previous coming recedes but is echoed in a veiled way in the reference to the "vine of David" (9:2) and in the hosanna cry of 10:6 at least.

The *Didache* liturgy is all the more clearly directed towards the future Parousia. The prayer for the gathering of the Church into the kingdom (9:4 and 10:5) and for the hastening of the Parousia in 10:6 attest this. There the community implores: "Let grace come and let the world pass away!" Further "*Maranatha!*" These prayers/cries relate primarily to the future event of the fulfillment of salvation, but nevertheless still have a second dimension of meaning, which even though it is not overt should still not be mistaken: they indicate that the future Parousia event, the future coming of Jesus, experiences a foretaste and anticipation here and now in the event of the Lord's Supper. The coming of grace implored for in 10:6 has in mind the eschatological fulfillment of salvation. It should not be overlooked, however, that χάρις in the ancient church could be on the one hand a title of Christ[96] and on the other hand also an equivalent for eu-charist.[97] The word is perhaps already chosen with respect to the latter. If we take all of this into account and further add the fact that the prayer for the coming of grace happens in the context of the Lord's Supper, then it can be concluded concerning the conviction of faith that the coming of the fulfillment of salvation, and more precisely the future coming of Christ, is experienced beforehand in this sacramental meal.

Similarly, a double meaning should be recognized in *maranatha*.[98] Even grammatically it allows for two meanings. The

---

[95] Cf. Betz, *Die Eucharistie* II.1, pp. 173-180.

[96] The Coptic version reads, "Let the Lord come!" As a title for Christ χάρις also appears in *Acts of John* 94 and 98, as well as in the *Odes of Solomon* 19. On this matter see F. J. Dölger, *Sol salutis* (Münster: Aschendorff, 1920) pp. 154ff; Lietzmann, *Mass and Lord's Supper*, p. 193 fn. 2.

[97] Cf. Heb 10:29; 12:15; 13:9; on this Betz, *Die Eucharistie* II.1 Index; for Patristic attestations see J. Betz, "Der Abendmahlskelch im Judenchristentum" in M. Reding (ed), *Abhandlungen über Theologie und Kirche (Festschrift für K. Adam)* (Düsseldorf: Patmos, 1952) p. 133.

[98] See K. G. Kuhn, TDNT IV, pp. 466ff; W. Kramer, *Christos Kyrios Gottessohn* (Zürich: Zwingli, 1963) pp. 95-103.

imperative, "Our Lord, come!" (*manana tha*) is suggested by the parallel line, "Let grace come!", and is shown to be certainly—but not necessarily exclusively—a primitive Christian conception. The indicative "Our Lord has come" or "is here" (*maran atha*) is philologically also possible and is attested by the Coptic version. One would not be wrong in the assumption that the oldest community could have consciously intended this double meaning and made it serve the purposes of their belief concerning the Lord's Supper. But even if one only allows the imperative as the grammatical clarification of the cry, it still retains its reference to the sacramental event.[99] For *maranatha* is indeed the answer of the community to the warning of the liturgist that only the holy should come to the sacrament. The coming of the Lord is anticipated in the elements of the meal. The eucharist functions as the bridge between the first and the second Parousia.

So the eschatological world is projected into and works in this sacrament and qualifies its elements. They are thus acknowledged as "spiritual food and (spiritual) drink" in an old formula attested also in 1 Cor 10:3 and so related to that sphere in which the Resurrected One lives (cf. 1 Cor 10:45). So it is not surprising if "life in the new aeon" is ascribed to it as its consequence.[100] It all leads however to a significant conclusion in the history of dogma: It was not hellenistic thought about substance which first accorded the sacramental elements a particular ontic character, but already Jewish Christian belief.

The eschatological tendency of the pre-*Didache* Lord's Supper also shows itself, as we have already seen, in the repeated prayer for the gathering of the church into the kingdom (9:4 and 10:5). Jesus had proclaimed the latter in the picture of a universal festal meal uniting all the elect (Mt 8:11; 22:1-14) and the Lord's Supper as the foretaste and anticipation of the same (Lk 22:16-18; Mk 14:25). This eschatological outlook and prayer has however still other roots. The thought of the gathering of the church is bound up with the Old Testament expectation of salvation, that the Diaspora of Israel would be gathered. This idea penetrates the Old Testament since Jeremiah[101] and also has a firm place in Jewish prayers.[102] Also the prophet says of the sprout of Jesse, that is of

---

[99] Cf. Lietzmann, *Mass and Lord's Supper*, p. 193; Dibelius, "Die Mahlgebete", p. 40; O. Cullmann, *The Christology of the New Testament*[2] (London: SCM, 1963) pp. 208-216.

[100] Audet's text εἰς ζωὴν αἰώνιον attributes the life of the new aeon as a direct consequence of the spiritual gifts of the meal. Even if one had to read καὶ ζ. α., nevertheless this formulation, that the life should follow on the gifts of the meal, still suggests the idea that the latter follows out of these.

[101] There is a good summary in Clerici, *Einsammlung der Zerstreuten*, pp. 65-102.

[102] Cf. the tenth benediction of the *Shemoneh Esreh*, "Sound the great horn for our freedom; lift up an ensign to gather our exiles (Balyolonian recension "from the

the Davidic messianic Son of David, that he will gather the scattered of Israel and bring together the dispersed of Judah (Is 11:10-12). So there is a connection between the thought of the benediction of the cup and the prayer for gathering. More immediately still, and more clearly, this is bound up with the prayer over the bread in 9:4, and it does this in two respects. First, inasmuch as the eucharistic bread is the renewed gift of paradise and so the partial and preliminary outworking of the end time salvation. The beginning however calls for fulfillment, the partial for the total realization of the eschatological salvation, the sign for the genuine thing. The urgent cry μνήσθητι in 10:5 also brings to expression thoughts of the fulfillment of the beginning. It is a formula already coined in Judaism and reminds Yahweh of the fulfillment of his previous redemptive acts, of the complete realization of his promises.[103] Secondly, the prayer for gathering in 9:4 utilizes the natural symbolism[104] of the bread inasmuch as it is made into one out of many grains scattered over the mountains. This unity of the bread is a sign of the eschatological unity of the church. What is even more interesting in this comparison is that the metaphorical aspect of the image (*Bildhälfte*) of bread is already provided by the terminology of the content of the image (*Sachhälfte*), since the expressions used of the bread διασκορπίζειν and συνάγειν are not the technical terms of agriculture, but of Jewish Diaspora theology for the gathering in of the scattered of Israel.[105] This terminological peculiarity is indeed hardly accidental, and makes it more probable that the eucharistic bread is already the foretaste and anticipation of the end time unification of Christians. It is however still also a representation of their already existing unity, inasmuch as the community prepares and shares in this bread. The *Didache* does not expressly mention this thought, but Paul does. For him the sharing in the eucharistic bread is not only a sign but the reason for the present unification of the many participants in the one body of Christ (1 Cor 10:17). In the *Didache*, however, the perspective is directed much more strongly towards the coming

---

four corners of the earth"). Blessed are you, O Lord, who gathers the banished ones of your people Israel." (cf. Strack-Billerbeck, *Kommentar* IV, p. 213).

[103] See Clerici, *Einsammlung der Zerstreuten*, pp. 48-64.

[104] E. R. Goodenough, "John a Primitive Gospel", *JBL* 64 (1945) pp. 145-182; C. F. D. Moule, "A Note on Didache 9,4", *JTS* ns 6 (1955) pp. 240-243. L. Cerfaux ("La multiplication des pains dans la liturgie de la Didachè", *Bib* 40 [1959] pp. 943-958) understand the picture in 9:4 not as a natural symbol of bread, but as a reference to the gathering of fragments left over in the miraculous multiplication of loaves by Jesus into one place. This thesis is refuted by H. Riesenfeld (see below note 105).

[105] Recognized by H. Riesenfeld, "Das Brot von den Bergen. Zu Did. 9,4", *Er* 54 (1956) pp. 142-150, esp. 145f.

unity.

The post-communion prayer (10:5) takes up this concern again, underlines its importance and shows how much the eucharist was experienced as an essential fulfillment of the church on its pilgrimage to final perfection. One prays God to save the church from all evil,[106] to perfect it in his love,[107] to gather it from the four winds into his kingdom, which he has prepared for it, that is has determined in his predestination. That is realized in the Parousia of Christ which 10:6 so emphatically proclaims.

We come to the end. Previous research has arrived at the reasoned conclusion that the two meal chapters *Didache* 9-10, in their present form, refer to a primitive Christian celebration in which a sacramental eucharist (10:6) follows an agape (9:1-10:5). However a closer examination led us to the conclusion that the bulk of the present agape text, except for 10:1, 3a, was itself originally intended as an independent eucharistic celebration. Only a eucharistic interpretation will really do justice to them. In conclusion, however, the question has now to be asked: What were the motives which led to the revaluation of the original eucharistic prayers into agape prayers? In answer to this question we have to rely on simple conjectures. One can first of all question whether the change of meaning in the text was caused by the change of ritual which the primitive Christian cultic meal had already undergone in the first decades. It is well known that it quickly abandoned the original sequence bread-meal-cup, drew the two eucharistic acts of bread and wine together and put them at the end of the celebration. This sequence is reflected in the present general conception of the two meal chapters.[108] But why did it not apply the old eucharistic material to the eucharistic part of 10:6 but instead to the agape part? A plausible interpretation cannot be provided only by the changes in the ritual, which in the *Didache* still shine through when it places the cup first. The reason must therefore be sought elsewhere.

A different consideration, starting from the theological content of the prayers, may well claim more probability. These describe the eucharistic event in Old Testament categories and are, in terms of soteriology, directed towards the coming of Jesus in the incarnation and above all in the Parousia; they are silent however about the death of Jesus, about his body given and his blood poured out. The latter are, however, the decisive perspectives and

---

[106] There is a parallel to this in 2 Tim 4:18.

[107] Two explanations are possible: God should perfect the Church in its love for him (Gen. object.) (as in Clerici, *Ensammlung der Zerstreuten*, pp. 65-102) or: God in his love (Gen. subject.) should perfect the Church.

[108] Just as in Mk 14:22-25 and Mt 26:26-29.

content of the accounts of the institution. The *Didache* prayers are formed by a preference for Old Testament motifs; they refer too little to the New Testament special material, to the facts declared in the institution words of Jesus, namely the memorial of his death and his resurrection. The old prayers are thus too one-sidedly eschatological in their direction towards the Parousia, too little informed by anamnesis looking back to the salvation-historical act of redemption. This forces us to the conclusion that these texts were found to be insufficient in the long run, because they did not describe the eucharistic events broadly and extensively enough. This conviction could gain all the more ground, when Paul found a hearing for his theology of the cross. From there on it can be understood that the original Lord's Supper prayers though not swept from the table were nevertheless forced out into the agape. So the history of the Lord's Supper in this respect only shares in the general development of the oldest church: a conduct and theology all too strongly and one-sidedly directed towards the Parousia was more and more completed and balanced by the reference to the work and word of the historical Jesus.

Moreover a similar development to that found in the *Didache* appears also to lie before us in the Lukan report of the Lord's Supper in Lk 22:15-20. H. Schürmann has shown it to be probable that verses 15-18, originally not directed to the Jewish but to the Christian Passover, were eucharistic sayings, as shown particularly by the terminology of the cup in verse 17.[109] This group of verses is likewise quite eschatologically orientated, and also does not mention anything about the body and blood and death of Jesus. So it did not, argues Schürmann, express the deepest and unique essence of the eucharist clearly enough, and was found to be insufficient. It was then completed and interpreted by an insertion which spoke clearly of the body and blood of Jesus. The combination arising in this way, however, now gives the impression that verses 15-18 refer to the previous Jewish Passover meal and only verses 19-20 to the new eucharist. According to this interpretation the old, now unsatisfactory, text was not completely erased, but applied to the description of the analogous Passover Meal. That would then provide a parallel to the fate of the *Didache* text.

For the preservation of the primitive eucharistic texts in the *Didache* we cannot be thankful enough. They provide us with a deep insight into the early history of the Lord's Supper in its liturgical form and also into the belief and piety of the oldest community. They open a wide salvation-historical horizon from Paradise to the Parousia of Christ. Their pronounced eschatological orientation can also be useful for our understanding of faith.

---

[109] Schürmann, *Der Paschamahlbericht Lk 22,(7-14)*, pp. 15-18.

DIDACHE 9-10: ELEMENTS OF A EUCHARISTIC INTERPRETATION

ENRICO MAZZA
Milan

Introduction

A long time has passed since Connolly admitted that he was unable to explain why the term "eucharist" introduced the eucharistic prayers of *Didache* 9-10.[1] Here is the relevant text[2]:

Chapter 9

1. Concerning the eucharist give thanks as follows.
2. First concerning the cup:
We give thanks to you, our Father, concerning the holy Vine of David your servant, which you have revealed to us through Jesus your servant.
To you be glory for ever.

3. And concerning the broken (bread):
We give thanks to you our Father for the life and knowledge which you have revealed to us through Jesus your servant.
To you be glory for ever.
4. Just as this broken (bread) was scattered upon the mountains and reunited has become one, so let your Church be reunited into your kingdom from the ends of the earth because yours is the glory and the power through Jesus Christ for ever.
5. Let no one eat or drink from your eucharist except those baptized in the name of the Lord; for indeed concerning this the Lord has said: "Do not give what is holy to the dogs."

Chapter 10

1. After you have eaten your fill, give thanks thus:

2. We give thanks to you holy Father
for your holy Name which you have made to dwell in our hearts and for the knowledge, faith and immortality which you have revealed to us through Jesus your servant;
To you be glory for ever.
3. You Lord almighty have created everything for the sake of your Name;
you have given human beings food and drink to partake with enjoyment so that they might give thanks;
but to us you have given the grace of spiritual food and drink and of eternal life through your servant.
4. Above all we give you thanks because you are mighty.
To you be glory for ever.
5. Remember Lord your Church, to preserve it from all evil and to make it perfect in your love.
And, sanctified, gather it from the four winds into your kingdom which you have prepared for it.
Because yours is the power and the glory for ever.

---

[1] R. H. Connolly, "Agape and eucharist in the Didache", *DRev* 50 (1937) pp. 447ff.

[2] The text of the eucharistic prayers of the Didache is in a footnote in the original Italian article, but is included, for convenience, in the body of the text here.

6. Let grace come and let this world
pass.
Hosanna to the God of David.
If one is holy let him come, if not let
him be converted.
Maranatha. Amen.
7. Afterwards, let the prophets give
thanks as they please.

This issue has been finally resolved by the work of J-P. Audet on
the literary genre of the Jewish blessing, [3] corrected by the observations of Talley who criticized his excessive schematization,
which on the one hand simplifies and on the other partly violates
the Jewish data on which the research is based.[4]

Another element which we are sure of today is the essential
relationship between the thanksgiving prayer and the development
of the Jewish meal in its various ritual forms. But what is still
much discussed is which amongst the various kinds of sacred
meals of Judaism could be the form-type that has given rise to the
Christian eucharist and to the eucharistic anaphora.[5] Characteristic
is the position of Dom B. Botte, in which he denies that one can
exactly identify the Jewish liturgy from which the Christian
anaphora is directly derived.

Equally sure is the essential relationship between *Didache* 10
and the *birkat ha-mazon*,[6] a thanksgiving prayer at the end of the
Jewish supper. The comparative work done by Finkelstein[7] and
Dibelius[8] is already known and needs no further demonstration.

The consequence of all this is that the explanation of chapters
9-10 of the *Didache* will necessarily have to begin from the Jewish
practice of the ritual meal.

For the interpretation of the eucharistic prayers of the
Didache recognition of this fact is necessary but not sufficient.
One is, in fact, dealing with Christian or rather Jewish-Christian

[3] J.-P. Audet, *La Didaché, Instructions des apôtres* (Paris: Gabalda 1958) pp.
372-410; also, "Esquisse du genre littéraire de la bénédiction juive et de
l'eucharistie chrétienne", *RB* 65 (1958) pp. 371-399.

[4] T. J. Talley, "De la "berakah" à l'eucharistie, une question à réexaminer", *La
Maison-Dieu* 125/1 (1976) pp. 11-39. An English version appears in "From
Berakah to *Eucharistia*: A Reopening Question", *Worship* 50/2 (1976) pp. 115-137.

[5] L. Ligier, "Les origines de la prière eucharistique", *Questions Liturgiques* 53
(1972) pp. 181-202; H. Cazelles, "Eucharistie, bénédiction et sacrifice dans
l'Ancien Testament", *La Maison-Dieu* 123 (1975/3) pp. 7-28.

[6] K. Hruby, "La "birkat ha-mazon"", in *Mélanges Liturgiques offerts au R. P.
dom Bernard Botte* (Louvain: Abbaye du Mont César, 1972) pp. 205ff; L. Ligier,
"Origines", p. 194; W. Rordorf, "The Didache", in *The Eucharist of the Early
Christians* (New York: Pueblo 1976) pp. 8-9.

[7] L. Finkelstein, "The "birkat ha-mazon"", *JQR* 19 (1928-1929) pp. 211-263.

[8] M. Dibelius, "Die Mahl-Gebete der Didache", *ZNW* 37 (1938) pp. 32-41.

texts, and so the gospel message must be the principal guide, the reading grid for their correct interpretation.

This relationship with the New Testament has been undervalued too often. We do not entirely support the assertion of Middleton who claims that the work of the writer of *Didache* was, in effect, a "Christianization of the Jewish prayer".[9] Instead we would say that the work of the Didachist was a profound re-elaboration of the Jewish theology expressed in the meal prayer, to convey the soteriological themes of the New Testament, even though in the initial phase of their elaboration and theological genesis.

It is above all the *method* of this comparison with the New Testament that needs to be changed. If our text is actually contemporary with the elaboration of the various redactions of some NT texts, it will not simply be a case of looking for NT themes in the *Didache* but rather the opposite;[10] in any case, the working hypothesis must not be rejected *a priori*.[11] We hope to find this treatment in the edition of the *Didache* that Rordorf and Tuilier have prepared for the collection *Sources Chretiennes*.[12]

In fact, nearly all the critics admit that these two chapters of the *Didache* are prior to the final editing of the work and have been integrated in the body of the work at a later date.[13] This has been ably demonstrated by both Audet[14] and Gibbins;[15] the latter

---

[9] R. D. Middleton, "The eucharistic prayers of the Didache", *JTS* 36 (1936) p. 266.

[10] We must suppose that the Christian community had immediately begun to live according to the message of Christ in continuity with what the apostles had experienced in living with him. Under the influence of the Spirit his teaching matured in them and the memory of Jesus became the source from which they drew all that the community required by way of regulation for the growth of the faith. On the other hand, the community gathered together for the "breaking of the bread" which could not be omitted from the message and proclamation of Jesus. Hence we believe that there is both an interaction and a reciprocal conditioning between the way of life of the first Christians, with their pastoral requirements, and the redaction of the gospel texts in their various phases and stages.

[11] Here it seems that Audet eliminated this possibility too quickly, almost *a priori*: "If the *Teachings of the Apostles* have seen the light of day in Antioch, and if they could have been earlier than a part of the New Testament writings, it would not be impossible *a priori* that the latter carried to some extent the trace of their existence...But, in fact (sic!), neither in the Pauline letters nor elsewhere has the little collection of the *Teachings of the Apostles* left any trace" (*Didachè*, p. 213).

[12] W. Rordorf & A. Tuilier, *La Doctrine des douze Apôtres (Didachè)*, Paris: Les Éditions du Cerf, 1978 (SC 248). This article was published before its appearance in print.

[13] W. Rordorf, "Didache", p. 2.

[14] *Didache*, pp. 174ff, 189-190.

[15] H. J. Gibbins, "The problem of the liturgical section of the Didache", *JTS* 36 (1935) pp. 373-386. Cf. specially the synthesis of pp. 385-386.

gives the origin of *Didache* 9-10 as 30-70, and is even prepared to accept the earlier part of this period.[16]

I. THE DATE

1) To determine the date of the eucharistic prayers in the *Didache*, Audet uses various arguments; one of these exemplifies his method.

Audet argues that "Hosanna to the House of David" (Did 10:6) is an acclamation almost unthinkable after the events of 70 C.E.[17] He compares this concept of the salvation of Israel with the events of 70 C.E. We will compare Did 9:2 with the sense of the so-called Council of Jerusalem in the same way, in order to get a date, as a *terminus ad quem*:

> We give thanks to you, our Father, concerning the holy Vine of David your servant, which you have revealed to us through Jesus your servant.

The wine brings to mind the vine whose hidden sense has been revealed through Jesus. This vine of David is distinct from Jesus, who is only its revealer; we cannot identify Jesus and the vine of David: the object or *anamnesis* of the "blessing" is the vine on its own. This object of "blessing" will be one of the *great works* which God has completed, the meaning of which has been revealed in the work of Jesus.

Rordorf[18] has documented the fact that inside Judaism there was emphasis on "a current of ideas that represented the kingdom of David in the form of a vine";[19] so it follows that the *great work* of God, object of the thanksgiving of Did 9:2 is the kingdom of David, or rather the saving economy which is achieved in the history of Israel. This economy reaches its fullness in the "revelation" of Jesus, who through the title, $\pi\alpha\hat{\iota}\varsigma$, is in a sense compared to David as protagonist of the saving work of God. The

---

[16] The argument, based above all on the use of *klasma*, does not seem particularly convincing, given that it involves the thorny problem of the meaning and dating of the various accounts of the multiplication of the bread both within the Johannine tradition and in the synoptic tradition.

[17] *Didachè*, pp. 189ff. There is no need to provide a discussion of the reading "house of David" in place of "God of David", today considered preferable. Audet has made his choice on the basis of the *lectio difficilior*.

[18] W. Rordorf, "La vigne et le vin dans la tradition juive et chrétienne", in *Annales de l'Université de Neuchâtel 1969-1970* (Neuchâtel: Université de Neuchatel 1971) pp. 131-146. Reprinted in *Liturgie, foi et vie des premiers chrétiens. Études patristiques* (Paris: Beauschesne, 1986 [ThH 75]) pp. 493-508.

[19] It seems that Rordorf's interpretation is better motivated than that accepted by J. Jeremias drawn from R. Eisler: "$\dot{\upsilon}\pi\dot{\varepsilon}\rho$ $\tau\hat{\eta}\varsigma$ $\dot{\alpha}\gamma\dot{\iota}\alpha\varsigma$ $\dot{\alpha}\mu\pi\dot{\varepsilon}\lambda o\upsilon$ $\Delta\alpha\upsilon\dot{\iota}\delta$ $\tau o\hat{\upsilon}$ $\pi\alpha\iota\delta\dot{o}\varsigma$ $\sigma o\upsilon$, "of whom David, thy servant, speaks" (i.e., in Ps. 80:8ff.)." J. Jeremias, art. $\pi\alpha\hat{\iota}\varsigma$ $\theta\varepsilon o\hat{\upsilon}$, in *TDNT* V, p. 700.

kingdom of David is presented as the fulfillment of the divine promise in the gift of the land, which in the Old Testament is the most important theme. David is the "blessed" of God and "wherever he went, God gave him victory" (2 Sam 8:14). Above all, we note that the victories of David are crowned with the taking of Jerusalem, which will be called the City of David, and so David and the House of Israel form a single people around their God. All this has, through Christ, a new sense and a deeper meaning, which nevertheless does not separate itself nor oppose itself to the salvation history of Israel.[20]

From this point of view Christianity presents itself as a development and explication of Judaism, within which it remains. Effectively, an incipient Christology could well conceive Christ as a son of Israel, who has remained within Judaism, showing its true nature, without necessarily constructing something different. Even if Jesus has shown a certain liberty as regards the prescriptions of the ancients in the matter of keeping the law, he has nevertheless remained within the channel of practicing Judaism: like every pious Jew of his time, he regularly participated in the temple cult, the pilgrimages at the festivals and in the synagogue cult of the Sabbath. "In this his reforming will is found to be in precise continuity with the prophetic tradition."[21] The temple is the house of his Father; here he teaches, and the possibility of its destruction brings tears to his eyes.[22] The same may be said for the weeping over Jerusalem because of its rejection of his invitation to gather together its children (Lk 13:34).

In an incipient Christology it is logical to have the "blessing" of God for the kingdom of David of which Jesus has shown us the fulfillment. Revealed in this way by Jesus, the kingdom of David is an object of blessing as a historical reality, which has retained its saving power even in the new economy.[23]

The Council of Jerusalem[24] is intended to be a reply to the problem posed by the "Judaizers" in Acts 15:1: "If you do not become circumcised according to the Law of Moses, you will not

---

[20] R. Motte, "David", in *Vocabulaire de théologie biblique* (Paris, 1962) p. 191.

[21] P. Grelot, "Liturgie", in M. Viller, F. Cavallera & J. de Guibert (eds.) *Dictionnaire de spiritualité, ascetique et mystique, doctrine et histoire*, (Paris: Beauchesne, 1976) vol. 9, col. 877.

[22] *Ibid.*

[23] Properly speaking, there is only one economy; therefore, our benediction would become a unique oddity because the controversy with the Judaizers forced the Church to separate from Judaism, constituted as if in a "new" distinct economy, even if not opposed to the kingdom of David.

[24] We say *Council of Jerusalem* leaving open the problem of the relation between the apostolic decree and the epistle. For a discussion of this, cf. J. Dupont, *Etudes sur les Actes des Apôtres* [Paris: Editions du Cerf, 1967 (Lectio Divina 45)] pp. 56-75).

be saved". It became necessary to discuss the question of soteriology which required the clarification of the relationship between the Torah and faith in Jesus.

The reply of the apostles is that in order to be Christian it is not necessary to become a Jew. However, some Jewish observances are enforced to avoid unnecessary motives for conflict between Jewish-Christians and Hellenic Christians. The decree is the fruit of a proposal by James. It is natural, therefore, that it represents the needs of the Jewish-Christians;[25] nevertheless, the affirmation of Peter is not contested: "We believe that it is by the grace of the Lord Jesus that we are saved, and in the same way them also." (Acts 15:11)

The *T.O.B.* comments that Peter is favourable towards an integral *status quo*: the Jew must continue to accept the Law, but the gentile is not bound by it.[26] Furthermore, the soteriological affirmation of Peter is very clear and precise and must have been an already existing formula, given that freedom from the Law—its natural consequence—was part of a missionary practice already applied in Antioch and approved by Jerusalem (Acts 11:22-24).

In Luke's intentions, this text has considerable importance, given the fact that he repeats it three times like the other stories he considers important for the development of the divine plan.[27] Besides this, we see that Paul proclaims the decree even outside of the geographical confines indicated in the letter of Jerusalem: Antioch, Syria, Cilicia. This shows that Luke intends to provide an exemplary model for the encounter of diverse groups on the clear basis of concessions made by Hellenic Christians towards any relevant norms for the Jewish Christians.

The decision made at Jerusalem was not purely a question of discipline or ecclesial politics; already the Christological consciousness of the Church has matured and has applied to Jesus the title of "Lord", making him the principle of salvation for Jews as for others. It follows that faith in Christ is what saves, not the law of Moses which we could call the kingdom of David.

We do not believe that the conception of Did 9:2 is compatible with the theology represented by the Council of Jerusalem and, therefore, we propose the Council of Jerusalem as the latest date for the two eucharistic texts of the *Didache*.[28]

---

[25] C. M. Martini, "Il decreto del concilio di Gerusalemme", in *Fondamenti biblici della teologia morale* (Brescia, 1973) p. 349.

[26] *Traduction Oecuménique de la Bible: Le Nouveau Testament* (Paris: Les Éditions du Cerf, 1973) *ad loc.*

[27] C. M. Martini, "Il decreto", p. 350.

[28] The decision of the Council of Jerusalem intervenes to resolve the problem existing between Jewish-Christians and Hellenistic Christians, who were still a united community of believers: and it was because of this unity that the problem and the polemic emerged. We cannot think that Did 9-10 could have been composed

Using the method of dating that J-P. Audet proposes in
respect of Did 10:6, it would seem that the theology underlying
Did 9:2 could not have been conceived after the Council of
Jerusalem, which critics place in 48[29] or 49[30] C.E., with margin
of error on either side.

In the text of chapters 9 and 10, the same date should be
given to the verses which share the same theology as 9:2: without
a doubt that applies to the verses which end with "through Jesus
your servant". For other verses, such as 10:5, there are no particular reasons to attribute them to a different editorial strata, whilst
for 9:4 and 9:5 there appear to be sufficient elements to exclude
them from the date when Did 9:2 was edited. But it is worth
returning to this with an appropriate study.

2) The theology of the *Vine of David* shows a close relationship
between Judaism and Christianity which perhaps may help to
obtain a more accurate chronology.

Putting the holy *Vine of David* as object of the anamnesis of
the "benediction", we have a substantial unity of faith between
Judaism and Christianity. If we examine the praxis shown in the
NT and look for an analogous situation to the *unity of faith*
expressed in Did 9:2, we can find something in the summary of
the Acts: "Day after day, with one heart, they faithfully visited the
temple and broke bread in their homes." (2:46).

Here one is describing the custom of the primitive Christian
community; next to the "breaking of the bread" is placed frequent
visitation of the temple,[31] which indicates full participation of the

---

by Jewish Christian dissidents after the Council of Jerusalem given that, in such a
case, our text would have to show traces of an emphasis and of an insistence on the
Torah as a basis for salvation, whereas Did 9-10 has the Jewish material as calm
and everyday occupation, with elements indeed visible of its having been superseded (10:3). The later insertion into the text of the Didache (to turn strongly
polemic against Judaism), makes one think that the two eucharistic prayers must
have continued to be considered not philo-Judaic but an expression of a use of traditional signs of an *archaic* soteriology. This means that they were seen to be—in
spite of their decidely Jewish flavour—in harmony with the new attitude that the
Church has assumed with respect to the Torah. This would not have been possible
if their origin lay in a late Jewish-Christian reversion.

[29] G. Bornkamm, *Paul*, trns. D. M. G. Stalker (London: Hodder & Stoughton,
1971) p. 31.

[30] L. Cerfaux (ed.), Introduction to *La Bible de Jérusalem. Les Actes des
Apôtres* (Paris: Les Éditions du Cerf, 1958²) p. 26.

[31] It is worth the trouble to record that the vine forms part of a widely diffused
symbol in Jewish decorative art, on the evidence of the mural paintings. In the
temple of Herod, before the destruction of 70, there was a grand vine of heavy gold
above the entrance. In the description of Flavius Josephus the bunches of grapes
were as big as a man and, according to the Mishnah, it took three hundred priests to
carry them. Rordorf rules out the possibility that this deals with a pious fraud. In

Christian community in the cultural life of the Jewish community. The first faithful did not consider themselves dissidents, but Israelites in the full sense of the word, what is more the true Israel to whom had been entrusted the duty to be the leaven in the midst of the people.[32] Certainly, forced by persecution and the aftermath of the case of Stephen, the temple was slowly abandoned,[33] at least as a systematic cultic practice.

In conclusion then, we would say that in the summaries of the Acts, we find a way of life which would justify in Did 9:2 the custom of giving thanks for the holy vine of David. The parallelism is quite suggestive.

On the historical value of the summaries, P. Rasco concludes, "The summaries..., even taking into account their limits, are of great importance in order to know the early conditions of the Christian life. Luke has not only conserved in them the primitive and ideal image of the community, but has also proposed an example."[34]

Concluding our consideration of the problem of the date of composition of Did 9-10, we would say that we are dealing with texts seemingly earlier than the Council of Jerusalem, dated 48/49 C.E. These texts describe a type of faith in the primitive community which find a parallel in the summary of Acts 2:46; therefore, the ideal epoch for the life of a community which expresses itself in terms of the theology of Did 9-10, would be in the first three or four years after the death and resurrection of Christ.

II. THE EUCHARISTIC NATURE OF DIDACHE 9-10

1) The Problem

On the meaning of the eucharist of *Didache* 9-10, there have been many interpretations, none of which are outstanding. It is a matter of determining whether the liturgy described in these two texts represents the celebration of the eucharistic sacrifice or not. In the case of the latter one is dealing with an explanation of the sense of this particular eucharist.

Another element to determine is the relationship with Did 14, where the Sunday eucharistic celebration is described. There are no such doubts about the sacramental significance of chapter 14.

Judaism the picture of the vine expresses all the messianic expectation of the people of Israel. See the documentation in W. Rordorf, "La vigne et le vin", p. 136.

[32] Cf. Acts 3:12ff, which shows Peter in the temple while he preached Christ.

[33] E. Rasco, *Actus Apostolorum*, II (lecture notes) (Rome, 1968) p. 314.

[34] *Ibid.*, pp. 327ff.

The arguments of those who deny the sacramentality of Did 9-10 are mostly treatments of the contents of the two eucharistic texts, whilst the arguments of those who affirm the sacramentality are mostly taken either from the use that the later tradition has made of our two texts, putting them together with the anaphora, or from the relationship that they have with the first eight chapters of the *Didache* dealing with the Christian initiation, which cannot but develop into the eucharist. The different nature of the arguments and the diverse method used, sufficiently explain the impossibility of an agreement in the argument.

As a result of these diverse criteria for evaluation, P. Ligier could say that about 30 years ago the commentators hesitated between "agape" and "eucharist proper" and were divided more or less in equal parts between the two interpretations. In the last 30 years, however, it is generally agreed ...that one is dealing with a eucharist proper."[35]

Professor Rordorf is of the opposite opinion. Announcing his own intention to show that one is not dealing with a eucharist proper, he concludes: "This is indeed the most common view today."[36]

The opinion of Rordorf presents Did 10 as the equivalent of the preface to the Roman mass, the introduction to the eucharistic liturgy proper.[37] One is dealing with a sophisticated variation of the opinion of Audet who speaks of a *minor eucharist* (distinct from the *agape*) and a *major eucharist*. Here we have an ingenious interpretation which, however, presents us with serious questions. What is the minor eucharist, other than an interesting expression. One is not dealing with the ritual meal of Judaism, given that the texts of the *Didache* are decidedly Christian, so we have to think of a ritual meal not Christocentric enough to represent obedience to the injunction of Christ ("Do this in memory of me..."). Then the question is: what is meant by "sufficiently Christocentric"? We must not forget that we are at the beginnings of the Christian community and that the Christology of our texts is a nascent Christology which is beginning to form itself around the title παῖς of God.[38] This is an archaic title which will quickly be abandoned in subsequent developments, but we cannot speak of "insufficiency" judging the past in the name of what follows it.

---

[35] L. Ligier, *Il Sacramento dell'Eucarestia* (from the manuscript, Rome, 1971) p. 99.

[36] W. Rordorf, "The Didache", p. 6.

[37] *Ibid.*, pp. 13f.

[38] Hence the importance of the work of dating; on the basis of a more developed Christology, the text of the *Didache* is indeed inadequate as a celebration of the mystery of Christ.

If παῖς represents the Christological reflection of the first moments of the Christian community, one cannot understand how it can be called insufficient to the "memory" of Christ articulated on παῖς. Even if we wanted to accept this liturgy as a *minor eucharist* (to which even Jews who were not Christians but only sympathizers would have access), we would have to ask ourselves in what way the *major eucharist* would be different from it, given that the Christology could not be different. The so called "major eucharist" would itself be "minor" also and so we would reach the conclusion that the first Christian community had a Christological understanding which did not yet allow them full obedience to the command of Christ, "Do this in memory of me."

With appropriate adaptations these observations are valid also for the positions of Rordorf. In fact, if Did 10 is like a Preface, in what would the eucharistic celebration consist? And what would follow on from this preface? Certainly the liturgy of chapter 14, which defines itself as "sacrifice" three times in three verses; but how would this be conducted and with what *eucologia* would it have consisted? If we are at the beginning of the development of Christological reflection it is legitimate to think that reflection on the sacraments would be in the same situation.

This is what we would like to suggest.

2) Agape

The authors who, for various reasons, could not recognize in chapters 9 and 10 of the *Didache* a true eucharist, explained this liturgy as an *agape*. The dilemma has always been: "eucharist or agape?"

In order to explain what an *agape* was, they fell back on Tertullian[39] and on the *Apostolic Tradition* of Hippolytus.[40] In these texts the eucharist is absolutely distinct from *agape* and between the two there could be no confusion of any kind. A. Hamman has made an exhaustive study on the *agape*, to which we go back. He inserts into the outline already presented by Vööbus and Audet,[41] an outline that interprets the *agape* as an institution born in a pagan land sharply distinct from the eucharist, which-- despite the analogies--was never identified with the *fractio panis* of Jewish origins. It is distinguished by its profound inspiration and the different religious sense given to the meal. Hamman

---

[39] *Apology* 39 (CC 8, pp. 152f).

[40] B. Botte, *La tradition apostolique de Saint Hippolyte, Essai de reconstruction* (Munster: Aschendorfsche Verlagsbuchhandlung, 1963) pp. 67ff.

[41] *La Didachè*, p. 406; A. Vööbus, *Liturgical traditions in the Didache* (Stockholm: Estonian Theological Society in Exile, 1968) pp. 69-70.

argues also from the use of terminology: the expression *fractio panis* was never used by the authors who come from paganism to define the *agape*, and *vice versa*, the ritual meal was never called *agape*. Unfortunately, Hamman reads the praxis of the primitive church in the same way as Audet and speaks of a ritual meal which *introduces* the eucharist[42] of the first Christian community.

After the church began to spread and develop in pagan lands, this ritual meal ceased to be that and was transformed into a love-meal, which took the name of *agape*. Between the two there is a strict continuity, but one cannot speak of identity. Ritual meal and eucharist are polarized around the invisible Christ, the expected guest at the table, and not around the fellowship which must bind the disciples with each other, the constitutive element of *agape*. For this reason one should ban the word *agape* when one is speaking of the ritual meal; over and above any other consideration, we should eliminate every ambiguity and not project a later institution into an earlier ritual belonging to a diverse cultural area.

To sum up: the *agape* has its roots in the eucharist, but was only able to emerge when the latter separated from the ritual meal of Judaism in which it was set and with which it formed one united body. After the eucharist diverged from it and became independent of the liturgy of the meal, the latter continued to exist in a different form, the *agape*,[43] which conserved from the primitive eucharistic liturgy the character of a meal and the social and religious significance of *koinonia*. The ritual meal did not survive but lost its proper original Jewish component throughout the church. In fact it was too tied to the historical experience of Israel and to its own particular cultural area to survive being transplanted into the world of the gentiles without undergoing profound transformations.[44]

On the basis of these elements--however summary--it does not seem correct to impose on the problem of Did 9-10 the classical formula: "eucharist or agape?", precisely for methodological reasons.

Once we have rejected the liturgy of the *agape* and the word itself, we have to find meaning for the two eucharistic texts of the *Didache* within the world of Judaism. Ligier offers a good exam-

---

[42] According to Hamman, the eucharistia does not constitute a *corpo unico* with the ritual meal, almost interwoven or confused in essence: it would already be an autonomous reality in juxtaposition to the paschal ritual to which it is the introduction. Cf. A. Hamman, *Vie liturgique et vie sociale* (Paris: Les Éditions du Cerf, 1968) pp. 225-226; *Id.*, *La vie quotidienne des premiers chrétiens* (Paris: Hachette, 1971) pp. 202-207; *Id.*, "Liturgie, prière et famille dans les trois premiers siècles chrétiens", *Questions Liturgiques* 57 (1976) pp. 87f.

[43] A. Hamman, "Liturgie, prière et famille", p. 87.

[44] J.-P. Audet, *Didachè*, p. 406.

ple of the application of this method of systematic research into the Jewish sources, even if we have had to point out a terminological *lapsus* in the use he makes of the word *agape*.[45]

3) The Jewish Ritual Meal

This reality can only be understood from the perspective of the biblical concept of *dabar*.

"For the Palestinian *Elohim*, gesture and word are the same act. It is *dabar*. His word raises something into being from nothing".[46] The analogy with the human word underlies this concept; with a word someone enters into your life: here is the first given of our experience of the human word. The word is action, interpersonal action. The ritual meal of Judaism is woven together with words: man blesses God, retelling and celebrating his "great works" undertaken to redeem and build Israel, on the basis of whose accomplishment Israel lives. Israel rejoices in its existence and summarizes this reality in a formal way in the ritual meal, the enjoyment of which becomes "real symbolism" of the enjoyment of God's works. On this and because of this, man blesses God in the celebration of his "works" in the ritual meal. The word of "blessing" and telling of the works of God merges with the actual actions of the supper until it constitutes a single unity with it. The actions of the meal and the prayer of benediction, which is inserted into it, become a new *single reality*: celebration of the "blessings" of God. With the Jews, the meal has thus a religious and sacred character which escapes our secular mentality. The religious aspect of the meal, although in a global and confused manner, is intrinsic to the actual meal; and is intrinsic in *every* meal and does not depend on ritual or eucological elements.

On this basic religiosity the real ritual meal may be articulated and developed as a celebration of the "great works" of God and their enjoyment.

The sacrality of the ritual meal is intrinsic to the synthesis between the eucological elements and the food itself, without being able to attribute to any one moment that which one might call "consecrating power". The problem of the validity of the consecration is a problem which does not exist in the Jewish concept of the ritual meal.

The problem is legitimate in itself, but it cannot be posed in the case of the Jewish ritual meal in terms of a correct methodology. But the methodological correctness takes nothing away

---

[45] L. Ligier, "Origines", pp. 181-202.

[46] M. Jousse, *L'antropologie du geste*, vol. I (Paris: Gallimard, 1969) pp. 110, 126ff.

from the sacrality of the ritual meal; it only prevents us from projecting our own concept of the "sacred" into a reality which cannot hold it because of its different cultural and religious environment.[47] The sacred meal is sacred by virtue of its *anamnesis* of the *mirabilia Dei*. This is formally expressed in the *berakot* which accompany and articulate the development of the various ritual meals; these are not to be reckoned among the *mirabilia Dei*, almost a *new* intervention of God in history; on the other hand, they are not an *anamnesis* only as far as the past is concerned, but the actualization today of what tomorrow will be in the final *consummatio*. The basic meaning of the *berakah* is described for us by Rabbi Simeon, quoted by El Zohar: "The pious Jew who recites all the *berakot* prescribed by the liturgical tradition of Judaism, prepares in everything a dwelling for the *shekinah*."[48] In other words, God is present amongst us thanks to the *berakah*, and so His presence is the source of sanctification.

At the beginning of the meal we have the *qiddush* with the two blessings of the wine and of the bread, fruit of the earth, which is the first fundamental gift of God to his people. At the end of the meal, with the last chalice, one blesses God who sustains the universe, and gives the earth, food and the benefits of the covenant; the supplication for Jerusalem ends this benediction, the *berakot ha-mazon*, which is divided into three parts.

These are the elements underlying the ritual meal; depending on the occasion, the *berakot* may receive various developments or be enriched by a more complex ritual, as in the case of the Passover *seder*.

In the text and in the structure of the *berakot* and of the Jewish supper we do not find any allusion to the consecration of the food. There is no invocation to the power of God to bless the food and drink. The pious Jew does not say: "bless and consecrate this food" but rather: "blessed are you, Lord...who brought forth the fruit of the vine". It is a conception of "consecration" (if we wish to call it this) different from the Catholic and Byzantine one, but it is just as much a prospective consecration.

The Pauline text of 1 Tim 4:4f presents this clear Jewish conception of the sacredness of the meal:

> For everything created by God is good, and nothing is to be rejected if it is received with thanksgiving (μετὰ εὐχαριστία); for then it is consecrated (ἁγιάζεται γὰρ) by the word of God and prayer.

---

[47] In our modern perspective, *sacrality* would be concerned with not so much the action, as the "ojbect", in other words the food and drink; the *sacred* stands for what is consecrated.

[48] If Did 9-10 edited the Jewish ritual meal appertaining to the same cultural and religious milieu, it does not follow that this beginning still applies for the Didache.

The *berakah* expresses and actuates by recognition the relationship between the thing and God and, in it, also our relationship
with God. Now a relationship which is expressed in the structure
of the *berakah* cannot be anything but sanctifying.[49] If we
understand this point of view, we understand the implications of
the expression of Justin: εὐχαριστήθεις ἄρτος, "eucharistized
bread".[50]

For Paul, the sanctification comes from the word of God and
from the prayer,[51] which is carried by the *berakah*; the Pauline
text quoted above does not yet concern the celebration of the
Lord's Supper, but only the ritual of the meal meant as a
sanctification, and in this text Paul is a good witness to the Jewish
mentality with respect to the ritual implications of the *berakah*.[52]

4) The Account of the Institution of the Lord's Supper

If we ask ourselves what is missing from the *Didache* in order for
it to be accepted as a celebration of the eucharistic mystery, we
receive the obligatory response: it lacks the account of the institution.[53]

a) The Fact

The presence of the account of the institution in the anaphora is a
continuous and constant fact and cannot be in doubt. On the other
hand, there exist various exceptions to the rule: one is dealing
with very interesting texts which, as a general rule, are to be
noted for their archaic nature. E. Lanne concludes his examination
of the problem in this way: "Up until now, this problem has not
received any solution of an *apodictic* nature. Therefore we can

---

[49] R. J. Ledogar, *Acknowledgment. Praise-verbs in the early greek anapphora*
(Rome, 1968) pp. 129-130.

[50] 1Apol 65:5 (cf. 66:2).

[51] R. J. Ledogar, *Acknowledgment*, p. 130; L. Maldonado, *La plegaria
eucarística* (Madrid, 1967) pp. 80ff; R. J. Galvin, "Addai and Mari revisited: the
state of the question", *EphLiturg* 87 (1978) p. 410; P. M. Gy, "Eucharistie et
"ecclesia" dans le premier vocabulaire de la liturgie chrétienne", *La Maison-Dieu*
130 (1977) p. 23. An analogous point of view in G. Dix, *The Shape of the Liturgy*
(London: SPCK, 1964) pp. 274-275.

[52] So says R. Levi: "In accordance with Psalm 21:1, the earth and all that it contains belongs to God. But when (the products of the earth) are sanctified by a
benediction, the human being obtains the privilege of rejoicing, in accordance with
Psalm 115:6" (bBer 36a). Other elements in K. Hruby, "La notion de "berakah"
dans la tradition et son charactère anamnétique", *Questions Liturgiques* 52 (1971) p.
167; *Id.*, "Le geste de la fraction du pain ou les gestes eucharistiques dans la tradition juive", in *Gestes et paroles dans les diverses familes liturgiques: (Conférences
St.-Serge, XXIVᵉ Semaine d'Etudes Liturgiques)* (Rome, 1978) pp. 123-133.

[53] L. Ligier, *Magnae orationis eucharisticae seu anaphorae origo et significatio*
(in manuscript, Rome, 1964) p. 63.

propose this hypothesis, that, for the entire Orient, the account and the words of the Lord were not asked for *ad efficacitatem*, at least at the beginning."[54]

Amongst these anaphora, the most famous is the anaphora of *Addai and Mari*. Scholars have discussed at length whether its original form had the account of the institution or not, leaving the problem wide open.

After Macomber had published the text of the anaphora, attested by the manuscript *Mar Eshaᶜya (10/11 century)*, the discussion ended; there never was, in fact, an "original form" of the anaphora of *Addai and Mari* which was then transformed into the present form.

The anaphora of *Addai and Mari* has not undergone any degenerative process; it has always been as it is now, without the account of the institution. The problem of the presence or absence of the account of the institution is now moved from the anaphora of *Addai and Mari* to its origins—a text now lost—from which it would have received both the present form of our text[55] and the Maronite anaphora of St. Peter the Apostle (third), commonly called *Sharar*. This has the account of the institution; hence the problem whether the text-source, the "mother" anaphora, had it or did not have it. The discussion is too recent for certain results.[56]

Another interesting text is the anaphora of the *Testamentum Domini*,[57] which carries only the words on the bread from the account of the institution; for the chalice, it is limited to an affirmation of its sacred nature: *dedit in typum sanguinis qui effusus est pro nobis*.[58]

---

[54] E. Lanne, *De anaphoris orientalibus praelectiones* (in manuscript, Rome, 1966) p. 62. The italics are my own.

[55] D. Webb, "La liturgie nestorienne des apôtres Addai et Mari dans la tradition manuscrite", in B. Botte et (eds.), *Eucharisties d'Orient et d'Occident: Semaine liturgique de l'Institut Saint Serge* II (Paris: Les Éditions du Cerf, 1970) p. 44.

[56] W. F. Macomber, "The oldest known text of the anaphora of the apostles Addai and Mari", *OrChrP* 32 (1966) pp. 335-371; *Id.* "The Maronite and Chaldean Version of the Anaphora of the Apostles", *OrChrP* 37 (1971) pp. 55-84; *Id.*, "A Theory on the Origins of the Syrian, Maronite and Chaldean Rites", *OrChrP* 39 (1973) pp. 235-242; E. J. Cutrone, "The Anaphora of the Apostles", *ThSt* 34 (1973) pp. 624-642; J. M. Sanchez-Caro, "La anáphora de Addai y Mari y la anáfora maronita "sharar": intento de reconstrucción de la fuente primitiva commún", *ThSt* 43 (1977) pp. 41-69; B. D. Spinks, "The original form of the Anaphora of the Apostles: A Suggestion in the Light of Maronite Sharar", *EphLiturg* 91 (1977) pp. 146-161.

[57] A. Hänggi-I. Pahl, *Prex eucharistica* (Freiburg: Universitätsverlag Freiburg-Schweiz, 1968), p. 220.

[58] The matter is all the more surprising because the *Testamentum Domini* has the same source as the anaphora of Hippolytus which contains the account of the insitution complete in all its parts.

The sixth century anaphora contained in the *Codex Brit. Mus. Add. 14669* is probably without the account of institution.[59] Besides this, the texts of the account of institution which present it in forms which are lacking or unusual are also part of our problem. P. Raes catalogues these texts in five categories.[60]

b) The Significance
Over and above the historical problem, there is the fact that the church of Malabar celebrated its own eucharist with an anaphora which does not contain the account of the institution. After the Synod of Diamper, requested by the Portuguese, the account of the institution was introduced into the eucharistic celebration and located in the rite of the *fractio*; but the anaphora still is without the account. Theologically speaking, there is no church without the eucharist: how can one refuse the ecclesial character of the Malabarese community because of the absence of the "words of consecration" in their anaphora? Above all, we must consider the fact that the Jesuits did not modify the text of the anaphora, but were content to insert the "words of consecration" in the *fractio*.[61]

What is the sense and the true function of the account of the institution in terms of the rite of the anaphora? Only as a result of this can one speak of consecratory words.

The account of the institution is closely tied to the *anamnesis* through the *command* (*mandatus*) of Christ, "Do this in memory of me". It is the whole *block*, centred on the *command*, which will give an answer to our question as to the sense and function of the account of institution. With the *anamnesis* the Church undertakes a theological reflection on the action taking place in the celebration. The church proclaims to the Father that what is celebrated is no other than *obedience* to and *execution* of the *command* of Christ, "Do this in memory of me." In other words: what is being celebrated corresponds to what has been established and instituted by the Lord. With the *anamnesis*, the Church establishes a line of continuity between our celebration and what happened in the Upper Room (*cenaculum*) at the Last Supper. This is the fundamental point.

The "line of continuity" is deepened and made more explicit with the concrete narration of what happened in the Upper Room when the Lord said, "Do this in memory of me." Recounting the "Supper" that the Lord made as a *proclamation* (*annuncio*) of his

---

[59] R. H. Connolly, "Sixth-century Fragments of an East-Syrian Anaphora", *OrChr* n.s. 12-14 (1925) pp. 99-128.

[60] A. Raes, "Les paroles de la consécration dans les anaphores syriennes", *OrChrP* 3 (1937) pp. 485-504.

[61] H. Manders, "Sens et fonction du récit de l'institution", *Questions Liturgiques* 53 (1972) pp. 203-218.

coming death, the Church calls on what Jesus himself has done in order to justify and give meaning to our own present celebration.

If our celebration conforms to the Lord's Supper, it will be the *proclamation* of his death and resurrection. In this "conformity" lies the guarantee that the Church is acting truly in the memory of the Lord dead and risen. The entire celebration is a true memorial of the Lord only if it is, in fact, in conformity with what he did, and therefore what he instituted; the Church makes this conformity its theme, by telling of what he has instituted and by explicitly pronouncing its own obedience to his *command*.

From this standpoint we can conclude that every account of the institution, however mutilated and incomplete, is sufficient to qualify our celebration as in conformity with the *command* of Christ; this is because the telling explains the connection between the celebration of the Church and the *command* of Christ. If this is the sense of the account of the institution, we would say that its consecratory validity is in fact in the *connection* (*nexus*) under discussion. But one can also say something else: from this point of view there is the true eucharistic celebration each time that this *connection* is firmly guaranteed, independently of the way in which it is expressed. In this way the anaphora of *Addai and Mari* is no longer an *extra chorum* text, given that the connection with the Upper Room and the command of the Lord is guaranteed with clear evidence, not from the extended *account* of the institution, but from the clear mention of them: *Et nos...accepimus per successionem formam quae a te est*.[62] In this text which lacks the account of the institution, the mention of it expresses in an unequivocal way the relation that the celebration of the church has with what the Lord did in the Upper Room; a model of our *proclamation* of the death and resurrection of Christ.[63]

When this relation is evident and the intention to do what Christ has done and which he would like us to do is also clear, we have a true and sacramental eucharist.

In Conclusion: the (sacramental) validity of the eucharist in a text of the anaphora is measured by its teleological function, in other words by the meaning (*sensus*) of the account of the institution, not by its simple presence or absence. In the case of absence, its teleological function may be supplemented or guaranteed by other elements for reflection, inside each single text, that is, by each single eucharistic prayer.

---

[62] Anaphora of *Addai and Mari* (*pro anamnesi*); in W. F. Macomber, "Addai and Mari", pp. 367-369.

[63] Cf. also G. Dix, *Shape of the Liturgy*, p. 181.

3. The Case of the Didache

The case of the *Didache* is not addressed by the above argument which has been used to solve the problem of the anaphora of *Addai and Mari* and of other analogous texts. In fact, the *Didache* does not refer to the institution of Christ, either through the telling of it, or, at least at first glance, through a simple *reference* to it. Usually, in order to accredit a fully eucharistic reading of chapters 9 and 10 of the *Didache*, people refer to the eucharistic use made of these texts in later documents. As in the case of the anaphora of the seventh book of the *Apostolic Constitutions*,[64] which the manuscripts call *Gratiarum actio mystica*. This text is based directly on *Didache* 9-10, retaining its structure and amplifying its source to a considerable extent.[65] Obviously we do not have the account of the institution, but we do have a clearly expressed *reference* to it: *cum ipse nobis constituerit (diatassi) mortem illius annuntiare.*

Must we consider this text as a correct interpretation of the *Didache*? Is one dealing with a true explanation? Is one dealing with a true explanation of the eucharistic value of the *Didache* or with an addition that transforms the same *Didache* into a true eucharist? The *command (diatassi)* of Christ may be expressed in various ways: we can have only the mention of it, or can we also have its reinforcement through the introduction of various elements of the account of the institution, as, in this case, the *command*, or its content: "to proclaim his death". This last is the case of the *Gratiarum actio mystica*. With the process of "reinforcement" of the theme, the simple *reference* enriches it even to form the whole account of the institution, made up, usually, of a synthesis between the elements taken from the synoptics and from Paul.[66]

---

[64] *...Pro praetioso sanguine Jesu Christi effuso nostra causa et pro praetioso corpore cuius haec antitypa celebramus cum ipse nobis constituerit mortem illius annuntiare.* Cf. M. Metzger, "Les deux prières eucharistiques des Constitutions Apostoliques", *RSR* (1971) pp. 59ff.

[65] M. Metzger, "The Didascalia and the Constitutiones Apostolorum", in Rordorf et al (eds.), *The Eucharist of the Early Christians, op.cit.*, pp. 205-6.

[66] The account of the institution presented in the anaphora does not co-incide with any of the four redactions contained in the New Testament: it simply provides a free composition which embellishes the basic framework of the connection with elements drawn from the New Testament itself or creates *ex novo*.

It is possible that some texts, instead of drawing on the account of the Upper Room contained in the Synoptics or in Paul, have made use of the eucharistic words' of the Johannine theology. This is the case with the anaphora *Sharar* which links the command with the theme "Bread of Life": *"in commemoratione corporis tui et sanguinis tui quae offerimus tibi super altare tuum vivum et sanctum, quaemadmodum tu spes nostra docuisti nos per evangelium tuum sanctum et dixisti: "Ego sum panis vivus qui de coelo descendi" ut vitam habeant per me mortales".*

After this passage there follows immediately the account of the institution, of Pauline workmanship, introduced in a substantially identical way: *Facimus, Domine, memoriam passionis tuae sicut docuisti nos: nocte qua tradebaris...his est*

If we examine the pluriformity of the anaphoric texts, we see that the account of the institution is not born in them *ex abrupto*, but is the fruit of a progressive development of the *diatassi* of Christ.

We believe we can substantiate the hypothesis that the same developmental principle also governed the rise of the simple *reference* to the institution. In other words, in the eucharist of Did 9-10 we have (*de facto*) conformity with the *command* of Christ, even if this conformity is not formulated in an explicit *reference* to the institution he made. Therefore we believe the argument which is limited to documentation of the eucharistic use of these texts in the seventh book of the *Apostolic Constitutions* to be insufficient; it is, in fact, necessary to demonstrate that this text explains and formulates the conformity of Did 9-10 to the *command* of Christ. One can allow that the Church of earliest times was aware of the "conformity" of its own eucharist to the Lord's Supper, without feeling the need to explain or formulate this *conformity* by making direct *reference* to the institution. In fact, because it was so close in time to the religious customs and the protagonists, because the celebration of the Church was so close in time to the Lord's Supper itself, it felt no need to formulate its conformity. The celebration itself, with all its elements, spoke on its own of its conformity with the Lord's Supper, without needing to make the theme explicit.

This awareness would become formal and explicit only when the problem had actually been identified; as we know, that happened almost at once; it is the case in 1 Cor 11, in which Paul accuses the Corinthians that theirs is no longer the Lord's Supper. The problem is born. From now on people felt the need to refer to the Supper in an explicit and thematic way, so as to guarantee the value of their own eucharist.

The thing is even more evident for the non-Jewish communities which, in terms of time, mentality and religious custom, are the most distant from the celebration of Jesus. The more the Church distances itself from Judaism, and its concept of sacred meal, the more the theme of conformity becomes utilized and secures for itself an entire sector of the anaphoric text; the account of the institution thus becomes a rite within a rite.[67]

---

panis corpus meum illud quod pro vita vita mundi frangitur et datur...; accipite manducate ex hoc et erit vobis in vitam aeternam (*Anaphora Sancti Petri Apostoli (tertia)*, care and subject of study of J. M. Sauget, in *Anaphorae Syriacae*, vol. II, fasc. III [Rome, 1973] p. 301). In fact, it is a matter of parallel references to the institution. We believe that the origin of the account of the institution or of the mention of it could be the result of the prevailing influence of a prospective eucharist derived from John or from the Synoptic-Pauline line. The argument is certainly complex, but cannot, for this reason, be avoided *a priori*.

[67] L. Ligier, "Origines", pp. 196-198.

4. Didache 10:3: Account of the Institution of the Jewish Meal and the Christian "Innovation"

Professor Rordorf finds in Did 10:3 a transparent allusion to the type of eucharist which gives to the believer the pledge of eternal life.[68] He notes that the Jews praised God, king of the universe, for the food given to every creature and in particular to humankind. Did 10:3 is directly inspired by this theme: in the first part of the verse one commemorates the food given to all human beings and in the second part one commemorates the food given to Christians. For the latter, one is dealing with food and drink that have received a new characteristic revealed by Jesus and unknown to the Jews: they are "spiritual".

With reference to this verse, one can argue that $\pi\nu\epsilon\upsilon\mu\alpha\tau\iota\kappa\acute{o}\varsigma$ illuminates the parallel text of 1 Cor 10:14, following Feuillet[69] with respect to the parallel with the sapiental literature. From our point of view, we prefer to go another road linked to the problem of the institution.

In the Last Supper the Lord concluded his celebration with a command, "Do this in memory of me." He did not say, "Do anything[70] in memory of me," he said, "Do *this*." What is "this"?

a) Perhaps one was dealing with the Passover Meal, perhaps with another Jewish ritual at which he was guest and Lord, which is to say at the centre of the action.

The supper of Jesus spoke of him in every moment; it was a prophecy and a parabolic gesture of his imminent passion as a return to the Father. In it, rather, the whole parable of the life of Jesus given for humanity was developed. The self-revelation of Jesus reached its fullness as he offered to his disciples the events which were about to happen; in this way the disciples took part in those conclusive events which he was about to achieve and which he lived in anticipation through the prophetic gestures of the supper. For this reason, the supper, loaded with these structures, was *proclamation* of the death of the Lord. This content was objectively inside the supper, even if the events had not yet happened historically. It belongs to the logic of the parable that there is the possibility of containing in itself something which is superior to itself and irreducible in itself: something which has its actualization elsewhere.

---

[68] W. Rordorf, "The Didache", p. 10; *Id.*, *art.cit.* in *Eucharisties d'Orient et d'Occident* I, p. 76.

[69] A. Feuillet, *Le Christ sagesse de Dieu* (Paris: Librairie Lecoffre, 1966) pp. 87-111.

[70] The problem is conceived in this way by J. Pascher. Cf. J. Ratzinger, "Forma e contenuto della celebrazione eucaristica", *Communio* 6/35 (1977) 19.

b) Two elements had to guide the disciples in their obedience to the command of the Lord. The first concerns the celebration of the ritual meal typical of the Jewish world; the second concerned the new content of this meal: the anamnesis of the *mirabilia Dei* had to be carrier of a new fact, that is of the new *work* (*opera*) which Jesus had accomplished.

If the Lord's Supper had been a Passover Supper, as many authors claim,[71] it must be admitted that it has left very few traces of the Passover in the liturgical and anaphoric tradition which was born from it. Against the Passover interpretation there is the fact of the continual reiteration (or ability to be reiterated) of the Christian eucharist, compared with the annual performance of the Jewish Passover ritual.

c) Faced with the command, *"Do this"*, the disciples cannot have understood that they should do anything different to what they had celebrated and lived with Jesus. A *Jew* (Jesus) asks *Jews* (the disciples) to perform a *Jewish* ritual meal in his memory.

Consequently, the ritual meal of the Jews, with its structure and its typical *berakot*, must have continued to exist in the new-born Christian community. There would have been a new dimension, given that its *berakot* would develop into the "mystery of Christ", and this would be obedience to the command which the disciples received.

The *command*, "Do this", finds its obedience in the celebration of the sacred meal typical of Judaism; "in memory of me", in its turn, finds its obedience in the *berakot*: these—commemorations of the *magnalia Dei*—will be transformed by having a Christological dimension. These Christological valences will then be reflected from the primitive kerygma and will represent the initial stages of the Christology of the new born Church; the title παῖς will be obligatory.

d) If we examine Did 9-10, we will see that the criteria outlined above will have a consequence.

Did 9 is parallel to the *qiddush*, the opening rite of the Jewish supper, and Did 10 is parallel to the *birkat ha-mazon*, the giving of thanks at the end of the supper. But the two texts of the *Didache* are profoundly Christological: besides the Christo-centric clauses "through Jesus your παῖς", we see an interesting phenomenon. The *magnalia Dei* which are announced are not drawn so much from the Old Testament, as from the message and function of Jesus as will be evident later in the Gospel of John. Here we have the motive for the thanksgiving: faith, knowledge, life, immortality, eternal life and the presence of the Holy Name

---

[71] Cf. J. Jeremias, *The Eucharistic Words of Jesus* (London: SCM 1966) pp. 15-88.

in our hearts. God is called "our Father", "holy Father" and in the place of Jerusalem we have "your" Church. In the entire salvation economy, Jesus is the one through whom the Father "has been made known"; Jesus as prophet is another characteristic of the Fourth Gospel.[72]

Already we can conclude that chapters 9 and 10 of the *Didache* present us with a Christian liturgy which sufficiently fulfils the requirement of the Church's obedience to the *command* of the Lord.

e) The argument may be further strengthened by an examination and comparison of the two parts of Did 10:3. Here, strictly speaking,[73] we do not have the substitution of the Jewish theme of "praise for creation and for food" with the spiritual dimension given to it by the Christians. Instead we have both themes, and the second is developed form the first: it is a development in organic continuity with it:

Didache 10:3(a)	Didache 10:3(b)
To human beings	To us then
You have given ($\check{\varepsilon}\delta\omega\kappa\alpha\varsigma$)	you have given grace ($\dot{\varepsilon}\chi\alpha\rho\acute{\iota}\sigma\omega$)
food and drink	of spiritual food and drink
for their enjoyment so that they	And eternal life
might give you thanks	through your servant

Verse 3(a) is a typical feature of the Jewish meal and it is based on Dt 8:10: "You will eat and be satisfied ($\dot{\varepsilon}\mu\pi\lambda\eta\sigma\theta\acute{\eta}\sigma\eta$) and will bless ($\varepsilon\dot{\nu}\lambda\sigma\gamma\acute{\eta}\sigma\varepsilon\iota\varsigma$) the Lord your God for the good earth which he has given you ($\delta\acute{\varepsilon}\delta\omega\kappa\acute{\varepsilon}\ \sigma\varepsilon$)." This is the logic which governs the Jewish meal and which makes it a sacred meal. And this is the logic behind the discourse of Paul on the sacredness of the meal;[74] we can say that in Dt 8:10 we have the account of the institution of the Jewish ritual meal, which Did 10:3(a) explicitly commemorates through the connection: "so that they might give you thanks".

f) Through the two halves of this anamnesis, Christians share with the Jews the sacrality of the ritual meal which they see instituted in Dt 8:10, but the addition of Did 10:3(b) sets in motion a significant development as a result of which the Christian meal can no longer be reduced to its Jewish ancestor. The juxtaposition is exact: the receiver changes (human beings/us); the verb changes ($\check{\varepsilon}\delta\omega\kappa\alpha\varsigma/\dot{\varepsilon}\chi\alpha\rho\acute{\iota}\sigma\omega$); the gift changes (food and drink/spiritual food

---

[72] M. de Jonge, "Jesus as Prophet and King in the Fourth Gospel", *EThL* 49 (1973) pp. 160-177.

[73] Cf. the position of K. Hruby, "La "birkat ha-mazon"", p. 216.

[74] 1 Tim 4:4-5.

and drink); the goal changes: the purpose in the first thanksgiving (for their enjoyment so that they might give you thanks) is transformed by the mention of a new gift (eternal life); the modality of the gift changes: from the perspective of Dt 8:10, God gives food from the fertility of the earth, and for this one must also give thanks, whilst for the Christians the new gift is given through the παῖς of God.

It is no accident, therefore, that Did 9-10 lacks any reference to the "promised land": one is dealing with a precise separation from the tie that the Jew has with the land.[75] Although still remaining within the milieu of the Jewish ritual meal, the eucharist of the *Didache* is the bearer of a new revelatory content and gift (ἐχαρίσω) from Jesus the παῖς of God. We must affirm both the elements: the new content and the tight continuity of ritual with the Jewish religious meal[76] which, according to the rabbinic tradition, has been instituted by God himself.

g) Given this rabbinic tradition, we must conclude that the thematic and verbal closeness between Dt 8:10 and Did 10:3(a) makes us think of the latter as a kind of "*reference* to the institution" of the Jewish religious meal. However, it is a precise recollection of the "command" of God of which the entire ritual meal is a realization with its *berakot*. To this memory and mention of the *mandatum* of God is linked as counterweight, the theme peculiar to Christians, "To us then you have given grace of spiritual food and drink and eternal life through your servant."

What has been instituted in Deuteronomy continues to be celebrated, but with a new significance, the origin of which is in Jesus himself; this is precisely tied to the evocatory recall of the institution of Dt 8:10.

---

[75] The benediction for the promised land is replaced by the thanksgiving for the dwelling of the holy Name in us, and by the knowledge, faith and immortality revealed by Jesus.

[76] Did 10:1 begins with "after you are satisfied with food", where ἐμπλησθῆναι directly recalls—almost as a technical term—the expression of Dt 8:10: καὶ φαγῇ καὶ ἐμπλησθήσῃ. Some authorities argue from this verb for a negative "sacramental" valuation of the *Didache*, given that ἐμπίπλημι signifies properly the material repletion of a meal and ill fits the spiritual significance proper to the eucharistic food. The motivation is correct: proof of it is that *Const* VII.26 replaces this term with μετάληψις. The conclusion is incorrect, given that, according to our hypothesis, this eucharist co-incides with the ritual structure of the meal; this, pure eucharistic essence (spiritual food and drink), is also a true and appropriate meal and hence conserves the consequent "satisfaction": if this were not so, it would not be based on Dt 8:10, and hence would not be a ritual meal either. In the Jewish meal the *birkat ha-mazon* was said after people had eaten and become satisfied; if the text of Did 10 is parallel to the *birkat ha-mazon*, it would not be surprising that it would come to be proclaimed at that very moment, namely after the meal was completed. Hence *empiplemi* indicates the moment in the meal and not the eucharistic communion.

In fact, Jesus has not come to abolish it but to bring it to fruition and in the Last Supper he has left a command, expressed in
the words, "Do this", which does not introduce his disciples to a
new meal characterized by a new ritual different to the logic of the
Jewish religious meal (or even of the Passover Meal).

The innovation is in the new content which he has prescribed
for his disciples: the anamnesis of this ritual action must have
been Christological. Therefore it is the Christological element
which constitutes what is new in what Christ instituted, not the
ritual meal, which, in itself, already existed in Israel, indeed was
directly instituted by God in Deuteronomy.

h) As we can see, we find in Did 10:3 the same relationship
with Judaism already evident in Did 9:2, dealing with the life of
David: Judaism retains all its validity but finds its fullness only in
Jesus who brings to fruition the ancient promise. In this primitive
stage of the life of the Church nothing is un-Jewish, not even the
eucharist, and neither is its institutor, Jesus.

Therefore, given the particular relationship between
Christianity and Judaism in the *Didache*, we can conclude that Did
10:3, in its two moments a) and b), represents a sufficiently evident tie with the institution command of Christ.

i) The account of the institution of the eucharist as it has been
handed down to us by the New Testament, will become a necessary element in the anaphora only when it changes its relationship
with Judaism, so that it is no longer possible to see Dt 8:10 as the
ultimate foundation of the logic of the Jewish sacred meal, matrix
of the Christian eucharist. Consequently, we cannot search in the
Didache for our account of the institution or even the simple
reference to it in another religious and cultural environment. The
Didache, in fact, already contains "its own" reference to the
institution, although in a particular form all its own, which it owes
to that relationship—also all its own—with Judaism, which the
Church had in the first years of its existence.

In this way, we believe our argument for the full
sacramentality of the eucharistic liturgy of Did 9-10 to be well
grounded; in fact it is contained in the peculiar mention of the
institution which replaces the institutive fact of the Jewish meal
(Dt 8:10) with the event of Christ: "but to us you have given the
gift of spiritual food and drink and eternal life *through your servant.*"

The Christ event is a development growing organically out of
the reference to Dt 8:10 and therefore, as such, participates in the
logic of the "institution".

MINISTERS IN THE DIDACHE

† ANDRÉ DE HALLEUX
Louvain-la-Neuve

In 1884, less than a year after the *editio princeps* of the *Didache*, Harnack thought he had discovered in this testimony the missing link between 1 Corinthians and the Pastorals in the evolution of the spiritual and ecumenical ministries of the Word towards the local monarchical episcopate. It thus provided an unexpected confirmation of the current consensus among historians of primitive Christianity about the theory elaborated by Lightfoot and Hatch to explain the birth of the "Catholic" institutional system. More recently, the theses of Käsemann, Bornkamm and their disciples on prophetic ministry in the New Testament have brought to the fore the opposition of the charismatic and the hierarchical, and the ecclesiology of H. Küng has contributed to it.

But what of the interpretation of the *Didache*? This "spoiled child of criticism", which Harnack imprudently announced would finally make all things clear, has itself long ago been transformed into such an irritating "enigma" that few researchers flatter themselves any more that they can elucidate it. On the question of ministries, however, the critiques which could have been addressed from Hort to Audet, to the advocates of the received opinion, do not appear to have shaken the assurance of those who continue to seek in this "first Christian catechism" a master key to the initial developments. Let us read, for example, the pages dedicated to the subject in the remarkable introduction to the recent *Sources chrétiennes* edition.[1]

We are led to believe that the apostles, prophets and teachers in the *Didache* represent the itinerant and charismatic ministries which essentially formed the hierarchy of the first Christian assemblies, according to the tradition of Antioch and western Syria, in the first century of our era.[2] Chapters 11-13 do not know of the existence of a ministerial hierarchy properly speaking, that is to say, of fixed ministers in the local church.[3] The election of bishops and deacons does not occur until ch. 15, which is a later addition to the disciplinary part of the *Didache*.[4] The innovation of local ministers, who needed to be substituted because of the decline in the quality and numbers of itinerant ministers, did not

---

[1] W. Rordorf & A. Tuilier, *La Doctrine des Douze Apôtres* (Paris: Les Éditions du Cerf, 1978 [SC 248]).
[2] *Ibid.*, pp. 57, 60, 62.
[3] *Ibid.*, pp. 63-64.
[4] *Ibid.*, pp. 49-64.

happen without a struggle, but still needed to be done quickly.[5] Therefore he also dates ch. 15 early, especially as it does not yet mention the monarchical episcopate, but comes from the same geographical milieu as the authentic letters of Ignatius of Antioch.[6]

Setting aside the date, place of origin and dual authorship, this essentially repeats the theory of Harnack on the evolution of ministers in the *Didache*. The exegesis has become so natural that it is no longer distinguished from the text itself, onto which it was imposed on the basis of other presuppositions. Would it be possible to dispel the misunderstanding by a demystificatory reading? Let us force ourselves to go back to the passages of the disciplinary section where ministries are spoken of (10:7-15:2), without the distorting spectacles of received opinion. When we allow the texts to speak for themselves, excluding all other extraneous data, the historical picture no doubt loses its neatness, but the critical foundations of the evidence perhaps gain in solidity.

However, two other methodological options suggest themselves at the outset. First: can one trust the text of the sole manuscript of the *Didache*, duly restoring the evident lapses of the copyist? It is true that the value of this witness of the eleventh century has been diversely appreciated. For if some consider it as an authority superior to the great biblical uncials of the fourth and fifth centuries,[7] or at least as a very good popular edition, unpretentious but careless,[8] others do not wish to see here any more than a late recension, intentionally amplified, abridged or corrupted.[9] Yet even to take the worst case, the ancient versions of the *Didache* and the parallel *Duae viae* do not permit us to reconstitute the archetype of the former with a reasonable degree of assurance, and the sceptical philologist is reduced, in spite of himself, to the ingenuity of conjecture. It is better then to respect the only known text than imprudently to forge an amalgam which probably never existed in the tradition.[10] In any case, no major textual correction has been proposed for the section in hand.

It is true that the critical literature raises questions of a very serious complexity. The author of the *Didache* has undeniably also

---

[5] *Ibid.*, pp. 72-73.

[6] *Ibid.*, p. 78.

[7] *Ibid.*, pp. 104-107.

[8] J.-P. Audet, *La Didachè* (Paris: Gabalda, 1958) pp. 77-78.

[9] B. H. Streeter, "Origin and Date of the "Didache"", in *The Primitive Church: Studied with Special Reference to the Origins of the Christian Ministry* (London: Macmillan, 1930), pp. 281-3; E. Peterson, "Über einige Probleme der Didache-Überlieferung", in *Frühkirche, Judentum und Gnosis: Studien und Untersuchungen* (Rome: Herder, 1959) pp. 146-182, esp. 146, 181-2.

[10] S. Giet, *L'Énigme de la Didachè* (Paris: Ophrys, 1970 [PFLUS 149]) pp. 32-33.

used sources, not necessarily written ones. But, unlike the *Duae viae* of ch. 1-6, for which there are related witnesses, the analysis of 7-16 can only rest on internal criticism, that is to say on indices of style, which are rarely decisive, and on the criteria of content, where the preconceived idea that the interpreter has of the institutional development of primitive Christianity plays a key rôle. It is not surprising then that the dissections into redactional stages which have been proposed so far often appear very artificial.[11]

With the undeniable mark of robust health, the *Didache* has always resisted these successive and contradictory attempts to co-opt one or another of its sections. The author was certainly not the creator of the traditions that he reports; but interpretation cannot confer on those heterogeneous elements a higher significance than the Didachist conferred on them when he collected them. A respectful approach to the unity of the writing could then prove the more plausible by virtue of its economy. Recent editors have wisely refused to retain in the *Didache* any addition, revision or interpolation other than the work of the continuator that they believe they can discern in ch. 14-15.[12] However, the reading which is proposed here shows that this last concession to hyper-criticism is not necessary either: the whole of 11-15 can be read, without internal contradiction, as a product of the same historical situation.

****

10.7 As for the prophets, let them give thanks as much as they will.

This instruction follows immediately on from the famous thanksgiving prayers of 9-10, on whose nature there is very little agreement. But it does not matter whether they accompanied the agape, the eucharist, or both together: what we should explain here is the presence at the same time of the identity and of the distinction, suggested respectively by the use of the same verb (9:1; 10:1; 10:7) and by the particle δέ (10:7), between the thanksgiving of the prophet and that of the preceding prayers.

The prophets of the *Didache* are often considered as the presidents of the cultic assembly[13] and some find this confirmed in the name "high priests" which they are given in 13:3.[14] But this

---

[11] Audet, *Didachè*, pp. 104-115; Giet, *L'énigme*, pp. 234-236, 239-244, 260-263; G. Schille, "Das Recht der Propheten und Apostelgemeinderechtliche Beobachtungen zu Didache Kapitel 11-13" in P. Wätzel and G. Schille (eds.), *Theologische Versuche* I (Berlin: Evangelische Verlag-Anstalt, 1966) pp. 84-103.

[12] Rordorf & Tuilier, *La Doctrine*, pp. 49, 63-4, 72-8.

[13] *Ibid.*, p. 41 n. 2.

[14] Schille, "Das Recht", p. 93.

implies that the prayers of 9-10—taken as a whole, however much they may represent the reworkings of sources—represent the "part" of the assembly of the faithful. It is true that they are composed in the first person plural; but must one infer their collective recitation? What more natural, on the contrary, than that a delegate, a president, should have pronounced in the name of all!

One might object to this that the Didachist has not mentioned any minister for baptism (ch. 7) nor for the agape/eucharist (ch. 9-10); but this is an unacceptable argument from silence. In fact, the disciplinary directives of the *Didache* are addressed to the community as a whole, without distinction of laity and clergy; but they do not presuppose a disorganized assembly, since the instructions concerning the dominical synaxis allow one to see the bishops and the deacons as those responsible for its good order (chs. 14-15:2).

Why then should the prayers of chs. 9-10 not have been compiled for the use of the presidents of the agape/eucharist? From this point of view, one can easily see the contrast and the similarity between their thanksgiving, presented as fixed formularies, and that of the prophets who are allowed an unconstrained liberty. The right accorded to the prophets corresponds, indeed, to the spontaneity of unpredictable inspiration, whereas the preceding formularies are normally addressed to the ministers charged with assuring the regular unfolding of the cultic weekly meeting (ch.14-15:2). Nothing would have prevented a bishop having been a prophet as well, certainly; but the way in which these two functions are contrasted in ch.15:1-2 discourages us from thinking that such a case was common in the community of the Didachist. The latter then tried, so to speak, to prevent the "institution" from suppressing the "event", so as not to "quench the Spirit".

Nothing designates the prophets of 10:7 as itinerant ministers, passing guests rather than permanent members of the community. And their free thanksgiving can hardly be imagined to be ecstatic prayer. Indeed, if the prophetic act *par excellence* that constitutes the "eulogy", is given under the inspiration of the Spirit (cf. Lk 1:67-8), it is not that the πνεῦμα eclipses the νοῦς, for the *Amen* of the listeners implies that they were aware of the sense of the prayer (cf. 1 Cor 14:16). One can then think of a "eucharist" intelligibly pronounced by the prophet, fully conscious and in possession of himself, but with "inspiration", in the sense given to this word today to describe an orator or an authentic poet, and of which the first Christian hymns have left some traces (cf. Eph 5:19).

****

11.1 If then someone comes and teaches you all these things which have
been said, receive him. 2. But if he who teaches changes and teaches
another teaching to destroy, do not listen to him; but if it is to add to
righteousness and fear of the Lord, receive him as the Lord.

The author again wishes to speak about the prophets, if the "then"
of v.1 refers back to 10:7. This of course presupposes that the
prayer over the perfume, or myrrh, inserted at the corresponding
point of the Coptic version and the Apostolic Constitutions (7:27)
is not the original text,[15] but is a later addition to this.[16] In fact,
we shall soon discover (10:10) that besides his role in the
eucharistic prayer, the prophet exercised a teaching function as
well.

However that may be, nothing allows one to read here (11:1-
2) the specific designation "teacher",[17] which will appear only
later (13:2; 15:1-2), since the subject given for v.2, ὁ διδάσκων
only repeats the indeterminacy of v.1, ὃς ἂν ἐλθὼν διδάξῃ. The
words of the διδάσκειν family accumulated in these two verses go
back to the instruction of the *Duae viae* (2:1; 6:2), and they have
perhaps contributed to the inspiration of the title of the *Didache*.
Doubtless "the one who teaches", αὐτὸς ὁ διδάσκων (11:2), has
acquired a right to teach in the community, but this function could
very well belong to the persons who will be presented in what follows in ch.11. And this is already a rule of *dokimasia* which the
Didachist expresses here, of the same order as that which he will
establish for prophets: for how should one discern the intention
(εἰς) of the teaching, whether it is destructive or edifying (11:1-2),
other than by examining the "way of life" of the one who teaches
(11:8)?

The second part of v.2 should not be taken as a simple repetition of v.1. It is therefore striking that the author does not monopolize the *didache* to his profit, however confident he may be,
incidentally, of his rectitude (6:1), but, on the contrary, he orders
the community to receive the person who teaches something different as if he were the Lord, provided that this teaching has in
mind the building up of the Church. By whom should "the one
who teaches" be dispensed from the doctrine of the Didachist
(11:1), if not by spiritual authority? Nothing then prevents us from
seeing the persons in vv.1-2 as prophets, enjoying the same
privilege in their activity as teacher as they were accorded in
prayer (10:7). And the Didachist could well have intended to indicate, at the same time, that he himself should not be considered a

---

[15] Peterson, "Probleme", pp. 156-68.
[16] A. Adam, "Erwägungen zur Herkunft der Didache" *ZKG* 68 (1957) pp. 1-47,
esp. 8-11.
[17] Rordorf & Tuilier, *La Doctrine*, pp. 54, 183.

charismatic; the use of the verb στρέφειν (11:2), which serves him elsewhere to refer to false eschatological prophets (16:3), then shows the extent of the respect with which he circumscribes the freedom of the authentic prophet.

The teaching prophets in view here are presented as coming from outside (ἐλθών 11:1), but nothing allows us to consider them as itinerant ministers, like the apostles or ordinary guests (ἐρχόμενος 11:3; 12:1). The necessity of discernment normally concerns strangers, not members of the community known to all. Unless, however, the latter changes his teaching, as is envisaged by v.2, which seems then to imply that the one who teaches has already been adopted by his church.

****

11.3 As regards the apostles and prophets, according to the precept of the gospel, act in this way: 4. let every apostle who comes to you be received as the Lord. 5. But he shall [only] stay one day and, if it is necessary, the following [day]; if he stays three [days], he is a false prophet. 6. When he leaves, let the apostle not receive anything except bread for the day's journey; if he asks for money, he is a false prophet.[18]

The way apostles are treated here shows that it is no longer a matter of the Twelve Apostles, as in the second title of the *Didache*, chosen by Jesus and envoys after his resurrection, but of itinerant ministers as the ones who are attested in the most ancient Christian literature,[19] and which have sometimes been considered as the ministerial model of the former,[20] sometimes on the contrary as their successors.[21] One could think, *mutatis mutandis*, of the preachers of the "popular mission" of yesterday, visiting the communities of those already converted. The author gives nothing concrete on the function of these missionaries, not so much because he no longer knew their apostolate[22] as because he knew that his public was warned and because his only concern was to unmask the false prophets.

The evangelical norm to which v.3 looks back recalls the mission discourse in Mt 10:9-14. But the "dry little code"[23] of the Didachist aims less to instruct the missionaries than to warn the

---

[18] Cf. Tuilier in Rordorf & Tuilier, *La doctrine*, p. 185.

[19] *Ibid.*, pp. 58-9.

[20] G. Saß, "Die Apostel in der Didache" in W. Schmauch, *In memoriam Ernst Lohmeyer* (Stuttgart: Evangelisches Verlagswerk, 1951) pp. 233-239.

[21] R.A. Kraft, "Vom Ende der urchristlichen Prophetie" in J. Panagopoulos (ed.), *Prophetic Vocation in the New Testament and Today* (Leiden: Brill [*NT.E* 45]) pp. 162-185, esp. 172.

[22] Streeter, *The Primitive Church*, p. 147; Schille, "Das Recht", pp. 85, 88.

[23] "Petit code assez sec", Hemmer, p. liv.

communities. The principle of a favourable disposition towards apostles certainly continues to hold for him, since they must be given the assistance due to those who come in the name of the Lord (11:4; 12:2). Having said this, the two criteria of parasitism and self-interest distinguish the charlatan: to stay longer than two days contravenes the rules of hospitality (11:5; 12:2-3); to ask for money would be contrary to the evangelical precept (11:6; cf. Mt 10:9-10). These two rules presuppose a certain degree of nomadism and poverty; but one should not twist their sense by interpreting them as an ascetic life[24] or as asocial vagabondage.[25]

Could the haziness which has shrouded the silhouette of the apostle in the *Didache* have arisen because it really only referred to the appearance of one ministry, because it only described one function exercized in many ways?[26] Among other indications which lead one to think so, one notes first that the order to receive him as the Lord, applied to the apostle in v.4, takes up again the same things that v.2 has said of "the one who teaches". The apostle, then, would here have a responsibility of teaching, but without any fixed attachment, as an itinerant teacher.

In the second place, it is striking that the apostle who abuses the hospitality or the generosity of a church is described twice not as a false apostle, but as a false prophet (11:5-6). The explanations that have been given for this anomaly[27] are not fully convincing; for, even if the words made up with ψευδο- had become interchangeable,[28] how can one prove that the term ψευδοπροφήτης has momentarily prevailed to the point of excluding the ψευδ-απόστολος attested by 2 Corinthians 11:13 (cf. Rev 2:2) and by the Fathers of the second century like Justin and Hegesippus?

It is important, finally, to notice in v.3 the absence of the repetition of the article in the clause περὶ δὲ τῶν ἀποστόλων καὶ προφητῶν. If this fact is often hidden by the translation "the prophets and the apostles",[29] it is perhaps because of the unconscious influence of the prejudice in favour of the ministerial trilogy of apostles, prophets and teachers. To suppose that the for-

---

[24] G. Kretschmar, "Ein Beitrag zur Frage nach dem Ursprung frühchristlicher Askese", *ZThK* 61 (1964) pp. 27-67, esp. 36-7.

[25] G. Theissen, "Wanderradikalismus. Literatursoziologische Aspekte der Überlieferung von Worten Jesus im Urchristentum", *ZThK* 70 (1973) pp. 245-271, esp. 252-3.

[26] Streeter, *The Primitive Church*, pp. 146-7; G. Dix, "The Ministry in the Early Church c. A.D. 90-410", in K. E. Kirk (ed.), *The Apostolic Ministry, Essays on the History and the Doctrine of the Episcopacy* (London: Hodder & Stoughton, 1946) pp. 240-1.

[27] Rordorf & Tuilier, *La Doctrine*, p. 52.

[28] J. Reiling, *Hermas and Christian Prophecy. A Study of the Eleventh Mandate* (Leiden: Brill, 1973 [NovTest.S 37]) pp. 60-61.

[29] Rordorf & Tuilier, *La Doctrine*, p. 185.

mula of the Didachist is inspired by Ephesians 2:20[30] is a gratu-
itous hypothesis and cannot settle anything, since Ephesians itself
can oscillate between distinct characters (4:11) and functions
united in the same person (3:5). That the latter case is exactly that
of the *Didache* in ch. 11:3 as well as in 15:1-2, is confirmed by
the fact that the author repeats the article where he designates two
clearly distinct persons (7:4; 11:8), whereas when he does not
repeat it the things he describes are contained in a hendiadys,
however different they remain in themselves (9:3; 10:2). One
must then doubtless understand the καί of 11:3 in the explicative
sense and not the additive sense: "On the subject of the apostles
who are also prophets", that is to say on the subject of the
prophets of the apostolic genre.

So then the Didachist only seems to be interested in the missionary itinerants insofar as their function bore in a certain way on
"inspired" teaching, able to build up but also to "destroy" the
community. After all, the remainder of ch 11 and 13 deals exclusively with prophets, beginning immediately (11:7) without any of
the particles which would normally suggest a change of subject, if
there had been one, as one would be led to think by the *"par ail-
leurs"* of the translation of Tuilier.[31]

****

11:7 And you shall not tempt or discern any prophet who speaks in a
spirit. For every sin will be forgiven, but this sin will not be. 8. Whoever
speaks in a spirit is not a prophet, unless he has the way of life of the
Lord. So one recognizes the false prophet and the prophet by their way of
life. 9. Every prophet who orders a table in a spirit shall abstain from
eating from it, or else he is a false prophet. 10. And every prophet who
teaches the truth, without doing what he teaches, is a false prophet. 11.
But every prophet proven, true, who acts with a view to the mystery of
the Church in the world, but who does not teach anyone to do everything
which he does himself, shall not be judged by you; for it is with God that
he has [his] judgment. For it is so that the prophets of old acted. 12. But
whoever says to you in a spirit: Give me money, or anything else, you
shall not listen to him; but if he tells you to give for others, who are in
need, let no-one judge him.[32]

This pericope contains many obscurities, which the most ingenious hypotheses have not sufficed to explain convincingly.
What is shown clearly by the whole passage, is the high esteem
the Didachist held for the prophet, an opinion all the more
unselfish as we have already seen (11:2) that he probably did not

---

[30] G. Schille, "Das Recht", p. 88.
[31] Rordorf & Tuilier, *La doctrine*, p. 185.
[32] Cf. Tuilier in Rordorf & Tuilier, *La doctrine*, pp. 185-187.

consider himself one. If it is again a matter of distinguishing the
true prophet from the false, it is done, it seems, with more
sympathy than in the case of the apostle (11:3-6). The author
appears concerned to save the prophetic "institution" by disentan-
gling it from its counterfeits, so that it would not be discredited by
its abuses.

Its general principle does not have the incoherence which it
has often been taken to show.[33] It seems to be the case that if the
community had to authenticate the prophet by means of his
behaviour (11:8), it had no right to inspect the doctrinal content of
his message (11:7). It is by the "way of life" that one discerns the
false prophet from the true, who is only authenticated as such if he
has the τρόπους κυρίου (11:8), that is to say if he "does" the truth
that he teaches (11:10). The parallelism in the sequence of ideas
of vv.7-8 and Mt 12:31-33 allows us, perhaps, to infer that the
Didachist knew the saying that the tree is judged by its fruit (cf.
Mt 7:15-16).

The examples of vv.9-12 concretize the ethic of the prophet
in the sense of the disinterest required of the "apostles" (11:5-6).
But this test, this *dokimasia* one could say (11:11; cf. 1 Thess
5:21), has nothing to do either with a "temptation", nor even with
the discernment of the prophet speaking in a spirit (11:7). One can
understand that once tested by his conduct, the authentically
spiritual prophet, was not under any other jurisdiction, except perhaps that of another spiritual person (cf. 1 Cor 2:15); far from
contradicting 1 Cor 14:29,[34] where οἱ ἄλλοι could incidentally
designate prophets,[35] the Didachist could then be functioning here
in a Pauline way. So great is his respect for the charism, that the
diakrisis of any true prophet is held to be unforgivable sin, that is
to say that it represents the sin against the Spirit (11:7; cf. Mt
12:31). The interpretation according to which the Didachist
simply wished to prevent one from interrupting an inspired
prophet[36] does not take proper account of such a solemn warning.

This respect for the Christian prophets is confirmed in v.11,
which sets them on the same footing as their Old Testament
predecessors. The sense of the expression ποιεῖν εἰς μυστήριον
κοσμικὸν ἐκκλησίας, related to Eph 5:32, has not ceased to
intrigue exegetes,[37] in which some have seen a symbolic action or

---

[33] *Ibid.*, pp. 87-8; Kraft, "Vom Ende", p. 181.

[34] I. Panagopoulos, Ἡ Ἐκκλησία τῶν προφητῶν. Τὸ προφητικὸν χάρισμα ἐν τῷ
Ἐκκλησίᾳ τῶν δύο πρώτων αἰώνων (Athens, 1979) p. 284.

[35] H. Greeven, "Propheten, Lehrer, Vorsteher bein Paulus. Zur Frage der
"Ämter" im Urchristentum", *ZNW* 44 (1952-1953) pp. 1-43, esp. 6.

[36] Rordorf & Tuilier, *La Doctrine*, p. 53 n. 3; cf. Greeven, "Propheten", pp.
13-14.

[37] Cf. Rordorf, *La Doctrine*, pp. 186-188 n. 5.

an acted-out apocalyptic drama, others have seen an ascetic and celibate life, anticipating the eschatological kingdom in this world, others on the contrary have seen spiritual syzygy of the prophet with a sister, recalling the celebrated case of Hosiah, of Moses and Rahab. What the text shows, in any event, is that not "doing" the truth which one teaches is the same as being a false prophet (11:10); the true prophet, morally tested, can be permitted a symbolic action which might be shocking for some reason, and this action cannot be judged by any human tribunal, as long as the prophet does not teach anyone to imitate it (11:11). In other words, since the mission of the true prophet places him outside the communal norms, he has the right to originality, even to a certain lawlessness, like his predecessors of the Old Testament, without being subject to anyone other than God.

Everything indicates that the Didachist roots the authority of the prophet in his "spiritual" being. But what is meant by speaking ἐν πνεύματι (11:7-12)? It is apparently not the Holy Spirit, warranted by the tradition, that he designates by this formula,[38] since he also affirms that the false prophet speaks in a spirit in the same way (11:8; 11:12), perhaps under the inspiration of demons who knew the future and the hidden things;[39] hence the caution of the translators, who write here "*esprit*" ("spirit") without a capital.[40] Does it then mean a state of unconsciousness and ecstatic agitation, midway between glossolalia and prophecy in the Pauline sense?[41] The examples of v.9-12 are certainly not very clear. However, if v.9 envisages the organization of a meal for the poor,[42] or even a eucharistic meal,[43] one cannot very well see the prophet acting, in this event, in somnambulance or ecstasy. Likewise, the enigmatic symbolic action of v.11, able to be taught and liable to judgment before the divine tribunal, is likely to cover a conscious and voluntary proceeding. Again, it would be hard to imagine the false prophet unconscious of all trickery when he asks for a gift of money ἐν πνεύματι (11:12). If one adds this case to that of the liturgical thanksgiving called for earlier (10:7), one envisages a particular authority, either explicitly claimed in the name of the spirit, or simply marked by the inspired tone of the discourse or by the assurance of the action.

---

[38] Panagopoulos, Ἐκκλησία, p. 284.
[39] Reiling, *Hermas*, p. 69.
[40] Rordorf & Tuilier, *La Doctrine*, pp. 185-9.
[41] A. von Harnack, *Die Lehre der zwölf Apostel nebst Untersuchungen zur ältesten Geschichte der Kirchenverfassung und des Kirchenrechts* (Leipzig: Hinrich's, 1884, pp. 122, 40-3.
[42] Rordorf & Tuilier, *La Doctrine*, p. 186 n. 3.
[43] Schille, "Das Recht", p. 93.

The prophet is not an ecstatic mystic; he has a message to communicate.[44] His functions, such as we can reconstruct them from the examples of 10:7 and 11:7-12, consisted of prayer, teaching and charity. All of this accords ill with an itinerant ministry; clearly the author was not thinking any more here of the "apostles" of 11:3-6, and if ch.12 repeats the law of Christian hospitality, the return to prophets in ch.13 explicitly presupposes them to be settled.

****

13.1 But every true prophet, who wishes to settle down among you, is worthy of his food. 2. ὡσαύτως διδάσκαλος ἀληθινός ἐστιν ἄξιος καὶ αὐτὸς ὥσπερ ὁ ἐργάτης τῆς τροφῆς αὐτοῦ. 3. You shall take, therefore, all the firstfruits of the produce of the winepress, of the threshingfloor, of cattle and of sheep, to give them as firstfruits to the prophets, for they indeed are your high-priests. 4. And if you do not have any prophet, give them to the poor. 5. If you make bread, take the first-fruits of it and give them according to the commandment. 6. In the same way, if you make a jar of wine or oil, take the first-fruits of it and give them to the prophets. 7. Of your money and of your clothing and of all your goods, take the first-fruits, as it seems good to you, and give them according to the commandment.[45]

Ch.12 presupposed that the ordinary visitor, who wished to settle in a community had to exercise his trade and in no way live in idleness. Here (13:1) it is stipulated, on the contrary, that every true prophet, that is to say every prophet tested by the way he lives (cf. 11:8; 11:11), deserves to be supported by the community in which he has decided to settle. It would be a false interpretation to see θέλων καθῆσθαι as inferring a nomadic prophetic ministry in the process of settling down. If the Didachist only mentions prophets who are strangers to the community, it is because the question of whether they should earn their keep was only posed in their case. The apostle-prophet of ch.11:3-6 was itinerant inasmuch as he was an apostle, and his character as a true prophet must again be submitted to the ethical test of the evangelical rule. Here the prophet is no longer a missionary, he is already assumed to have been tested, and the only thing which remains to be regulated by the community of his adoption is the way he should be treated.

But aside from the prophet, does the Didachist not present the teacher as a distinct ministry? This is how v.2 has been understood, "In the same way [as every true prophet] the true

---

[44] Reiling, *Hermas*, p. 18.
[45] Cf. Tuilier in Rordorf & Tuilier, *La doctrine*, p. 191.

teacher also deserves his food, like the workman".[46] This translation, the most obvious one, requires an interruption in the teaching
of ch.13, which is entirely devoted to the prophets; therefore some
critics, noting that the noun διδάσκαλος is only found here and in
ch.15:1-2, that is to say in a section which they regard as the
work of a continuator, are led to consider the verse in question as
an interpolation by the same hand.[47]

However, the unity of ch.13 can be saved by means of
another reading of v.2, which is only surprising at first sight, for
it is grammatically correct and offers a perfectly satisfying sense.
We understand the adverb ὡσαύτως as announcing not the addition of a parallel case (cf. 13:6), but the simple explication of
what precedes (cf. 11:11); we interpret the words διδάσκαλος
ἀληθινός, which occur without any specification and at the head
of the proposition, as an attribute and not as the subject; and we
relate καὶ αὐτός, taken as the subject of v.2, to the subject of v.1,
"every true prophet". We then translate as follows: "It is for this
reason that [inasmuch as he is] a true teacher, [the prophet] also is
worthy of his food, like the workman". The Didachist did not
wish then at all to enumerate a second category of pensionaries of
the church; he simply indicated the reason that the prophet
deserved to be supported, namely in virtue of his "social utility",
of the service that he provided as teacher. Put another way, it is
the teaching of the *didache* which puts the prophet in the category
envisaged by the evangelical principle, "the workman is worthy of
his food" (cf. Mt 10:10). Is not every "true" prophet indeed a
"true" teacher, inasmuch as he "teaches the truth" (11:10)?

The sequence of ch.13:3-7 specifies the rules of the first
fruits, ἀπαρχή, which the author does not call a tithe, δεκάτη,
perhaps because the amount was left to the estimation of the donor
(13:7). These verses seem to be composed as a doublet, in which
some have believed they can discern a trace of an evolution in the
condition of the prophet from ancient domestic catechist (vv.5-7)
to ecclesiastical functionary (vv.3-4).[48] This is an over-subtle
interpretation, since it could be that we simply have, for that matter, a double gloss on the traditional references to Deut 14:22-29.
The transition from "you" (sg.) to "you" (pl.) does not force one
to think of v.4 as an interpolation (of the second degree according
to Audet[49]), since it is possible that the first-fruits were not taken
individually to their beneficiaries, but collected together and
shared out in the name of the church.

---

[46] Rordorf & Tuilier, *La Doctrine*, p. 191.
[47] Giet, *L'énigme*, pp. 227-8; Rordorf, *La Doctrine*, p. 190 n. 2.
[48] Schille, "Das Recht", pp. 90-1, 100.
[49] *Didachè*, p. 458.

One notices that v.3 and 4 presuppose, like 10:7, the existence of several prophets in one community (v.3), while others did not have any (v.4). From the fact that the first fruits must then be distributed to the poor, people often infer that the churches of ch.7-13 did not yet have fixed local ministries of the kind spoken of in ch.15.[50] In fact, nothing prevents one from thinking that these ministers, where they had traditionally existed, could not have had their subsistence assured in another way, as we shall see, so that the author did not have to mention them here.

The description of the prophets as ἀρχιερεῖς in v.3 does not necessarily envisage a liturgical function.[51] It can be just a simple implicit, purely formal, comparison:[52] in the same way that the first fruits were due to the priests, so this same commandment (13:5; 13:7) of the Old Testament or, perhaps, an evangelical ordinance (cf. 1 Cor 9:14), demands of Christians that they give them to their prophets. Nevertheless the transposition of the title of "priests" and of "high priests" remains intriguing. The *Apostolic Constitutions* identify, in an analogous context (2.26.3), the high priests with the bishops, the priests with the presbyters and the Levites with the deacons. Perhaps the Didachist thought, for his part, of the charismatic prophecy with which Jewish tradition credited the high priest (cf. Jn 11:51; Josephus, *AJ* 13.229 etc.).

****

15.1 Elect for yourselves, therefore, bishops and deacons worthy of the Lord, men who are gentle, not anxious for gain, honest and tested; for they indeed replenish for you the service of the prophets and teachers 2. Therefore do not scorn them, for these are the people to whom you owe honour, together with the prophets and teachers.[53]

Does this pericope present us with the birth certificate of the local ministries of bishops and deacons, successors of the three ancient universal ministries of apostles, prophets and teachers—at least for the poorly evolved churches addressed by the Didachist[54]? And is it necessary, consequently, to attribute ch. 14-15 to a continuator of the *Didache*, who described a more developed institutional state of affairs than ch. 11-13?[55]

It is, in any case, not possible that the "bishops" of ch. 15 already reflect the system of the monarchical episcopate, as the

---

[50] Giet, *L'énigme*, p. 262; Rordorf & Tuilier, *La Doctrine*, p. 191 n. 5.
[51] Schille, "Das Recht", p. 93; Rordorf & Tuilier, *La Doctrine*, p. 53.
[52] Giet, *L'énigme*, p. 229.
[53] Cf. Tuilier in Rordorf & Tuilier, *La doctrine*, pp. 193-195.
[54] Streeter, *The Primitive Church*, pp. 144-145; 149-152.
[55] Rordorf & Tuilier, *La Doctrine*, pp. 63-4.

paraphrase in the *Apostolic Constitutions* supposed (7.31.1) by inserting presbyters between bishops and deacons. The Jewish roots of the *Didache* make it indeed a little strange that presbyters do not appear in place of bishops. Does this indicate Paulinism,[56] or that the author wrote for Christians coming out of paganism and not for converted Jews?[57] The fact remains that the repeated plural of vv.1-2 presupposes an episcopal college. Like the deacons, the bishops are elected democratically, by a vote of hands raised in the assembly (15:1), which does not exclude however a consecration of the newly elected by the laying on of hands by their peers. In short, everything leads one to believe that the bishops and deacons of the *Didache* reflect a very ancient situation, perhaps analogous to that attested by Philippians 1:1.

But it is not necessary to interpret the text as if it required the churches to begin a tradition of designating its ministers, still less as if it required the prophets to consecrate them.[58] The emphasis rightly falls on the qualities of the bishops and the deacons who are needed for a "liturgy" (15:1), and accords them the same honour (15:2) as the prophets and the teachers.

One notices here, as above for the apostles and prophets (13:3), but this time at second hand, that the article is not repeated in the phrase τῶν προφητῶν καὶ διδασκάλων, which dissuades us from distinguishing between these different titles. In fact, it is striking to confirm that the virtues required of the bishops and deacons (15:1) are the same ones that ch.11 required of the prophet. First, summarized in the expression ἀξίους τοῦ κυρίου, which recites the τρόπους κυρίου (11:8) characteristic of the true prophet, those qualities are specified in the four adjectives which follow. The last two, ἀληθεῖς καὶ δεδοκιμασμένους, repeat almost to the letter the qualification of the προφήτης δεδοκιμασμένος ἀληθινός (11:11). With respect to the second, ἀφιλαργύρους, it reminds one that the question of money also constituted one of the criteria for discerning the false prophet (11:6; 11:12). As for gentleness, evoked above all by the adjective πραεῖς, it appears in the *Duae viae* (5:2) as a virtue leading to the defence of the poor and the oppressed, and then particularly appropriated for the bishops and deacons in their social activity; but this was also one of the attributes of the prophet (11:9; 11:12). Finally, one notes that if ch.15:1 seems to relate the election of bishops and deacons to the dominical synaxis mentioned in ch.14, where one imagines that the bishops presided served by the deacons,[59] ch. 10:7

---

[56] Greeven, "Propheten", pp. 40-1, 43 n. 103.
[57] Rordorf & Tuilier, *La Doctrine*, pp. 75-6.
[58] Panagopoulos, Ἐκκλησία, p. 407.
[59] Dix, "The Ministry", pp. 246-7; Rordorf & Tuilier, *La Doctrine*, p. 74.

allowed the prophets to give thanks freely. The common "liturgy" (15:1) then was as much cultic as charitable; these two dimensions were also perhaps found linked in the practice of the weekly agape/eucharist.

Nothing then supports the thesis that a continuator of ch.11-13 required, in ch. 15, the same duties and the same respect for the two types of ministry, because that of the bishops and deacons was in the process of replacing an ancient itinerant hierarchy of apostles, prophets and teachers.[60] The historical context of the *Didache* appears, on the contrary, perfectly homogeneous and does not require dual authorship. What seems to be causing problems for the Didachist, was rather the simultaneous exercise (καὶ αὐτοί 15:1) of a similar "liturgy" by two categories of ministers. Even excellent pastors, the bishops and deacons, can be despised because they are non-charismatic, *vis-à-vis* the prophets, who gave thanks, taught and acted "in the spirit". The author, who shows the highest respect for the prophetic charism, is none the less anxious for the good order of the community. That is why he takes up here the defence of the bishops and the deacons, by ordering them to make sure after their election that they present the same moral guarantees as the true prophets (15:1), and by requiring that they be shown the same honour as the latter.

It would be interesting to note that in the only other place where the Didachist has used the verb τιμᾶν there is an echo of the Jewish principle of honouring the one who speaks the word of God (4:1; cf. 11:2; Heb 13:7). The honour due to the bishops and deacons would come to them because they also announce the word, even if it is not with the spiritual authority of the prophets. Could one think here, among other things, of the "eucharist" of ch.9-10 provided for the presidents of the assembly, and which, in its turn, he now found himself defending as equal to the free inspiration of the prophets (10:7)?

****

Did the above reading of ch.10:7-15:2 of the *Didache*, interpreted in the final stage of its redaction, confirm the existence of the charismatic and itinerant ministries, "characteristic of the missionary centre of Antioch and of its period of full activity, around the years 50-60",[61] if not even of the primitive community of Jerusalem?[62] Nowhere does the Didachist unite the titles of

---

[60] Kraft, "Vom Ende", pp. 178-179.

[61] "Charactéristiques du centre missionnaire d'Antioche et de sa période de pleine activité, aux environs des années 50-60"; A. Lemaire, *Les ministères aux origines de l'Église* (Paris: Les Éditions du Cerf, 1971 [*Lectio divina* 68]) p. 182.

[62] Kraft, "Vom Ende", pp. 166, 168-9.

apostle, prophet and teacher in a trilogy. This can only be found by combining the two pairs "apostles and prophets" (ch.11) and "prophets and teachers" (ch.13 & 15). But these two pairs could be reduced, in their turn, to a single figure, that of the prophet,[63] considered occasionally in his itinerant or missionary form in the apostle (11:3-6), but essentially in his praying (10:7; 15:1-2) and above all, teaching rôle (11:1-2; 11:7-12; 15:1-2).

It is, therefore, with very great circumspection that we come to treat the other witnesses cited to support the "Antiochene trilogy" (if not Palestinian) by those who try and trace it not only in Acts (13:1; 14:4, 14) but also in the Matthean tradition (Mt 10:40-1; 23:34).[64] The New Testament evidence never requires that the apostolate, prophecy and teaching constituted specialized ministries which could not be held by the same person, at least for two of them. The text seemingly most favourable to separating the three functions, that of 1 Corinthians 12:28-30, which incidentally needs to be corrected by Romans 12:6-8, was intended perhaps less to enumerate a list of distinct ministers than to show the rich variety of the gifts of the Spirit, of which each member of the ecclesial body has received his share.[65] The titles of apostle, prophet and teacher could then always have been applied to three modes of exercise of the same gospel ministry.

The prophets-teachers of the *Didache* hardly resemble the Syrian charlatans of the second century caricatured by Lucian and Celsus, and the Didachist was attempting to defend their reputation.[66] Nowhere are they presented as the marginals of society, ascetic vagabonds and sexual ascetics, idealists of *Wanderradikalismus*.[67] Nothing more suggests that he wished to encourage the itinerant prophets to settle down in the communities in order to become the equivalent of a monarchical bishop.[68] Rather, the prophets whom he has in mind appear to be already normally resident in their churches, even if he was particularly interested in the case posed by the installation of a non-local prophet. And their ministry seems to constitute a permanent office in these churches, so that one would willingly speak of an institutional order, were it not for its exclusively personal nature; indeed it could be that the choice of the Spirit, manifested by the prophetic charism, has dispensed the community from all need for ordination[69] and succes-

---

[63] Dix, "The Ministry", pp. 241-2.
[64] Cf. E. Cothenet, "Le prophétisme dans le Nouveau Testament" in *Supplément au Dictionnaire de la Bible* VIII (Paris, 1971) cc. 1222-1337, esp. 1271-1275.
[65] Dix, "The Ministry", p. 239; Greeven, "Propheten", pp. 28-9, 31, 38.
[66] Dix, "The Ministry", p. 241.
[67] Theissen, "Wanderradikalismus", pp. 252-3, 262.
[68] Streeter, "The Primitive Church", pp. 150-1.
[69] Dix, "The Ministry", p. 238.

sion,[70] so that in the end they only needed the guarantee of the "way of life".

Were these prophets living in the local churches without ministerial responsibility for pastoral organization? Actually, the author never suggests that the bishops and deacons did not coexist traditionally with the prophets-teachers (15:1-2). The charismatic type of ministry exercised "in the spirit" sufficiently explains the eventual disappearance of the prophets-teachers in certain communities, where their absence could not have provoked any crisis of structure. So nothing suggests a situation of institutional transformation from ch. 11-13 to ch. 15 and, consequently, nothing requires us to see ch. 15 as the addition of a continuator.

One could not fail to be struck by the positive attitude of the Didachist with respect to the prophet. Whatever his requirement for order in the "liturgy" of the community, he refuses to constrain the liberty of prophecy (10:7), in which he sees the model for pastoral ministers (15:1-2). Once tested by the moral criterion, the prophet must not only be fed by the community (ch.13), but the contents of his teaching and his action, even if they scandalize, are to be exempt from all criticism (11:7; 11:11). The reason for this singular respect lies clearly in the spiritual dignity of the prophet: it is because he speaks and acts "in a spirit" that any attempt to anticipate his judgment by God (11:11) constitutes the unforgivable sin (11:7)

****

However, this evidence about the prophetic ministry would radically change in its significance if the author only depicted an archaizing utopia. But, if there is no longer any suggestion today that the *Didache* is a later imposture, some critics continue to interpret it as the apology of a Montanist around the year 200, who was trying to convince the Great Church of the apostolic character of the "New Prophecy" by composing a fictitious picture of the primitive community from a *florilegium* of the New Testament and other early Christian writings.[71]

The partisans of this interpretation have clearly seen the central role of prophecy in the disciplinary section of the *Didache*, but their theory is none the less difficult to sustain, because of the incredible success that it attributes to a vulgar trickery.[72] One of their major reasons consists in the date to which they assign the

---

[70] Panagopoulos, Ἐκκλησία, pp. 305-6.

[71] F. E. Vokes, *The Riddle of the Didache: Fact or Fiction, Heresy or Catholicism* (London: SPCK, 1938) pp. 7-8, 136-145, 161-5, 209-19.

[72] Streeter, *The Primitive Church*, pp. 284-6.

writing, on the basis of a dependence on *Barnabas*, the *Shepherd* of Hermas and Justin, and the utilization of just about the whole New Testament canon.[73] But the most careful analyses tend to explain the literary parentage of the *Duae viae* of 1-6 by a descent from common ancestors[74] and to attribute the supposed citations of the New Testament to a gospel writing close to the Matthean tradition, but at a stage earlier than the form in which we know it.[75] An "antiquary" of the end of the second century would have cited the received texts in a more servile manner.

But the inner coherence of the writing similarly resists the hypothesis of a forger, however clever one might think him to be. For if the supposed "antiquary" created his "montage" starting from the *Pastoral Epistles*, fully cognizant already of the system of the monarchical episcopate with apostolic succession,[76] why did he not speak of the bishop in the singular (1 Tim 5:17; Tit 1:7) and why did he not treat the apostles with more reverence (13:3-6)? And what archaizing scruple would have led him to join to the prophets, whom alone he wished to set in honour, the apostles and teachers of 1 Corinthians 12:28 and Ephesians 4:11,[77] since he does not understand these three titles as a trilogy of separate ministries?

Finally, and above all, the two major indications that could have given credence to a Montanist origin of the *Didache* give every indication themselves of being authentically ancient traits. What is extraordinary in the existence of stipendiary prophets[78] in certain churches of a sub-apostolic period, since prophecy is already more than sufficiently attested! There is nothing suspect in the instruction to fast on Wednesdays and Fridays (8:1)[79], far from it! The Jewish fast on Mondays and Thursdays is attested in the *Mishnah*, which codified the earlier customs at the end of the second century; one easily understands then that in a region where Christians were in contact with the "hypocrites" (8:1-2), they wanted to distinguish themselves, in fasting as in prayer.[80]

This detail joins itself to many other traces of Jewish *halakah* that one can discover in the content, the form and the structure of the *Didache*: two ways, baptism of proselytes, *berakot*, casuistic style, the sequence of the grand mishnaic "orders",[81] as one of the

---

[73] Vokes, *The Riddle of the Didache*, pp. 27-119.

[74] Giet, *L'énigme*, pp. 71, 152.

[75] H. Köster, *Synoptische Überlieferung bei den apostolischen Vätern* (Berlin: Akademie-Verlag, 1957) pp. 159-241.

[76] Vokes, *The Riddle of the Didache*, pp. 164, 171, 215.

[77] *Ibid.*, pp. 117, 142, 154, 166.

[78] *Ibid.*, pp. 171, 164-5, 172.

[79] *Ibid.*, pp. 136-145.

[80] Adam, "Erwägungen", p. 42.

[81] F. Manns, *Essais sur le judéochristianisme* (Jerusalem, 1977 [SBFA 12]) pp. 117-129.

best indicators of the authentic archaism of the writing, and perhaps also of its links to Palestinian, Antiochene or Mesopotamian Syria, even if Egypt cannot be entirely excluded,[82]around the end of the first century of our era.

****

One then has every reason for considering the *Didache* to be true to life, and not a nostalgic idealization of the ministerial structures that it intended to codify. But here a last objection arises from the picture that certain contemporary exegetes have drawn of prophets as heads of the first communities of which they would have elaborated the tradition and formulated the law.[83] Could one not perhaps imagine that the Didachist, a "prophet" himself but already acting as an official, only published his code to take away from the communities their traditional right to test and judge the spiritual leaders democratically, so as to place himself beyond any control?[84] In that case his testimony, however ancient it might be, still shows the evolution of prophecy towards monarchical episcopate.[85]

Such a reading rests on a subtle reconstruction of redactional stages, in part determined by the strange theory of the prophetic functionary, ancient itinerant catechist and domestic become subsidized ecclesiastical agent.[86] It also presupposes that the prophet installed himself in an anarchic—in the etymological sense of the word, i.e. ruling itself in a purely spontaneous democracy—community, to take control of it, whereas the churches addressed by the Didachist doubtless traditionally contained bishops and deacons.

In fact, the coexistence of the "ancient rules" (11:3-6; 11:9-10), recognizing the right of the assembly to test its charismatics, and the new norms, dispossessing them of this privilege,[87] would have been a strange thing; for why would the functionary prophet have preserved the denunciatory procedure of the ancient custom which he wished to abolish? After all, the "recent layers" (11:1-2; 11:8-10; 11:12) also afford to the community the moral *dokimasia* or testing of the prophet-teacher; and we have seen how the latter would not have been opposed to the prohibition of the *diakrisis* of the tested prophet (11:7; 11:11).[88]

---

[82] Rordorf & Tuilier, *La Doctrine*, pp. 97-9.
[83] Cothenet, "Le prophétisme", cc. 1265-7; 1285-7.
[84] Schille, "Das Recht", pp. 97-8, 102-3.
[85] Streeter, *The Primitive Church*, pp. 150-1.
[86] Schille, "Das Recht", pp. 86, 90-1, 100.
[87] *Ibid.*, p. 88.
[88] *Ibid.*, pp. 87-8.

Is it then conceivable that the Didachist would have tried to monopolize to his profit the right of discernment which he denies to the community? This implies that he would have exempted himself from the "unforgivable sin" (11:7) and given himself the power of judgment reserved for God (11:11). But such audacity fits ill with the modesty with which he instructs the churches to receive another teaching than his own, if it is to add to righteousness and the knowledge of the Lord (11:2).

The *Didache* represents, in primitive Christian literature, perhaps a unique case of discretion: the author does not try to build up his authority, either by apocalyptic scenery setting or by an apostolic pseudepigraphy. To be sure, the presentation of the writing as "Teaching of the Twelve Apostles" must have been very ancient to guarantee it, perhaps from the second century, a quasi-canonical reception in Egypt and Syria.[89] Yet, even if one retains only the shorter of the two titles, correcting it in accordance with the Patristic tradition to διδαχαὶ τῶν ἀποστόλων,[90] this design again contrasts too much, for a conception of apostolic authority inspired by Acts 2:42, with the low esteem accorded itinerant apostles in 11:3-6[91], for one could consider it as authentic and for the apostolate thus to correspond to the Didachist's own view of himself.[92]

But what the titles rightly understood is that the writing does indeed represent a διδαχή, which implies that it properly has a Didachist for its author, i.e. a διδάσκαλος. And indeed, as soon as the compiler emerges timidly from the traditions which he transmits and betrays something of his identity, it is in order to appear as the messenger of a "teaching", in other words as a teacher (1:3; 2:1; 6:1; 11:1-2). However, unlike the prophet, an inspired teacher who receives revelations from on high and penetrates the secrets of the heart, the humble teacher is a man of tradition, of *halakah*, only concerned with faithfulness in the transmission of the past.[93] That our Didachist fits into this last category, stands out clearly from the content and style of all he has written, and the appeal to the prophet as guardian of the traditional doctrine of the church, sanctioned by the Spirit,[94] would not here be an abuse of language. In removing the authentic prophet from every human tribunal, he paid him a homage more sincere

[89] Streeter, *The Primitive Church*, pp. 284-6.

[90] Audet, *Didachè*, pp. 91-103; 116-120.

[91] Saß, "Die Apostel", pp. 233-6; 238-9.

[92] P. Vielhauer, *Geschichte der urchristlichen Literatur* (Berlin: de Gruyter, 1975) pp. 723-5.

[93] Greeven, "Propheten", pp. 9-10, 17, 29.

[94] Panagopoulos, Ἐκκλησία, p. 286.

because he knew himself to be without this charism; and could one not find a supplementary indication of his complete impartiality in the fact that he has not thought it necessary to make any law on the subject of his peers, the teachers to whom he perhaps addressed his writing as a testament?

The Christian teacher who composed the *Didache* around the end of the first century, perhaps having in mind certain communities in the hinterland of Antioch, does not show the anxious zeal of orthodoxy and of its norms, which already characterized his contemporaries: the false prophets whom he denounced are not false teachers (2 Pe 2:1), that is to say that their falsehood is not a matter of their teaching but of their pretension to a title for which their conduct disqualifies them (11:10). But the halachist, this ancestor of the canonists, uniquely preoccupied by the orthopraxis of the moral and disciplinary way (4:13), is not in love with law and order to the point of quenching the Spirit by condemning any other *didache* than his own (11:2). On these two points, his attitude contrasts with the dogmatism and intolerance of the Johannine author who takes up the criterion of the *dokimasia* in the christological confession, and who demands that anyone who does not carry this *didache* to the community should be expelled as the Antichrist (1 Jn 4:1-6; 2 Jn 7-10).

AN EXAMINATION OF THE DEVELOPMENT OF ITINERANT RADICALISM IN THE ENVIRONMENT AND TRADITION OF THE DIDACHE

KURT NIEDERWIMMER
Vienna

There are grounds for assuming that the beginning of post-Easter Christianity manifested itself in certain areas of the Palestinian-Syrian area in two very different social forms: besides local Christians we find groups of homeless missionaries and prophets of the new movement who travelled from place to place. Without exaggerating, it might perhaps even be stated in the opposite manner: besides the itinerant charismatics, as the real bearers of the new movement, individual groups of settled Christians formed, from whom, in the course of development, the local communities originated.

Recently, the phenomenon of the "itinerant charismatics" or "itinerant ascetics" has repeatedly been the subject of research.[1] It is likely that the origin of this phenomenon is to be found in the early Palestinian church among missionaries and prophets who, in their own way, attempted to develop an analogous continuation of discipleship in the changed conditions of the post-Easter period.[2] In my opinion, the first "enthusiastic" mission in the Palestinian-Syrian region was also related to the itinerant charismatics. After this, the movement appears to have continued in rural and small-

---

[1] G. Kretschmar, "Ein Beitrag zur Frage nach dem Ursprung frühchristlicher Askese", *ZThK* 61 (1964) pp. 27-67; now also in: K. S. Frank, *Askese und Mönchtum in der alten Kirche* (Darmstadt: Wissenschaftliche Buchgesellschaft, 1975 [WdF 409]) pp. 129-179 (The following is cited according to the first edition); G. Kretschmar, "Das christliche Leben und die Mission in der frühen Kirche", in H. Frohnes & U. W. Knorr (eds), *Kirchengeschichte als Missionsgeschichte I: Die Alte Kirche* (München: Kaiser, 1974) pp. 94ff; G. Theissen, "Wanderradikalismus. Literatursoziologische Aspekte der Überlieferung von Worten Jesu im Urchristentum", *ZThK* 70 (1973) pp. 245-271 (Eng. "Itinerant Radicalism: The Tradition of Jesus Sayings from the Perspective of the Sociology of Literature", trans. A. Wire, *RadRel* 2 [1976] pp. 84-93); G. Theissen, "Legitimation und Lebensunterhalt: Ein Beitrag zur Soziologie urchristlicher Missionare", *NTS* 21 (1974/75) pp. 192-221 (Eng. "Legitimation and Subsistence: An Essay on the Sociology of Early Christian Missionaries" in G. Theissen, *The Social Setting of Pauline Christianity: Essays on Corinth*, trans. J. H. Schütz [Philadelphia: Fortress, 1982] pp. 27-67).

[2] G. Theissen ("Wanderradikalismus", p. 252 n. 20) takes the position of Kretschmar one step further and raises the question as to the true identity of those tradents of Jesus-tradition propagating ethical radicalism. For Theissen these itinerant ascetics are the tradents; in their own way they attempt literally to fulfil Jesus' demand for homelessness, renunciation of marriage and renunciation of possessions ("Wanderradikalismus", pp. 249ff). Theissen conceives of the itinerant charismatics' asceticism as an authentic continuation of the τρόποι κυρίου and Jesus himself as the first itinerant charismatic (p. 257).

town areas of Syria. From that point there appears to have been a
development leading finally to the early east Syrian church, or at
least to particular traditions within it. In this fashion an independent branch of early Christianity's developmental history emerges,[3]
important among other things for casting light upon the transition,
in this region delayed for a particularly long time, from the
original atmosphere of eschatological immediacy to the early
catholic mentality.

Within this development, the relevant sayings of the
Didache's community rule assume a key position. Can a picture
be drawn of the developmental stage depicted by the rules of the
Didache?[4] In my opinion, to this end an attempt must be made to
distinguish clearly between traditional material and the
"Didachist" even within the community rule. That will be
attempted in the following. That all assertions about the *Didache*
bear merely hypothetical character, in view of the condition of our
Didache tradition, has rightly been emphasized time and again.[5] It
goes without saying that this applies in even stronger measure to
tradition-historical differentiations, which are, of course, unavoidable.

---

[3] As far as the ascetic motives at work are concerned, it is necessary to remember that here only one particular aspect comes to light, only one of the lines of
development of the history of the primitive and early Christian asceticism.

[4] This presupposes that the composer of the *Didache* wrote at the beginning of
the second century C.E. for Syrian communities in the village or small town milieu.
For the arguments about the date, see J. Quasten, *Patrology I: The Beginnings of
Patristic Literature* (Utrecht: Spectrum, 1975[5]) p. 36-7; B. Altaner, *Patrology*,
trans. H. C. Graef (Freiburg: Herder, 1960[7]) p. 51; P. Vielhauer, *Geschichte der
urchristlichen Literatur. Einleitung in das Neue Testament, die Apokryphen und die
Apostolischen Väter* (Berlin: de Gruyter, 1975) p. 737. An early date is not justified, in my opinion. For the arguments about the place, cf. Quasten, *Patrology*, p.
37 (probably Syrian); O. Bardenhewer, *Geschichte der altkirchlichen Literatur* I
(Freiburg, 1913[2]; Darmstadt: Wissenschaftliche Buchgesellschaft, 1962 [Reprint])
p. 96 (probably Syrian or Palestinian); Altaner, *Patrologie*, p. 81 (Syrian-
Palestinian); with caution Vielhauer, *Geschichte*, p. 737. For the arguments about a
rural or small town milieu cf. 13:3-7; R. Knopf *Die Lehre der zwölf Apostel. Die
zwei Clemensbriefe* (Tübingen: Mohr, 1920 [HNT.E 1]) p. 34; Kretschmar,
"Askese", p. 41 n. 35; Vielhauer, *op.cit.*, p. 737.—A. Adam, "Erwägungen zur
Herkunft der Didache", *ZKG* 68 (1957) pp. 1ff, 37ff and *passim* argues for a Syrian
origin. His thesis: the primitive form of the Didache was written as a church order
for the young communities in east Syria toward establishing their community life.
Hypothetical conclusion concerning the date: between 90 and 100; as place of composition Adam suggests Pella. There is a critique of Adam in Vielhauer
(*Geschichte*, p. 737).

[5] Vielhauer, *Geschichte*, pp. 734, 737. Instructive (but excessive in its overall
judgment of the Bryennios text) is the scepticism of E. Peterson, "Über einige
Probleme der Didache-Überlieferung", now in *Frühkirche, Judentum und Gnosis.
Studien und Untersuchungen* (Rome: Herder, 1959) pp. 146-182. (He argues that
the Bryennios text is merely a late recension of the Didache, p. 181!).

I.

The literary analysis, with which we begin, presents the following picture: 11:1f concludes the section 7-10 (instructions about the cult) and introduces the following community rule (11-15). In my opinion the Didachist is at work in 11:1f, for 11:1f forms the transition[6] to the new theme: the community's attention is brought to teachers arriving from without, who are consequently to be tested as to whether they teach what has been set forth in the preceding text or not. In the negative case the community should not listen to them, in the positive case the teachers should be received. Thus the subject of the following section is set forth.[7]

The composition of the following is not, of course, immediately transparent.[8] In 11:3 a section is introduced περὶ δὲ τῶν

---

[6] Vielhauer, *Geschichte*, p. 735, rightly *contra* J.-P. Audet, *La Didachè. Instructions des apôtres* (Paris: Gabalda, 1958 [ÉBib]) p. 111, who understands 11:2 as the conclusion of D1. Audet distinguishes between D1, D2 and the Interpolator. He argues that D2 was only added after the conclusion of D1 and under the pressure of recent conditions (p. 111), but probably derives from the same—apostolic!—author (cf. pp. 104ff, 110ff, 119f). Vielhauer (*Geschichte*, p. 735) is critical of Audet's distinction of D1 and D2.

[7] M. Dibelius, *Geschichte der urchristlichen Literatur* (Berlin: de Gruyter, 1975 [ThB 58]) pp. 151f, and also, *Die Pastoralbriefe* (Tübingen: Mohr, 1966 [HNT 13]) pp. 5f (Eng. *The Pastoral Epistles*, trans. P. Buttolph & A. Yarbro [Philadelphia: Fortress, 1972]). The edition of the latter completed by H. Conzelmann, wants to see in Didache 7-15 a scheme of composition present also in 1 Tim 2 and 3. What is characteristic of this scheme, he maintains, is the sequence of instructions on prayer (cf. *Did* 7-10; 1 Tim 2:1ff), ethical conditions for the worship service (*Did* 14; 1 Tim 2:8ff) and community organization (*Did* 15:1f; 1 Tim 3:1ff). The instructions of *Did* 11-13 then depart from this scheme: according to Dibelius, they must have been from a later date, inserted at this point for the occasion. There is agreement from Vielhauer (*Geschichte*, p. 727). But the thesis is not compelling, the parallels are not exact, and the wholesale assumption that *Did* 11-13 was from a later date is, in my opinion, unjustified. Even supposing that the Didachist really broke a pre-existing literary scheme in 11-13, he could nevertheless have worked also with older traditional material in dealing with the question at hand; i.e. in 11-13 can be found both old and redactional material. And that is in fact the case, as I hope to show.

[8] It has often been suggested that *Did* 11-13 does not represent a unity. Cf. Knopf, *Die Lehre*, p. 33; according to Audet (*Didachè* pp. 111f) 11:3ff comes from D2 (cf. also *Didachè* p. 435); 13:3, 5-7 is attributed to the Interpolator (pp. 105ff, 457; cf. p. 453), 13:4 is a gloss (p. 458). W. Schmithals (*Das kirchliche Apostelamt. Eine historische Untersuchung* [Göttingen: Vandenhoeck & Ruprecht, 1961 (FRLANT 79)] p. 171 n. 373) thinks that the tradition taken over in 11:3-6 could be older than the final redaction (Eng. *The Office of Apostle in the Early Church*, trans. J. E. Steely (London: SPCK, 1971). According to Schmithals (*Apostelamt*, p. 172) "dürfte das von der Didache verwertete Material, in dem von Aposteln die Rede ist, noch im 1.Jahrhundert fixiert worden sein." G. Schille tries to provide our text with a (somewhat over-complicated) history of tradition, in "Das Recht der Propheten und Apostel—gemeinderechtliche Beobachtungen zu Didache Kapitel 11-13" in P. Wätzel & G. Schille (eds.), *Theologische Versuche* I (Berlin:

ἀποστόλων καὶ προφητῶν, which, strictly speaking, can only
extend to 11:12. Besides apostles and prophets, chapter 12 names
a third group for which we are not prepared by the superscript in
11:3: ordinary itinerant Christians. Chapter 13 returns once again
to the prophets, whose case had seemed extensively and finally
treated in 11:7-12. One cannot, however, make 13:1 follow
11:12,[9] since chapter 13 is too clearly bound to 12:3ff by the
catch-phrase θέλων καθῆσθαι πρὸς ὑμᾶς. 13:1 is thus the logical

---

Evangelische Verlagsanstalt, 1966) pp. 84ff. In the beginning, according to him, it
was the right of the community to test the charismatics; this right of the community
was gradually eroded; finally the author (=the Didachist) forbade the testing of the
charismatics (who meanwhile had become community officials). Schille tries to support his concept of the history of the tradition by distinguishing between casuistical
rules, apodictic decrees and declarative formulae (pp. 89ff). Important decisions he
makes on the basis of the history of tradition are: 11:4-6, framed in the style of the
declarative formula, belongs to old tradition (4 is of course explained as "die
anredende Gesetzesparänese des Autors", p. 92 n. 31; here a decree has intruded
into a declarative formula, p. 91 n. 25,5); likewise 11:9f belongs to old tradition.
The remarks on testing (11:11a; 13:1f; p. 88) demonstrate a later stage (although
the rule 11:11 may still be older than the "Anstellungsformel" in 13:1f; cf. Schille,
p. 101). 11:12 "ist eine erweichte Spätform der Apostel-Unterhaltsregel 11:6 ohne
Titel" (!? p. 88). The author of the Didache marks the final stage, forbidding the
testing of the charismatics attempting to justify this in 11:8 (p. 87).—The proposal
for the tradition history of chapters 12 and 13 is just as complicated: for 12:1a, 2b,
5a (!) Schille proposes older tradition (p. 95 n. 53); 13:3-7 consists (p. 90f) of an
older executive formula (5-7) and a later introductory formula (3f). He argues that
this section contains casuistical rules; one can, however, no longer speak of a
purely casuistical style. "Die kasuistische Form ist in den dekretalen Bereich
eingeschmolzen" (p. 91). Cf. further under n. 60—The main considerations speaking against the analysis of Schille (though he makes valuable observations with
respect to details): 1. The prohibition against the testing charismatics (11:7) is
certainly not the latest tradition, but on the contrary the oldest tradition. It is found
already in 1 Cor 2:15 (to which Schille himself, with restrictions, refers: p. 87 n.
11). The proximity of the prohibition against testing and the formation of criteria
need not be separated out into different temporal stages of the tradition (cf. under n.
37). Therefore I cannot follow the notion that the right to test the charismatics was
successively taken away from the community either, during the development of the
Didache tradition. 2. The distinction made among text types of a legal character fit
the text itself only laboriously. Schille has to concede that in part mixed forms are
present (pp. 91, 94). 3. The subject of the Didache tradition is not the successive
"Entmündigung der Gemeinde" (p. 102), but the co-existence of two different social
forms of the Christian life, which led at the time of the Didachist to the attempt to
integrate the itinerant charismatics.—After the conclusion of this manuscript, G.
Kretschmar, kindly made available to me the text of his contribution to the
Festschrift for Rousseau, "Die innerkirchlichen Dienste und das Amt der Kirche in
der Welt. Strukturen der frühen Christenheit". Kretschmar distinguishes different
layers of the Didache (cf. already his "Askese", p. 37). For our context it is also
significant among other things that he attributes the instruction of 15:1 to the last
layer of the Didache and sets it off against the preceding elaborations about the
itinerant charismatics.

    [9] As Knopf (Die Lehre, p. 33) does.

sequence to 12:3-5 and presupposes this section. Neither may 13:1f together with 12:1-5, be immediately subsumed under the catch-phrase "Brethren, who wish to settle",[10] for 12:1f does not treat this question yet. Furthermore, it is conspicuous that in the superscript 11:3 only apostles and prophets are mentioned and in the following only their situations are dealt with; there is no mention of the διδάσκαλοι.[11] In spite of this, the teachers emerge in 13:2 (even if only tangentially), and form in 15:1f (together with the prophets) the complement to the local church officials (there, on the other hand, the apostles are missing completely from the ranks of the charismatics).[12] These observations might be explained by assuming that an older tradition was available to the author of the *Didache* in 11:4ff. This older tradition speaks of itinerant apostles and itinerant prophets (and only of these), and in particular of how such charismatics are to be received by local Christians (11:4-12). The itinerant teachers are not yet mentioned here. The Didachist has (for this occasion) reproduced this older material, though it may remain open whether the author had formulated material before him or whether he formulated the wording of the elements of tradition himself in archaizing fashion, the latter being less likely. In any case, the section 11:4-12 represents a situation older than that of the author of the *Didache* and which must differ substantially in certain respects from conditions in the

---

[10] Audet, *Didachè*, p. 453. For Audet 12:1-5 and 13:1f belong together. The caesura lies between 13:2 and 3. Audet attributes the section 13:3, 5-7 to the Interpolator. Cf. above n. 8.

[11] Audet (*Didachè*, p. 442) explains it as follows: the teachers were most probably not itinerant teachers, and for this reason are missing in 11:3-12, but are present on the other hand in 12:1-13:2. Hardly correct.

[12] So too Schille, "Recht", p. 85: the title of apostle is limited to 11:4-6 and absent in the further rules.—Another question is whether one can make an argument on the basis of the dissent between the term apostle in 11:4ff and the title of the Didache, especially considering that the wording and genuineness of the title are contested. Audet (*Didachè*, pp. 91ff) has good grounds for making the assertion that the *Didache* originally only had the shorter wording as title, in which the mention of the Twelve is missing. Audet sees no dissent between the superscript (the short title) and 11:3-6 (p. 119). Cf. also G. Klein, *Die zwölf Apostel. Ursprung und Gehalt einer Idee* (Göttingen: Vandenhoeck & Ruprecht, 1961 [FRLANT 77]) pp. 80ff. According to J. Roloff, *Apostolat-Verkündigung-Kirche. Ursprung, Inhalt und Funktion des kirchlichen Apostelamtes nach Paulus, Lukas und den Pastoralbriefen* (Gütersloh: Mohn, 1965) p. 82 n. 138, a dissent still, of course, remains, inasmuch as Roloff assumes that the title refers to a limited number of apostles, even if the Twelve are not mentioned, and thus apparently contradicts the usage of "apostle" in chapter 11. Vielhauer (*Geschichte*, pp. 723ff), on the other hand, sees the problem differently. Vielhauer emphasizes the material difference between the short title and the apostle concept in chapter 11. "Die 'Apostel' in 11,3-6 sind keine unbestrittene Lehrautorität wie die 'Apostel' im Titel" (p. 724). Vielhauer concludes from this, that even the short title does not come from the Didachist, but rather from a later hand.

author's day. In reproducing the tradition, the author provided it with an introduction (11:3; the expression of δόγμα τοῦ εὐαγγελίου is certainly typical of the redaction of the *Didache*)[13] and accommodated it to the circumstances of his time by constructing two appendices (12:1-5; 13:1ff). That 13:3, 5-7 is a later interpolation, as argued by Audet,[14] is not in my opinion demonstrable. On the other hand, Audet is correct in his assumption that a later gloss is present in 13:4,[15] revealing a later time when local prophets have also become scarce. Incidentally, the reference to the ἐντολή (the ἐντολὴ κυρίου which the author quotes in 13:1 and repeats in 13:2 is probably meant) is characteristic of the redaction. And lastly the mention of διδάσκαλοι (13:2) in this section is no accident, since we know from 15:1f that they are present next to and after the prophets as charismatics in the communities of the Didachist.

If these assumptions are correct, then we have to reckon with the following structure for the section:

11:1f	Transition (redactor)
11:3	Introduction to the ancient tradition (redactor)
11:4-12	Concerning the reception of itinerant apostles and itinerant prophets (tradition)[16]

---

[13] 11:3 is a rubric from the pen of the Didachist, cf. H. Köster, *Synoptische Überlieferung bei den Apostolischen Vätern* (Berlin: Akademie-Verlag, 1957 [TU 65]) p. 10; Schille, "Recht", p. 88. The reference to the "gospel" (four times in *Did* 8:2; 11:3; 15:3, 4) is, in my opinion, typical of the redactor. On εὐαγγέλιον in Didache, cf. *TDNT* II, p. 736 (Friedrich); Köster, *Synopt. Überl.* pp. 10f, 209ff; H. von Campenhausen, *Die Entstehung der christlichen Bibel* (Tübingen: Mohr, 1968 [BHTh 39]) pp. 142ff [Eng. *The Formation of the Christian Bible*, trans. J. A. Baker [Philadelphia: Fortress]); P. Stuhlmacher, *Das paulinische Evangelium I: Vorgeschichte* (Göttingen: Vandenhoeck & Ruprecht, 1968 [FRLANT 95]) pp. 60f; A. Sand, *Kanon. Von den Anfängen bis zum Fragmentum Muratorianum* (Freiburg: Herder, 1974 [HDG I, 3a,1]) pp. 55f. As Köster (pp. 10f, 209ff, 239f) has shown, "Evangelium" means for the Didachist a written gospel, referring his readers to it without citing it literally. Oral and written gospel tradition did not compete with one another at the time of the *Didache* (more precisely: even into the Didachist's day). See also von Campenhausen, *Entstehung*, p. 144.—In terms of content, "gospel" for the Didache consists of a collection of rules and instructions. In the "gospel" the reader finds the commands of the Lord—and indeed in respect of right prayer (8:2), right almsgiving (15:4), in respect of conduct with the erring brethren (15:3)—and even in respect of the pressing questions for the area in which the *Didache*-tradition arose, namely concerning proper conduct toward itinerant charismatics (which 11:3 proposes).—(According to the as yet unpublished paper of G. Kretschmar, cf. above n. 8, it is assumed that all of the layers of the *Didache* were reworked, presumably in the second half of the second century [?]; for this reworking the reference to "the gospel" is typical).

[14] *Didachè*, pp. 105ff, 457; cf. 453.

[15] *Didachè*, p. 458. The gloss must of course be old. *Const* 7:29 appears already to presuppose it.

[16] In terms of genre, the piece of tradition belongs to the "Gemeinderegeln für den Umgang mit wandernden Charismatikern" (Theissen, "Legitimation", p. 192;

12:1-5	First appendix: Concerning the reception of non-charismatic travelling brethren (redactor)
13:1-3, 5-7	Second appendix: Concerning the duty to support prophets (and teachers), who wish to settle in the community (redactor)[17]
(13:4	Later gloss)

The Didachist returns to the subject of the prophets and teachers in 15:1ff—characteristically in the context of the question about the right relation between local church officials and those charismatics who have settled in the community. The tendency is the same as the one dominating chapters 11-14 (and which in fact the older tradition 11:4ff also already displays): the aim is to establish an intelligible relation between the two groups (the itinerant charismatics and the local Christians).[18] The standpoint of the Didachist (and already of the tradition) is that of the local Christians. It is not a representative of the itinerant charismatics speaking here, but a representative of those Christians bound to a particular place.[19] With that observation, however, we have already arrived at the question of content.

---

yet Theissen applies these sayings to Didache 11 as a whole; cf. Mt 10:40-42 on the matter).—The inner structure of the section is apparent:
  (1) 11:4-6   Concerning itinerant apostles
      (a) 11:4 The dignity of the apostle
      (b) 11:5f Criteria for distinguishing the true apostle from the false prophet
  (2) 11:7-12   Concerning the itinerant prophets
      (a) 11:7 The dignity of the prophet
      (b) 11:8 The criterion for distinguishing the true prophet from the false prophet
      (c) 11:9-12 Three particular cases
[17] Structure:
  (1) 12:1-5 First Appendix: Concerning the reception of non-charismatic brethren who arrive
      (a) 12:1a The right of the arrivals to hospitable reception
      (b) 12:1b The testing of immigrants
      (c) 12:2 Those travelling through
      (d) 12:3-5 The new arrival who wishes to settle
  (2) 13:1-3, 5-7 Second Appendix: Concerning the duty to support prophets (and teachers), who wish to settle in the community
      (a) 13:1f The right of the prophets (and teachers) to settle
      (b) 13:3, 5-7 The duty of the community to provide support
[18] The Christians in the area of the Didachist's tradition lived in two social forms, as itinerant charismatics and as local communities of Christians. Within the structure of the *Didache* this is reflected by the fact that the community rule consists of two parts: instructions about the conduct toward itinerant Christians (chapters 11-13), instructions about the conduct of the local community (chapters 14-15). It should also be noted, however, that the first of the two parts is determined from the standpoint of the local Christian community.
[19] The occasion for the reception of the old tradition (11:4-12) by the Didachist was thus provided by the fact that even in his time the institution of the itinerant charismatics still existed—even if (as we will see) in an altered form. The Didachist also still knew the two forms of Christian existence: the παροικοῦντες, living in an

II.

First we will try to recognize the situation presupposed by the old tradition in 11:4-12. At first glance, it appears that itinerant charismatics and local Christians represent two independent forms of Christian existence clearly distinguished from each other. The problem is the relationship of the two groups to one another.

We learn little about the local Christians from 11:4-12. 11:5 presupposes a dense network of individual Christian houses already existing in the area for which the tradition speaks: the itinerant apostle can thus reckon with arriving at the next Christian house, or in the next Christian group, in a day's journey (probably in one of the neighbouring villages or in one of the small towns).

Itinerant Christians sought accommodation with these local Christians for a short time. What is envisaged is obviously not an isolated event, but a repeated and regular one. The arrivals are themselves without permanent residence, without a living, they are dependent on the support of the local Christians.[20] The arrivals are characterized as charismatics.[21] The two titles used (apostle and prophet) point to two different forms of itinerant charismatics. *Peregrinatio* is common to both. It is clearly an intrinsic requirement of the apostles in *Didache* 11:4ff. It is unthinkable for an apostle to take up permanent residence, since his stay with the local brethren is limited to one day, or two at need (11:5).[22]

---

eschatologically stringent manner, and the local Christians. However, the two groups did not co-exist without conflict: there were also false prophets, swindlers and frauds among the visiting itinerant charismatics, against whom the communities must be warned; furthermore, at the time of the Didachist the itinerant charismatics also came into conflict with the local officials. In this situation the author of the Didache returned to the old traditional elements and adapted them for his own time by additions.

[20] Cf. 3 Jn 7f, where it says of the itinerant brethren: ὑπὲρ γὰρ τοῦ ὀνόματος ἐξῆλθαν μηδὲν λαμβάνοντες ἀπὸ τῶν ἐθνικῶν. ἡμεῖς οὖν ὀφείλομεν ὑπολαμβάνειν τοὺς τοιούτους.

[21] Note that they are neither community founders nor community organizers. Their interest does not lie with the historical existence of a Christian group within the framework of existing society, but rather with the eschatological exodus out of the society of their day. Thus, they can hardly be conceived of as the charismatic "officials" of the global church as compared with the local officials; rather they conceive of themselves as the consistent followers of Jesus *in conspectu regni coelorum.*—On the differentiation between the two types of primitive Christian itinerant preachers (the type of itinerant preacher presented here that was at home in the rural milieu and the type of the church organizer, doing mission work in the cities) cf. Theissen, "Wanderradikalismus", pp. 264ff; Theissen, "Legitimation", pp. 193ff.

[22] H reads: οὐ μενεῖ δὲ ἡμέραν μίαν. εἰ μή should be inserted before ἡμέραν (A. Harnack, *Lehre der zwölf Apostel nebst Untersuchungen zur ältesten Geschichte der Kirchenverfassung und des Kirchenrechts* [Leipzig: Hinrichs (Reprint), 1893 (TU

Moreover, the prophet (despite the absence of a similarly rigorous instruction concerning the length of their stay) is also thought of as a homeless charismatic, travelling from place to place. Next to homelessness we find renunciation of property,' which again is conceived of particularly stringently in the apostle's case. The apostle lives exclusively from the support of local Christians. When the apostle comes, he is of course a guest; if he continues his journey on the following day, then he has a claim to a daily ration for the coming day;[23] if, however, he demands money, he is immediately unmasked (11:6).[24] It is not directly stated that the prophet of Did. 11:7ff lived without any possessions. Nevertheless the warnings in 11:9, 12 show that the true prophet also knows poverty and need. Renunciation of marriage is not mentioned here *verbo tenus*, nevertheless one may confidently assume it to be the rule. On the other hand, 11:11 appears to allude to the custom of *matrimonium spirituale*. We know from Ps.Clem, *AdVir* 1:10 that this custom was widespread among the later forms of itinerant asceticism in Syria.[25]

Didache 11:3ff clearly distinguishes between itinerant apostles and itinerant prophets.[26] The instructions concerning the

---

2,1-2)] p. 39).

[23] τὸν ἄρτον λαμβάνειν = to receive rations (*BAGD*, s.v. ἄρτος). ἕως οὗ αὐλισθῇ shows that by ἄρτος is meant simply the ration for the coming day.—Incidentally, the instruction 11:6a contradicts Mt 6:8.

[24] Cf. Lk 10:4 (Q?): μὴ βαστάζετε βαλλάντιον, Mk 6:8: μὴ εἰς τὴν ζώνην χαλκόν, Mt 10:9: μὴ κτήσησθε χρυσὸν μηδὲ ἄργυρον μηδὲ χαλκὸν εἰς τὰς ζώνας ὑμῶν.

[25] The practice is there condemned; here (Did. 11:10f) it is defended with reservations.

[26] It is certainly right to draw together closely the apostles and prophets of Did. 11:3-12 (a strict distinction of "offices" on the basis of "canonical law" is, of course, not present; cf. Audet, *Didachè*, pp. 440f). Yet neither can one equate ἀπόστολος and προφήτης (as in Kretschmar, "Askese", p. 37; Roloff, *Apostelamt*, p. 82; more differentiated: Schille, "Recht", p. 86; he holds that "prophet" designates the charisma, "apostle" the function; primarily only the matter of the prophet is being discussed here: p. 93). On the other hand, the use of the term ψευδοπροφήτης in the section on apostles (11:6) is not conclusive (Roloff, p. 82, note 139; Schille, "Recht", p. 93). For the use of the term in 11:6 is simply a verbal improvisation! The word ψευδαπόστολος is apparently unknown to the tradent. It is not attested prior to 2 Cor 11:13 and there probably represents an *ad hoc* creation of Paul (cf. *TDNT* I, p. 446, line 1ff [Rengstorf]; Schille, "Recht", p. 93 n. 33). It was probably formed on the analogy to ψευδοπροφήτης. The apostolic fathers do not have the word ψευδαπόστολος. It first emerges again in Hegesippius (Eusebius, *HE* 4.22:6), Justin, *Dial* 35:3 and Ps.Clem., *Hom* 16:21,4; after that frequently. (It is typical that when the same subject is mentioned in Rev 2:2, the word is missing!) The term ψευδοπροφήτης, on the other hand, was common (LXX, Philo, NT; *HermMan* 11:1, 2, 4, 7; the term then naturally plays a role in the quarrel between the catholic church and the montanist prophets; *TDNT* VI, pp. 860f [Friedrich].

apostles are by far the more rigorous. Unfortunately there is no discussion about the term "apostle". It is clear that a delineated circle of apostles, that is the δώδεκα, is not being referred to here.[27] What is meant here is a numerically unspecified group of itinerant charismatics and missionaries, who sojourn with local resident sympathizers. *Didache* 11:4ff appears not to know any other kind of apostles than itinerant ones. This much is clear: the apostle of the *Didache* appears as emissary, as representative of the Kyrios (for which reason he is also to be received like the Kyrios: 11:4).[28] The background is provided by the first, enthusiastic mission in the Palestinian and Syrian region. Only from this perspective, only as a later derivative of this movement, can one understand the apostle of *Didache* 11:4ff, in my opinion—whereby it cannot be ascertained to what degree the expectation of the imminent end still plays a key rôle. We can assume the function of the apostle according to the *Didache* tradition: eschatological proclamation, call to repentance, exorcism. Just like his proclamation, so too the life-style of the apostle is eschatologically motivated. Homelessness, renunciation of possessions and renunciation of marriage (?) represent the eschatological existence. The apostle proclaims and intentionally lives the radical renunciation of the world. According to his self-understanding, his rôle as social outsider[29] manifests the eschatological ἀπόταξις.[30]

---

[27] The question as to the historical setting of the concept of the apostle present here within the framework of the general history of the primitive apostolate cannot be discussed here, and has not yet, in my opinion, been convincingly solved. Cf. only G. Sass, "Die Apostel in der Didache", in W. Schmauch (ed), *In memoriam Ernst Lohmeyer* (Stuttgart: Evangelisches Verlagswerk, 1951) pp. 235ff; Klein, *Zwölf Apostel*, pp. 50ff, 80ff; Schmithals, *Apostelamt*, pp. 42f, 170ff, 212ff, 242; F. Hahn, "Der Apostolat im Urchristentum. Seine Eigenart und seine Voraussetzungen", *KuD* 20 (1974) pp. 54ff, esp. 60f.

[28] δεχθήτω ὡς κύριος is, of course, not attested in the Ethiopian and Coptic versions, but the Coptic does not offer a reliable witness for the assumption that δεχθήτω ὡς κύριος is a later interpolation. For more precise information on the problems of the Coptic text in this passage see L.-Th. Lefort, *Les pères apostoliques en copte* (Louvain: Durbecq, 1952 [CSCO 135 (ScrCop 17)]) p. 33 n. 15; (Louvain: Durbecq, 1952 [CSCO 136 (ScrCop 18)]) p. 27 n. 19. The expression (attested: H georgian) is probably original.—By κύριος naturally Jesus is meant (Audet's scruples are unnecessary, *Didachè*, p. 443).—By the way, it should not be ruled out that the redactor anticipated the use of the expression δεχθήτω ὡς κύριος in his transition (11:2). What the tradition relates specifically to the apostles, the redactor then generalized.

[29] See Theissen, "Wanderradikalismus", pp. 261ff.

[30] Concerning the social and economic factors of primitive Christian itinerant radicalism, see Theissen, "Legitimation", pp. 193ff. In this case it is indeed not a matter of explaining origins in a reductionist manner, but of analyzing mutual relationship between a social situation and religious motivation.—On the phenomenon of the similarity of the primitive Christian itinerant charismatic to the Cynic itinerant philosopher, see Theissen, "Wanderradikalismus", pp. 255ff; esp. concerning the difference, pp. 258f.

The other groups of itinerant ascetics (next to and following
the apostles in rank)[31] are the prophets, itinerant spirituals, whose
gift is the λαλεῖν ἐν πνεύματι (cf. 11:7, 8), that is, ecstatic
speech.[32] It should be noted that the prophets of the *Didache* are
itinerant pneumatics who come from outside. The *Didache* does
not mention prophets who come from the local community. The
prophets of the tradition in 11:7-12 are wanderers, who
temporarily make their home among the local Christians and then
continue on afterwards. Of significance is the remark that one
recognizes the genuine prophets by the τρόποι κυρίου (11:8).[33] We
do not obtain a more exact picture of the manner and content of
their spiritual, ecstatic speech from 11:7ff, since what we learn
from 11:9 and 12 is perhaps not representative. In the first
instance apocalyptic, esoteric proclamation should be assumed. A
reference to this is perhaps made in 11:11.[34] If the prophet lives in

---

[31] Although the ranking should, of course, not be viewed as one already firmly
established according to canon law. Audet's polemical elaborations (Audet,
Didachè, pp. 439ff) are instructive (even if Audet here—differently from ourselves—still thinks of the triad, apostle-prophet-teacher).

[32] Glossolalia is apparently not intended (cf. 11:9f, 12).

[33] Obviously Jesus is intended. The deliberations of Audet (*Didachè*, p. 450) are
unnecessary.

[34] The well-known crux (ποιῶν εἰς μυστήριον κοσμικὸν ἐκκλησίας) is still best
understood, if one accepts the interpretation of Harnack: it was a matter of sexual
asceticism, probably of "spiritual marriages" in particular (*Lehre*, pp. 44ff). So also
Knopf, *Die Lehre*, pp. 32f; *TDNT* IV, p. 824 lines 40ff (Bornkamm); H. von
Campenhausen, *Kirchliches Amt und geistliche Vollmacht in den ersten drei
Jahrhunderten* (Tübingen: Mohr, 1963² [BHTh 14] p. 78 n. 10 (Eng. *Ecclesiastical
Authority and Spiritual Power in the Church of the First Three Centuries*, trans. J.
A. Baker [London: Black, 1969]); Adam, *Herkunft*, p. 20; Kretschmar, "Askese",
p. 34 n. 18; K. Niederwimmer, *Askese und Mysterium. Über Ehe, Ehescheidung
und Eheverzicht in den Anfängen des christlichen Glaubens* (Göttingen: Vandenhoeck & Ruprecht, 1975 [FRLANT 113]) p. 191. This behaviour is then probably
motivated by *syzygy* speculations, alluded to by the text. The nearest parallel to the
current speculation is provided by 2 Clement 14. On *syzygy* speculation in general,
cf. Niederwimmer, *Askese*, pp. 186ff and *passim*.—The belief underlying our passage would then be this: the earthly spiritual marriage (the μυστήριον κοσμικόν) is a
reflection and re-enactment of the heavenly *syzygy* between Christ and the Church
(It is to be understood in this way and stands as a correction to my mistaken interpretation in *Askese*, 191). The tradent is determined to justify, under certain conditions, the spiritual marriage of prophet and prophetess, which clearly gave offence
to the local Christians in some cases (on the other hand cf. Ps. Clem *de vir.* and the
later development!).—Other, older interpretations of the passage in F. X. Funk,
Patres apostolici I (Tübingen: Laupp, 1901²) pp. 28f.—Adam begins from the Coptic text (cf. Lefort, CSCO 135, p. 34), which differs strongly from H, as is well
known. Adam translates, "Jeder Prophet, wahrhaftig, der erprobt, der lehrt und
bezeugt eine weltliche Überlieferung in der Kirche, der soll bei euch nicht gerichtet
werden..." ("Herkunft", p. 6). Adam posits ("Herkunft", p. 7) a Syrian original:
Both the ποιεῖν of the Greek version and the ΠΑΡΑΔΟΣΙΣ of the Coptic version
can be explained, he argues, from the Syriac *'ašlem*. The assumption that the Coptic
version no longer understood or no longer wanted to understand the Greek text (as
generally also the Ethiopian) seems to me to be simpler. One must start, in my

matrimonium spirituale with the προφῆτις (a surprising innovation over against the original tradition!), then this is (apparently) based on esoteric speculation.[35]

Yet neither the apostle nor the prophet is described in 11:4ff. Whatever an apostle or prophet was, in the sense of the speech usage of the group addressed, is clearly presupposed as known. The intention of the rules of 11:4ff pursues a quite different direction. The local Christians are threatened by impostors and swindlers, who represent themselves as apostles and prophets, without being such.[36] One must bear in mind that the wanderers arriving in the community could have been unknown to the local Christians at first, and indeed this was probably the usual case. It became necessary to establish criteria for distinguishing the true apostle from the impostor, the *propheta verus et probatus* from the *propheta falsus*. A dominant catch-word of the section is consequently ψευδοπροφήτης (11:5, 6, 8, 9, 10). Yet the dominant intention is not of a polemical, but rather of an apologetic nature. The instructions follow the same scheme in both cases: first the right and the dignity of the charismatics is set out (11:4 for apostles, 11:7 for the prophets),[37] and only then are particular criteria formulated which serve to distinguish the genuine apostles from the false, the true prophets from the pseudo-prophets.[38] Or

---

opinion, from the Greek text of H, which is confirmed by the Georgian text (apart from two small, unimportant changes). Audet, *Didachè*, p. 451.—Audet's own attempt at interpretation is not very convincing.—Harnack's explanation leaves open the sense of the expression ὡσαύτως γὰρ ἐποίησαν καὶ οἱ ἀρχαῖοι προφῆται (11c). Here it is best to understand the Old Testament prophets (cf. also Funk, *Patres apostolici*, pp. 29f and Knopf, *Die Lehre* p. 33). *AJ* 12:413; Lk 9:8; *TDNT* I, p. 487 (Delling).

[35] The foundation for such speculation was provided by Gen 1:27; 2:24. Cf. Niederwimmer, *Askese*, Index.

[36] By way of illustration: Mt 7:15ff; *HermMan* 11; with differences: Lucian, *PergMort* 11-13; Origen, *Cels* 7:9, 11. On the decline of primitive Christian prophecy in the first half of the second century: M. Dibelius, *Die Apostolischen Väter IV: Der Hirt des Hermas* (Tübingen: Mohr, 1923 [HNT.E 4]) pp. 538ff.

[37] The dignity of the apostle is based on his rôle as representative of the Kyrios (11:4), the dignity of the prophet on his inspiration (11:7). The structure of 11:4/5f and 11:7/8ff is, in my opinion, parallel. Traditio-critical distinctions are not appropriate (*contra* Schille, cf. above n. 8).—Is there a contradiction between 11:7 and 11:8? The tradent wishes to hold on to both, to the unimpeachableness of the prophets (11:7) and to the need to be able to distinguish the true prophets from the false. Similarly Paul, cf. 1 Cor 2:15 with 14:29, 37f. The tradent's solution: the unimpeachableness is valid only for the *propheta verus* (11:8a). Harnack, *Lehre*, p. 43; von Campenhausen, *Kirchliches Amt*, p. 78.

[38] It is noteworthy that the pseudo-prophets are nowhere expressly branded as false teachers. Cf., on the other hand, the characterisation in the concluding apocalypse 16:3! (Schmithals, *Apostelamt*, p. 171, has in mind gnostic pneumatics).

stated differently: despite the signs of decay that had set in within the institution of itinerant charismatics, the local Christians should not doubt the institution of itinerant charismatics itself.[39] The independence and special rank of the itinerant charismatics (inasmuch as it is a matter of genuine apostles and true prophets!) is uncontested in the tradition.

Then again, both groups, the "itinerant" and the "settled" Christians, are undoubtedly dependent on each other. The itinerant charismatics cannot maintain their lifestyle without the permanent support of the brethren in the villages and small towns. They are dependent on lodging with them, on being provided with the most basic and meagre necessities and on being equipped by them for the following day (as far as the prophets are concerned: for the day of their onward travel). What they offer the local Christians, or for that matter the local communities, in exchange, is—not a material gift, but the charisma which has been given to them. It is questionable, in my opinion, whether one should really speak of a "leadership" of the "community" by the itinerant ascetics (in the case of the circumstances presented in 11:4ff). Itinerant charismatics are *eo ipso* not suitable for the leadership of a local community, nor are they predestined for it by virtue of their self-understanding. Beyond this it is even questionable to what extent we may already speak of constituted local communities for the relations presupposed by *Didache* 11:4ff. Then again, while present as guests, the charismatics would naturally have dominated the smaller or larger Christian groups in which they were received. Moreover, the Kyrios himself appears in the apostle (11:4) and the spirit-inspired word of the pneumatic is regarded as a command (11:9, 12). What the local Christians do for the itinerant charismatics is not to be understood as reward or payment. The local Christians only do their duty of supporting the itinerant ascetics by offering the Lord's emissary shelter, a place to sleep and food as he passes through on his "holy journey". It is more a matter of "archaic" motives, transformed by the motivational horizon of eschatological motivation, playing a rôle here.

III.

The situation presupposed by the Didachist (11:1-3; 12; 13; 15), paints a quite different picture.

Firstly, in view of 11:4ff, doubt remains whether clearly delineated local communities are already being presupposed (or whether one should not think rather of isolated groups not yet constituted into communities); for the situation of the redactor,

---

[39] von Campenhausen, *Kirchliches Amt*, p. 78.

however, all such doubt is ruled out. 15:1f presupposes constituted local communities, which are on the point of choosing
functionaries out of their own ranks. In the following we shall discuss what consequences that has for their relation to the itinerant
charismatics.

Furthermore, just as the groups of local Christians changed,
so also did the groups of the *peregrini*. Among other things, attention needs to be drawn above all to the fact that, besides the
itinerant charismatics, "ordinary" itinerant brethren are also visiting the community (12:1ff), that is, Christians who make no
charismatic claim—whereby some of them come intending to
settle[40] in the new place with the support of the communities
(12:3-5). Here too the community has to be protected from
impostors. The instructions of the Didachist seek in a casuistic
manner to counteract the danger of exploitation by dubious elements.[41]

Yet the immigration of itinerant charismatics did not cease.
The fact that the Didachist takes up the tradition of 11:4ff at all,
implies indeed that the problem it addressed still existed, in one
form or another, in his situation. In fact the institution of itinerant
charismatics is as alive for the Didachist as it ever was. Of course
fundamental changes have taken place. No mention is made of
itinerant apostles. The group of spirituals no longer consists of
apostles and prophets together (as in 11:4-12), but of prophets and
teachers (13:1-7; 15:1f). Within that group, the Didachist's chief
interest clearly lies with the prophets.

The teachers[42] are only mentioned beside and after them in
13:2, merely, in a hasty and somewhat incidental manner (13:3

---

[40] H reads καθῆσθαι in 12:3. Harnack, *Lehre*, p. 49, emends: καθίσαι. So too
13:1 (*Lehre*, p. 50). Yet καθῆσθαι can also have the reflexive meaning in LXX and
primitive Christian literature. *BAGD* s.v. καθῆσθαι; *BDF* §100.101.

[41] 12:1 formulates the basic rule: before any testing, the newcomer claiming to
be a Christian is to be accorded the right to hospitality. Only after the primitive
duties of initial hospitable reception have been fulfilled, should the new arrival be
tested (ἔπειτα δέ ... 1b). 12:2ff then goes into various cases. In the first case
(12:2): the guest is travelling through; he is to be received, to be supported, yet he
should make the claim to hospitality for no longer than two to three days (and that
only in case of need). In the second case (12:3-5): the new arrival wishes to settle.
The relevant instructions allow one to see something of the bad experience of the
local communities with various strange "brethren". The instruction deals with three
possibilities: (a) if the arrival has learnt a trade (in this case the community has no
duty to support him, he can take responsibility for himself: 12:3); (b) if the new
arrival has not learnt any trade, that is (as we are to understand) he is a day
labourer or a beggar (in this case the community should clearly try to find a job for
him: 12:4); (c) if the arrival is not prepared to take a job (in this case a harsh
refusal is given to him: 12:5).

[42] Most likely itinerant teachers are meant. Audet (*Didachè*, pp. 442, 456) thinks
otherwise.

immediately returns once again to the prophets).[43]

In addition, in the Didachist's day (and in his area) a change took place in the institution of itinerant prophecy.[44] 13:1ff deals with the case where a prophet (of course a *propheta verus!*) expresses the wish to settle, not temporarily but permanently, i.e. to give up his homelessness (the case is dealt with following another in which a non-charismatic Christian is desirous of permanent residence in the local community: 12:3ff). The Didachist considers it necessary to regulate the question as to what should happen if a previously homeless prophet wants to become resident—apparently this is not a run of the mill case, and apparently no consensus prevails as to what the local community should do. As the context shows, the special problem which surfaces in this is not that of becoming resident as such, but the question of the community's duty to support the prophet! For there is no doubt that the itinerant prophets have the right to reception and support. There were, however, certain doubts as to whether the prophet (like the ordinary Christian), who became resident, was exempted from the rule ἐργαζέσθω καὶ φαγέτω (12:3) or μὴ ἀργὸς μεθ' ὑμῶν ζήσεται Χριστιανός (12:4). The decision which the Didachist arrives at, is of great significance for the definition of his position. The settlement of the *propheta verus* is accepted, although *his original exceptional situation is preserved*. The προφήτης ἀληθινός (just like the διδάσκαλος ἀληθινός) should not be constrained to live from the work of his own hands (13:1f),[45] rather he is privileged with the right to the first fruits (13:3; applied to the small town situation in 13:5-7).[46] The

---

[43] As far as the διδάσκαλοι are concerned, the text only reveals this much: (1) They were missing in the old traditional material 11:4ff. (2) They play, on the other hand, a rôle in the conditions which the Didachist presupposes. (3) They are probably itinerant teachers; they belong in any case together with the prophets, form together with them a group standing over against the group of locally resident "clerics". (4) The teachers come in the rank after the prophets.

[44] Audet, *Didachè*, pp. 455f, thinks otherwise; Schille, "Recht", p. 86, correctly. Yet it seems to me that the expressions "Gemeinde-Beamtete" and "Anstellungsregelung" (with respect to 13:1) are not entirely appropriate.

[45] Cf. Mt 10:10b/Lk 10:7b (Q?). It cannot be proven that the redactor cites a written gospel. See Köster, *Überlieferung*, pp. 212f. Cf. further 1 Tim 5:18. Perhaps Paul in 1 Cor 9:14 also plays on the word. Originally it was a matter of a general maxim of Jewish *chokma* (Billb. I, p. 569; III, pp. 379ff, 400f), that was received by the Christian tradition and used particularly to justify the duty of supporting the apostle (Q), the prophet (Did.), the presbyter (1 Tim). It is to be noted that, in terms of the history of development (though not necessarily chronologically!), the use of the logion in the *Didache* represents an older stage than the use in 1 Tim.

[46] 13:5-7 extends the thinking of 13:3. The question of the offerings is more closely elaborated in a circumstantial manner. The content of 5-7 does not completely agree with 3. Knopf (*Die Lehre*, p. 35): "Offensichtlich werden jetzt auch die berücksichtigt, die keine eigene Landwirtschaft haben, sondern ihre Vorräte einkaufen, die von Handwerk, Gewerbe und Handel leben." Another interpretation

rationale for the decision is characteristic. It is given, on the one hand, by a recourse to the Old Testament tradition (13:3: the ἀπαρχή belongs to the prophets, because they assume the same position of honour as the ἀρχιερεῖς received in the old covenant;[47] it is difficult to reconcile a *munus sacerdotale* of the prophets with that!); and, on the other hand, the decision is justified by an appeal to the Jesus tradition (cf. the logion which he cites in 13:1f, framing it as a command of the Lord in 13:5, 7).[48]

Lastly, the changed situation shows itself in a still further, yet just as significant, place. In connection with instructions concerning the regular community gathering (chapter 14), the Didachist commands that the communities should elect out of their midst ἐπίσκοποι καὶ διάκονοι,[49] after which the conditions, which a candidate in order to assume such a function must bring, are enumerated (15:1).[50] This is not the place to go into the involved history of the development of these two terms;[51] for our context it suffices for the moment to recognize that the named officials (or better: functionaries) are representatives of the local communities.[52] This evidences once more the changed situation as

---

is given by Schille, "Recht", pp. 90f, 99f; cf. above n. 8. The (older) usage (13:5-7) represents, according to Schille ("Recht", p. 100), "eine Unterhaltsregelung für beschränkte Zeit"; and in particular the temporary stay of the catechist in the catachumen's home is being referred to. The later formula (3f) indicates "einen tiefgreifenden Wandel". The prophets are now employees of the local communities, and the transitory duty to support the prophets has, he argues, been raised to a standing duty (*Ibid.*). Lastly, the double rule 13:1f attests "das werdende Anstellungsrecht" (p. 100).

[47] The allusion is to the levitical gifts: Dt 18:4 cf. 16:2,10f; Num 18:8ff; Neh 10:32ff; Ez 45:13-16.

[48] A later glossator (cf. above n. 15) has interpolated the text in 13:4. The development has proceeded in the meantime. Now there is already an occasional lack of prophetic charismatics. In this case the community should bestow their contributions on the poor.

[49] The officials were apparently chosen by the whole community. χειροτονεῖν refers here to a "democratic" election in contrast to an authoritarian appointment. Cf. 2 Cor 8:19; Ign. *Phld* 10:1; *Smy* 11:2; *Pol* 7:2.—χειροτονεῖν is used differently in Acts 14:23; cf. Tit 1:9 vl. Here the term means not "elect" but "nominate", Lohse, *TDNT* IX, p. 437.

[50] Did. 15:1 names four conditions: ἄνδρας πραεῖς καὶ ἀφιλαργύρους καὶ ἀληθεῖς καὶ δεδοκιμασμένους. The instructions belong in the same literary genre as 1 Tim 3:1ff; Tit 1:5ff; 1 Pet 5:1ff; Ign. *Polyc* 5:2; 6:1. It is noteworthy how brief the elaborations in the *Didache* are.

[51] We can also not here go into the subject of the transition to the title "presbyter", which is not omitted here by co-incidence (in *Const* 7.31.1 it is has been added).

[52] The bishops and deacons are in any case no itinerant charismatics, but members of the local community. They were not called to discipleship in the narrower sense (like the charismatic apostles and prophets), but chosen and appointed by the community for a particular function in the regions of the local community.

compared to 11:4ff, not only in respect of the groups of local Christians (whose advanced stabilization resulted in the need for functionaries to lead and serve the community!), but also in respect of the rôle of the charismatics. For not only the local group of Christians appears in opposition to the charismatics, but also the charismatics who were in the process of settling must compete with the representatives and functionaries of the local community.[53] In 11:4ff we find the following dialectic: itinerant charismatics vs. the local Christians; here, however: charismatics in the process of settling vs. the functionaries of the local community. The expression λειτουργεῖν, λειτουργίαν (15:1)[54] alludes perhaps to the matter of carrying out and conducting the community worship service. The somewhat obscure text does not allow an accurate picture of the situation with any certainty. Only the intention of the Didachist is clear: the instruction in 15:1f obviously attempts to clarify the relationship of the two leading groups to the local community (and so naturally to each other). The Didachist is clearly intent on reconciliation. He does not wish to oust the charismatics, who are in the process of settling, from their dominant position; at the same time, however, he awards the same right to the emerging local "clergy" (*sit venia verbo*).[55] Both groups (the local functionaries as well as the pneumatics, who have become resident in the community) serve the local church by carrying out the "holy service".[56] The bishops and deacons are those honoured (by God!)[57] together with (15:2) the prophets and teachers.[58] That obviously means that the execution and the lead-

---

[53] The development which emerges here is valid initially only for the area of the tradition of the *Didache*. Generalizing hypotheses are not justified in my opinion.

[54] The expression is not unequivocal. For general observations on the word-group, see *TDNT* IV, pp. 226ff (Strathmann), where reference is made to Did. 15:1 only in passing (p. 229 line 1f).

[55] The way of the pneumatics (as far as the tradition area of the *Didache* is concerned) thus begins with a relative independence apart from the local Christians (as still in 11:4ff), leads to the incorporation into the local community (in which only they at first played a dominant rôle), and ends up in equality status with the local office-bearers (15:1f). In the end, the local clerics came to take over their functions entirely, and the idea and reality of the itinerant spirituals slip into the heterodox milieu.

[56] Harnack depicted it in this way: the bishops and deacons, originally active mostly in organization and administration, assume the teaching rôle of the charismatics as the latter recede or die out (*Lehre*, pp. 56ff, 137ff). Similarly: R. Knopf, *Das nachapostolische Zeitalter. Geschichte der christlichen Gemeinden vom Beginn der Flavierdynastie bis zum Ende Hadrians* (Tübingen: Mohr, 1905) pp. 156ff; Dibelius, *Geschichte*, p. 152. Against the idea of the rise of the stewards to spiritual functions: von Campenhausen, *Kirchliches Amt*, p. 79 n. 6. It is, in fact, a question whether the bishops and deacons called for in Did. 15:1f exercised merely organizational-practical functions.

[57] Harnack, *Lehre*, p. 58; Knopf, *Die Lehre*, pp. 37f.

[58] They stand on the same level as the charismatics.—Typically, there is, however, no obligation to support the local functionaries. The duty to support is

ership of the worship service, functions which had lain in the
hands of the pneumatics since the establishment of spirituals in the
community, should now be shared by the groups of functionaries
coming from the local communities themselves.[59] Or expressed
differently, the charismatics are being integrated into the local
community (without losing their exceptional status), while the
local community is producing functionaries who are assuming the
leadership functions of the charismatics. Incidentally, all of this
does not necessarily imply that the "officials" had come to restrict
or even rob the community of its autonomy. The warnings and
instructions are still directed to the whole community.[60] It is the
community that is called on to conduct itself properly toward the
different groups of immigrants (12:1 σύνεσιν γὰρ ἕξετε δεξιὰν
καὶ ἀριστεράν!);[61] it is considered capable of deciding for itself
(12:4) in cases which cannot be determined casuistically from the
outset, and it is the community, finally, which must elect
functionaries out of its ranks (15:1).

---

still limited to the charismatics.

[59] That this was to occur in proportion to the failure of prophets in the communities (Harnack, *Lehre*, p. 58; cf. p. 146; *TDNT* VI, p. 859 [Friedrich];
Kretschmar, "Askese", p. 38 n. 26) is of course not alluded to in 15:1f and can
only be concluded from 13:4—yet the latter probably depicts later conditions.

[60] Cf. von Campenhausen, *Kirchliches Amt*, pp. 78ff.—Schille ("Recht", pp.
102f and *passim*) judges otherwise, indeed he also reconstructs a quite different history of development and history of tradition. Cf. above n. 8. According to Schille,
his reconstruction is based on "die Diskussion um zwei entgegengesetzte Geist-
Konzeptionen" (p. 102), namely "die täuferische Behauptung einer vollgültigen
Geistbegabung aller Getauften", on the one hand, and "der Glaube an die her-
vorgehobene Stellung des Propheten als des Charismatikers im Vollsinne" on the
other (*Ibid.*). "Das deklarative Rechtsgebaren" (*Ibid.*) is characteristic of the first
group, "die dekretale Aufrichtung des eschatologischen Rechtes" is typical of the
second (p. 103.). In the area of the tradition of Did. 11-13, the prophetic charisma
was originally subordinate to the baptismal charisma, according to Schille; only
later, according to Schille, has the charisma of office, "kraft der angestammten
Selbständigkeit die Fesseln zerrissen und das Taufcharisma zur Laienbegabung
herabgewürdigt" (p. 103). While this interpretation clearly recognizes that two different groups stood opposed to each other, it fails, in my opinion, to see the social
dialectic separating the two groups (itinerant charismatics—local Christians) and the
course of the development.

[61] The phrasing in 12:1b is abbreviated (cf. Jonah 4:11 LXX), the use of
γνώσεσθε without an object is striking. Perhaps σύνεσιν γὰρ ἕξετε is to be
understood here parenthetically (Harnack, *Lehre*, p. 48). The sense is, however,
clear. On the terminology cf. *TDNT* II, p. 38 lines 19ff (Grundmann).

IV.

Obviously the stages of development indicated here are none other than stages in the development of the "process of catholicization", though at the time of the composition of the *Didache* this process has not been finalized, but is still completely in flux (It was first concluded in characteristic manner in the course of reworking of the *Didache* in the *Apostolic Constitutions!*). With respect to *Didache* 11-13, 15, the process of catholicization presents itself as *a process of successive incorporation of eschatologically motiv- ated itinerant asceticism into the association of "settled" Christ- ians, the local communities that are in turn becoming successively stabilized.* The dialectic evoked by the development is here (as elsewhere) that of the eschatological ἀπόταξις on the one hand and accommodation to the prevailing historical-social conditions on the other. *What leads to the early catholic solution, is the trend towards the stabilization of the group.* One should note, more- over, (once again, here as elsewhere) that the early catholic solu- tion (in this case the integration of the itinerant charismatics into the local communities) is not willing to surrender the eschatologi- cal motivation. The solution does not lie in the disappearance of the eschaton as motivation, but in finding ways of living that allow for eschatological motivation on the one hand and life under the conditions of social reality on the other hand. It is clear that the otherworldly charismatic institution of the itinerant apostles and prophets corresponds more closely to the original eschatological immediacy than the lifestyle of the local communities; it is just as clear that with the loss of the original immediacy, the institution of itinerant charismatics also must either become perverted or trans- formed into another social form. *For the eschaton can only become a historical force if it is communicated historically.* The future of the Church did not lie with the itinerant charismatics but with the individual local communities—but that does not mean, conversely, that a Church in the process of stabilizing itself rejected the charisma of the itinerant prophets. Rather the com- munities in the process of stabilization sought to integrate the charismatics, thus aiding not only the old institution of itinerant charismatics but also themselves in developing a new structure. The subsequent history of itinerant radicalism has shown that (in this case) no conclusive solution was found.

TORAH AND TROUBLESOME APOSTLES IN THE
DIDACHE COMMUNITY[1]

JONATHAN A. DRAPER

Pietermaritzburg

I. INTRODUCTION

The *Didache* has long been one of the most puzzling of the early Christian writings. It is routinely left out of consideration when an analysis of the evolution of early Christianity is attempted. Alternatively, it is relegated to some rural backwater out of the mainstream of development. J.P. Meier, for instance, throws in the towel and declines to use the *Didache* at all in his reconstruction of the development of Antiochene and Syrian Christianity, concluding that:

> We are left with something of a paradoxical situation: while some of the theological and liturgical traditions of the *Didache* show expansion upon and perhaps decline from those of Matthew's gospel, the church structure remains more primitive than that of Ignatius.[2]

Meier sees the *Didache* as the product of an isolated rural community, yet its influence is too widespread and early for this marginal origin[3]. J.-P. Audet's[4] attempt at a redactional analysis of the *Didache* is more convincing[5], as is his early dating for the writing, although his reconstruction is speculative and unlikely. In this paper, I will be attempting to follow one *trajectory* through

---

[1] This is a development of a paper presented to Dr. E. Bammel's Seminar on Christian Origins in Cambridge, while the author was on sabbatical leave sponsored by the Human Sciences Research Council.

[2] J.P. Meier & R.E. Brown, *Antioch and Rome: New Testament Cradles of Christianity* (London: Chapman, 1983) p. 84.

[3] Even the textual evidence argues against this, since texts or fragments of the *Didache*, have been found in Egypt, Ethiopia, Asia Minor and Syria. It has been used by a wide variety of secondary authors and was by some regarded as "Scripture".

[4] J.-P. Audet, *La Didachè: Instructions des Apôtres* (Paris: Gabalda, 1958). The multi-layered redactional nature of the *Didache* has been accepted also by R.A. Kraft (*Barnabas and the Didache* [New York: Nelson, 1965 (*AF* 3)] pp. 1-3, 76), M. E. Boring (*Sayings of the Risen Jesus: Christian Prophecy in the Synoptic Tradition* [Cambridge: University Press, 1982] pp. 47-48), and W. Rordorf & A. Tuilier (*La Doctrine des Douze Apôtres* [Paris: Les Éditions du Cerf, 1978 (SC 248)] pp. 17-21).

[5] It is in the nature of a community rule to be constantly updated, in accordance with the changing situation of the community. The manifest redactions of the *Manual of Discipline* are a contemporary example of such an ongoing process. For a convincing analysis of this process in 1QS, see J. M. O'Connor's analysis ("La Genèse Litteraire de la Règle de la Communauté", *RB* 76 [1969] pp. 528-549).

the *Didache*, namely the question of false apostles, and the threat they posed to the community. This represents the situation of the community at a particular stage of its development, which has been superseded by the final redaction of the text.

Form criticism seeks, by isolation and delineation of a literary form, to determine the life situation of the community which uses the form. On the other hand, since it is in the redaction of a text or tradition that the developing interests of a community at any particular stage of its history can be determined, particular care needs to be taken to map out the different layers of a developing tradition.[6] This article seeks, on the one hand, to make certain deductions concerning the *Sitz im Leben* of the *Didache* on the basis of the form of *instructions* given in a community rule, and on the other hand, to draw conclusions on the basis of the redaction of this form and its contents in the face of changing circumstances and controversy. The tradition concerning apostles and its redaction represent a historical dynamic, which is analysed in terms of its relation to the use of the same traditional material in Matthew's gospel.

II. THE FORM AND REDACTION HISTORY OF *DIDACHE* 11:1-6

While, as we have seen, it has often been noted before that *Didache* 11 is a patchwork of differing redactional stages[7], the process of development it represents needs further examination. The recent commentary by K. Niederwimmer[8] rightly sets a redactional analysis at the centre of its interpretation, but envisages the redaction in terms of composition by a single

---

[6] H. Conzelmann succinctly sums up the methodology with regard to the gospel material in *Theology of St. Luke*, trans. G. Buswell (San Francisco: Harper & Row, 1960) p. 12: "The first phase in the collection of the traditional material ...has been clarified by form criticism. Now a second phase has to be distinguished, in which the kerygma is not simply transmitted and received, but itself becomes the subject of reflection...This new stage is seen both in the critical attitude to tradition as well as in the positive formation of a new picture of history out of those already current, like stones used as parts of a new mosaic".

[7] Failure to take account of these stages has created confusion in the use G. Theissen makes of this passage in his theory of *Wanderradikalismus* (*The First Followers of Jesus* [London: SCM, 1978] pp. 7-30). This confusion is present also in the study of G. Kretschmar ("Ein Beitrag zur Frage nach dem Ursprung frühchristlicher Askese", *ZTK* 61 (1964) pp. 27-67, esp. 37-38), who sees apostles, prophets and teachers all as charismatics, who can be subsumed under the generic title "prophet".

[8] *Die Didache* (Göttingen: Vandenhoeck & Ruprecht, 1989). This builds on his important article, "Zur Entwicklungsgeschichte des Wanderradikalismus im Traditionsbereich der Didache", *Wiener Studien* 11 (1977) pp. 145-167, esp. 148-153.

author. This seems to fly in the face of the way a community rule evolves by trial and error, by erasing words or phrases, by inserting new words or phrases above the line or in the margin, which are later incorporated into the text. This process is graphically displayed in the manuscript of the *Community Rule* from Qumran.[9] Certainly whole new sections may have been added from time to time, but one should not hypothesize a wholesale, consistent composition for every change.

C.N. Jefford[10] also sets out a consistent redactional theory, in which an original core of 1-5(6) was revised by a first correction consisting of 7-10, and then by 11-15 as a second correction. However, he also notices contradictions in the instructions on apostles and prophets, which he attributes to "an even later hand". The result of this overview is that Jefford sees the final version of the *Didache* as reflecting "a mixture of world-views that ultimately were deemed to be useless by later religious communities" which "soon led to its rejection within the evolving church".[11] It seems, however, that the *Didache* continued to be modified and used, particularly by the communities of the *Apostolic Constitutions*, the *Liber Graduum* and the Coptic and Ethiopic churches. Jefford sees Matthew and the *Didache* as representing divergent trends from a common starting point. This article argues for a closer dialectic between the two texts, in which Matthew utilizes and ultimately undermines the need for the community rule, by taking up key elements of the community rule into the gospel form. The rule is then subordinated in the community to "gospel".

A certain perplexity also results from a fallacious use of the concept of "decline" which seems to influence many New Testament scholars, who view the *Didache* as a "decline" from the heights of Matthew's gospel.[12] This begs the question in assuming that a work inside the canon of Scripture must be prior to a work outside it. It is more likely that teachings emerge out of the concrete life-situations of a community in a rudimentary and unattractive form, and are later developed and refined theologically into a consistent whole.

The confusion over the *Didache* is also partly due to the failure to see that the instructions on the prophets represent the latest

---

[9] See especially 1QS 7 and 8, where numerous erasures, additions and corrections have been made. E.g. increasing problems in the community lead to the increase of a penalty from six months to one year, written above the line.

[10] *The Sayings of Jesus in the Teachings of the Apostles* (Leiden: Brill, 1989) p. 109.

[11] Jefford, *Sayings of Jesus*, pp. 117-118.

[12] E.g. E. Peterson, "Über einige Probleme der Didache-Überlieferung", in *Frühkirche, Judentum und Gnosis* (Rome: Herder, 1959) pp. 146-182.

redactional phase of the text, and not the earliest.[13] The instructions concerning the apostles show a different formal construction and a different temper to those concerning the prophets. I have argued elsewhere[14] that the instructions concerning apostles in 11:3-6 are from the earliest stage of the text. It is no accident that the *Didache* is associated with "the apostles" in its title uniformly through the tradition.[15] It is not that apostles are a thing of the past when the instructions were written.[16] There would be no need to write instructions regulating a dead institution, unless one posits an elaborate fraud to reconstruct an archaic document.[17]

Moreover, this instruction concerning apostles corresponds to the form of the instructions which precede it. Each set of instructions is prefaced by the same formula: περὶ δὲ τῶν...οὕτω ποιήσατε.[18] Only one subject appears in the title of each section

---

[13] This is related to the idea of "decline", in that it is assumed that the earliest Christian communities were "free and spontaneous" in their patterns of life and worship, and that this then declined into the formalism and authoritarianism of *Frühkatholizismus*. This is more a product of the Reformation and Liberal Protestantism than of historical verification. There is little evidence that a Jewish group in Palestine in the first century, nor its first successors in Syria, would have worshipped in such a manner. Pneumatic or ecstatic worship was more widely known and practised in the Hellenistic cults and may well have influenced the development of Christian worship as it moved out from its Palestinian heartland (Cf. Kretschmar, "Frühchristliche Askese", p. 38 n. 26). It is significant that it is above all Luke's picture of the development of the Church that supports such a picture.

[14] This is the subject of a paper presented at the 1989 meeting of the Society of Biblical Literature, Anaheim, entitled "Weber, Theissen and the Wandering Charismatics of the *Didache*", which is as yet unpublished.

[15] See Audet, *La Didachè*, pp. 91-103.

[16] Niederwimmer ("Entwicklungsgeschichte", pp. 149-150) argues that the "Didachist" composed the section out of older traditions. However, if the *Didache* is indeed a community rule, there would be no "Didachist", but only an ongoing process of correction and updating by a community.

[17] Such an elaborate process is posited by F. E. Vokes (*The Riddle of the Didache. Fact or Fiction, heresy or Catholicism?* (London: SPCK, 1938); cf. J. A. Robinson, *Barnabas, Hermas and the Didache* (London: SPCK, 1929), and R. H. Connolly, "The Didache in Relation to the Epistle of Barnabas", *JTS* 24 (1923) pp. 147-157. However, late pseudonymous works usually mention the apostles by name and add biographical detail real or invented to support the fiction. The *Ecclesiastical Cannons*, with their attribution of individual sayings to each of the apostles, or the *Didascalia*, with its elaborate description, show how such a "fraud" would operate. There is nothing in the *Didache* which indicates such a dynamic. Few critics today follow the "English School" in their radical rejection of the authenticity of the work.

[18] Compare περὶ δὲ τῆς βρώσεως, ὃ δύνασαι βάστασον (6·3); περὶ δὲ τοῦ βαπτίσματος, οὕτω βαπτίσατε (7·1); πρὸ δὲ τοῦ βαπτίσματος προνηστευσάτω (7·4); περὶ δὲ τῆς εὐχαριστίας, οὕτως εὐχαριστήσατε (9·1); μετὰ δὲ τὸ ἐμπλησθῆναι, οὕτως εὐχαριστήσατε (10·1); περὶ δὲ τῆς εὐωδίας, οὕτως εὐχαριστήσατε (10:8, in *Const* and the Coptic version, but absent from *H*). For a thorough examination of the Hellenistic background to the use of περὶ δέ, see M. M. Mitchell, "Concerning ΠΕΡΙ ΔΕ in 1 Corinthians", *NovT* 31/3 (1989) pp. 229-

introduced in this way, with the exception of 11:3, where the introduction of prophets into the title seems to be a redaction made at a time when instructions concerning prophets were added. The reference to the δόγμα τοῦ εὐαγγελίου also marks this as a later interpolation, as we have seen. The original title probably read περὶ δὲ τῶν ἀποστόλων, οὕτω ποιήσατε. The instructions of 11:3-6 show the same casuistic development and the same brevity as the other instructions in the section 6:2-10:6. The instructions on prophets are in marked contrast: detailed, self-contradictory in places and vivid. The instructions concerning prophets have tended, for this reason, to dominate discussion on the *Didache*.

Nevertheless, there are signs of controversy surrounding the institution of apostles in the *Didache* too.[19] Here I wish to focus particularly on 11:1-2. K. Niederwimmer sees this passage as a composition of the "Didachist", connecting the liturgical tradition of 9-10 with further traditional material concerning apostles.[20] However, the form of *instructions* does not require such connecting links between sections, which are simply introduced by περὶ δέ. Thus 11:1-2 should not be seen as a connecting link but as a later redaction, modifying the instructions on apostles in 11:3-6 in the light of new circumstances in the community:

11.1 Ὃς ἂν οὖν ἐλθὼν διδάξῃ ὑμᾶς ταῦτα πάντα τὰ προειρημένα, δέξασθε αὐτόν·
2. ἐὰν δὲ αὐτὸς ὁ διδάσκων στραφεὶς διδάσκῃ ἄλλην διδαχὴν εἰς τὸ καταλῦσαι, μὴ αὐτοῦ ἀκούσητε· εἰς δὲ τὸ προσθεῖναι δικαιοσύνην καὶ γνῶσιν κυρίου, δέξασθε αὐτὸν ὡς κύριον.

3. Περὶ δὲ τῶν ἀποστόλων [καὶ προφητῶν, κατὰ τὸ δόγμα τοῦ εὐαγγελίου] οὕτως ποιήσατε· 4. πᾶς [δὲ ἀπόστολος ἐρχόμενος πρὸς ὑμᾶς δεχθήτω [ὡς κύριος]· 5. [οὐ μενεῖ εἰ μὴ] ἡμέραν μίαν· ἐὰν δὲ ᾖ χρεία, καὶ τὴν ἄλλην. τρεῖς δὲ ἐὰν μείνῃ, ψευδοπροφήτης ἐστίν.
6. ἐξερχόμενος δὲ ὁ ἀπόστολος μηδὲν λαμβανέτω εἰ μὴ ἄρτον ἕως οὗ αὐλισθῇ. ἐὰν δὲ ἀργύριον αἰτῇ, ψευδοπροφήτης ἐστί.

---

256. Note also, however, the Semitic background in the use of על or ועל in CD 9:8; 10:10, 14; 16:10, 13, and עליו, נאמר, על זה in the Rabbinic writings (W. Bacher, *Die exegetische Terminologie der jüdischen Traditionsliteratur* [Darmstadt, 1899] Vol. I, pp. 5f; Vol. II pp. 148).

[19] *Contra* K. Wengst (*Didache (Apostellehre) Barnabasbrief, Zweiter Klemensbrief Schrift an Diognet* [Darmstadt: Wissenschaftliche Buchgesellschaft, 1984] p. 37), who argues that the problem here is not dogmatic but one of charlatans. This comes from confusing the instructions concerning apostles with those concerning prophets.

[20] *Die Didache*, pp. 212-214. Niederwimmer recognizes that the formula is itself part of the tradition. On the other hand, he rightly observes that the reference to the "gospel" is characteristic of the last stage of the redaction, so that he sees the whole section coming from the pen of the redactor. We argue here that if the introduction and the following instructions are both provided by the tradition, then the work of the redactor is more likely to be in the form of an interpolation between the introduction and the instruction, to link this traditional instruction on apostles with

The text presents several problems. In particular, the phrase ὡς κύριον in 11:4 is missing in the Coptic and Ethiopic versions. However, the omission in the Coptic occurs in the break between folio I and II, where the manuscript contains five indecipherable letters. This indicates that the scribe was aware of making an omission.[21] The Ethiopic omits not only ὡς κύριος but δεχθήτω and οὐ...εἰ μὴ as well, which seems to indicate a deliberate revision. The text given above is found in the Jerusalem manuscript, and is supported by the revision found in the *Apostolic Constitutions*, ὡς Χριστοῦ μαθητήν. The latter indicates a smoothing over of a theological problem which may also be behind the omission of ὡς κυρίος in Coptic and Ethiopic, namely the scandal of according the same treatment to a human teacher as to the Lord. The *Apostolic Constitutions* takes the teaching as referring to the correct way to say the eucharist, and proceeds to omit the whole of 11:2-6. Clearly the idea of receiving anyone "as the Lord" was problematic, given the development of a heightened Christology and the experience of imposters. The Coptic retains the phrase in 11:2, in agreement with the Jerusalem text. Thus ὡς κύριος should be retained in 11:4.[22] δέ is present in 11:4 in the Jerusalem text, but absent in Coptic and Ethiopic and should be omitted. Its absence is a further indication that at one stage there was no mention of prophets in the superscription.

The passage 11:1-2, then, is connected to what follows by the *Stichwort* ὡς κύριον. The problem relates to the instruction that the apostle is to be received "as if he were the Lord himself". This is, of course, the proper function of an apostle, according to the Jewish legal institution of the שליח.[23] The instructions in 11:1-

---

instructions on prophets.

[21] See L. T. Lefort, *Les Pères Apostoliques en copte* (Louvain, 1952 [CSCO]) p. 33; *contra* C. Schmidt, "Das koptische Didache-Fragment des British Museum", *ZNW* 24 (1925) pp. 81-99, esp. 87.

[22] As in Rordorf & Tuilier, *Doctrine*, p. 184; *contra* Wengst, *Didache (Apostellehre)*, p. 82.

[23] The principle is that "A man's *shaliach* is as himself" (שליחו אדם כמותו *m.Ber* 5:5; *b.Ned* 72b; *b.Qid* 41b; *b.Hag* 10b; *b.Naz* 12b; *b.BM* 96a; *b.Men* 93b). The Christian apostle's function is essentially *representative* of the Lord who sends him, whereas the prophet claims direct revelation through the Spirit. This is argued in detail in my SBL paper "Weber, Theissen and Wandering Charismatics". Whether or not a Jewish *office* of apostle existed in Jesus' lifetime is, of course, a matter of dispute. J. B. Lightfoot ("The Name and Office of an Apostle" in *St. Paul's Epistle to the Galatians* [London: Macmillan, 1865] pp. 93-94]), A. Harnack (*The Mission and Expansion of Christianity* I [London, 1908] pp. 327ff) and K. H. Rengstorf ("ΑΠΟΣΤΟΛΟΣ", *Theological Dictionary of the New Testament*, ed. G. Kittel, trns. G. W. Bromiley [Grand Rapids: Eerdmans, 1964] pp. 407-447; cf. Niederwimmer, *Die Didache*, p. 213) argue for the existence of such an office. Against its existence are A. Ehrhardt (*The Apostolic Succession in the First Two Centuries of the Church* [London: Lutterworth, 1953] p. 17), W. Schmithals (*The*

2 do not relate to anything in the instructions concerning prophets, but only to those concerning apostles. This is significant, in light of our contention that the instructions concerning prophets come from the latest phase of the text's development. Moreover, 11:1-2 must have been written *after* 11:3-6, since this formula *introduces* the instruction on apostles (περὶ δέ). Here in 11:1-2 we have to do with an intermediate phase, a redaction of the instruction concerning the reception of apostles by the community at a time when they were a very real institution, but apostles had come to feature in doctrinal dispute(s).

The problem with which the instructions deal is that of false teaching given by people claiming to be apostles. This teaching is fundamentally subversive of the foundational instruction of the community, reflected in *Didache* 1-10 (ταῦτα πάντα τὰ προειρημένα). We would be in a position to know a lot more about the mysterious *Didache* community if we could only know what dispute is hidden behind this brief redactional insertion in 11.1-2. To paraphrase a German proverb, "Tell me who you're fighting, and I'll tell you who you are"[24].

III. THE THREAT TO THE COMMUNITY OF THE *DIDACHE*

The Relation between Didache and Matthew
Fortunately, there is a clue provided by Matthew's Gospel, to which the *Didache* is closely related. The *Didache* is a "Q" community, and draws on the same traditions as does Matthew, although it cannot be shown to be dependent on Matthew as we have it.[25] The relationship of the *Didache* with the "Q" tradition is

---

Office of Apostle in the Early Church [London: SPCK, 1971] pp. 98-110) and J. H. Schütz (*Paul and the Anatomy of Apostolic Authority* [Cambridge: University Press, 1975] pp. 28-29). The argument in favour of its existence seems strong, and it may be that the evidence against it is artificially strengthened by Paul's statements, when Paul himself is concerned to play down the significance of the "office" of apostle for his own reasons. In any case, for the purpose of this paper, it is only necessary to establish that the *function* of apostle is clearly differentiated from the *function* of prophet.

[24] My translation. Taken from E. Bammel, "Sadduzäer und Sadokiden", *ETL* 55 (1979) pp. 107-115, esp. 107.

[25] See J. A. Draper, "The Jesus Tradition in the Didache", in *Gospel Perspectives V: The Jesus Tradition Outside the Gospels*, ed. D. Wenham (Sheffield: JSOT, 1985) pp. 269-289; cf. R. Glover, "The Didache's Quotations and the Synoptic Gospels", *NTS* 5 (1958-1959) pp. 12-29. The opposite view is held by H. Köster (*Synoptische Überlieferung bei den Apostolischen Väter* [Berlin: Akademie Verlag, 1957 (*TU* 65)] pp. 159-241), B. Layton ("The Sources, Dates and Transmission of Didache 1:3b-2:1", *HTR* 61 [1968] pp. 343-383) and E. Massaux (*The Influence of the Gospel of Saint Matthew on Christian Literature before Saint Irenaeus*, trns. N. J. Belval & S. Hecht [Macon, Ga: Mercer University Press, 1990-1993 (NGSt 5,1-3)]).

complex. It appears as if this "Q" material gradually penetrated an existing community rule, especially in the catechetical section of chapters 1-6, where 1:2-6 is clearly an insertion. Chapters 8 and 15 also seem to be a later layer in the tradition, in which "gospel" gradually comes to replace "*didache*". In particular, 15:4 is subversive of the whole community rule, since it subordinates its teaching to the emerging gospel tradition, which may, perhaps, already be a written document at this stage[26]: τὰς δὲ εὐχὰς ὑμῶν καὶ τὰς ἐλεημοσύνας καὶ πάσας τὰς πράξεις οὕτω ποιήσατε, ὡς ἔχετε ἐν τῷ εὐαγγελίῳ τοῦ κυρίου ἡμῶν. One may well ask, if all of this teaching is already in a written gospel, what need of the *Didache*.

On the other hand, while the Jesus tradition of "Q" represents a gradual intrusion, other points of contact between Matthew and the *Didache* are not related to "Q", but seem to have their original *Sitz im Leben* in instruction concerning community problems and discipline. Other factors apart, it would seem more likely that these points of contact originate in a community rule, which then influence the arrangement of the "Q" material in Matthew's redaction, since the Sermon on the Mount is that writer's own creation, ordering originally independent material (found partially scattered in Luke) according to a grand design.[27] In this study the attempt will be made to show that the *Didache*, at least in an early form, lies behind the composition of parts of Matthew. Like Audet[28], I believe that the *Didache* comes from the same community as Matthew, namely from Antioch[29], although this is not the place to argue that in detail.[30] If both documents emerge

---

[26] Cf. H. Köster, "Überlieferung und Geschichte der frühchristlichen Evangelienliteratur" (in W. Haase, *Aufstieg und Niedergang der Römischen Welt: Geschichte und Kultur Roms im Spiegel der Neueren Forschung* II.2,) pp. 1463-1542, esp. 1466.

[27] This design may well have been catechetical, which would provide a further link with *Didache*. See the discussion on δικαιοσύνη below.

[28] *La Didachè*, pp. 211-219.

[29] For a summary of the evidence, see W. D. Davies & D. C. Allison, *The Gospel according to Matthew* I (Edinburgh: Clark, 1988 [*ICC*]) pp. 143-147). A Syrian background to *Didache* is also accepted, with variations, by E. Peterson ("Einige Probleme", pp. 146-182), A. Adam ("Erwägungen zur Herkunft der Didache", *Zeitschrift für Kirchengeschichte* 68 [1957] pp. 1-47) and G. Kretschmar ("Frühchristliche Askese", pp.29-32).

[30] I have studied this connection more thoroughly in *The Didache: its Text, its Nature and its Community. A Study in the Relationship of Literary Form, Redaction and Society. Final Report to the Human Sciences Research Council on Specialized Research Abroad, at Cambridge University, September 1988 to January 1989* (Unpublished).

from the same community, one need not see the relationship
between them as a one way literary dependence, but as a dialectic
in which each influenced the development of the other. In the end,
however, the gospel *genre* replaced the *genre* of the community
rule. The *genre* of the community rule or church order did survive
on the periphery, but without the authority of Scripture.

The Instructions of Didache 11:1-2 and Matthew 5:17-20

The implication of the instructions in 11:1-2 is that some
(apostles) are going around teaching something different to what is
contained in *Didache* 1-10. What is particularly interesting here,
is the close relationship of the language of *Didache* 11:1-2 to the
polemic in Matthew 5:17-20:

Didache 11:1-2

ὃς ἂν οὖν ἐλθὼν διδάξῃ ὑμᾶς ταῦτα
πάντα τὰ προειρημένα, δέξασθε αὐτόν.
ἐὰν δὲ αὐτὸς ὁ διδάσκων στραφεὶς
διδάσκῃ ἄλλην διδαχὴν εἰς τὸ
καταλῦσαι, μὴ αὐτοῦ ἀκούσητε, εἰς δὲ τὸ
προσθεῖναι δικαιοσύνην καὶ γνῶσιν
κυρίου, δέξασθε αὐτὸν ὡς κύριον

Matthew 5:17-20

Μὴ νομίσητε ὅτι ἦλθον καταλῦσαι τὸν
νόμον ἢ τοὺς προφήτας· οὐκ ἦλθον
καταλῦσαι ἀλλὰ πληρῶσαι. ἀμὴν γὰρ
λέγω ὑμῖν· ἕως ἂν παρέλθῃ ὁ οὐρανὸς
καὶ ἡ γῆ, ἰῶτα ἓν ἢ μία κεραία οὐ μὴ
παρέλθῃ ἀπὸ τοῦ νόμου, ἕως ἂν πάντα
γένηται. ὃς ἐὰν οὖν λύσῃ μίαν τῶν
ἐντολῶν τούτων τῶν ἐλαχίστων καὶ
διδάξῃ οὕτως τοὺς ἀνθρώπους,
ἐλάχιστος κληθήσεται ἐν τῇ βασιλείᾳ
τῶν οὐρανῶν· ὃς δ' ἂν ποιήσῃ καὶ διδάξ
οὗτος μέγας κληθήσεται ἐν τῇ βασιλεί
τῶν οὐρανῶν. Λέγω γὰρ ὑμῖν ὅτι ἐὰν μ
περισσεύσῃ ὑμῶν ἡ δικαιοσύνη πλεῖον τ
γραμματέων καὶ Φαρισαίων, οὐ μὴ
εἰσέλθητε εἰς τὴν βασιλείαν τῶν
οὐρανῶν.

The wording is so close that some kind of literary relationship
between the two writings seems to be required. The problem
seems to be the same in both. In Matthew, the problem is the
abiding validity of the Torah[31]: heaven and earth will pass away,
but not one least part of the Torah ἕως ἂν πάντα γένηται. R.
Bultmann sees reflected here the debate between Matthew's community and the Hellenistic church.[32] E. Schweizer takes ἕως ἂν

---

[31] Cf. W. G. Kümmel, "Jesus und der jüdische Traditionsgedanke", *ZNW* 33
(1934) pp. 129f; G. Barth, "Matthew's Understanding of the Law", in G.
Bornkamm, G. Barth & H. J. Held, *Tradition and Interpretation in Matthew*
(London: SCM, 1960) pp. 58-164, esp. 62-73.

[32] R. Bultmann, *History of the Synoptic Tradition* (Oxford: Blackwell, 1972) pp.
146f. Cf. G. Barth, who argues that "one cannot therefore avoid seeing behind the
opponents attacked here the apostle Paul, whatever the distance" ("Matthew's
Understanding", p. 161).

πάντα γένηται, seen as the work of the evangelist redacting received tradition, as the key to understanding the passage. The phrase then makes the validity of the Torah conditional and points forward to its fulfilment in God and neighbour love in the teaching of Jesus.[33]

W.D. Davies[34] sets these words solely on the lips of the historical Jesus, so that they refer to the death of Jesus and the inauguration of the new Covenant. According to him, the legalism belongs to Jesus and not to Matthew, so that any reference to Paul and legal controversy in the community is ruled out. However, we shall argue that this passage draws its meaning from the whole context of 5:17-48, and is intended to function as instruction for Matthew's community.

For Matthew, the man who teaches one to break the Torah (διδάξῃ οὕτως) is the least in the kingdom[35], although with this, he is still recognized as a fellow Christian. Clearly this is the language of internal polemic in the Christian community. In the *Didache*, the one who is teaching claims to be an apostle, but must not be received by the community. Still further detail is provided concerning this kind of apostle: he is one who has "turned" (στραφείς). He once was acceptable, but his present teaching makes him unacceptable, because it is regarded as threatening the foundational norms of the community.

The uncommon word καταλῦσαι seems to have a technical reference to undermining Torah[36], as it is used in Matthew (καταλῦσαι τὸν νόμον). This is confirmed by its use in 2 Maccabees 2:22 (καταλύεσθαι νόμους), Josephus (*AJ* XVI.35 καταλῦσαί τι τῶν πατρίων; *BJ* II.393 σπουδὴ γὰρ ὑμῖν μία τὸ μὴ τῶν πατρίων τι καταλῦσαι; cf *BJ* IV.382) and Philo (*SpecLeg* III.182).[37]

A further parallel with the *Didache* injunction comes in the demand that Christian righteousness (δικαιοσύνη) must exceed that of the Pharisees and Scribes (περισσεύσῃ ...πλεῖον). Since G.

[33] E. Schweizer, "Matth. 5,17-20: Anmerkungen zum Gesetzesverständnis des Matthäus" in *Neotestamentica* (Stuttgart: Zwingli Verlag, 1963) pp. 399-406. Cf. G. Bornkamm, "End-Expectation and Church in Matthew" (in Bornkamm, Barth & Held, *Tradition and Interpretation*, pp. 31-32, 70-71; J. Gnilka, *Das Matthäus-evangelium* (Freiburg: Herder, 1986) pp. 140-149.

[34] W. D. Davies, *The Setting of the Sermon on the Mount* (Cambridge: University Press, 1964) pp. 334-336.

[35] Note the ironic interplay between "least commandment" and "least in the kingdom" observed by J. Gnilka, *Matthäus-evangelium*, pp. 195-196.

[36] Cf. F. Büchsel "ΛΥΩ" (*TDNT* IV) pp. 335-338, esp. 336, 338.

[37] See also Tatian, resident of Antioch from AD c166 until his death, cited by Clement of Alexandria, *Stromata* III.12 (81.2ff), also in connection with the debate over the Law: πλὴν οὐχ ᾗ βούλεται ἐκεῖνος καταλύων τὸν νόμον ὡς ἄλλου θεοῦ. Cf. Gnilka, *Matthäus-evangelium*, p. 143.

Strecker[38], it is widely agreed that δικαιοσύνη reflects a particular redactional emphasis in Matthew, occurring at seven key points (3:15; 5:6, 10, 20; 6:1, 33; 21:32).[39] The use of δικαιοσύνη in 5:20 and 6:1 is particularly emphatic, in that it introduces and concludes a section of legal interpretation. In particular, 6:1 refers to actual conduct which can be observed or not observed.

This indicates that an ethical interpretation of the term is correct, and that it has its basis in observation of the Torah according to its interpretation within the Christian community.[40] So the *Didache* suggests that one should receive the teacher who interprets the Torah in this way, who "adds to righteousness", but not one who advocates the abolition of the Torah! Matthew amplifies what this means, since the following verses (5:21-47) take the five commandments of the second tablet of the Decalogue and heighten each of them in turn, to "add to righteousness".[41] This procedure is then summarized by the injunction to perfection, a key word also for the *Didache*: ἔσεσθε οὖν ὑμεῖς τέλειοι ὡς ὁ πατὴρ ὑμῶν ὁ οὐράνιος τέλειός ἐστιν (Mt 5:48; cf *Did* 1:4; 6:2; c.f. in verbal form 10:5; 16:2). The whole section shows Matthew collecting together catechetical material into a carefully constructed unit, in a way which matches the much briefer statement of the *Didache*.

Nothing in all of this suggests that the *Didache* is drawing on the text of Matthew. There is no mention of the "gospel" until 11:3, and here in what we have argued is a redactional insertion linked to the material on prophets. On the other hand, there are some features which suggest that Matthew may be drawing on *Didache* 11.1-2. Here it occurs in the form of *instruction*, where it has a clear setting in life in the community. Gnilka argues that the dispute over the Torah was a *past* debate by the time of the final redaction of the tradition in Matthew's gospel, although the text shows signs of the debate in different redactional layers.[42] In the final resolution, the Law is re-affirmed, but subordinated to the organizing principle of God and neighbour love, or the Golden Rule. It is important to note that the same solution is adopted by the *Didache*, where these very things are inserted into the Two Ways (1:2) and become the *first* principle of the Way of Life

---

[38] *Der Weg der Gerechtigkeit* (Göttingen: Vandenhoeck & Ruprecht, 1966 [FRLANT 82]). Cf. G. Bornkamm, "End-Expectation", pp. 30-31.

[39] The debate, which is well summarized by W. Popkes recent article ("Die Gerechtigkeitstradition in Matthäus-Evangelium", *ZNW* 80 [1989] pp. 1-23, esp. 1-3), has largely concerned whether Matthew holds a view of "righteousness" as grace or works or both.

[40] See, for example, Phil 3:6, κατὰ δικαιοσύνην τὴν ἐν νόμῳ γενόμενος ἄμεμπτος. Cf. Bornkamm, "End-Expectation", p. 25.

[41] Cf. Gnilka, *Matthäus-evangelium*, p. 141.

[42] *Ibid.*, pp. 147-148.

(πρῶτον). The original interpretation of the Two Ways consisted of haggadic expansion of the moral sections of the Torah, especially the Decalogue. This now becomes the *second* principle (2:1).[43] The new "first" interpretation is then further defined by the addition of material drawn from the "Q" tradition in 1:3-6.[44] Seemingly, in the *Didache* we can observe the development still in process, which comes to full theological expression in Matthew.

A recent contribution to the δικαοσύνη-tradition within Matthew by W. Popkes, taking up a suggestion of G. Braumann,[45] has argued persuasively that the *Sitz im Leben* of the tradition lies in instruction for neophytes.[46] If he is correct, then this would tend to highlight the cnnection of the tradition in Matthew with the *Didache*, which contains such catechetical instruction in chapters 1-6, followed by instructions concerning baptism.

Matthew represents a development of the material by means of theological reflection, and its authority is guaranteed by setting it on the lips of Jesus himself.[47] The development is essentially *Christological*, in that the material on the abiding validity of the Torah is bracketed between the "I"-Sayings of vv 17 and 20. "The consistent and radical acceptance of the law (in its actual intention) thus stands for Matthew in the closest connexion with his Christology".[48] The *Didache*, on the other hand, shows little,

---

[43] Cf. Draper, "Jesus Tradition", pp. 271-272.

[44] The relegation of this material to the footnotes by Wengst (*Didache (Apostellehre)*, pp. 66-68), while he retains the insertions of the Jesus tradition in chapters 8 and 15, seems to me to be inconsistent and misleading. No-one would deny that the passage was missing in the original Two Ways teaching, but it is present in every witness to the *Didache* which we possess.

[45] "Zum traditionsgeschichtlichen Problem der Seligpreisungen Mt V 3-12", *NT* 4 (1960) pp. 253-260.

[46] Popkes states the problem in helpfully precise terms, "Zudem fällt auf, daß Matthäus das Wort nirgendwo näher erläutert oder kommentiert, vielmehr als Interpretament verwendet und somit offenbar als bekannt voraussetzt. Es signalisiert anscheinend für Matthäus und seine Leser eine spezielle Vorgeschichte. Die Frage ist: welche?" ("Die Gerechtigkeitstradition", pp. 4-5). J. Jeremias raises the same question, with his insistence that particular sayings in the Sermon on the Mount can only be understood on the presupposition that "it was preceded by something else" (*The Sermon on the Mount*, trns. N. Perrin [Philadelphia: Fortress, 1963] p. 26). *Didache*, it seems, offers the social historian a glimpse of that particular pre-history of the tradition in Matthew. More recently, Gnilka (*Matthäus-evangelium*, p. 142) argues that the mention of entry into the kingdom of heaven in Matthew 5:19 indicates a catechetical *Sitz im Leben*.

[47] Although it is hazzardous to make comparisons, one might say of Matthew, as Bultmann says of Paul's relation to the Hellenistic church, that he "raised the theological motifs that were at work" in the Antioch community "to the clarity of theological thinking" (*Theology of the New Testament* I, trans. K. Grobel [London: SCM, 1952] p. 187).

[48] Bornkamm, "End-Expectation", p. 37. Cf. Barth, "Matthew's Understanding", pp. 147-153.

if any, interest in Christological speculation, which is usually seen
by critics as a sign of late development of the tradition. The quarrel within the Christian community concerning the observation of
the Torah seems to have receded somewhat in Matthew, and to be
replaced by hostility to the Scribes and Pharisees. *Didache* 8:1-2,
on the other hand, while it advocates separation of its community
from other Jewish groups, whom it describes as ὑποκριτῶν, shows
no other trace of hostility towards them. Yet it shows great
hostility towards Christians who advocate the abolition of the
Torah. These two features in Matthew represent a movement
towards rapprochement between his community and the Pauline
churches, and a corresponding movement away from the Jewish
community, a movement which is more fully represented by
Luke-Acts. Increasingly, the abiding validity of the Torah is
related to Jesus Word as interpretation and fulfilment. In Matthew
24:35, the words of Jesus (οἱ δὲ λόγοι μου) replace the Torah in
the same saying in 5:18. The *Didache* seems to represent the earlier stage of development.

In Matthew it is not false apostles who represent a threat, but
false prophets (7:15-20). This would, according to the redactional
analysis offered above, align Matthew with the latest redaction of
the *Didache* instructions, where prophets replace apostles as the
burning issue in the community.

IV. THE "WHOLE YOKE OF THE LORD" (*DIDACHE* 6:2)

A further identifying mark of the *Didache* community, which
relates to the instructions on false apostles in 11:1-2, and provides
a clue to the solution of the puzzle, is *Didache* 6:1-3:

6:1 Ὅρα, μὴ τίς σε πλανήσῃ ἀπὸ ταύτης τῆς ὁδοῦ τῆς διδαχῆς, ἐπεὶ
παρεκτὸς θεοῦ σε διδάσκει.
2. Εἰ μὲν γὰρ δύνασαι βαστάσαι ὅλον τὸν ζυγὸν τοῦ κυρίου, τέλειος ἔσῃ·
εἰ δ' οὐ δύνασαι, ὃ δύνῃ, τοῦτο ποίει.
3. Περὶ δὲ τῆς βρώσεως, ὃ δύνασαι βάστασον· ἀπὸ δὲ τοῦ εἰδωλοθύτου
λίαν πρόσεχε· λατρεία γάρ ἐστι θεῶν νεκρῶν.

Here again, there is a concern to preserve the foundational teaching of the community against false teachers. The perspective is
markedly different, however, in the absence of a Christological
reference: it is not a matter here of ὡς κύριος, but of παρεκτὸς
θεοῦ. 6:1 is part of the Two Ways teaching and acts as a final
warning to preserve its integrity.[49] 11:1 represents a later stage of

---

[49] *Contra* Jefford (*The Sayings of Jesus*, pp. 93-96), who sees it as a late transi-
tional section by "some redactor other than the Didachist".

the redaction of the *Didache*, and shows a significant Christological development.

Although traces of 6:2-3 remain in the Two Ways tradition,
it is only in the *Didache* that this text occurs in this form[50]. This is
an indication that it was found to be objectionable by redactors
and compilers. A. von Harnack[51] and, after him, R. Knopf[52],
have seen here the teaching of Christian asceticism, which divided
Christians into the "perfect", who abstain from carnal pleasures,
and the bulk of Christians, who do the best they can. There is
certainly evidence that the passage came to be used in this way[53],
indeed, it may be that the text only survived at all because Tatian
introduced encratism into Antioch, but there is no evidence that
this is its original meaning.[54] There is little, if any, trace of
asceticism in the rest of the document, except for the lifestyle of
the prophets, which reflects a later state of development in the
community. Even here, the evidence for asceticism is implied
rather than stated.[55]

Moreover, 6:3 clearly refers to the question of idol worship
and belongs in the realm of Jewish ritual food laws. The sub-title
of the *Didache* in the Jerusalem manuscript gives the setting: "The

---

[50] Although note the presence of at least 6:3 in the Ethiopian Church Order in a
garbled form (G. Horner, *The Statutes of the Apostles* [London: Williams &
Norgate, 1904] p. 129 lines 4-6). Textual critics of the Didache do not seem to have
noticed this fact.

[51] *Die Lehre der Zwölf Apostel* (Leipzig: Hinriche, 1896 [*TU* 2/1-2]), pp. 19-22.

[52] *Die Lehre der Zwölf Apostel. Die Zwei Clemensbriefe* (*HzNT. Die Apostolischen Väter* I, Tübingen: Mohr, 1920), pp. 20-21.

[53] The sermon *De Centesima*, published by R. Reizenstein ("Eine fruhchristliche
Schrift von der dreierlei Fruchten des christlichen Lebens", *ZNW* 15 [1914] pp. 60-
90), uses the passage in this way. Eusebius uses similar language in *Demonstration*
I.8 concerning the δυο βιον of the "more perfect form (ἐντελής) of the Christian
life". Above all, it is the Fourth Century *Liber graduum* (ed. M. Kmosko,
Patrologia Syriaca III [Paris: Firmin -Didot, 1926]), for which *Didache* is
"Scripture" (*kthîb*, e.g. VII.20), which best reflects this trend. Its compatibility
with this ascetic usage is probably the reason for the survival of the Didache.

[54] Cf. Rordorf & Tuilier (*La Doctrine*, pp. 32-33) and Kretschmar
("Frühchristliche Askese", pp. 61-62).

[55] Unless the μυστήριον κοσμικόν ἐκκλησίας (11:11) is taken to refer to
"syzygy", the ascetic union between a prophet and a virgin, as suggested by
Harnack (*Die Lehre*, pp. 44-48), Adam ("Erwägungen zur Herkunft", pp. 20f), H.
von Campenhausen ("Early Christian Asceticism" in *Tradition and Life in the
Church* [London: Collins, 1968] pp. 90-122, esp. 117 n. 190) and Kretschmar
("Frühchristliche Askese", p. 34), or ascetic renunciation of marriage, as suggested
by Knopf (*Lehre der Zwölf Apostel*, pp. 32-33). The evidence for such an assumption is slight, and the reference could also be to unconventional symbolic actions of
the prophets (Audet, *La Didachè*, pp. 451-453; cf. Rordorf & Tuilier, *La Doctrine*,
p. 187). The contention of A. Broek-Utne ("Eine schwierige Stelle in einer alten
Gemeindeordnung, Did. 11:11", *ZKG* 54 [1935] pp. 576-581) that it refers forward
to almsgiving in 11:12, is possible but unlikely.

Teaching of the Lord through the twelve apostles to the Gentiles".
This title implies the teaching of a basically Jewish church to
Gentile converts, and there is no reason to doubt that it is intended
literally. A. Stuiber[56] has argued convincingly that the reference
of "the whole yoke of the Lord" is to the Torah as the yoke of
Yahweh, which is the final step for the Gentile proselyte, although
he sees this as a purely Jewish text. C. Deutsch, in a recent study
of Matthew 11:25-30,[57] has re-affirmed the necessary connection
between the metaphorical use of "yoke" and Torah (or at least of
"Wisdom...which is to be equated with Torah"[58]) in Jewish thinking.

If, however, *Didache* 6:2 were a "purely Jewish text", the
problem would be: why should any Christian document continue
to advocate such a Jewish teaching? The reference certainly seems
to be to the Torah as the "yoke", but understood now as the yoke
"of the Lord". There is no example of such terminology in the
Jewish texts, where it is "the yoke of Heaven" or "the yoke of the
kingdom". If the reference of "yoke" in the *Didache* is to the
Torah, as seems likely, it refers to the Torah *as interpreted by the
Lord, i.e. by the Christian community under the influence of the
Jesus tradition.*

The use of ζυγός in the New Testament
A study of the expression δύνασαι βαστάσαι ὅλον τὸν ζυγὸν τοῦ
κυρίου confirms this background to the text. Of the five occur-
rences of ζυγός in the New Testament, one refers literally to a
yoke (1 Tim 6:1), and the others all relate to the Torah.

In Acts 15:10, the question concerns the obligation of the
Gentiles to accept the full Jewish Torah, arising out of the crisis in
Antioch[59]:

---

[56] See A Stuiber, "Das ganze Joch des Herrn (Did. 6:2-3)" in *Studia Patristica*
IV (Berlin: Akademie Verlag, 1961 [*TU* 79]) pp. 323-329. Stuiber sees the passage
as Jewish in origin, rather than Jewish Christian, but this cannot explain the con-
tinuance of such a passage in an early Christian text, if it refers so unequivocally to
the Jewish Torah. Audet (*La Didachè*, pp. 352-357) also sees the reference to the
Torah, though as the work of a Christian interpolator who reflects the situation of
Acts 15. Cf. also G. Kretschmar, "Frühchristliche Askese", pp 47-48.

[57] C. Deutsch, *Hidden Wisdom and the Easy Yoke: Wisdom, Torah and Discipleship in Matthew 11.25-30* (Sheffield: JSOT, 1987 [*JSNT Supp.* 18]) esp. pp.
126-128; 133-135.

[58] *Ibid.*, pp. 115-116.

[59] This connection between 6:3 and the Council of Jerusalem was explored by
W. Telfer ("The Didache and the Apostolic Synod of Antioch", *JTS* 40 (1939) pp.
133-146, 258-271; cf. Kraft, *Barnabas and the Didache*, p. 163), who sees *Didache*
as relaxing the severity of Acts. See more recently, Jefford's similar suggestion that
Didache may reflect the Council decision independently of Acts (*The Sayings of
Jesus*, pp. 96-98).

Now then, why do you test God, by laying a yoke (ζυγός) on the neck of the disciples, which neither our fathers nor we ourselves have been able to bear (ἰσχύσαμην βαστάσαι).

Note here the same combination of ζυγός and being able to bear, βαστάσαι, and a solution similar to that in the *Didache*: If the Gentiles are not "able" to "bear the yoke" of the Torah, the minimum obligation laid on them largely concerns ritual food laws (despite the ethicising attempt of the Western Text!): keep from what has been offered to idols, from what has been strangled, and from [meat which has] blood.[60] Although Luke suggests that the argument at the "Jerusalem Council" was over "circumcision" only, Paul makes it quite clear in Galatians 2:11-13, that the observation of the food laws was at the heart of the problem. The minimum requirement was intended to enable the Gentile Christians to continue worshipping with Jewish Christians, avoiding ritual impurity which could render them unclean. This probably continues the practice of the Diaspora synagogue. The language is certainly to be found in Rabbinic texts, for example the saying of Nehunya b. Ha-Kanah (T 1-2):

He that takes upon himself yoke of the Law (כל־המקבל עליו עול תורה), from him shall be taken the yoke of the kingdom and the yoke of worldly care (*m.Abot* 3:5)[61]

Acts links this solution to the problem of relationships between Jewish and Gentile Christians with Antioch, after the intervention of emissaries from Jerusalem. What must be questioned in Luke's account is his contention that Paul was present at the "Jerusalem Council" and was party to the agreement.[62] This creates almost insuperable problems in understanding Paul's letter to the Galatians—except, of course, by juggling the timing of it all.

---

[60] καὶ τῆς πορνείας seems a little out of place in this theory. It is omitted by P45, while the Syriac Didascalia reads πορκείας; either of these would retain the sole reference to the food laws. If the original reading were indeed "pork", then this would explain both the other readings. However, the external evidence is very slight. In view of the manifest ethicising tendency of the tradition, the introduction of "fornication" could be seen as an early scribal gloss. Certainly there is evidence that Christians in the second and third centuries were still observing the prohibition against food offered to idols and meat with the blood in it. See also the *Martyrs of Lyons*. On the other hand, the confusion may have been introduced into the evidence by Luke himself, who was concerned to downplay observance of the food laws, since, for him, God had declared all foods clean (Acts 10:9-16).

[61] Compare *m.Abot* 6:2; *b.BM* 85b.

[62] P. Achtemeier, *The Quest for Unity in the New Testament Church* (Philadelphia: Fortress, 1987).

Paul uses the word ζυγός polemically in Gal 5:1, against those Gentile Christians who want to be circumcised and keep the Torah: μὴ πάλιν ζυγῷ δουλείας ἐνέχεσθε. The context is an attempt by envoys from outside the community, probably from Jerusalem, to persuade Gentiles in Paul's communities to keep the Law. Interestingly, Paul's defense against them is a rehearsal of the events of the Antioch crisis, in which he defends his own role. Peter and Barnabas succumb to pressure from James and the Judaizing party. Part of Paul's polemic seems to be a reworking of the Two Ways teaching—both parenesis and the schema in which the two ways become the way of flesh (presumably associated with the way of circumcision) and the way of the Spirit (the way of salvation by faith apart from works of Torah).

The image of the yoke recurs in Matthew 11:29-30, where again the symbolism probably relates to the Torah[63], with Jesus as the new Law-giver like Moses, as in the Sermon on the Mount.[64] The new law of Jesus is an easy yoke to bear, unlike the oral Torah of the Pharisees who "tie up heavy loads and put them on men's shoulders, but they themselves are not willing to lift a finger to move them" (23:4).[65] This is how it was understood by Cyprian (ad Quirinum III.119), who argues: "That the yoke of the Law was heavy, which is cast off by us, and that the Lord's yoke is easy, which is taken up by us".[66]

The "yoke" in the Fathers
In the early Christian writings outside the New Testament, most occurences of ζυγός simply reflect the influence of Mt 11:29-30. Otherwise the metaphorical use of ζυγός is not common. Those texts which do use the word use it to refer to the Torah. In particular, Barnabas 2:6 rejects the Torah as ζυγόν ἀνάγκης and in its place puts the "new law of our Lord Jesus Christ" (ὁ καινὸς νόμος). Justin, *Dial* 53:1, also refers to the Torah as the yoke of the Jews, who are like a harnessed ass (ὄνον ὑποζύγιον), contrasted with the Gentiles who are like an unharnessed foal until they receive the yoke of the Word (τὸν ζυγὸν τοῦ λόγου). So too *Didascalia* LII.17-35 differentiates between the Torah given on

---

[63] Deutsch, *Hidden Wisdom*, pp. 40-44.

[64] The background to this concept is well depicted by W. D. Davies (*Setting of the Sermon on the Mount*, pp. 25-108), although he denies that Mt. envisaged Jesus unambiguously as a new Moses giving a new Torah. His caution is taken further by T. L. Donaldson, *Jesus on the Mountain: A Study in Matthean Theology* (Sheffield: JSOT, 1985 [*JSOT Supp.* 8]) pp. 111-118. Donaldson argues that Moses typology is absorbed by "christologically re-interpreted Zion eschatology" (*Ibid.*, p. 118).

[65] My translation.

[66] Translation from A. Roberts & J. Donaldson, *The Ante-Nicene Fathers* V [Grand Rapids: Eerdmans, 1957] p. 556.

Sinai, which remains binding on the Church, and is the ζυγός of the eternal Law, and the laws given after the golden calf as a punishment for idolatry, which are the "Deutero Legislation", no longer binding. Justin takes a similar line in his *Dialogue*.[67]

All of this seems to confirm the supposition that the "yoke of the Lord" in the *Didache* refers to the Torah, as maintained and interpreted in the Christian community.

V. BECOMING "PERFECT" ACCORDING TO *DIDACHE* 6:2

The word τέλειος also has its roots in Jewish debate concerning the Torah.[68] In particular the Dead Sea Scrolls use תמים as the qualification of the Way of Light. "Perfection" means keeping the Torah according to the community *halakoth* (e.g. 1QS 1:8f; 2:2; 3:9f; 8:1f). So here in the *Didache*, it is only by keeping the whole Torah, according to the Christian *halakoth* (the new law of Christ, which is an "easy yoke"), that one would become perfect in the way of life. Presumably, then, if Paul was understood as advocating the abolition of the Torah, he would be understood as teaching contrary to God's will (παρεκτὸς θεοῦ 6:1). This is the whole issue of Galatians writ large from the other side.

The use of the word τέλειος in Matthew 5:48 confirms this reference to Torah. For, after the passage concerning the abiding application of the Torah, which must mean greater δικαιοσύνη for the Christian than for the Scribes and Pharisees, Matthew gives an example of what he means by this. Each of the five ethical commands of the Decalogue are given a more stringent application in 5:21-47. The concluding comment, which recaps and restates the principle, is ἔσεσθε οὖν ὑμεῖς τέλειοι ὡς ὁ πατὴρ ὑμῶν ὁ οὐράνιος τέλειός ἐστιν. For Matthew, at least, the word τέλειος summarizes the Christian approach to Torah[69]: the Torah remains intact and the Christian *halakah* represents a legal "righteousness" which exceeds that of the Scribe and Pharisee!

Matthew 19:16-22 has often been used to argue for an ascetic background to the word τέλειος, since the rich young man is asked by Jesus to sell his possessions and give to the poor.

---

[67] See also M. Simon, *Verus Israel: A Study of the Relations between Christians and Jews in the Roman Empire, 135-425*, trans. M. McKeating (Oxford: University Press, 1986) pp. 114-117.

[68] Cf. Kretschmar, "Frühchristliche Askese", pp. 49-54.

[69] See G. Barth, "Matthew's Understanding", pp. 97-103. Barth, however, seems unaware of the parallel to Matthew's usage in the *Didache*, since he argues that, "This use of τέλειος is found nowhere else in the LXX, the New Testament or the post-New Tstament writings" (*Ibid.*, p. 98). Cf. Gnilka (*Matthäus-evangelium*, p. 141), who claims that, "Man darf vermuten, daß die Volkommenheit am Ende des 5. Kapitels ein Zielpunkt is, auf den hin die Gedankenführung verläuft".

However, the context again indicates that Matthew understands the term as a reference to Torah in Christian interpretation ("adding to righteousness").[70] Where Mark 10:17-22 makes the pericope revolve around the Christological question of who Jesus is, "Why do you call me good? No-one is good except God alone", Matthew makes the pericope revolve around the correct fulfillment of the Torah. The man asks, "What good thing must I do?" and receives the answer, "Why do you ask me concerning what is good? There is only One who is good...Keep the commandments!" ($\tau\acute{\eta}\rho\eta\sigma ο\nu\ \tau\grave{\alpha}\varsigma\ \grave{\epsilon}\nu\tau ο\lambda\acute{\alpha}\varsigma$). The question is pushed further, "Which commandments?" The answer is the five ethical commandments of the Decalogue, together with the golden rule (found also in *Didache* 1:2) which Matthew adds to Mark. Finally, when the man claims to have kept all these, Jesus responds to the question of what is still "lacking" with the statement about how to be "perfect"—again a Matthean addition $\epsilon\grave{\iota}\ \theta\acute{\epsilon}\lambda\epsilon\iota\varsigma\ \tau\acute{\epsilon}\lambda\epsilon ο\varsigma\ \epsilon\grave{\hat{\iota}}\nu\alpha\iota$.

The "perfect" ($\tau\acute{\epsilon}\lambda\epsilon ο\varsigma$) or complete Christian in the *Didache*, then, is the one who keeps the whole Torah according to Christian *halakah*. The food laws were the minimum legal requirement to ensure table fellowship between the "perfect" and the uncircumcised Gentiles.[71] The community of the *Didache* remains within the ambit of faithful Torah-observant Jewish Christianity,[72] but takes an understanding line on the problems of Gentile believers, who are not excluded from the Christian community, just relegated to the status of second class Christians.[73]

On the other hand, the *Didache* takes a harsh line on those who oppose this instruction: anyone who teaches differently is teaching contrary to God himself! *Didache* 6:1 is connected to 6:2 by $\gamma\grave{\alpha}\rho$, indicating a causal connection. The implication is that there are people who teach that one can be "perfect" without taking up the whole yoke [of the Torah], and these must be understood as teaching contrary to God's will. Further, the emphasis in the instruction seems to fall on $\acute{ο}\lambda ο\nu$, which has a

---

[70] Cf. Kretschmar, "Frühchristliche Askese", pp. 54-61.

[71] Cf P. J. Donahue, "Jewish Christianity in the Letters of Ignatius of Antioch" (*VigChr* 32 [1978]) pp. 81-92, esp. 90.

[72] Kretschmar sees Mt as remaining within the ambit of the Synagogue and Jewish people, but the *Didache* as presupposing a separation, but does not argue for this beyond a general supposition that no community rule would be necessary if Christians remained within Judaism. However this idea that a community rule would only be needed after a separation from Judaism is based on a naïve picture of a monolithic Judaism. Qumran, at least, saw the need for a *Manual of Discipline*.

[73] G. Barth ("Matthew's Understanding", pp. 99-102) argues persuasively that the use of $\tau\acute{\epsilon}\lambda\epsilon ο\varsigma$ by Matthew does not imply a two-level ethic, but the way the term is used in *Didache* must raise questions about this assertion.

polemical edge. This teaching on the Torah was an inseparable part of what was taught to all converts before their baptism: "Having said all these things [beforehand], baptize in this way" (7:1).

In any case, their baptism would admit them only to partial fellowship with Jewish Christians, and they would know from the start that the goal of the Christian life was full compliance with the Jewish Torah, under the aegis of the Messiah. The question of admission to table fellowship in the Christian eucharist is raised in 9:5, where baptism not Torah is affirmed as the criterion, so the debate seems to have continued. This passage reflects the same world of Jewish ritual concern as 6:2-3.

VI. THE ESCHATOLOGICAL TEACHING OF *DIDACHE* 16

The full implications of this understanding of the Torah as the goal of the Christian life for Gentile converts may be gauged from the eschatological exhortation in 16:2. The whole time of the proselyte's life will not avail unless he/she be found "perfect" or "perfects him/herself" (τελειωθῆτε) in the last time! The word τελειωθῆτε is commonly used in the mystery religions to mean "to be consecrated" or "initiated"[74]. The connection of the noun τέλειος with Torah, which has been examined above, seems to indicate that final acceptance of the Torah by Gentiles is at issue here, as the final mark of initiation.

In other words, the *Didache* allows the proselyte flexibility about the timetable, but at the end of the day, it is required of him/her that he/she become a full Jew in order to attain salvation. Of course, the way this was understood would have been modified in the course of time, but this may well have been its original reference.

A parallel to this attitude is provided by the words of a Jew to the godfearer Flavius Clemens, who faces martyrdom for his conversion to Judaism: "Pity the ship that sails [towards the harbour] without paying the tax" (b.AZ 10b; DeutR ii.24). The demand is that the godfearer be circumcised before he dies or forfeit his right to eternal life. When Flavius is circumcised, Ketiah b. Shalom says, "Thou has paid the tax, thou wilt enter [paradise]". This puts maximum pressure on the Gentile Christian to become a Jew. Meanwhile he/she must keep a minimum ritual purity, particularly with regard to the food laws. The Law was given to Israel, and only Israelites were obligated to keep it; the

---

[74] W. Bauer, W. F. Arndt & F. W. Gingrich, *A Greek-English Lexicon of the New Testament* (Chicago: University Press, 1957) p. 818.

moral law was sufficient for God-fearing Gentiles who wished to attend the worship of the community, but the hope was that eventually the Gentile would become a Jew. This is the environ of the Diaspora Jewish synagogue, where a גר תושב [75] is admitted to worship in the hope that he/she will eventually become a גר צדק.

The close connection of *Didache* 16 with *Didache* 6:2 and 11:1 has not been noticed before. Certain features indicate that it has an underlying thread of polemic. In the first place, the negative formulation of οἱ λύχνοι ὑμῶν μὴ σβεσθήτωσαν καὶ αἱ ὀσφύες ὑμῶν μὴ ἐκλυέσθωσαν (16:1) differs from the positive formulation of Luke 12:35, which follows Exodus 12:11 (LXX). The positive form derives from Passover tradition, but the negative form indicates a community facing a threat. This threat could be interpreted in terms of a waning of eschatological ardour certainly, but what makes this less likely is that the threat concerns their "life" (ὑπὲρ τῆς ζωῆς ὑμῶν, 16:1), which ties the thinking to the Two Ways teaching of 1-6. It concerns the individual's faithfulness to the teaching of the Way of Life, which includes faithfulness to the Torah. Thus the warning re-iterates 6:1 ὅρα μὴ τις σε πλανήσῃ ἀπὸ τῆς ὁδοῦ τῆς διδαχῆς.

16:2 urges frequent meetings to inquire about τὰ ἀνήκοντα ταῖς ψυχαῖς ὑμῶν, although it does not specify further what the things required might be. The context suggests that they are the things which would make it possible for the reader to be "perfect", since the warning which follows is connected to it by γάρ. The whole time of faith will be of no avail unless on the last day he/she is "perfected". This would seem to imply that τὰ ἀνήκοντα refers to instruction in the Christian *halakah*.

The threat to the community does not come from outside but from within, from false prophets (πληθυνθήσονται οἱ ψευδοπροφῆται) and corrupters, from sheep who have turned into wolves (καὶ στραφήσονται τὰ πρόβατα εἰς λύκους, καὶ ἡ ἀγάπη στραφήσεται εἰς μῖσος)—those who were once seemingly faithful members have turned against the community. The word ψευδοπροφῆται could well refer to the false apostle(s) of 11:1-2, since the instructions of 11:3-6 call false apostles ψευδοπροφῆται. Notice also the link with στραφείς in 11:2. The perspective of the Matthew 7:15 is somewhat different, since the wolves come from outside the community *clothed* as sheep (οἵτινες ἔρχονται πρὸς ὑμᾶς ἐν ἐνδύμασιν προβάτων). The memory of the concrete

---

[75] See Tractate *Gerim* 3:1, "What is a "resident proselyte"? Whoever undertakes to abstain from idolatry, in the view of R Meir; R Judah said, "Whoever undertakes not to eat flesh that has not been ritually slaughtered"" (Translated by A. Cohen, *The Minor Tractates of the Talmud* [London: Soncino, 1965]). Cf Juvenal, *Sat.* 14:96-106; *ApocZeph.* 10:8f.

origin of the saying in a betrayal by a particular member(s) of the community found in the *Didache* (στραφήσονται) is absent in Matthew. This seems to be parallel to the softer line taken by the Gospel on the apostle who teaches that one need not keep the Torah (5:19), and to indicate a development of the tradition. In the *Didache* love, which once existed between the false apostles / prophets and the community, is turned into hatred.

The reason is again given in what follows, connected by a causal γάρ: αὐξανούσης γὰρ τῆς ἀνομίας μισήσουσιν ἀλλήλους καὶ διώξουσι καὶ παραδώσουσι. The disastrous betrayal by former members is caused by an increase in "lawlessness", ἀνομία. The signs are that ἀνομία should be given a more specific reference than general license. It refers here to those who put aside the νόμος and advocate καταλῦσαι (11:1). Again, Matthew 7:23 preserves the tradition that the root of the conflict over true and false prophecy is ἀνομία, since Jesus says ἀποχωρεῖτε ἀπ᾽ ἐμοῦ οἱ ἐργαζόμενοι τὴν ἀνομίαν.

At this time the "world deceiver" is to appear (16:4), into whose evil hands the world has been given (for a time). Significantly, he is described as υἱὸς θεοῦ who even does signs and wonders, like the false prophets of Matthew 7:21-23. This seems to indicate that the title "world deceiver" is polemical and linked to the disputes within the Christian movement. The temptation to ἀνομία, under the influence of false teaching by former members of the community subjects present members to a fiery ordeal and many will stumble and be lost (σκανδαλισθήσονται πολλοὶ καὶ ἀπολοῦνται).

In this situation those who endure in their faith will be saved ὑπ᾽ αὐτοῦ τοῦ καταθέματος (16:5). This strange phrase has never been satisfactorily explained. The word καταθέματος is a rare word found only in Christian writings, usually in the context of polemic against heretics (apart from the cursing of Peter in Mt 26:74 and those writings dependent on it[76]). There is an interesting use of the verbal form in Justin's depiction of Jews and Jewish Christians in *Dial* 47:4, where cursing is the means by which such people hope to escape from the fire (ὅπως τύχωσι τῆς σωτηρίας καὶ τῆς τιμωρίας τῆς ἐν τῷ πυρὶ ἀπαλλαγῶσιν).

Another echo in this passage of Justin is found in the strange phrase ἐπ᾽ αὐτὸν τοῦτον τὸν Χριστὸν, which is reminiscent of ὑπ᾽ αὐτοῦ τοῦ καταθέματος in *Didache* 16:5. It is likely that the same context of Judaizing polemic lies behind both passages. It has often been suggested that the expression means "by him who was cursed", ie by Jesus who became a curse by "hanging upon a

---

[76] Perhaps, even here, there is an implication of apostasy in the community forming the *Sitz im Leben* of the story as Mt. tells it.

tree" (Dt 21:23). That is the argument of Paul in Galatians 3:13f, that the goal of this curse was "that the blessing given to Abraham might come to the Gentiles through Christ Jesus". But Paul is here engaging in polemic against Judaizing Christians. He argues that "all who rely on observing the law are under a curse (ὑπὸ κατάραν)" (3:10) and that "Christ redeemed us from the curse of the law (ἐκ τῆς κατάρας τοῦ νόμου) by becoming a curse for us" (3:13). If the *Didache* is in some way connected with the conflict between Paul and the Judaizing party at Antioch, and originates in Antioch, then it could be that the phrase ὑπ᾽ αὐτοῦ τοῦ καταθέματος is a polemic against Paul and refers to the "curse of the Law". This may have been a proverbial expression. The date of the Rabbinic proselyte tractate *Gerim* is uncertain, but it may contain ancient material. Here the proselyte is first initiated into the disadvantages of the Torah:

> If a man wishes to become a proselyte he is not accepted at once but they say to him, "Why do you want to become a proselyte? Do you not see that this people are debased, oppressed and degraded more than all other peoples, that diseases and chastisements come upon them and they bury their children and children's children, that they are slaughtered for [observing] circumcision, immersion and the other precepts [of the Torah] and cannot hold up their heads like other people". If he says, "I am not worthy to place my neck under the yoke (ליתן צוארי בעול)...".[77]

The instruction in the *Didache* would then remind the community that they are saved by the very thing which they find brings a curse on them, namely the Torah. It is to this that they must hold fast if they are to be perfect on the last day.

VII. CONCLUSION

A study of the enemies of the *Didache* community seems to indicate that it is a community still living within the ambit of the Torah, though threatened by those former members of the community who are, in its view, advocating the abolition of the law.[78] If our redactional study is accepted, then 11:1-2 represents a development of the original instructions on apostles found in 11:3-6, under the pressure of historical developments. The one(s) who

---

[77] Translation from A. Cohen, *The Minor Tractates of the Talmud* (London: Soncino, 1965) p. 603; Hebrew text from G. Polster, "Der kleine Talmudtraktat über die Proselyten (Text und Übersetzung)", *Angelos* 2 (1926) pp. 2-38. Compare the different, but perhaps not unrelated idea of the "curses of the Covenant" at Qumran, based on Dt 30.

[78] Although, if the Pauline mission is in mind, it would refer rather to his ruling that *Gentiles* should not observe the Torah. In the view of the *Didache* community, this was nothing less than ἀνομία.

is advocating abolition of the Torah claim(s) to be an apostle. He is to be excluded from the community. He is like a sheep who has turned into a wolf and will destroy the community if left inside it. This is to be compared with the position of Matthew that such a one is "least in the Kingdom", but not outside of it. In comparison to this, the *Didache* represents the more severe ruling, Matthew indicates the beginning of rapprochement. It is not difficult to extrapolate from the scenario which has emerged from our study, that the false apostle who advocates abolition of the Torah is Paul, and that the community of the *Didache* is Antioch. This clearly calls for further investigation.

What has also emerged from this study is that this redactional stratum of the text of the *Didache* shares with Matthew's gospel not just the "Q" sayings of the Jesus tradition, but also a common theological and structural conception. That they originate in the same community is hard to deny; they breathe the same air and reflect the same historical development. What must remain a matter of debate is the question of priority. Our contention here is that the *Didache* is the community rule of the Matthean community, constantly in process of development. Naturally, if this is so, some of its parts will reflect a situation pre-supposed by Matthew's gospel, other parts may reflect a situation after its composition. Only a careful redactional analysis can indicate in which way the influence runs in a specific instance. In the matter of the instructions on apostles, however, it seems that the text of the *Didache* forms the source of the material in Matthew.

PATTERN AND PROTOTYPE OF DIDACHE 16

ERNST BAMMEL

Cambridge

The *Teaching of the Twelve Apostles* or *Didache* consists of three scarcely connected parts, a Two-Ways-Schema, a community manual of discipline and an eschatological conclusion. The first complex dates back—there is broad consensus about this—to a particular textual pattern or schema and in the end back to a Jewish prototype (*Vorlage*).[1] While the direct and indirect witnesses for Two-Ways-Catechisms reach up to chapter 6, only uncertain traces of the following chapters have been found.[2] Hence the maximal extent of the schema seems to be precisely delineated. Only A. von Harnack, taking up certain suggestions of C. Taylor[3], considered whether the Jewish model might have contained more material which would be analogous to what is found in the second part of the *Didache*, but he did not follow up this consideration on the grounds that it was too hypothetical.[4] Harnack argued on the basis of the content, and it is in fact possible to draw connections between the first and the second part. A continuation of the one into the other is easily conceivable. But in that case the third part appears to be all the more mysterious. What is an eschatological perspective doing at the end of a manual of discipline for life and community?

But the situation is not unique. Comparable formations are recognizable in the Jewish tradition. Pseudo-Phocylides, at the end of his admonitions, describes the gate of life through which the approved one will walk.[5] The *Testament of Asher*, probably the oldest testimony to the two ways, ends[6] with a short description of

---

[1] For a recent contrary opinion, see W. Michaelis, *TDNT* V, 58-60, 93-96. The German word *Vorlage* in the original paper is particularly difficult to translate, but has been rendered consistently by the English word "prototype".

[2] On the quotation contained in the Pseudo-Cyprianic tract *De aleatoribus* (Hartel III, 92f), read *Didache* 14:2 and compare A. Harnack, *Die Lehre der zwölf Apostel* (Leipzig: Hinrichs 1884 [TU 2,1-2]) pp. 20f. Number 9 of the *Teaching of the Eleven Apostles* reconstructed by T. Schermann (= prototype of the *Apostolic Church Order*) perhaps presupposes a knowledge of *Didache* 10:3.

[3] *The Teaching of the Twelve Apostles* (Cambridge: Deighton Bell, 1886), pp. 49ff.

[4] *Die Apostellehre und die jüdischen beiden Wege* (Leipzig: Hinrichs, 1896[2]), p. 29, cf. p. 30.

[5] Contained in *SibOr* 2.149-54. Concerning the priority of this version over against the one printed by J. Bernays (*Über das phokylideische Gedicht* [Berlin, 1856] reprinted in *Gesammelte Abhandlungen* I [Berlin:Hertz, 1885 (reprinted Hildesheim: Olms, 1971)] pp. 192-261), cf. A. Kurfess, "Das Mahngedicht des sogenannten Phokylides", *ZNW* 38 (1939) pp. 171-181.

[6] Is ch.7 a later addition?

the reception of the righteous by an angel of peace at the door to heaven, and of the remainder by an evil spirit.[7] The *Damascus Rule* ends in the Cairo recension with a description of the future victory of the faithful of the sectarian community and the expected redemption.[8] However, remains of a similar ending are also recognizable in Rabbinic literature. In the *Tosephta* tractate *t.Berakoth*, a passage which supplements the rules in the mishnaic material follows this pattern; it concludes as follows: the angel of Yahweh encamps around those who fear him and delivers them.[9] The quotation from Psalm 34:8 is not connected to what precedes, it has been added as an eschatological conclusion.

The passage has been included as a whole in the Jerusalem Talmud, *j.Berakhoth* 9. But the closing quotation is drawn into the text as a secondary addition to another quotation that serves as a scripture reference, and says nothing in that context. Instead a different ending has been abruptly added,[10] that deals in a quite uneschatological way with peace, in that it proceeds from the Rabbis. Its purpose is obviously to take the place of the original ending, either because it was not understood any more or, more probably, to neutralize it.—In the Babylonian Talmud *b.Berakoth* 64a, the sentences found in the Tosephta 7:24-25 are missing as a whole; only the last sentence of the Jerusalem Talmud has been taken in and has been paraphrased and extended by means of additional sentences.[11]

The complex from Tosephta *t.Berakoth* 7:25 is taken into *b.Menahoth* 43b as a *Baraitha*. Yet the closing Psalm quotation is missing in this later version. This ending may have been intentionally omitted, but it is more likely that it still belonged to the *Baraitha* and from there was placed at the end of a saying which was added only during the final redaction of the Talmud. This saying originates from the same period as the saying of Meir and is identical with part of it, as far as its meaning is concerned.[12]

In the Midrash *Tehillim* to Psalm 6, par. 1 (29b), the development of *j.Berakoth* 9 has continued in that Psalm 34:8 appears

---

[7] *t.Ash* 6:4-6.

[8] CD 20:27ff.

[9] *t.Ber* 7:25 (Zuckermandel, p. 17 lines 26ff). See the way of life also in the Targum to Dt 3:15.

[10] R. Eleazar says in the name of R. Ḥanina: "The wise bring much peace into the world. Why? All your sons are scholars of God and overflowing is the peace of your sons."

[11] Perhaps the last of them has an eschatological component. Yet it is more likely that this one also was already meant to be understood as edifying.

[12] The ending did not originally belong to this saying ascribed to Eleazer b. Jacob, for that is established adequately by the quotation of Ec 4:12. In the present context therefore it seems to be an addition.

altogether in place of 119:164, and hence is used in a different way. A new ending is not added, since the passage is fitted firmly into the whole context.

Outside of the context of Tosephta tractate *t.Berakoth*, Ps 34:8 is only quoted in the Babylonian Talmud tractate *b.Jebamoth* 102b. There the liberation is referred to the Judgment of Gehinnom, hence it is interpreted in an individualized eschatological way.[13]

In *m.Sota* a list of apocalyptic signs follows the regulations for divorce (up to 9:8 [10]) which ends[14] in the threefold formula: on whom else shall we depend than on our Father who is in Heaven.[15] And the corpus of the Mishnah is closed with the saying of Simeon b. Ḥalafta that originates from Psalm 29:11: "the Lord will give power to his people, the Lord blesses his people with peace."[16]

These single references[17] are confirmed by the fact that the Jewish proselytic catechism had an eschatological ending, which has been discovered by Alfred Seeberg[18] and clarified by G. Klein[19] and D. Daube.[20] Its structure may be controversial,[21] but there are no disagreements about the ending. Hence one may conclude that, in contemporary Judaism, there was already a com-

---

[13] Here it must be considered that the individual interpretation developed from חלץ = "to pull" is stressed for the sake of the argument. Hence the eschatological relation of the verse seems to be the precondition of the specific interpretation.

[14] *m.Sot* 9:15.

[15] Attributed to Phinehas b. Jaïr or Eliezer the Great. This text has made its way into the *Sefer ha-Likkutim*, cf. G. Klein, *Der älteste christliche Katechismus und die jüdische Propagandaliteratur* (Berlin: Reimer, 1909), p. 238.

[16] *m.Uktzin* 3:12. It is clear that עז לעמו יתן has an eschatological meaning from the preceding saying of Joshua b. Levi ("then will the Holy One, blessed be He, give 310 worlds to every single just person"). The passage is missing in a part of the textual tradition (as in the Munich manuscript). But the saying as such is old (read *b.San* 100a: cf. Jub 32:18f; *SibOr* 3.769) and a later suppression of the passage from this striking position is more likely than an addition.

[17] An eschatological reference for the Two Ways is a precondition in the two stories attributed to Eliezer and Joḥanan b. Zakkai. as well.—To what extent pretalmudic material is present in *Tanna debe Eliahu*, a medieval text with an eschatological ending (as Klein, *Katechismus*, pp. 66ff), or whether it expresses nothing more than the new apocalyptic wave of the Islamic period, cannot be discussed further here.

[18] *Der Katechismus der Urchristenheit* (Leipzig: Andreas Deichert, 1903; reprinted, with an introduction by F. Hahn, Munich: Kaiser Verlag, 1966); *Die Didache des Judentums und der Urchristenheit* (Leipzig: Andreas Deichert, 1908).

[19] *Studien über Paulus* (Stockholm, 1918 [Beiträge zur Religionswissenschaft 3]), p. 20.

[20] *The New Testament and Rabbinic Judaism* (London: University of London, Athlone Press, 1956), pp. 118ff, 135ff.

[21] Cf. the different prototypes suggested by Seeberg (*op.cit.* fn. 18) and by Daube in *NT and Rabbinic Judaism*.

parable scheme: a rule of conduct with an eschatological ending. Did this scheme play a role in the past history of the *Didache*?

It is significant that, the Two-Way-Catechisms show connections precisely to chapter 16. The *Freising Fragment* found by Schlecht closes with an apostrophe to *spes*.[22] *Didache* 16:2 is quoted in the *Doctrina Severini*: *(Lauda veritatem et) quae animae prosint discere elabora*.[23] Maybe in the fifteenth speech of Bonifatius another part of the same verse has been taken up: *Ad ecclesiam convenite orantes*.[24] What is important, is that these forms are not found in the witnesses of the stylized *Instruction of the Eleven Apostles*, but in the real representatives of the Two Ways-Teaching.

Similar things show up in the treatment of the Two-Ways-Catechism. The form taken up in the *Apostolic Church Order* closes with a reference to the nearness of the End, which means both judgment and reward.[25] In the edition of *Barnabas*[26] this is

---

[22] J. Schlecht, *Doctrina XII Apostolorum, die Apostellehre in der Liturgie der katholischen Kirche* (Freiburg im Breisgau: Herder, 1901) pp. 104f; cf. p. 65. Close to it is the fragment of the Arabic version, a previously unknown version of the first part of the *Teaching of the Apostles*, discussed by L. E. Iselin and translated by A. Heusler (*Eine bisher unbekannte Version des ersten Teiles der "Apostellehre"* [Leipzig: Heusler, 1895 (TU 13,1b)] p. 9). Admittedly there it deals with the end of the Way of Life (a very short summary of the way of death follows).

[23] Schlecht, *Doctrina XII Apostolorum*, p. 93.

[24] *Ibid.*, p. 78. Schlecht notes as a parallel only Didache 14:1 and hesitates to draw conclusions from that—unlike J. R. Harris, *The Teaching of the Apostles* (London: Clay/ Baltimore: John Hopkins University Press, 1887), p. 60: "The Teaching must have been his (Bonifatius') text-book". Only tangentially, the enigmatic *Cod. papyr. Vatican. 146* may be noted, although it contains an individual eschatological ending (text in Schlecht, *Doctrina XII Apostolorum*, p. 96); this has nothing in common with Didache 16.

[25] 1:14. It is interesting to note that in *Cod. Mosquensis*, one of the oldest of all the witnesses to the Two-Ways-Schema, this chapter follows ch. 11, i.e. it is at the end of the chapters taken from the positive part of the Two-Ways-Schema. Ch. 12 and 13 contain parts of Didache 4:1f, 3-8; 10:3; 13:1f. Apparently the character of the old ending as a conclusion was still so clear when they were inserted that it was relocated accordingly. The version of the *Cod. Ottonianus* then represents the final stage of the textual history, where the eschatological passage has fallen away altogether, in favour of a full recital of the Way of Life in the form it takes in the Didache (cf. the omission of nearly the whole of ch. 8!).—If this is correct, then the order of *Cod. Mosq.* is at the same time an indication for an older form, in which the subdivision into individual discourses by each of the apostles had not yet taken place (for a different point of view see T. Schermann, *Die allgemeine Kirchenordnung* III [Paderborn: Ferdinand Schöningh, 1916 (SGKA.E)], p. 599) and which is highly significant for the reconstruction of the Jewish archetypes (for a different point of view see Harnack, *Die Lehre der zwölf Apostel*, p. 221f, whose solution seems simple, but is actually problematic)

[26] Probably only 21:1bα belongs to the text *Barn* draws from the tradition.

intensified still further.[27]

These are only traces. In assessing them one must consider: a) the common tendency to modify final sentences or directly change them, b) a certain restraint with respect to eschatological descriptions after the end of the second century.[28] Therefore one must assume that the ending would have changed in any case (where changes could still have been made much later), so that only edited forms of the ending have been passed on to us. But still the facts of the matter remain remarkable. For, in any case, a totally different and, in fact, secondary development is perceivable, namely the tendency to insert eschatological expressions into the rules themselves[29], or to insert them at the beginning.[30] So one can state almost definitely: the Two-Ways-Catechism had an eschatological ending right from the beginning. Does it follow that *Didache* 16 belongs to the schema of the *Teaching of the Twelve Apostles*? Not necessarily. Because what is ancient as a *type* can be fairly late in its actual form. The previous research does not provide a clue as to how things really stand in this matter. The chapter is felt by some to lack any specifically Jewish characteristics[31] and by others to be totally Jewish.[32] Hence argumentation on basis of the content does not get one very far. But still, perhaps one can gain some circumstantial evidence for the origin of the chapter.

If one takes a closer look at the endings of the Two-Ways-Catechisms it becomes clear that they do not all have the same structure, but go back to two different types. The one type is directed towards the blissful goal, the other points to judgment and only in that context to the $\mu\iota\sigma\theta\delta\varsigma$. The former has its natural position as the conclusion of the description of the Way of Life—and it does in fact occupy this position in the Arabic fragment.[33] The latter would be most likely to be found at the end of a

---

[27] The structure of the Syriac *Didascalia* is probably comparable: it concludes with an ecclesiastical form of eschatology (ch. 25).—Ch. 26 is a postscript, as the distinctive preaching style and the special form of address proves (cf. also the almost complete absence of parallels to the *Didache* in ch. 26; the material is from C. Holzhey, "Die Abhängigkeit der syrischen Didaskalie von der Didache", in: *Compte rendu du 4º congr. scient. des Catholiques* [Freiburg-im-Üchtland, 1898], *passim*).

[28] Cf. Harnack, *Lehrbuch der Dogmengeschichte* I (Tübingen: Mohr, 1909⁴), p. 188.

[29] *Barn* 19:10f; 20:2.

[30] *Barn* 18:2; 20:1.

[31] Harnack, *Beiden Wege*, p. 15.

[32] Harris, *Teaching of the Apostles*, p. 90: "Judaic in matter and manner".—Cf. also the interesting theory of V. W. H. Tubesing, *Die ὁδός der Apostelgeschichte und die Διδαχὴ τῶν ἀποστόλων* (Leipzig: Pöschel & Trepte, 1902), p. 17f.

[33] P. 256, A.5.

Two-Ways-Schema. So it is in *Barnabas*. So it was apparently also in the prototype of the *Apostolic Church Order*: The beginning (chapter 4) and—this is little less certain—the ending[34] show, that the excerpt did not include the teachings of the Way of Death. One can only think that the first type was added secondarily at the end of *each* of the ways.[35]

Didache 16 belongs without doubt to the second type. The literal correspondence between *Did.* 16:2 and *Barn.* 4:8 marks the common affiliation. But on the other hand the chapter contains passages which have no parallels in the related texts: the information on the κοσμοπλανής and the coming of the κύριος. And yet indeed this special material again breathes the Jewish atmosphere in a special way. Surely it is related to Matthew 24 and 2 Thessalonians 2. But both these passages seem to be taken from a Jewish prototype. Again the facts of the matter are ambivalent at first glance.

A glance at the joint between the two passages takes us further. Verse 2b ἐν τῷ ἐσχάτῳ καιρῷ leads to verse 3a ἐν γὰρ (!) ταῖς ἐσχάταις ἡμέραις πληθυνθήσονται; the importance of the last time for the verdict obviously requires a description of the judgment itself, to provide direction in the decisive hour.[36] This is the bridge from eschatologically determined ethics to a description of the cosmic eschatology. But which one, then, is primary?

Both are old. But verse 2b is throughout materially the most thorough and obvious[37] development of the predominant type of conclusion.[38] So one must look at it also as the foundation for *Did* 16. The material logic of the thought in 2b, namely that ethical righteousness is to be determined only in the time of the apocalyptic events, led then to a digression[39] (first signs of the same

---

[34] πονηρῷ (*ACO* 14) is probably to be taken substantively and can only be understood against the background of *Barn* 4:10; 18:1, 2; 20:1; i.e. the representation of a metaphysical determination of this Way. Did *Did* 5:1 originally have πονηροῦ?

[35] Did this happen only at the time of the redaction of the *Didache*? 6:1 fits well after 4:13 (v.14 is a later addition).

[36] The motif of the last hour as the decisive moment is paralleled by the assumption, present in James in 2:10, that a deviation from the law in one particular point implies the trespassing of the whole law.

[37] Ez 33:17ff; *m.Both* 2:10. Cf. H. Windisch, *Die Barnabasbrief* (Tübingen: Mohr, 1920 [HNT.E 3]), p. 324, on *Barn* 4:9.

[38] Harnack could not know that and therefore saw v.2b as an isolated sentence, which he was only able to explain as taken directly from *Barn* and which in that way became the main point for his theory of the dependency of *Did* on *Barn* (*Geschichte der altchristlichen Literatur* II.1 [Leipzig: Hinrichs, 1958²], p. 436).—H adds that the logical connection with *Barn* 4:9 would be better. This is correct, but the overlapping of the thoughts in *Did* 16 only results because in v.2a a motif has been included that follows *Barn* 4:10b.

[39] It is however not an inclusion *en-bloc* of an eschatological saying. As single characteristics—like v.5c (ἐν τῇ πίστει αὐτῶν)—prove, neither has the catechetical

process can be seen in Mt 7:13ff).[40] It remains predominant until the end. The description of the eschatological events has thus prevailed over the ethical teaching and supplanted the representation of the eschatological goal. The proper conclusion, which takes up again the ethical thread and which still appears in a reworked form in *Barn* 21:1bα, 3, has fallen out of the Bryennios text.

One would have to see in this deviation from the Two-Ways-Schema the characteristic of the *Didache*, if it were not for the fact that the conclusion of the prototype of Bryennios was so altogether puzzling[41] and that the Georgian version[42] offers a text which is fully connected to the thought process of the Two-Ways-Schema. Since it can be derived neither from Mt 24[43] nor from 2 Thess 2, nor does it show recognizable signs of a secondary origin,[44] one must seek the original conclusion in a formula close to the Georgian version.[45] A specifically theological understanding

---

situation been lost sight of here. However, that no original connection to the first part exists, is shown by the different use of φθορεῖς in 5:2 and ψευδοπροφῆται in 11:5.

[40] The eschatological conclusion of the Sermon on the Mount begins with the picture of the gates current from the Two Ways-Literature (cf. *SibOr* 2.150) and thus appears to correspond entirely to the Jewish prototype. Yet, in actual fact, it is not at all unified. V.22f is a matter of a reworking of the ethical content of v.21 with reference to magical speculation about names (in the eschatological period?). V.15 has no inherent connection with the preceding, but is a warning description of apocalyptic abuses. V.16 (17)-20; v.13 (v.14 is an augmentation) reflects an older layer. Only v.21 reflects an original saying of Jesus (without μοί) and perhaps vv.24-27 (in which the Lucan version is to be preferred). In a comparable way, the redactor of *SibOr* has connected the ethical eschatology of Ps.Phocylides with an apocalyptic description (2.154ff), which for its part derives from a Jewish prototype, though without being entirely Jewish (cf. 2.242f).

[41] See J.-P. Audet, *La Didachè: Instructions des Apôtres* (Paris: Gabalda, 1958) 73f. Did the scribe of the Bryennios text know of two versions and does this explain the striking omission on p. 80b of his script (cf. the photographic plate provided in the edition of J. R. Harris, *Teaching of the Apostles*, plate X)? A. J. McLean (editor of second edition of C. Bigg, *The Doctrine of the Twelve Apostles* [London: SPCK, 1922²] p. 46) thinks that a page went missing from the archetype.

[42] Edited by G. Peradse, "Die "Lehre der zwölf Apostel" in der georgischen Überlieferung." *ZNW* 31 (1932) pp. 111-116. The text is also provided by F. E. Vokes, *The Riddle of the Didache* (London: Church Historical Society, 1938 [ns. 32]) 25f and by Audet, *La Didachè*, p. 49.

[43] Where the χρονίζειν is the problem.

[44] Christian insertions are: "our Lord Jesus Christ, who is Son of God", "before the whole human race and before the angels."

[45] Cf. *Const* 7.32: ἀποδοῦναι ἑκάστῳ κατὰ τὴν πρᾶξιν αὐτοῦ, a formulation in agreement with the Georgian text. The compiler of the *Const* had a version of the whole of the *Didache* before him. That accounts for the fact that his conclusion departs entirely from the Two-Ways-Schema and instead of this a new conclusion emerges at the end of the description of the Way of Life (ch. 17).

of the eschatological events, as it is already expressed in Phil 2:11; Col 2:15, has then given the text a different direction, perhaps receiving occasion from v.8.[46] It comes close in this way to the type of liturgical conclusion beloved from an early time.[47]

If verses 3-8 are almost entirely Jewish in content, nevertheless it is a matter here of a Christian intersertion.[48] Despite the common origin, the taking over also means a material shift. In other words, this apocalyptic propping up stands in a certain tension with another development which is already demonstrable in Judaism. The *Manual of Discipline* (1QS 4) deals with the metaphysical predetermination of the final destinies of human beings. From this the Ways developed very quickly.[49] The Two-Ways-Schema is taken up in this way in in *Barnabas* 18:1f.[50] However this does not mean that the predominantly ethical tone of the Two-Ways-Catechism is abolished, but rather is endangered. It is significant that one does not meet a particular δοκιμασία in the texts which have been reworked in this way. *Didache* 16 is free from such speculative elaboration. For this reason, the apocalyptic material is taken up in a variant reading, in which the evil culminates in a historical appearance, which becomes an ethical problem. To this extent, the ethical theme of the Two Ways-Teaching is preserved more purely in the reworking it has received in the *Didache* 16, than was the case in the parallel reformulations.

The Jewish form of conclusion[51] underwent a double development in the first century: national eschatology emerged in place of individual eschatology. But this developed schema is only just

---

[46] Κόσμος refers to a world hostile to God, as in John, which allows itself to be described as the consequence of a demonstrative act like that in Phil 2:10f.

[47] Harnack thought that the eschatological conclusion did not show the ardour demonstrated by the composer of the prayers which have been handed on ("Die Apostellehre und die beiden jüdischen Wege" [*RE*] p. 24; similarly in *Geschichte der altchristlichen Literatur* II.1 [Leipzig: Hinrichs, 1958] p. 435). One would have to explain this as a secondary reworking.

[48] V.7 perhaps followed first. Cf. the absence of 7a in *Const.* Concerning a Christian element in v.6f, see E. Stommel, "Σημεῖον ἐκπετάσεως (Didache xvi,6)." *RQ* 48 (1953) pp. 21-42, esp. 39.

[49] Briefly formulated in 1 En 91:18f; 94:1, 3; cf S. Wibbing, *Die Tugend- und Lasterkataloge im Neuen Testament und ihre Traditionsgeschichte unter besonderer Berücksichtigung der Qumran-Texte* (Berlin: de Gruyter, 1959 [BZNW 25]) p. 39.

[50] Cf. *HermMan* 6.

[51] It entirely possible, that as G. Klein thought (*Der älteste christliche Katechismus und die jüdische Propagandaliteratur* [Berlin: Reimer, 1909] pp. 137ff), the use of Psalm 34 was important for the edification of Catechism and its conclusion. It appears that for the concluding section v.23 was exegeted directly and after the destruction of the Temple v.8 emerged at this point. Cf. the striking use of Psalm 34 in 1 Pet, concerning which see W. Bornemann, "Der erste Petrusbrief—eine Taufrede des Sylvanus", *ZNW* 19 (1919-1920): 143-165, esp. 146ff.

recognizable.[52] The tendency is overpowered by another, namely to be silent altogether about eschatology.[53] (The peace formula at the end is introduced as a substitute). For this process, besides opportunistic considerations, the controversy with Christianity has been especially relevant.[54]

It was in two stages that the old schema was reshaped in the sphere of Christianity as well. The outlook on the fate of the individual is completed or replaced by a universalistically oriented apocalyptic description. And the success of this change was favoured by another restraining interest in a shaping out of eschatology generally. The stages of development are still visible in the elements of *Didache* 16, in the different versions of the conclusion to the Two Ways-Teaching which have come down to us.[55]

---

[52] Therefore the rabbinic evidence, introduced, is secondary to that of the Two Ways-Teaching. Also in bYeb 47, the form of eschatology indicated by the formula for Proselyte baptism, is already reworked in this direction and therefore cannot without more ado be viewed as characteristic for the New Testament period.

[53] Hence the brevity of the formulation which has come down to us. Hence the attempt to move it to less exposed positions. From this tendency one can explain the history of the use of the last section of *Tosephta Berakoth* in rabbinic literature (see above). R. Löwe (Oxford) directed me to *b.Shab 31a*. In this saying attributed to Rabbah, the national hope emerges in another form.

[54] See Daube, *NT and Rabbinic Judaism*, p. 135.

[55] The author had the opportunity to discuss particular questions with Professors E. Stauffer and D. Daube.

CONSIDERATIONS ON THE BACKGROUND AND PURPOSE OF THE APOCALYPTIC CONCLUSION OF THE DIDACHE

HANS REINHARD SEELIGER
Siegen

The apocalyptic conclusion of the *Didache* has received little attention in the most recent literature on the subject and, in my opinion, not as much as it rightly deserves.[1] This small chapter shares this fate with many other apocalyptic texts, which have for a long time caused perplexity (*Ratlosigkeit*), as the title of a book in 1970 puts it.[2] The situation has changed fundamentally since then; the attention paid to the texts and themes of apocalyptic in research has strengthened as two congresses, the one in Rome in 1977[3] and especially the one in Uppsala in 1979,[4] bear witness. With respect to the state of research into *Didache* 16, we have not, of course, got beyond the debate about questions of the history of traditions, which this short apocalyptic conclusion poses, and no unity has been achieved even in this matter.[5]

---

[1] An example is already A. Harnack, *Lehre der Zwölf Apostel nebst Untersuchungen zur ältesten Geschichte der Kirchenverfassung und des Kirchenrechts* (Leipzig: Hinrichs (reprint), 1893 [TU 2,1-2]) passim, as well as recently G. Schöllgen's otherwise perceptive investigation, "Die Didache als Kirchenordnung", *JAC* 29 (1986) pp. 5-26, esp. 20 fn. 117: Chapter 16 "bringt im wesentlichen eine eschatologische Ermahnung zur Wachsamkeit (Vv. 1-2), verbunden mit einer kleinen Apokalypse, und fällt damit aus dem Rahmen der Didache in der abschließenden Einschärfung der Einzelbestimmungen der Schrift." A short commentary is provided by P. Vielhauer in E. Hennecke & W. Schneemelcher, *New Testament Apocrypha* II (Philadelphia: Westminster 1965) pp. 626-629, and A. P. O'Hagan, *Material Re-creation in the Apostolic Fathers* (Berlin: Akademie-Verlag, 1968 [TU 100]) pp. 25-30. In greater detail: O. Giordano, "L'escatologia nella Didache", *Oikoumene. Studi paleocristiani in onore del Concilio Ecumenico Vaticano II* (Catania: Università di Catania, 1964) pp. 121-39, who examines the apocalyptic motifs of the Did especially with respect to their New Testament background. The scholarly debate up until now has been more extensively summarized in the commentary of K. Niederwimmer (*Die Didache* [Göttingen: Vandenhoeck & Ruprecht, 1993 (KAV 1)] pp. 247-269).

[2] K. Koch, *Ratlos vor der Apokalyptik. Eine Streitschrift über ein vernachlässigtes Gebiet der Bibelwissenschaft und die schädlichen Auswirkungen auf Theologie und Philosophie* (Gütersloh: Gütersloher Verlaghaus, 1970). The English translation of this book by M. Kohl changes the title to *The Rediscovery of Apocalyptic: A Polemical Work on a Neglected Area of Biblical Studies and its Damaging Effects on Theology and Philosophy* (London: SCM, 1972 [StBibTh 22]).

[3] *VI Incontro di Studiosi dell' Antichità cristiana* (Roma: Maggio, 1977): "Studi sull'Escatologia", *Augustinianum* 18 (1978) pp. 5-278.

[4] *Apocalypticism in the Mediterranean World and the near East: Proceedings of the International Colloquium on Apocalypticism, Uppsala, August 12-17, 1979*, ed. by D. Hellholm (Tübingen: Mohr, 1983).

[5] See E. Stommel, "Σημεῖον ἐκπετάσεως (Didache 16,6)", *RQ* 48 (1953) pp. 20-42; B. C. Butler, "The Literary relations of Didache, CH. XVI", *JTS* ns. 11

The following reflections aim at a modest goal: they are intended, besides reflection on some considerations of (a) the form of apocalyptic theology and (b) an important condition for understanding it, to (c) draw attention to some particular aspects of apocalyptic, which the *Didache* offers, and finally to (d) formulate a hypothesis concerning the purpose of the concluding chapter.

I

One fruit of the recent discussion about apocalyptic texts is the attempt to define the literary genre of apocalypses more precisely. Most convincing here is the definition of John J. Collins, given in the context of the work of the Genres Project of the American Society of Biblical Literature: "'Apocalypse' is a genre [*Gattung*][6] of revelatory literature with a narrative framework, in which a revelation is mediated by an otherworldly being to a human recipient, disclosing a transcendent reality which is both temporal, insofar as it envisages eschatological salvation, and spatial, insofar as it involves another, supernatural world."[7] Those familiar with the attempts at definition will confirm that an attempt is made here to get beyond the systematization of different elements of the style of apocalyptic (pseudonymity, accounts of visions, revelations and keys, overviews of history, paraenesis, prayers etc.)[8] to a comprehensive description of the full literary form "Apocalypse".

(1960) pp. 265-83; E. Bammel, "Schema und Vorlage von Didache 16", *StPat* IV,2, ed. F. L. Cross (Berlin: Akademia-Verlag, 1961 [TU 79]), pp. 253-62; H. Köster, *Synoptische Überlieferung bei den Apostolischen Vätern* (Berlin: Akademie-Verlag, 1965 [TU 65]) pp. 179-90; R. A. Kraft, *Barnabas and the Didache (The Apostolic Fathers: A New Translation and Commentary* 3) (New York: Thomas Nelson, 1965) pp. 12-6, 175-7: A. Stuiber, "Die drei Σημεῖα von Didache XVI", *JAC* 24 (1981) pp. 42-4.

[6] On the problems of the use of "genre" and "*Gattung*" as synonymous terms in Anglo-American and German literature, see L. Hartmann, "Survey of the Problem of Apocalyptic Genre", in Hellholm, *Apocalypticism*, pp. 329-43, here p. 330.

[7] J. J. Collins, "Towards the Morphology of a Genre", *Semeia* 14 (1979) pp. 1-19, esp. 9. See also L. Hartmann, in Hellholm, *Apocalypticism* p. 338 and K. Rudolph, "Apokalyptik in der Diskussion", *Ibid.*, pp. 771-89, esp. 774f.

[8] P. Vielhauer, *Geschichte der urchristlichen Literatur* (Berlin: de Gruyter, 1975) pp. 487-9; J. Lebram, art. "Apokalypsen II", *TRE* 3 (1978) p. 192; Collins, *"Morphology"*, pp. 6-8; following Vielhauer also M. Krause, "Die literarischen Gattungen der Apokalypsen von Nag Hammadi", in Hellholm, *Apocalypticism*, pp. 621-37, esp. 622f; K. Rudolph, *ibid.*, pp. 776f; K. Koch, Introduction to K. Koch & J. M. Schmidt (eds.), *Apokalyptik* (Darmstadt: Wissenschaftliche Buchgesellschaft, 1982 [*Wege der Forschung* 365]) pp. 1-29, esp. 14f; H. Stadelmann, "Biblische Apokalyptik und heilsgechichtliches Denken", in H. Stadelmann (ed.), *Epochen der Heilsgeschichte. Beiträge zur Förderung heilsgeschichtlicher Theologie* (Wuppertal: Brockhaus, 1984) pp. 86-100, esp. 87f.

Obviously this does not mean that the comprehensive full literary form, above all one in book form, should have already existed at the beginning of apocalyptic literature, which indeed is not limited to apocalypses in the defined sense. But apocalyptic revelation theology in the form of the "Apocalypse" is nevertheless easily discernible since the second century B.C. (1 En 1-36 and Dan 2, 7-11).[9]

Its great phase in the realm of Christian and Jewish theology lasted then until the end of the 2nd century C.E.[10] But besides apocalypses in the defined sense, apocalyptic motifs and apocalyptic theology also entered into other literary genres at the same time; the apocalyptic categories in Pauline theology can only be referred to briefly.[11] In our context, it is important to notice that, inside Christian literature at the time when apocalypses in the narrow sense were still being written, apocalyptic theology was pursued in other ways besides the complete literary form as such: besides the *Epistle of Barnabas*,[12] one should refer to Papias,[13] to Justin,[14] and to Irenaeus,[15] as well as to apocalyptic traces in the early martyr acts[16] and in the commentaries to the canonical apocalypses, in all probability beginning with Melito of Sardis.[17]

For the evaluation of the apocalyptic conclusion of the *Didache* this means first of all that we do not have an apocalypse according to the definition before us. The narrative framework is missing, as is also any information about the revealer and receiver

---

[9] Cf. Collins, "Morphology", pp. 30-2; 37f.

[10] Christian: Mk 13 par; Rev; *ApocPet*; *Herm*; 5 Esra; *AscIsa*; Jewish: 2 Bar; 4 Esra; *Fragments of Elchsai*; on this latter, cf. G. P. Luttikhuizen, *The Revelation of Elchsai. Investigations into the Evidence for a Mesopotamian Jewish Apocalypse of the Second Century and his Reception by Judeo-Christian Propagandists*, (Tübingen: Mohr, 1985 [TSAJ 8]). Concerning the time span within which apocalypses emerged, cf. Koch, in Koch & Schmidt, *Apokalyptik*, p. 13f.

[11] For the "doctrine of Aeons" see 1 Cor 10:11, 2 Cor 4:17; for the "new creation" see 2 Cor 5:17, Rom 8:17-30.

[12] *Barn* 4, 7 (F. X. Funk, K. Bihlmeyer & W. Schneemelcher, *Die Apostolischen Väter: Neubearbeitung der Funkschen Ausgabe* [Tübingen: Mohr (SQS II 1,1³)] pp. 12f, 18f).

[13] *Fragments of Papias*, (ed) R.M. Hübner = J. Kürzinger, *Papias von Hierapolis und die Evangelien des Neuen Testaments* (Regensburg: F. Pustet, 1983 [*Eichstätter Materialien 4*]) pp. 89-138.

[14] *Dial* 32:3f; 49:3; 80:5-81:3; 109:1-111:1; (E. J. Goodspeed, *Die ältesten Apologeten* [Göttingen: Vandenhoeck & Ruprecht, 1984] pp. 126f, 147f, 192f, 225-7).

[15] *AdvHaer* V.24-36 (V. A. Rousseau, L. Doutreleau & C. Mercier, *Irénée de Lyon: Contre les hérésies* II [Paris: Les Éditions du Cerf (SC 153)] pp. 294-466).

[16] E.g. *Martyrdom of Perpetua and Felicitas* (SQF ns. 3, pp. 39-41 Knopf-Krüger-Ruhbach).

[17] Evidence for the lost commentary is *HE* IV.26:2 (*GCS* 9,1, 382,6f Schwartz); the oldest commentary on Rev is Hippolytus, *In Dan* (*GCS* 1,1 Bonwetsch).

of an apocalyptic message, as well as any information about the manner of the revelation. It rather reports an apocalyptic message, which already appears to have been issued; nothing is revealed here in the sense of the apocalyptic genre, but what is already known is repeated for the deepening of knowledge. In view of the other apocalyptic literature mentioned above, it is not surprising to find that sort of thing. Yet it appears to me that we have a special case before us in the *Didache*.

The *Didache* as a whole is, as Georg Schöllgen has recently shown, only a "selective church order", whose "loose composition" on the one hand presents little difficulty to those interpolating additional instructions into the text in the face of newly arising problems, but whose greater openness of structure at the same time makes it correspondingly "difficult for the historian to prove such an insertion decisively."[18] The history of research into the *Didache* is a faithful picture of this problematic situation.[19]

I am proceeding on the assumption that the apocalyptic part of the conclusion is not a later addition, as has been often claimed or suspected.[20] This is because one finds here again a stylistic element or structuring principle often found in the *Didache*: the association of terms or catch-words.[21] From the warning in 16:2b that "for the whole time of your faith will profit you nothing, if you do not become perfect", the author proceeds directly in 16:3 to the description of what is to be expected ἐν ταῖς ἐσχάταις ἡμέραις.[22] What comes next is certainly so different in background and form from the ethical instructions of the Two Ways Teaching that it cannot have formed its conclusion, as Rordorf rightly insisted.[23] The question is thus posed all the more acutely as to how this

---

[18] Schöllgen, *"Didache als Kirchenordnung*, p. 22.

[19] Compare the work of J.-P. Audet, *La Didachè. Instructions des apôtres* (Paris: Gabalda, 1958) pp. 104-20 and G. Schille, "Das Recht der Propheten und Apostel—gemeinderechtliche Beobachtungen zu Didache Kapitel 11-13", P. Wätzel & G. Schille, *Theologische Versuche* (Berlin: Evangelisches Verlags-Anstalt, 1966) pp. 84-103, both of whom present theories of interpolation which make precise differentiations.

[20] Köster, *Synoptische Überlieferung*, pp. 160, 173, 189f; Kraft, *Barnabas and the Didache*, p. 7; W. Rordorf & A. Tuilier, *La Doctrine des Douze Apôtres* (Paris: Les Éditions du Cerf [SC 248], 1978) p. 83 (subsequent quotations are from this edition); Schöllgen, "Didache als Kirchenordnung", p. 20 fn. 117.

[21] Vielhauer, *Geschichte*, p. 727; Schöllgen, "Didache als Kirchenordnung", pp. 9, 20.

[22] Rordorf & Tuilier, *La Doctrine*, pp. 194, 196f. The observation is already made by Bammel, "Schema und Vorlage", p. 259.

[23] Rordorf & Tuilier, *La Doctrine*, p. 82. This thesis does not mean to deny, however, that the *Didache* is part of a broader literary background, as argued by K. Baltzer, *Das Bundesformular* (Neukirchen: Neukirchen-Vluyn, 1964² [WMANT 4]) pp. 132-7.

piece of apocalyptic theology can be interpreted, providing, as it does, the final chord to the *Didache*, a selective church order.

II

In the interpretations offered up to now, people have been satisfied to point out that "the eschatological conclusion merely has the function of strengthening the warning to the reader to obey the instructions given in what precedes. The eschatology directed towards retribution in the end time becomes thus a subordinate aspect of the ethical instruction, and for the rest is a simple piece of teaching 'about the last things'."[24]

Egon Brandenburger has rightly argued that because the *jus talionis* plays an important rôle inside the apocalyptic thought model, according to which the returning Lord will repay to each according to his work,[25] it cannot be deduced that it is the concept of judgement which positions enactment of law theologically.[26] He argues that nowhere in New Testament or early Jewish apocalyptic is there a law based on judgment or expectation of the end. "It has long been known in what the law consists—but now, in this time of the world, it is prevented from its genuine appearance, held back, pushed down. It is precisely this which characterizes this aeon among other things as evil. The law belongs in the realm of the Creator, who has so ordered the world that it is oriented to himself and to life."[27] The parenesis, which is only partly bound up with apocalyptic,[28] brings the laws of life to remembrance, but it does not serve as their sanction. The sanctioning instance is the Judge who appears at the End, who re-instates the *old* order. It is however only *one* element in apocalyptic theology. Anyone who plays parenesis against apocalyptic in interpretation, runs into the

---

[24] K. Wengst in the Introduction to his edition of the *Didache* (*Didache (Apostellehre), Barnabasbrief, Zweiter Klemensbrief, Schrift an Diognet* [Darmstadt: Wissenschaftliche Buchgesellschaft (SUC 2), 1984] p. 60); according to Schöllgen ("Didache als Kirchenordnung", p. 20 fn. 117), the function of Ch. 16 lies "möglicherweise...in den abschließenden Einzelbestimmungen der Schrift." Niederwimmer (*Die Didache*, pp. 258f) interprets the chapter as a whole simply as concluding parenesis.

[25] The lost conclusion of *Did* 16 can indeed be reconstructed following the implications of the framework of judgment, as is well known. Compare Wengst, *Didache (Apostellehre)*, p. 90; more carefully Rordorf & Tuilier, *La Doctrine*, p. 199.

[26] E. Brandenburger, *Markus 13 und die Apokalyptik* (Göttingen: Vandenhoeck & Ruprecht, 1984 [FRLANT 134]) pp. 135-9, in debate with E. Käsemann.

[27]*Ibid*, p. 138.

[28] One of the apocalypses without parenesis is e.g. Dan. See C.H. Lebram, "The Piety of the Jewish Apocalyptists" in Hellholm, *Apocalypticism*, pp. 171-210 esp. 178f.

danger of overlooking important aspects of what it is intended to communicate.

III

Probably because of that, it has been maintained on more than one occasion that the *Didache* contains no theological debate,[29] i.e. has no interest in dogmatic questions.[30]

On the other hand it is striking that Did 16:7 expressly attacks the assumption that there will be a general resurrection of the dead, as attested by Jn 6:28f, but about which Lk 20:35 still has reservations. According to the *Didache*, expressly, only the saints are saved. It differs thus also from the thought model of Revelation, which links the assumption of the general resurrection with that of the second death of the evil doers (Rev 20:11-21:8), and so mediates between the competing assumptions of a general or an exclusive resurrection of the dead.[31] The *Didache* only allows the latter model,[32] and so we get into relatively old traditions in the history of the development of theology, which have to be linked to the exclusive resurrection-belief of the Maccabbean Martyrs, and are also found in Paul (1 Thess 4:16; Rom 6:5; 8:11), the Gospel of John (3:36), Ignatius (*Trall* 9:2) and Polycarp (*Phil* 2:2),[33] but differ from the chronologically or ontologically graded orders of resurrection, as later in Hippolytus,[34] in mil-

---

[29] Wengst, *Didache (Apostellehre)*, p. 17.

[30] Schöllgen, "Didache als Kirchenordnung", p. 5.

[31] On the resurrection in Rev see G. Kegel, *Auferstehung Jesu - Auferstehung der Toten. Eine traditionsgeschichtliche Untersuchung zum Neuen Testament* (Gütersloh: Mohn, 1970) pp. 107f. Cf. in general: T.H.C. van Eijk, *La resurrection des morts chez les pères apostoliques* (Paris: Beauchesne, 1974 [ThH 25]), pp. 19-28 refer to the *Didache* in particular.

[32] The idea of a *general* judgement *after* the resurrection, which is specifically *restricted* to the saints alone, as it results from one reconstruction of the conclusion of *Didache* 16 (compare fn. 25), is not without tensions! It would be profitable to research the early Christian conceptions of the resurrection with respect to whether they depart in every case from a *general* resurrection, or whether they do not more commonly than is accepted depart from an *exclusive* resurrection of believers.

[33] T. Baumeister, *Die Anfänge der Theologie des Martyriums* (Münster, 1980 [Münsterische Beiträge zur Theologie 45]) pp. 44, 248. Ignatius (SUC 11, p. 178, lines 1-3 Fischer); Polykarp (Ibid. p. 250, lines 7-12). A late witness to a belief in an exclusive resurrection is found in the apocryphal 3 Cor 3:24 (Greek: A. v. Harnack, *Apocrypha IV. Die apokryphen Briefe des Paulus an die Laodiceer und Korinther* (KlT 12; Bonn ²1912, repr. Berlin: de Gruyter, 1931) p. 17; Coptic: C. Schmidt, *Acta Pauli aus der Heidelberger koptischen Papyrushandschrift Nr.1.* (Leipzig, 1904, repr. Hildesheim: Olms, 1965) p. 43, lines 14-8, and is rejected as heretical in *ActsPaulThec* 12f (Greek: R.A. Lipsius, *Acta apostolorum apocrypha* 1, Leipzig, 1981, Reprint 1959, p. 244; Schmidt, *ibid.*, p. 8, line 26 to p. 9, line 1, a new edition of the *Acts of Paul* is currently being prepared by W. Rordorf).

[34] P. Prigent, "Hyppolyte, commentateur de l'Apocalypse", *TZ* 28 (1972) pp. 391-412, esp 403f.

lenarian context in Irenaeus,[35] and in gnostic context in the
Treatise on Resurrection addressed to Rheginos in NgH I,4.[36]

The description of the Saviour as κατάθεμα (curse)[37] also
points to a very old tradition. It reminds one of Christ "made into
sin" of 1 Cor 5:21 and stands directly parallel to the saying of Gal
3:13, that he has become a curse (κατάρα) for our sake as the
crucified, since everyone who is hanged on a tree is cursed
(ἐπικατάρατος). *Barnabas*[38] also describes him as the crucified
Accursed One, who "on that day" will come again in the purple
royal robe (7:9), and all these are reflections on the verdict of Dt
21:23,[39] according to which anyone hanged on a pole is cursed by
God. Paul, *Barnabas* and the *Didache* use this idea in the sense of
a paradox christology: the one apparently accursed is in reality the
future Saviour, who, as Paul then worked it out theologically, has
broken the curse of the Law.[40]

We have all the grounds for the conclusion that we see here
one of the oldest layers of christology, which experiences the
Easter event as a revelation of the future quality as Judge of the
one so shamefully crucified and did not yet use the title "Son of
Man" for this purpose, which then makes the apocalyptic
reference of this revelation very clear.[41]

---

[35] *AdvHaer* V.35:4 (SC 153, pp. 438-40). In my opinion, one cannot detect the
millenarian context in *Did*, which O'Hagan (*Material Recreation*, pp. 28-30)
cautiously indicates.

[36] *De resurrectione* (*Ep. ad Rheginum*) NHC 1, 45,32-46,2 (*Bibliotheque copte
de Nag Hammadi*, Section "Textes" 12, pp. 46-8 Ménard). Compare also the commentary of the editor there, pp. 65-7, and in M. L. Peel, *Gnosis und Auferstehung.
Der Brief des Rheginus von Nag Hammadi* (Neukirchen: Neukirchener Verlag,
1974) pp. 82-4. The English text can be found in J. M. Robinson, *The Nag Hammadi Library in English* (Leiden: Brill, 1977) pp. 50-53).

[37] From κατανάθεμα. Butler ("Literary Relations", pp. 275f) confirms the correctness of this version.

[38] 7:9 (Funk, Bihlmeyer & Schneemelcher, *Apostolischen Väter*, p. 19, lines
10f).

[39] Correct correspondingly the detail "Dt 27:26" in Wengst, *Didache* (*Apostellehre*, p. 99 fn. 137! For the interpretation of this verse compare the *Temple Scroll*,
11QTemp 64:9-13 (ed. Y. Yardin, *The Temple Scroll 2: Text and Commentary*
[Jerusalem: Israel Exploration Society, 1983] pp. 290f). Note also the introduction
by the same author in *The Temple Scroll 1: Introduction* [Jerusalem: Israel Exploration Society, 1983] pp. 373-9, and *The Temple Scroll: The Hidden Law of the Dead
Sea Sect* (London: Weidenfeld and Nicolson, London, 1985) pp. 204-217.

[40] Cf H. W. Kuhn, "Jesus als Gekreuzigter in der frühchristlichen Verkündigung
bis zur Mitte des 2. Jahrhunderts", *ZThK* 72 (1975) pp. 1-46, esp. 35-7; G.
Friedrich, *Die Verkündigung des Todes Jesu im Neuen Testament* (Neukirchen:
Neukirchener Verlag, 1982 [BSt 6]) pp. 122-30. There may be a connection
between this paradox christology and the idea of the elevation of Jesus directly from
the cross, attested especially by Jn 3:14.

[41] Compare the reflections in P. Hoffmann, art. "Auferstehung" II/1, *TRE* 4
(1979) pp. 496, 19-47.

The above two observations on *Didache* 16, which refer us
to different ancient layers of early theology do not now, however,
go along with the conception of imminent expectation. Rather the
ideas about the World Deceiver, who will appear like a son of
god,[42] and about the fire of testing,[43] take up a relatively large
amount of space. It is striking that, in contrast to the apocalypses
in the narrower sense, the spatial dimension of a transcendent
world is here completely missing, and only the future perspective
of the temporal dimension plays a role. Since it is not a case of an
originally apocalyptic revelation as such, which takes place in an
transcendent world, but rather a repetition of long revealed traditional material, it is self-evident why only the temporal dimension
plays a quintessential role: the world events climax in a dramatic
development, which will allow the parousia to appear all the more
triumphally.[44] In this parousia a change is expected; the conclusion of the *Didache* projects a discontinuous development of history.[45] In view of this, the formula generally accepted in critical
scholarship, that the imminent expectation of early Christianity
has passed over into a continuing expectation, is false for sure, if
by continuing expectation the idea of a continuing course of history is implied.

IV

But why did the *Didache* at its conclusion hand on traditional
material into which have flowed clearly theological assumptions
from different stages of tradition?

It is conspicuous that the apocalyptic tradition in 16:3 begins
with the warning about the false prophets in the last days. So it
warns about them, and offers criteria in 11:5f, 8-10 for their
exposure. Such warnings also introduce the apocalyptic chapters
in Mk 13:22 and Mt 24:24. Precisely because the *Didache* is a
selective church order, it cannot be without significance that this
is the case here also. The reference to the false prophets must be
more than just a traditional motif.

Both apostles (11:6) and prophets (11:9) can turn out to be
false prophets.[46] Now it has indeed legitimately been said that,

---

[42] 16:4 (Rordorf & Tuilier, *La Doctrine*, p. 196, line 12); the translation
"appear as *the* Son of God" in Wengst (*Didache (Apostellehre)*, p. 89) is misleading.

[43] 16:5 (Rordorf &Tuilier, *La Doctrine*, p. 196, line 15).

[44] For the signs connected to the parousia see especially the posthumous essay of
A. Stuiber, "Die drei Σημεῖα", pp. 42-44.

[45] On these fundamental characteristic thought patterns of apocalyptic literature
see Lebram, "Piety", p. 173 fn. 10.

[46] One cannot deduce from this, without further ado, that the apostolic and
prophetic offices in the Didache are the same: K. Niederwimmer, "Zur Entwicklungsgeschichte des Wanderradikalismus im Traditionsbereich der Didache", *WSt*

despite many statements, the *Didache* does not allow one to recognize anything exact about the task of the apostle or the prophet.[47] If this cannot be determined from the *Didache* with the help of inner criteria, then one may and must bring in other sources to clarify what they are, in view of the fact that these officials are so important that a false apostle or prophet is considered to be very dangerous.

Without being able here to go into the origin of apocalyptic from prophecy[48] and the difficult questions about the identity of the prophetic and the teaching office[49], and indeed about the prophetic and apostolic office[50] in the New Testament, nevertheless it seems to me to be very significant that both canonical apocalypses of the Bible, which undisputedly represent this genre of revelation literature in the narrow sense, are there themselves designated as prophetic.[51] So apocalyptic proclamation was considered to be prophetic. And without claiming to describe the prophetic activity comprehensively in this way, it can indeed be reckoned as part of the prophetic activity.

I thus come to the thesis that the apocalyptic conclusion of the *Didache*, directed against the false prophets, preserves an important part of the preaching of the prophets attested in the *Didache*. Even if it was scarcely a norm of prophetic preaching, since the speech of the prophet was not subject to anyone's judgment.[52] It is, however, conceivable on the other hand, that here the most important content of prophetic preaching is repeated for

---

ns. 11 (1977) pp. 145-167, esp. 155 note 26; Rordorf & Tuilier, *La Doctrine*, p. 52; for a contrary view see A. de Halleux, "Les ministères dans la Didachè", *Irenikon* 53 (1980) pp. 5-29, esp. 13.

[47] Schöllgen, "Didache als Kirchenordnung", pp. 12f.

[48] On the development of research Rudolph in Hellholm, *Apocalypticism*, p. 782: Koch, *Apokalyptik*, pp. 20f.

[49] Brandenburger, *Markus 13 und die Apokalyptik*, p. 140.

[50] Cf 1 Cor 12:29; Eph 2:20: A de Halleux, "Les ministères", pp. 10f; on this Schöllgen, "Didache als Kirchenordnung", p. 12 fn. 55.

[51] Daniel as a prophet: Mt 24:15; Rev as prophecy: Rev 11:3; 22:7, 10, 18f. In this context it is significant that the apocalypses in Mk 13 and Mt 24 begin with warnings about pseudo-prophets (Mk 13:22; Mt 24:24).

[52] 11:7 (Rordorf & Tuilier, *La Doctrine*, p. 184 lines 13f); criteria for the assessment of a prophet emerge only from his deeds: cf Schöllgen, "Didache als Kirchenordnung", pp. 13f. Because of the understanding that fasting and prayer are to be regarded as pre-requisites for the visionary, prophetic experience (cf. K. Koch, "Vom profetischen zum apokalyptischen Visionsbericht" in Hellholm, *Apocalypticism*, pp. 413-46, esp. 430), the inclusion of commandments on prayer and fasting among the selected themes of the *Didache* may perhaps become understandable, as something that must of necessity be regulated by the congregations, since it emerged from the spiritual practice of the prophets and belonged to their parenesis.

the communities that have no prophet.[53] In the face of the danger
of the false prophets, true prophecy, which means apocalyptic,
however, is preserved in its basic concepts. That is unnecessary if
one has a prophet. But if one does not have one, it becomes a matter of urgency. So it is not surprising that the apocalyptic conclusion of the *Didache* appears as a reference to a genre of
revelation-literature; nevertheless is itself no apocalypse, but only
an *aide-mémoire* of apocalyptic theology.

---

[53] 13:4 (Rordorf & Tuilier, *La Doctrine*, p. 191, lines 7f) formulates a rule for
these communities.

WORKS CITED

Achtemeier, P. *The Quest for Unity in the New Testament Church*. Philadelphia: Fortress, 1987.

————. *"Omne Verbum Sonat:* The New Testament and the Oral Environment of Late Western Antiquity", *JBL* 109/1 (1990) pp. 3-27.

Adam, A. "Grundbegriffe des Mönchtums in sprachlicher Sicht", *ZKG* 65 (1953/4): 209-239.

————. "Erwägungen zur Herkunft der Didache", *ZK* 68 (1957): 1-47.

————. *Lehrbuch der Dogmengeschichte I: Die Zeit der alten Kirche*. Gütersloh: Mohr, 1965.

Albeck, C. "Die vierte Eulogie des Tischgebets", *MGWJ* 78 (1934): 430-437.

Alfonsi, L. "Aspetti della struttura letteraria della Διδαχή." In *Studi classici in onore di Q. Cataudella* 2, 465-81. Catania: Università di Catania, 1972.

Alon, G. "[דידאכי] ההלכה שבתורת י"ב השליחים." In *Studies in Jewish History in the Times of the Second Temple, the Mishna and the Talmud* I, 274-94. Tel Aviv: Hakibbutz Hameuchad, 1958.

Altaner, B. "Zum Problem der lateinischen Doctrina apostolorum", *VgChr* 6 (1952): 1-47.

————. *Patrology*, trans. H. C. Graef. Freiburg: Herder, 1960[7].

Andersen, A. "Das Abendmahl in den zwei ersten Jahrhunderten nach Christus", *ZNW* 3 (1902): 115-141.

Arbesmann, R. "Fasttage", *RAC* 7 (1969): 500-524.

Ascough, R.S. "An Analysis of the Baptismal Tirual of the *Didache*", *StLiturg* 24 (1994): 201-213.

Audet, J.-P. "Affinités littéraires et doctrinales du "Manuel de Discipline"", *RB* 59 (1952): 219-238.

————. "Esquisse du genre littéraire de la bénédiction juive et de l'eucharistie chrétienne", *RB* 65 (1958): 371-399.

————. *La Didachè. Instructions des Apôtres*. Paris: Gabalda, 1958 [ÉBib].

————. "Literary Forms and Contents of a Normal Εὐχαριστία in the First Century", in *Studia Evangelica*, 643-62. Berlin: Akademie-Verlag, 1959 [TU 73].

————. "Genre littétaire et formes cultuelles de l'Eucharistie. 'Nova et Veteras'", *EphLiturg* 80 (1966): 353-385.

Aune, D.E. *Prophecy in Early Christianity and the Ancient Mediterranean World*. Grand Rapids, Mich.: Eerdmans, 1983.

Bacher, W. *Die Agada der Tannaiten* II. Strassbourg: Trübner, 1890.

Bacher, W. *Die Agada der Tannaiten* I. Strassbourg: Trübner, 1903.

————. *Die exegetische Terminologie der jüdische Traditionsliteratur* Vol. I & II. Darmstadt: Wissenschaftlicher Buchgesellochaft, 1905.

Baltzer, K. *Das Bundesformular*. Neukirchen: Neukirchner Verlag, 1964[2] [WMANT 4].

Bammel, E. "Schema und Vorlage von Didache 16" in *Studia Patristica* IV, ed. F. L. Cross, 253-62. Berlin: Akademie-Verlag, 1961 [TU 79].

―――――. "Sadduzäer und Sadokiden", *ETL* 55 (1979): 107-115.

Bardenhewer, O. *Geschichte der altkirchlichen Literatur* I. Freiburg, 1913². Reprint. Darmstadt: Wissenschaftliche Buchgesellschaft, 1962.

Barnard, L.W. "The Epistle of Barnabas and the Tannaitic Catechism", *AThR* 41 (1959): 177-190.

Barnikol, E. "Die triadische Taufformel: Ihr Fehlen in der Didache und im Matthäusevangelium und irh altkotholischer Urspring", *ThJ* 4-5 (1936-1937): 144-152.

Barth, G. "Matthew's Understanding of the Law", in *Tradition and Interpretation in Matthew*, ed. G. Bornkamm, G. Barth & H. J. Held, 58-164. London: SCM, 1960.

Barth, G. *Die Taufe in Frühchristliche Zeit*. Neukirchen-Vluyn: Neukirchener-Verlag, 1981.

Bartlet, J.V. "The Didache Reconsidered", *JTS* 22 (1921): 239-249.

Batiffol, P. *Études d'histoire et de théologie positive II: L'Eucharistie*. Paris: Lecoffre, 1920.

Bauckham, R.J. "Synoptic Parousia Parables and the Apocalypse", *NTS* 23 (1976-1977): 162-176.

―――――. "Synoptic Parousia Parables Again", *NTS* 29 (1983): 129-134.

―――――. "The Lord's Day", in *From Sabbath to Lord's Day*, ed. D. Carson. Grand Rapids: Academie, 1985 pp. 221-250.

―――――. "The Two Fig-Tree Parables in the Apocalypse of Peter", *JBL* 104 (1985): 271-273.

Bauer, W., Arndt, W.F. & Gingrich, F.W. *A Greek-English Lexicon of the New Testament*. Chicago: University Press, 1957.

Baumeister, T. *Die Anfänge der Theologie des Martyriums*. Münster: Aschendorff, 1980 [Münsterische Beiträge zur Theologie 45].

Baus, K. *Handbook of Church History I: From the Apostolic Community to Constantine*, ed. H. Jedin & J. Dolan. London: Burns & Oates, 1965.

Becker, J. *Untersuchungen zur Entstehungsgeschichte der Testamente der zwölf Patriarchen*. Leiden: Brill, 1970.

Bellinzoni, A. *The Sayings of Jesus in the Writings of Justin Martyr*. Leiden: Brill, 1967 [NT.S 17].

Benoit, A. *Le Baptême Chrétien au Second Siècle*. Paris: Presses Universitaires de France, 1953.

―――――. "Review of J.-P. Audet, *La Didachè*, Paris, 1958", *RB* 68 (1959): 594-600.

Berger, K. *Die Gesetzesauslegung Jesu. Ihr historischer Hintergrund im Judentum und im Alten Testament*. Neukirchen-Vluyn: Neukirchener Verlag, 1972 [WMANT 40].

Bernays, J. *Gesammelte Abhandlungen* I-II. Berlin: Hertz, 1885. Reprint. Hildesheim: Olms, 1971.

Betz, H.D. *Essays on the Sermon on the Mount*. Philadelphia: Fortress, 1985.

Betz, J. "Der Abendmahlskelch im Judenchristentum." In *Abhandlungen über Theologie und Kirche (Festschrift für K. Adam)*, ed. M. Reding. Düsseldorf: Patmos, 1952.

————. *Die Eucharistie in der Zeit der griechischen Väter I: Die Aktualpräsenz der Person und des Heilswerkes Jesu im Abendmahl nach der vorephesinischen griechischen Patristik.* Freiburg: Herder 1955.

————. *Die Eucharistie in der Zeit der griechischen Väter. II.1: Die Realpräsenz des Leibes und Blutes Jesu im Abendmahl nach dem Neuen Testament.* Freiburg: Herder, 1964.

————. "Die Eucharistie in der Didache", *ALW* 11 (1969): 10-39.

Bigg, C. *The Doctrine of the Twelve Apostles.* London: SPCK, 1898.

Bihlmeyer, K. *Die Apostolischen Väter.* Tübingen: Mohr, 1956³.

Billerbeck, P. *Kommentar zum Neuen Testament* IV. München: Beck, 1922.

Blau, L. *Das altjüdische Zauberwesen.* Budapest, 1898. Reprint. Graz: Äkademishe Druck und Verlaganstallt, 1974.

Böcher, O. "Wölfe im Schafspelzen: zum religionsgeschichtlichen Hintergrund von Matth. 7,15", *TZ* 24 (1968): 405-426.

Boismard, M.É. "Une liturgie baptismale dans la Prima Petri", *RB* 63 (1956): 182-208.

————. "Une liturgie baptismale dans la Prima Petri", *RB* 64 (1957): 161-183.

Bonnard, P. *L'Évangile selon St. Matthieu.* Neuchatel: Delachaux & Niestlé, 1970.

Bonsirven, J. *Palestinian Judaism in the Time of Jesus Christ.* New York: Holt, Rinehart & Winston, 1964.

Borgen, P. *Bread from Heaven.* Leiden: Brill, 1965.

————. "Cataalogues of Vices, the Apostolic Decree and the Jerusalem Meeting." In *The Social World of Formative Christianity and Judaism: Festschr. H. C. Kee*, ed. J. Neusner, P. Borgen, E. S. Frerichs, R. Horsley, 126-41. Philadelphia: Fortress, 1988.

Borig, R. *Der wahre Weinstock. Untersuchungen zu Jo 15,1-10.* München: Kösel, 1967 [SANT 16].

Boring, M.E. *Sayings of the Risen Jesus: Christian Prophecy in the Synoptic Tradition.* Cambridge: University Press, 1982.

Bornemann, W. "Der erste Petrusbrief—eine Taufrede des Sylvanus", *ZNW* 19 (1919-1920): 143-165.

Bornkamm, G. "End-Expectation and Church in Matthew" in *Tradition and Interpretation in Matthew*, ed. G. Bornkamm, G. Barth & H. J. Held. London: SCM, 1960.

————. *Überlieferung und Auslegung im Matthäusevangelium.* Neukirchen-Vluyn: Neukirchner Verlag, 1965⁴ [WMANT 1].

————. *Paul*, trns. D. M. G. Stalker. London: Hodder & Stoughton, 1971.

Botte, B. *La tradition apostolique de Saint Hippolyte, Essai de reconstruction.* Munster: Aschendorfsche Verlagsbuchhandlung, 1963.

Bousset, W. "Eine Judische Gebetsammlung im siebenten Buch der apostolischen Konstitutionen" *NGG.PH* (1915): 435-489. Reprinted in: *Reli-*

gionsgeschichtliche Studien. Aufsätze zur Religionsgeschichte des hellenistischen Zeitalters, ed. A.F. Verheule, 231-285. NovTestSup, vol. 50. Leiden: E.J. Brill, 1979.

Bouyer, L. L'eucharistie. Théologie et spiritualité de la prière eucharistique: Spiritualité d'hier et d'aujour'hui. Tournai: Descleé, 1966 [BiblTh].

Bradshaw, P.F. Daily Prayer in the Early Church. London: SPCK, 1981.

Brandenburger, E. Markus 13 und die Apokalyptik. Göttingen: Vandenhoeck & Ruprecht, 1984 [FRLANT 134].

Braun, H. Qumran und das Neue Testament II. Tübingen: Mohr, 1966.

Broek-Utne, A. "Eine schwierige Stelle in einer alten Gemeindeordnung, Did. 11:11", ZKG 54 (1935): 576-581.

Bryennios, P. Διδαχὴ τῶν δώδεκα ἀποστόλων. Constantinople: S. I. Boutura, 1883.

Bruyne, D. de "Une traité gnostique sur les trois récompenses", ZNW 15 (1914): 280-284.

Büchler, A. Studies in Sin and Atonement in the Rabbinic Literature of the First Century. Oxford: Oxford University Press, 1928 [Jews' College Publications 11]. Reprint. NY: KTAV, 1967.

Bultmann, R. Theology of the New Testament I, trans. K. Grobel. London: SCM, 1952.

————. The History of the Synoptic Tradition, trns. J. Marsh. Oxford: Basil Blackwell, 1972.

Burchard, C. "Das doppelte Liebesgebot in der frühen christlichen Überliefering." In Der Ruf Jesu und die Antwort der Gemeinde, Festschrift für Joachim Jeremias, ed. E. Lohse et al, 39-62. Göttingen: Vandenhoeck & Ruprecht, 1970.

Burnett, F.W. The Testament of Jesus-Sophia: a redaction-critical study of the eschatological discourse in Matthew. Washington: University Press of America, 1979.

Butler, B.C. "The Literary Relations of Didache, Ch. XVI", JTS 11 (1960): 265-283.

————. "The 'Two Ways' in the Didache", JTS 12 (1961): 27-38.

Campenhausen, H. von Kirchliches Amt und geistliche Vollmacht in den ersten drei Jahrhunderten. Tübingen: Mohr, 1963² [BHTh 14] (Eng. Ecclesiastical Authority and Spiritual Power in the Church of the First Three Centuries, trans. J. A. Baker. London: Black, 1969).

————. Die Entstehung der christlichen Bibel. Tübingen: Mohr, 1968 [BHTh 39] (Eng. The Formation of the Christian Bible, trans. J. A. Baker. Philadelphia: Fortress, 1972).

————. "Early Christian Asceticism." In Tradition and Life in the Church, 90-122. London: Collins, 1968.

————. "Taufen auf den Namen Jesu", VigChr 25 (1971): 1-16.

————. The Formation of the Christian Bible. Philadelphia: Fortress, 1972.

Carleton-Paget, J. The Epistle of Barnabas: Outlook and Background. Tübingen: Mohr, 1994 [WUNT ns. 64].

Carrington, P. *The Primitive Christian Catechism. A Study in the Epistles.* Cambridge: Cambridge University Press, 1940.

Casel, O. "The Mystery of Christian Worship and Other Writings", *JLw* 9 (1930): 1-19.

―――. *Prophetie und Eucharistie*, trns. B. Neunheuser. Westminster, Md: Darton, Longman & Todd, 1963.

Catchpole, D.R. "Jesus and the Community of Israel--The Inaugural Discourse in Q" in *BJRL* 68 (1986): 296-316.

Cayré, P. *Patrologie et Histoire de la Théologie* I. Paris: Desolée, 1953.

Cazelles, H. "Eucharistie, bénédiction et sacrifice dans l'Ancien Testament", *La Maison-Dieu* 123 (1975/3): 7-28.

Cerfaux, L. Introduction to *La Bible de Jérusalem. Les Actes des Apôtres.* Paris: Cerf, 1958.

Cerfaux, L. "La multiplication des pains dans la liturgie de la Didachè", *Bib* 40 (1959): 943-958.

Charlesworth, J.H., ed. *The Old Testament Pseudepigrapha* I: *Apocalyptic Literature and Testaments.* Garden City, NY: Doubleday, 1983

Clerici, L. *Einsammlung der Zerstreuten. Liturgiegeschichtliche Untersuchung zur Vor- und Nachgeschichte der Fürbitte für die Kirche in Did. 9:4 und 10:5.* Münster: Westfalen, 1966 [LQF 44].

Cohen, A. *The Minor Tractates of the Talmud.* London: Soncino, 1965.

―――. *The Minor Tractates of the Talmud* II. London: Soncino, 1971.

Collins, J.J. "Towards the Morphology of a Genre", *Semeia* 14 (1979): 1-19.

Coneybeare, F. "The Eusebian Form of the Text of Matthew 28,29". *ZNW* 2 (1901): 275-288.

Connolly, R.H. "The Use of the Didache in the Didascalia", *JTS* 24 (1923): 147-157.

―――. "Sixth-century Fragments of an East-Syrian Anaphora", *OrChr* 12-14 (1925): 99-128.

―――. "The Didache in Relation to the Epistle of Barnabas", *JTS* 33 (1932): 327-353.

―――. "Agape and Eucharist in the Didache", *DR* 55 (1937): 477-489.

―――. "Canon Streeter on the Didache", *JTS* 38 (1937): 364ff.

―――. "The Didache and Montanism", *DRev* 55 (1937): 339-347.

Conzelmann, H. *Theology of St. Luke*, trans. G. Buswell. San Francisco: Harper & Row, 1960.

Coquin, R.-G. *Les Canons d'Hippolyte. Edition Critique de la version arabe. Introduction et traduction franc aise.* Paris: Firmin-Didot, 1966 [*Patrologia Orientalis* 31/2].

Cothenet, E. "Le prophétisme dans le Nouveau Testament." In *Supplément au Dictionnaire de la Bible* VIII, ed. L. Pirot. Paris: Létouzey & Ané, 1971.

Creed, J.M. "The Didache", *JTS* 39 (1938): 370-287.

Crossan, J.D. *The Historical Jesus: The Life of a Mediterranean Jewish Peasant.* San Francisco: Harper & Rowe, 1991.

Cross, F.L. *I Peter. A Paschal Liturgy*. London: Mowbray, 1954.

Cullmann, O. *The Christology of the New Testament*. London: SCM, 1963².

———. *La foi et le culte de l'Église primitive*. Paris: Delachaux & Niestlé, 1963 [Bibliotheque théologigue].

———. *Salvation in History*. London: SCM, 1967.

Cutrone, E.J. "The Anaphora of the Apostles", *ThSt* 34 (1973): 624-642.

Danby, H. *The Mishnah*. Oxford: Oxford University Press, 1933.

Daniélou, J. "Une source de la spiritualité chrétienne dans les manuscrits de la Mer Morte: la doctrine des deux esprits", *DViv* 25 (1953): 127ff.

———. "La communanté de qumrân et L'organisation de l'église ancienne", *RHPhR* 35 (1955): 104-115.

———. *The Dead Sea Scrolls and Primitive Christianity*, trns. S. Athanasio. Baltimore, Md: Helicon, 1958.

———. *A History of Early Christian Doctrine Before the Council of Nicaea I: The Theology of Jewish Christianity*. London: Darton, Longman & Todd, 1964.

———. *The Christian Centuries I: The First Six Hundred Years*, trns. V. Cronin. London: Darton, Longman & Todd, 1964.

———. *La catéchèse aux premiers siècles*. Paris: Fayard-Marne, 1968.

———. "Bulletin d'histoire des origines chrétiennes", *RSR* 59 (1971): 37-74.

———. "Le traité de centesima, sexagesima, tricesima et la judéo-chretianisme latin avant Tertullien", *VigChr* 25 (1971): 171ff.

Daube, D. *The New Testament and Rabbinic Judaism*. London: University of London, Athlone Press, 1956.

Davies, W.D. *The Setting of the Sermon on the Mount*. Cambridge: Cambridge University Press, 1964.

———. & Allison, D.C. *A Critical and Exegetical Commentary on the Gospel according to Saint Matthew* I. Edinburgh: T. & T. Clark, 1988.

Dehandschutter, B. "The Text of the *Didache*: Some Comments on the Edition of Klaus Wengst." In *The Didache in Context: Essays on its Text, History and Transmission*, ed. C.N. Jefford, 37-46. Leiden: Brill, 1995.

del Verme, M. *Giudaismo e Nuovo Testamento: Il Caso delle Decime* (Naples: D'Auria, 1989) pp. 216-228

———. "Medio giudaismo e *Didaché*: il caso della comunione dei beni", *VetChr* 32 (1995) pp. 293-320.

Deussen, G. "Weisen der Bischofswahl im 1 Klemensbrief und in der Didache", *TheolGl* 62 (1972): 131-134.

Deutsch, C. *Hidden Wisdom and the Easy Yoke: Wisdom, Torah and Discipleship in Matthew 11.25-30*. Sheffield: JSOT, 1987 [*JSNT Supp.* 18].

Dibelius, M. *Die Apostolischen Väter IV: Der Hirt des Hermas*. Tübingen: Mohr, 1923 [HNT.E 4].

———. "Die Mahl-Gebete der Didache", *ZNW* 37 (1938): 32-41.

————. *Die Pastoralbriefe*. Tübingen: Mohr, 1966 [HNT 13]. (Eng. *The Pastoral Epistles*, trans. P. Buttolph & A. Yarbro. Philadelphia: Fortress, 1972).

————. *Geschichte der urchristlichen Literatur*. Berlin: de Gruyter, 1975 [ThB 58].

————. *James: A Commentary on the Epistle of James*, revised H. Greeven; translated M. A. Williams, and edited H. Koester. Philadelphia: Fortress 1976.

Dihle, A. *Die goldene Regel*. Göttingen: Vandenhoeck & Ruprecht, 1962 [StAW 7].

Dix, G. *The Shape of the Liturgy*. Westminster: Dacre, 1945. Reprint. London: SPCK, 1964.

————. "The Ministry in the Early Church c. A.D. 90-410." In *The Apostolic Ministry, Essays on the History and the Doctrine of the Episcopacy*, ed. K. E. Kirk. London: Hodder & Stoughton, 1946.

Dodd, C.H. "The primitive Catechism and the Sayings of Jesus." In *New Testament Essays.Studies in Memory of Thomas Walter Manson 1893-1958*, ed. A.J.B. Higgins, 106-18. Manchester: Manchester University Press, 1959.

————. *Gospel and Law: the Relation of Faith and Ethics in Early Christianity*. Cambridge: Cambridge University Press, 1965⁶.

Dölger, F.J. *Der Exorzismus im altchristlichen Taufritual*. Schöningh: Paderborn, 1909 [SGKA III,1-2].

————. *Sol salutis*. Münster: Aschendorff, 1920.

————. "Nilwasser und Taufwasser", *ACh* 5 (1936): 175-183.

————. *Die Sonne der Gerechtigkeit und der Schwarze*. Münster: Aschendorff, 1971².

Donahue, P.J. "Jewish Christianity in the Letters of Ignatius of Antioch", *VigChr* 32 (1978): 81-92.

Donaldson, T.L. *Jesus on the Mountain: A Study in Matthean Theology*. Sheffield: JSOT, 1985 [*JSOT Supp.* 8].

Draper, J.A. *A Commentary on the Didache in the Light of the Dead Sea Scrolls and Related Documents*. Unpublished Cambridge PhD Dissertation, 1983.

————. "The Jesus Tradition in the Didache." In *Gospel Perspectives V: The Jesus Tradition Outside the Gospels*, ed. D. Wenham, 269-89. Sheffield: JSOT, 1985.

————. "The Social Milieu and Motivation of Community of Goods in the Jerusalem Church of Acts." In *Church in Context*, ed. C. Breytenbach, 77-88. Pretoria: NG Boekhandel, 1988.

————. "Weber, Theissen and the Wandering Charismatics of the *Didache*", Unpublished Paper presented at the 1989 meeting of the Society of Biblical Literature, Anaheim.

————. "The Development of the "Sign of the Son of Man" in the Jesus Tradition", *NTS* 39 (1991): 1-21.

————. "Torah and Troublesome Apostles in the *Didache* Community", *NovT* 33/4 (1991): 347-372.

————. "Christian Self-definition against the "Hypocrites" in *Didache* VIII.*" In *Society of Biblical Literature: 1992 Seminar Papers (No. 31, 128th Annual Meeting, San Francisco, November 21-24, 1992)*, ed. E.H. Lovering, 362-77. Atlanta, Ga.: Scholars Press, 1992.

————. "Barnabas and the Riddle of the Didache Revisited", *JSNT* 58 (1995): 89-113.

————. "Social Ambiguity and the Production of Text: Prophets, Teachers, Bishops,and Deacons and the Development of the Jesus Tradition in the Community of the *Didache.*" In *The Didache in Context: Essays of Its Text, History and Transmission*, ed. C. N. Jefford, 284-313. Leiden: Brill, 1995 [*NT.E* 77].

————. "Resurrection and Zechariah 14.5 in the Didache Apocalypse", *JEC*: forthcoming.

Drews. P. "Untersuchungen zur Didache", *ZNW* 5 (1904): 53-79.

Dugmore, C.W. *The Influence of the Synagogue upon the Divine Office.* London: Alcuin, 1964².

Dujarier, M. *Le parrainage des adultes aux trois premiers siècles de l'Eglise.* 1962.

Dupont, J. *Etudes sur les Actes des Apôtres.* Paris: Editions du Cerf, 1967 [Lectio Divina 45].

Ehrhardt, A. *The Apostolic Succession in the First Two Centuries of the Church.* London: Lutterworth, 1953.

Eijk, T.H.C. van *La resurrection des morts chez les pères apostoliques.* Paris: Beauchesne, 1974 [ThH 25].

Eisler, R. "Das letzte Abendmahl", *ZNW* 25 (1926): 6-12.

Elbogen, I. *Der jüdische Gottesdienst in seiner geschichtlichen Entwicklung.* Frankfurt a. M.: Kauffmann, 1924².

Farmer, W.R. *The Synoptic Problem.* Dillsboro NC.: Wester, 1976².

Farrar, F.W. "The Teaching of the Lord by the Twelve Apostles to the Gentiles", *The Contemporary Review* 45 (1884): 698-706.

Feuillet, A. *Le Christ sagesse de Dieu.* Paris: Librairie Lecoffre, 1966.

Finkelstein, L. "The "birkat ha-mazon"", *JQR* 19 (1928-1929): 211-263.

Fischer, J.A. "Review of Audet *La Didachè*, Paris, 1958" in *ThLZ* 85 (1960): col. 524-526.

Fitzmyer, J.A. *The Gospel according to Luke I-IX.* New York: Doubleday, 1981 [Anchor 28].

————. *The Gospel according to Luke X-XXIV.* New York: Doubleday, 1985 [Anchor 28A].

Flusser, D. *Jewish Sources in Early Christianity.* Tel Aviv: Sifriat Poalim, 1979 (in Hebrew).

————. "The Two Ways." In *Jewish Sources in Early Christianity*, 232-52. Tel Aviv: Sifriat Poalaim, 1979.

————. & Safrai, S. "Das Aposteldekret und die Noachistischen Gebote." In *Wer Tora vermehrt mehrt Leben: Festgabe für Heinz Kremers zum*

60. Geburtstag, 173-92. Neukirchen-Vluyn: Neukirchener-Verlag, 1986.

————. "Paul's Jewish Christian Opponents in the Didache." In *Gilgul: Essays on Transformation, Revolution and Permanence in the History of Religions: Dedicated to R. J. Zwi Werblowsky*, eds. S. Shaked, D. Shulman & G. G. Stroumsa, 71-90. Leiden: Brill, 1987.

————. "The Ten Commandments and the New Testament." In *The Ten Commandments in History and Tradition*, ed. B. Segal, 219-246. Jerusalem: Magnes, 1990.

Frank, A. *Studien zur Ekklesiologie des Hirten, 2 Klemems, der Didache und der Ignatiusbriefe mit besonderer Berücksichtigung der Idee einer präexistenten Kirche*. Dissertation: Munich, 1975.

Friedrich, G. *Die Verkündigung des Todes Jesu im Neuen Testament*. Neukirchen: Neukirchener Veralg, 1982 [BTS 6].

Fuller, R.H. "The Double Commandment of Love: A Test Case for the Criteria of Authenticity." In *Essays on the Love Commandment*, ed. R.H. Fuller, 41-56. Philadelphia: Fortress, 1978.

Funk, F.X. *Doctrinae duodecim apostolorum, Canones ecclesiastici ac reliquae doctrinae duarum viarum expositiones veteres*. Tübingen: Henrici Laupp, 1887.

————. "Der Barnabasbrief und die Didache", *ThQ* (1897): 617ff.

————. *Patres apostolici* I. Tübingen: Laupp, 1901².

————. *Didascalia et Constitutiones apostolorum* II. Paderborn: F. Schöningh, 1906.

————., Bihlmeyer, K. & Schneemelcher, W. *Die Apostolischen Väter: Neubearbeitung der Funkschen Ausgabe*. Tübingen: Mohr, 1970 [SQS II 1,1³].

Gaechter, P. *Das Matthäusevangelium*. Münich: Tyrolia-Verlag, 1964.

Galvin, R.J. "Addai and Mari revisited: the state of the question", *EphLiturg* 87 (1978): 383-414.

Gavin, F. *The Jewish Antecedents of the Christian Sacraments*. London: SPCK, 1928.

Gebhardt, O. von "Ein übersehenes Fragment der Didache in alter lateiner Übersetzung." In *Die Lehre der zwölf Apostel*, ed. A. von Harnack, 275-86. Leipzig: Hinrichse, 1884 [TU 2].

Geffcken, J. *Die Oracula Sibyllina*. Leipzig: Hinrichs, 1902 [GCS 8].

Gerhardt, M. *Das Leben und die Schriften des Lactantius*. Erlangen: Thesis, 1924.

Gibbins, H.J. "The problem of the liturgical section of the Didache", *JTS* 36 (1935): 373-386.

Giet, S. "Coutume, évolution, droit canon. A propos de deux passages de la "Didaché"", *RDC* 16 (1966): 118-132. Reprinted in *L'énigma de la Didachè*, 192-97. Paris: Ophrys, 1970 [PFLUS].

————. "La Didachè, enseignement des douze apôtres?", *Melto* 3 (1967): 223-236.

————. *L'Énigme de la Didachè*. Paris: Ophrys, 1970 [PFLUS 149].

Giordano, O. "L'escatologia nella Didache." In *Oikoumene. Studi paleocristiani in onore del Concilio Ecumenico Vaticano II*, 121-39. Catania: Università di Catania, 1964.

Glover, R. "The Didache's Quotations and the Synoptic Gospels", *NTS* 5 (1958): 12-29.

————. "Patristic Quotations and Gospel Sources", *NTS* 31 (1985): 234-251.

Gnilka, J. *Das Matthäus-evangelium*. Freiburg: Herder, 1986.

Goguel, M. *L'Eucharistie des origines á Justin Martyr*. Paris: Fischbacher, 1910.

————. *Jésus et les origines du Christianisme III: L'Église primitive*. Paris: Payot, 1947 (Eng. *The Primitive Church*, trns. H. C. Snape. London: Allen & Unwin, 1964).

Golz, E. von der *Tischgebete und Abendmahlsgebete in der altchristlichen und in der griechischen Kirche* Leipzig: Hinrichs, 1905 [TU n.s. 14,2b].

Goodenough, E.R. "John a Primitive Gospel", *JBL* 64 (1945): 145-182.

Goodspeed, E.J. "The Didache, Barnabas and the Doctrina", *AThR* 27 (1945): 228-247.

————. *A History of Early Christian Literature*. Chicago: University of Chicago Press, 1942.

————. *Die ältesten Apologeten*. Göttingen: Vandenhoeck & Ruprecht, 1984.

Goppelt, L. *Die apostolische und nachapostolische Zeit* (Eng. *Apostolic and Post-Apostolic Times*, trns. A. Guelich. London: Black, 1970).

Goulder, M.D. *Midrash and Lection in Matthew*. London: SPCK, 1974.

Green, H.B. "The Command to Baptize and Other Matthaean Interpolations." In *SE* 4. Berlin: Akademie-Verlag, 1968 [TU 102].

Greeven, H. "Propheten, Lehrer, Vorsteher bein Paulus. Zur Frage der "Ämter" im Urchristentum", *ZNW* 44 (1952-1953): 1-43.

Greiff, A. *Das älteste pascharituale der Kirche, Did. 1-10, und das Johannesevangelium*. Paderborn: Ferdinand Schöningh, 1929 [JS 1].

Grenfell, B.-P. & Hunt, A.S. *The Oxyrhynchus Papyri* 15. London: Egyptian Exploration Society, 1922.

Guelich, R.A. *The Sermon on the Mount*. Waco: Word, 1982.

Gundry, R.H. *Matthew: A Commentary on his Literary and Theological Art*. Grand Rapids, Mich.: Eerdmans, 1982.

Gy, P.-M. "Eucharistie et "ecclesia" dans le premier vocabulaire de la liturgie chrétienne", *La Maison-Dieu* 130 (1977): 19-34.

Hagner, D.A. *The Use of the Old and New Testament in Clement of Rome*. Leiden: Brill, 1973 [NT.S 34].

————. "The Sayings of Jesus in the Apostolic Fathers and Justin Martyr." In *Gospel Perspectives V*, ed. Wenham, 233-68. Sheffield: JSOT, 1985.

Hahn, F. "'Einführung' to A. Seeberg." In *Der Katechismus der Urchristenheit*. Munich: Kaiser, 1966.

————. "Der Apostolat im Urchristentum. Seine Eigenart und seine Voraussetzungen", *KuD* 20 (1974): 54ff.

————. "Die Rede von der Parusie des Menschensohnes Markus 13." In *Jesus und der Menschensohn* (Fs. Anton Vögtle), ed. R. Pesch & Schnakenburg, 240-56. Freiburg: Herder 1975.

Halleux, A. de "Les ministères dans la Didachè", *Irenikon* 53 (1980): 5-29.

Hamman, A. *Vie liturgique et vie sociale*. Paris: Les Éditions du Cerf, 1968.

————. *La vie quotidienne des premiers chrétiens*. Paris: Les Éditions du Cerf, 1971.

————. "Liturgie, prière et famille dans les trois premiers siècles chrétiens", *Questions Liturgiques* 57 (1976): 87f.

Hammond, N.G.L. & Scullard, H.H. *The Oxford Classical Dictionary*. Oxford: Clarendon, 1970².

Harnack, A. von *Die Lehre der zwölf Apostel nebst Untersuchungenzur ältesten Geschichte der Kirchenverfassung und des Kirchenrechts*. Leipzig: Hinrichs, 1884 [TU 2,1/2].

————. *Die Apostellehre und die jüdischen beiden Wege*. Leipzig: J. C. Hinrichs, 1886, reprint 1896².

————. *Lehrbuch der Dogmengeschichte* I. Tübingen: Mohr, 1909⁴.

————. *Apocrypha IV. Die apokryphen Briefe des Paulus an die Laodiceer und Korinther*. Bonn 1912², repr. Berlin: de Gruyter, 1931 [KIT 12].

————. *Die Mission und Ausbreitung des Christentums in den ersten drei Jahrhunderten* I. Leipzig: Hinrichs, 1924⁴. (Eng. *The Mission and Expansion of Christianity in the First Three Centuries*. London: William & Norgate, 1908).

————. *Geschichte der altchristlichen Literatur* II.1. Leipzig: Hinrichs, 1958².

Harris, J.R. *The Teaching of the Apostles*. London: Clay / Baltimore: John Hopkins University Press, 1887.

Harrison, E.F. "Some Patterns of New Testament Didache", *Biblia Sacra* 119 (1962): 118-128.

Hatch, E. & Redpath, H.A. *A Concordance to the Septuagint and the Other Greek Versions of the Old Testament* II. Oxford: Clarendon, 1897.

Heinemann, I. *Philons griechische und jüdische Bildung*. Hildesheim: Olms, 1962.

Henderson, I.H. "*Didache* and Orality in Synoptic Comparison", *JBL* 111 (1992): 283-306.

Henderson, I.H. "Style-switching in the *Didache*: Fingerprint or Argument." In *The Didache in Context: Essays of Its Text, History and Transmission*, ed. C.N. Jefford, 177-209. Leiden: Brill, 1995 [*NT.E* 77].

Hengel, M. *Judaism and Hellenism*. London: SCM, 1974.

Hennecke, E. "Die Grundschrift der Didache und ihre Rezensionen", *ZNW* 2 (1901): 58-72.

————. *Neutestamentliche Apokryphen.* Tübingen: Mohr, 1964.

Hilgenfeld, A. *Novum Testamentum extra canonem receptum, Evangeliorum* 4,2. Leipzig: Weigel, 1884.

Hoffmann, P. *Studien zur Theologie der Logienquelle.* Münster: Aschendorff, 1972 [NTA 8].

————. "Auferstehung" II/1, *TRE* 4 (1979) pp. 496.

————. "Tradition und Situation. Zur 'Verbindlichkeit' des Gebots der Feindesliebe in der synoptischen Überlieferung und in der gegenwärtigen Friedensdiskussion." In *Ethik im Neuen Testament,* ed. K. Kertelge, 50-118. Freiburg: Herder, 1984.

Holtz, T. "Der antiochenische Zwischenfall (Galater 2:11-14)", *NTS* 32 (1986): 321-343.

Holtzmann, O. "Das Abendmahl im Urchristentum", *ZNW* 5 (1904): 89-120.

————. "Die täglichen Gebetsstunden im Judentum und Urchristentum", *ZNW* 12 (1911): 90-107.

————. *Der Tosephtatraktat Berakot.* Gießen: Topelmann, 1912.

Holzapfel, H. *Die sittliche Wertung der körperlichen Arbeit im christlichen Altertum.* Würzburg: Rita-Verlag, 1941.

Holzhey, C. "Die Abhängigkeit der syrischen Didaskalie von der Didache", in *Compte rendu du 4º congr. scient. des Catholiques.* Freiburg-im-Üchtland, 1898.

Horner, G. *The Statutes of the Apostles or Canones Ecclesiastici.* London: Williams & Norgate, 1904.

————. "A New Fragment of the Didache in Coptic", *JTS* 25 (1924): 225-231.

Horn, F.W. *Glaube und Handeln in der Theologie des Lukas.* Göttingen: Vandenhoeck & Ruprecht, 1983 [GTA 26].

Horovitz, S. & Rabin, J.A. (eds.) *Mechilta de-Rabbi Ishmael.* Jerusalem, 1970.

Horsley, R.A. *Sociology and the Jesus Movement.* New York: Crossroad, 1989.

Hruby, K. "La notion de "berakah" dans la tradition et son charactère anamnétique", *Questions Liturgiques* 52 (1971): 155-170.

————. "La "birkat ha-mazon"." In *Mélanges Liturgiques offerts au R.P. dom Bernard Botte: à l'occasion du cinquantième anniversaire de son ordination sacerdotale (4 Juin 1972).* Louvain: Abbaye du Mont César, 1972.

————. "Le geste de la fraction du pain ou les gestes eucharistiques dans la tradition juive." In *Gestes et paroles dans les diverses familes liturgiques: (Conférences St.-Serge, XXIVᵉ Semaine d'Etudes Liturgiques),* 123-33. Rome, 1978.

Iselin, L.E. *Eine bisher unbekannte Version des ersten Teiles der "Apostellehre".* Leipzig: Heusler, 1895 [TU 13,1b].

————. *Texte und Untersuchungen* 13,1b. Leipzig: Hinrichs, 1895.

Jefford, C.N. *The Sayings of Jesus in the Teaching of the Twelve Apostles.* Leiden: Brill, 1989 [*VigChr.E* 11].

———. & Patterson, S.J. "A Note on *Didache* 12.2a (Coptic)", *SecCent* 7 (1989-1990): 65-75.

———. "An Ancient Witness to the Apostolic Decree of Acts 15?" In *Proceedings: Eastern Great Lakes and Midwest Biblical Societies* 10 (1990): 204-213.

———. "Tradition and Witness in Antioch: Acts 15 and Didache 6." In *Perspectives on Contemporary New Testament Questions*, ed. E. V. McKnight, 409-19. Lewiston: Mellen, 1992 [Perspectives in Religious Studies 19].

Jeremias, J. "Das Brotbrechen beim Passahmahl und Mc 14,22 par.", *ZNTW* 33 (1934): 203-204.

———. *Infant Baptism in the First Four Centuries.* London: SCM, 1960.

———. *The Sermon on the Mount*, trns. N. Perrin. Philadelphia: Fortress, 1963 [*Biblical Series* 2].

———. *The Eucharistic Words of Jesus.* London: SCM, 1966.

———. *The Prayers of Jesus.* London: SCM [StBTh 2,6].

Jones, F.S. & Mirecki, P.A. "Considerations on the Coptic Papyrus of the *Didache* (British Library Oriental Manuscript 9271)." In *The Didache in Context: Essays of Its Text, History and Transmission*, ed. C. N. Jefford, 47-87. Leiden: Brill, 1995 [*NT.E* 77].

Jonge, M. de "Jesus as Prophet and King in the Fourth Gospel", *EThL* 49 (1973): 160-177.

Jouon, P. "YPOKRITES dans l'Evangile et hebreux HANEF", *RSR* 20 (1930): 312-316.

Jousse, M. *L'antropologie du geste*, vol. I. Paris: Gallimard, 1969.

Jungmann, J.A. *Missarum Sollemnia* I. Freiburg: Herder, 1962⁵ (Eng. *The Eucharistic Prayer: A Study of the Canon Missae*, trns. R. L. Batley. London: Challoner, 1956).

———. *The Mass: An Historical, Theological and Pastoral Survey.* Collegeville, Minn.: Liturgical Press, 1976.

Kamlah, E. *Die Form der katalogischen Paränese im Neuen Testament.* Tübingen: Mohr, 1964 [WUNT 7].

Kegel, G. *Auferstehung Jesu - Auferstehung der Toten. Eine traditionsgeschichtliche Untersuchung zum Neuen Testament.* Gütersloh: Mohn, 1970.

Kelly, J.N.D. "Review: *La Didache: instructions des Apotres.* By J.-P. Audet" *JTS* 12 (1961): 329-333.

Kertelge, K. "Der sogennante Taufbefehl Jesu (Mt 28,19)." In *Zeichen des Glaubens. Studien zu Taufe und Firmung (Fst* B. Fischer), 29-40. Freiburg im Breisgau: Einsiedeln, 1972.

Kilpatrick, G.D. *The Origins of the Gospel according to St. Matthew.* Oxford: Oxford University Press, 1946.

Kirsten, H. *Die Taufabsage.* Berlin: Evangelische Verlagsanstalt, 1960.

Klauser, T. "Taufet in Lebendigem Wasser! Zum religions- und kulturges-chichtlichen Verständnis von Didache 7,1-3." In *Pisciculi. Studien zur Religion und Kultur des Altertums (Fst. F. J. Dölger)*, ed. T. Klauser & Rükker, 157-64. Münster: Aschendorff, 1939. Reprinted in: *Gesammelte Arbeiten zur Liturgiegeschichte, Kirchengeschichte und Christlichen Archäologie*, ed. E. Dassmann, 177-83. Münster: Aschendorff, 1974 [JAC.E 3].

Klein, G. "Die Gebete in der Didache", *ZNW* 9 (1908): 134-144.

⸻. *Der Älteste Christliche Katechismus und die Jüdische Propaganda-Literatur*. Berlin: Reimer, 1909.

⸻. *Studien über Paulus*. Stockholm, 1918.

⸻. *Die zwölf Apostel. Ursprung und Gehalt einer Idee*. Göttingen: Vandenhoeck & Ruprecht, 1961 [FRLANT 77].

Klijn, A.F.J. "The Pseudo-Clementines and the Apostolic Decree", *NT* 10 (1968): 305-312.

Kloppenborg, J.S. "Didache 16:6-8 and Special Matthean Tradition", *ZNW* 69-70 (1978-1979): 54-67.

⸻. "The Transformation of Moral Exhortation in *Didache* 1-5." In *The Didache in Context: Essays of Its Text, History and Transmission*, ed. C.N. Jefford, 88-109. Leiden: Brill, 1995 [*NT.E* 77].

Knopf, R. *Das nachapostolische Zeitalter. Geschichte der christlichen Gemeinden vom Beginn der Flavierdynastie bis zum Ende Hadrians*. Tübingen: Mohr, 1905.

⸻. *Die Lehre der zwölf Apostel; Die zwei Clemensbriefe*. Tübingen: Mohr, 1920 [HNT.E 1].

Koch, K. Introduction to Koch, K. & Schmidt, J.M. (eds.), *Apokalyptik*. Darmstadt: Wissenschaftliche Buchgesellschaft, 1982 [*Wege der Forschung* 365]) pp. 1-29.

Koch, K. *Ratlos vor der Apokalyptik. Eine Streitschrift über ein vernach-lässigtes Gebiet der Bibelwissenschaft und die schädlichen Auswirkungen auf Theologie und Philosophie*. Gütersloh: Gütersloher Verlaghaus, 1970. (Eng. *The Rediscovery of Apocalyptic: A Polemical Work on a Neglected Area of Biblical Studies and its Damaging Effects on Theology and Philosophy*, trans. M. Kohl. London: SCM, 1972 [StBibTh 22]).

⸻. "Vom profetischen zum apokalyptischen Visionsbericht." In *Apocalypticism in the Mediterranean World and the near East: Proceedings of the International Colloquium on Apocalypticism, Uppsala, August 12-17, 1979*, ed. by D. Hellholm, 413-46. Tübingen: Mohr, 1983.

Köhler, W.D. *Die Rezeption des Matthäusevangeliums in der Zeit vor Irenäus*. Tübingen: Mohr, 1987 [WUNT 2/24].

Kosmala, H. "The Conclusion of Matthew", *ASTI* 4 (1965): 132-147.

Köster, H. *Synoptische Überlieferung bei den apostolischen Vätern*. Berlin: Akademie-Verlag, 1957 [TU 65].

⸻. "Überlieferung und Geschichte der frühchristlichen Evangelienliteratur." In *Aufstieg und Niedergang der Römischen Welt: Geschichte und Kultur Roms im Spiegel der Neueren Forschung* II.2, ed. W. Haase, 1463-1542. Berlin: de Gruyter, 1972.

Kraft, R.A. *Barnabas and the Didache. The Apostolic Fathers: A New Translation and Commentary* 3. New York: Thomas Nelson, 1965 [AF 3].

————. *The Apostolic Fathers III: Barnabas and the Didache.* London: Nelson, 1965.

————. "Vom Ende der urchristlichen Prophetie." In *Prophetic Vocation in the New Testament and Today*, ed. J. Panagopoulos, 162-185. Leiden: Brill [*NT.E* 45].

Kramer, W. *Christos Kyrios Gottessohn.* Zürich: Zwingli, 1963.

Krause, M. "Die literarischen Gattungen der Apokalypsen von Nag Hammadi." In *Apocalypticism in the Mediterranean World and the near East: Proceedings of the International Colloquium on Apocalypticism, Uppsala, August 12-17, 1979*, ed. by D. Hellholm, 621-37. Tübingen: Mohr, 1983.

Krawutzcky, A. "Über die sogenannte Zwölfapostellehre, ihre hauptsächlichsten Quellen und ihre erste Ausnahme", *TQ* 4 (1884): 547-606.

Kretschmar, G. *Studien zur frühchristlichen Trinitätstheologie.* Tübingen: Mohr, 1956.

————. "Ein Beitrag zur Frage nach dem Ursprung frühchristlicher Askese", *ZThK* 61 (1964): 27-67. Reprinted in: *Askese und Mönchtum in der alten Kirche*, ed. K. S. Frank, 129-79. Darmstadt: Wissenschaftliche Buchgesellschaft, 1975 [WdF 409].

————. "Die Geschichte des Taufgottesdienstes in der alten Kirche", *Leiturgia* 5 (1970): 64f.

————. "Das christliche Leben und die Mission in der frühen Kirche." In *Kirchengeschichte als Missionsgeschichte I: Die Alte Kirche*, eds. H. Frohnes & U. W. Knorr, 94ff. München: Kaiser, 1974.

Kuhn, H.W. "Jesus als Gekreuzigter in der frühchristlichen Verkündigung bis zur Mitte des 2. Jahrhunderts", *ZThK* 72 (1975): 1-46.

Kühschelm, R. *Jüngerverfolgung und Geschick Jesu.* Klosterneuburg: Verlag Österreichisches Katholisches Bibelwerk, 1983 [ÖBS 5].

Kümmel, W.G. "Jesus und der jüdische Traditionsgedanke", *ZNW* 33 (1934): 129f.

————. *Introduction to the New Testament.* London: SCM, 1975.

Kurfess, A. "Das Mahngedicht des sogenannten Phokylides", *ZNW* 38 (1939): 171-181.

Kürzinger, J. *Papias von Hierapolis und die Evangelien des Neuen Testaments.* Regensburg: F. Pustet, 1983 [*Eichstätter Materialien 4*].

Ladd, G. *The Eschatology of the Didache.* Unpublished Harvard Thesis, 1949.

Lake, K. *The New Testament in the Apostolic Fathers.* Oxford: Oxford University Press, 1905.

Lambrecht, J. *Die Redaktion der Markus-Apokalypse. Literarische Analyse und Structuruntersuchung.* Rome: Pontifical Biblical Institute, 1967 [AB 28].

———. "The Parousia Discourse. Composition and Content in Mt XXIV-XXV." In *L'Evangile selon Matthieu,* ed. M. Didier. Gembloux: Duculot, 1972 [BETL 29].

Lampe, G.W.H. *A Patristic Greek Lexicon.* Oxford: Clarendon, 1961.

———. *The Seal of the Spirit.* London: SPCK, 1967².

Lanne, E. *De anaphoris orientalibus praelectiones.* Rome: unpublished, 1966.

Laufen, R. *Die Doppelüberlieferungen der Logienquelle und des Markusevangeliums.* Bonn: Hanstein, 1980 [BBB 54].

Layton, B. "The Sources, Dates and Transmission of Didache 1:3b-2:1", *HTR* 61 (1968): 343-383.

Leaney, A.R.C. *The Rule of Qumran and its Meaning.* London: SCM, 1966.

Lebram, J. "Apokalypsen II", *TRE* 3 (1978): 192ff.

Lebram, C.H. "The Piety of the Jewish Apocalyptists." In *Apocalypticism in the Mediterranean World and the near East: Proceedings of the International Colloquium on Apocalypticism, Uppsala, August 12-17, 1979,* ed. by D. Hellholm, 171-210. Tübingen: Mohr, 1983.

Leclercq, H. "Didache." In *Dictionnaire d'archeologie chrétienne et de liturgie* 4,1, ed. F. Cabrol & H. Leclercq, 772-98. Paris: Letouzey and Ané, 1913-1953.

Ledogar, R.J. *Acknowledgement: Praise Verbs in the Early Greek Anaphoras.* Rome: Herder, 1968.

Lefort, L.-Th. *Les pères apostoliques en copte.* Louvain: Durbecq, 1952 [CSCO 135 (ScrCop 17)].

Lemaire, A. *Les ministères aux origines de l'église: Naissance de la triple hierarchie: eveques, presbytres, diacres.* Paris: Les Éditions du Cerf, 1971 [*Lectio divina* 68].

Lessig, H. *Die Abendmahlsprobleme im Lichte der ntl. Forschung seit 1900.* Bonn: dissertation, 1953.

Lewy, H. *ZNW* (1934): 117-132.

L'Hour, J. *La morale de l'alliance.* Paris: Gabalda, 1966 [CahRB 5].

Liebaert, J. *Les enseignements moraux des Pères apostoliques.* Gembloux: Duculot, 1970 [Recherches Syntheses Sc.relig.]

Lieberman, S. *Hayerushalmi Kiphshuto.* Jerusalem: Darom, 1934.

Lietzmann, H. "Die liturgischen Angaben des Pliniusbriefs." In *Geschichtliche Studien für A. Hauck zum 70. Geburtstag,* 34ff. Leipzig: Hinrichs, 1916.

———. *Messe und Herrenmahl: Eine Studie zur Geschichte der Liturgie.* Bonn: Marcus & Weber, 1926 (Eng. *Mass and Lord's Supper: A Study in the History of the Liturgy,* trns. D. H. G. Reeve. Leiden: Brill, 1953-1964).

Lightfoot, J.B. "The Name and Office of an Apostle." In *St. Paul's Epistle to the Galatians.* London: Macmillan, 1865.

———. *The Apostolic Fathers.* London: Macmillan, 1893.

Ligier, L. *Magnae orationis eucharisticae seu anaphorae origo et significatio*. Rome: unpublished, 1964.

――――. *Il Sacramento dell'Eucarestia*. Rome: Pont. Univ. Gregoriana, Fac. di Teologia, 1971.

――――. "Les origines de la prière eucharistique", *Questions Liturgiques* 53 (1972): 181-202

Lilje, H. *Die Lehre der Zwölf Apostel*. Hamburg: Furche, 1956².

Lipsius, R.A. *Acta apostolorum apocrypha: Post Constantinum Tischendorf* 1. Leipzig, 1891, Reprint Aldesheim: Olms, 1972.

Lohmeyer, E. "Vom urchristlichen Abendmahl", *Theologische Rundschau* 9 (1937): 302ff.

――――. "Mir ist gegeben alle Gewalt!" In *In Memoriam Ernst Lohmeyer*, ed. W. Schmauch, 22-49. Stuttgart: Evangelisches Verlagswerk, 1951.

――――. *The Lord's Prayer*. London: Collins, 1965.

Löwenich, von W. *Das Johannesverständnis im zweiten Jahrhundert*. Gießen: Töpelmann, 1932.

Lührmann, D. "Liebet eure Feinde (Lk 6,27-36/Mt 5,39-48)", *ZTK* 69 (1972): 412-438.

Luttikhuizen, G.P. *The Revelation of Elchsai. Investigations into the Evidence for a Mesopotamian Jewish Apocalypse of the Second Century and his Reception by Judeo-Christian Propagandists*. Tübingen: Mohr, 1985 [*Texte und Studien zum Antiken Judentum* 8].

Luz, U. *Matthew 1-7: A Continental Commentary*. Minneapolis: Fortress, 1989.

Macomber, W.F. "The oldest known text of the anaphora of the apostles Addai and Mari", *OrChrP* 32 (1966): 335-371.

――――. "The Maronite and Chaldean Version of the Anaphora of the Apostles", *OrChrP* 37 (1971): 55-84.

――――. "A Theory on the Origins of the Syrian, Maronite and Chaldean Rites", *OrChrP* 39 (1973): 235-242.

Maldonado, L. *La plegaria eucarística*. Madrid: Bibl. de autores cristianos, 1967.

Manders, H. "Sens et fonction du récit de l'institution", *Questions Liturgiques* 53 (1972): 203-218.

Manns, F. *Essais sur le judéochristianisme*. Jerusalem: Franciscan, 1977 [SBFA 12].

Manson, T.W. *The Sayings of Jesus*. London: SCM, 1949.

――――. "The Lord's Prayer", *BJRL* 38 (1955-1956): 99-113.

Margalioth, M. *(ed.), Encyclopedia of Talmudic and Geonic Literature*. Tel Aviv: Tsetsig, 1960 (Hebrew).

Marshall, I.H. *The Gospel of Luke*. Exeter: Paternoster, 1977.

Martini, C. M. "Il decreto del concilio di Gerusalemme." In *Fondamenti biblici della teologia morale*, ed. M. Adinolfi. Brescia: Paideia Ed., 1973.

Marxsen, W. "The Lord's Supper as a Christological Problem" in *The*

Beginning of Christology, trns. P. Achtemeier & L. Nieting. Philadelphia: Fortress, 1979.

Massaux, E. *Influence de l'Évangile de saint Matthieu sur la littérature chrétienne avant saint Irénée*. Louvain, 1950. (Eng. *The Influence of the Gospel of Saint Matthew on Christian Literature before Saint Irenaeus I: The First Ecclesiastical Writers*, trns N. J. Belval & S. Hecht. Leuven: Peeters; Macon, Ga: Mercer University Press, 1990-1993 [NGSt 5,1-3]).

Mattioli, U. *Didachè—Dottrina dei dodici apostoli: Introduzione, traduzione e note*. Rome: Edizioni Paoline, 1980³.

Mazza, E. "Didaché IX-X: Elementi per una interpretazione Eucaristica", *Ephemerides Liturgicae* 92 (1979): 393-419.

———. *The Origins of the Eucharistic Prayer*. Collegeville, Minnesota: The Liturgical Press, 1995 [Pueblo].

McLean, A. J. (ed.), C. Bigg, *The Doctrine of the Twelve Apostles*. London: SPCK, 1922².

Meeks, W.A. & Wilken, R.L. *Jews and Christians in the First Four Centuries of the Christian Era*. Missoula, Mont.: Scholars, 1978.

Mees, M. "Die Bedeutung der Sentenzen und ihrer Auxesis für die Formung der Jesuworte nach Didache 1:3b-2:1", *VetChr* 8 (1971): 55-76.

Meier, J.P. & Brown, R.E. *Antioch and Rome: New Testament Cradles of Christianity*. London: Chapman, 1983.

Merklein, H. *Die Gottesherrschaft als Handlungprinzip. Untersuchung zur Ethik Jesu*. Würzburg: Echter-Verlag, 1978 [FzB 34].

Metzger, M. "Les deux prières eucharistiques des Constitutions Apostoliques", *RSR* (1971): 59ff.

———. "The Didascalia and the Constitutiones Apostolorum." In *The Eucharist of the Early Christians*, ed. W. Rordorf *et al*. New York: Pueblo, 1978.

Michaelis, W. "Die Davidssohnschaft Jesu als historisches und kerygmatisches Problem." In *Der historische Jesus und der kerygmatische Christus*, ed. H. Ristow & K. Mattiae, 317-30. Berlin: Evangelische-Verlagsanstalt, 1962².

Middleton, R.D. "The eucharistic prayers of the Didache", *JTS* 36 (1936): 266.

Milavec, A. "The Pastoral Genius of the Didache: An Analytical Translation and Commentary." In *Religious Writings and Religious Systems* II, ed. J. Neusner, E. S. Frerichs, & A. J. Levine, 105-10. Atlanta: Scholars, 1989 [BStR]).

———. "The Saving Efficacy of the Burning Process in *Didache* 16.5." In *Didache in Context: Essays of Its Text, History and Transmission*, ed. C.N. Jefford, 131-55. Leiden: Brill, 1995 [NT.E 77].

———. "The Social Setting of "Turning the Other Cheek" and "Loving One's Enemies" in the Light of the *Didache*", *BTB* 25 (1995): 131-143.

Mingana, A. (ed.) *Woodbrooke Studies* I. Cambridge: Heffer & Sons, 1927.

Mitchell, M.M. "Concerning ΠΕΡΙ ΔΕ in 1 Corinthians", *NovT* 31/3 (1989): 229-256.

Mohrlang, R. *Matthew and Paul*. Cambridge: Cambridge University Press, 1984 [SNTS MS, 48].

Moll, H. *Die Lehre von der Eucharistie als Opfer*. Köln: Hanstein, 1975 [*Theophaneia* 26].

Moore, G. *Judaism in the First Centuries of the Christian Era* I. New York: Schocken, 1958.

————. *Judaism in the First Centuries of the Christian Era: The Age of the Tannaim* II. New York: Schocken, 1958.

Motte, R. "David." In *Vocabulaire de théologie biblique*, ed. J. Duplacy. Paris: Leon-Dufour, 1962.

Moule, C.F.D. "A Note on Didache 9:4", *JTS* 6 (1955): 240-243.

Muilenburg, J. *The Literary Relations of the Epistle of Barnabas and the Teaching of the Twelve Apostles*. Marburg: Yale Dissertation, 1929.

Nautin, P. "La composition de la "Didachê" et son titre", *RHR* 78 (1959): 191-214.

Neirynck, F. *The Minor Agreement of Matthew and Luke against Mark*. Leuven: Leuven University Press, 1974 [BETL 37].

————. "John and the Synoptics." In *Evangelica: Collected Essays*. Leuven: Leuven University Press, 1982 [BETL 60].

————. "Paul and the Sayings of Jesus." In *L'Apôtre Paul*, ed. A. Vanhoye, 265-321. Leuven: Leuven University Press, 1986 [BETL 73].

Niederwimmer, K. *Askese und Mysterium. Über Ehe, Ehescheidung und Eheverzicht in den Anfängen des christlichen Glaubens*. Göttingen: Vandenhoeck & Ruprecht, 1975 [FRLANT 113].

————. "Zur Entwicklungsgeschichte des Wanderradikalismus im Traditionsbereich der Didache", *WSt* 11 (1977): 145-167.

————. "Textprobleme der Didache", *WSt* 95 (1982): 116-119.

————. *Die Didache*. Göttingen: Vandenhoeck & Ruprecht, 1989 [KAV 1].

————. "Der Didachist und seine Quellen." In *The Didache in Context: Essays on its Text, History and Transmission*, ed. C.N. Jefford, 15-36. Leiden: Brill, 1995.

Nissen, A. *Gott und der Nächste im antiken Judentum*. Tübingen: Mohr, 1974 [WUNT 15].

O'Connor, J.M. "La Genèse Litteraire de la Règle de la Communauté", *RB* 76 (1969): 528-549.

Oesterley, W.O.E. *The Jewish Background of the Christian Liturgy*. Oxford: Clarendon, 1925.

O'Hagan, A.P. *Material Recreation in the Apostolic Fathers*. Berlin: Akademie-Verlag, 1968 [TU 100].

Ong, W. J. *Orality and Literacy: the Technologizing of the Word*. London / New York: Methuen, 1982

Ortiz de Urbina, I. "Review of Audet, *La Didachè*, Paris, 1958", *OChrP* 25 (1959): 186-7.

Pahl, A. & Hänggi-I. *Prex eucharistica*. Freiburg: Universitätsverlag Freiburg-Schweiz, 1968.

Panagopoulos, I. Ἡ Ἐκκλησία τῶν προφητῶν. Τὸ προφητικὸν χάρισμα ἐν τῷ Ἐκκλησίᾳ τῶν δύο πρώτων αἰώνων. Athens: St. Vasilopoulos, 1979.

Pardee, N. "The Curse that Saves (*Didache* 16.5)." In *The Didache in Context: Essays of Its Text, History and Transmission*, ed. C.N. Jefford, 156-76. Leiden: Brill, 1995 [*NT.E* 77].

Patterson, S.J. "*Didache* 11-13: The Legacy of Radical Itinerancy in Early Christianity." In *The Didache in Context: Essays of Its Text, History and Transmission*, ed. C. N. Jefford, 313-29. Leiden: Brill, 1995 [*NT.E* 77].

Pearson, B. "Friedländer Revisited: Alexandrian Judaism and Gnostic Origins." In *Gnosticism, Judaism, and Egyptian Christianity*, 10-28. Minneapolis: Fortress, 1990 [*Studies in Antiquity and Christianity*].

Peel, M.L. *Gnosis und Auferstehung. Der Brief des Rheginus von Nag Hammadi*. Neukirchen: Neukirchener Verlag, 1974.

Peradse, G. "Die "Lehre der zwölf Apostel" in der georgischen Überlieferung", *ZNW* 31 (1932): 111-116.

Perdue, L.G. "The Social Character of Paraenesis and Paraenetic Literature", *Semeia* 50 (1990): 2-39.

Pesch, R. *Naherwartungen. Tradition und Redaktion in Mk 13*. Dusseldorf: Patmos, 1968.

———. *Das Markusevangelium II. Teil*. Freiburg: Herder, 1980².

Peterson, E. "Über einige Probleme der Didache-Überlieferung", *RivAC* 27 (1951): 37-68. Reprinted in: *Frühkirche, Judentum und Gnosis: Studien und Untersuchungen*, 146-82. Rome: Herder, 1959.

———. "Einige Beobachtungen zu den Anfängen der christlichen Askese." In *Frühkirche, Judentum und Gnosis: Studien und Untersuchungen*, 209-20. Rome: Herder, 1959.

Philonenko, M. *Joseph et Aséneth*. Leiden: Brill, 1968.

Pillinger, R. "Die Taufe nach der Didache", *WSt* 88 (1975): 152-160.

Piper, J. *Love Your Enemies. Jesus' Love Command in the Synoptic Tradition and the Early Christian Paraenesis*. Cambridge: Cambridge University Press, 1979 [SNTS 38].

Polster, G. "Der kleine Talmudtraktat über die Proselyten (Text und Übersetzung)", *Angelos* 2 (1926): 2-38.

Ponthof, J. "La signification religieuse du "Nom" chez Clément de Rome et dans la Didachè", *EThL* 35 (1959): 359ff.

Popkes, W. "Zum traditionsgeschichtlichen Problem der Seligpreisungen Mt V 3-12", *NT* 4 (1960): 253-260.

———. "Die Gerechtigkeitstradition in Matthäus-Evangelium", *ZNW* 80 (1989): 1-23.

Poschmann, B. *Paenitentia secunda*. Bonn: Hanstein, 1940 [*Theophaneia* 1].

Prigent, P. *Les testimonia dans le christiniasm primitif. L'épître de Barnabé I-XVI*. Paris: Études bibliques, 1961.

————. & Kraft, R.A. *Epître de Barnabé*. Paris: Les Éditions du Cerf, 1971 [SC 172].

————. "Hyppolyte, commentateur de l'Apocalypse", *Theol.Zschr.* 28 (1972): 391-412.

Puzicha, M. *Christus peregrinus. Die Fremdenaufnahme (Mt 25:35) als Werk der privaten Wohltätigkeit im Urteil der Alten Kirche*. Münster: Aschendorff, 1980.

Qimron, E. & Strugnell, J. "An Unpublished Halachic Letter from Qumran." In *Biblical Archaeology Today*. Jerusalem: Israel Exploration Society, 1985.

Quasten, J. *Patrology I: The Beginnings of Patristic Literature*. Utrecht: Spectrum, 1975⁵.

Rabinowitz, Z.W. *Shᶜare Torat Eretz Jisrael: Notes and Comments on the Yerushalmi*, ed. E. Z. Melammed. Jerusalem: Jewish Theological Seminary of America, 1940.

Raes, A. "Les paroles de la consécration dans les anaphores syriennes", *OrChrP* 3 (1937): 485-504.

Rasco, E. *Actus Apostolorum*, II. Lecture notes: Rome, 1968.

Ratzinger, J. "Forma e contenuto della celebrazione eucaristica", *Communio* 6/35 (1977): 19.

Rauschen, G. *Eucharistie und Bußsakrament in den ersten sechs Jahrhunderten*. Freiburg: Herder, 1919³.

Reed, J. "The Hebrew Epic and the *DIDACHE*." In *The Didache in Context: Essays of Its Text, History and Transmission*, ed. C.N. Jefford, 213-25. Leiden: Brill, 1995 [*NT.E* 77].

Reicke, B. *Diakonie, Festesfreude und Zelos in Verbindung mit der altchristlichen Agapefeier*. Uppsala: Lundequistska Bokhandeln, 1951.

Reiling, J. *Hermas and Christian Prophecy. A Study of the Eleventh Mandate*. Leiden: Brill, 1973 [*NT.E* 37].

Reitzenstein, R. "Eine frühchristliche Schrift von den dreierlei Früchten des christlichen Lebens", *ZNW* 15 (1914): 60-90.

————. *Die Vorgeschichte der christlichen Taufe*. Darmstadt: Wissenschaftlicher Buchgeseloch, 1929.

Resch, A. *Das Aposteldekret nach seiner ausserkanonischen Textgestalt Untersucht*. Leipzig: Hinrich's, 1905 [TU 13, 3].

Riesenfeld, H. "Das Brot von den Bergen. Zu Did. 9,4", *Er* 54 (1956): 142-150.

Rietschel, G. & Graff, P. *Lehrbuch der Liturgik*. Göttingen: Vandenhoeck & Ruprecht, 1951²².

Riggenbach, E. *Der trinitarische Taufbefehl Matth. 28:19 nach seine ursprünglichen Textgestalt und Authentie untersucht*. Gütersloh: Bertelsmann, 1903 [BFCTh 7].

Riggs, J. W. 1984. "From Gracious Table to Sacramental Elements: The Tradition-History of Didache 9 and 10", *Second Century* 4 (1984): 83-102.

—————. "The Sacred Food of Didache 9-10 and Second Century Ecclesiologies." In *The Didache in Context: Essays of Its Text, History and Transmission*, ed. C. N. Jefford, 256-83. Leiden: Brill, 1995 [*NT.E* 77].

Roberts, A. & Donaldson, J. *The Ante-Nicene Fathers* V. Grand Rapids: Eerdmans, 1957.

Robillard, E. "L'Epître de Barnabé: trois époques, trois théologies, trois rédacteurs", *RB* 78 (1971): 184-209.

Robinson, J.A. "The Problem of the Didache", *JTS* 13 (1912): 339-356.

—————. *Barnabas, Hermas and the Didache: Being the Donnellan Lectures Delivered before the University of Dublin in 1920.* London: SPCK, 1920.

—————. "The Epistle of Barnabas and the Didache", *JTS* 35 (1934): 113-146, 225-248.

Robinson, J.A.T. *Redating the New Testament.* London: SCM, 1976.

Robinson, J.M. *The Nag Hammadi Library in English.* Leiden: Brill, 1977.

Roloff, J. *Apostolat-Verkündigung-Kirche. Ursprung, Inhalt und Funktion des kirchlichen Apostelamtes nach Paulus, Lukas und den Pastoralbriefen.* Gütersloh: Mohn, 1965.

Romestin, H. de *The Teaching of the Twelve Apostles.* ΔΙΔΑΧΗ ΤΩΝ ΔΩΔΕΚΑ ΑΠΟΣΤΟΛΩΝ *With Introduction, Translation, Notes and Illustrative Passages.* Oxford & London: Parker, 1884[1].

Rordorf, W. *Der Sonntag: Geschichte des Ruhe- und Gottesdienstages im ältesten Christentum.* Zürich: Zwingli, 1962 [AThANT 43].

—————. "La vigne et le vin dans la tradition juive et chrétienne", in *Annales de l'Université de Neuchâtel 1969-1970.* Neuchâtel: Université de Neuchâtel, 1971.

—————. "Un chapitre d'éthique judéo-chretienne. Les deux voies", *RSR* 60 (1972): 109-128.

—————. *Sabbat und Sonntag in der Alten Kirche.* Zürich: Theologische Verlag, 1972 [Traditio Christiana].

—————. "Le baptême selon la Didachè." In *Mélanges liturgiques offerts au R. P. Dom B. Botte O.S.B. de l'Abbaye du Mont César à l'occasion du cinquantième anniversaire de son ordination sacerdotale (4 Juin 1972)*, 499-509. Louvain: Abbaye du Mont César, 1972.

—————. "La rémission des péchés selon la Didachè", *Irénikon* 46 (1973): 283-297.

—————. "L'eucharistie selon la *Didachè*." In *L'eucharistie des premiers chrétiens*, eds. W. Rordorf *et al.*, 7-28. Paris: Beauchesne, 1976 [PoTH 17]. (Eng. "The Didache." In *The Eucharist of the Early Christians*, eds. W. Rordorf *et al*, 1-23. New York: Pueblo, 1978).

—————. & Tuilier, A. *La doctrine des Douze Apôtres (Didachè).* Paris: Les Éditions du Cerf, 1978 [SC 248].

————. "Le problème de la transmission textuelle de "Didachè" 1:3b-2:1." In *Überlieferungsgeschichtliche Untersuchungen*, ed. F. Paschke, 499-513. Berlin: Akademie-Verlag, 1981 [TU 125]. Reprinted in: *Liturgie, foi et vie des premiers chrétiens. Études patristiques*. Paris: Beauchesne, 1986 [ThH 75].

————. *Liturgie, foi et vie des premiers chrétiens. Études patristiques*. Paris: Beauchesne, 1986 [ThH 75].

————. "Does the Didache Contain Jesus Tradition Independently of the Synoptic Gospels?" In *Jesus and the Oral Gospel Tradition*, ed. H. Wansbrough, 394-423. Sheffield: Sheffield Academic Press, 1991 [JSNTSupp 64].

Rousseau, V.A., Doutreleau, L. & Mercier, C. *Irénée de Lyon: Contre les hérésies* II. Paris: Les Éditions du Cerf, 1969 [SC 153].

Rudolph, K. *Die Mandäer II: Der Kult*. Göttingen: Vandenhoeck & Ruprecht, 1961.

Sabatier, P. ΔΙΔΑΧΗ ΤΩΝ ΙΒ´ ΑΠΟΣΤΟΛΩΝ: *La Didaché ou l'Ensignement des douze apôtres*. Paris: Noblet, 1885.

Salmon, G. *A Historical Introduction to the Study of the Books of the New Testament*. London: Murray, 1894[7].

Sanchez-Caro, J.M. "La anáphora de Addai y Mari y la anáfora maronita "sharar": intento de reconstrucción de la fuente primitiva commún", *ThSt* 43 (1977): 41-69.

Sand, A. *Kanon. Von den Anfängen bis zum Fragmentum Muratorianum*. Freiburg: Herder, 1974 [HDG I, 3a,1].

Sandt, H. von de "Didache 3,1-6: A Transformation of an Existing Jewish Hortatory Pattern", *JSJ* 23 (1992): 21-41.

Saß, G. "Die Apostel in der Didache." In *In memoriam Ernst Lohmeyer*, ed. W. Schmauch, 233-39. Stuttgart: Evangelisches Verlagswerk, 1951.

Sauer, J. "Traditionsgeschichtliche Erwägungen zu den synoptischen und paulinischen Aussagen über Feindesliebe und Wiedervergeltungsverzicht", *ZNW* 76 (1985): 1-28.

Savi, P. *La dottrina degli apostoli. Richerche critiche sull'origine del testo con una not intorno all'eucharistia*. Rome, 1893.

Schaff, P. *The Oldest Church Manual Called the Teaching of the Twelve Apostles*. Edinburgh: Clark, 1885.

Schermann, T. *Eine Elfapostelmoral oder die Christliche Rezension der "beiden Wege"*. München: Lentner, 1903 [SGKA.E 3].

————. *Die allgemeine Kirchenordnung, frühchristliche Liturgien und kirchliche Überliefering* III. Paderborn: Ferdinand Schöningh, 1916 [SGKA.E].

Schille, G. "Erwägungen zur Hohepriesterlehre des Hebräerbriefes", *ZNW* 46 (1955): 81-109.

————. "Die Basis des Hebräerbriefes", *ZNW* 48 (1957): 270-280.

————. "Zur urchristlichen Tauflehre. Stilistische Beobachtungen am Barnabasbrief", *ZNW* 49 (1958): 31-52.

————. "Katechese und Taufliturgie: Erwägungen zu Hbr 11", *ZNW* 51 (1960): 112-131.

————. "Das Recht der Propheten und Apostelgemeinderechtliche Beobachtungen zu Didache Kapitel 11-13." In *Theologische Versuche* I, ed. P. Wätzel & G. Schille, 84-103. Berlin: Evangelische Verlag-Anstalt, 1966.

Schlecht, J. *Doctrina XII Apostolorum, die Apostellehre in der Liturgie der katholischen Kirche*. Freiburg im Breisgau: Herder, 1901.

Schlosser, J. *Le Dieu de Jésus*. Paris: Les Éditions du Cerf, 1987 [LD 129].

Schmid, J. *Matthäus und Lukas*. Freiburg: Herder, 1930 [BSt 23/2-4].

Schmidt, C. *Acta Pauli aus der Heidelberger koptischen Papyrushandschrift Nr.1*. Leipzig, 1904. Reprint. Hildesheim: Olms, 1965.

————. "Das koptische Didache-Fragment dere British Museum", *ZNW* 24 (1925): 81-99.

Schmithals, W. *Das kirchliche Apostelamt. Eine historische Untersuchung*. Göttingen: Vandenhoeck & Ruprecht, 1961 (FRLANT 79) (Eng. *The Office of Apostle in the Early Church*, trans. J. E. Steely. London: SPCK, 1971).

Schnackenburg, R. *The Gospel According to St John* I. London: Burns & Oates, 1968.

Schöllgen, G. "Die Didache—ein frühes Zeugnis für Landgemeinden?", *ZNW* 76 (1985): 140-143.

————. *Ecclesia sordida? Zur Frage der sozialen Schichtung frühchristlicher Gemeinden am Beispiel Karthagos zur Zeit Tertullians*. Münster: Aschendorff, 1985 [*JAC.E* 12].

————. "Monepiskopat und monarchischer Episkopat", *ZNW* 77 (1986): 146-151.

————. "Die Didache als Kirchenordnung", *JAC* 29 (1986): 5-26.

————. "Die literarische Gattung der syrischen Didaskalie." In *IV. Symposium Syriacum 1984. Literary Genres in Syriac Literature*, eds. H. J. W. Drijvers *et al*, 149-59. Rome: Pontifical Institutum Studiarum, 1987 [OCA 229].

————. "Wandernde oder seßhafte Lehrer in der Didache?", *Biblische Notizen* 52 (1990): 19-26.

————. *Didache—Zwölf-Apostel-Lehre. Einleitung, Übersetzung und Kommentar*. Freiburg: Herder, 1991 [FC 1].

————. "Pseudapostolizität und Schriftgebrauch in den ersten Kirchenordnungen. Anmerkungen zur Begründung des frühen Kirchenrechts." In *Stimuli. Exegese und ihre Hermeneutik in Antike und Christentum: Festschrift Ernst Dassmann*, 96-121. Münster, 1996 [*JbAC Erg.-Bd* 23].

————. "Der Abfassungszweck der frühen Kirchenordnungen. Anmerkungen zu den Thesen Bruno Steimers", *JbAC* 40 (1997): forthcoming.

Schottroff, L. "Gewaltverzicht und Feindesliebe in der urchristlichen Tradition. Mt 5,38-48; Lk. 6,26-27." In *Jesus Christus in Historie und Theologie: Fs. H. Conzelmann*, 197-221. Tübingen: Mohr, 1975.

Schrage, W. *Die konkreten Einzelgebote in der paulinischen Paränese.* Gütersloh, Mohr, 1961.

Schroeder, D. *Die Haustafeln des Neuen Testamentes.* Hamburg: Dissertation, 1959.

Schulz, S. *Q--Die Spruchquelle der Evangelisten.* Zürich: Theologische Verlag, 1972.

Schümmer, J. *Die altchristliche Fastenpraxis. Mit besonderer Berücksichtigung der Schriften Tertullians.* Münster, 1933 [LQF 27].

Schürer, E., Vermes, G., Millar, G. & Goodman, M., *The History of the Jewish People in the Age of Jesus Christ (175 B.C.-A.D. 135)* III.1. Edinburgh: T & T Clark, 1986.

Schürmann, H. *Der Paschamahlbericht Lk 22,(7-14).* Münster: Aschendorff, 1953 [NTA 19,5].

————. *Das Lukasevangelium.* Freiburg: Herder, 1969 [HTKN 3/1].

Schütz, J.H. *Paul and the Anatomy of Apostolic Authority.* Cambridge: University Press, 1975.

Schweizer, E. "Matthew 5:17-20: Anmerkungen zum Gesetzesverständnis des Matthäus." In *Neotestamentica,* 399-406. Stuttgart: Zwingli Verlag, 1963.

Seeberg, A. *Der Katechismus der Urchristenheit.* Leipzig: Deichert, 1903.

————. *Das Evangelium Christi.* Leipzig: Deichert, 1905.

————. *Die Beiden Wege und das Aposteldekret.* Leipzig: Deichert, 1906.

————. *Die Didache des Judentums und der Urchristenheit.* Leipzig: Deichert, 1908.

Seeliger, H.R. "Erwägungen zu Hintergrund und Zweck des apokalyptischen Schlusskapitels der *Didache.*" In *Studia Patristica 21: Papers presented to the Tenth International Conference on Patristic Studies held in Oxford 1987,* ed. E.A. Livingstone, 185-92. Leuven: Peeters, 1989.

Segelberg, E. *Masbuta. Studies in the Ritual of the Mandaean Baptism.* Uppsala: Almqvist & Wiksell, 1958.

Seidensticker, P. *Die Gemeinschaftsform der religiösen Gruppen des Spätjudentums und der Urkirche.* Jerusalem: Franciscan Press, 1959 [SBFLA].

Selwyn, E.G. *The First Epistle of St. Peter.* London: Macmillan, 1947[2].

Shepherd, M.H. "Smyrna in the Ignatian Letters. A Study in Church Order", *JR* 20 (1940): 141-159.

Shukster, M.B. & Richardson, P. "Temple and *Bet Ha-midrash* in the Epistle of Barnabas." In *Anti-Judaism in Early Christianity 2: Separation and Polemic,* ed. S.G. Wilson, 17-31. Waterloo, Ont.:Wilfrid Laurier University Press, 1986 [*Studies in Christianity and Judaism* 2].

Simon, M. "The Apostolic Decree and its setting in the Ancient Church", *BJRL* 52 (1969-1970): 437-460.

————. *Verus Israel: A Study of the Relations between Christians and Jews in the Roman Empire, 135-425,* trans. M. McKeating. Oxford: University Press, 1986.

Skehan, P.W. "Didache 1:6 and Sirach 12:1", *Bib* 44 (1963): 533-536.

Smith, M. A. "Did Justin Know the Didache?", *StPatr* 7 (1966): 287-290.

Spence, Ca. *The Teaching of the Twelve Apostles. Διδαχὴ τῶν δώδεκα Ἀποστόλων. A Translation with Notes; And Excursus (I. to IX.) Illustrative of the "Teaching;" and the Greek Text.* London: Nisbet, 1885.

Spinks, B.D. "The original form of the Anaphora of the Apostles: A Suggestion in the Light of Maronite Sharar", *EphLiturg* 91 (1977): 146-161.

Stadelmann, H. "Biblische Apokalyptik und heilsgechichtliches Denken." In *Epochen der Heilsgeschichte. Beiträge zur Förderung heilsges-chichtlicher Theologie*, ed. H. Stadelmann, 86-100. Wuppertal: Brock-haus, 1984.

Stählin, G. "Die Geschichte und Lehre des evangelischen Gottesdienstes", in *Leiturgia. Handbuch des evangelischen Gottesdienst* I, ed. K. F. Müller & W. Blankenburg. Kassel: Stauda, 1954.

Stegemann, W. "Vagabond Radicalism in Early Christianity?: A Historical and Theological Discussion of a Thesis Proposed by Gerd Theissen." In *God of the Lowly*, eds. W. Schottroff & W. Stegemann, 148-68. Maryknoll: Orbis, 1984.

Steidle, B. *Die Regel St. Benedikts.* Beuron/Hohenzoller: Beuroner Kunstver-lag, 1952.

Steimer, B. *Vertex Traditionis. Die Gattung der altchristliche Kir-chenordnungen.* Berlin/New York: de Gruyter, 1992 [BZNW 63].

Stempel, H.A. "Der Lehrer in der "Lehre der zwölf Apostel", *VigChr* 34 (1980): 209-217.

Stendahl, K. *The School of St. Matthew and its Use of the Old Testament.* Philadelphia: Fortress, 1954.

Stenzel, A. *Die Taufe: eine genetische Erklärung der Taufliturgie.* Innsbruck: Rauch, 1958 [FGThUL 7/8].

Stevenson, J. *A New Eusebius.* London: SPCK, 1957.

Stommel, E. "Σημεῖον ἐκπετάσεως (Didache xvi,6)." *RQ* 48 (1953): 21-42.

Strack, H.L. & Billerbeck, P. *Kommentar zum NT aus Talmud und Midrasch* II. München: C. H. Beck, 1926⁴.

Strecker, G. "Die Kerygmata Petrou." In *New Testament Apocrypha* II, ed. E. Hennecke & W. Schneemelcher. Philadelphia: Westminster, 1965.

————. *Der Weg der Gerechtigkeit.* Göttingen: Vandenhoeck & Ruprecht, 1966 [FRLANT 82].

————. "Die Antithesen der Bergpredigt", *ZNW* 69 (1978): 36-72.

————. *Die Bergpredigt: Ein Exegetischer Kommentar.* Göttingen: Vandenhoeck & Ruprecht, 1984.

Streeter, B.H. "Origin and Date of the 'Didache'" in *The Primitive Church*, 279-87. London: Macmillan, 1929.

————. *The Four Gospels: A Study of Origins.* London: Macmillan, 1936.

————. "The Much Belaboured Didache", *JTS* 37 (1936): 369-374.

Stuhlmacher, P. *Das paulinische Evangelium I: Vorgeschichte.* Göttingen: Vandenhoeck & Ruprecht, 1968 [FRLANT 95].

Stuiber, A. "Das ganze Joch des Herrn (Didache 6:2-3)." In *Studia*

Patristica IV, ed. F. L. Cross, 323-29. Berlin: Akademie-Verlag, 1961 [TU 79].

————. "Die drei Σημεῖα von Didache XVI", *JAC* 24 (1981): 42-4.

Suggs, M.J. "The Christian Two Ways Tradition: Its Antiquity, Form, and Function." In *Studies in New Testament and Early Christian Literature: Essays in Honor of Allen P. Wikgren*, ed. D.E. Aune, 60-74. Leiden: Brill, 1972 [NovTestSupp 33].

Swete, H.B. *The Holy Spirit in the Ancient Church.* London: Macmillan, 1912.

Talley, T.J. "De la "berakah" à l'eucharistie, une question à réexaminer", *La Maison-Dieu* 125/1 (1976): 11-39. (Eng. "From *Berakah* to *Eucharistia*: A Reopening Question", *Worship* 50/2 [1976]: 115-137).

————. "The Eucharistic Prayer: Tradition and Development." In *Liturgy Reshaped*, ed. K. Stevenson. London: SPCK, 1982.

————. "The Literary Structure of Eucharistic Prayer", *Worship* 58 (1984): 404-420.

Taylor, C. *The Teaching of the Twelve Apostles, with illustrations from the Talmud.* Cambridge: Deighton Bell, 1886.

————. *An Essay on the Theology of the Didache.* Cambridge: Deighton Bell, 1889.

Telfer, W. "The Didache and the Apostolic Synod of Antioch", *JTS* 40 (1939): 133-146, 258-271.

Theissen, G. "Wanderradikalismus. Literatursoziologische Aspekte der Überlieferung von Worten Jesu im Urchristentum", *ZThK* 70 (1973): 245-271. Reprinted in: *Studien zur Soziologie des Urchristentums*, 70-105. Tübingen: Mohr, 1979 [WUNT 19]. (Eng. "Itinerant Radicalism: The Tradition of Jesus Sayings from the Perspective of the Sociology of Literature", trans. A. Wire, *RadRel* 2 [1976]: 84-93).

————. "Legitimation und Lebensunterhalt: Ein Beitrag zur Soziologie urchristlicher Missionare", *NTS* 21 (1974/75): 192-221 (Eng. "Legitimation and Subsistence: An Essay on the Sociology of Early Christian Missionaries." In G. Theissen, *The Social Setting of Pauline Christianity: Essays on Corinth*, trans. J. H. Schütz, 27-67. Philadelphia: Fortress, 1982).

————. *Soziologie der Jesus bewegung.* Munich: Kaiser Verlag, 1977 (Eng. *The First Followers of Jesus: a sociological analysis of earliest Christianity.* London: SCM, 1978).

————. "Gewaltverzicht und Feindesliebe (Mt 5,38-48/Lk 6,27-38) und deren sozialgeschichtlicher Hintergrund." In *Studien zur Soziologie des Urchristentums*, 160-97. Tübingen: Mohr, 1979 [WUNT 19].

Tissot, Y. "Les prescriptions des presbytres [Acts 15:41 D]", *RB* 77 (1970): 321-346.

Tubesing, V.W.H. *Die ὁδός der Apostelgeschichte und die Διδαχὴ τῶν ἀποστόλων.* Leipzig: Pöschel & Trepte, 1902.

Tuckett, C.M. "1 Corinthians and Q", *JBL* 102 (1983): 607-619.

————. "The Beatitudes: A Source-Critical Study", *NT* 25 (1983): 193-207.

————. *The Revival of the Griesbach Hypothesis*. Cambridge: Cambridge University Press, 1983 [SNTS MS 44].

————. "Paul and the Synoptic Mission Discourse?" *ETL* 60 (1984): 376-381.

————. "Synoptic Tradition in the Didache." In *The New Testament in Early Christianity*, ed J.-M. Sevrin, 197-230. Louvain: Louvain University Press, 1989 [BEThL 86].

Tuilier, A. "Didache", *TRE* 8 (1981): 731-736.

————. "Une nouvelle édition de la Didachè (Problèmes de méthode et de critique textuelle)." In *Studia Patristica* 15, 31-36. Berlin: Adademie-Verlag, 1984 [TU 128].

Turck, A. *Evangélisation et catéchèse aux deux premiers siècles*. Paris: Les Éditions du Cerf, 1962.

Turner, C.H. "The Early Christian Ministry and the Didache." In *Studies in Early Church History*, 1-31. Oxford: Oxford University Press, 1912.

Turner, V. *The Ritual Process*. Ithaca: Cornell University, 1967.

Unnik, W.C. van "Die Motivierung der Feindesliebe in Lukas VI 32-35", *NT* 8 (1966): 288-300.

Vielhauer, P. "The Final Chapter of the Didache." In *New Testament Apocrypha* II, eds. E. Hennecke & W. Schneemelcher, 626-29. Philadelphia: Westminster 1965.

————. *Geschichte der urchristlichen Literatur. Einleitung in das Neue Testament, die Apokryphen und die Apostolischen Väter*. Berlin: de Gruyter, 1975.

Vincent, L.H. "Découverte de la 'synagogue des affranchis' à Jérusalem", *RevBib* 30 (1921): 247-277.

Vögtle, A. *Die Tugend- und Lasterkataloge im Neuen Testament*. Münster: Aschendorff, 1936.

Vokes, F.E. *The Riddle of the Didache. Fact or Fiction, heresy or Catholicism?* London: SPCK, 1938.

————. "The Didache Re-examined", *Theol* 58 (1955): 12-16.

————. "The *Didache* and the Canon of the New Testament." In *Studia Evangelica* 3, 427-36. Berlin: Akademie-Verlag, 1964 [TU 88].

————. "The Didache—Still debated", *ChQR* 3 (1970): 58f.

Völker, K. *Mysterium und Agape*. Gotha: Klotz, 1927.

Vööbus, A. "Celibacy a Requirement for Admission to Baptism in the Early Syrian Church", *ETSE* 1 (1951).

————. *History of Asceticism in the Syrian Orient* I. 1958 [CSCO 184 = subs. 14].

————. *Liturgical Traditions in the Didache*. Stockholm: Estonian Theological Society in Exile, 1968 [PETSE 16].

Walker, J.H. "An Argument from the Chinese for the Antiochene Origin of the Didache." In *Studia Patristica* 8, ed. F. L. Cross, 44-50. Berlin: Akademie-Verlag, 1966 [TU 93].

Walters, B.S. *Didachè (ΔΙΔΑΧΗ ΤΩΝ ΔΩΔΕΚΑ ΑΠΟΣΤΟΛΩΝ) The Unknown Teaching of the Twelve Apostles.* San Jose: Bibliographics, 1991.

Webb, D. "La liturgie nestorienne des apôtres Addai et Mari dans la tradition manuscrite." In *Eucharisties d'Orient et d'Occident* II: *Semanie liturgique de l'Institut Saint Serge*, ed. B.Botte *et al.* Paris: Les Éditions du Cerf, 1970.

Weeden, T.J. *Mark--Traditions in Conflict.* Philadelphia: Fortress, 1971.

Wegenast, K. *Das Verständnis der Tradition bei Paulus und in den Deuteropaulinen.* Neukirchen-Vluyn: Neukirchner Verlag, 1962 [WMANT 8].

Weinfeld, M. "The Charge of Hypocrisy in Matthew 23 and in Jewish Sources", *Immanuel* 24-25 (1990): 52-58.

Weiss, J. *Earliest Christianity* I-II. New York: Harper, 1959.

Wengst, K. *Tradition und Theologie Des Barnabasbriefes.* Berlin: de Gruyter, 1971.

————. *Didache (Apostellehre), Barnabasbrief, Zweiter Klemensbrief, Schrift an Diognet.* Darmstadt: Wissenschaftliche Buchgesellschaft, 1984 [SUC 2].

Wenham, D. "A Note on Matthew 24:10-12", *TynB* 31 (1980): 155-162.

————. *The Rediscovery of Jesus' Eschatological Discourse.* Sheffield: JSOT, 1984.

Westermann, C. *Das Loben Gottes in den Psalmen.* Göttingen: Vandenhoeck & Ruprecht, 1963³.

Wibbing, S. *Die Tugend-und Lasterkataloge im Neuen Testament und ihre Traditionsgeschichte unter besonderer Berücksichtigung der Qumran-Texte.* Berlin: de Gruyter, 1959 [BZNW 25].

Windisch, H. *Die Barnabasbrief.* Tübingen: Mohr, 1920.

Wlosok, A. *Laktanz und die philosophische Gnosis.* Heidelberg: Winter, 1960 [Abhandlungen der Heidelberger Akadamie der Wissenschaften Phil-hist. Klasse 2].

Wohleb, L. *Die lateinische Übersetzung der Didache kritisch und sprachlich untersucht.* Paderborn: F. Schöningh, 1913 [SGKA 7].

Wordsworth, J. "Christian Life, Ritual, and Discipline at the Close of the First Century", *The Guardian* 39/1998 (1884): 422-423.

Wrege, H.T. *Die Überlieferungsgeschichte der Bergpredigt.* Tübingen: Mohr, 1968 [WUNT 9].

Yardin, Y. *The Temple Scroll 1: Introduction.* Jerusalem: Israel Exploration Society, 1983.

————. *The Temple Scroll 2: Text and Commentary.* Jerusalem: Israel Exploration Society, 1983.

————. *The Temple Scroll: The Hidden Law of the Dead Sea Sect.* London: Weidenfeld and Nicolson, London, 1985.

Zeller, D. *Die weisheitlichen Mahnsprüche bei den Synoptikern.* Würzburg: Echter-Verlag, 1977 [FzB 17].

Zeller, F. *Die Apostellehre, 6-16.* München: Kösel, 1918 [BKV 35]

I. JEWISH LITERATURE

4. Rabbinic Literature

4.1. Babylonian Talmud

II. EARLY CHRISTIAN LITERATURE

3. Other Early Christian Literature

III. GREEK AND ROMAN LITERATURE

IV. MODERN AUTHORS

DATE DUE